The History of Reading

The History of Reading offers an engaging, accessible overview of this fast developing subject from the rise of literacy through to the current trend for 'book clubs'. The editors offer a variety of extracts crucial to the understanding of the history of reading and to its social, political and cultural implications.

Divided into seven sections, each with a useful introduction, this *Reader* collects together key primary extracts written by leading scholars in the field to:

- summarise the main debates and perspectives shaping the field
- introduce key theorists such as Iser, Fish and Bakhtin
- survey influential works and outline important studies on mass reading
- focus on specific communities such as Welsh miners, African American library users and settlers in the American frontier
- look at individual readers from a variety of countries, classes and historical periods
- explore new approaches to research in the history of reading.

Providing both a clear introduction to the history of the field and a taster of the breadth, diversity and vitality of current debates, *The History of Reading* is an essential resource for undergraduates, graduates and researchers.

Shafquat Towheed is a Lecturer in English at the Open University, where he is also Project Supervisor and Co-Investigator for *The Reading Experience Database, 1450–1945* (RED). He is the editor of *The Correspondence of Edith Wharton and Macmillan, 1901–1930* (2007) and *New Readings in the Literature of British India, c.1780–1947* (2007), and co-editor of *Publishing in the First World War: Essays in Book History* (2007).

Rosalind Crone is Lecturer in History at the Open University, where she is a Co-Investigator on the AHRC-funded project, *The Reading Experience Database, 1450–1945* (RED). She has published widely on popular culture, crime and literacy in the nineteenth century, and is co-editor of *New Perspectives in British Cultural History* (2007).

Katie Halsey is Lecturer in the Literature of the Long Eighteenth Century at the University of Stirling. She has published a large number of articles on Jane Austen. Other interests include the history of reading, literature and print culture in the eighteenth and nineteenth centuries, more broadly. She is the co-editor of *The Concept and Practice of Conversation in the Long Eighteenth Century* (2007) and is currently writing a monograph about Jane Austen's readers.

Routledge Literature Readers

Also available

Literature and Globalisation

For further information on this series visit: www.routledgeliterature.com/books/series

The History of Reading

A Reader

Edited by

**Shafquat Towheed, Rosalind Crone and
Katie Halsey**

Routledge
Taylor & Francis Group

LONDON AND NEW YORK

First published 2011
by Routledge
2 Park Square, Milton Park, Abingdon, Oxon OX14 4RN

Simultaneously published in the USA and Canada
by Routledge
270 Madison Avenue, New York, NY 10016

Routledge is an imprint of the Taylor & Francis Group, an informa business

Typeset in Perpetua and Bell Gothic by
RefineCatch Limited, Bungay, Suffolk
Printed and bound in Great Britain by
TJ International Ltd, Padstow, Cornwall

British Library Cataloguing in Publication Data
A catalogue record for this book is available from the British Library

Library of Congress Cataloging-in-Publication Data
The history of reading / edited by Shafquat Towheed, Rosalind Crone and
Katie Halsey—1st ed.
    p. cm.
    1. Reading—History.   2. Literacy—History.   I. Towheed, Shafquat, 1973–.
    II. Crone, Rosalind.   III. Halsey, Katie.
    LB1050.H58 2010
    418'.409—dc22   2010005179

ISBN 10: 0-415-48420-0 (hbk)
ISBN 10: 0-415-48421-9 (pbk)

ISBN 13: 978-0-415-48420-6 (hbk)
ISBN 13: 978-0-415-48421-3 (pbk)

Contents

Acknowledgements

The publisher and the editors would like to thank the following for permission to reprint material under copyright:

Section 1: Defining the Field: What is the History of Reading?

Q. D. Leavis, excerpt from *Fiction and the Reading Public* (London: Pimlico, 2000, part of the Random House Group, original publication – London: Chatto & Windus, 1932). Reproduced by kind permission of the executor of the Mrs Q. D. Leavis Literary Estate. Copyright © Q.D. Leavis 1932

Robert Darnton, excerpts from 'First Steps Towards a History of Reading' From *The Kiss of Lamourette*. Copyright © 1990 by Robert Darnton. Used by permission of W.W. Norton and Company. Inc. and by permission of Faber and Faber Ltd.

Exerpts from Roger Chartier, excerpts from 'Preface' to *The Order of Books*, by Roger Chartier, translated by Lydia G. Cochrane, Copyright © 1994 Polity Press English translation. Reproduced with permission.

Reinhard Wittmann, excerpts from 'Was there a Reading Revolution at the End of the Eighteenth Century?', in Guglielmo Cavallo and Roger Chartier (eds), *A History of Reading in the West* (Cambridge: Polity Press, 1999). Reproduced with permission. Copyright © this translation Polity Press 1999.

John Moorhead, excerpts from 'Reading in Late Antiquity', in Carl Deroux (ed), *Studies in Latin Literature and Roman History* (Brussels: Latomus, 2008). Reproduced with the kind permission of the publishers and the author.

Section 2: Theorising the Reader

Jauss, Hans Robert, excerpts from "Literary History as a Challenge to Literary Theory," trans. Elizabeth Benzinger, New Literary History 2.1 (1970), 7–37. © New Literary History, University of Virginia. Reprinted with permission of New Literary History.

Iser, Wolfgang, excerpts from "The Reading Process: A Phenomenological Approach." New Literary History 3.2 (1972), 279–299. © New Literary History, University of Virginia. Reprinted with permission of New Literary History.

Judith Fetterley, excerpts from 'On the Politics of Literature' in *The Resisting Reader: A Feminist Approach to American Fiction* Copyright © 1978 by Judith Fetterley, reproduced with permission of Indiana University Press.

Stanley Fish, excerpts from 'What Makes an Interpretation Acceptable?' reprinted by permission of the publisher from IS THERE A TEXT IN THIS CLASS?: THE AUTHORITY OF INTERPRETATIVE COMMUNITIES by Stanley Fish, pp. 338–345, 347–355, Cambridge, Mass: Harvard University Press, Copyright © 1980 by the President and Fellows of Harvard College.

Reproduced with permission. Excerpts from THE DIALOGIC IMAGINATION: FOUR ESSAYS by M. M. Bakhtin, edited by Michael Holquist, translated by Caryl Emerson and Michael Holquist, Copyright © 1981. By permission of the University of Texas Press.

Extracts from Paul Saenger, 'Silent Reading: its impact on Late Medieval Script and Society', *Viator* 13 (1982). 2.6. Baltimore, MD: The Johns Hopkins University Press, 1982. See also Saenger, *Space Between Words: The Origins of Silent Reading*, Stanford University Press, 2000. Reproduced by kind permission.

Michel de Certeau, 'Reading as Poaching' in *The Practice of Everyday Life*, trans. Steven Rendall (Berkeley, Los Angeles and London: University of California Press, 1988 Copyright © 1984 by the Regents of the University of California. Reproduced by kind permission.

Section 3: Researching and Using Literacy

Margaret Spufford, excerpts from 'Literacy, trade and religion in the commercial centres of Europe' in Karel Davids and Jan Lucassen (eds), *A Miracle Mirrored: the Dutch republic in European perspective*, Cambridge: Cambridge University Press, 1996. © Cambridge University Press 1995, reproduced with permission.

Roger S. Schofield, excerpts from 'Dimensions of illiteracy in England, 1740–1850', *Explorations in Economic History* 10. Copyright © 1973 by The Kent State University Press. Reproduced with permission.

David Vincent, excerpts from 'Reading and Writing' in *The Rise of Mass Literacy: Reading and Writing in Modern Europe* (Cambridge: Polity, 2000). Reproduced with permission.

Carl F. Kaestle, 'Studying the History of Literacy' in Carl Kaestle et al (eds),

Literacy in the United States: Readers and Reading since 1880, New Haven: Yale University Press, 1991. Copyright © 1991 by Yale University Press. All rights reserved, reproduced by kind permission.

Richard Hoggart, excerpts from 'Summary of present tendencies in mass culture' in *The Uses of Literacy* (London: Chatto & Windus, 1957). Reproduced by kind permission of The Random House Group Ltd.

Section 4: Reading the Masses

Kevin Sharpe, excerpts from *Reading Revolutions: the Politics of Reading in Early Modern England,* New Haven, CT and London: Yale University Press, 2000, Copyright © 2000 by Kevin Sharpe. Reproduced by kind permission.

Anne E. McLaren, excerpts from 'Constructing New Reading Publics in Late Ming China' in Cynthia J. Brokaw and Kai-wing Chow (eds), *Printing and Book Culture in Late Imperial China* (University of California Press, 2005) Berkeley, Los Angeles and London: University of California Press, 2005 (Regents of the University of California) © 2005 by the Regents of the University of California. Reproduced with permission.

William St. Clair, excerpts from 'At the Boundaries of the Reading Nation' in *The Reading Nation in the Romantic Period*, pp.339–356, 2004 © William St. Clair 2004, published by Cambridge University Press, reproduced with permission.

Anindita Ghosh, excerpts from 'Contesting Print Audiences' in *Power in Print: popular publishing and the politics of language and culture in a colonial society, 1778–1905* (New Delhi: Oxford University Press, 2006). Reproduced by permission of Oxford University Press India, New Delhi.

Jeffrey Brooks, excerpts from 'The Literature of the Lubok' in *When Russia Learned to Read: Literacy and Popular Literature, 1861–1917*, 2nd edition, (Northwestern University Press, 2003) Evanston, IL: Northwestern University Press, 2003. Copyright © 2003 by Jeffrey Brooks. First published 1985 by Princeton University Press. All rights reserved, reproduced by kind permission.

Excerpts reproduced by permission of Oxford University Press Australia from *Australian Readers Remember* © Martin Lyons and Lucy Taska, 1992, Oxford University Press, www.oup.com.au. Reproduced by kind permission.

Section 5: Reading Communities

Armando Petrucci, excerpts from 'Reading in the Middle Ages' in Charles M. Radding (ed. and trans.), *Writers and Readers in Medieval Italy: Studies in the History of Written Culture*, New Haven: Yale University Press, 1995. Copyright © 1995 by Yale University. Reproduced by kind permission.

Jonathan Rose, excerpts from 'The Welsh Miners' Libraries' in *The Intellectual Life of the British Working Classes*, New Haven: Yale University Press, 2001, © 2001 by Jonathan Rose. Reproduced by kind permission.

Excerpts reprinted from *Reading on the Middle Border: The Culture of Print in Late-Nineteenth-Century Osage, Iowa* by Christine Pawley. Copyright © 2001 by University of Massachusetts Press and published by the University of Massachusetts Press. Reproduced by kind permission.

Excerpt reprinted from *Institutions of Reading: The Social Life of Libraries in the United States* by Elizabeth McHenry. Copyright © 2007 by University of Massachusetts Press and published by the University of Massachusetts Press. Reproduced by kind permission.

Section 6: Individual Readers

Anthony Grafton and Lisa Jardine, '"Studied for Action": How Gabriel Harvey read his Livy', *Past and Present* (1990) 129, extracts pp. 30–78, by permission of Oxford University Press.

Baggerman, Arianne. Excerpts from 'The Cultural Universe of a Dutch Child: Otto van Eck and his Literature'. *Eighteenth-Century Studies* 31:1 (1997), 129–133. © 1997 The American Society for Eighteenth-Century Studies. Reprinted with permission of The Johns Hopkins University Press.

Stephen Colclough, excerpts from '"R R, A Remarkable Thing or Action": John Dawson as a Reader and Annotator', *Variants* 2:3 (2004) Amsterdam & New York, Rodopi, 2004. Reproduced with the kind permission of the publisher.

James A. Secord, excerpts from 'Self-Development' in *Victorian Sensation: the extraordinary publication, reception and secret authorship of* Vestiges of the Natural History of Creation (Chicago: University of Chicago Press, 2003 revised edition). © 2000 by the University of Chicago. Reproduced with permission.

Section 7: New Directions and Methods in the History of Reading

Teresa Gerrard, excerpts from 'New Methods in the History of Reading: "Answers to Correspondents" in *The Family Herald*, 1860–1900', *Publishing History*, 43 (1998). Cambridge: Chadwyck-Healey, 1998. Reproduced with the kind permission of Pro-Quest and author.

Excerpts from : 'No longer left behind: Amazon.com, reader-response, and the changing fortunes of the Christian novel in America', by Paul Gutjahr. *Book History* 5, pp.210–227, 2002. Copyright © 2002 The Society for the History of Authorship, Reading and Publishing. Reproduced by permission of Penn State Press.

Excerpts from HOFMEYR, ISABEL: THE PORTABLE BUNYAN. Princeton University Press reprinted by permission of Princeton University Press. Copyright © 2004 by Princeton University Press.

Danielle Fuller, excerpts from 'Listening to the Readers of "Canada Reads"', *Canadian Literature* 193 (2007). Vancouver: University of British Columbia, 2007. Reproduced with permission.

Updated essay based on Mary Hammond, 'The Reading Experience Database 1450–1945', in Robin Myers, Michael Harris and Giles Mandelbrote (eds),

Owners, Annotators and the Signs of Reading (New Castle: Oak Knoll Press and the British Library, 2005), 175–187. Reproduced with the cooperation of the author and the permission of the publisher.

Editors' Acknowledgements

The editors would like to thank Routledge's anonymous external readers for their generous advice in shaping the project; The British Academy, Arts and Humanities Research Council, and The Open University for continued financial support for our work; and colleagues and students at the Institute of English Studies (University of London), The Open University, the University of Cambridge, and the University of Stirling for their interest in this project. We owe a debt to the editorial and production team at Routledge for bringing this book into being. Finally, two people deserve a special mention for independently suggesting the viability of a reader such as this in the first place: Stephen Colclough and Mary Hammond.

GENERAL INTRODUCTION

If not a single book were published from this moment on, it would still take 250,000 years for us to acquaint ourselves with those books already written.

— Gabriel Zaid, *So Many Books* (London, 2004, p.30)

On the wall at the side of the chimney Dad put up the bookshelves which Dodie began to fill with secondhand penny books. Over the years we had Conrad and Wodehouse, Eric Linklater and Geoffrey Farnol, Edgar Wallace, Jane Austen, Thomas Hardy, Mark Twain, Arnold Bennett, Robert Louis Stevenson, John Buchan, and a host of others, good, bad and awful, and we read the lot, some of them over and over.

— Rose Gamble, *A Chelsea Child* (London, 1979, p.143)

AS A SUBJECT, THE HISTORY OF READING presents an essential paradox. On one hand, in an age of mass literacy, reading is both too ordinary an activity to warrant our attention, and too ubiquitous for us to ignore. On the other, it is often the most deeply engaged act in the construction of an individual's identity. For the Mexican writer and essayist Gabriel Zaid, the overwhelming freight of published material provokes anxiety, solipsism, and a strategy for reading. His calculation is based on a person reading as a full time occupation, at the rate of four books per week, 200 per year, and 10,000 over 50 years, confronted with the reality of the over 50 million titles in existence. In such a world – our own – no person can ever hope to have read even the smallest percentage of the collective output of humanity. For Zaid, the only response to such a predicament is to reinvest, emotionally and personally, in each individual act of reading: 'the measure of our reading should therefore be, not the number of books we've read, but the state in which they leave us' (*So Many Books*, 24). Zaid, like so many writers dealing with the history of reading (Benedict Anderson, Nicholas Basbanes, Anne Fadiman, Alberto Manguel, Margaret Willes, to name but a few) rightly invokes the transformative capacity of the book, and just as readily, the investment in the act of reading made by the reader. While Zaid postulates the dilemma of an ideal reader, with unlimited time and access to books, for the vast majority of readers through history, a reading practice clustered around a small number of easily accessible books and often involving reading aloud, was the norm. For Rose Gamble, growing up in the book hungry deprivation of an urban slum in London in the period between the two world wars, the transformative capacity of books, however cheap or humble, was never in doubt. Each act of reading was invested with value and a sense of self-identification; Gamble read for pleasure as much as for self-improvement. The second-hand penny paperbacks were housed next to the family hearth, and they were all nurtured through repeated reading, even when she had achieved sufficient literary discernment to make value judgements ('good, bad and awful, and we read the lot') between them.

These two musings on the act of reading, both clearly intensely autobiographical, present two poles in approaches to the history of reading: the macro-analytical, and the micro-analytical. The impossibility that any individual could read even a small proportion of the cumulative human output of books implicitly urges us to engage with the broader issue of collecting the quantitative, statistical evidence of reading, a methodology that allows us to examine broader trends in reading practices, and make sense of the mind-boggling weight of extant titles and their possible readers. While an individual reader's engagement can tell us little about the broader trends and patterns of *how* a particular text was consumed, collating a range of quantifiable data, such as that offered by print runs, library circulation records, literacy figures, sale prices, average incomes, distribution networks, and advertising, can accurately reconstruct the environment for reading in a particular period and territory. Such a macro-analytical approach is taken by William St. Clair in his exemplary study of British readers during the Romantic period (Section 4, extract 20), and to a lesser degree, by Christine Pawley in her analysis of library users in Sage, Iowa in the late nineteenth-century (Section 5, extract 26).

Social historians and scholars of literacy have also often adopted a macro-analytical methodology to assess literacy in a wide range of territories and historical periods, from rural Mexico to Northern Greenland, and from Early Modern Holland to Apartheid-era South Africa. By systematically collating and analysing data such as census returns and marriage registers (for evidence of the ability to write as well as read), they have been able to map the spread of literacy, its distribution in a given population, and alert us to the various intermediate stages between illiteracy and literacy (literacy and illiteracy are not simply binary opposites). Margaret Spufford's work (Section 3, extract 13) demonstrates the ways in which literacy spread due to the specific occupational needs of an emerging mercantile class, while Roger Schofield shows the extent to which the collated data of marriage registers in England over the span of a century yields evidence of the inequalities of the acquisition of this key skill, depending upon location, class, income, and gender (Section 3, extract 14). Quantitative macro-analysis allows social historians to map out with some sophistication the changing dimensions of the reading public, and therefore, that population's engagement with textual matter. As David Vincent demonstrates (Section 3, extract 15), oral and literate (or semi-literate) cultures were coextensive through most of the nineteenth-century in Britain, despite the increasing number of newly literate adults, and a similar pattern has been described by François Furet and Jacques Ozouf in France in a slightly earlier and longer historical period.

However, while it can empirically map out the metrics of the domain of reading, quantitative macro-analysis cannot offer us a complete picture of how individual readers interacted with specific books. The Gamble family's habit of buying cheap second-hand books, a practice still widespread for example, on the footpaths of that great clearing house of hand-me-down books, College Street in Kolkata, India, is unlikely to have been recorded in book sales' catalogues or store inventories, and would slip beneath the radar of such a quantitative survey. Nor does this kind of statistical approach adequately account for Rose Gamble's considerable investment of leisure time in the books themselves; a macro-analytical study cannot tell us how many times she read these books, why she chose them, or indeed, how she responded to them, on an intellectual or an emotional level.

Between the approaches of quantitative macro-analysis and qualitative micro-analysis in the history of reading, and writing prior to both of them, theorists of reading have proposed a variety of models for reading practices, and extrapolated a range of broader changes over time. Paul Saenger has argued for the transition from reading aloud to silent reading in Europe in the Middle Ages, demonstrated visibly in manuscripts and later in printed books, by the evolution of spaces between words rather than continuous script (Section 2, extract 11), while Hans Robert Jauss (Section 2, extract 6) has reminded us that all texts carry with them implicit assumptions about how they should be read; readers have protocols for reading, including cultural, aesthetic and ideological assumptions, the 'horizon of expectations', that they bring to the act of reading itself. While Wolfgang Iser, Stanley Fish, and Mikhail Bakhtin (Section 2, extracts 7, 9 and 10) argue for the construction of meaning taking place in the engagement between reader and text, Judith Fetterley's feminist approach to reader response (Section 2, extract 8) provides us with a welcome warning against complacently assuming the passivity of readers. Readers can actively resist the codes implicit in the text, for they are individuals with the potential for agency. Moreover, readers are inherently both selective, and as Michel de Certeau (Section 2, extract 12) so memorably put it, 'impertinent': they may or may not subscribe to the protocols of reading, the message of the author, the ideology of the state, or the expectations we might have of them. These theoretical models have essentially been hypotheses, which research will eventually prove, disprove, or modify. They do, however, remind us of the importance of individual responses in the act of reading. The vitality of debate amongst theorists in the history of reading over the last thirty-five years strongly indicates the need for continuing empirical research of the subject. Indeed, theoretical models of reading practice have been highly influential in shaping scholarship in the subject.

Approaches to the history of reading can be predominantly either text centred, or reader centred, nor are these two foci mutually incompatible. James Secord (Section 6, extract 31) maps out the life of a Victorian bestselling text, Robert Chambers' *Vestiges of the Natural History of Creation* (1844), through its readers, especially one Thomas Hirst; in narrating the life of a book, he wonderfully illuminates the reading community of Halifax, West Yorkshire. A converse perspective is offered by John Brewer's reader centred study, 'Reconstructing the reader: prescriptions, texts and strategies in Anna Larpent's reading' (in James Raven, Helen Small and Naomi Tadmor, *The Practice and Representation of Reading in England* Cambridge, 1996, pp.226–245: not included in this Reader). Brewer's deft unpicking of Larpent's varied and highly sophisticated reading practices refutes the grand claims of a 'reading revolution' (the shift from the intensive reading of a few books, to the extensive reading of many books) proposed by theorists such as Rolf Engelsing, by demonstrating that Larpent engaged in both types of reading, and many others besides (such as reading aloud). Of course, studies in the history of reading can be *both* text *and* reader centred. Anthony Grafton and Lisa Jardine (Section 6, extract 28) have famously examined the reading of one text (Livy's *Histories*) by one man (Gabriel Harvey) from the perspective of a particular type of professionalised reader (the 'facilitator'), to propose a model of politically engaged, humanist reading as a form of advocacy in Elizabethan England. Qualitative micro-analytical studies can provide us with the kind of detailed information about how individual readers actually read and responded to texts that other approaches cannot. Increasingly, research projects in the history of reading, such as the *Reading Experience Database* project based at the Open University (Section 7, extract 36), consciously accommodate *both* qualitative micro-analysis, and the broader trends offered up by quantitative macro-analysis. Finally, it is worth considering the extent to which research in the history of reading is still in its infancy. We have yet to see historians of reading systematically engaging with the history of art (and visual representations of reading), or with the history of music; not all reading material, after all, is textual, and annotated musical scores offer a wealth of information of reading and use. National, regional and thematic studies outside Western Europe and North America are still surprisingly scarce. The physiology, psychology and neurology of reading as an evidence based inquiry is still in its infancy; one might want to draw a parallel here with the emergence of the neurology of music as a research field. We are only scratching the surface in our examination of the reading of material other than the printed book: ephemera, pamphlets, advertising hoardings, timetables, maps, tombstones and so on. And finally, the sheer scale of the evidence of reading and response to published (both printed and electronic) texts in archived e-mails, the blogosphere, computer hard drives, and social networking sites is only now beginning to be comprehended, let alone scrutinised.

Sections, selections, and further reading

This volume brings together 36 short extracts from some of the leading scholarship in the histories of reading, literacy, and the book to have been published in the last 80 years.

The aim of this Reader is to provide teachers, students, and researchers with a representative overview of the major developments in the scholarship in the history of reading, as well as to indicate particular intellectual or methodological approaches that we felt were especially worth of attention and would likely encourage future research. As a matter of consistency and to aid comprehensibility, we have kept graphs, charts and diagrams to a minimum, and have only included these where they are essential to the point being made. Each section introduction provides a précis of the argument of each extract, as well as a wider consideration of the perspective, theme or methodological approach being examined in that section; the indicative bibliography guides readers towards issues for further research. We have divided this Reader into seven sections, each of which can be read or studied independently of the others, but all of which are arranged in a specific, cumulative pattern. Section 1, 'Defining the Field: What is the History of Reading?' deals with the tentative emergence of the history of reading, from the context of the history of the book, economic and social history and literary criticism and theory, into an increasingly discreetly defined field of study. This is an ongoing process, and the ways in which the history of reading overlaps (or not) with for example, the history of the book, is still a subject for considerable debate. While Q.D. Leavis wrote *Fiction and the Reading Public* without any sense of the history of reading as an academic field (her training was squarely in English Literature), Robert Darnton has repeatedly drawn our attention to how this sub-discipline has emerged, and how it might develop. Section 2 surveys the major theoretical models of reading, from Jauss' 'horizon of expectations' to Fish's 'interpretive communities', and from de Certeau's construction of the reader as poacher, to Fetterley's hypothesis of the feminist reader's resistance to patriarchy and the protocols of reading.

Section 3 displays the ways in which research in literacy can accurately map the changing size and nature of the reading public. While the extracts selected are from Western Europe and North America, researching literacy has an exceptionally well developed international and comparative aspect. If section 3 identifies and quantifies the literate masses, section 4 seeks to uncover their complex and sometimes contradictory engagement with print. The chosen extracts cover India, Russia, China, Australia and England, and demonstrate both the appetite for reading amongst the newly literate masses, and their close proximity to a vital and creative oral culture. Section 5 narrows the focus from mass reading, to the engagement of specific reading communities with textual matter. While the masses in section 4 are defined through their entry into the world of print, the reading communities in section 5 define themselves through their active participation in reading – whether in lending libraries in Iowa, Welsh miners' institutes, African-American reading rooms, or the private homes and public educational spaces of Renaissance Florence. In section 6, individual readers – de Certeau's 'poachers' – come to the fore, with four extracts closely assessing the intensive and at times transformative relationship between readers and their books. These studies may well be of exemplary, even elite readers, for they all left considerable evidence of their reading for posterity – not an activity in which the average reader participated. Finally, section 7 showcases some of the more important recent developments in the history of reading, shaped by technological developments, new literary critical or theoretical perspectives, and the increasing interdependence of different types of media and cultural content.

The History of Reading is organised along a clearly marshalled intellectual trajectory. A consideration of the evolution of the discipline in Section 1 leads to Section 2, which offers an assessment of theoretical models for the practice of reading. These theoretical models are interrogated by the largely quantitative methods used to research and analyse literacy, the range of key skills which characterise populations of readers, in Section 3. Sections 4, 5 and 6 offer us a representative sample of case studies in the history of reading, organised telescopically, from a macro- to a micro-perspective. Thus Section 4 assesses the masses, while Section 5 defines and studies specific reading communities, and Section 6 devotes itself to examining individual readers. Finally, Section 7 yields a highly attractive selection of new methodologies and interpretative approaches to the history of reading, suggestively indicating some of the ways in which the field might develop in the coming decades.

Not all studies or approaches can be easily summarised and anthologised, and there are some books and articles of particular significance to the subject that we would like to mention here. The first is *The Practice and Representation of Reading* (Cambridge, 1996), edited by James Raven, Helen Small, and Naomi Tadmor, a volume which, as much as any other, has inspired a new generation of researchers in the field. This is a remarkably rich resource for the study of the history of reading practices in Britain, and all 14 chapters in this edited collection are highly significant contributions to the subject. John Brewer's seminal case study of Anna Larpent's reading in the Romantic period, Helen Small's bravura examination of Dickens and the mid-Victorian reading public, and Jan Fergus' careful excavation of the reading of provincial servants in the eighteenth century are perhaps the highlights, but we would unhesitatingly recommend reading this volume in its entirely. The second is Leah Price's essay, 'Reading: the state of the discipline', *Book History* 7 (2004), 303–320, which provides the best brief summary of the scholarship in the history of reading to date. Kate Flint's *The Woman Reader, 1837–1914* (Oxford, 1993) and H.J. Jackson's *Marginalia: Readers Writing in Books* (London, 2001) provide the most detailed and compelling accounts of nineteenth-century British women readers and the importance of marginalia to the history of reading respectively, and they have yet to be superseded. Alberto Manguel's *A History of Reading* (London, 1996) remains an immensely readable and informative popular history of the subject, while two very recent, and more overtly scholarly works by historians of France in the long eighteenth and nineteenth centuries respectively, Robert Darnton's *The Case for Books: Past, Present and Future* (Philadelphia, 2009) and Martyn Lyons' *A History of Reading and Writing in the Western World* (Basingstoke, 2009), provide very timely rejoinders of how far the history of reading has come, and also where it may be heading. Both Darnton and Lyons have been highly influential figures in the history of reading in the last quarter century, and these books advocate radically different departures for future scholarship in this area. All these works are readily available in affordable paperback editions or digital download; they are listed in the comprehensive bibliography (organised according to each section) at the end of the volume, which also serves to provide a comprehensive map of scholarship in this developing subject area.

Global literacy, the digital revolution and the future of the history of reading

At the end of the first decade of the twenty-first century, it might be worth reflecting upon the nature of reading as an activity today. Sven Birkerts has argued that in the shift to a saturated digital media environment, a particular type of literary reading has been lost forever; in his view, the 'single-track concentration' of reading has been put under unbearable pressure by the 'restless, grazing behaviour of clicking and scrolling' (*The Gutenberg Elegies*, p.xiv). There is a clear parallel here with the shift, caused by Gutenberg and print capitalism, from manuscript, *lectio* and intensive contemplation, to printed books and silent humanist reading in Early Modern Europe. But while Birkerts views the newly digitally empowered masses as mindless herbivores rather than contemplative ruminants, his dire vision of reading in danger is belied by the astonishing and undiminished appetite of humans for literacy as a skill, and reading as a practice. Nearly a millennium after Bi Sheng's invention of first wooden and then porcelain movable type in Song Dynasty China (c.1040), almost eight centuries after the development of metal movable type in Korea (c.1240), and some 555 years after Gutenberg's use of metal type to produce the first printed Bible in Europe (c.1455), are we finally on the cusp of both global literacy and widespread, democratic access to reading matter?

The statistics certainly seem to support such a view. World illiteracy halved between 1970 and 2005, and according to UNESCO's most recent statistics issued for International Literacy Day, 84% of the world's 6.6 billion population are literate, a figure which is expected to rise to 90% by 2015; this means that although there are currently some 774 million people (20% of the world's adult population) who are still unable to read and write (http://portal.unesco.org/en/, accessed 15/11/2009), the total elimination of illiteracy is now for the first time, a realistic goal. With the prospect of mass literacy becoming a reality in almost every country within the next few decades, our twenty-first century will undoubtedly be the reading century *par excellence*. However, we should not be complacent about the inevitability of the spread of literacy always resulting in the formation of a mass literary culture. Readers cannot be coerced to engage with books, and recent evidence from the developed world indicates a small, but growing population of non-readers and illiterates, increasingly divorced from the world of print.

Not only will more people have the ability to read than ever before, but they will be accessing their reading material through an ever increasing array of printed and digital sources – from print on demand books, to educational content browsed through 3G mobile phones, Apple's iPad, and from wireless digital e-Readers (like Amazon's Kindle, the Barnes and Noble nook, and Sony's Reader), to mass reprints of the classics (such as the 1 million free copies of Cervantes' *Don Quixote* distributed by Hugo Chavez's government in Venezuela in 2005). As Danielle Fuller's article on 'Canada Reads' demonstrates (Section 7, extract 35), technological developments have increasingly embedded the act of reading in a range of other multimedia interactions, from television and the blogosphere, to celebrity endorsements and cinema adaptations, but despite the competition of other media, and fears over the apparent tyranny of the visual over the textual, the popular appetite for reading of all kinds and for a range of reasons seems to be undiminished. Beneath the visual array of images on the internet lies a hidden continent of textual matter, expressed as machine-read (and increasingly machine-designed) code. Similarly, the forensic analysis of computer hard drives might yield us valuable information about still developing digital reading and editorial practices, such as the evidence of reading embedded in extant and deleted e-mail correspondence, as Matthew Kirschenbaum's fascinating study *Mechanisms: New Media and the Forensic Imagination* (2008) has suggestively illuminated. It may well be the case that future artificial intelligence will learn to read as fluently and contextually as we do, in the same way that it has been trained to process binary code (in which case an AI history of reading will surely have to be written).

New technologies require new forms of gathering and assessing the evidence of reading, as Paul Gutjahr's analysis of reviews posted on Amazon.com indicates (Section 7, extract 33); this use of readers' responses on Amazon has since been developed further by Timothy Aubry in his study of the American readership of Khalid Hosseini's post-9/11 Afghan bestseller, *The Kite Runner* (2003). While scholars of the reading revolution in the Romantic period in Western Europe examined print runs, library borrowings, the inventories of private collections, and the circulation of clandestine books in order to assess social change expressed through the act of reading, their colleagues examining twenty-first century reading will need to quantify digital download data, web statistics, file sharing, the impact of social networking and reviewing, and utilise technology that can track the movement of the eye across the screen, thereby offering us real-time information about the act of reading *in situ*. The increasing use of mobile 3G devices (e-readers, mobile phones and iPods) as digital readers may well usher in another 'reading revolution', replicating the late eighteenth and early nineteenth century explosion of cheap printed books. While we must rely on the material textual evidence that historical readers have chosen to leave behind for posterity in order to reconstruct their reading world, the data collected by networked mobile digital reading devices and Global Positioning Systems can potentially offer us new evidence of each individual act of reading: not just what is being read, but where, when, for how long, whether statically or in motion, and how many times. In the increasingly dematerialised digital twenty-first century, individual readers' qualitative responses to their reading will still be exceptionally valuable for historians of reading; while technology can map out the mechanics and trends of reading, it cannot generate value judgements (aesthetic, emotional or literary-critical) about the content itself. For that, as ever, we must consider the individuality and autonomy of each reader.

The exponential rise in the digitisation of previously printed material, both for commercial and non-commercial purposes, has massively increased the number of titles available to readers, but it also implicitly changes the ways in which they access and read these texts. *Google Books* (http://books.google.com/) now has 10 million scanned titles (including Birkerts' jeremiad *The Gutenberg Elegies*, ironically in 'snippet view'), with 1 million offered with fully viewable content, the *Internet Archive* (www.archive.org) has digitised over 1.7 million texts for open access, while the Chinese language only *Super Star Digital Library* (www.chinamaxx.net/) has scanned over 700,000 volumes on a commercial subscription basis (and to a higher optical character recognition standard than its American counterparts). These and other future digitisation, subscription and live streaming services promise to make an unprecedented number of previously printed books available to readers, offering the possibility of an almost infinite 'long tail' of out of copyright material. Ironically, twenty-first century readers now have access to far more titles from pre-twentieth century periods than readers who actually lived during those times. For a new, primarily digitally literate readership, one that will have greater expertise in web browsing and using third and fourth generation digital devices to read than in the continuous, uninterrupted reading practice promoted by the printed book, this freight of digitised material represents both an opportunity, and a challenge of comprehension. Indeed, for many current and future readers, the twenty-first century may well prove to be a tipping point between printed and digital material, perhaps replicating the transition from a manuscript to a largely print society in Western Europe between the fifteenth and eighteenth centuries. Such a digital modification of the familiar codex is suggested by the cover illustration of Robert Darnton's robustly optimistic musing on this transition, *The Case for Books: Past, Present and Future* (2009), which features a hardback book with several USB ports and a power cable. Or mass digitisation may not represent a tipping point, and the continuities of reading practices might be greater than the changes. As Martyn Lyons cogently reminds us, 'every society since ancient Egypt has been an "information society", in the sense that those who control and restrict access to knowledge in any given society thereby control a key component of power' (*A History of Reading and Writing in the Western World*, p.1). This relationship between hegemonic power and knowledge is a sobering reminder in a century where the world's largest reading nation (and the one with the largest number of internet users) remains entirely committed to restricting what its citizens can read.

Technology may well change *how* we access and read textual material, and it can clearly be used to show us how previous generations responded to reading in the past, with digital projects like *The Reading Experience Database* (see Section 7, extract 36) offering valuable macro- and micro-analyses of reading, but it remains to be seen whether it will actively change *what* we read in the future. Indeed, early surveys of reading in China, the country with the fastest increase in the number of people accessing the internet, and the largest absolute number of newly literate people, suggest that the preference for a particular type of content, or reason for reading, is slow to change. Despite the surge (increasing by 40 million, or 13.4%, every six months) in the volume of people accessing the internet, especially through their mobile phones, the percentage of adults who read printed books went up from 48.8% in 2007 to 49.3% in 2009 ('Survey of Reading Behaviour', *China Press and Publishing Journal*, 24 April 2009). Fiction remains popular in China, and the bestselling novel in July 2009 was Eileen Chang's semi-autobiographical *Little Reunion* (2009); four of the ten bestselling fiction titles were translations from English, indicating once again the tremendous ability of the novel throughout history to cross cultural, geographical and political boundaries ('Open Book', http://www.openbook.com.cn/).

The extracts in this Reader and the evolving scholarship in the history of reading strongly indicate that we should never consider the readers of the future to be merely passive consumers of digital content in a world with too many books and too little time, nor should we think of new technology as simply deleting the old. The printed codex in paperback form will still be with us for some centuries to come, despite the rise of Amazon's Kindle and other, yet to be invented devices. Studies in the history of reading have repeatedly reminded us of the extent to which readers through the centuries have contested, shaped, rejected, or transformed reading material, and the rise in literacy and access to books across the globe will only intensify this engagement on both an individual and a collective basis. We as readers will still need to negotiate that path between the alienating anxiety of too many books and too little time, and the comforting identity-affirming familiarity of well-thumbed cheap paperbacks, furnishing our homes and nourishing our minds.

SECTION 1

Defining the field: what is the history of reading?

INTRODUCTION

FOR SUCH A UBIQUITOUS activity, the rise of the academic study of reading as a practice, and indeed, the understanding that it has a unique and complex history worth telling, has been a relatively recent development. Surprisingly, all these extracts were first published within the last 80 years, and four of them within the last 20 years. Indeed, while thinkers in the nineteenth century and earlier (going back to Saint Augustine) were deeply interested in how reading took place and what it signified, there were no systematic attempts to investigate reading as a sociological phenomenon until the early twentieth century; perhaps the earliest example was Lady Bell's study of Middlesbrough life, *At the Works* (1907). Q.D. Leavis' *Fiction and the Reading Public* emerged from her doctoral dissertation at Cambridge, and is generally considered to be the first concerted attempt systematically to classify and analyse reading practices in Britain in the interwar period. Drawing upon quantitative methods, such as the statistics of library borrowings and book production figures from the *Publishers' Circular*, as well as amassing qualitative information ('I can't read Conrad, sea-stories bore me') gleaned from participant observation and questionnaires, Leavis provides an overview of what material was available to British readers, how they might access it, and what their personal or group preferences might have been. Leavis' study has since been castigated for its doctrinaire approach to good literature versus bad, as well as its unquestioning endorsement of the relationship between class stratification and reading, but her study still remains immensely valuable, for it is the first detailed investigation of how ordinary readers engaged with (primarily) cheap fiction. You may want to compare Leavis' approach with Richard Hoggart's examination of working class reading two decades later (section 3, *Researching and Using Literacy*, extract 17).

The greatest leaps forward in the development of the history of reading as a concerted area for academic research took place in two specific phases, that ran parallel to the rise of the history of the book as a subject: the late 1950s with the rise of the French *annaliste* school and their work on the *Bibliographie de la France*, and the late 1980s and early 1990s, with the work of scholars (mainly social historians) such as Roger Chartier, Robert Darnton, Guglielmo Cavallo, Armando Petrucci, James Raven, Helen Small, Naomi Tadmor and others, working on reading in Europe between the sixteenth and the end of the eighteenth centuries. While Leavis examined the practice of reading without a clear sense of the develop- ment of a discipline, both Robert Darnton and Roger Chartier make assertive claims for an emerging field of study. Darnton's essay explicitly steers its readers from the history of the book to the history of reading. He acknowledges that while book historians have offered us a 'great deal of information about the external history of reading', the 'whys' and 'hows' of reading practice (both individual and collective) have been neglected. Darnton draws our attention to the fact that the quantitative statistical analysis ('macroanalysis') of book pro- duction, circulation and library borrowing can yield valuable information about wider social trends, but he also highlights how the detailed investigation of a single reader, text, or reading community ('microanalysis') provides actual evidence of reading rather than theoretical extrapolation.

While Darnton's model is implicitly consumption-led, Roger Chartier invokes the presence of the author in his study *The Order of Books*, a detailed cultural history of the change in reading material and practices in Western Europe from the end of the Middle Ages to the eighteenth century. In the preface extracted here, he argues that the rise of print and the expansion of readers (and reading as an activity) necessitated the 'invention of the author as the fundamental principle for the designation of a text'. For Chartier, any investigation of reading must take on board the 'constraints and obligations' accompanying each text, and negotiated by every reader. Darnton is happy to examine the broader trends offered up by macro-analysis, but Chartier cogently reminds us that reading is 'by definition, rebellious and vagabond'; readers construct meaning through an engagement with the text, and they have the ability to overthrow the order imposed upon them by books, authors, and regimes (you can follow up this issue through the de Certeau, Fetterley, Fish and Bakhtin extracts in section 2, *Theorising the Reader*).

Engaging both macro- and micro-analysis, Reinhard Wittmann in his study of the *Leserevolution* ('reading revolution') in German speaking *Mitteleuropa* in the eighteenth cen- tury investigates the claim that this linguistic region, like France and England at the same time, experienced a transition from reading as a minority to a mass participatory activity, and that this was largely mediated through the rise of fiction. Wittmann carefully compares the statistics for literacy, book print runs, and the demography of occupations to assess the size of the potential readership for books. Wittmann assesses the rising appetite for fiction through two specific best-selling works, Klopstock's *The Messiah* (1749) and Goethe's *The Sorrows of Young Werther* (1774); like Darnton and Chartier, he argues that examining the history of reading offers us vital information about social and historical change.

This section of the reader brings together five representative extracts demonstrating particular phases and arguments in the development of the history of reading as a field of study. The first four extracts are from works which have already become hugely influential in shaping research in the history of reading; the fifth specifically articulates how the field is changing and developing in unexpected and exciting ways. The history of reading is an evolving field. It is developing outwards geographically, from its start as a primarily European subject, as well as backwards and forwards in time, taking in the era before Gutenberg, the printing press, and the development of the codex, as well as the internet, e-readers and digital download. The extract from John Moorhead's essay on reading in late antiquity, a process mediated through an oral culture dependent on hearing, listening, and the active construction of texts, demonstrates the extent to which both the analyses and methodologies that have emerged in the last 80 years are now being vigorously applied to other disciplines and areas of study.

Chapter 1

Q. D. Leavis

THE BOOK MARKET

IN TWENTIETH-CENTURY ENGLAND not only every one can read, but it is safe to add that every one does read. Though the Report on Public Libraries (1927) states that not more than 11 per cent. of the population make use of the public library books, yet the number of Sunday newspapers sold will correct any false impression these figures may give. On the day of leisure even the poorest households take a newspaper, though it may be of a different type from that favoured by the educated. A Sunday morning walk through any residential district will reveal the head of the family 'reading the paper' in each front window; in the poorest quarters the *News of the World* is read on the doorstep or in bed; the weekly perusal of the *Observer* or the *Sunday Times*, which give a large proportion of their contents to book-reviews and publishers' advertisements, is in many cases the only time that even the best-intentioned business man or schoolmaster can spare for his literary education.

The *Advertiser's A B C* for 1929 gives the total net sales of eight of the chief Sunday papers alone as nearly ten million, and there exist others nearly as popular for which figures are not available. If one remembers that a newspaper is usually assumed to be read by five people, and that the entire population of Great Britain is forty-three million, it seems reasonable to conclude the existence of an inveterate general reading habit. The more interesting question, What do they read? cannot be answered without first indicating where and how the reading matter is obtained.

The striking peculiarity of the situation is that while, as demonstrated above, the entire population above the school age has acquired reading habits, shops existing solely to sell books are rare outside the university towns of Oxford, Cambridge, and Edinburgh, certain parts of London and a few big cities. Serious book-buying has not increased in proportion to literacy,[1] the bulk of the public does not buy many books[2] but borrows or hires them, in the former case from the not very satisfactory municipal or endowed libraries, in the latter from subscription libraries of various kinds. The investigation made in 1924 into the stocks and issues of urban libraries revealed that while they had 63 per cent. of non-fiction works on an average to 37 per cent. of fiction, only 22 per cent. of non-fiction was issued in comparison with 78 per cent. of fiction, while the county libraries, which stocked 38 per cent. of non-fiction to 62 per cent. of fiction, issued only 25 per cent. non-fiction.[3] This, considering that the 11 per cent. minority which takes advantage of its right to borrow books from the public libraries is probably the more enterprising section of the poorer reading public, shows convincingly enough the supremacy of fiction and the neglect of serious reading which characterise the age.

The fiction shelves of a public library commonly contain the classics and hardy popular novels of the past, representative works of all the most popular contemporary novelists, and (more rarely) the 'literary' novels of the age,[4] but seldom what is considered by the critical minority to be the significant work in fiction—the novels of D. H. Lawrence, Virginia Woolf, James Joyce, T. F. Powys, and E. M. Forster. Apart from the fact that three out of the five are held by the majority to be indecent,[5] a fact suggestive in itself, four out of the five would convey very little, if anything, to the merely literate. A librarian who has made the experiment of putting 'good' fiction into his library will report that no one would take out *South Wind* or *The Garden Party*, whereas, if he were to put two hundred more copies of Edgar Wallace's detective stories on the shelves, they would all be gone the same day. Attached to the public library is a reading-room, where a number of people can always be seen looking through the newspapers, periodicals and magazines provided.

The public library, then, is the chief source for the poorer class of reading-matter in book form. For those who can afford an annual subscription the Times Book Club and Mudie's Library exist in London (and send out boxes of books to their country clients), Messrs. W. H. Smith's bookstalls provide handy circulating libraries at railway termini and junctions, while in every town of any size Messrs. Boots, the multiple chemists, run similar libraries at very low rates. At these libraries, for the lowest payment (it need not be more than half a guinea a year), the subscriber may borrow such novels and works of history, biography, travel, essays, etc., as the library chooses to provide for him, while for a larger payment he may order what he wishes (except that by three of these firms a strict moral censorship is enforced). No figures are available,[6] and no information forthcoming from these libraries on application, but as a result of spending many hours at different branches of each and at different times of the day, the writer was able to conclude that the proportion of 'guaranteed' or 'on demand' subscriptions is not very great; that is, that in general those who are enterprising and affluent enough to subscribe to a circulating library are prepared to have their reading determined for them. And 'reading' in this case means fiction.[7] It is not an exaggeration to say that for most people 'a book' means a novel. This becomes apparent if one watches the process of selection, in which the assistant is generally consulted in some such formula as 'Another book like this one, please,' or 'Can you recommend me a nice book?' The assistant glances at the novel held out and produces another novel which is accepted without question. She may ask 'Have you read this?' and the answer will be 'I can't remember, but I'll take it.' Where criticism is offered, it almost invariably betrays a complete ignorance of values, *e.g.* a common complaint: 'I can't read Conrad, sea-stories bore me,' or alternatively: 'I like Conrad because I'm so fond of stories about the sea.' In the better districts the subscribers bring lists of novels they have copied out from the newspaper advertisements or reviews.

Undoubtedly there are subscribers who use the circulating libraries to supplement and direct their book-buying. But no one who has made a point of frequenting London and provincial branches of the book-clubs for the past few years can avoid concluding that the book-borrowing public has acquired the reading habit while somehow failing to exercise any critical intelligence about its reading. It is significant that the proportion of fiction to non-fiction borrowed is overwhelmingly great, that women rather than men change the books (that is, determine the family reading), and that many subscribers call daily to change their novels. This, along with the information volunteered by a public librarian that many take out two or three novels by Edgar Wallace a week, and the only other books they borrow are 'Sapper's' or other 'thrillers', suggests that the reading habit is now often a form of the drug habit. In suburban side-streets and even village shops it is common to find a stock of worn and greasy novels let out at 2d. or 3d. a volume; and it is surprising that a clientèle drawn from the poorest class can afford to change the books several times a week, or even daily; but so strong is the reading habit that they do.

An article in the *Publishers' Circular*[8] called 'Pushing a Lending Library' shows the kind of fiction in demand at such places. It was apparently a small suburban circulating library, which charged 3d. a week. Its regular advertisement was—

BOOKS!

Good selection by

'Sapper'	Edgar Wallace
Sax Rohmer	William Le Queux
Zane Grey	Margaret Pedler
E. M. Dell	Margaret Peterson
May Christie	Kathlyn Rhodes
	Olive Wadsley

These were the regular authors advertised, with the addition of Rider Haggard, Ruby M. Ayres, and Oppenheim, and the advertisement is reported as being highly successful. [It will be noticed that by the heading 'Books' is meant novels.]

In the case of such tuppenny dram-shops the choice of reading is determined in effect by the supply, which is the shopkeeper's attempt to provide attractive reading, but even in the great subscription libraries the client is as passive. The writer of 'a *bona-fide* experience' relates in the *Manchester Evening News*[9] how when he went into Mudie's to change a novel for his wife the assistant produced 'a detective story by J. S. Fletcher and a romantic adventure by W. J. Locke,' explaining that 'if a woman is taken up with a house all day, she doesn't want tales about married problems or misunderstood wives—she knows enough about these already; she can't be bothered with dialect after a day's work, and historical novels aren't alive enough. What she enjoys is something that is possible but outside her own experience—you see if I'm not right.' The writer adds 'And she was.'

The effect of all this upon taste will be examined later on in this study; the effects on the book market are thus described by Mr. Stanley Unwin the publisher in his important work, *The Truth About Publishing*:

> Circulating libraries are amongst the biggest buyers upon whom the town traveller calls, and here we enter upon a very thorny subject. There are some publishers who defend the circulating libraries; some who would like to see them abolished root and branch. In so far as they promptly and efficiently supply the public with the particular books for which the public asks, it is difficult to see that serious objection can be reasonably taken to them; but unfortunately the conditions here laid down are applicable only to what is known as 'guaranteed subscriptions,' and, although I have no statistics before me, I imagine that guaranteed subscribers form a tiny minority. There is no certainty that what other subscribers ask for they will be given. . . .
>
> The present system tends to assist the circulation of indifferent and bad books, and to retard the circulation of really good books, especially those by writers who have not yet established reputations. . . . There is one circulating

library that makes a boast of the extent to which it can force its subscribers to take what is given them, which means, in that particular case, what the library can buy cheapest. . . . The remedy for all this is not necessarily the abolition of circulating libraries (the circulating-library habit has become far too engrained in England for that), but the educating of the public to see that they get the books they ask for and not substitutes. . . . I feel strongly that any form of subscription other than a guaranteed subscription is pernicious.

Without going here into the question of what Mr. Unwin means by the terms 'bad books' and 'really good books', one can at least point out that the provision of novels by the commercial libraries for their subscribers means a provision for the widest common level of taste, since it pays better to buy (at a substantial discount) three hundred copies of one novel that every one will be willing to read than a few each of a hundred different books that will not circulate throughout the clientèle. Any bookseller if asked why people don't buy books will inevitably reply that the circulating libraries are responsible—'look at France, where the only way to read a book is to buy it, and haven't book-sales increased in France three- or four-fold since the war?' But though the facts are correct, the explanation is inadequate. The English public will not pay for books as freely as it pays for clothes and entrance to the cinema, but it does buy the work of the journalist—magazines (at a shilling or more a month), and any number of newspapers to a family. The French buy books because France has an educated public,[10] the English buy journals and periodicals.

Scattered liberally throughout every district, even the poorest, are newsagents' shops whose function is to supply the neighbourhood's reading; these explain the absence of bookshops. An analysis of the stock of typical newsagents[11] yielded the following representative list:

1.   Periodicals. [(A) after a title signifies American.]

   (a)   Daily and weekly newspapers in great variety.[12]
   (b)   A few cultural weeklies of different levels, ranging from the *New Statesman* and *Nation* (neither obtainable unless ordered) to *John o' London's*, which contains literary gossip, and articles about books and authors by popular writers.[13] In between comes such a paper as *Everyman* or the *Week-End Review*, that sets out to tell its readers which books they will like, or the *Listener*, published by the B.B.C.
   (c)   Weekly humorous papers such as *Punch* (based on the middle-class prejudices) and the *Humorist* (lower class).
   (d)   Seven or eight luxurious shilling illustrated news magazines with a *Punch* orientation,[14] e.g. the *Tatler, Sphere, Sketch, Sporting and Dramatic, Bystander.*
   (e)   An occasional representative of the literary periodicals (see below).
   (f)   More than a score of substantial story magazines, 6d. or 1s. monthly—*e.g.* the *Strand, Happy, Hush Magazine, Nash's, Wide World* ('The Magazine for Men'), *True Story, World Stories of Thrills and Adventure*, and several devoted to detective stories, one at least, *Black Mask*, American.
   (g)   Women's magazines—*i.e.* magazines containing stories as in class (f) but specially designed for a feminine public by means of articles on home-furnishing, housekeeping, clothes, cookery, and beauty, with a heavy cargo of advertisements.
          Twelve of these are stocked regularly—*e.g.* representative titles are *Modern Woman* ('It specialises in the *personal touch*'), *Good Housekeeping* (A), *Ideal Home,*

Delineator (A), *Woman and Beauty*, the most popular of all being American. These frequently boast of supplying 'first-class fiction.'

(*h*) Nine film magazines—not technical but filled with fiction and articles of film interest, and film publicity designed to create 'film-fans.' Of these nine, seven are American, with such names as *Motion Picture Classics* (A) ('The Magazine with a Personality'), *Screen Romances* (A), *Screen Play Secrets* (A), *Screenland* (A) ('America's Smartest Screen Magazine'), the *Motion Picture* (A), the *Picturegoer*.

A newsagent, asked of this section 'And do they sell?' replied 'Vastly.' Perhaps here should be mentioned *College Humour* (A), an American magazine devoted to articles, stories, and jokes on college life.

(*i*) 2d. weekly papers in magazine form containing the crudest marketable fiction— *e.g. London Novels* ('Was He Her Husband?'), *Love Stories* ('Only a Painted Doll'), *Peg's Paper, Eve's Own*—at least a dozen.

2. A large stock of 6d., 9d., and 1s. paper novels[15] (by popular writers such as Oppenheim, Edgar Wallace, Baroness Orczy).

3. Benn's Sixpenny Library (light educational pamphlets).

4. A selection of Benn's Sixpenny *Augustan Poets*.

5. A row or two of Nelson's 1s. 6d. Classics and a few more of 2s. popular novels.

6. An assortment of children's books, dictionaries, and cookery books.

7. A number of sixpenny novels published by the Readers' Library and the Novel Library.

The proportions may vary slightly—class 5 may be absent, or it may swell in an affluent district to include more expensive popular novels and such safe 7s. 6d. or even half-guinea works as the Forsyte volumes, *The Good Companions, The Week-End Book*, the latest P. G. Wodehouse and Ethel M. Dell, or classes 3 and 4 may not be represented. But nevertheless the significant facts emerge, that books are not generally bought but magazines are, that of these there is an enormous steady sale at all levels and prices, although there is not enough demand for serious papers to make it worth the newsagents' while to stock them on chance,[16] and that what Mr. Oliver Madox Hueffer found in his recent investigation of a poor South London suburb is largely true of the book market all over the country:

> Literature was confined to chemists' or to drapers' shops and devoted chiefly to fiction and the cheaper magazines. The few free public libraries strove, not unworthily, to cater for more serious readers, but lack of funds prevented the acquisition of new works to any useful extent and their contents were too miscellaneous to be of great value to the student.[17]

Moreover, certain reading habits have been formed and stabilised by the kind of matter provided by the magazine and the manner of its presentation. Some indication of the general trend will be found in the popularity of women's and film magazines, especially those published in America and consequently in an idiom hitherto foreign to the English periodical.

Another point to be made here is that classes (*a*), (*c*), (*d*), (*f*), (*g*), and (*h*) contain at least as much advertisement as letterpress, and when the cost of printing and illustrating the paper and the rates of payment to writers and staff are considered, it becomes evident that the price which the retailer pays for the paper or magazine is a good deal less than the cost of production. That is to say, the periodical is virtually dependent upon the advertiser,[18] so that its policy is to consider the advertisers' interests above all, and (since it only pays to advertise where sales are greatest) to sacrifice everything to a large circulation.

There is one other agent whose influence upon the book market must not be over-looked. If the Times Book Club and Mudie's serve the upper middle-class and Boots' the lower middle-class, while the news-agent's represents the bookshop for most people, there is the bookshop of the working-class to consider. Where multiple stores have a branch there is usually to be found a bazaar of the American firm, Messrs. Woolworth; here for 3d. or 6d. nearly everything necessary to existence may be bought, including literature. It is all fiction, and of three kinds. There is a counter for 2d., 3d., and 6d. paper novels by Gene Stratton Porter and the English equivalents. There is another labelled 'Yank Magazines: Interesting Reading,' where American magazines are remaindered at 3d., and of these there is presumably a steady sale, as the stock changes frequently. There is, moreover, a brisk trade done in the Readers' Library and similar 6d. cheap editions, first introduced to the public by these stores. The Foreword to each volume explains the object of the series in these terms:

> The READERS' LIBRARY is intended to bring the best-known novels of the world within the reach of the millions, by presenting at the lowest possible price per copy, in convenient size, on excellent paper, with beautiful and durable binding, a long series of the stories, copyright and non-copyright, which every one has heard of and could desire to read.
>
> Nothing of the kind has ever before been possible, even in the days when book production has been least expensive.[19] To render it possible now it will be necessary that each volume should have a sale of hundreds of thousands of copies, and that many volumes of the series should in due course find their way into nearly every home, however humble, in the British Empire.
>
> The publishers have the utmost confidence that this end will be achieved, for already, in less than five years that these books have been on the market, upwards of fifty million copies have been sold in Great Britain alone.
>
> The novels of the READERS' LIBRARY will be selected by one of the most distin-guished of living men of letters,[20] and a short biographical and bibliographical note on the author and his works will be appended to each volume.

The editor started off by choosing the popular classics (*Uncle Tom's Cabin, The Last Days of Pompeii, Pilgrim's Progress, Westward Ho!*, etc.) and writing a critical introduction to each; but soon a new principle became apparent: whenever a super-film was released—*Love* (film-version of *Anna Karenina*), *Ben Hur*, *His Lady* (film of *Manon Lescaut*), *The Man Who Laughs* (film-version of *L'Homme Qui Rit*)—'the book of the film' was published too (and advertised as such on the dust-cover, with photo-gravures from the film inside). This sold so well that the next stage was to produce an eponymous book of the film or play, when none existed, put together by a hack. These, with thrillers and very popular novelettes, now hold the field and acknowledge the frank commercialisation of a series which was hailed warmly on its appearance in 1924 by statesmen and bishops. The distinguished man of letters descended in his introductions from critic to apologist, then to a champion of popular taste,[21] last of all he contented himself with a few facts about author and story.

The latest stage is the appearance of the Readers' Library Film Edition with this Foreword:

> The Readers' Library Film Edition has been instituted to meet a real modern demand. Interest in a film is by no means exhausted merely by seeing it. The two arts, or forms of expression, the picture and the written word in book

form, react one on the other. . . . In a word, the filmgoer wishes also to read the book of the film, and the reader to see the picture.

   To meet this undeniable call for literature associated with the film, it would not be enough to produce books of inferior quality. . . . *Publication will coincide with the appearance of each new and important film.*[22]

The distinguished man of letters has been dropped in favour of the American film-producer, a change all the easier since the 'talkie' furnishes ready-made dialogue. The introductory paragraph is now significantly directed away from literature, and the appeal to the reader is focussed on the film-star:

'The Rogue Song,' based on the popular romantic musical comedy 'Gipsy Love,' is one of the most colourful achievements of the talking screen. The story makes a gripping novel, and Mr. Val Lewton's style has captured all the melody and romance of the film, which has for its star Lawrence Tibbett, America's greatest baritone. . . . This heart-throbbing romance of a gypsy bandit's love for a beautiful princess forms one of the most delightful film novels we have yet published.

There appears to be money in 'literature associated with the film', for the Novel Library ('For Fiction Lovers') has similarly gone over to the talkies. Starting, like the Leisure Library Ltd. and the Detective Story Club Ltd.,[23] as a close imitation of the Readers' Library, it has stopped publishing Wells and Galsworthy for the masses and now produces the book of the talkie:

Welcome Danger is introduced to the public in the language of the talkies—'Know Harold Lloyd? Sure. Seen him in "College Days" and "Safety Last"? Sure. Well, you haven't laughed until you've seen him in "Welcome Danger"—the funniest thing he's done yet. And you'll be tickled to death when you read the book, for in it you get right close up to Harold,' etc.

   The effect of the increasing control by Big Business—in which it would hardly be unreasonable, on the strength of the evidence above, to include the film interests—is to destroy among the masses a desire to read anything which by the widest stretch could be included in the classification 'literature', and to substitute something which is best described by the title-page of a specimen:

'The Girl from China'
   novelized by Karen Brown.
Adapted from
   John Cotton's
      DRIFTING
         Universal Picture
      Starring MARY NOLAN.

A selection of the Readers' Library is now sold by most newsagents, but the chief sale of these libraries is still at the bazaars. Here, while passing from counter to counter to buy cheap crockery, strings of beads, lamp-shades, and toffee, toys, soap, and flower-bulbs, and under the stimulus of 6d. gramophone records filling the air with 'Headin' for Hollywood' and 'Love Never Dies', the customer is beguiled into patronising literature. If it is a country town, the bazaar is packed on market-day with the country folk who come in once a week to do their shopping, so that Woolworth literature supplies the county with reading,[24] if it is a city, the housewives of the district make their regular tour on Saturdays, though a constant stream passes along the counters handling the goods throughout the week. So paper-covered novels by Nat Gould, Charles Garvice and Joseph Hocking,[25] P. C. Wren, Sabatini and Phillips Oppenheim; American magazines—*Ranch Romances* ('Love Stories of the Real West'), *Far-West Stories, Love Romances* ('Gripping clean love stories'), *The Popular Magazine* ('America's Best and Brightest Fiction Magazine'), *Marriage Stories, Detective Classics, Black Mask* ('Detective Fiction'), *Gangster Stories* ('A Magazine of Racketeers and Gun Molls'); and sixpenny books—*Harem Love* ('by Joan Conquest, author of *Desert Love*'), *Officer* ('An Underworld Thriller by Hulbert Footner'), *The King of Kings* (the story of the super-film of Christianity); all go home in the shopping baskets.

References

1   Whearas a German publisher only spends 3 per cent. to 4 per cent. of the *cost of production* on advertising, the English publisher spends about 6 per cent. of his *turnover* in advertisement, while the American publisher George H. Doran claims to spend 10 per cent. of his *gross income* on 'promotion'. This information, obtained from the article 'Publishing' in the *Ency. Brit.* (14th ed.), of course proves nothing, but it does suggest the general proposition that the more cultured a country the less its publishers would have to spend in forcing books on the public attention.

2   A really popular-at-all-levels novel like *The Constant Nymph*, which was the book of the year 1924–25, has only sold a million copies, and those largely in the 6d. Readers' Library edition.

3   These figures are taken from the Report on Public Libraries (1927). It has been suggested to me by an eminent and experienced public librarian that the relative percentages of fiction and non-fiction would be even more disproportionate were it not that librarians, actuated presumably by local patriotism, endeavour to equalise matters by transferring such sections as 'Juvenile Fiction' and 'Classical Novels' over to the non-fiction classifications.

4   By 'literary novels' is meant those contemporary novels which the general public accepts as 'literature'. I will anticipate for the reader's convenience by stating here that it includes the works of Willa Cather, Thornton Wilder, John Galsworthy, and David Garnett, among others.

5   The head of a big public library (and in a University town), when asked why there were no novels by D.H. Lawrence on the shelves, replied indignantly: 'I've always tried to keep this library *clean*.'

6   Arthur Waugh, *A Hundred Years of Publishing* (1930), says there are 340 branches of Boots' Library, with a quarter of a million subscribers.

7   When these libraries sell off their out-of-date stock several times a year, the novels are generally worn and shabby, while the other books are 'good as new.'

8   August 6th, 1927.

9   February 22nd, 1926.

10   A random instance from the *Times* (June 24th, 1930): 'In honour of the centenary of the French Romantic movement, the western façade of Notre Dame was brilliantly illuminated by floodlighting on Sunday evening.' The English general public has never heard of the English Romantic movement, and the governing classes who possibly would not in any case think of taking up a serious attitude to it. Cf. too the space given in any French newspaper to the death of a man of letters and a purely literary event with the absence of such an interest in England. Also the two main features of English journalism, the Sunday paper and the large-circulation newspaper, are both unknown in France. In contrast to the responsible interest in literature so evident in the French Press, that little attention is paid by the English journalist to the recent appointment of a Poet Laureate is significant. The announcement was made on a Saturday, and an inspection of the next day's newspapers showed that not one of the popular Sunday organs thought the news worth mentioning (one published a photograph of the new Laureate without comment), though the appointment was what might be called a popular one.

11   Taken as common to a majority of the following: a flourishing shop in the centre of a market

town, a back-street 'paper-shop,' the contents of the periodicals rack in a Boots' store, a W.H. Smith shop, a suburban newsagent's.

12   A foreigner's opinion of the English Press is illuminating. The intelligent and open-minded Dibelius (*England*, Cape, 1930) comments on the superior appearance and good workmanship of English newspapers, and concludes: 'In this respect the English standard is very high indeed, certainly higher than the German. But a different picture is given by a comparison of the contents of the newspapers of the two countries. While, in this respect, the better-class English newspaper, like the *Morning Post, Manchester Guardian*, or *Daily Chronicle* [now defunct], certainly does not give its readers any more than the *Deutsche Allgemeine, Vossische*, the *Frankfurter Zeitung* or *Hamburger Fremdenblatt*, the great mass of English newspapers, even in the metropolis, are incredibly thin and empty. Most of them, in sharp contrast to the half-dozen or so papers with an international reputation, have practically no foreign news, little or no literary or general information, and no magazine page; they are made up of leaders, telegrams, local gossip, and a mass of sporting news. In the provinces, there is the *Scotsman* and *Glasgow Herald* in Scotland, and, in the industrial areas, the *Birmingham Daily Post, Liverpool Daily Post*, the *Yorkshire Post*, and the admirable *Manchester Guardian*; but outside this half-dozen there is an almost unbelievable dullness. No one who has not been condemned to read a local sheet of that sort regularly can understand the empty chatter that does duty as the average play or the popular novel . . .'

13   In the *Advertiser's ABC* it describes itself in these terms: 'John O'London's Weekly has unique powers of appeal. It is not a paper only for women or only for men; it is a paper for both; for the whole family, and it is calculated to make a direct appeal to clear-thinking people of educated tastes and a discriminating standard of comfort.

14   The scope of these is best suggested by their own advertisements in the *Advertiser's ABC* (1929): 'It exists to remind its readers that life is not all work and worry; that there is a more leisurely, laughing side, which contributes so much to make it worth living. The Editorial policy of the Tatler embraces all the lighter interests of the well-to-do Englishman – Sport, Society, Motoring, Art, the Theatre. It is found in every club and regimental mess, in every doctor's waiting room, hotel lounge.' 'The Sphere is representative of all that is best in English life. The Sphere is read by the very rich, the moderately rich, and by the ordinary well-to-do folk of intelligence and culture throughout the Empire. It is in the Empire's Illustrated Weekly Journal, and is found, not only in club-rooms, hotels and libraries, but in the homes of the best people throughout the English-speaking world.' 'The Sketch was the first expression of an entirely new idea in British Illustrated Journalism. Before its appearance, in 1893, illustrated newspapers devoted themselves almost exclusively to the more serious of current happenings . . . It sets itself to provide cheery entertainment for the smoking room and boudoir, and to illustrate the subjects most commonly discussed when men and women meet after the serious business of the say is done. Its instant and signal success is a matter of history. Inevitably it had many imitators,' etc.

15   It may be useful to point out here that there is no reason for supposing that novelettes are bought exclusively by the uneducated and the poor. A list kindly made for me of the private reading-matter in a high-class establishment states that the young men own all varieties of film and detective-story magazine mentioned above, 3s. 6d. and 7s. 6d. novels by Rider Haggard, Baroness Orczy, John Buchan, Edgar Wallace, Freeman Willis Crofts, and also, 'There are a great number of 9d. and 1s. paper novels circulating among them, most of them by Edgar Wallace and Oppenheim.'

16   The writer has vainly tried to buy the *Nation and Athenæum, New Statesman*, and *Times Literary Supplement* all over south-western England, and obtained them only (but not invariably) at the bookstalls at big railway junctions. The newsagents in many cases showed no knowledge of the names even. It is worth remembering that in France there are at least three serious literary weekly *newspapers* (*i.e.* literary journals in newspaper form which review intelligently all the notable poetry and criticism that appear as well as lighter works, and have leading articles on literary movements by distinguished writers), and they can all be bought in the ordinary way in the little provincial towns (and are usually sold out on the day of issue).

17   *Some of the English* (1930), by Oliver Madox Hueffer, p. 291.

18   For illustration see *Is Advertising To-Day a Burden or a Boon?* (The New Advertiser's Press, 1930).

19   On the contrary, for before the war Messrs. Nelson published pocket editions of the classics and

good copyright novels (*e.g.* Jane Austen, George Eliot, Thackeray, the Brontës, in Nelson's Classics, the early Wells, and Henry James and Conrad, in Nelson's Library) at 6d. and 7d. each, that really were well printed and bound.

20   The Manager of the Readers' Library Publishing Co. Ltd., when requested to put the writer into communication with the editor of the series, regretted that he was unable to do so or to furnish any information, so that not only the identity of this distinguished man of letters, but also the principle on which he chooses the volumes for publication, must remain a dark secret.

21   'Edgar Wallace, although so immensely successful in his own line of work, is too modest a man to claim that the mystery story necessarily belongs to the highest form of literature, although some of its examples are assuredly among the best.' – From the introduction to *The Melody of Death*, 'the first book by Edgar Wallace the READERS' LIBRARY has had the honour to publish' (1927).

22   The italics are mine.

23   All three are sold along with the Readers' Library.

24   'Before I conclude this letter, I cannot help observing that the sale of books in general has increased prodigiously within the last twenty years. According to the best estimate I have been able to make, I suppose that more than four times the number of books are sold now than were sold twenty years since. The poorest sort of farmers, and even the poor country people in general, who before that period spent their winter evenings in relating stories of witches, ghosts, hobgoblins, &c. now shorten the winter nights by hearing their sons and daughters read tales, romances, &c., and on entering their houses you may see Tom Jones, Roderick Random, and other entertaining books stuck up on their bacon racks, &c. If *John* goes to town with a load of hay, he is charged to be sure not to forget to bring home "Peregrine Pickle's Adventures"; and when *Dolly* is sent to market to sell her eggs, she is commissioned to purchase "The history of Pamela Andrews." '—*Memoirs of the first forty-five years of The Life of James Lackington, Bookseller*, written by himself, 2nd ed. 1792, p. 386.

25   It is interesting to notice that Woolworth fiction has revived 'best sellers' of the last generation with considerable success: Garvice and Hocking appear to sell nearly as well as P.C. Wren and Edgar Wallace.

Chapter 2

Robert Darnton

FIRST STEPS TOWARDS A HISTORY OF READING[1]

BOTH FAMILIAR AND FOREIGN, [reading] is an activity that we share with our ancestors yet can never be the same as what they experienced. We may enjoy the illusion of stepping outside of time in order to make contact with authors who lived centuries ago. But even if their texts have come down to us unchanged—a virtual impossibility, considering the evolution of layout and of books as physical objects—our relation to those texts cannot be the same as that of readers in the past. Reading has a history. But how can we recover it?

We could begin by searching the record for readers. Carlo Ginzburg found one, a humble miller from sixteenth-century Friulia, in the papers of the Inquisition. Probing for heresy, the inquisitor asked his victim about his reading. Menocchio replied with a string of titles and elaborate comments on each of them. By comparing the texts and the commentary, Ginzburg discovered that Menocchio had read a great deal of biblical stories, chronicles, and travel books of the kind that existed in many patrician libraries. Menocchio did not simply receive messages transmitted down through the social order. He read aggressively, transforming the contents of the material at his disposition into a radically non-Christian view of the world. Whether that view can be traced to an ancient popular tradition, as Ginzburg claims, is a matter of debate; but Ginzburg certainly demonstrated the possibility of studying reading as an activity among the common people four centuries ago.[2]

I ran across a solidly middle-class reader in my own research on eighteenth-century France. He was a merchant from La Rochelle named Jean Ranson and an impassioned Rousseauist. Ranson did not merely read Rousseau and weep: he incorporated Rousseau's ideas in the fabric of his life as he set up business, fell in love, married, and raised his children. Reading and living run parallel as leitmotifs in a rich series of letters that Ranson wrote between 1774 and 1785 and show how Rousseauism became absorbed in the way of life of the provincial bourgeoisie under the Old Regime. Rousseau had received a flood of letters from readers like Ranson after the publication of *La Nouvelle Héloïse*. It was, I believe, the first tidal wave of fan mail in the history of literature, although Richardson had already produced some impressive ripples in England. The mail reveals that readers everywhere in France responded as Ranson did and, furthermore, that their responses conformed to those Rousseau had called for in the two prefaces to his novel. He had instructed his readers how to read him. He had assigned them roles and provided them with a strategy for taking in his novel. The new way of reading worked so well that *La Nouvelle Héloïse* became the greatest best seller of the century, the most important single source of romantic sensibility. That sensibility is now extinct. No modern reader can weep his way through the six volumes of *La Nouvelle Héloïse* as his predecessors did two centuries ago. But in his day, Rousseau captivated an entire generation of readers by revolutionizing reading itself.[3]

The examples of Menocchio and Ranson suggest that reading and living, construing texts and making sense of life, were much more closely related in the early modern period than they are today. But before jumping to conclusions, we need to work through more archives, comparing readers' accounts of their experience with the protocols of reading in their books and, when possible, with their behavior.

[. . .]

In each case the fiction could be fleshed out and compared with documents—actual suicide notes, diaries, and letters to the editor. The correspondence of authors and the papers of publishers are ideal sources of information about real readers. [. . .]

In short, it should be possible to develop a history as well as a theory of reader response. Possible, but not easy; for the documents rarely show readers at work, fashioning meaning from texts, and the documents are texts themselves, which also require interpretation. Few of them are rich enough to provide even indirect access to the cognitive and affective elements of reading, and a few exceptional cases may not be enough for one to reconstruct the inner dimensions of that experience. But historians of the book have already turned up a great deal of information about the external history of reading. Having studied it as a social phenomenon, they can answer many of the "who," "what," "where," and "when" questions, which can be of great help in attacking the more difficult "whys" and "hows."

Studies of who read what at different times fall into two main types, the macro- and the microanalytical. Macroanalysis has flourished above all in France, where it feeds on a powerful tradition of quantitative social history. Henri-Jean Martin, François Furet, Robert Estivals, and Frédéric Barbier have traced the evolution of reading habits from the sixteenth century to the present, using long-term series constructed from the *dépôt légal*, registers of book privileges, and the annual *Bibliographie de la France*. One can see many intriguing phenomena in the undulations of their graphs: the decline of Latin, the rise of the novel, the general fascination with the immediate world of nature and the remote worlds of exotic countries that spread throughout the educated public between the time of Descartes and Bougainville. The Germans have constructed a still longer series of statistics, thanks to a peculiarly rich source: the catalogues of the Frankfurt and Leipzig book fairs, which extend from the mid-sixteenth to the mid-nineteenth century. (The Frankfurt catalogue was published without interruption from 1564 to 1749, and the Leipzig catalogue, which dates from 1594, can be replaced for the period after 1797 by the *Hinrichssche Verzeichnisse*.) Although the catalogues have their drawbacks, they provide a rough index to German reading since the Renaissance; and they have been mined by a succession of German book historians since Johann Goldfriedrich published his monumental *Geschichte des deutschen Buchhandels* in 1908–09. The English-reading world has no comparable source; but for the period after 1557, when London began to dominate the printing industry, the papers of the London Stationers' Company have provided H. S. Bennett, W. W. Greg, and others with plenty of material to trace the evolution of the English book trade. Although the British tradition of bibliography has not favored the compilation of statistics, there is a great deal of quantitative information in the short-title catalogues that run from 1475. Giles Barber has drawn some Frenchlike graphs from customs records. And Robert Winans and G. Thomas Tanselle have taken the measure of early American reading by reworking Charles Evans's enormous

American Bibliography (eighteen thousand entries for the period 1638–1783, including, unfortunately, an undetermined population of "ghosts").[4]

All this compiling and computing has provided some guidelines to reading habits, but the generalizations sometimes seem too general to be satisfying. The novel, like the bourgeoisie, always seems to be rising; and the graphs drop at the expected points—most notably during the Thirty Years' War at the Leipzig fair, and during World War I in France. Most of the quantifiers sort their statistics into vague categories like "arts and sciences" and "belles-lettres," which are inadequate for identifying particular phenomena like the Succession Controversy, Jansenism, the Enlightenment, or the Gothic Revival—the very subjects that have attracted the most attention among literary scholars and cultural historians. The quantitative history of books will have to refine its categories and sharpen its focus before it can have a major impact on traditional strains of scholarship.

Yet the quantifiers have uncovered some significant statistical patterns, and their achievements would look even more impressive if there were more of an effort to make comparisons from one country to another. For example, the statistics suggest that the cultural revival of Germany in the late eighteenth century was connected with an epidemic-like fever for reading, the so-called *Lesewut* or *Lesesucht*. The Leipzig catalogue did not reach the level it had attained before the Thirty Years' War until 1764, when it included 1,200 titles of newly published books. With the onset of *Sturm und Drang*, it rose to 1,600 titles in 1770; then 2,600 in 1780 and 5,000 in 1800. The French followed a different pattern. Book production grew steadily for a century after the Peace of Westphalia (1648)—a century of great literature, from Corneille to the *Encyclopédie*, which coincided with the decline in Germany. But in the next fifty years, when the German figures soared, the French increase looks relatively modest. According to Robert Estivals, requests for authorization to publish new books (*privilèges* and *permissions tacites*) came to 729 in 1764, 896 in 1770, and only 527 in 1780; and the new titles submitted to the *dépôt légal* in 1800 totaled 700. To be sure, different kinds of documents and standards of measurement could produce different results, and the official sources exclude the enormous production of illegal French books. But whatever their deficiencies, the figures indicate a great leap forward in German literary life after a century of French domination. Germany also had more writers, although the population of the French- and German-speaking areas was roughly the same. A German literary almanac, *Das gelehrte Teutschland*, listed 3,000 living authors in 1772 and 4,300 in 1776. A comparable French publication, *La France littéraire*, included 1,187 authors in 1757 and 2,367 in 1769. While Voltaire and Rousseau were sinking into old age, Goethe and Schiller were riding a wave of literary creativity that was far more powerful than one might think if one considered only the conventional histories of literature.[5]

Cross-statistical comparisons also provide help in charting cultural currents. After tabulating book privileges throughout the eighteenth century, François Furet found a marked decline in the older branches of learning, especially the humanist and classical Latin literature that had flourished a century earlier according to the statistics of Henri-Jean Martin. Newer genres such as the books classified under the rubric "arts and sciences" prevailed after 1750. Daniel Roche and Michel Marion noticed a similar tendency in surveying Parisian notarial archives. Novels, travel books, and works on natural history tended to crowd out the classics in the libraries of noblemen and wealthy bourgeois. All the studies point to a significant drop in religious literature during the eighteenth century. They confirm the quantitative research in other areas of social history—Michel Vovelle's on funeral rituals, for example, and Dominique Julia's investigation of clerical ordinations and teaching practices.[6]

The thematic surveys of German reading complement those of the French. Rudolf Jentzsch and Albert Ward found a strong drop in Latin books and a corresponding increase in novels in the fair catalogues of Leipzig and Frankfurt. By the late nineteenth century, according to Eduard Reyer and Rudolf Schenda, borrowing patterns in German, English, and American libraries had fallen into a strikingly similar pattern: 70–80 percent of the books came from the category of light fiction (mostly novels); 10 percent came from history, biography, and travel; and less than 1 percent came from religion. In little more than two hundred years, the world of reading had been transformed. The rise of the novel had balanced a decline in religious literature, and in almost every case the turning point could be located in the second half of the eighteenth century, especially in the 1770s, the years of the *Wertherfieber*. *Die Leiden des jungen Werthers* produced an even more spectacular response in Germany than *La Nouvelle Héloïse* had in France or *Pamela* in England. [. . .]

Thus for all their variety and occasional contradictions, the macroanalytical studies suggest some general conclusions, something akin to Max Weber's "demystification of the world." That, however, may seem too cosmic for comfort. Those who prefer precision may turn to microanalysis, although it usually goes to the opposite extreme—excessive detail. We have hundreds of lists of books in libraries from the Middle Ages to the present, more than anyone can bear to read. Yet most of us would agree that a catalogue of a private library can serve as a profile of a reader, even though we don't read all the books we own and we do read many books that we never purchase. To scan the catalogue of the library in Monticello is to inspect the furnishings of Jefferson's mind.[7] And the study of private libraries has the advantage of linking the "what" with the "who" of reading.

The French have taken the lead in this area, too. Daniel Mornet's essay of 1910, "Les Enseignements des bibliothèques privées," demonstrated that the study of library catalogues could produce conclusions that challenged some of the commonplaces of literary history. After tabulating titles from five hundred eighteenth-century catalogues, he found only one copy of the book that was to be the bible of the French Revolution, Rousseau's *Social Contract*. The libraries bulged with the works of authors who had been completely forgotten, and they provided no basis for connecting certain kinds of literature (the work of the philosophers, for example) with certain classes of readers (the bourgeoisie). Seventy years and several refutations later, Mornet's work still looks impressive. But a vast literature has grown up around it. We now have statistics on the libraries of noblemen, magistrates, priests, academicians, burghers, artisans, and even some domestic servants. The French scholars have studied reading across the social strata of certain cities—the Caen of Jean-Claude Perrot, the Paris of Michel Marion—and throughout entire regions—the Normandy of Jean Quéniart, the Languedoc of Madeleine Ventre. For the most part, they rely on *inventaires après décès*, notarial records of books in the estates of the deceased. So they suffer from the bias built into the documents, which generally neglect books of little commercial value or limit themselves to vague statements like "a pile of books." But the notarial eye took in a great deal in France, far more than in Germany, where Rudolf Schenda considers inventories woefully inadequate as a guide to the reading habits of the common people. The most thorough German study is probably Walter Wittmann's survey of inventories from the late eighteenth century in Frankfurt am Main. It indicates that books were owned by 100 percent of the higher officials, 51 percent of the tradesmen, 35 percent of the master artisans, and 26 percent of the journeymen. Daniel Roche found a similar pattern among the common people of Paris: only 35 percent of the salaried workers and domestic servants who appear in the notarial archives around 1780 owned books. But Roche also discovered many indications of familiarity with the written word. By 1789 almost all the domestic servants could sign their names on the inventories. A great many owned desks, fully equipped with writing implements and packed with family papers. Most artisans and shopkeepers spent several years of their childhood in school. Before 1789 Paris had five hundred primary schools, one for every thousand inhabitants, most of them free. Parisians were readers,

Roche concludes, but reading did not take the form of the books that show up in inventories. It involved chapbooks, broadsides, posters, personal letters, and even the signs on the streets. Parisians read their way through the city and through their lives, but their ways of reading did not leave enough evidence in the archives for the historian to follow closely on their heels.[8]

He must therefore search for other sources. Subscription lists have been a favorite, though they normally cover only rather wealthy readers. From the late seventeenth to the early nineteenth century, many books were published by subscription in Britain and contained lists of the subscribers. Researchers at the Project for Historical Biobibliography at Newcastle upon Tyne have used these lists to work toward a historical sociology of readership. Similar efforts are under way in Germany, especially among scholars of Klopstock and Wieland. Perhaps a sixth of new German books were published by subscription between 1770 and 1810, when the practice reached its peak. But even during their *Blütezeit*, the subscription lists do not provide an accurate view of readership. They left off the names of many subscribers, included others who functioned as patrons instead of as readers, and generally represented the salesmanship of a few entrepreneurs rather than the reading habits of the educated public, according to some devastating criticism that Reinhard Wittmann has directed against subscription-list research. The work of Wallace Kirsop suggests that such research may succeed better in France, where publishing by subscription also flourished in the late eighteenth century. But the French lists, like the others, generally favor the wealthiest readers and the fanciest books.[9]

The records of lending libraries offer a better opportunity to make connections between literary genres and social classes, but few of them survive. The most remarkable are the registers of borrowings from the ducal library of Wolfenbüttel, which extend from 1666 to 1928. According to Wolfgang Milde, Paul Raabe, and John McCarthy, they show a significant "democratization" of reading in the 1760s: the number of books borrowed doubled; the borrowers came from lower social strata (they included a few porters, lackeys, and lower officers in the army); and the reading matter became lighter, shifting from learned tomes to sentimental novels (imitations of *Robinson Crusoe* went over especially well). [. . .]

The microanalysts have come up with many other discoveries—so many, in fact, that they face the same problem as the macroquantifiers: how to put it all together? The disparity of the documentation—auction catalogues, notarial records, subscription lists, library registers—does not make the task easier. Differences in conclusions can be attributed to the peculiarities of the sources rather than to the behavior of the readers. And the monographs often cancel each other out: artisans look literate here and unlettered there; travel literature seems to be popular among some groups in some places and unpopular in others. A systematic comparison of genres, milieux, times, and places would look like a conspiracy of exceptions trying to disprove rules.

So far only one book historian has been hardy enough to propose a general model. Rolf Engelsing has argued that a "reading revolution" *(Leserevolution)* took place at the end of the eighteenth century. From the Middle Ages until sometime after 1750, according to Engelsing, men read "intensively." They had only a few books—the Bible, an almanac, a devotional work or two—and they read them over and over again, usually aloud and in groups, so that a narrow range of traditional literature became deeply impressed on their consciousness. By 1800 men were reading "extensively." They read all kinds of material, especially periodicals and newspapers, and read it only once, then raced on to the next item. Engelsing does not produce much evidence for his hypothesis. Indeed, most of his research concerns only a small sampling of burghers in Bremen. But it has an attractive before-and-after simplicity, and it provides a handy formula for contrasting modes of reading very early and very late in European history. Its main drawback, as I see it, is its unilinear character.

Reading did not evolve in one direction, extensiveness. It assumed many different forms among different social groups in different eras. Men and women have read in order to save their souls, to improve their manners, to repair their machinery, to seduce their sweet-hearts, to learn about current events, and simply to have fun. In many cases, especially among the public of Richardson, Rousseau, and Goethe, the reading became more intensive, not less. But the late eighteenth century does seem to represent a turning point, a time when more reading matter became available to a wider public, when one can see the emergence of a mass readership that would grow to giant proportions in the nineteenth century with the development of machine-made paper, steam-powered presses, linotype, and nearly universal literacy. All these changes opened up new possibilities, not by decreasing intensity but by increasing variety.[10]

I must therefore confess to some skepticism about the "reading revolution." Yet an American historian of the book, David Hall, has described a transformation in the reading habits of New Englanders between 1600 and 1850 in almost exactly the same terms as those used by Engelsing. Before 1800, New Englanders read a small corpus of venerable "steady sellers"—the Bible, almanacs, the *New England Primer*, Philip Doddridge's *Rise and Progress of Religion*, Richard Baxter's *Call to the Unconverted*—and read them over and over again, aloud, in groups, and with exceptional intensity. After 1800 they were swamped with new kinds of books—novels, newspapers, fresh and sunny varieties of children's literature—and they read through them ravenously, discarding one thing as soon as they could find another. Although Hall and Engelsing had never heard of one another, they discovered a similar pattern in two quite different areas of the Western world. Perhaps a fundamental shift in the nature of reading took place at the end of the eighteenth century. [. . .]

The "where" of reading is more important than one might think, because placing the reader in his setting can provide hints about the nature of his experience. In the University of Leyden there hangs a print of the university library, dated 1610. It shows the books, heavy folio volumes, chained on high shelves jutting out from the walls in a sequence determined by the rubrics of classical bibliography: *Jurisconsulti, Medici, Historici,* and so on. Students are scattered about the room, reading the books on counters built at shoulder level below the shelves. They read standing up, protected against the cold by thick cloaks and hats, one foot perched on a rail to ease the pressure on their bodies. Reading cannot have been comfortable in the age of classical humanism. In pictures done a century and a half later, "La Lecture" and "La Liseuse" by Fragonard, for example, readers recline in chaises longues or well-padded armchairs with their legs propped on footstools. They are often women, wearing loose-fitting gowns known at the time as *liseuses*. They usually hold a dainty duodecimo volume in their fingers and have a faraway look in their eye. From Fragonard to Monet, who also painted a "Liseuse," reading moves from the boudoir to the outdoors. The reader backpacks books to fields and mountaintops where, like Rousseau and Heine, he can commune with nature. Nature must have seemed out of joint a few generations later in the trenches of World War I, where the young lieutenants from Göttingen and Oxford somehow found room for a few slim volumes of poetry. One of the most precious books in my own small collection is an edition of Hölderlin's *Hymnen an die Ideale der Menschheit*, inscribed "Adolf Noelle, Januar 1916, nord-Frankreich"—a gift from a German friend who was trying to explain Germany. I'm still not sure I understand, but I think the general understanding of reading would be advanced if we thought harder about its iconography and accoutrements, including furniture and dress.[11]

Of course, one cannot take pictures literally, as a depiction of how people actually read. But they can reveal hidden assumptions about what people thought reading should be or the atmosphere in which it should take place.

[. . .]

[F]or the common people in early modern Europe, reading was a social activity. It took place in workshops, barns, and taverns. It was almost always oral but not necessarily edifying.

[. . .]

The most important institution of popular reading under the Old Regime was a fireside gathering known as the *veillée* in France and the *Spinnstube* in Germany. While children played, women sewed, and men repaired tools, one of the company who could decipher a text would regale them with the adventures of *Les quatre fils Aymon, Till Eulenspiegel*, or some other favorite from the standard repertory of the cheap, popular chapbooks. Some of these primitive paperbacks indicated that they were meant to be taken in through the ears by beginning with phrases such as, "What you are about to hear . . .". In the nineteenth century, groups of artisans, especially cigar makers and tailors, took turns reading or hired a reader to keep themselves entertained while they worked.

[. . .]

Reading was a more private experience for the minority of educated persons who could afford to buy books. But many of them joined reading clubs, *cabinets littéraires*, or *Lesegesellschaften*, where they could read almost anything they wanted, in a social atmosphere, for a small monthly payment. Françoise Parent-Lardeur has traced the proliferation of these clubs in Paris under the Restoration, but they went back well into the eighteenth century. Provincial booksellers often turned their stock into a library and charged dues for the right to frequent it. Good light, some comfortable chairs, a few pictures on the wall, and subscriptions to a half-dozen newspapers were enough to make a club out of almost any bookshop. Thus the *cabinet littéraire* advertized by P. J. Bernard, a minor bookseller in Lunéville: "A large, comfortable, well-lit, and well-heated house, which will be open every day from nine in the morning until noon and from one o'clock until ten in the evening, will provide members with two thousand volumes; and the stock will be increased by four hundred each year. . . . A room on the ground floor and another on the second floor will be reserved for conversation; all the others will be placed at the disposition of readers of newspapers and books." By November 1779, the club had two hundred members, mostly officers from the local *gendarmerie*. For the modest sum of three livres a year, they had access to five thousand books, thirteen journals, and special rooms set aside for socializing.[12]

German reading clubs provided the social foundation for a distinct variety of bourgeois culture in the eighteenth century, according to Otto Dann. They sprang up at an astounding rate, especially in the northern cities. Martin Welke estimates that perhaps one of every five hundred adult Germans belonged to a *Lesegesellschaft* by 1800. Marlies Prüsener has been able to identify well over four hundred of the clubs and to form some idea of their reading matter. All of them had a basic supply of periodicals supplemented by uneven runs of books, usually on fairly weighty subjects like history and politics. They seem to have been a more serious version of the coffee-house, itself an important institution for reading, which spread through Germany from the late seventeenth century. By 1760, Vienna had at least sixty coffeehouses. They provided newspapers, journals, and endless occasions for political discussions, just as they had in London and Amsterdam for more than a century.[13]

Thus we already know a good deal about the institutional bases of reading. We have some answers to the "who," "what," "where," and "when" questions. But the "whys" and "hows" elude us. We have not yet devised a strategy for understanding the inner process by which readers made sense of words. We do not even understand the way we read ourselves, despite the efforts of psychologists and neurologists to trace eye movements and to map the hemispheres of the brain. Is the cognitive process different for Chinese, who read pictographs, and for Westerners, who scan lines? For Israelis who read words without vowels moving from right to left and for blind people who transmit stimuli through their fingers?

For Southeast Asians whose languages lack tenses and order reality spatially and for American Indians whose languages have been reduced to writing only recently by alien scholars? For the holy man in the presence of the Word and for the consumer studying labels in a supermarket? The differences seem endless, for reading is not simply a skill but a way of making meaning, which must vary from culture to culture. It would be extravagant to expect to find a formula that could account for all those variations. But it should be possible to develop a way to study the changes in reading within our own culture. I would like to suggest five approaches to the problem.

First, I think it should be possible to learn more about the ideals and assumptions underlying reading in the past. We could study contemporary depictions of reading in fiction, autobiographies, polemical writings, letters, paintings, and prints in order to uncover some basic notions of what people thought took place when they read. Consider, for example, the great debate about the craze for reading in late eighteenth-century Germany. Those who deplored the *Lesewut* did not simply condemn its effects on morals and politics. They feared it would damage public health. In a tract of 1795, J. G. Heinzmann listed the physical consequences of excessive reading: "susceptibility to colds, headaches, weakening of the eyes, heat rashes, gout, arthritis, hemorrhoids, asthma, apoplexy, pulmonary disease, indigestion, blocking of the bowels, nervous disorder, migraines, epilepsy, hypochondria, and melancholy." On the positive side of the debate, Johann Adam Bergk accepted the premises of his opponents but disagreed with their conclusions. He took it as established that one should never read immediately after eating or while standing up. But by correct disposition of the body, one could make reading a force for good. The "art of reading" involved washing the face with cold water and taking walks in fresh air as well as concentration and meditation.

No one challenged the notion that there was a physical element in reading, because no one drew a clear distinction between the physical and the moral world. In the eighteenth and nineteenth centuries, readers attempted to "digest" books, to absorb them in their whole being, body and soul. A few extremists took to reading-as-digestion literally: thus the case of a woman in Hampshire, England, who "ate a New Testament, day by day and leaf by leaf, between two sides of bread and butter, as a remedy for fits." More often the devouring of books took the form of a spiritual exercise, whose physicality still shows on the surviving pages. The volumes from Samuel Johnson's library, now owned by Mrs. Donald F. Hyde, are bent and battered, as if he had wrestled his way through them.[14]

Reading as a spiritual exercise predominated in the sixteenth and seventeenth centuries. But how was it performed? One could look for guidance in the manuals of Jesuits and the hermeneutical treatises of Protestants. Family Bible readings took place on both sides of the great religious divide. And as the example of Restif de la Bretonne indicates, the Bible was approached with awe, even among some Catholic peasants. Of course, Boccaccio, Castiglione, Cervantes, Erasmus, and Rabelais had developed other uses of literacy for the elite. But for most people, reading remained a sacred activity. It put you in the presence of the Word and unlocked holy mysteries. As a working hypothesis, it seems valid to assert that the farther back in time you go the farther away you move from instrumental reading. Not only does the "how-to" book become rarer and the religious book more common; reading itself is different. In the age of Luther and Loyola, it provided access to absolute truth.

On a more mundane level, assumptions about reading could be traced through advertisements and prospectuses for books. Thus some typical remarks from an eighteenth-century prospectus taken at random from the rich collection in the Newberry Library: a book seller is offering a quarto edition of the *Commentaires sur la coutume d'Angoumois*, an excellent work, he insists, for its typography as much as its content: "The text of the *Coutume* is printed in *gros-romain* type; the summaries that precede the commentaries are printed in *cicéro*; and the commentaries are printed in *Saint-Augustin*. The whole work is made from very beautiful paper manufactured in Angoulême."[15] No publisher would dream of mentioning paper and type in advertising a law book today. In the eighteenth century advertisers assumed that their clients cared about the physical quality of books. Buyers and sellers alike shared a typographical consciousness that is now nearly extinct.

The reports of censors also can be revealing, at least in the case of books from early modern France, where censorship was highly developed if not enormously effective. A typical travel book, *Nouveau voyage aux isles de l'Amérique* (Paris, 1722) by J.-B. Labat, contains four "approbations" printed out in full next to the *privilège*. One censor explains that the manuscript piqued his curiosity: "It is difficult to begin reading it without feeling that mild but avid curiosity that impels us to read further." Another recommends it for its "simple and concise style" and also for its utility: "Nothing in my opinion is so useful to travelers, to the inhabitants of that country, to tradesmen, and to those who study natural history." And a third simply found it a good read: "I had great pleasure in reading it. It contains a multitude of curious things." Censors did not simply hound out heretics and revolutionaries, as we tend to assume in looking back through time across the Inquisition and the Enlightenment. They gave the royal stamp of approval to a work, and in doing so they provided clues as to how it might be read. Their values constituted an official standard against which ordinary readings might be measured.

But how did ordinary readers read? My second suggestion for attacking that problem concerns the ways reading was learned. In studying literacy in seventeenth-century England, Margaret Spufford discovered that a great deal of learning went on outside the schoolroom, in workshops and fields, where laborers taught themselves and one another. Inside the school, English children learned to read before they learned to write instead of acquiring the two skills together at the beginning of their education as they do today. They often joined the work force before the age of seven, when instruction in writing began. So literacy estimates based on the ability to write may be much too low, and the reading public may have included a great many people who could not sign their names. The disparity between reading and writing stands out even more sharply in Sweden, where the archives are rich enough to provide reliable statistics. By 1770, according to Egil Johansson, Swedish society was almost fully literate. Church records show that 80–95 percent of the population could both read and respond satisfactorily when interrogated about the meaning of religious texts. Yet only 20 percent could write, and only a tiny fraction had ever gone to school. A vast literacy campaign had taken place in homes, without the aid of professional teachers, in response to a church law of 1686, which required that everyone, and especially children, farm hands, and domestic servants, should "learn to read and see with their own eyes [i.e., be able to understand] what God bids and commands in His Holy Word."[16]

[. . .]

If the experience of the great mass of readers lies beyond the range of historical research, historians should be able to capture something of what reading meant for the few persons who left a record of it. A third approach could begin with the best-known autobiographical accounts—those of Saint Augustine, Saint Theresa of Avila, Montaigne, Rousseau, and Stendhal, for example—and move on to less familiar sources. J.-M. Goulemot has used the autobiography of Jamerey-Du-val to show how a peasant could read and write his way up through the ranks of the Old Regime, and Daniel Roche discovered an eighteenth-century glazier, Jacques-Louis Ménétra, who read his way around a typical tour de France. Although he did not carry many books in the sack slung over his back, Ménétra constantly exchanged letters with fellow travelers and sweethearts. He squandered a few sous on broadsides at public executions and even composed doggerel verse for the cere- monies and farces that he staged with the other workers. When he told the story of his life, he organized his narrative in picaresque fashion, combining oral tradition (folk tales and the stylized braggadocio of male bull sessions) with genres of popular literature (the novelettes of the *bibliothèque bleue*). Unlike other plebeian authors—Restif, Mercier, Rousseau, Diderot, and Marmontel—Ménétra never won a place in the Republic of Letters. He showed that letters had a place in the culture of the common man.[17]

That place may have been marginal, but margins themselves provide clues to the experience of ordinary readers. In the sixteenth century marginal notes appeared in print in the form of glosses, which steered the reader through humanist texts. In the eighteenth century the gloss gave way to the footnote. How did the reader follow the play between text and paratext at the bottom or side of the page? Gibbon created ironic distance by masterful deployment of footnotes. A careful study of annotated eighteenth-century copies of *The Decline and Fall of the Roman Empire* might reveal the way that distance was perceived by Gibbon's contemporaries. John Adams covered his books with scribbling. By following him through his copy of Rousseau's *Discourse on the Origin of Inequality*, one can see how radical Enlightenment philosophy looked to a retired revolutionary in the sober climate of Quincy, Massachusetts.

[. . .]

Christiane Berkvens-Stevelinck has found an excellent site for mapping the Republic of Letters in the marginalia of Prosper Marchand, the bibliophile of eighteenth-century Leyden. Other scholars have charted the currents of literary history by trying to reread great books as great writers have read them, using the annotations in collector's items such as Diderot's copy of the *Encyclopédie* and Melville's copy of Emerson's essays. But the inquiry needn't be limited to great books or to books at all. Peter Burke is currently studying the graffiti of Renaissance Italy. When scribbled on the door of an enemy, they often functioned as ritual insults, which defined the lines of social conflict dividing neighborhoods and clans. When attached to the famous statue of Pasquino in Rome, this public scribbling set the tone of a rich and intensely political street culture. A history of reading might be able to advance by great leaps from the Pasquinade and the Commedia dell'Arte to Molière, from Molière to Rousseau, and from Rousseau to Robespierre.[18]

My fourth suggestion concerns literary theory. It can, I agree, look daunting, especially to the outsider. It comes wrapped in imposing labels—structuralism, deconstruction, hermeneutics, semiotics, phenomenology—and it goes as rapidly as it comes, for the trends displace one another with bewildering speed. Through them all, however, runs a concern that could lead to some collaboration between literary critics and historians of the book—the concern for reading. Whether they unearth deep structures or tear down systems of signs, critics have increasingly treated literature as an activity rather than an established body of texts. They insist that a book's meaning is not fixed on its pages; it is construed by its readers. So reader response has become the key point around which literary analysis turns.

In Germany, this approach has led to a revival of literary history as *Rezeptionsästhetik* under the leadership of Hans Robert Jauss and Wolfgang Iser. In France, it has taken a philosophical turn in the work of Roland Barthes, Paul Ricœur, Tzvetan Todorov, and Georges Poulet. In the United States, it is still in the melting-pot stage. Wayne Booth, Paul de Man, Jonathan Culler, Geoffrey Hartman, J. Hillis Miller, and Stanley Fish have supplied ingredients for a general theory, but no consensus has emerged from their debates. Nonetheless, all this critical activity points toward a new textology, and all the critics share a way of working when they interpret specific texts.[19]

[. . .]

Writers have devised many other ways to initiate readers into stories. A vast distance separates Melville's "Call me Ishmael" from Milton's prayer for help to "justify the ways of God to men." But every narrative presupposes a reader, and every reading begins from a protocol inscribed within the text. The text may undercut itself, and the reader may work against the grain or wring new meaning from familiar words: hence the endless possibilities of interpretation proposed by the deconstructionists and the original readings that have shaped cultural history—Rousseau's reading of *Le Misanthrope*, for example, or Kierkegaard's reading of Genesis 22. But whatever one makes of it, reading has reemerged as the central fact of literature.

If so, the time is ripe for making a juncture between literary theory and the history of books. The theory can reveal the range in potential responses to a text—that is, to the rhetorical constraints that direct reading without determining it. The history can show what readings actually took place—that is, within the limits of an imperfect body of evidence. By paying heed to history, literary critics may avoid the danger of anachronism; for they sometimes seem to assume that seventeenth-century Englishmen read Milton and Bunyan as if they were twentieth-century college professors. By taking account of rhetoric, historians may find clues to behavior that would otherwise be baffling, such as the passions aroused from *Clarissa* to *La Nouvelle Héloïse* and from *Werther* to *René*. I would therefore argue for a dual strategy, which would combine textual analysis with empirical research. In this way it should be possible to compare the implicit readers of the texts with the actual readers of the past and, by building on such comparisons, to develop a history as well as a theory of reader response.

References

1   This essay was first published in the *Australian Journal of French Studies* 23 (1986): 5–30.

2   Carlo Ginzburg, *The Cheese and the Worms: The Cosmos of a Sixteenth-Century Miller*, translated by Anne and John Tedeschi (Baltimore, 1980).

3   Robert Darnton, "Readers Respond to Rousseau: The Fabrication of Romantic Sensitivity," in Darnton, *The Great Cat Massacre and Other Episodes of French Cultural History* (New York, 1984), pp. 215–56.

4   As examples of this literature, which is too vast to cite in detail here, see Henri-Jean Martin, *Livre, pouvoirs et société à Paris au XVIIIe siècle (1598–1701)* (Geneva, 1969), 2 volumes, Robert Estivals, *La Statistique bibliographique de la France sous la monarchie au XVIIIe siècle* (Paris and The Hague, 1965); Frédéric Barbier, "The Publishing Industry and Printed Outputs in Nineteenth-Century France" in *Books and Society in History: Paper of the Association of College Research Libraries Rare Books and Manuscripts Preconference, 24–28 June, 1980, Boston, Massachusetts* (New York and London, 1983), pp. 199–230; Johann Goldfriedrich, *Geschichte des deutschen Buchhandels* (Leipzig, 1886–1913), 4 volumes; Rudolf Jentzsche, *Der deutsch-lateinische Büchermarket nach den Leipziger Ostermesskatalogen von 1740, 1770 und 1800 in seiner Gliederung und Wandlung* (Leipzig, 1912); H.S. Bennett, *English Books and Readers 1558 to 1603* (Cambridge, 1965); Bennett, *English Books and Readers 1603 to 1640* (Cambridge, 1970); Giles Barber, "Books from the Old World and for the New: the British International Trade in Books in the Eighteenth Century," *Studies on Voltaire and the Eighteenth Century* 151 (1976):185–224; Robert B. Winanas, "Bibliography and the Cultural Historian: Notes on the Eighteenth Century Novel," in *Printing and Society in Early America*, edited by William L. Joyce, David D. Hall, Richard D. Brown, and John B. Hench (Worcester, Mass., 1983), pp. 174–85; and G. Thomas Tanselle, "Some Statistics on American Printing, 1764–1783," in *The Press and the American Revolution*, edited by Bernard Bailyn and John B. Hench (Boston, 1981), pp. 315–64.

5   Estivals, *La Statistique bibliographique*, p. 309; Paul Raabe, "Buchproduktion und Lesepublikum in Deutschland 1770–1780," *Philobiblion. Eine Vievteljahrsschrift für Buch- und Graphiksammler* 21 (1977): 2–16. The comparative statistics on writers are based on my own calculations.

6   François Furet, "La Librairie du royaume de France au 18e siècle," in Furet et al., *Livre et société dans la France du XVIIIe siècle (1750–1759)* (Paris, 1965), pp. 3–32; Daniel Roche, "Noblesses et culture dans la France du XVIIIe: Les Lectures de la noblesse," in *Buch und Sammler: Private und*

öffentliche Bibliotheken im 18. Jahrhundert. Colloquium der Arbeitsstelle 18. Jahrhundert Gesamthochschule Wuppertal Universität Münster vom 26.-28 September 1977 (Heidelberg, 1979), pp. 9–27; Michel Marion, *Rescherches sur les bibliothèques privées à Paris au milieu du XVIIIe siècle (1750–1759)* (Paris, 1978); Michel Vovelle, *Piété baroque et déchristianisation en Provence au XVIIIe siècle: Les Attitudes deant la mort d'apres les clauses des testaments* (Paris, 1973).

7   For Jefferson's model of a minimal library for an educated but not especially scholarly gentleman, see Arthur Pierce Middleton, *A Virginia Gentleman's Library* (Williamsburg, Va., 1952).

8   Daniel Mornet, "Les Enseignements des bibliothèques privées (1750–1780)," *Revue d'histoire littéraire de la France* 17 (1910): 449–96. For an overview of the French literature with bibliographic references, see Henri-Jean Martin and Roger Chartier, eds., *Histoire de l'édition française* (Paris, 1982–), of which the first two volumes, covering the period up to 1830, have appeared. Walter Wittmann's study and related works are discussed in Scenda, *Volk ohne Buch*, pp. 461–67. On the Parisian common reader, see Daniel Roche, *Le Peuple de Paris: Essai sur la culture populaire au XVIIIe siècle* (Paris, 1981), pp. 204–41.

9   Reinhard Wittmann, *Buchmarkt und Lektüre im 18. Und 19. Jahrhundert. Beiträge zum literarischen Leben 1750–1880* (Tübingen, 1982), pp. 46–68; Wallace Kirsop, "Les Mécanismes éditoriaux," in Martin and Cartier, eds., *Histoire de l'édition française*, II:31–32.

10   Robert Engelsing, "Die Perioden der Lesergeschichte in der Neuzeit: Das statische Ausmass und die soziokulturelle Bedeutung der Lektüre, *'Archiv für Geschichte des Buchwesens* 10 (1969): cols. 944–1002; and Engelsing, *Der Bürger als Leser: Lesergeschichte in Deutschland 1500–1800* (Stuttgart, 1974).

11   For similar observations on the setting of the reading, see Roger Chartier and Daniel Roche, "Les Pratiques urbaines de l'imprimé," in *Histoire de l'édition française*, II: 403–29.

12   Françoise Parnt-Lardeur, *Les Cabinets de lecture: La Lecture publique à Paris sous la Restauration* (Paris, 1982). The description of Bernard's *cabinet littéraire* comes from his dossier in the papers of the Société typographique du Neuchâtel, Bibliothèque publique et universitaire, Neuchâtel, Switzerland.

13   The studies by Dann, Welke, and Prüsener, along with other interesting research, are collected in Otto Dann, ed., *Lesegesellschaften und bürgerliche Emanzipation: ein europäischer Vergleich* (Munich, 1981).

14   Heinzmann's remarks are quoted in Helmut Kreuzer, "Gefährliche Lesesucht? Bemerkungen zu politischer Lektürekritik im ausgehenden 18. Jahrhundert," in *Leser und Lesen im 18. Jahrhundert. Colloquium der Arbeitsstelle Achtzehntes Jahrhundert Gesamthochschule Wuppertal, 24–26. Oktober 1975,* edited by Rainer Gruenter (Heidelberg, 1977). Bergk's observations are scattered througout his treatise, *Die Kunst Bücher zu Lesen* (Jena, 1799), which also contains some typical remarks about the importance of "digesting" books: see its title page and page 302. On eating the New Testament and other ritualistic uses of books, see David Cressy, "Book Totems in Seventeenth-Century England and New England," *The Journal of Library History* 21 (1986): 99.

15   Newberry Library, Case Wing Z. 45.18 ser. 1a, no. 31.

16   Margaret Spufford, "First Steps in Literacy: The Reading and Writing Experiences of the Humblest Seventeenth-Century Autobiographers," *Social History* 4 (1979): 407–35; and Spufford, *Small Books and Pleasant Histories: Popular Fiction and Its Readership in Seventeeth-Century England* (Athens Ga., 1981). On reading in England from the sixteenth through the eighteenth century, see Keith Thomas, "The Meaning of Literacy in Early Modern England," in *The Written Word: Literacy in Transition*, edited by Gerd Baumann, (Oxford, 1986), pp. 97–131. On popular reading in nineteenth- and twentieth-century England, see R.K. Webb, *The British Working Class Reader* (London, 1955); and Richard D. Altick, *The English Common Reader: A Social History of the Mass Reading Public 1800–1900* (Chicago, 1957). Egril Johansson has summarized much of his remarkable research in "The History of Literacy in Sweden in Comparision with Some Other Countries," *Educational Reports: Umeå* (Umeå, Sweden: 1973).

17   Valentin Jamerey-Duval, *Mémoires: Enfance et éducation d'un paysan au XVIIIe siècle*, edited by Jean-Marie Goulemot (Paris: 1982).

18   Adam's margin notes are quoted in Zoltán Haraszti, *John Adams and the Prophets of Progress* (Cambridge, Mass., 1952), p. 85. On glosses and footnotes, see Lawrence Lipking, "The Marginal Gloss," *Critical Inquiry* 3 (1977): 620–31; and G.W. Bowersock, "The Art of the Footnote," *The American Scholar* 53 (1983–84); 54–62. On the Prosper Marchand manuscripts, see the two articles by Christiane Berkvens-Stevelinck, "L'Apport de Prosper Marchand au 'système des

libraires de Paris' " and "Prosper Marchand, 'trait d'union' entre auteur et éditeur," *De Gulden Passer* 56 (1978): 21–63, 65–99.

19   For surveys and bibliographies of reader-response criticism, see Susan Suleiman and Inge Crosman, eds., *The Reader in the Text: Essays on Audience and Interpretation* (Princeton, N.J., 1980); and Jane P. Tompkins, ed., *Reader-Response Criticism: From Formalism to Post-Structuralism* (Baltimore, 1980). One of the most influential works from this strain of criticism is Wolfgang Iser, *The Implied Reader: Patterns of Communication in Prose Fiction from Bunyan to Beckett* (Baltimore, 1974).

Chapter 3

Roger Chartier

PREFACE TO *THE ORDER OF BOOKS*

[H]OW DID PEOPLE IN WESTERN EUROPE between the end of the Middle Ages and the eighteenth century attempt to master the enormously increased number of texts that first the manuscript book and then print put into circulation? Inventorying titles, categorizing works, and attributing texts were all operations that made it possible to set the world of the written word in order. Our own age is the direct heir of this immense effort motivated by anxiety. It was in those decisive centuries, when the hand-copied book was gradually replaced by works composed in movable type and printed on presses, that the acts and thoughts that are still our own were forged. The invention of the author as the fundamental principle for the designation of a text, the dream of a universal library, real or imaginary, containing all the works that have ever been written, and the emergence of a new definition of the book that made an indissoluble connection between an object, a text, and an author – these are some of the innovations that transformed people's relationship with texts, both before and after Gutenberg.

That relationship typically contains an internal contradiction. On the one hand, every reader has to deal with an entire set of constraints and obligations. The author, the bookseller-publisher, the commentator, and the censor all have an interest in keeping close control over the production of meaning and in making sure that the text that they have written, published, glossed, or authorized will be understood with no possible deviation from their prescriptive will. On the other hand, reading, by definition, is rebellious and vagabond. Readers use infinite numbers of subterfuges to procure prohibited books, to read between the lines, and to subvert the lessons imposed on them.

The book always aims at installing an order, whether it is the order in which it is deciphered, the order in which it is to be understood, or the order intended by the authority who commanded or permitted the work. This multi-faceted order is not all-powerful, however, when it comes to annulling the reader's liberty. Even when it is hemmed in by differences in competence and by conventions, liberty knows how to distort and reformulate the significations that were supposed to defeat it. The dialectic between imposition and appropriation, between constraints transgressed and freedoms bridled, is not the same in all places or all times or for all people. Recognizing its diverse modalities and multiple variations is the first aim of a history of reading that strives to grasp – in all their differences – communities of readers and their 'arts of reading'.

The order of books has still another meaning. Whether they are in manuscript or in print, books are objects whose forms, if they cannot impose the sense of the texts that they bear, at least command the uses that can invest them and the appropriations to which they are susceptible. Works and discourses exist only when they become physical realities and are inscribed on the pages of a book, transmitted by a voice reading or narrating, or spoken on the stage of a theatre. Understanding the principles that govern the 'order of discourse' supposes that the principles underlying the processes of production, communication, and reception of books (and other objects that bear writing) will also be deciphered in a rigorous manner. More than even before, historians of literary works and historians of cultural practices have become aware of the effects of meaning that material forms produce. In the case of the book, those forms constitute a singular order totally distinct from other registers of transmission of the canonical works as ordinary texts. This means that [. . .] keen attention should be paid to the technical, visual, and physical devices that organize the reading of writing when writing becomes a book.

[. . .]

Works – even the greatest works, especially the greatest works – have no stable, universal, fixed meaning. They are invested with plural and mobile significations that are constructed in the encounter between a proposal and a reception. The meanings attributed to their forms and their themes depend upon the areas of competence or the expectations of the various publics that take hold of them. To be sure, the creators (or the 'powers' or the 'clerics') always aspire to pin down their meaning and proclaim the correct interpretation, the interpretation that ought to constrain reading (or viewing). But without fail reception invents, shifts about, distorts.

Works are produced within a specific order that has its own rules, conventions, and hierarchies, but they escape all these and take on a certain density in their peregrinations – which can be in a very long time span – about the social world. Deciphered on the basis of mental and affective schemes that constitute the 'culture' (in the anthropological sense) of the communities that receive them, works turn the tables and become a precious resource for thinking about what is essential: the construction of social ties, individual subjectivity, and relationship with the sacred.

Conversely, any work inscribes within its forms and its themes a relationship with the manner in which, in a given moment and place, modes of exercising power, social configurations, or the structure of personality are organized. Thought of (and thinking of himself or herself) as a demiurge, the writer none the less creates in a state of dependence. Dependence upon the rules (of patronage, subsidy, and the market) that define the writer's condition. Dependence (on an even deeper level) on the unconscious determinations that inhabit the work and that make it conceivable, communicable, and decipherable.

To consider in this way that all works are anchored in the practices and the institutions of the social world is not to postulate any general equivalence among all the products of the mind. Some, better than others, never exhaust their significative force. If we try to understand this by invoking the universality of beauty or the unity of human nature we will fall short of the truth. The essential game is being played elsewhere, in the complex, subtle, shifting relationships established between the forms (symbolic or material) proper to works, which are unequally open to appropriation, and the habits or the concerns of the various publics for those works.

What any cultural history must take into consideration today is the paradoxical articulation between a *difference* – the difference by means of which all societies, with varying modalities, have separated out from daily practice a particular domain of human activity – and *dependencies* – the dependencies that take a variety of ways to inscribe aesthetic and intellectual invention within the conditions of possibility and intelligibility. This problematic connection is rooted in the very trajectory that gives works their most powerful meanings – meanings constructed on the aesthetic or reflective transfiguration of ordinary experiences, grasped on the basis of practices proper to those works' various publics.

Reflection on how the figure of the author was constructed, on the rules for the formation of communities of readers, or on the significance invested in the building of libraries (with or without walls) may perhaps contribute to focusing a few of the questions that currently inhabit the disciplines of knowledge and public debate. By reintroducing variation and difference where the illusion of universality spontaneously springs up, such reflection may help us to get rid of some of our over-sure distinctions and some over-familiar truisms.

Chapter 4

Reinhard Wittmann

WAS THERE A READING REVOLUTION AT THE END OF THE EIGHTEENTH CENTURY?

The world of readers

WE CAN ONLY GIVE A suggestion of the varied and closely interwoven conditions and premises of reading in the eighteenth century, together with the political, economic, sociological and cultural changes it underwent. The population of the German linguistic area must have almost doubled between 1700 and 1800, to about 25 million (excluding the Habsburg Empire), reaching a high point in the last third of the century. At the same time, a clear, if initially only gradual, trend toward urbanization began, even though around 80 per cent of the population continued to live on the land. In all the territories belonging to the politically very fragmented Holy Roman Empire of the German nation, the social status and structure of the nobility and peasantry remained largely unchanged until the end of the century, but within the bourgeoisie situated in between there were important processes of transformation, emancipation and differentiation that ultimately led to the breakup of feudal society.

[. . .]

Jürgen Habermas has outlined this change in consciousness, using his theory of the 'structural transformation of the public sphere'. According to this theory, bourgeois identity emerged with a new public sphere that was independent of the courts, a 'sphere of private people assembled into a public' that questioned the monopoly of information and interpretation enjoyed by the authorities of Church and State, and developed new, anti-feudal structures of intercourse and communication, initially through literature but then politically too. Individual identity replaced status bestowed by birth. It was first and foremost within the intellectual sphere that this identity sought to win and maintain the autonomy to which it aspired. The characteristic feature of this bourgeois individuality was the way it discovered and liberated subjectivity, and strove toward constant communication, in order to expand its restricted sphere of experience.

No medium could perform this function better than the printed word. Written culture and literature became the training ground for self-understanding and reasoning, while books and reading acquired a new status in the public consciousness. For the first time the bourgeoisie now had at its disposal enough time and purchasing power for reading. Reading acquired an emancipatory function, and became a productive social force: it expanded one's moral and intellectual horizon. It made of the reader a useful member of society, allowed him to command his range of duties better, and was even an aid to his social career. The printed word became the vehicle of bourgeois culture.

In previous centuries, the book had been principally regarded as an authoritarian medium with an impersonal claim to power. It was seen as an indispensable factor of social discipline imposed by the State and the Church. It was not until the general change in attitudes in the eighteenth century that people recognized the capacity of printed matter to 'completely penetrate the reader's subjective life'.[1] Precisely because the mechanically duplicated text could be read in its complete uniformity, far more automatically than any manuscript, it drew new readers hook, line and sinker into the imagined world of the book. To do so, of course, there was a fundamental prerequisite: namely, literacy.

Without even approximate figures for the whole of Europe, the extent of reading and writing at the end of the eighteenth century can only be guessed at. What are the criteria for selection? What use are rough approximations of an 'elementary reading ability', deduced from a limited school education, if during a whole lifetime this ability is never converted into reading *practice*? Do we count among 'readers' people who are able to scribble their signature at the bottom of a bill of sale? Or those who pore over their catechism in an effort to decipher it? Or could 'readers' include any illiterate person who listens eagerly and attentively to another person who is reading aloud? We must take gender differences between readers into account (female literacy centred more on reading than writing), differences in religion, but in particular differences between readers in the town and those in the country.

[. . .]

We have at our disposal more accurate statistics for the number of actual readers in the duchy of Württemberg, which can serve as a case study (albeit not as a representative one). In his study of *Das gelehrte Württemberg* in 1790, Balthasar Haug conducted a careful census of the class of dignitaries within the duchy who for the most part must also have been the agents of literary culture in their society: 834 clerics, 388 curates and scholarship-holders in Tübingen, 452 lawyers (who probably included higher-ranking officials), 218 doctors and apothecaries, 300 officers (two-thirds of them from the nobility), around 200 graduate students, 75 merchants in Stuttgart and around 450 in the country, and finally, 1,324 *Schreiber* ('clerks') – that is, middle-ranking officials without a university education.[2] If we add to these 4,000 members of the property-owning and educated bourgeoisie a further 2,000 women and young people and a few hundred nobles, we arrive at a figure of around 7,000 'extensive' readers in Württemberg in the last years of the eighteenth century – a little over 1 per cent of the population as a whole. Those who practised the traditional mode of reading continued to revert to the edifying 'old solaces', the Bible, the catechism and the calendar.

However, it would be a mistake for us to assign only a marginal role, culturally or within society as a whole, to the regularly reading public in Germany, which numbered approximately 300,000 people, or 1.5 per cent of the adult population. For this (initially very small) ferment of new readers started some momentous cultural and political chain reactions.

Old and new forms of reading in the eighteenth century

How did reading evolve in the eighteenth century? To answer this question, we would need to have a more sophisticated model of the history of readers to work with, one that took account of both the diachronic sequence of events, together with its intermediate stages, *and* instances of synchronic overlap. Reading evolved into an individual process independent of social class. The class to which people belonged scarcely determined their access to reading any more [. . .]

The most widespread form of interaction with the printed word continued to be 'unruly' reading, a mode of reading that was naïve, non-reflexive and undisciplined, and for the most part performed aloud. It constituted the sole form of reading among the rural population and a large section of the urban lower classes too. Given that they worked week in, week out, from sunrise to sunset, six days a week, there was neither the time nor the motivation for these people to read. For the static world of the rural populace, from the stable-boy to the large farm-holder, reading was a social practice or technique of domination that was superfluous to their daily lives. If they had a rudimentary reading ability, they applied it to reading blood-letting tables, rules for the weather and sowing, and devotional works sold at market and by pedlars, as well as chapbooks both spiritual and secular in character. Many provincial publishers, particularly those in Germany, published dozens of these little chapbooks [. . .] [W]ith time the contents of these booklets underwent textual modifications that anticipated the change in reading habits.

This 'unruly' form of reading could, however, be linked to a collective 'alfabetismo di gruppo' (Italo Sordi) – in other words, a well-developed capacity to listen, implying an indirect 'literalization' without any literacy education. It was promoted by a hierarchical form of communication, the lecture: in most family circles, religious texts were recited by the father of the house or the children, while in public places such as inns or markets, those who could read, including teachers and priests, distributed political and other new publications. In the last years of the eighteenth century, Enlightenment thinkers largely failed in their intensive efforts to transform 'unruly' reading into a socially integrative 'useful' form of reading among the rural population using an authoritarian method of teaching people to read.

This situation underwent a permanent change following the trauma of the French Revolution. An elementary interest in the sensational news about freedom, equality and fraternity began to spread beyond the towns. Backstreet lawyers, schoolmasters who had abandoned their duties, rebellious students, ecclesiastical reformers, innkeepers and coach-house owners read newspapers aloud in schools or taverns, and encouraged noisy debate. All this helped considerably to motivate people to learn to read for themselves (measures taken by the counter-revolutionary authorities to control opinion had much the same effect), to the discomfort of the leading political and social classes, who were increasingly determined to oppose this intellectual emancipation.

A quicker and earlier change in reading habits occurred among the urban classes than in the rural lower and middle classes, in particular among domestic workers, lackeys and barbers, chambermaids, employees in trade and craft industries, and among the middle ranks and some lower ranks in the army. This group possibly constituted up to a quarter of the urban population. It also enjoyed the necessary pre-conditions for reading: namely, that precious resource, light, together with brief times for reading throughout the day, and often when there were free meals and lodging, a small budget for a lending library too. By emulating the ruling class, the workers also acquired its fashionable reading habits, in particular its extensive consumption of *belles-lettres*. In the city the printed word was a natural component part of daily urban life: posters on houses, public notices on walls, town criers and market criers with their declarations, the ubiquitous newspapers in the smoke rooms and taverns. [. . .] In 1781 a Viennese author noted a true passion for *belles-lettres* among chambermaids: 'Not satisfied with this alone, they also play the part of sentimental souls, demand the rights to *belles-lettres*, read comedies, novels and poems conscientiously, and learn entire scenes, passages or verses off by heart, and even argue about the sorrows of young Werther.' These reading tastes could no longer be disciplined by a moralizing work like the *Little Book of Morals for the People* (Lavater, 1773). Long hours of idleness on guard duty encouraged reading in the urban army, as one observer lamented in 1780: 'Even the musketeers in the large towns have library books brought to them at the main guardroom.' Apart from novels, the preferred reading materials in the garrisons were racy stories and pamphlets.

Socially, 'unruly' reading was in decline, but in percentage terms it was still prevalent. Its opposite had always been 'scholarly' reading. Among the intellectual elites a 'modern', cursory reading to gain information was not the only current form. An extensive, poly-historical and encyclopaedic mode of reading had also become established by the seventeenth century. However, from the middle of the eighteenth century onwards, the scholarly bookworm who remained oblivious to the world as he pored over his folios was looked upon as a figure of ridicule. His knowledge of books, which stubbornly resisted any form of pragmatism, was contrary to the enlightened bourgeois world-view. The ponderous, pedantic thinker reading within the confines of his room was replaced by the learned and versatile 'petit maître' who was more superficial in his pursuit of the sciences.

Enlightenment ideology, on the other hand, propagated 'useful' reading for both traditional and new agents of culture. Between 1720 and 1750 the main vehicles of this reading propaganda were the *Moralische Wochenschriften* ('moral weeklies') that appeared principally in the commercial towns of the Protestant north. In addition to Leipzig, Hamburg played the decisive role as the gateway for British Enlightenment thought. Following the model of the 'moral weeklies' such as the *Spectator*, *Tatler* and *Guardian*, these publications disseminated a specifically bourgeois 'message of virtue' and the cultural ideal of the Enlightenment, opposed to the *galant* life-style of the court. Using such programmatic titles as *Der Patriot*, *Der Weltbürger*, *Der Vernünftler*, *Der Biedermann*, *Der Menschenfreund*, *Der Freygeist*, *Der Gesellige* and *Die vernünftigen Tadlerinnen* and the reader-oriented strategies of the earlier edifying books, they now conveyed secular information from this world, in an effort to pass the time in an entertaining way. For both the well-to-do tradesman and the ambitious student, the well-mannered woman and the honest official, reading material that was both socially useful and at the same time promoted individual morality was no idle pleasure but actually a moral duty.

This strategy was particularly effective among the female reading public. With their increasing economic prosperity, the wives and daughters of the bourgeoisie had more free time available for reading. Up to the beginning of the eighteenth century, their reading canon had been almost exclusively confined to edifying religious writings (even if such restrictions were not always effective), but it was now allowed to expand. The 'moral weeklies' recommended several 'women's libraries', which were not intending to educate any 'femme savante', but merely presupposed a 'relative education, narrowly confined to a range of domestic duties'. However, they undoubtedly quenched the female thirst for knowledge with travel stories and fables, even with British family novels. The teaching of literacy skills to youngsters was pursued with a similar level of commitment. As childhood was now recognized as a properly defined stage in life, greater attention was given to what children and young adults actually read. From 1760 onwards, an intensive method of teaching the young generation of the bourgeoisie to read was implemented. This had scarcely any impact among young students, who did not have very much time and who had always had a more extensive and secularized mode of reading.

This 'useful' form of reading not only considered the text as a moralizing allegory; as a guide to achieving the perfection of the individual, it later developed within the rising bourgeois public, thanks in particular to the institution of the reading society (see below), into a form of reading oriented toward communication and reflection, with the aim of shaping the social identity of the bourgeoisie through reading.

[. . .]

[T]his kind of reading was regarded even by some German Enlightenment thinkers as an act of liberation from a feudal obscurantism. On the part of the bourgeoisie it promoted a new, collective self-understanding that was based on a secular argumentation and was freeing itself from the religious and legal doctrinaire discourse of the feudal structures of the *ancien régime*. The bourgeois individual was thus able to keep his sense of direction, and gain a new corporative, social and cultural identity. Obviously, this 'rational' way of reading was a male preserve. With their growing economic prosperity, men had more and more time for reading. They were interested not only in information related to their trade or profession, but also in new political publications and works of diversion.

The role played by the German nobility in all this was relatively minor. We have clearly to distinguish their reading habits, which we have only little knowledge of, even today. In France, right up to the end of the century, the landed gentry still possessed very few books. Similarly, in Germany the 'Krautjunker' (country nobleman), whose homes contained perhaps several dozen books, faced a small circle of educated patrons of literature, who, like the educated bourgeoisie, modernized their roles as readers. Among the courtly nobles and especially the landed gentry, the number of book lovers who had amassed valuable collections was extremely small. None of them played more than a minimal role in the 'reading revolution'.

As previously mentioned, the process of modernizing reading habits sprang not so much from the residences and courts as from the Protestant commercial towns of northern and central Germany. The Catholic regions of the Empire did not begin to participate in the process until later. Unlike the Protestants, they lacked the tradition of individual Bible reading, a quasi-religious act providing a fundamental stimulus to reading.

[. . .]

[E]ven among the Catholic population, popular mass-market publications such as calendars and leaflets were in circulation, and it was not strictly forbidden for laymen to pore over the Bible. However, in contrast to the early Protestant argument, which held that writing prevailed over tradition (*sola scriptura*), here oral mediation via the authority of teaching had absolute precedence. Nevertheless, for the role of the popular book, this only applied to the wider strata of religious believers. The clergy and the monasteries, by contrast, had always constituted a literary public *sui generis*. Libertine reading matter was especially popular in religious cities, as it was in France. But a far more significant role was played by the monastic libraries, which, right up to the period of secularization at the beginning of the nineteenth century, were the locus of a late and prestigious burgeoning of scholarly life.

[. . .]

While Bible reading among Protestants became increasingly rare, first in the towns, the processes of acculturation and de-regionalization and the 'reading mania' spread among Catholics, including those in the metropolises. A perfect example of this was Josephinian Vienna, with its deluge of anticlerical pamphlets. Clergymen who were hostile to reading resorted in their sermons and pamphlets to the old Baroque model for criticizing this reading mania. They feared, not without justification, that reading would lead to a general process of secularization and de-Christianization.

[. . .]

The 'reading mania'

Around 1770 even this model of reading, one which fitted with Enlightenment doctrine, and in which the social aspect of education played a central role, changed and became more sophisticated. Through a rapid process of modernization which also began to break free of the constraints of rationalism, the criteria for its reception, which were both authoritarian and academic, became more emotional and individual. This marked the beginning of a particularly decisive phase in the history of reading, one that remained especially virulent for several decades: that of a 'sentimental' or 'empathetic' form of reading. This form of reading was mid-way between, on the one hand, an individual passion that isolated the reader from society and his environment and, on the other, a hunger for communication through reading. [. . .] The isolation and anonymity felt by the reader who was emotionally aroused yet isolated was compensated by his awareness that reading made him part of a community of like-minded people. Undeniably, this form of reading was – in the sense of a 'revolution' in reverse – far more 'intensive' than before, and not in the least 'extensive'.

In Britain, France and Germany respectively, this culturally very significant process is specifically associated with the names Richardson, Rousseau, Klopstock and Goethe. At the root of the new relationship that existed between author, text and reader was Samuel Richardson (1689–1761). His novels *Pamela, or Virtue Rewarded* (1740) and *Clarissa* (1747–8) were received with greater enthusiasm than any representative of this literary genre before him. [. . .]

In France, too, this reading matter created a considerable stir, as Diderot's *Éloge de Richardson* (1761) showed. But it was not until the work of Jean Jacques Rousseau (1712–78) appeared that the passion kindled by Diderot's book turned into a conflagration. Rousseau demanded to be read:

> as if he were a prophet of divine truth . . . What set the reading of Rousseau apart from his religious forebears – be it Calvinist, Jansenist or pietist reading – was the invitation to read the most suspect kind of literature, the novel, as if it were the Bible . . . Rousseau . . . wanted to penetrate life through literature, his own life and that of his reader.[3]

Conversely, his readers hungered for this kind of reading matter, 'not in order to enjoy literature, but better to master life, in particular family life, and precisely according to Rousseau's ideas'.[4]

La Nouvelle Héloïse (1761), probably the top bestseller of the *ancien régime* and reprinted at least seventy times by 1800, unleashed an overwhelming response, including floods of tears and extreme despondency.

[. . .]

In Germany this revolution took place in a significant intermediate stage. Here, the female readership in particular needed a link between purely religious and purely worldly reading material. This was Friedrich Gottlieb Klopstock's (1724–1803) biblical epic *The Messiah*, published after 1749. It dealt with an edifying and, even for women, perfectly permitted subject, that of the life of Christ, but it did so from a sentimental perspective and in a boldly subjective way. Readers seized upon it at the moment they were preparing to emancipate themselves from traditional scholarly and religious reading materials, and it was abandoned immediately this emancipation was achieved, at which point they dealt with poetry and *belles-lettres* so naturally and casually that they no longer comprehended how 'Klopstock's Messiah could have once meant so much to them'.[5] The success enjoyed by C. F. Gellert's works is similarly explained. In the first bourgeois novel in Germany, his *Life of the Swedish Countess of G* (1746), the author's moral and religious intention was above all suspicion, which allowed the reader to devour the story's events all the more greedily.

A crucial breakthrough ultimately came in 1774, with Goethe's bestseller *The Sorrows of Young Werther*, the young Napoleon's favourite book. In contrast to Rousseau, however, its author placed not the slightest value on any kind of intimacy with the reader. Nevertheless, a proportion of his largely youthful reading public interpreted this tragic love story, in which bourgeois morality on earth was no longer propagated but exposed, as something other than a work of art. In line with the traditional concept of the 'useful' and edifying text, they constructed it as an invitation to emulate. A wave of suicides among *Werther* readers was the disastrous consequence of this misinterpretation. However, the great majority of readers were content to identify with the hero on a merely superficial level, turning Werther's clothing (a blue tailcoat and yellow breeches) into a symbol of rebellious youth, and bought cult objects such as the famous Werther cup. Finally, a small minority succeeded in objectifying the story aesthetically, distinguishing between the world of reading and everyday reality.

The example of *Werther* illustrated the sophistication of the new reading public who were trying out various forms of interaction with literary texts, new modes and rituals of reading. Both social and solitary forms of reading assumed new functions. The main reading public for *belles-lettres*, namely women, preferred a mode of collective reading that for them was a means of direct communication. However, the authoritative, 'frontal' method of reading aloud used by the *paterfamilias*, priest or teacher was now replaced by a gregarious-ness legitimized and formalized by reading, whose significance lay in the 'experience of empathetic role-playing',[6] or in other words a controlled and disciplined common mastering of literary texts. An exemplary case was a day described by Luise Mejer in 1784, in a letter to her friend Heinrich Christian Boie. She worked as a lady's companion at Tremsbüttel in Holstein, at the residence of the Countess of Stolberg, whose husband and brother-in-law were successful writers:

> Breakfast is at ten o'clock. Then Stolberg reads out a chapter from the Bible, and a song from Klopstock's *Lieder*. Everyone retires to his or her bedroom. Then I dip into the *Spectator* or *Physiognomy*, and a few books the Countess has given me. She comes downstairs while Lotte translates, and I spend an hour reading her Lavater's *Pontius Pilate*. While she has her Latin lesson, I copy for her or read myself until dinner is served. After dinner and coffee, Fritz reads from the *Lebensläufen*, then Lotte comes downstairs and I read Milton with her for an hour. Then we go back upstairs and I read to the Count and Countess from Plutarch until teatime at around nine o'clock. After tea Stolberg reads a chapter from the Bible and one of Klopstock's *Lieder*, then it's 'goodnight'.[7]

Luise Mejer assessed this excessive kind of reading, which was both intensive and extensive in character, as follows: 'Here people are stuffed with reading matter in the same way that geese are stuffed with noodles.'

As a counterpart to the gregarious and communicative form of reading, solitary reading too assumed new qualities, characterized by quiet, peaceful appreciation. The body as a medium of textual experience was relegated to second place, and 'unruly' reading was disciplined. Quiet and relaxation while reading were now regarded as bourgeois virtues and as the prerequisite for aesthetic appreciation. By no longer putting himself at the mercy of the text, the reader remained master of himself and consequently free to interact with the text in a controlled way.[8] The immobility required from then on when reading at one's desk posed difficulties for more than just a few men, who continued to prefer the most casual positions. Literacy teaching at the end of the eighteenth century regarded the physically accentuated practice of reading aloud solely from a dietetic viewpoint, describing 'the acting of walking, in which the effort required causes the blood to circulate, prevents the bodily fluids from coagulating, and wards off illnesses and feelings of weariness. During rainy or unhealthy weather, or when we are ill, we have to take refuge in reading aloud as a substitute for the pleasures and benefits of a walk in the open air.'[9] Furthermore, as it internalized all emotions, quiet reading itself encouraged the reader to withdraw into the realm of the imagination.

The intensity conferred by closeted reading was further heightened by the 'sentimental' practice of reading in natural surroundings, in the open countryside, which for a time became a popular setting for the academically educated bourgeoisie, as an ostentatious retreat from society. It reflected the bourgeoisie's precarious position between, on the one hand, its revolt against the norms of late feudal society and, on the other, its humiliating consciousness of the fragility of its social prestige. This pointed escape from society, from the unreasonable demands of the court, from the town and from daily duties, into a sentimental retreat with a literary vade-mecum, conferred a particular intensity to the experience of reading by creating an interplay between the idyll of the surrounding land-scape and imagined destinies. Readers liked to enjoy 'beautiful places' to the full by reading beautiful passages.

However, the principal location for reading continued to be the private domestic sphere, the bourgeois living space. The new cultural practice was integrated into daily life. Hitherto, the only people who had spent the hours of darkness unhealthily bent over folios had been scholars. Now, however, the evenings and nights also became available as free time for the literary public to enjoy reading. A change came about in the bourgeois attitude to time: once the day and time were structured and 'departmentalized', people gradually learned to alternate effortlessly between the imaginative world of reading and daily life, and the risk of confusing separated spheres of life with each other was reduced.[10]

The manufacturers of luxury items made 'reading furniture' available for the first time: *chaises longues* with an inbuilt reading desk, convertible furniture for the lady of rank, furniture that could serve simultaneously as a dressing table, a dining table, a desk for reading and writing, comfortable 'English chairs for reading or sleeping', and many others.[11] Women could procure clothing to match: the *liseuse*, a warm yet light house-frock or two-piece for imaginative journeys. For *galant* rococo ladies the boudoir had been a private space to which they could retire, but for the new bourgeois woman it was a 'closet' for reading, a refuge of female independence. It coupled the act of withdrawing from society with that of giving free rein to feelings. It 'was not used to conceal lovers, but to keep them out'.[12] It no longer contained courtly decorations, just reading materials and a writing desk, complete with letter-writing equipment. Just as popular among the female reading public was the habit of reading in bed, as can be inferred from contemporary accounts (often containing highly erotic allusions).

By the end of the eighteenth century, only a small proportion of the reading public had succeeded in achieving the highest, 'adult' stage in the literary culture of reading, namely 'by effecting the transition to the fictional world solely through the imagination',[13] and in integrating reading into everyday reality. They read hermeneutically, as an autonomous artistic practice, no longer in order to confirm already familiar truths within the range of their own expectations, but to discover new and unknown ones. These competent readers of classical national literature were few in number, and have remained so right up to the present day. This was why Friedrich Schiller rejected the search for a 'Volksdichter' (national poet): 'There is now a very large gap between the *élite* of a nation and its *masses*.' Jean Paul referred to a similar division, describing German readers around 1800 as follows:

> In Germany there are three types of reading public: 1. the broad, almost completely uncultured and uneducated one of libraries, 2. the learned scholarly public consisting of professors, students and critics, and 3. the cultured public

consisting of men of the world and educated women, artists and members of the upper classes, among whom at least frequent contact and journeys form the rudiments of an education. (Of course, these three categories of public often communicate with one another.)[14]

The great majority of readers practised a quasi-pubescent variant of sentimental reading, a 'narcotic' (as the philosopher J. G. Fichte put it) and often escapist 'reading mania'. This practice was at the heart of contemporary discussions.

Around 1780 this new epidemic began to spread rapidly, again emanating from central and northern Germany outwards, and particularly among the younger, female audience. The debate in the newspapers and journals, sermons and pamphlets, at the end of the century even detected it 'among classes who otherwise did little or no reading, and who even now do not read in order to teach and educate themselves, but do so simply for the purpose of personal entertainment' (in the words of the Bavarian Enlightenment thinker L. Westenrieder).

The authorities of Church and State were not alone in taking offence at the new reading mania. Even progressive Enlightenment thinkers regarded it as a principal obstacle to the emancipation they were striving to bring out in a disciplined and rational way. This socially harmful practice would, they believed, lead to vices that conflicted with the bourgeois, Protestant work ethic, and belonged within the world of the nobility and the court: idleness, luxury, boredom. Initially, however, the case against reading was brought mainly on dietetic and sociomedical grounds. While Tissot's *On the Health of Scholars* (1786) merely warned of the health risks to scholars who spent all their time in their rooms, in the pedagogues' tracts of the late eighteenth century the 'masturbation' debate was linked to the debate about reading. Both were counted among the harmful 'secret sins of youth':

> the obligatory position, the lack of all physical movement when reading, com-
> bined with the violent alternation of imaginings and feelings [create] limpness,
> bloatedness and constipation of the intestines, in a word hypochondria, which
> has a recognized effect on the genitals of both sexes, particularly of the female
> sex [and creates] coagulations and defects in the blood, excitation and exhaus-
> tion of the nervous system, as well as conditions of languor and weakness in
> the whole body.[15]

Instructions on reading in the late Enlightenment condemned reading as a socially useless diversion: 'To read a book merely in order to kill time is an act of high treason toward humanity because one is belittling a medium that was designed for loftier purposes.'[16]

[. . .]

Reading tastes and the book trade

The fundamental changes in the cultural practice of reading naturally had direct effects on the book trade that modernized both its forms of communication and its products. From the second half of the eighteenth century onwards, the book was consistently regarded as a cultural commodity, and with the transition from the barter economy that until then had been dominant to a monetary economy, the market was realigned according to capitalist principles. Starting with Leipzig and the booksellers of Saxony and northern Germany, the trend toward strictly sales-oriented book production led to a new market of demand, and even to new forms of advertising. The number of booksellers in the provincial towns also increased conspicuously, and a new generation of publishers pursued Enlightenment as a business. For this they were denounced by conservative publicists as the principal cause of the reading revolution.

At the same time the role of the author became professional, and in Germany the 'freier Schriftsteller' (freelance writer) emerged, on the one hand insisting on the autonomy of his creativity, and on the other having to subordinate himself to the laws of the emergent anonymous traffic in goods. This necessity for self-prostitution on the market before an anonymous public induced the author to have intensive contact with the recipient of his work, and vice versa, leading to a spiritual community created by the book.

The book market now tended to deal with a reading public that was unlimited, heterogeneous and anonymous, whose reading tastes and needs were becoming increasingly sophisticated, and who were interested in both specialist books for advancing their professional careers and political information, in bloody horror stories and spiritual comfort. Nevertheless, these special, overlapping interests were matched by the homogenization of reading tastes transcending former class boundaries. The same moving family story was read both by the noblewoman and by her maids-in-waiting; the same horror story was read by the high-ranking official in the judiciary and the tailor's apprentice alike. However, they were all able to rise to the level of the canonized national literature. While the anonymous reader was at the mercy of market supply, he also made collective demands of this market that could not be ignored without risk of commercial failure.

The fluctuations in the market and reading tastes are (despite inadequate statistics) reflected in the Leipzig book fair catalogue that represented the transregional book trade throughout the entire century. The sheer expansion in the volume of production after 1760 shows the remarkable growth in a public hungry for reading matter. In 1765 the book fair catalogue recorded 1,384 titles; in 1775, 1,892 titles; in 1785, 2,713; in 1790, 3,222; in 1795, 3,257; and in 1800, 3,906 titles. Total annual production may have comprised almost double that number around 1800. The growth in the number of new publications was matched by the rapid decline in Latin, which for centuries had been the dominant language among scholars. At the book fairs the proportion of titles written in Latin fell from 27.7 per cent in 1740 to 3.97 per cent in 1800. Similarly there was a change in the hierarchy of subject areas: the overwhelming superiority of theology and religion rapidly diminished, indicating both the secularization of learning and the disaffection of the Protestant reading public with the edifying literature of the time. At the same time, there was an increase in the percentage of modern subjects like geography, natural history, politics, education and above all belles-lettres. The latter, which in 1740 had constituted only 6 per cent of the book supply at the fairs, had increased to 16.5 per cent by 1770, and to 21.45 per cent by 1800, reaching the highest position of all subjects. This increase was mostly attributable to the novel, whose market share more than quadrupled from 2.6 per cent of the book supply in 1740 to 11.7 per cent in 1800.

It was not only the number of titles that increased, but also the number of copies. Of course, average print runs did not increase to the same extent, owing to the reprinting of titles and the growth of lending libraries. Far larger print runs were achieved by newspapers than by books at the very end of the century, following the trauma of the French Revolution: the renowned Hamburgischer Correspondent reached 25,000 copies in 1798, rising to as many as 51,000 copies in 1801. At an average of ten readers per copy, this would have amounted to half a million readers. The print runs for more sophisticated literary journals, on the other hand, were lower by far (for instance, Wieland's Teutscher Merkur, with its 1,500 copies).

In the last third of the eighteenth century, book prices proved to be an obstacle to the rapid expansion of the reading public, especially the prices of the much sought-after belles-lettres. During this period, prices increased around eight- or ninefold, which was attributable to bookseller's practices, net retailing and low break-even quantities, but also to ever-increasing demand. For the price of one novel, a family in Germany (like Britain) could afford to feed itself for two weeks. For this reason most people among the newly emerging reading public, including the ranks of the bourgeois middle classes, switched to the lending libraries and reading societies in order to satisfy their reading requirements, or at least bought the reprinted editions that were produced in the south of the Empire and were far cheaper than the original editions printed in northern and central Germany.

[. . .]

In an effort to promote an extensive and quick form of reading, progressive publishers tried in vain to introduce the elegant roman type in place of Gothic print, those 'ghastly runes' and that 'angular, scroll-filled monks' script' (as J. J. Bertuch described it). Such attempts to modernize largely failed, making the readers of *belles-lettres* all the more eager for the texts to have an elegant and pleasing appearance. They had to be provided with a number of copper plates and vignettes, decorations and tailpieces. An integral part of the gripping novel was the illustration, best of all those by Daniel Chodowiecki, the incomparably talented portrayer of bourgeois life. The aversion to thick tomes grew: 'books create scholars, pamphlets create human beings' went the new motto.

The beginning of the bourgeois culture of reading in the age of Enlightenment also saw the introduction of the octavo format. Throughout the following decades, books became slimmer and slimmer, and the octavo, duodecimo and even the dainty sextodecimo grew to be the preferred formats for readers of *belles-lettres*. The content matched the dainty exterior most perfectly in the case of almanacs. The poetry chapbook was the medium of a literary culture that, in line with the French model, gave rise to over 2,000 of these often pleasantly, even luxuriously, produced little volumes: literary chapbooks, scientific ones for the popular and specialist markets, and political and satirical ones.

[. . .]

It was not the educative and informative literature of 'real facts', the travelogues and works of natural history, that occupied the highest position in the public taste and simultaneously constituted the main objects of the critics of the reading mania; it was rather the principal new genres of 'extensive' reading, the periodicals and novels. The latter in particular encouraged a 'rapid, inattentive, almost unconscious kind of reading habit'.[17] However, it may seem paradoxical that 'the most powerful vicarious identification of readers with the feelings of fictional characters that literature had seen should be produced by exploiting the qualities of print, the most impersonal, objective, and public of the media of communication'.[18]

As is well known, the polemic against the reading of novels has a long tradition stretching back to the *Amadis de Gaule*, though it is always described as a perversion confined to a privileged minority. However, with the multiplication of the production and reception of the novel in the late eighteenth century, the mania for reading novels assumed a sociopolitical dimension for the first time. In Germany the Easter trade fair of 1803 alone launched no fewer than 276 new novels, a figure that neither France nor Britain could come near. The deluge of novels covered all nuances of taste. In 1805 the *Allgemeine Literatur-Zeitung* took stock of the main trends in the production of novels in Germany since 1775, the year Johann Martin Miller's *Siegwart* was published: the sentimental, the comical, the psychological, the era of the passion novel, the chivalric or visionary romance, the ghost story, the magic novel, the novel of secret orders and courtly cabals, the domestic era, the era of the brigand, the thief and the rogue. A substantial proportion (around 40 per cent) of these new publications consisted of translations, primarily from English. An entire generation seemed to have caught the 'reading bug', that very generation that was meant to be continuing the struggle for bourgeois emancipation, yet was spending its time indulging in the narcotic habit of reading. Moral criticism thus acquired an eminently political dimension. Some progressive authors deplored the fact that, in the case of young students and men, such reading material destroyed the autonomy of reason and the desire for emancipation – 'and without the slightest indignation they watch the murdering of freedom of thought and the press'. By exciting and unleashing the power of the imagination, reading released the reader from concrete sensory perception and the world of experience, at the risk of total disillusionment, even nihilism. Women with a passion for novels were reproached for escaping into passive and sentimental pleasures at the very moment when the bourgeois family was assigning a new and important range of duties to them. Complaints were also heard from conservative quarters in innumerable variations that such novels stimulated the reader's imagination, corrupted his sense of morality, and distracted him from his work. Immanuel Kant stated it succinctly: 'Besides causing many other upsets to a person's nature, reading novels also makes a habit of diversion.'

Besides novels, the reading matter preferred by the new reading public was periodicals. There had already been complaints about the 'untimely new newspaper craze' since the end of the seventeenth century, but even this now assumed a new dimension. The desire for daily news, for journalistic information about topical political and ecclesiastical, literary and economic events, spread far beyond the bourgeois classes. This was also true of pamphlets, in so far as the barriers of censorship gave way. When the reforming emperor Joseph II introduced press freedom in Austria, the consequence was a unique 'thaw', due to more than 1,200 brochures, pamphlets and loose sheets that were published in the years 1781 and 1782 alone. By the end of the century, the absolute dominance of politics united all strata of readers according to the conditions specific to each group. The lower classes had the sensational new publications read to them in the markets and the inns, while the upper classes devoured them at the commercial notice stalls, or else discussed them in a well-mannered way at reading societies.

[. . .]

In Germany the revolution in reading literature did not prevent the formation of a political consciousness. On the contrary, it promoted anti-feudal, anti-Church and altogether anti-authoritarian tendencies that manifested themselves in fashionable *belles-lettres* just as frequently as they did in the political commentaries. Unfortunately the role played by clandestine reading in Germany has not yet been fully explored. As Robert Darnton has shown, using the rich sources of the *Société typographique* in Neuchâtel, obscene and irreligious books were particularly sought after in France, even among the middle class of officials and administrators.

References

1   I. Watt, *The Rise of the Novel* (Harmondsworth: Penguin, 1957), p. 174.

2   B. Haug, *Das gelehrte Württemberg* (Stuttgart, 1790), pp. 26–32.

3   R. Darnton, 'Readers respond to Rousseau: the fabrication of romantic sensitivity', in Darnton, *The Great Cat Massacre and Other Episodes in French Cultural History* (New York: Basic Books, 1984), p. 226.

4   Ibid., p. 234.

5   R. Engelsing, 'Die Perioden der Lesergeschichte in der Neuzeit', *Archiv für Geschichte des Buchwesens*, 10 (1970): 143.

6   E. Schön, *Der Verlust der Sinnlichkeit oder die Verwandlungen des Lesers: Mentalitätswandel um 1800* (Stuttgart: Klett-Cotta, 1987), p. 327.

7   L. Mejer, letter to H. C. Boie of 1 January 1784; quoted in Ilse Schreiber (ed.), *Ich war wohl klug, daß ich dich fand. H. C. Boies Briefwechsel mit Luise Mejer 1777–1785* (Munich, 1961), p. 275.

8   Cf. Schön, *Der Verlust der Sinnlichkeit*, p. 326.

9   J. A. Bergk, *Die Kunst, Bücher zu lesen: Nebst Bemerkungen über Schriften und Schriftsteller* (Jena: Hempel, 1799), p. 69.

10   Cf. Schön, *Der Verlust der Sinnlichkeit*, p. 328.

11   Cf. Eva Maria Hanebutt-Benz, ed., *Die Kunst des Lesens: Lesemöbel und Leseverhalten vom Mittelalter bis zur Gegenwart*, exhibition catalogue (Frankfurt am Main, 1985), pp. 109ff.

12   Watt, *Rise of the Novel*, p. 213.

13   Schön, *Der Verlust der Sinnlichkeit*, p. 167.

14   Jean Paul, *Briefe und bevorstehender Lebenslauf: Konjektural-Biographie, sechste poetische Epistel*; quoted from Jean Paul, *Werke*, ed., Norbert Miller, vol. 4 (Munich: Hanser, 1962), p. 1070.

15   Karl G. Bauer, *Über die Mittel, dem Geschlechtstrieb eine unschädliche Richtung zu geben* (Leipzig, 1791), p. 190.

16   Bergk, *Die Kunst, Bücher zu lesen*, p. 59.

17   Watt, *Rise of the Novel*, p. 54.

18   Ibid., p. 234.

Chapter 5

John Moorhead

READING IN LATE ANTIQUITY

IN THE FOLLOWING PAGES we shall consider evidence for the style of reading practised in late antiquity, centuries old by then, suggesting that it was one of orality, and indeed aurality, point to signs of this in what may be unexpected places, and consider the practice of memorizing texts, which would have come much more easily to those who read in this way. In conclusion we shall consider two authors of a slightly later period, some of whose works point to an expectation on the part of those who wrote them that they would be accessed in a way quite different to that anticipated by Latin fathers writing on similar topics in the preceding centuries.

One aspect of the earlier style of reading which its authors took for granted was that it could be done in public, for there is considerable evidence for the reading of books to groups of people.[1] Octavia is said to have broken down when she heard the words "tu Marcellus eris" read out from the *Aeneid*; some four centuries later, Augustine and his companions at Cassiciacum were accustomed to listen to half a volume of Vergil before dinner.[2] Books which one might expect to have been the objects of solitary study were read before groups. In his commentary on Ezekiel, Jerome found it necessary to set out in its entirety a long passage (capitulum) being commented upon, in case he violated the understanding of a reader and the division of the material into parts disturbed the understanding of a hearer;[3] Augustine envisaged the books of his *De Trinitate* being listened to, transcribed and read,[4] and a perception by well educated Christians that, when Augustine's works against the Manichaeans were read out, the ignorant understood them not at all or with difficulty, led him to write another work at a different level.[5] Gregory the Great's *Moralia in Iob* was read out in public in Ravenna; while the pope did not approve, it was the audience rather than the practice to which he objected.[6] Public readings could be part of what we would now see as the process of publication: the author of a text attributed to Vigilius of Thapsus wanted it read out to a group of learned and sensible people who were unaware of who wrote it before copies of it were made,[7] while during the spring of 544, the subdeacon Arator read out his poem on the Acts of the Apostles, which ran to over two thousand lines of hexameters, over four days in the church of S Peter ad vincula in Rome.[8] Even the reading of a letter from one person to another could be a public event: Paulinus of Nola professed fear that people would laugh when a letter he wrote to Augustine was read.[9] When bishop

Nicetius of Lyon died in 573 his will was read out by a judge in the forum, with crowds of people standing around.[10] Modern scholarship has developed the helpful notion of textual communities which were not confined to the literate,[11] and readings of texts to wide groups, such as took place when a work of a Marcionite or similar tendency was read to a large and appreciative audience in a square by the sea at Carthage,[12] gave many people access to ideas expressed in writing, no less than readings before restricted groups, as occurred in the case of an illiterate beggar known to Gregory the Great who bought codices of the Bible and had visitors to his home read them out.[13] Indeed, an author could seek to create the impression of having read his work before a live audience when this had not occurred.[14]

Such a manner of reading suggests that when readers in late antiquity picked up a book to read, whether to themselves or before others, they would have looked for qualities in the writing very different to those we appreciate. The ease with which a text could be negotiated by the tongue was highly regarded. Hence an aspect of the style of bishop Remigius of Reims which Sidonius Apollinaris praised: his writing was "easy and smooth and completely rounded, letting the reader's tongue run on gracefully without impediment and not bothered by harsh word-connections which make the voice stutter as it rolls around the arched palate."[15] Such a style of reading, which stressed the operation of the mouth, made the metaphor of eating perfectly applicable to the activity.[16] The metaphor was easily applied to the text of Scripture, which a reader could assimilate in the same way one did the bread of the Eucharist.[17] But it could be used in other contexts, as when Paulinus of Nola wrote to Augustine describing his feeling on receiving a letter from him:

> So the certain expectation of a feast in store allowed me, as often occurs, to curb the hunger of my mind, though it was greedy. The sure hope of obtaining my fill (for the loaves that I longed for were in my hand, in the form of the letter which I was soon to devour, and which later tasted most sweet to my mouth and stomach when I devoured it) allowed me easily to postpone my gluttony, which gaped open mouthed at the honeycomb of your letter, until I could set out from Rome and devote a whole day to the task. This I did at Formiae, so that I feasted on the spiritual delicacies of your letter.[18]

(That a whole day could be devoted to reading a letter suggests that this was a serious business.) The metaphorical passage from reading to eating is very clear.

It is therefore not surprising that much of the writing of the period has a remarkably oral quality which is often lost on modern readers. This is particularly true of the works of Gregory the Great, for even in his pieces of formal writing which did not originate from oral discourse he often gives the impression that he expected his words to be heard. His famous image of the Bible being a river in which a lamb may walk and an elephant swim is expressed in Latin with a lovely run of vowels (*fluvius . . . in quo agnus ambulet et elephas natet*), and the pairs of words in which sounds recur correspond exactly to units of sense.[19] And his observation that the water of the sea is bitter, while that of a river is sweet, while perhaps trivial, is given beautiful expression in which, again, the sounds and the units of meaning correspond perfectly (aqua enim maris amara est, fluminis dulcis).[20] He thought of Job's misfortunes as being turned towards a fervour of virtue (in fervorem virtutis vertitur),[21] while his famous bringing together of the words picture and scripture (pictura, scriptura) in a letter to bishop Serenus of Marseilles recurred elsewhere.[22] The hissing sound of the word "serpens" offered no end of possibilities for satisfying alliteration.[23] Such effects are not peculiar to Gregory, for they occur very frequently in patristic writing.[24] Augustine, for example, often contrasts things known in reality and in hope (in re . . . in spe). It is not surprising that the jingle occurs in his sermons, but it can also be found in the *De Civitate Dei* and *De Doctrina Christiana*.[25] Rather than interpreting such repetition of sounds within a passage as reflecting a mannered style, we would do well to see it as a device which appealed to the ear rather than the eye,[26] and having been written with the intention of providing pleasure to those who encountered the text as they heard it.

But traits of this kind were not merely designed to please the reader of a text. They also directly reflect the voice of their authors, as books in this period were generally dictated or originated in addresses to groups of listeners, and so stood very close to living speech. Hence Possidius on Augustine's literary output: "So many works were dictated and produced by him, so many of his discussions in church excerpted and revised, whether they were composed against heretics or expounded from the canonical books for the building up of the holy children of the church."[27] This summary breaks Augustine's output into two parts, one dictated against heresies and another which, having been spoken in church, was copied and revised; in both cases, the initial delivery was oral, as that of Gregory the Great was thought to have been when he was depicted in the act of dictating.[28] Towards the end of a letter he wrote to the emperor Theodosius after the massacre at Thessaloniki on 390, Ambrose stated that the final passage was being written in his own hand for the emperor's eyes alone ("postremo scribo manu mea quod solus legas"), implying that the earlier part of the letter would have been dictated by its author and then read aloud in the presence of the emperor.[29] Whereas modern authors and their readers operate in silence, in the time of the fathers of the church, a text was usually heard by both.

That texts were written and read in this way made it more than a convention to assume that as one read a piece of writing one could hear the voice of the person who wrote it. Augustine suggestively moves from the case of not remembering what you have heard someone say to that of a reader coming to the end of a page or a letter and not knowing what he had read.[30] It seems to have been a topos that the communication one enjoyed through a letter was of the same kind as one would enjoy conversing with someone who was present: "For when I am dictating and wholly concentrating on you, I speak as if we were face to face after a long separation."[31] Augustine held that the letters of the alphabet had been invented to allow us to speak with those who were absent; they were signs of spoken utterances.[32] From this it is a short jump to hearing God speaking through the words of Scripture, quotations from which patristic authors tend to introduce with verbs of speech in the present tense, such as "dicit." Readers of the sacred text could be expected to hear the words they read being spoken. Hence, Gregory the Great can envisage someone who hated his enemy reading the Bible. He would read "Love your enemies" and "Bless and do not curse" and "Not rendering evil for evil, nor curse for curse," yet fail to observe the precepts he had heard.[33] Injunctions which one heard as the Bible was read out could be taken as acts of speech addressed to oneself. Such, famously, was the case of Antony, who went into church one day: "and just then it happened that the Gospel was being read, and he heard the Lord saying to the rich man . . . ."[34] As Augustine understood it, Antony took what was being read as though it were being spoken to himself.[35] Similarly, the opening words of the Rule of St Benedict invite the person to whom they are addressed to "hear" the words of the master, and it is clear from what follows that the words Benedict has in mind are those of God, which can be heard in the Bible;[36] we may note too in passing that a tendency to interpret the Psalms as having been uttered in the voice of Christ, or that of the church, inclined people to detect a speaker uttering the words of the psalter.

The assumption that written texts would be heard as they were read out is reflected in a wide range of media, for many of the ways in which writing was used in the period imply that the words were intended to be heard as they were enunciated. Mosaics frequently show Christ holding a book open at declarative passages from S John's Gospel beginning with the words "ego sum . . ."; those who pronounced these words would hear Christ speaking about himself.[37] Similarly, portrayals of the Annunciation containing the words spoken by Gabriel to Mary, "Hail full of grace, the Lord is with thee," prompt those who view them "to read the inscription aloud and address the Virgin with the angel's words of greeting."[38] The tituli which Venantius Fortunatus supplied for pictures in the cathedral at Tours have been interpreted as providing a "voice-over" for each image.[39] Ancient inscriptions frequently address their readers, apparently in the expectation of being read out. Perhaps the best known case is the epitaph quoted by Possidius at the end of his biography of Augustine,[40] but many of the inscriptions which pope Damasus placed in Rome towards the end of the fourth century function in a similar way, and come close to accosting the person who reads them. For example, four of them begin "si quaeris," and one of them allows us to hear Damasus himself speaking: "Supplicis haec Domini vox est: venerare sepulchrum. . . ."[41] Similarly, many of the inscriptions the antiquarian Agnellus was able to gather at Ravenna in the ninth century speak directly to their reader,[42] and the early medieval inscriptions at San Vincenzo at Volturno have been held to suggest that writing on books and scrolls was used "as a means of incorporating the act of speech into the mute medium of painting, and here the Prophets were represented calling out their prophecies in succession."[43] The tendency is frequently encountered in Germanic artefacts, as in the inscription on the Alfred Jewel which represents it as speaking: "Alfred made me."[44] In a picture, now destroyed, of himself and his parents which Gregory the Great had made, his mother held a Psalter open at words expressing her feelings: "vivit anima mea et laudabit te et iudicia tua adiuvabant me."[45] This is not to say that portions of writing incorporated in non-literary media in this period were not often descriptive, but it is noteworthy how many of them take on the persona of a person in the act of speech, which would in turn be assumed by the voice of the person reading them out.

Writing, then, was widely intended for oral performance. A final indicator of this are the devices of punctuation which were used in the patristic period. Whereas modern punctuation interprets the sense and meaning of a passage of writing on behalf of a silent reader, that used in the ancient world did not have this function, so that some passages in the Bible were left open to more than one interpretation.[46] Seen in terms of the liberal arts, such punctuation as was used in the time of the Fathers, rather than helping a reader interpret the text in accordance with dialectic, gives the impression of having operated as an aid to rhetoric. Hence, the text of the Vulgate was laid out in short units of "cola et commata," which were combined to form periods. Such units were thought in terms of speech, both that of the person whose words the text expressed, so that the prophet Hosea, for example, could be imagined as speaking in commas,[47] and that of the person who was reading it, which Isidore of Seville understood in terms of breathing: he connected a comma with exhaling, and felt that it ought not to take longer than one breath to give utterance to a period.[48] More elaborate systems of punctuation, which involved the use of marks in the text, were also understood in terms of the assistance they provided for people reading out loud. Cassiodorus writes of three of these, the media, the subdistinctio and the plena, and holds that they were invented so that a person's breathing, made tired by speaking at length, might regain its strength at discrete intervals,[49] while Alcuin saw marks of punctuation as having been designed to aid a person reading to others in church.[50]

That people would access texts by reading or hearing others reading made it possible for authors to target their audiences in a way it is hard to imagine modern authors doing, and evidence a little later than most of that we have been considering shows there was more than one way in which this could be done. While the two versions of the Life of Willibrord by the Carolingian scholar Alcuin were addressed to different audiences, people who read a book and those who heard it being read could be envisaged as forming separate audiences of the one work, which would be catered for in different ways. A passage in the prefatory letter to king Ceolwulf which stands at the head of Bede's *Historia Ecclesiastica* is worth more attention than it has generally received:

> If history relates good things about good people, the anxious hearer is stimulated to imitate the good; if it recounts bad things of wicked people, no less is the religious and pious hearer or reader incited, from avoiding what is harmful and perverse, to pursue more carefully the things which he knows are good and worthy of God.[51]

These words suggest that Bede envisaged two kinds of people who would learn from his work: those who heard it, and would benefit from learning of good things, and those who heard it or read it, a group qualified as being "religious and pious" (*religiosus ac pius*) and hence presumably monastic or clerical, for whom both good and bad things were recounted. This antithesis is sustained in the letter to Ceolwulf, and it is possible to show that, while Bede wrote in a formally correct Latin, the class of hearers, whom he may well have expected to gain knowledge of his work through translation,[52] was important to him. He goes on to list the chief sources for his work, "to take away from hearers or readers any reason for doubting this history." Bede is almost certainly imitating at this point a passage in the prologue to the Dialogues of Gregory the Great, in which the pope said he would list his authorities "to take away from readers any reason for doubt;"[53] Bede's addition of the category of "hearers" to Gregory's "readers" certainly suggests that he envisaged a broader audience for his work than Gregory did for his. The only story in the *History* Bede specifically indicates he is telling for the benefit of his readers and hearers concerns the fate of a damned layperson (5.13), but he states that the story of the prisoner whose chains fell off when masses were sung (4.22), which we may take as a narration of a good things about good people, led many people, presumably lay, to adopt new practices. Fittingly, stories involving bad religious are aimed at readers (4,25, 5.14), as is a account of the Holy Land, presumably of interest to religious professionals (5.17, 319) and his telling the good qualities of the monk Aidan was for the benefit of his readers (3.17, 161). Bede, no less than Augustine, was familiar with quite difficult works being read out to an audience, although in his case this would have been mediated by translation. The Carolingian scholar Hincmar of Reims moved in another direction, by placing marks in the margin of his Life of Remigius which indicated the portions suitable for being recited to the people and those to be read to people described as enlightened, instructed and devoted to study (*illuminatis, instructioribus, studiosioribus*).[54] But in the case of Bede's History, those capable of reading the book themselves, and those who would hear it being read, could as it were be envisaged as sharing the one book, while being expected to gain different things from it or being exposed to different parts of it.

[. . .]

Memory was central in the society of late antiquity, just as it had been in the ancient world.[55] Cicero, having quoted a few words from the *Twelve Tables*, can go on: "You know what comes after, for when we were boys we learned the twelve as something which had to be sung (*carmen necessarium*), things which no-one learns now."[56] A boyhood friend of Augustine could recite Vergil and Cicero starting from a given point, moving either forwards or backwards; astonishingly, the biographer of Fulgentius of Ruspe asserts that he had committed all of Homer to memory.[57] But not surprisingly, given the centrality of the Bible in patristic culture, this text was held in the mind to a far greater extent than any other. We are told that Didymus, blind from the age of five, had acquired astonishing learning through what he had heard, and that another Egyptian, the illiterate monk Antony, memorized the Bible through hearing it read out.[58] But within the Bible, one portion was central.

Someone joining a monastery would begin by memorizing "the whole sequence of Psalms,"[59] and this was only the beginning of the massive exposure to this text which a monk or nun would experience through the liturgy. For someone living according to the Rule of Benedict, which prescribed for the recitation of the complete Psalter across a week,[60] there must have come a time at which the text had penetrated very deeply into one's being; perhaps the so-called Gregorian Chant was designed to force those who sang it to concentrate upon the words and syllables of an all too familiar text. Caesarius of Arles encouraged monks to run through the Psalms in their memory frequently,[61] while the author of the *Regula Magistri* envisages people being able to recite from memory passages which were lacking in a text.[62] Such intimate knowledge of the Psalms underwrites the sometimes overwhelming density of formal quotation and indirect allusion to them in patristic and medieval writing. This can be seen in particular in works which were not based directly on Scripture but in which it was used to supply images and vocabulary in discussions of other things; of the vast number of biblical allusions in the *Confessions* of Augustine, for example, some three quarters are to Psalms.[63] These can sometimes be very subtle, as when Augustine described his decision to abandon his chair at Milan following his conversion. In writing of his wish not to sit for one hour in the chair of mendacity ("sedere in cathedra mendacii") he alludes to a phrase from the beginning of Psalm 1, describing the blessed man as not sitting in the chair of pestilence ("in cathedra pestilentiae non sedit," Vulgate).[64] Many reminiscences of this kind must have been unconscious, familiar words coming to mind without recollection of their source.

The central role of memory in this culture can be demonstrated in another way. It was taken for granted in late antiquity that the clergy memorized texts. Augustine had to specify that someone who had memorized the chants of a priest did not thereby become a priest![65] In particular, clergy could be assumed to have committed chunks of the Bible to memory. Not surprisingly, much of the evidence relates to the Psalter, which sometimes had to be memorized before someone was ordained, so that we hear of a young man who could recite the Psalter from memory being made a deacon[66] and of Gregory the Great refusing to consecrate men "ignorant of the Psalms."[67]

[. . .]

Doubtless most people were considerably less familiar with scripture than the clergy and monastics, but the "textual community" which formed around the Bible was huge. Augustine thought of his congregation committing passages of it to memory,[68] and Caesarius of Arles assumed that the greatest part of the human race held Psalm 103, "Sol cognovit occasum suum," in its memory.[69] It was therefore reasonable for African Donatists who were asked whether they possessed the Scriptures to seek to evade the question by replying that they had them in their hearts.[70] The first generation to sing Christian hymns in the West not only needed no hymn books, but found passages of hymns they had sung coming to their consciousness at odd times.[71] Congregations that heard words read committed them to memory, as was the case with a congregation in Africa that became agitated when Jerome's translation of Jonah was read out: it was, Augustine complained, "very different from the version enshrined in the memory and hearing of all and sung for so many generations."[72] The fact that Scripture was not only read out but also sung facilitated this process. Augustine writes of the pleasure he received when the words of God were chanted in a pleasant, trained voice. He goes on to discuss the Psalms, accusing himself of taking too much pleasure in the way they were sung, and agreeing with the practice of Athanasius of Alexandria, who had the reader of a Psalm pronounce it in such a way that it was closer to recited than sung, but it is highly likely that the initial reference to chanting applies to other parts of the Bible.[73] And so the contents of the Bible may have presented themselves to people in late antiquity via their memory as much as the reading or hearing of the written word.

There are many signs of patristic authors accessing the Bible through the use of memory.[74] Writing to Augustine about things in the Gospels which were hard to understand, Paulinus said that he lacked the time to look for things scattered through books or agitate his memory in recalling them to mind. His statement may have been no more than a conventional utterance or an excuse for laziness, but it suggests the two ways in which portions of a text could be summoned up: one could consult books or use one's memory.[75] We may consider an aspect of the mental processes of Gregory the Great. His allegorizing approach to the Scriptures involved assigning various significances to words in the Bible, and sometimes the one word could bear more than one meaning. Take the word "mons" (mountain). Gregory believed it could mean five different things. In various contexts, it stood for the incarnate Lord, the holy church, the testament of God, the apostate angel, and a heretic of some kind. In the plural, "montes" could refer to the apostles and angels in their height, or to the swelling of secular powers.[76] The word "gold" had five meanings, those of the brightness of the divinity, the shininess of the city above, love, the lustre of worldly glory, and the beauty of holiness.[77] Gregory provides an example of each meaning in a quotation from Scripture, in a sequence quite at variance with that of the books of the Bible from which they are taken, although elsewhere, when he adduced a series of passages in the Bible to exemplify one point, he brought them forward in a sequence very similar to the order in which they are found in the Bible.[78] Given that Gregory cannot have summoned up occurrences of a particular word in the Bible by using a concordance, for the system of chapters and verses needed for a concordance would only be invented hundreds of years after his time, and that he can hardly have scanned the entire Bible looking for occurrences of particular words, we may assume that his statements of the various significances one word could bear were made on the basis of memory. Very often, a series of quotations from the Bible in patristic writing will be linked by the recurrence of words rather than ideas, in a process which has been seen to reveal an author's "sheer joy in the potentialities of his own word-play."[79] Word summons word, or in some cases it may be no more than a sound summoning a similar sound from the vast treasure house of memory. Doubtless the ability to operate in this way could be facilitated by the systematic memorization of passages of text. But the process of memorization, and the mulling over of texts which had been lodged in the memory, need not have been fully conscious.

[. . .]

Slow, oral reading, and the sense of a potentially series of meanings which a non-literal approach to texts allowed, found natural expression in a discursive response to the content of one's reading. Doubtless this was chiefly the concern of religious professionals, such as the nuns for whom Caesarius of Arles prescribed that sisters were to read until the third hour, after which meditation on the word of God and prayer from the heart would not cease.[80] But the practice was open to people in the world, and Augustine commends it to the members of his congregation. Discussing the words "And those who will dwell safely in the desert will sleep by the streams" [cf Ez 34.25], he applies the metaphor of moving water to a mind as it processes scripture:

> In that inner solitude are certain streams of memory flowing, distilling divine essences from the mind of one who retains and mulls over the scriptures. You see, if you entrust what you have read, what you have heard to your memory, then when you begin to rest in that inner desert or solitude, in a good conscience, it seeps from the inner recesses of your mind, and recollection of the word of God starts flowing somehow or other . . .[81]

And so, according to Jerome, by persistent reading and lengthy meditation one could turn one's breast into a Bible ("biblioteca," perhaps "library") of Christ.[82] Indeed, it was said that, for Antony, memory took the place of a book.[83]

But expectations that texts would be accessed not merely by private readers but by those who heard them being read, and committed passages to memory, were not to last. Indeed, there were already works which seem to have been designed to be consulted as efficiently as possible by a private reader seeking a particular piece of information,[84] and a series of works by an author of the sixth century point to expectations that a book would be read in a way quite different to those we have been considering. All the manuscripts of Cassiodorus' *De anima* begin with a list of the eighteen capitula into which the work is divided, and we may assume that it was provided by the author when he wrote, in c.540. The first of these capitula provides another list, which itemized twelve things to be learned about the soul.[85] Readers of another work of Cassiodorus, the *Institutiones*, would not have been surprised to learn from its author that it contained teachers of an earlier period who were always at the ready, but their mode of instruction may have been unexpected, for they would teach "not so much by their tongues as by your eyes."[86] The two parts of this work, respectively devoted to divine and secular letters, each begin with a table of contents; as has been well said concerning it, "[t]he text is no longer composed to be read aloud and listened to, but rather studied and examined by the individual reader directly from the manuscript."[87] Again, the preface to the long commentary on the Psalms which Cassiodorus wrote in two versions across the second and third quarters of the sixth century concludes with a list of the twelve parts of the "ordo dicendorum."[88] This commentary, in turn, has been seen as the first work in Latin antiquity presented with the expectation of being read privately and in silence,[89] and it is indeed full of technical explanations of points of rhetoric and dialectic, etymological explanations, and discussions of the significance of the number of each Psalm which would be appropriate for a solitary, scholarly reader; not surprisingly, Cassiodorus often envisages the Bible as being read as well as heard.[90]

Cassiodorus' exposition of the Psalms in this manner is very different to the mode employed by such commentators on this text as Ambrose, Hilary and Augustine, for while the knowledge that their words were being written could influence the way these bishops treated the text,[91] their works present us with material substantially in the form in which it was preached to congregations; perhaps any novelty in Cassiodorus' procedure simply reflected a style of composition being applied to a work which had hitherto been generally treated in other ways, rather than a radically new way of writing about a text, in which case the difference between him and his predecessors may be his choice of a different genre rather than a development across time from one way of commentating to another. But it would be wrong to distinguish sharply between these two possibilities, for as time passed formal commentaries on Scripture were increasingly products of the study rather than the pulpit. Perhaps atrophy in the practice of preaching lay behind this tendency, for while Caesarius and then Gregory devoted attention to preaching on readings from the Bible to lay audiences, and Caesarius encouraged others to preach,[92] the practice seems to have become less common after the sixth century. Proper consideration of this development, which would involve considerations of the relation of spoken language to that of the Bible, both its development away from formal Latin in the Romance speaking areas and the need to preach in a language in which the Bible was not available where Germanic languages were spoken, would take us beyond the scope of this paper, but for whatever reason the pastoral concerns which underwrote the expositions of the fathers of the classical period came to find less expression in preaching, so the field was left open to relatively bookish productions, con-siderably more indebted to preceding works than expositors in pulpits could have been.

More general developments in education stood behind this shift. The purpose of education in antiquity had been to produce people who could speak in public, and such training in rhetoric underwrote the preaching of Ambrose and Augustine; the initial judgment the latter passed on the preaching of Ambrose was that of a fellow-professional who was interested not in what was said but how it was said.[93] But the skill was less relevant in the post-Roman world; the genre of panegyric, while still practiced by Cassiodorus and Boethius in Italy early in the sixth century, had little future. And as the purpose of education shifted away from producing orators towards enabling the mastery of key texts, the Bible in particular, books moved in accordance with the trend. Hence, in the Greek-speaking, world the *Apophthegmata Patrum* were organized alphabetically during the sixth century, while in the early seventh century Isidore of Seville produced his *Etymologiae*, surely aimed at a solitary, silent reader.[94]

[. . .]

That a text would be read orally, whether by a solitary reader or before a group, is a practice which itself mirrored the way the text had been delivered by its author, and that those who had heard books would sometimes be able to use what they had heard to access their contents through the exercise of memory, was generally taken for granted. The readers of late antiquity sought qualities in books quite alien to those we seek; conversely, and perhaps disturbingly, few of us read books written in the period in the way their authors took it for granted they would be read.

* Standard abbreviations:

ACW   Ancient Christian Writers
CCSL   Corpus Scriptorum Series Latina
CSEL   Corpus Scriptorum Ecclesiasticorum Latinorum
FC   The Fathers of the Church
MGH   Monumenta Germaniae Historica
LL   Leg Leges
SRM   Scriptores Rerum Merovingicarum
PL   Patrologia Latina
SChr   Sources Chrétiennes

References

1   On the oral performance of works in an earlier period, Moses Hadas, *Ancilla to Classical Reading*, Morningside Heights, NY, 1954, p. 50–64.

2   Octavia: *Vita Donati*, in C. Hardie, ed., *Vitae Vergilianae Antiquae*, Oxford, 1966, ll. 113–15 (13). Augustine and companions: *De ordine* 1.8.26 (PL 32:989).

3   *Commentarii in Ezechielem* 14.47.6 (CCSL 75:713).

4   Ep. 174 (PL 33:758), but note "quisquis haec legit . . . qui ea quae scribo legunt . . . quisquis ergo cum legit . . ." (*De Trinitate* 1.3.5, CCSL 50:32). Compare "cum leguntur et audiuntur" in the Confessions (10.3.4); "legenti vel audienti" *De doctrina christiana* 4.31.64 (CCSL 32:167).

5   *De Genesi contra Manichaeos* 1.1.1 (PL 34:173).

6   *Registrum epistularum* 12.6 (CCSL 140A:975f).

7   PL 62:466; I owe the reference to Paul Meyveart, "Medieval Notions of Publication: the 'unpublished' Opus Caroli Regis contra synodum and the Council of Frankfort (794)", in *Journal of Medieval Latin* 12, 2002, p. 78–89 at 79.

8   See on this work Richard Hillier, *Arator on the Acts of the Apostles*, Oxford, 1993; Arator's writings are ed. CSEL 72.

9   Paulinus ep. 50.1 (ed. CSEL 30:404).

10   Gregory of Tours, *Vita patrum* 8.5 (MGH SRM 1:695).

11   On textual communities, the work of Brian Stock is fundamental. Note that a statement by the author of a medieval saint's life in the vernacular that the work was based on a Latin source need not mean that he, or she, had read such a source: "It may very well be that he had heard the story read to him, or just that he had heard it read, in church perhaps; or again, perhaps someone told him the story": E. B. Vitz, *From the Oral to the Written in Medieval Saints' Lives*, in R. Blumenfeld-Kosinsky and T. Szell, ed., *Images of Sainthood in Medieval Europe*, Ithica, NY, 1991, p. 97–114 at 100.

12   Augustine, *Retractationes* 2.58 (CCSL 57:136).

13   Gregory the Great, *Dialogues* 4.15.3 (SChr 265:60); Caesarius of Arles envisages people paying others to read the Bible to them, *serm.* 6.8 (CCSL 103:36).

14   Deborah Mauskopf Deliyannis, *The Book of the Pontiffs of the Church of Ravenna*, Washington, DC, 2004, p. 60–65.

15   Sidonius Apollinaris, ep. 9.7, transl. W. B. Andersen (Loeb edn), p. 527.

16   Hence Gregory the Great's discussion of the command given to Ezekiel to eat a book: *Homiliae in Hiezechielem* 1.10.2–13 (SChr 327: 382–96).

17   See for example PS. Jerome, PL 26:1256f.

18   Paulinus, ep. 45.1 (CSEL 29:380); transl. P. G. Walsh, ACW 36:245. Another of Augustine's correspondents had a similar response: "sermonibus tuis pascar" (Augustine, ep. 152.3; PL 33. 653).

19   *Moralia in Iob, ep. ad Leandrum* 4 (CCSL 143:6).

20   *Moralia in Iob* 12.7.10 (CCSL 143A:634).

21   *Moralia in Iob, praef.* 2.6 (CCSL 143:12). See on all this John Moorhead, *Gregory the Great*, London and New York, 2005, p. 45f.

22   With Gregory *Registrum* 11.10 (CCSL 140:874), compare an interpolated version of 9.148 (1111). Isidore of Seville was not so encouraging: "Pictura autem dicta quasi fictura" (*Etymologiae* 19.16.1, ed. W. M. Lindsay, Oxford, 1911)! See too the Council of Paris (825): "ipsa pictura pro scriptura haberetur" (MGH Leg 3 Concilia 2/2, 479, line 18).

23   "Astutia serpentis" (*Regula pastoralis* 3.11, SChr 382:316; perhaps for reasons of sound, Gregory avoids the "prudentia" suggested by the "prudentes" of Matt 10:16, which he has just quoted, although he retains "simplicitas" as a characteristic of the dove); "serpens prava suggessit" (*Regula pastoralis* 3.29, 474, line 89); "inmanissimae asperitatis serpentem" (*Dialogi* 3.35.2, SChr 260:404); "serpens suasit" (*Moralia in Iob* 4.27.49, CCSL 143:193); "serpens insidians" (*Moralia in Iob* 17.15.21, CCSL 143A:864); "serpentis suasione" (*Moralia in Iob* 24.4.7, CCSL 143B:1193).

24   It is hard to go past Ambrose's condemnation of usury: "Nihil interest inter funus et faenus, nihil inter mortem distat et sortem: personat, personat funebrem ululatum faenebris usura" (*De Tobia* 10.36).

25   *Serm.* 9.3, 27.4, 47.1, 117.10 (PL 38:77, 180, 295, 670) etc, with *De Civitate Dei* 13.4, 15.18, 21 (CCSL 47:388, 481, 487), *De Trinitate* 14.18.24 (CCSL 50A:456).

26   Mannered style: A. Loyen, *Sidoine Apollinaire et l'ésprit précieux en Gaule*, Paris, 1943. Appealing to ear: G. M. Cook, *The Life of Saint Epiphanius by Ennodius*, Washington, DC, 1942, p. 19.

27   Possidius *Vita Augustini* 18 (PL 32:49). The word 'edita,' here translated 'produced,' is rendered as 'published' in the translation of M. D. Muller and R. J. Deferrari (FC 15:95), but this cannot be correct: Meyvaert "Medieval Notions" (cit. above n. 15), 79f. Jerome's practice in dictating has been investigated by E. Arns, *La technique du livre d'après Saint Jérôme*, Paris, 1953, p. 37–51, concluding that Jerome's frequent references to "dictare" generally refer to dictation.

28   See for example H. Schnitzer, "Hieronymus und Gregor in der Ottonischen Kölner Buchmalerei," in Wolfgang Braunfels, ed., *Kunstgeschichtliche Studien für Hans Kauffmann*, Berlin, 1956, p. 11–18. A famous picture of Gregory in this style executed by an artist based in Trier towards the end of the tenth century is conveniently reproduced by Henry Mayr-Harting, *Ottonian Book Illumination*, London, 1991, ill. 13.

29   *Ep. Ext. coll.* 11.14 (letter 51 in the Maurist enumeration; ed. M. Zelzer, *Sancti Ambrosii Episcopi Mediolanensis Opera* 21: 238.) The recipient of a letter could be expected to identify the author's handwriting in the subscription, but apparently this alone: Augustine ep. 72.2.3 (PL 33:244). Compare S Paul's supplying a greeting in his own hand ("mea manu," Vulgate) at the end of epistles (1 Cor 16.21, 2 Thess 3.17).

30   *De Trinitate* 11.8.15 (CCSL 50:352).

31   Paulinus ep. 5.20 (CSEL 29:38); transl. Walsh, ACW 35:68. Compare: "Welcome me, and look on me as I speak, as if I were standing next to you and talking face to face" (ibid 13.2: CSEL 29:85, ACW 35:119); "quanto magis quod ad te scribitur, ubi tanquam praesenti loquar," Augustine ep. 200.3 (PL 33: 926–7); "quasi ille loquitur quando codex eius titulatus nomine legitur", *S. Fulgentii episcopi Ruspensis Vita* prol. 2 (PL 65:117; note too a following reference to a book in which Fulgentius "absens loquitur", 118).

32   *De Trinitate* 15.10.19 fin (CCSL 50A: 486).

33   *Moralia in Iob* 22.12.25 (CCSL143A:1110).

34   *Vita Antonii* 2 (SChr 400:132.); transl. R. C. Gregg, London 1980). Compare "nos itaque sic audiamus evangelium quasi praesentem Dominum": Augustine *Tractatus in Evangelium Iohannis* 30.1 (CCSL 36:289, FC 88:22).

35   *Confessiones* 8.12.29.

36   "Obsculta, o fili, praecepta magistri" (*Benedicti Regula, prol.* 1); on the identity of the master, John Moorhead, "Hearing the Bible in St Benedict", in *Studia monastica* 27, 2005, p. 7–17. P. Tombeur has gathered evidence for the importance of hearing in hagiographical narratives: *«Audire» dans le thème hagiographique de la conversion*, in *Latomus* 42, 1965, p. 159–65 (discussion not entirely convincing).

37   *Ego sum via veritas et vita* in the archbishop's chapel in Ravenna (F. W. Deichmann, *Ravenna Hauptstadt des spätantiken Abendlandes* 3, Wiesbaden, 1958, ill. 217); *Ego sum via veritas et vita qui credit in me vivet* in S Peter's Rome, early eighth century (M. Oakeshott, *The Mosaics of Rome from the Third to the Eighteenth Centuries*, London, 1967, ill. 111); *Ego sum lux ego sum vita ego sum resurrectio* in S Marco, from the time of pope Gregory IV (828–44) (ibid, pl. XXIII).

38   Ann van Dijk, *The Angelic Salutation in early Byzantine and Medieval Annunciation Imagery*, in *The Art Bulletin* 81, 1999, p. 420–36; the words quoted are from 425.

39   P. Brennan, *Text and Image Reading the Walls of the sixth-century Cathedral at Tours*, in *Journal of Medieval Latin* 6, 1996, p. 65–83 at 72f.

40   Vivere post obitum vatem vis nosse viator Quod legis ecce loquor vox tua nempe mea est: Possidius *Vita Augustini* 31 (PL 32:164); note the alliteration in the first line.

41   A. Ferrua ed. *Epigrammata Damasiana*, Rome, 1942, p. 291 s.v. 'quaero'; 46 line 11. There are signs of this tradition in *Venantius Fortunatus*, as: "Qui celerare paras, iter huc deflecte, viator" (*carm* 1.5.1, ed. M. Reydellet, Paris, 1994, p. 24), and "Si Hilarium quaeris qui sit cognoscere, lector" (*carm* 2.15.1, p. 71).

42   D. Deliyannis, "The Liber Pontificalis Ecclesiae Ravennatis Critical Edition and Commentary" (unpublished PhD thesis, University of Pennsylvania, 1994); see for example inscriptions cast in the first person (ch. 27; p. 470), using the imperative (28, 42; p. 471, 493), and addressing the reader in the vocative (41; p. 492).

43   John Mitchell, "Literacy Displayed: The Use of Inscriptions in the Monastery of San Vincenzo al Volturno in the early Ninth Century", in R. McKitterick ed. *The Uses of Literacy in Early Medieval Europe*, Cambridge, 1990, p. 186–225 at 194; note too references to open books with writing in the first person, 193.

44   +*Aelfred mec heht gewyrcan*: reproduced in Alfred P. Smyth, *King Alfred the Great*, Oxford, 1995, plate 2.

45   According to John the Deacon, *Vita Gregorii* 4.83 (PL 75:230). An engraving made in 1597 represents the first word as "vivet," in conformity with the Vulgate: G. B. Ladner, *Die Papstbildnisse des Altertums und des Mittelalters* 1, Vatican City, 1941, p. 70–75.

46   For example, in the words "Deus erat verbum hoc erat in principio apud Deum" (within John 1.1f), the word "verbum" could go either with the preceding or following words, and in the face of such ambiguity the meaning could only be settled by recourse to the "regula fidei": Augustine, *De doctrina christiana* 3.2.4 (CCSL 32:78; the following passage gives further examples of ambiguity which modern punctuation would have cleaned up). Augustine takes the words "ascendi recumbens" at Gen 49.9 as a phrase, contrary to the modern understanding (*sermo* 37.2.2); a similar problem arose with the word "hodie" in Luke 23.43, on which see CASSIAN *Conlationes* 1.14 (SChr 42:94f.)

47   "Osee commaticus est et quasi per sententias loquens:" *Prologus duodecim prophetarum*, in *Biblia Sacra iuxta Vulgatam Versionem*, ed. R. Weber, Stuttgart, 1983, p. 1374.

48   Comma: *Etymologiae* 1.20.3, but note that he sees a comma as a mark in the text. Period: *De*

rhetorica 18 (ed. Ch. Halm, *Rhetores Latini Minores*, Leipzig, 1863, p. 516. When Isidore wrote of cola, commata and periodi he meant something like musical pauses: Jacques Fontaine, *Isidore de Séville et la culture classique dans l'Espagne wisigothique*, Paris, 1959, p. 71–73.

49   *Institutiones* 1.15.12 (ed. R. A. B. Mynors, Oxford, 1937, p. 48f); Jerome's system in the Vulgate is mentioned at 1, *praef.* 9 (p. 8).

50   Alcuin *carm.* 69.183–86, 94.7–10 (MGH Poetae 1:292, 320.). The context in which such reading took place, however, is unclear: Lawrence Nees, "Problems of Form and Function in early medieval Illustrated Bibles from northwest Europe", in John Williams, ed., *Imaging the Early Medieval Bible*, University Park, PA, 1999, p. 121–77 at 132f; see further on Alcuin J. Vezin, "Les divisions du texte dans les Evangiles jusqu'à l'apparition de l'imprimerie", in A. Maierù, ed., *Grafia e interpunzione del Latino nel medioevo*, Rome, 1987, p. 53–68 at 59.

51   *Historia Ecclesiastica*, (ed. Ch. Plummer, Oxford, 1896, overall still of greater utility than the edition of B. Colgrave, Oxford, 1969), p. 5. It occurs to me to wonder whether a phrase of Augustine, "pudicus et religiosus lector vel auditor" (*De Civitate Dei* 14.23; CCSL 47:446), does not lie behind Bede's "religiosus ac pius auditor sive lector."

52   The very long and technical letter of Abbot Ceolfrid to king Nechtan (*Historia ecclesiastica* 5.21, ed. Plummer p. 333–45) is described as having been read out in the presence of Nechtan and many of his learned men (p. 345). Such a practice of reading out before a king a text which needed to be translated from Latin presumably lay behind Pope Honorius' otherwise inexplicable advice to king Edwin of Northumbria to be frequently employed in the reading ("lectio") of Gregory the Great: Bede *Historia ecclesiastica* 2.17 (119); there is no need to see literacy on Edwin's part as being taken for granted by the pope, as does George Henderson, *From Darrow to Kells the Insular Gospel Books 650–800*, London, 1987, p. 11

53   "Ut . . . auditoribus sive lectoribus huius historiae occasionem dubitandi subtraham" (ed. Plummer, p. 6); "ut dubitationis occasionem legentibus subtraham" Gregory *Dialogues* 1 prol. 10 (SChr 260:16); note as well in BEDE "legentes sive audientes" (ed. Plummer, p. 8). Such an amendment of Gregory by Bede may have implications for the way he regarded his work in relation to that of his predecessor.

54   MGH SRM 3:258f.

55   The study of Mary Carruthers, *The Book of Memory A Study of Memory in the Middle Ages*, Cambridge, 1990, is fundamental, although she emphasizes deliberate memorization, whereas in what follows I shall place more emphasis on this occurring unconsciously. Note too a tendency in this book to over-interpret texts, sometimes seeing mnemonic significance where none was intended: Laura Kendrick, *Animating the Letter: The Figurative Embodiment of Writing from late antiquity to the Renaissance*, Columbus, OH, 1999, p. 8f. Carol Gibson-Wood, "The Utrecht Psalter and the art of memory", in *Revue d'art canadienne/Canadian art review* 14, 1987, p. 9–15, has seen a famous set of illustrations as intended to aid memorization (also discussed by Carruthers, *Book of Memory*, 226f), but against this argument we may note the de luxe nature of the volume, scarcely in keeping with a teaching aid.

56   *Legibus* 2.23.59.

57   Augstine's friend: *De natura et origine animae*, 4.7.9 (CSEL 60:389); admittedly, this was seen as a spectacular feat. Fugentius: *S Fulgentii episcopi Ruspensis Vita* 1.4. (PL 65:119).

58   He was known to the Greek ecclesiastical historians of the fifth century (Socrates 4.25; Sozomen 3.15; Theodoret 4.26) and Jerome (*De viris illustribus* 109, PL 23:743f). It was said of Antony that "memory took the place of books" (*Vita Antonii* 3; SC400:138).

59   As did Wilfrid at Lindisfarne, although before long he had to go to the trouble of memorizing another version: *Vita Wilfridi* 2f (ed MGH SRM 6:195f). Theodore of Sykeon memorized the Psalter within a few days: *Vie de Théodore de Sykeôn*, ed. and transl. A-J. Festugière, 2 vols, Brussels, 1970 (=*Subsidia Hagiographica* 48), 13. P. Riché sets a daunting agenda in noting that it would be interesting to study the influence of this first contact with the sacred text on medieval literature and spirituality: "Le Psautier, livre de lecture élémentaire d'après les vies des saints mérovingiens", in *Études Mérovingiennes*, Paris, 1953, p. 253–56 at 256.

60   *Benedicti Regula* 18.23 (CSEL 75:23).

61   *Sermo* 238.1 (CCSL 104:949f.)

62   "Hoc ideo constituimus ut frequentius aliqua meditentur et memoria teneant scripturas, fratres, ut quando in quovis loco codex deest textum lectionis vel paginae si opus fuerit memoria recitetur": *Regula Magistri* 44.11 (SChr 106:204).

63   See the list of Loci Sacrae Scripturae in the edition of M. Skutella, pp. 667–79.

64   Confessions 9.2.3, on which see G. N. Knauer, *Augustins Psalmenzitate*, Gottingen, 1955, p. 120, who concludes that Augustine must have known the Psalms by heart (p. 192).

65   *Contra litteras Petiliani* 2.68 (PL 43:281). Yet the ability of Sidonius Apollinaris to conduct a liturgy from memory after a book had been stolen was a source of wonder: Gregory of Tours *Libri Historiarum* 2.22 (p. 67).

66   *Vita Gaugerici* 4 (MGH SRM 3:653). Compare the case of John Chrysostum, who learned the two Testaments by heart over two years, prior to becoming a deacon: Palladius *Dialogue sur la vie de Jean Chrysostme* 5 (SChr 241:110).

67   *Registrum* 5.51, 14.11 (CCSL 140:345, 140A:1081).

68   "Audivi etiam hoc in sacra scriptura et commendavi cordi meo et in memoria mea reposui": *sermo* 41.3 (PL 38:248).

69   Caesarius of Arles, *sermo* 136.1 (CCSL 103:560).

70   PL 18:695f, 697C.

71   Hence Augustine's mother, "recognitis verbis quae suae memoriae penitus inhaerebant, et quasi vigilans": De Beata Vita 35 (PL 32:976; we shall return to the theme of "vigilans"); note too how verses of Ambrose came to Auguxtine's mind while he was lying in bed, *Confessiones* 9.12.32

72   "quam erat omnium sensibus memoriaeque inveteratum, et tot aetatem successionibus decan-tatum": Augustine *ep.* 71.3.5 (PL 33:242f, FC 12:327); cf Jerome ep. 112.22 (ed. Labourt).

73   *Confessiones* 10.33.49f. Other parts of the Bible: Jonah was "decantatum", see prec. footnote.

74   While coming from a period different to that we are considering, we may note that Thomas Aquinas did not pause to check references while dictating: Carruthers, *Memory*, p. 6.

75   Ep. 50.14.

76   *Moralia in Iob* 33.1.2 (CCSL 143B:1670f).

77   *Moralia in Iob* 34.15.26 (CCSL 143B: 1752f).

78   As in the case of the virtues of fathers of the Old Testament: *Moralia in Iob* 27.10.17 (CCSL 143B:1341–43).

79   C. Conybeare, *Paulinus Noster Self and Symbols in the Letters of Paulinus of Nola*, Oxford, 2000, p.123 (with reference to ep. 23).

80   Caesarius, *Regula ad virgines* 18 (PL 67:1109f); cf A. M. Mundó, "Las Reglas Monásticas Latinas del Siglo VI y la «lectio divina»", in *Studia Monastica* 9, 1967, p. 229–55, with the classic discussion of Leclercq, *Love of Learning* (cit. above, n. 8), p. 18–22.

81   Augustine, serm. 47.23, transl. Hill.

82   Ep. 60.10.9. On the significance of 'bibliotheca,' the argument of A. M. Mundó, "Bibliotheca Bible et lecture du carême d'après Saint Benoît", in *Revue Bénédictine* 60, 1950, p. 65–92, concerning *Benedicti Regula* 48.15 has neither been proved nor disproved; see further Harry Y. Gamble, *Books and Readers in the Early Church: A History of Early Christian Texts*, New Haven, 1995.

83   Above, n. 67. While he refused to learn letters, he paid attention to readings, keeping the fruit inside (1.2f).

84   The entries in Jerome's *Liber Interpretationis Hebraicorum Nominum* are arranged according to books of the Bible, and within this framework alphabetically according to the initial letter of each name (CCSL 72). Not surprisingly, Augustine assumes a reader for his *De Consensu Evange-listarum: Tractatus in evangelium Ioannis* 117.2 (CCSL 36:652). From an earlier period, one thinks of the massive first book of Pliny the Elder's *Historia Naturalis* is taken up with a list of the contents of the whole work, and at the conclusion of the dedicatory letter to Vespasian he explains its purpose: it will enable readers to find what they want.

85   CCSL 96: 533, 535.

86   "[N]on vos doceant tam suis linguis quam vestris potius oculis": *Institutiones praef.* 5 (ed. Mynors, p. 6).

87   M. Gorman, "The Diagrams in the Oldest Manuscripts of Cassiodorus' Institutiones", in *Revue Bénédictine* 110, 2000, p. 27–41, at 41. Tables of contents: ed. Mynors, p. 9–11, 93. On the complex history of this work, L. Holtz, "Quelques aspects de la tradition et de la diffusion des Institutions", in S. Leanza, ed., *Flavio Aurelio Cassiodoro*, Soveria Mannelli, 1986, p. 281–312. See too the somewhat diffuse study of Fabio Troncarelli, *Vivarium I libri, il destino*, Turnhout, 1998, envisioning a series of revisions by Cassiodorus himself, and, recently, Mark Vessey with James Halporn, *Cassiodorus Institutions of Divine and Secular Learning and On the Soul*, Liverpool, 2003, p. 39ff.

88   *Expositio psalmorum praef.* 17 (CCSL 97:24f).
89   M. Stansbury, *Early-medieval Biblical Commentaries, their Writers and Readers*, in *Frühmittelalterliche Studien* 33, 1999, p. 49–82, building on the work of J. W. Halporn, "Methods of Reference in Cassiodorus", in *Library Journal* 16, 1981, p. 71–91, who argues that the commentary on the Psalms was designed for individual readers, its notae serving as an index. I concur with this judgment despite Cassiodorus' referring to listeners of the commentary and his prayer that he might deserve to be heard and that speech would be granted to him: *Expositio Psalmorum praef* 17 (CCSL 97:24). Other works would have been composed with the expectation of being consulted in silence.
90   His use of the formula "sicut legitur" to cue biblical quotations is recurrent, as at 5.3.4 (CCSL 97:64), 12.6 (125), 18.2 (170), 18.7 (172), 25.2 (232).
91   "Non auditorem tantum sed et lectorem etiam cogitare debeamus": Augustine, *Enarrationes in psalmos* 51.1 (CCSL 39:623).
92   William E. Klingshirn, *Caesarius of Arles The Making of a Christian Community in Late Antique Gaul*, Cambridge, 1984, p. 147, 228–32.
93   *Confessiones* 5.14.24.
94   On the Apophthegmata, see J. Pauli in *Lexikon der Antiken Christlichen Literatur*, ed. S. Döpp and W. Geerlings, 3rd edn, Freiburg, 2002, p. 53.

SECTION 2

Theorising the reader

INTRODUCTION

THE SCHOLARLY FIELD OF enquiry now defined as the history of reading draws on a number of different disciplines and methods, as demonstrated in the previous section. Within literary theory, two related schools of thought that came to prominence in the 1970s and 1980s have been particularly influential: reader-response and reception theory. Their most significant proponents were respectively Stanley Fish and Wolfgang Iser, though the work of Roland Barthes, Mikhail Bakhtin, Michel de Certeau and Hans Robert Jauss was also important to both schools of thought. These theorists came from various disciplinary backgrounds — linguistics, sociology, history, philosophy and literature — and different cultures — continental Europe, Britain, the USA and the former USSR. They also drew on different philosophical traditions. What they had in common was an interest in the ways literature worked upon its readers. In contrast to the formalist or New Critical schools of theory, which focused on the qualities of the text irrespective of its effects on the reader, reader-response critics asked not what literature *is*, but what it *does*, and predicated their answers on an ideal or hypothetical reader, whose reactions were dictated by the linguistic and rhetorical features of the text.

In its early and purest form, reader-response theory therefore suggested a reader who encountered texts outside any sort of context, a Lockean *tabula rasa* who was influenced only by the textual strategies encountered in the particular work of literature under consideration at the time of the reading experience. Reception studies, however, took the focus on the reader a step further. As Jauss suggested as early as 1970, 'a literary work, even if it seems new, does not appear in an informational vacuum' (Jauss, 1970: 12). Jauss suggested that it was important to consider the 'horizon of expectations' of the hypothetical reader, in conjunction with the text's rhetorical strategies, in order to understand the ways in which the text might work on a particular reader in a particular time. In Jauss's model, it is the reader's understanding of literary conventions, such as the rules of genre, that creates his or her 'horizon of expectations' for the text. Such expectations are historically specific, because literary conventions and rules differ from age to age. For Jauss, understanding the 'horizon of expectations' of the reader was important because it would explain 'how the text is "properly" to be understood, that is according to its intention and its time' (Jauss, 1970: 19). Jauss's concept of the 'horizon of expectations' has proved important to historians of reading, who have taken the phrase to include more than just literary conventions. William St Clair, for example, suggests that the study of the 'horizon of expectation' of a historical reader should include the social, economic, cultural and legal issues that affected his or her reading experiences (St Clair, 2004: 268–292).

Reader-response theory and reception studies both have at their heart the desire to explicate or elucidate literary texts or other artworks. They are both, we might say, text-centred. The history of reading, on the other hand, encompasses a much wider range of material and approaches, and is often reader-centred. Historians of reading are interested in the transmission of texts through time, but they also believe it is important to understand the material conditions of reading in different historical periods. Readership historians believe that it is impossible to understand the influence of literature on its readers without thinking seriously about the factors that affect real readers when they engage with literary works.

The extracts in this section represent a range of theoretical approaches. Jauss and Iser are influential reception theorists. Fish, Bakhtin and de Certeau come from reader-response theory. Judith Fetterley is a feminist theorist, while Paul Saenger utilises an approach that combines historicist and reader-response theories. Iser sets out to record the phenomena that occur when a reader encounters a text. He describes the reading process as a dynamic encounter between text and reader. The text provides a prompt, and the reader 'sets the work in motion, and this very process results ultimately in the awakening of responses within himself' (Iser, 1974: 275). In Iser's frame of reference, then, the text does not actually exist in any meaningful way outside the encounter with the reader. His work spurred critics and theorists into giving the reading experience serious consideration.

Like Iser, Bakhtin sees dynamism as an inherent quality of literary prose. He insists that every utterance presupposes a hearer, and that literary language is by its nature polyphonic or multivalent. The word on the page 'reaches out' to the world beyond the text, and demands the active understanding and participation of the reader. An active understanding, Bakhtin suggests, 'assimilates the word under consideration into a new conceptual system, that of the one striving to understand', and 'establishes a series of complex inter-relationships, consonances and dissonances with the word and enriches it with new elements' (Bakhtin, 1981: 282).

The difficulty for the reader-response theorist who takes the position that meaning is only realised at the point of reception is the fact that all such meaning must therefore be individually and subjectively created. Any interpretation of a text could – hypothetically – therefore be considered to be valid, and so, critics of this position argue, no meaningful conclusions can be drawn. To counter this argument, Stanley Fish introduces the idea of an interpretive community. Members of an interpretive community share a common understanding of what is and is not 'acceptable' as an interpretation because they are able to recognise the textual strategies encoded in the text and arrive at a shared understanding of its meaning. Interpretive communities are self-constituted and self-perpetuating, and depend, Fish argues, on conventions of interpretation that are known or taught to all members of the community. Hence interpretations of a text are not entirely subjective or individual, but are bounded by the implicit rules of one's own interpretive community.

In her analysis of canonical American literature, Fetterley draws on reader-response theory's idea of the dynamism of the reading experience to theorise the female reader as being in constant opposition to the textual strategies she encounters. Fetterley argues that the female reader is 'co-opted into participation in an experience from which she is explicitly excluded; she is asked to identify with a selfhood that defines itself in opposition to her; she is required to identify against herself' (Fetterley, 1978: xii). Fetterley suggests that women's reading of American literature is characterised by powerlessness and self-division, and asserts that the first task of the feminist critic is to become a resisting reader – to read *against* the textual strategies that coerce her into identifying as male.

Michel de Certeau also theorises a resisting reader, one who is able to oppose hegemonic discourse and the seductions of mass culture. De Certeau reacts against the idea that a reader is a passive recipient of information and culture. Instead, he argues, readers actively take what they need from texts, reconfiguring what they discover through their reading for their own purposes. These versions of the active, powerful, resistant reader are also the focus of Paul Saenger's work on late Medieval readers. Saenger's article reconstructs implied readers and reading practices from the material aspects of the books under consideration. By tracing the change from reading aloud to silent reading in the late Medieval period, he makes a connection between silent reading, irony, cynicism and intellectual rigour. The study of the history of reading has been influenced by many of the methods used and the theories propounded by the writers in this section.

Chapter 6

Hans Robert Jauss

LITERARY HISTORY AS A CHALLENGE TO LITERARY THEORY

[. . .]

THE ANALYSIS OF THE LITERARY EXPERIENCE of the reader avoids the threatening pitfalls of psychology if it describes the response and the impact of a work within the definable frame of reference of the reader's expectations: this frame of reference for each work develops in the historical moment of its appearance from a previous understanding of the genre, from the form and themes of already familiar works, and from the contrast between poetic and practical language.

My thesis is opposed to a widespread skepticism that doubts that an analysis of the aesthetic impact can approach the meaning of a work of art or can produce at best more than a plain sociology of artistic taste. René Wellek directs such doubts against the literary theory of I. A. Richards. Wellek argues that neither the individual consciousness, since it is immediate and personal, nor a collective consciousness, as J. Mukarovsky assumes the effect of an art work to be, can be determined by empirical means.[1] Roman Jakobson wanted to replace the "collective consciousness" by a "collective ideology." This he thought of as a system of values which exists for each literary work as *langue* and which becomes *parole* for the respondent—although incompletely and never as a whole.[2] This theory, it is true, limits the subjectivity of the impact, but it leaves open the question of which data can be used to interpret the impact of a unique work on a certain public and to incorporate it into a system of values. In the meantime there are empirical means which had never been thought of before—literary data which give for each work a specific attitude of the audience (an attitude that precedes the psychological reaction as well as the subjective understanding of the individual reader). As in the case of every experience, the first literary experience of a previously unknown work demands a "previous knowledge which is an element of experience itself and which makes it possible that anything new we come across may also be read, as it were, in some context of experience."[3]

A literary work, even if it seems new, does not appear as something absolutely new in an informational vacuum, but predisposes its readers to a very definite type of reception by textual strategies, overt and covert signals, familiar characteristics or implicit allusions. It awakens memories of the familiar, stirs particular emotions in the reader and with its "beginning" arouses expectations for the "middle and end," which can then be continued intact, changed, re-oriented or even ironically fulfilled in the course of reading according to certain rules of the genre or type of text. The psychical process in the assimilation of a text on the primary horizon of aesthetic experience is by no means only a random succession of merely subjective impressions, but the carrying out of certain directions in a process of directed perception which can be comprehended from the motivations which constitute it and the signals which set it off and which can be described linguistically. If, along with W. D. Stempel, one considers the previous horizon of expectations of a text as paradigmatic isotopy, which is transferred to an immanent syntactical horizon of expectations to the degree to which the message grows, the process of reception becomes describable in the expansion of a semiological procedure which arises between the development and the correction of the system.[4] A corresponding process of continuous horizon setting and horizon changing also determines the relation of the individual text to the succession of texts which form the genre. The new text evokes for the reader (listener) the horizon of expectations and rules familiar from earlier texts, which are then varied, corrected, changed, or just reproduced. Variation and correction determine the scope, alteration, and reproduction of the borders and structure of the genre.[5] The interpretative reception of a text always presupposes the context of experience of aesthetic perception. The question of the subjectivity of the interpretation and the taste of different readers or levels of readers can be asked significantly only after it has been decided which transsubjective horizon of understanding determines the impact of the text.

The ideal cases of the objective capability of such literary frames of reference are works which, using the artistic standards of the reader, have been formed by conventions of genre, style, or form. These purposely evoke responses so that they can frustrate them. This can serve not only a critical purpose but can even have a poetic effect. Thus Cervantes in *Don Quixote* fosters the expectations of the old tales of knighthood, which the adventures of his last knight then parody seriously.[6] Thus Diderot in the beginning of *Jacques le Fataliste* evokes the expectations of the popular journey novel along with the (Aristotelian) convention of the romanesque fable and the providence peculiar to it, so that he can then confront the promised journey and love novel with a completely unromanesque "verité de l'histoire": the bizarre reality and moral casuistry of the inserted stories in which the truth of life continually denies the lies of poetic fiction.[7] Thus Nerval in *Chimères* cites, combines, and mixes a quintessence of well-known romantic and occult motives to produce the expectation of a mythical metamorphosis of the world only in order to show his renunciation of romantic poetry. The mythical identification and relationships which are familiar to the reader dissolve in the unknown to the same degree as the attempted private myth of the lyrical "I" fails; the law of sufficient information is broken and the darkness which has become expressive gains a poetic function.[8]

There is also the possibility of objectifying the expectations in works which are historically less sharply delineated. For the specific reception which the author anticipates from the reader for a particular work can be achieved, even if the explicit signals are missing, by three generally acceptable means: first, by the familiar standards or the inherent poetry of the genre; second, by the implicit relationships to familiar works of the literary-historical context; and third, by the contrast between fiction and reality, between the poetic and the practical function of language, which the reflective reader can always realize while he is reading. The third factor includes the possibility that the reader of a new work has to perceive it not only within the narrow horizon of his literary expectations but also within the wider horizon of his experience of life. [. . .]

If the horizon of expectations of a work is reconstructed in this way, it is possible to determine its artistic nature by the nature and degree of its effect on a given audience. If the "aesthetic distance" is considered as the distance between the given horizon of expectations and the appearance of a new work, whose reception results in a "horizon change" because it negates familiar experience or articulates an experience for the first time, this aesthetic distance can be measured historically in the spectrum of the reaction of the audience and the judgment of criticism (spontaneous success, rejection or shock, scattered approval, gradual or later understanding).

The way in which a literary work satisfies, surpasses, disappoints, or disproves the expectations of its first readers in the historical moment of its appearance obviously gives a criterion for the determination of its aesthetic value. The distance between the horizon of expectations and the work, between the familiarity of previous aesthetic experiences and the "horizon change"[9] demanded by the response to new works, determines the artistic nature of a literary work along the lines of the aesthetics of reception: the smaller this distance, which means that no demands are made upon the receiving consciousness to make a change on the horizon of unknown experience, the closer the work comes to the realm of "culinary" or light reading. This last phrase can be characterized from the point of view of the aesthetics of reception in this way: it demands no horizon change but actually fulfills expectations, which are prescribed by a predominant taste, by satisfying the demand for the reproduction of familiar beauty, confirming familiar sentiments, encouraging dreams, making unusual experiences palatable as "sensations" or even raising moral problems, but only to be able to "solve" them in an edifying manner when the solution is already obvious.[10] On the other hand, if the artistic character of a work is to be measured by the aesthetic distance with which it confronts the expectations of its first readers, it follows that this distance, which at first is experienced as a happy or distasteful new perspective, can disappear for later readers to the same degree to which the original negativity of the work has become self-evident and, as henceforth familiar expectation, has even become part of the horizon of future aesthetic experience. Especially the classic nature of so-called masterworks belongs to this second horizon change; their self-evident beauty and their seemingly unquestionable "eternal significance" bring them, from the point of view of the aesthetics of reception, into danger-ous proximity with the irresistable convincing and enjoyable "culinary" art, and special effort is needed to read them "against the grain" of accustomed experience so that their artistic nature becomes evident again. [. . .]

The relationship between literature and the public encompasses more than the fact that every work has its specific, historically and sociologically determined audience, that every writer is dependent upon the milieu, views and ideology of his readers and that literary success requires a book "which expresses what the group expects, a book which presents the group with its own portrait. . . ."[11] The objectivist determination of literary success based on the congruence of the intent of a work and the expectation of a social group always puts literary sociology in an embarrassing position whenever it must explain later or continuing effects. This is why R. Escarpit wants to presuppose a "collective basis in space or time" for the "illusion of continuity" of a writer, which leads to an astonishing prognosis in the case of Molière: he "is still young for the Frenchman of the 20th century because his world is still alive and ties of culture, point of view and language still bind us to him . . . but the ties are becoming ever weaker and Molière will age and die when the things which our culture has in common with the France of Molière die" (p. 117). As if Molière had only reflected the manners of his time and had only remained successful because of this apparent intention! Where the congruence between work and social group does not exist or no longer exists, as for example in the reception of a work by a group which speaks a foreign language, Escarpit is able to help himself by resorting to a "myth": "myths which are invented by a later period which has become estranged from the reality which they represent" (p. 111). As if all reception of a work beyond the first socially determined readers were only "distorted echoes," only a consequence of "subjective myths" (p. 111) and did not have its objective

a priori in the received work which sets boundaries and opens possibilities for later understanding! The sociology of literature does not view its object dialectically enough when it
determines the circle of writers, work and readers so one-sidedly.[12] The determination is
reversible: there are works which at the moment of their publication are not directed at any
specific audience, but which break through the familiar horizon of literary expectations so
completely that an audience can only gradually develop for them.[13] Then when the new
horizon of expectations has achieved more general acceptance, the authority of the changed
aesthetic norm can become apparent from the fact that readers will consider previously
successful works as obsolete and reject them. It is only in view of such a horizon change that
the analysis of literary effect achieves the dimension of a literary history of readers[14] and
provides the statistical curves of the historical recognition of the bestseller.

[. . .]

The reconstruction of the horizon of expectations, on the basis of which a work in the past
was created and received, enables us to find the questions to which the text originally
answered and thereby to discover how the reader of that day viewed and understood
the work. This approach corrects the usually unrecognized values of a classical concept of art
or of an interpretation that seeks to modernize, and it avoids the recourse to a general spirit
of the age, which involves circular reasoning. It brings out the hermeneutic difference
between past and present ways of understanding a work, points up the history of its
reception—providing both approaches—and thereby challenges as platonizing dogma the
apparently self-evident dictum of philological metaphysics that literature is timelessly
present and that it has objective meaning, determined once and for all and directly open to
the interpreter at any time.

The method of the history of reception[15] is essential for the understanding of literary
works which lie in the distant past. Whenever the writer of a work is unknown, his intent
not recorded, or his relationship to sources and models only indirectly accessible, the
philological question of how the text is "properly" to be understood, that is according to its
intention and its time, can best be answered if the text is considered in contrast to the
background of the works which the author could expect his contemporary public to know
either explicitly or implicitly.

[. . .]

The philological method of criticism is obviously not protected by its historical objectivity from the interpreter who, though supposedly eliminating his subjective evaluation,
unconsciously raises his preconceived aesthetic sense to an unacknowledged standard and
unwittingly modernizes the meaning of a text from the past. Whoever believes that the
"timeless truth" of a work must reveal itself to the interpreter directly and through simple
absorption in the text as if he had a point of view outside of history, disregarding all "errors"
of his predecessors and of the historical reception, "conceals the fabric of impact and history
in which historical consciousness itself stands;" he disavows the "preconditions, which are
neither intentional nor random but all-inclusive, which govern his own understanding," and
can only feign objectivity "which actually depends on the legitimacy of the questions."[16]

Hans Georg Gadamer, whose criticism of historical objectivism I am incorporating
here, described in *Wahrheit und Methode* the principle of the history of impact, which seeks to
show the reality of history in understanding itself[17] as an application of the logic of question
and answer to historical tradition. Continuing Collingwood's thesis that "one can only
understand a text when one understands the question which it answers,"[18] Gadamer suggests
that the reconstructed question can no longer stand in its original context because this
historical context is always surrounded by the context of our present: "Understanding
is always the process of fusion of such horizons which seem to exist independently."[19]
The historical question cannot exist independently; it has to be fused with another question

which will result from our attempt to integrate the past.[20] This logic of question and answer is the solution to what René Wellek described as the problem of literary judgment: should the philologist evaluate a literary work according to the perspective of the past, according to the viewpoint of the present, or according to the "judgment of the centuries?"[21] The actual criteria of the past could be so narrow that their use would only make a work, whose historical impact had a great potential, poorer. The aesthetic judgment of the present would favor a group of works which appeal to the modern taste and would evaluate all other works unjustly because their function in their own day is no longer evident. And the history of the impact itself, as instructive as it may be, is "as authority open to the same criticism as the authority of the writer's contemporaries."[22] Wellek argues that it is impossible to avoid one's own opinion; one must only make it as objective as possible by doing what every scholar does—"isolating the subject."[23] This view, however, is not a solution for the dilemma, but a relapse into objectivism. The "judgment of the centuries" of a literary work is more than just "the collected judgments of other readers, critics, audiences and even professors;"[24] it is the successive development of the potential meaning which is present in a work and which is gradually realized in its historical reception by knowledgable criticism. This judgment must, however, take place in contact with tradition and thus cause a controlled fusion of the horizons.

[. . .]

The impact of even the greatest literary work of the past cannot be compared either with an event which communicates itself automatically or with an emanation: the tradition of art presupposes a dialogue between the present and the past, according to which a past work cannot answer and speak to us until a present observer has posed the question which retrieves it from its retirement. In *Wahrheit und Methode*, when understanding—analogous to Heidegger's *Seinsgeschehen*—is thought of as "becoming part of a self-sufficient tradition in which the past and the present are continuously in mutual mediation,"[25] the "productive moment which lies in understanding"[26] must be short-changed. This productive function of progressive understanding, which necessarily also includes the criticizing and even forgetting of tradition, forms the basis of the aesthetics of reception of literary history outlined in the following chapter. This outline must consider the historical relevance of literature in three ways: diachronically in the relationship of literary works based upon reception, synchronically within the frame of reference of literature of the same period as well as in the sequence of such frames of reference and finally in the relationship of the immanent literary development to the general process of history.

[. . .]

The theory of the aesthetics of reception not only allows the understanding of the meaning and form of a literary work within the historical development of its reception. It also demands the ordering of the individual work in its "literary series" so that its historical position and significance in the context of literary experience can be recognized. Literary history based on the history of reception and impact will reveal itself as a process in which the passive reception of the reader and critic changes into the active reception and new production of the author, or in which—stated differently—a subsequent work solves formal and moral problems that the last work raised and may then itself present new problems.

How can the individual work, which determines chronological order in positivistic literary history and thereby superficially turns it into a "fact," be brought back into its historical order and thus be understood as an "event" again? The theory of the formalist school seeks to solve this problem with its principle of "literary evolution." In this theory the new work appears against a background of previous or competing works, reaches the "high ridge" of a literary epoch as a successful form, is reproduced and thereby continuously automated so that finally, when the next form has won out, it vegetates on as a worn-out genre and thus as a part of commonplace literature. If one analyzed and described a literary period according to this program which so far has hardly been begun,[27] one might expect a result far superior to the conventional literary history. It would relate the separate categories, which stand side by side unconnected or at least connected only by a sketchy general history (for example, works of one author, one direction, or one style, as well as different genres) to each other and disclose the evolutionary give and take of function and form.[28] Works either striking, related, or interdependent would appear as factors in a process which would no longer have to be aimed at one central point because, as a dialectic producing new forms, the process requires no teleology. Seen in this way, the dynamics of literary evolution would eliminate the dilemma of selective criteria. The unique criterion is the work entering the literary series as a new form, not the reproduction of worn-out forms, styles and genres which now move to the background until a new turn in the evolutionary development makes them perceptible again. Finally, in the formalist plan of literary history, which is understood as "evolution" and, contrary to the normal meaning of this term, rejects every directed course, the historical character of a work would remain the same as its artistic character. The evolutionary meaning and characteristics of a literary work presuppose innovation as the decisive feature just as does the tenet that the work of art is to be perceived against the background of other artistic works.[29]

The formalist theory of "literary evolution" is certainly one of the most significant beginnings in the renovation of literary history. The recognition that historical changes are also occurring within a system in the field of literature, the attempt to functionalize literary development, and last but not least the theory of automation, are achievements which must be retained, even if the one-sided canonization of the changes requires correction. Criticism has sufficiently pointed out the weaknesses of the formalist theory of evolution: mere opposition or aesthetic variation is not enough to explain the growth of literature; the question of the direction of the change of literary forms remains unanswered; innovation alone cannot assure artistic value; and the relationship between literary evolution and social change cannot be dispensed with by simple negation.[30] [. . .]

The description of literary evolution as a never-ending fight of the new with the old or as the alternation of canonizing and automation of forms reduces the historical character of literature to the one-dimensional reality of its changes and limits historical understanding to recognition of these changes. The changes of the literary order do not become a historical process until along with the opposition of old and new forms is recognized its specific mutual mediation. This mutual mediation, including the step from the old to the new form in the interaction of work and recipient (public, critic, new producer), past events and successive receptions, can be conceived of formally and substantially as the problem "which every work of art as a horizon of possible solutions creates and leaves behind."[31] But the mere description of the structural changes and new artistic means of a work does not necessarily lead to this problem, nor back to the work's function within the historical order. In order to determine this function, that is, in order to recognize the remaining problem which the new work answers in the historical succession, the interpreter must call upon his own experience, because the past horizon of old and new forms, problems and solutions, can only be recognized after it has been further mediated by the present horizon of the work. Literary history as "literary evolution" presupposes the historical process of aesthetic reception and production up to the observer's time as a condition for the communicating of all formal contrasts or "qualities of difference."[32]

Founding "literary evolution" on an aesthetics of reception not only restores its lost direction by making the position of the literary historian the temporary term of this process. This procedure also emphasizes the fundamentally historical dimension of literary experience by stressing the variable distance between the immediate and the potential meaning of a literary work. This means that the artistic character of a work, whose potential importance as criterion is reduced to that of innovation by formalism, does not by any means have to be immediately perceivable in the horizon of its first appearance, nor does it have to be exhausted by the opposition between old and new forms. The distance between the immediate first perception of a work and its potential meanings, or, to put it differently, the opposition between the new work and the expectations of its first readers, can be so great that a long process of reception is necessary in order to catch up with what first was unexpected and unusable. It can happen that the potential significance of a work may remain unrecognized until the evolution of a newer form widens the horizon and only then opens up the understanding of the misunderstood earlier form. Thus the dark lyrics of Mallarmé and his school prepared the way for a re-evaluation of baroque poetry, which had long been neglected and forgotten, and especially for the new philosophical interpretation and "rebirth" of Góngora. There are many examples of how a new literary form can open an approach to forgotten literature; they include the so-called "renaissances"—so-called because the term implies the appearance of an automatic rebirth and often obscures the fact that literary tradition does not transmit itself. That is, the literary past can only return when a new reception has brought it into the present again—whether it be that a different aesthetic attitude has intentionally taken up the past, or that a new phase of literary evaluation has expectedly illuminated past works.[33]

The new is not only an *aesthetic* category. It cannot be explained completely by the factors of innovation, surprise, surpassing, rearrangement and alienation, to which the formalist theory assigned utmost importance. The new becomes an historical category when the diachronic analysis of literature is forced to face the questions of which historical forces really make the literary work new, to what degree this newness is recognizable in the historical moment of its appearance, what distance, route, or circumlocution of understanding were required for its full realization, and whether the moment of this realization was so effective that it could change the perspective of the old and thereby the canonization of the literary past.[34] How the relationship of poetic theory and aesthetically productive practice appears in this light has already been discussed in another context.[35] Certainly the possibilities of the interaction between production and reception in the historical change of aesthetic attitude are not exhausted by these remarks. I only want to indicate the dimension into which a diachronic study of literature would move, since it can no longer remain satisfied with considering a chronological series of literary "facts" as the historical appearance of literature.

References

1   R. Wellek, "The Theory of Literary History,", *Études dediées au quatrième Congrès de linguists*, Travaux du Cercle Linguistique de Prague (Prague, 1936), p. 179.

2   In *Slovo a slovenost*, I, 192, cited by Welleck, "The Theory of Literary History," pp. 179 ff.

3   G. Buck, *Lernen and Erfahrung* (Stuttgart, 1967), p. 56, who refers here to Husserl (*Erfahrung und Urteil*, esp. § 8) but goes farther than Husserl in a lucid description of negativity in the process of experience, which is of importance for the horizon structure of aesthetic experience.

4   W.D. Stempel, *Pour une description des genres littéraires*, in: *Actes du XIIe congrès internat. de linguistique Romane* (Bucharest, 1968), also in *Beiträge zur Textlinguistik*, ed. by W.D. Stempel (Munich, 1970).

5   See also my treatment of this in *"Littérature medieval et théorie des genres,"* in *Poétique*, I (1970), 79–101, which will also shortly appear in an extended form in volume I of *Grundriss der romanischen Literaturen des Mittelalters*, (Heidelberg, 1970).

6   According to the interpretation of H.J. Neuschäfer, *Der Sinn der Parodie im Don Quijote*, Studia Romantica, V (Heidelberg, 1963).

7　According to the interpretation of R. Warning, *Allusion und Wirklichkeit in Tristram Shandy und Jacques le Fataliste*, Theorie and Geschichte der Literatur und der schönen Künste, IV (Munich, 1965), esp. pp. 80 ff.

8　According to the interpretation of K. H. Stierle, *Dunkelheit und Form in Gérard de Nervals "Chimères,"* Theorie und Geschichte der Literatur und der schönen Künste, V (Munich, 1967), esp. pp. 55 and 91.

9　See Buck, pp. 64 ff. about this idea of Husserl in *Lernen und Erfahrung*.

10　Here I am incorporating the results of the discussion of "Kitsch," as a fringe manifestation of aesthetics, which took place during the third colloquium of the "Forschungsgruppe Poetik und Hermeneutik" in the volume *Die nicht mehr schönen Künste – Grenzphänomene des Ästhetischen*, ed. H. R. Jauss (Munich, 1968). For the "culinary" approach, which presupposes mere light reading, the same thing holds true as for "Kitsch," namely, that the "demands of the consumers are *a priori* satisfied" (P. Beylin), that "the fulfilled expectation becomes the standard for the product" (W. Iser), or that "a work appears to be solving a problem when in reality it neither has nor solves a problem" (M. Imdahl), pp. 651–67.

11　R. Escarpit, *Das Buch und der Leser: Entwurf einer Literatursoziologie* (Cologne and Opladen, 1961; first German expanded edition of *Sociologie de la littérature* [Paris, 1958], p. 116.

12　K.H. Bender, *König und Vasall: Untersuchungen zur Chanson de Geste des XII. Jahrhunderts*, Studia Romanica, XIII (Heidelberg, 1967), shows which step is necessary in order to escape from this one-sided determination. In this history of the early French epic the apparent congruence of feudal society and epic ideality is represented as a process which is maintained through a continually changing discrepancy between "reality" and "ideology," that is between the historical constellation of feudal conflict and the poetic answers of the epic.

13　The much more sophisticated sociology of literature by Eric Auerbach brought to light this aspect in the variety of epoch-making disruptions of the relationship between author and reader. See also the evaluation of F. Schalk in his edition of E. Auerbach's *Gesämmelte Aufsätze zur romanischen Philologie* (Bern and Munich, 1967), pp. 11 ff.

14　See H. Weinrich, "Für eine Literaturgeschichte des Lesers," *Merker*, XXI (November, 1967). Just as the linguistics of the speaker, which was earlier customary, has been replaced by the linguistics of the listener, Weinrich pleads for a methodical consideration for the perspective of the reader in literary history and thereby supports my aims. Weinrich shows especially how the empirical methods of literary sociology can be supplemented by the linguitics and literary interpretation of the role of the reader, which is implicit in the work.

15　Examples of this method, which not only follows the fame, image, and influence of a writer through history but also examines the historical conditions and changes in his understanding, are rare. The following should be mentioned: G. F. Ford, *Dickens and His Readers* (Princeton, 1955); A. Nisin, *Les Oeuvres et les siècles* (Paris, 1960): discusses Vergil, Dante et nous, Ronsard, Corneille, Racine; E. Lämmert, "Zur Wirkungsgeschichte Eichendorffs in Deutschland," *Festschrift für Richard Alewyn*, ed. H. Singer and B. Von Wiese (Cologne and Graz, 1967). The methological problem of the step from the impact to the reception of a work is shown most sharply by F. Vodicka in *Die Problematik der Rezeption von Nerudas Werk* (1941, now in *Struktur vyvoje* [Prague, 1969]), where he discusses the changes of the work which are realized in its sucessive aesthetic perceptions.

16　H. G. Gadamer, *Wahrheit und Methode* (Tübingen, 1960), pp. 284–85.

17　*Ibid.*, p. 283.

18　*Ibid.*, p. 352.

19　*Ibid.*, p. 289.

20　*Ibid.*, p. 356.

21　Wellek, "Theory of Literary History," p. 184; *ibid.*, "Der Begriff der Evolution in der Literaturgeschichte," *Grundbegriffe der Literaturkritik* (Stuttgart, 1965), pp. 20–22.

22　Wellek, "Der Begriff der Evolution," p. 20.

23　*Ibid.*

24　*Ibid.*

25　*Wahrheit und Methode*, p. 275.

26　*Ibid.*, p. 280.

27　In the 1927 article, "Über literarische Evolution," by Jurii Tynjanov (*Die literarischen Kunstmittel und die Evolution in der Literatur* [Frankfort, 1967], pp. 37–60), this program is presented almost exactly. It was only partially fulfilled – as J. Striedter informed me – in the treatment of problems of structural change in the history of literary genres, as in the volume *Russkaja Proza, Voprosy poetiki*, VIII (Leningrad, 1926). See also J. Tynjanov, "Die Ode als rhetorische Gattung" (1922), *Texte der russischen Formalisten*, II, ed. J. Streider (Munich, 1970).

28   J. Tynjanov, "Über literarische Evolution," p. 59.

29   "A work of art is viewed as a positive value if it changes the structure of the preceding period; it is seen as a negative value if it adopts the structure without changing it," (J. Mukarovsky, cited by R. Wellek, "Der Begriff der Evolution," op. cit. pp. 42 ff.

30   See V. Erlich, *Russischer Formalismus*, pp. 284–287, and R. Welleck "Der Begriff der Evolution," op cit. pp. 42 ff. See also J. Streidter, *Texte der russischen Formalisten*, I, (Munich, 1969), Introduction, Section X.

31   H. Blumenberg in *Poetik und Hermeneutik*, III (see note 10) p. 692.

32   According to V. Erlich. *Russischer Formalismus*, p. 281, this concept means three things to the formalists: "on the level of the represention of reality 'quality of difference' stands for the 'avoidance' of the real, thus for creative deformation. On the level of language the expression means the avoidance of usual speech usage. On the level of literary dynamics finally . . . a change in the prevailing artistic standard."

33   For the first possibility the (anti-romantic) re-evaluation of Boileau and the classic *contrainte* poetics through Gide and Valéry can be introduced; for the second the tardy discovery of Hölderlin's Hymns or Novalis's concept of future poetry (for the last see H. R. Jauss in *Romantische Forschungen*, LXXVII [1965], 174–83).

34   Thus, since the reception of the "minor romantic" Nerval, whose *Chimères* only attracted attention under the influence of Mallarmé, the canonized "major romantics," Lamartine, Vigny, Musset and a large part of the "rhetorical" lyrics of Victor Hugo have been forced more and more into the background.

35   *Poetik und Hermeneutik*, II (*Immanente Aesthetik – Aesthetische Reflexion*), ed. W. Iser (Munich, 1966), esp. pp. 395–418.

Chapter 7

Wolfgang Iser

THE READING PROCESS:
A PHENOMENOLOGICAL APPROACH

THE PHENOMENOLOGICAL THEORY OF ART lays full stress on the idea that, in considering a literary work, one must take into account not only the actual text but also, and in equal measure, the actions involved in responding to that text. Thus Roman Ingarden confronts the structure of the literary text with the ways in which it can be *konkretisiert* (realized).[1] The text as such offers different "schematised views"[2] through which the subject matter of the work can come to light, but the actual bringing to light is an action of *Konkretization*. If this is so, then the literary work has two poles, which we might call the artistic and the esthetic: the artistic refers to the text created by the author, and the esthetic to the realization accomplished by the reader. From this polarity it follows that the literary work cannot be completely identical with the text, or with the realization of the text, but in fact must lie half-way between the two. The work is more than the text, for the text only takes on life when it is realized, and furthermore the realization is by no means independent of the individual disposition of the reader—though this in turn is acted upon by the different patterns of the text. The convergence of text and reader brings the literary work into existence, and this convergence can never be precisely pinpointed, but must always remain virtual, as it is not to be identified either with the reality of the text or with the individual disposition of the reader.

It is the virtuality of the work that gives rise to its dynamic nature, and this in turn is the precondition for the effects that the work calls forth. As the reader uses the various perspectives offered him by the text in order to relate the patterns and the "schematised views" to one another, he sets the work in motion, and this very process results ultimately in the awakening of responses within himself. Thus, reading causes the literary work to unfold its inherently dynamic character. That this is no new discovery is apparent from references made even in the early days of the novel. Laurence Sterne remarks in Tristram Shandy: ". . . no author, who understands the just boundaries of decorum and good-breeding, would presume to think all: The truest respect which you can pay to the reader's understanding, is to halve this matter amicably, and leave him something to imagine, in his turn, as well as yourself. For my own part, I am eternally paying him compliments of this kind, and do all that lies in my power to keep his imagination as busy as my own."[3] Sterne's conception of a literary text is that it is something like an arena in which reader and author participate in a game of the imagination. If the reader were given the whole story, and there were nothing left for him to do, then his imagination would never enter the field, the result would be the boredom which inevitably arises when everything is laid out cut and dried before us. A literary text must therefore be conceived in such a way that it will engage the reader's imagination in the task of working things out for himself, for reading is only a pleasure when it is active and creative. In this process of creativity, the text may either not go far enough, or may go too far, so we may say that boredom and overstrain form the boundaries beyond which the reader will leave the field of play.

The extent to which the "unwritten" part of a text stimulates the reader's creative participation is brought out by an observation of Virginia Woolf's in her study of Jane Austen:

> Jane Austen is thus a mistress of much deeper emotion than appears upon the surface. She stimulates us to supply what is not there. What she offers is, apparently, a trifle, yet is composed of something that expands in the reader's mind and endows with the most enduring form of life scenes which are outwardly trivial. Always the stress is laid upon character. . . . The turns and twists of the dialogue keep us on the tenterhooks of suspense. Our attention is half upon the present moment, half upon the future. . . . Here, indeed, in this unfinished and in the main inferior story, are all the elements of Jane Austen's greatness.[4]

The unwritten aspects of apparently trivial scenes and the unspoken dialogue within the "turns and twists" not only draw the reader into the action but also lead him to shade in the many outlines suggested by the given situations, so that these take on a reality of their own. But as the reader's imagination animates these "outlines," they in turn will influence the effect of the written part of the text. Thus begins a whole dynamic process: the written text imposes certain limits on its unwritten implications in order to prevent these from becoming too blurred and hazy, but at the same time these implications, worked out by the reader's imagination, set the given situation against a background which endows it with far greater significance than it might have seemed to possess on its own. In this way, trivial scenes suddenly take on the shape of an "enduring form of life." What constitutes this form is never named, let alone explained in the text, although in fact it is the end product of the interaction between text and reader.

[. . .]

The question now arises as to how far such a process can be adequately described. For this purpose a phenomenological analysis recommends itself, especially since the somewhat sparse observations hitherto made of the psychology of reading tend mainly to be psychoanalytical, and so are restricted to the illustration of predetermined ideas concerning the unconscious. [. . .]

As a starting point for a phenomenological analysis we might examine the way in which sequent sentences act upon one another. This is of especial importance in literary texts in view of the fact that they do not correspond to any objective reality outside themselves. The world presented by literary texts is constructed out of what Ingarden has called *intentionale Satzkorrelate* (intentional sentence correlatives):

> Sentences link up in different ways to form more complex units of meaning that reveal a very varied structure giving rise to such entities as a short story, a novel, a dialogue, a drama, a scientific theory. . . . In the final analysis, there arises a particular world, with component parts determined in this way or that,

and with all the variations that may occur within these parts—all this as a purely intentional correlative of a complex of sentences. If this complex finally forms a literary work, I call the whole sum of sequent intentional sentence correlatives the "world presented" in the work.[5]

This world, however, does not pass before the reader's eyes like a film. The sentences are "component parts" insofar as they make statements, claims, or observations, or convey information, and so establish various perspectives in the text. But they remain only "component parts"—they are not the sum total of the text itself. For the intentional correlatives disclose subtle connections which individually are less concrete than the statements, claims, and observations, even though these only take on their real meaningfulness through the interaction of their correlatives.

How is one to conceive the connection between the correlatives? It marks those points at which the reader is able to "climb aboard" the text. He has to accept certain given perspectives, but in doing so he inevitably causes them to interact. When Ingarden speaks of intentional sentence correlatives in literature, the statements made or information conveyed in the sentence are already in a certain sense qualified: the sentence does not consist solely of a statement—which, after all, would be absurd, as one can only make statements about things that exist—but aims at something beyond what it actually says. This is true of all sentences in literary works, and it is through the interaction of these sentences that their common aim is fulfilled. This is what gives them their own special quality in literary texts. In their capacity as statements, observations, purveyors of information, etc., they are always indications of something that is to come, the structure of which is foreshadowed by their specific content.

They set in motion a process out of which emerges the actual content of the text itself. In describing man's inner consciousness of time, Husserl once remarked: "Every originally constructive process is inspired by pre-intentions, which construct and collect the seed of what is to come, as such, and bring it to fruition."[6] For this bringing to fruition, the literary text needs the reader's imagination, which gives shape to the interaction of correlatives foreshadowed in structure by the sequence of the sentences. Husserl's observation draws our attention to a point that plays a not insignificant part in the process of reading. The individual sentences not only work together to shade in what is to come; they also form an expectation in this regard. Husserl calls this expectation "pre-intentions." As this structure is characteristic of all sentence correlatives, the interaction of these correlatives will not be a fulfillment of the expectation so much as a continual modification of it.

For this reason, expectations are scarcely ever fulfilled in truly literary texts. If they were, then such texts would be confined to the individualization of a given expectation, and one would inevitably ask what such an intention was supposed to achieve. Strangely enough, we feel that any confirmative effect—such as we implicitly demand of expository texts, as we refer to the objects they are meant to present—is a defect in a literary text. For the more a text individualizes or confirms an expectation it has initially aroused, the more aware we become of its didactic purpose, so that at best we can only accept or reject the thesis forced upon us. More often than not, the very clarity of such texts will make us want to free ourselves from their clutches. But generally the sentence correlatives of literary texts do not develop in this rigid way, for the expectations they evoke tend to encroach on one another in such a manner that they are continually modified as one reads. One might simplify by saying that each intentional sentence correlative opens up a particular horizon, which is modified, if not completely changed, by succeeding sentences. While these expectations arouse interest in what is to come, the subsequent modification of them will also have a retrospective effect on what has already been read. This may now take on a different significance from that which it had at the moment of reading.

Whatever we have read sinks into our memory and is foreshortened. It may later be evoked again and set against a different background with the result that the reader is enabled to develop hitherto unforeseeable connections. The memory evoked, however, can never reassume its original shape, for this would mean that memory and perception were identical, which is manifestly not so. The new background brings to light new aspects of what we had committed to memory; conversely these, in turn, shed their light on the new background, thus arousing more complex anticipations. Thus, the reader, in establishing these inter-relations between past, present and future, actually causes the text to reveal its potential multiplicity of connections. These connections are the product of the reader's mind working on the raw material of the text, though they are not the text itself—for this consists just of sentences, statements, information, etc.

This is why the reader often feels involved in events which, at the time of reading, seem real to him, even though in fact they are very far from his own reality. The fact that completely different readers can be differently affected by the "reality" of a particular text is ample evidence of the degree to which literary texts transform reading into a creative process that is far above mere perception of what is written. The literary text activates our own faculties, enabling us to recreate the world it presents. The product of this creative activity is what we might call the virtual dimension of the text, which endows it with its reality. This virtual dimension is not the text itself, nor is it the imagination of the reader: it is the coming together of text and imagination.

As we have seen, the activity of reading can be characterized as a sort of kaleidoscope of perspectives, preintentions, recollections. Every sentence contains a preview of the next and forms a kind of viewfinder for what is to come; and this in turn changes the "preview" and so becomes a "viewfinder" for what has been read. This whole process represents the fulfillment of the potential, unexpressed reality of the text, but it is to be seen only as a framework for a great variety of means by which the virtual dimension may be brought into being. The process of anticipation and retrospection itself does not by any means develop in a smooth flow. Ingarden has already drawn attention to this fact and ascribes a quite remarkable significance to it:

> Once we are immersed in the flow of *Satzdenken* (sentence-thought), we are ready, after completing the thought of one sentence, to think out the "continu-ation," also in the form of a sentence—and that is, in the form of a sentence that connects up with the sentence we have just thought through. In this way the process of reading goes effortlessly forward. But if by chance the following sentence has no tangible connection whatever with the sentence we have just thought through, there then comes a blockage in the stream of thought. This hiatus is linked with a more or less active surprise, or with indignation. This blockage must be overcome if the reading is to flow once more.[7]

The hiatus that blocks the flow of sentences is, in Ingarden's eyes, the product of chance, and is to be regarded as a flaw; this is typical of his adherence to the classical idea of art. If one regards the sentence sequence as a continual flow, this implies that the anticipation aroused by one sentence will generally be realized by the next, and the frustration of one's expect-ations will arouse feelings of exasperation. And yet literary texts are full of unexpected twists and turns, and frustration of expectations. Even in the simplest story there is bound to be some kind of blockage, if only because no tale can ever be told in its entirety. Indeed, it is only through inevitable omissions that a story gains its dynamism. Thus whenever the flow is interrupted and we are led off in unexpected directions, the opportunity is given to us to bring into play our own faculty for establishing connections—for filling in the gaps left by the text itself.[8]

These gaps have a different effect on the process of anticipation and retrospection, and thus on the *Gestalt* of the virtual dimension, for they may be filled in different ways. For this reason, one text is potentially capable of several different realizations, and no reading can ever exhaust the full potential, for each individual reader will fill in the gaps in his own way, thereby excluding the various other possibilities; as he reads, he will make his own decision as to how the gap is to be filled. In this very act the dynamics of reading are revealed. By making his decision he implicitly acknowledges the inexhaustibility of the text; at the same time it is this very inexhaustibility that forces him to make his decision. With "traditional" texts this process was more or less unconscious, but modern texts frequently exploit it quite deliberately. They are often so fragmentary that one's attention is almost exclusively occupied with the search for connections between the fragments; the object of this is not to complicate the "spectrum" of connections, so much as to make us aware of the nature of our own capacity for providing links. In such cases, the text refers back directly to our own preconceptions—which are revealed by the act of interpretation that is a basic element of the reading process. With all literary texts, then, we may say that the reading process is selective, and the potential text is infinitely richer than any of its individual realizations. This is borne out by the fact that a second reading of a piece of literature often produces a different impression from the first. The reasons for this may lie in the reader's own change of circumstances; still, the text must be such as to allow this variation. On a second reading familiar occurrences now tend to appear in a new light and seem to be at times corrected, at times enriched.

In every text there is a potential time sequence which the reader must inevitably realize, as it is impossible to absorb even a short text in a single moment. Thus the reading process always involves viewing the text through a perspective that is continually on the move, linking up the different phases, and so constructing what we have called the virtual dimension. This dimension, of course, varies all the time we are reading. However, when we have finished the text, and read it again, clearly our extra knowledge will result in a different time sequence; we shall tend to establish connections by referring to our awareness of what is to come, and so certain aspects of the text will assume a significance we did not attach to them on a first reading, while others will recede into the background. It is a common enough experience for a person to say that on a second reading he noticed things he had missed when he read the book for the first time, but this is scarcely surprising in view of the fact that the second time he is looking at the text from a different perspective. The time sequence that he realized on his first reading cannot possibly be repeated on a second reading, and this unrepeatability is bound to result in modifications of his reading experience. This is not to say that the second reading is "truer" than the first—they are, quite simply, different: the reader establishes the virtual dimension of the text by realizing a new time sequence. Thus even on repeated viewings a text allows and, indeed, induces innovative reading.

In whatever way, and under whatever circumstances the reader may link the different phases of the text together, it will always be the process of anticipation and retrospection that leads to the formation of the virtual dimension, which in turn transforms the text into an experience for the reader. The way in which this experience comes about through a process of continual modification is closely akin to the way in which we gather experience in life. And thus the "reality" of the reading experience can illuminate basic patterns of real experience:

We have the experience of a world, not understood as a system of relations which wholly determine each event, but as an open totality the synthesis of which is inexhaustible. . . . From the moment that experience—that is, the opening on to our *de facto* world—is recognized as the beginning of knowledge, there is no longer any way of distinguishing a level of *a priori* truths and one of factual ones, what the world must necessarily be and what it actually is.[9]

The manner in which the reader experiences the text will reflect his own disposition, and in this respect the literary text acts as a kind of mirror; but at the same time, the reality which this process helps to create is one that will be different from his own (since, normally, we tend to be bored by texts that present us with things we already know perfectly well ourselves). Thus we have the apparently paradoxical situation in which the reader is forced to reveal aspects of himself in order to experience a reality which is different from his own. The impact this reality makes on him will depend largely on the extent to which he himself actively provides the unwritten part of the text, and yet in supplying all the missing links, he must think in terms of experiences different from his own; indeed, it is only by leaving behind the familiar world of his own experience that the reader can truly participate in the adventure the literary text offers him.

[. . .]

We have seen that, during the process of reading, there is an active interweaving of anticipation and retrospection, which on a second reading may turn into a kind of advance retrospection. The impressions that arise as a result of this process will vary from individual to individual, but only within the limits imposed by the written as opposed to the unwritten text. In the same way, two people gazing at the night sky may both be looking at the same collection of stars, but one will see the image of a plough, and the other will make out a dipper. The "stars" in a literary text are fixed; the lines that join them are variable. The author of the text may, of course, exert plenty of influence on the reader's imagination—he has the whole panoply of narrative techniques at his disposal—but no author worth his salt will ever attempt to set the whole picture before his reader's eyes. If he does, he will very quickly lose his reader, for it is only by activating the reader's imagination that the author can hope to involve him and so realize the intentions of his text.

Gilbert Ryle, in his analysis of imagination, asks: "How can a person fancy that he sees something, without realizing that he is not seeing it?" He answers as follows:

> Seeing Helvellyn [the name of a mountain] in one's mind's eye does not entail, what seeing Helvellyn and seeing snapshots of Helvellyn entail, the having of visual sensations. It does involve the thought of having a view of Helvellyn and it is therefore a more sophisticated operation than that of having a view of Helvellyn. It is one utilization among others of the knowledge of how Helvellyn should look, or, in one sense of the verb, it is thinking how it should look. The expectations which are fulfilled in the recognition at sight of Helvellyn are not indeed fulfilled in picturing it, but the picturing of it is something like a rehearsal of getting them fulfilled. So far from picturing involving the having of faint sensations, or wraiths of sensations, it involves missing just what one would be due to get, if one were seeing the mountain.[10]

If one sees the mountain, then of course one can no longer imagine it, and so the act of picturing the mountain presupposes its absence. Similarly, with a literary text we can only picture things which are not there; the written part of the text gives us the knowledge, but it is the unwritten part that gives us the opportunity to picture things; indeed without the elements of indeterminacy, the gaps in the text, we should not be able to use our imagination.[11]

The truth of this observation is borne out by the experience many people have on seeing, for instance, the film of a novel. While reading *Tom Jones*, they may never have had a clear conception of what the hero actually looks like, but on seeing the film, some may say, "That's not how I imagined him." The point here is that the reader of *Tom Jones* is able to visualize the hero virtually for himself, and so his imagination senses the vast number of possibilities; the moment these possibilities are narrowed down to one complete and immutable picture, the imagination is put out of action, and we feel we have somehow been cheated. This may perhaps be an oversimplification of the process, but it does illustrate plainly the vital richness of potential that arises out of the fact that the hero in the novel must be pictured and cannot be seen. With the novel the reader must use his imagination to synthesize the information given him, and so his perception is simultaneously richer and more private; with the film he is confined merely to physical perception, and so whatever he remembers of the world he had pictured is brutally cancelled out.

[. . .]

The "picturing" that is done by our imagination is only one of the activities through which we form the *Gestalt* of a literary text. We have already discussed the process of anticipation and retrospection, and to this we must add the process of grouping together all the different aspects of a text to form the consistency that the reader will always be in search of. While expectations may be continually modified, and images continually expanded, the reader will still strive, even if unconsciously, to fit everything together in a consistent pattern. "In the reading of images, as in the hearing of speech, it is always hard to distinguish what is given to us from what we supplement in the process of projection which is triggered off by recognition . . . it is the guess of the beholder that tests the medley of forms and colours for coherent meaning, crystallizing it into shape when a consistent interpretation has been found."[12] By grouping together the written parts of the text, we enable them to interact, we observe the direction in which they are leading us, and we project onto them the consistency which we, as readers, require. This *Gestalt* must inevitably be colored by our own characteristic selection process. For it is not given by the text itself; it arises from the meeting between the written text and the individual mind of the reader with its own particular history of experience, its own consciousness, its own outlook. The *Gestalt* is not the true meaning of the text; at best it is a configurative meaning; ". . . comprehension is an individual act of seeing-things-together, and only that."[13] With a literary text such comprehension is inseparable from the reader's expectations, and where we have expectations, there too we have one of the most potent weapons in the writer's armory—illusion.

[. . .]

With regard to the experience of reading, Walter Pater once observed: "For to the grave reader words too are grave; and the ornamental word, the figure, the accessory form or colour or reference, is rarely content to die to thought precisely at the right moment, but will inevitably linger awhile, stirring a long "brainwave" behind it of perhaps quite alien associations."[14] Even while the reader is seeking a consistent pattern in the text, he is also uncovering other impulses which cannot be immediately integrated or will even resist final integration. Thus the semantic possibilities of the text will always remain far richer than any configurative meaning formed while reading. But this impression is, of course, only to be gained through reading the text. Thus the configurative meaning can be nothing but a *pars pro toto* fulfillment of the text, and yet this fulfillment gives rise to the very richness which it seeks to restrict, and indeed in some modern texts, our awareness of this richness takes precedence over any configurative meaning.

This fact has several consequences which, for the purpose of analysis, may be dealt with separately, though in the reading process they will all be working together. As we have seen, a consistent, configurative meaning is essential for the apprehension of an unfamiliar experience, which through the process of illusion-building we can incorporate in our own imaginative world. At the same time, this consistency conflicts with the many other possibilities of fulfillment it seeks to exclude, with the result that the configurative meaning is always accompanied by "alien associations" that do not fit in with the illusions formed. The first consequence, then, is the fact that in forming our illusions, we also produce at the same time a latent disturbance of these illusions. Strangely enough, this also applies to texts in which our expectations are actually fulfilled—though one would have thought that the fulfillment of expectations would help to complete the illusion. "Illusion wears off once the expectation is stepped up; we take it for granted and want more."[15] The experiments in *Gestalt* psychology referred to by Gombrich in *Art and Illusion* make one thing clear: ". . . though we may be intellectually aware of the fact that any given experience must be an illusion, we cannot, strictly speaking, watch ourselves having an illusion."[16] Now, if illusion were not a transitory state, this would mean that we could be, as it were, permanently caught up in it. And if reading were exclusively a matter of producing illusion—necessary though this is for the understanding of an unfamiliar experience—we should run the risk of falling victim to a gross deception. But it is precisely during our reading that the transitory nature of the illusion is revealed to the full.

As the formation of illusions is constantly accompanied by "alien associations" which cannot be made consistent with the illusions, the reader constantly has to lift the restrictions he places on the "meaning" of the text. Since it is he who builds the illusions, he oscillates between involvement in and observation of those illusions; he opens himself to the unfamiliar world without being imprisoned in it. Through this process the reader moves into the presence of the fictional world and so experiences the realities of the text as they happen.

In the oscillation between consistency and "alien associations," between involvement in and observation of the illusion, the reader is bound to conduct his own balancing operation, and it is this that forms the esthetic experience offered by the literary text. However, if the reader were to achieve a balance, obviously he would then no longer be engaged in the process of establishing and disrupting consistency. And since it is this very process that gives rise to the balancing operation, we may say that the inherent nonachievement of balance is a prerequisite for the very dynamism of the operation. In seeking the balance we inevitably have to start out with certain expectations, the shattering of which is integral to the esthetic experience.

[. . .]

As we work out a consistent pattern in the text, we will find our "interpretation" threatened, as it were, by the presence of other possibilities of "interpretation," and so there arise new areas of indeterminacy (though we may only be dimly aware of them, if at all, as we are continually making "decisions" which will exclude them). In the course of a novel, for instance, we sometimes find that characters, events, and backgrounds seem to change their significance; what really happens is that the other "possibilities" begin to emerge more strongly, so that we become more directly aware of them. Indeed, it is this very shifting of perspectives that makes us feel that a novel is much more "true-to-life." Since it is we ourselves who establish the levels of interpretation and switch from one to another as we conduct our balancing operation, we ourselves impart to the text the dynamic lifelikeness which, in turn, enables us to absorb an unfamiliar experience into our personal world.

As we read, we oscillate to a greater or lesser degree between the building and the breaking of illusions. In a process of trial and error, we organize and reorganize the various data offered us by the text. These are the given factors, the fixed points on which we base our "interpretation," trying to fit them together in the way we think the author meant them to be fitted. "For to perceive, a beholder must *create* his own experience. And his creation must include relations comparable to those which the original producer underwent. They are not the same in any literal sense. But with the perceiver, as with the artist, there must be an ordering of the elements of the whole that is in form, although not in details, the same as the process of organization the creator of the work consciously experienced. Without an act of recreation the object is not perceived as a work of art."[17]

The act of recreation is not a smooth or continuous process, but one which, in its essence, relies on *interruptions* of the flow to render it efficacious. We look forward, we look back, we decide, we change our decisions, we form expectations, we are shocked by their nonfulfillment, we question, we muse, we accept, we reject; this is the dynamic process of recreation. This process is steered by two main structural components within the text: first, a repertoire of familiar literary patterns and recurrent literary themes, together with allusions to familiar social and historical contexts; second, techniques or strategies used to set the familiar against the unfamiliar. Elements of the repertoire are continually back-grounded or foregrounded with a resultant strategic overmagnification, trivialization, or even annihilation of the allusion. This defamiliarization of what the reader thought he recognized is bound to create a tension that will intensify his expectations as well as his distrust of those expectations. Similarly, we may be confronted by narrative techniques that establish links between things we find difficult to connect, so that we are forced to reconsider data we at first held to be perfectly straightforward. One need only mention the very simple trick, so often employed by novelists, whereby the author himself takes part in the narrative, thus establishing perspectives which would not have arisen out of the mere narration of the events described. Wayne Booth once called this the technique of the "unreliable narrator,"[18] to show the extent to which a literary device can counter expectations arising out of the literary text. The figure of the narrator may act in permanent opposition to the impressions we might otherwise form. The question then arises as to whether this strategy, opposing the formation of illusions, may be integrated into a consistent pattern, lying, as it were, a level deeper than our original impressions. We may find that our narrator, by opposing us, in fact turns us against him and thereby strengthens the illusion he appears to be out to destroy; alternatively, we may be so much in doubt that we begin to question all the processes that lead us to make interpretative decisions. Whatever the cause may be, we will find ourselves subjected to this same interplay of illusion-forming and illusion-breaking that makes reading essentially a recreative process.

[. . .]

This entanglement of the reader is, of course, vital to any kind of text, but in the literary text we have the strange situation that the reader cannot know what his participation actually entails. We know that we share in certain experiences, but we do not know what happens to us in the course of this process. This is why, when we have been particularly impressed by a book, we feel the need to talk about it; we do not want to get away from it by talking about it—we simply want to understand more clearly what it is in which we have been entangled. We have undergone an experience, and now we want to know consciously *what* we have experienced. Perhaps this is the prime usefulness of literary criticism—it helps to make conscious those aspects of the text which would otherwise remain concealed in the subconscious; it satisfies (or helps to satisfy) our desire to talk about what we have read.

The efficacy of a literary text is brought about by the apparent evocation and subsequent negation of the familiar. What at first seemed to be an affirmation of our assumptions leads to our own rejection of them, thus tending to prepare us for a re-orientation. And it is only when we have outstripped our preconceptions and left the shelter of the familiar that we are in a position to gather new experiences. As the literary text involves the reader in the formation of illusion and the simultaneous formation of the means whereby the illusion is punctured, reading reflects the process by which we gain experience. Once the reader is entangled, his own preconceptions are continually overtaken, so that the text becomes his "present" while his own ideas fade into the "past;" as soon as this happens he is open to the immediate experience of the text, which was impossible so long as his preconceptions were his "present."

[. . .]

In our analysis of the reading process so far, we have observed three important aspects that form the basis of the relationship between reader and text: the process of anticipation and retrospection, the consequent unfolding of the text as a living event, and the resultant impression of life-likeness.

Any "living event" must, to a greater or lesser degree, remain open. In reading, this obliges the reader to seek continually for consistency, because only then can he close up situations and comprehend the unfamiliar. But consistency-building is itself a living process in which one is constantly forced to make selective decisions—and these decisions in their turn give a reality to the possibilities which they exclude, insofar as they may take effect as a latent disturbance of the consistency established. This is what causes the reader to be entangled in the text-*Gestalt* that he himself has produced.

Through this entanglement the reader is bound to open himself up to the workings of the text and so leave behind his own preconceptions. This gives him the chance to have an experience in the way George Bernard Shaw once described it: "You have learnt something. That always feels at first as if you had lost something."[19] Reading reflects the structure of experience to the extent that we must suspend the ideas and attitudes that shape our own personality before we can experience the unfamiliar world of the literary text. But during this process, something happens to us.

This "something" needs to be looked at in detail, especially as the incorporation of the unfamiliar into our own range of experience has been to a certain extent obscured by an idea very common in literary discussion: namely, that the process of absorbing the unfamiliar is labeled as the identification of the reader with what he reads. Often the term "identification" is used as if it were an explanation, whereas in actual fact it is nothing more than a description. What is normally meant by "identification" is the establishment of affinities between oneself and someone outside oneself—a familiar ground on which we are able to experience the unfamiliar. The author's aim, though, is to convey the experience and, above all, an attitude toward that experience. Consequently, "identification" is not an end in itself, but a strategem by means of which the author stimulates attitudes in the reader.

This of course is not to deny that there does arise a form of participation as one reads; one is certainly drawn into the text in such a way that one has the feeling that there is no distance between oneself and the events described. This involvement is well summed up by the reaction of a critic to reading Charlotte Brontë's *Jane Eyre*: "We took up *Jane Eyre* one winter's evening, somewhat piqued at the extravagant commendations we had heard, and sternly resolved to be as critical as Croker. But as we read on we forgot both commendations and criticism, identified ourselves with Jane in all her troubles, and finally married Mr. Rochester about four in the morning."[20] The question is how and why did the critic identify himself with Jane?

In order to understand this "experience," it is well worth considering Georges Poulet's observations on the reading process. He says that books only take on their full existence in the reader.[21] It is true that they consist of ideas thought out by someone else, but in reading the reader becomes the subject that does the thinking. Thus there disappears the subject-object division that otherwise is a prerequisite for all knowledge and all observation, and the removal of this division puts reading in an apparently unique position as regards the possible absorption of new experiences. This may well be the reason why relations with the world of the literary text have so often been misinterpreted as identification. From the idea that in reading we must think the thoughts of someone else, Poulet draws the following conclusion: "Whatever I think is a part of my mental world. And yet here I am thinking a thought which manifestly belongs to another mental world, which is being thought in me just as though I did not exist. Already the notion is inconceivable and seems even more so if I reflect that, since every thought must have a subject to think it, this *thought* which is alien to me and yet in me, must also have in me a *subject* which is alien to me. . . . Whenever I read, I mentally pronounce an *I*, and yet the *I* which I pronounce is not myself."[22]

But for Poulet this idea is only part of the story. The strange subject that thinks the strange thought in the reader indicates the potential presence of the author, whose ideas can be "internalized" by the reader: "Such is the characteristic condition of every work which I summon back into existence by placing my consciousness at its disposal. I give it not only existence, but awareness of existence."[23] This would mean that consciousness forms the point at which author and reader converge, and at the same time it would result in the cessation of the temporary self-alienation that occurs to the reader when his consciousness brings to life the ideas formulated by the author. This process gives rise to a form of communication which, however, according to Poulet, is dependent on two conditions: the life-story of the author must be shut out of the work and the individual disposition of the reader must be shut out of the act of reading. Only then can the thoughts of the author take place subjectively in the reader, who thinks what he is not. It follows that the work itself must be thought of as a consciousness, because only in this way is there an adequate basis for the author-reader relationship—a relationship that can only come about through the negation of the author's own life-story and the reader's own disposition. This conclusion is actually drawn by Poulet when he describes the work as the self-presentation or materialization of consciousness: "And so I ought not to hesitate to recognize that so long as it is animated by this vital inbreathing inspired by the act of reading, a work of literature becomes (at the expense of the reader whose own life it suspends) a sort of human being, that it is a mind conscious of itself and constituting itself in me as the subject of its own objects."[24] Even though it is difficult to follow such a substantialist conception of the consciousness that constitutes itself in the literary work, there are, nevertheless, certain points in Poulet's argument that are worth holding onto. But they should be developed along somewhat different lines.

If reading removes the subject-object division that constitutes all perception, it follows that the reader will be "occupied" by the thoughts of the author, and these in their turn will cause the drawing of new "boundaries." Text and reader no longer confront each other as object and subject, but instead the "division" takes place within the reader himself. In thinking the thoughts of another, his own individuality temporarily recedes into the background, since it is supplanted by these alien thoughts, which now become the theme on which his attention is focussed. As we read, there occurs an artificial division of our personality, because we take as a theme for ourselves something that we are not. Consequently when reading we operate on different levels. For although we may be thinking the thoughts of someone else, what we are will not disappear completely—it will merely remain a more or less powerful virtual force. Thus, in reading there are these two levels—the alien "me" and the real, virtual "me"—which are never completely cut off from each other. Indeed, we can only make someone else's thoughts into an absorbing theme for ourselves, provided the virtual background of our own personality can adapt to it. Every text we read draws a different boundary within our personality, so that the virtual background (the real "me") will take on a different form, according to the theme of the text concerned. [. . .]

In this context there is a revealing remark made by D. W. Harding, arguing against the idea of identification with what is read: "What is sometimes called wish-fulfilment in novels and plays can . . . more plausibly be described as wish-formulation or the definition of desires. The cultural levels at which it works may vary widely; the process is the same. . . . It seems nearer the truth . . . to say that fictions contribute to defining the reader's or spectator's values, and perhaps stimulating his desires, rather than to suppose that they gratify desire by some mechanism of vicarious experience."[25] In the act of reading, having to think something that we have not yet experienced does not mean only being in a position to conceive or even understand it; it also means that such acts of conception are possible and successful to the degree that they lead to something being formulated in us. For someone else's thoughts can only take a form in our consciousness if, in the process, our unformulated faculty for deciphering those thoughts is brought into play—a faculty which, in the act of deciphering, also formulates itself. Now since this formulation is carried out on terms set by someone else, whose thoughts are the theme of our reading, it follows that the formulation of our faculty for deciphering cannot be along our own lines of orientation.

Herein lies the dialectical structure of reading. The need to decipher gives us the chance to formulate our own deciphering capacity—i.e., we bring to the fore an element of our being of which we are not directly conscious. The production of the meaning of literary texts—which we discussed in connection with forming the *Gestalt* of the text—does not merely entail the discovery of the unformulated, which can then be taken over by the active imagination of the reader; it also entails the possibility that we may formulate ourselves and so discover what had previously seemed to elude our consciousness. These are the ways in which reading literature gives us the chance to formulate the unformulated.

References

1   Cf. Roman Ingarden, *Vom Erkennen des literarischen Kunstwerks* (Tübingen, 1968), pp. 49 ff.
2   For a detailed discussion of this term see Roman Ingarden, *Das literarische Kunstwerk* (Tübingen, 1960), pp. 270 ff.
3   Laurence Sterne, *Tristram Shandy* (London, 1956), II, 11:79.
4   Virginia Woolf, *The Common Reader*, First Series (London, 1957), p. 174.
5   Ingarden, *Vom Erkennen des literarischen Kunstwerks*, p. 29.
6   Edmund Husserl, *Zur Phänomenologie des inneren Zeitbewusstseins, Gesammelte Werke* (The Hague, 1966), 10:52.
7   Ingarden, *Vom Erkennen des literarischen Kunstwerks*, p. 32.
8   For a more detailed discussion of the function of "gaps" in literary texts see Wolfgang Iser, "Indeterminacy and the Reader's Response in Prose Fiction," *Aspects of Narrative* (English Institute Essays), ed. J. Hillis Miller (New York, 1971), pp. 1–45.
9   M. Merleau Ponty, *Phenomenology of Perception*, transl. Colin Smith (New York, 1962), pp. 219, 221.
10   Gilbert Ryle, *The Concept of Mind* (Harmondsworth, 1968), p. 255.
11   Cf. Iser, "Indeterminacy," pp. 11 ff., 42 ff.
12   E. H. Gombrich, *Art and Illusion* (London, 1962), p. 204.
13   Louis O. Mink, "History and Fiction as Modes of Comprehension," *New Literary History* 1 (1970): 553.
14   Walter Pater, *Appreciations* (London, 1920), p. 18.
15   Gombrich, *Art and Illusion*, p. 54.
16   Ibid., p. 5.
17   John Dewey, *Art as Experience* (New York, 1958), p. 54.
18   Cf. Wayne C. Booth, *The Rhetoric of Fiction* (Chicago, 1963), pp. 211 ff., 339 ff.
19   G. B. Shaw, *Major Barbara* (London, 1964), p. 316.

20   William George Clark, *Fraser's* (December, 1849); 692, quoted by Kathleen Tillotson, *Novels of the Eighteen-Forties* (Oxford, 1961), pp. 19 f.

21   Cf. Georges Poulet, "Phenomenology of Reading," *New Literary History* 1 (1969): 54.

22   Ibid., p. 56.

23   Ibid., p. 59.

24   Ibid.

25   D. W. Harding, "Psychological Processes in the Reading of Fiction," in *Aesthetics in the Modern World*, ed. Harold Osborne (London, 1968), pp. 313 f.

Chapter 8

Judith Fetterley

ON THE POLITICS OF LITERATURE

LITERATURE IS POLITICAL. It is painful to have to insist on this fact, but the necessity of such insistence indicates the dimensions of the problem. John Keats once objected to poetry "that has a palpable design upon us." The major works of American fiction constitute a series of designs on the female reader, all the more potent in their effect because they are "impalpable." One of the main things that keeps the design of our literature unavailable to the consciousness of the woman reader, and hence impalpable, is the very posture of the apolitical, the pretense that literature speaks universal truths through forms from which all the merely personal, the purely subjective, has been burned away or at least transformed through the medium of art into the representative. When only one reality is encouraged, legitimized, and transmitted and when that limited vision endlessly insists on its comprehensiveness, then we have the conditions necessary for that confusion of consciousness in which impalpability flourishes. It is the purpose of this book to give voice to a different reality and different vision, to bring a different subjectivity to bear on the old "universality." To examine American fictions in light of how attitudes toward women shape their form and content is to make available to consciousness that which has been largely left unconscious and thus to change our understanding of these fictions, our relation to them, and their effect on us. It is to make palpable their designs.

American literature is male. To read the canon of what is currently considered classic American literature is perforce to identify as male. Though exceptions to this generalization can be found here and there—a Dickinson poem, a Wharton novel—these exceptions usually function to obscure the argument and confuse the issue: American literature is male. Our literature neither leaves women alone nor allows them to participate. It insists on its universality at the same time that it defines that universality in specifically male terms. "Rip Van Winkle" is paradigmatic of this phenomenon. While the desire to avoid work, escape authority, and sleep through the major decisions of one's life is obviously applicable to both men and women, in Irving's story this "universal" desire is made specifically male. Work, authority, and decision-making are symbolized by Dame Van Winkle, and the longing for flight is defined against her. She is what one must escape from, and the "one" is necessarily male. In Mailer's *An American Dream*, the fantasy of eliminating all one's ills through the ritual of scapegoating is equally male: the sacrificial scapegoat is the woman/wife and the cleansed survivor is the husband/male. In such fictions the female reader is co-opted into participation in an experience from which she is explicitly excluded; she is asked to identify with a selfhood that defines itself in opposition to her; she is required to identify against herself.

The woman reader's relation to American literature is made even more problematic by the fact that our literature is frequently dedicated to defining what is peculiarly American about experience and identity. Given the pervasive male bias of this literature, it is not surprising that in it the experience of being American is equated with the experience of being male. In Fitzgerald's *The Great Gatsby*, the background for the experience of disillusionment and betrayal revealed in the novel is the discovery of America, and Daisy's failure of Gatsby is symbolic of the failure of America to live up to the expectations in the imagination of the men who "discovered" it. America is female; to be American is male; and the quintessential American experience is betrayal by woman. Henry James certainly defined our literature, if not our culture, when he picked the situation of women as the subject of *The Bostonians*, his very American tale.

Power is the issue in the politics of literature, as it is in the politics of anything else. To be excluded from a literature that claims to define one's identity is to experience a peculiar form of powerlessness—not simply the powerlessness which derives from not seeing one's experience articulated, clarified, and legitimized in art, but more significantly the powerlessness which results from the endless division of self against self, the consequence of the invocation to identify as male while being reminded that to be male—to be universal, to be American—is to be *not female*. Not only does powerlessness characterize woman's experience of reading, it also describes the content of what is read. [. . .] The final irony, and indignity, of the woman reader's relation to American literature, then, is that she is required to dissociate herself from the very experience the literature engenders. Powerlessness is the subject and powerlessness the experience, and the design insists that Rip Van Winkle/Frederic Henry/Nick Carraway/Stephen Rojack speak for us all.

The drama of power in our literature is often disguised. In "Rip Van Winkle," Rip poses as powerless, the henpecked husband cowering before his termagant Dame. Yet, when Rip returns from the mountains, armed by the drama of female deposition witnessed there, to discover that his wife is dead and he is free to enjoy what he has always wanted, the "Shucks, M'am, I don't mean no harm" posture dissolves. In Sherwood Anderson's "I Want to Know Why," the issue of power is refracted through the trauma of a young boy's discovery of what it means to be male in a culture that gives white men power over women, horses, and niggers. More sympathetic and honest than "Rip," Anderson's story nevertheless exposes both the imaginative limits of our literature and the reasons for those limits. Storytelling and art can do no more than lament the inevitable—boys must grow up to be men; it can provide no alternative vision of being male. Bathed in nostalgia, "I Want to Know Why" is infused with the perspective it abhors, because finally to disavow that perspective would be to relinquish power. The lament is self-indulgent; it offers the luxury of feeling bad without the responsibility of change. And it is completely male-centered, registering the tragedy of sexism through its cost to men. At the end we cry for the boy and not for the whores he will eventually make use of.

[. . .]

> But what have I to say of *Sexual Politics* itself? Millett has undertaken a task
> which I find particularly worthwhile: the consideration of certain events or
> works of literature from an unexpected, even startling point of view. Millett
> never suggests that hers is a sufficient analysis of any of the works she discusses.
> Her aim is to wrench the reader from the vantage point he has long occupied,

and force him to look at life and letters from a new coign. Hers is not meant to be the last word on any writer, but a wholly new word, little heard before and strange. For the first time we have been asked to look at literature as women; we, men, women and Ph.D.s, have always read it as men. Who cannot point to a certain over-emphasis in the way Millett reads Lawrence or Stalin or Euripides. What matter? We are rooted in our vantage points and require transplanting which, always dangerous, involves violence and the possibility of death.

—*Carolyn Heilbrun*[1]

The method that is required is not one of correlation but of *liberation*. Even the term "method" must be reinterpreted and in fact wrenched out of its usual semantic field, for the emerging creativity in women is by no means a merely cerebral process. In order to understand the implications of this process it is necessary to grasp the fundamental fact that women have had the power of *naming* stolen from us. We have not been free to use our own power to name ourselves, the world, or God. The old naming was not the product of dialogue—a fact inadvertently admitted in the Genesis story of Adam's naming the animals and the woman. Women are now realizing that the universal imposing of names by men has been false because partial. That is, inadequate words have been taken as adequate.

—*Mary Daly*[2]

Re-vision—the act of looking back, of seeing with fresh eyes, of entering an old text from a new critical direction—is for us more than a chapter in cultural history: it is an act of survival. Until we can understand the assumptions in which we are drenched we cannot know ourselves. And this drive to self-knowledge, for woman, is more than a search for identity: it is part of her refusal of the self-destructiveness of male-dominated society. A radical critique of literature, feminist in its impulse, would take the work first of all as a clue to how we live, how we have been living, how we have been led to imagine ourselves, how our language has trapped as well as liberated us; and how we can begin to see—and therefore live—afresh.

—*Adrienne Rich*[3]

A culture which does not allow itself to look clearly at the obvious through the universal accessibility of art is a culture of tragic delusion, hardly viable.

—*Cynthia Ozick*[4]

When a system of power is thoroughly in command, it has scarcely need to speak itself aloud; when its workings are exposed and questioned, it becomes not only subject to discussion, but even to change.

—*Kate Millett*[5]

Consciousness is power. To create a new understanding of our literature is to make possible a new effect of that literature on us. And to make possible a new effect is in turn to provide the conditions for changing the culture that the literature reflects. To expose and question that complex of ideas and mythologies about women and men which exist in our society and are confirmed in our literature is to make the system of power embodied in the literature open not only to discussion but even to change. Such questioning and exposure can, of course, be carried on only by a consciousness radically different from the one that informs the literature. Such a closed system cannot be opened up from within but only from without. It must be entered into from a point of view which questions its values and assumptions and which has its investment in making available to consciousness precisely that which the literature wishes to keep hidden. Feminist criticism provides that point of view and embodies that consciousness.

In "A Woman's Map of Lyric Poetry," Elizabeth Hampsten, after quoting in full Thomas Campion's "My Sweetest Lesbia," asks, "And Lesbia, what's in it for her?"[6] The answer to this question is the subject of Hampsten's essay and the answer is, of course, nothing. But implicit in her question is another answer—a great deal, for someone. As Lillian Robinson reminds us, "and, always, *cui bono*—who profits?"[7] The questions of who profits, and how, are crucial because the attempt to answer them leads directly to an understanding of the function of literary sexual politics. Function is often best known by effect. Though one of the most persistent of literary stereotypes is the castrating bitch, the cultural reality is not the emasculation of men by women but the *immasculation* of women by men. As readers and teachers and scholars, women are taught to think as men, to identify with a male point of view, and to accept as normal and legitimate a male system of values, one of whose central principles is misogyny.

One of the earliest statements of the phenomenon of immasculation, serving indeed as a position paper, is Elaine Showalter's "Women and the Literary Curriculum." In the opening part of her article, Showalter imaginatively recreates the literary curriculum the average young woman entering college confronts:

> In her freshman year she would probably study literature and composition, and the texts in her course would be selected for their timeliness, or their relevance, or their power to involve the reader, rather than for their absolute standing in the literary canon. Thus she might be assigned any one of the texts which have recently been advertised for Freshman English: an anthology of essays, perhaps such as *The Responsible Man*, "for the student who wants literature relevant to the world in which he lives," or *Conditions of Men*, or *Man in Crisis: Perspectives on the Individual and His World*, or again, *Representative Men: Cult Heroes of Our Time*, in which thirty-three men represent such categories of heroism as the writer, the poet, the dramatist, the artist, and the guru, and the only two women included are the Actress Elizabeth Taylor and The Existential Heroine Jacqueline Onassis. . . . By the end of her freshman year, a woman student would have learned something about intellectual neutrality; she would be learning, in fact, how to think like a man.[8]

Showalter's analysis of the process of immasculation raises a central question: "What are the effects of this long apprenticeship in negative capability on the self-image and the self-confidence of women students?" And the answer is self-hatred and self-doubt: "Women are estranged from their own experience and unable to perceive its shape and authenticity. . . . they are expected to identify as readers with a masculine experience and perspective, which is presented as the human one. . . . Since they have no faith in the validity of their own perceptions and experiences, rarely seeing them confirmed in literature, or accepted in criticism, can we wonder that women students are so often timid, cautious, and insecure when we exhort them to 'think for themselves'?"[9]

The experience of immasculation is also the focus of Lee Edwards' article "Women, Energy, and *Middlemarch*." Summarizing her experience, Edwards concludes:

> Thus, like most women, I have gone through my entire education—as both

student and teacher—as a schizophrenic, and I do not use this term lightly, for madness is the bizarre but logical conclusion of our education. Imagining myself male, I attempted to create myself male. Although I knew the case was otherwise, it seemed I could do nothing to make this other critically real.

Edwards extends her analysis by linking this condition to the effects of the stereotypical presentation of women in literature:

I said simply, and for the most part silently that, since neither those women nor any women whose acquaintances I had made in fiction had much to do with the life I led or wanted to lead, I was not female. Alien from the women I saw most frequently imagined, I mentally arranged them in rows labelled respectively insipid heroines, sexy survivors, and demonic destroyers. As organizer I stood somewhere else, alone perhaps, but hopefully above them.[10]

Intellectually male, sexually female, one is in effect no one, nowhere, immasculated.

Clearly, then, the first act of the feminist critic must be to become a resisting rather than an assenting reader and, by this refusal to assent, to begin the process of exorcizing the male mind that has been implanted in us. The consequence of this exorcism is the capacity for what Adrienne Rich describes as re-vision—"the act of looking back, of seeing with fresh eyes, of entering an old text from a new critical direction." And the consequence, in turn, of this re-vision is that books will no longer be read as they have been read and thus will lose their power to bind us unknowingly to their designs. While women obviously cannot rewrite literary works so that they become ours by virtue of reflecting our reality, we can accurately name the reality they do reflect and so change literary criticism from a closed conversation to an active dialogue.

In making available to women this power of naming reality, feminist criticism is revolutionary. The significance of such power is evident if one considers the strength of the taboos against it:

I permit no woman to teach . . . she is to keep silent.

—*St. Paul*

By Talmudic law a man could divorce a wife whose voice could be heard next door. From there to Shakespeare: "Her voice was ever soft,/Gentle, and low – an excellent thing in woman." And to Yeats: "The women that I picked spoke sweet and low/ And yet gave tongue." And to Samuel Beckett, guessing at the last torture, The Worst: "a woman's voice perhaps, I hadn't thought of that, they might engage a soprano."

—*Mary Ellmann*[11]

The experience of the class in which I voiced my discontent still haunts my nightmares. Until my face froze and my brain congealed, I was called prude and, worse yet, insensitive, since I willfully misread the play in the interest of proving a point false both to the work and in itself.

—*Lee Edwards*[12]

The experience Edwards describes of attempting to communicate her reading of the character of Shakespeare's *Cleopatra* is a common memory for most of us who have become feminist critics. Many of us never spoke; those of us who did speak were usually quickly silenced. The need to keep certain things from being thought and said reveals to us their importance. Feminist criticism represents the discovery/recovery of a voice, a unique and uniquely powerful voice capable of canceling out those other voices, so movingly described in Sylvia Plath's *The Bell Jar*, which spoke about us and to us and at us but never for us.

[. . .]

References

1   Carolyn Heilbrun, "Millett's *Sexual Politics:* A Year Later," *Aphra* 2 (Summer 1971), 39.
2   Mary Daly, *Beyond God the Father: Toward a Philosophy of Women's Liberation* (Boston: Beacon, 1973), p. 8.
3   Adrienne Rich, "When We Dead Awaken: Writing as Re-Vision," *College English* 34 (1972), 18.
4   Cynthia Ozick, "Women and Creativity: The Demise of the Dancing Dog," *Motive* 29 (1969); reprinted in *Woman in Sexist Society*, eds. Vivian Gornick and Barbara Moran (New York: Signet-New American Library, 1972), p. 450.
5   Kate Millett, *Sexual Politics* (Garden City: Doubleday, 1970), p. 58.
6   Elizabeth Hampsten, "A Woman's Map of Lyric Poetry," *College English* 34 (1973), 1075.
7   "Lillian Robinson, Dwelling in Decencies: Radical Criticism and the Feminist Perspective," *College English* 32 (1971), 887; reprinted in *Sex, Class, and Culture* (Bloomington: Indiana University Press, 1978), p. 16.
8   Elaine Showalter, "Women and the Literary Curriculum," *College English* 32 (1971), 855.
9   *Ibid.*, 856–57.
10   Lee Edwards, "Women, Energy and *Middlemarch*". *Massachusetts Review* 13 (1972), 226, 227.
11   Mary Ellmann, *Thinking About Women* (New York: Harcourt Brace Jovanovich, 1968), pp. 149–50.
12   Edwards, 230.

Chapter 9

Stanley Fish

WHAT MAKES AN INTERPRETATION ACCEPTABLE?

LAST TIME I ENDED BY SUGGESTING that the fact of agreement, rather than being a proof of the stability of objects, is a testimony to the power of an interpretive community to constitute the objects upon which its members (also and simultaneously constituted) can then agree. This account of agreement has the additional advantage of providing what the objectivist argument cannot supply, a coherent account of *dis*agreement. To someone who believes in determinate meaning, disagreement can only be a theological error. The truth lies plainly in view, available to anyone who has the eyes to see; but some readers choose not to see it and perversely substitute their own meanings for the meanings that texts obviously bear. Nowhere is there an explanation of this waywardness (original sin would seem to be the only relevant model), or of the origin of these idiosyncratic meanings (I have been arguing that there could be none), or of the reason why some readers seem to be exempt from the general infirmity. There is simply the conviction that the facts exist in their own self-evident shape and that disagreements are to be resolved by referring the respective parties to the facts as they really are. In the view that I have been urging, however, disagreements cannot be resolved by reference to the facts, because the facts emerge only in the context of some point of view. It follows, then, that disagreements must occur between those who hold (or are held by) different points of view, and what is at stake in a disagreement is the right to specify what the facts can hereafter be said to be. Disagreements are not settled by the facts, but are the means by which the facts are settled. Of course, no such settling is final, and in the (almost certain) event that the dispute is opened again, the category of the facts "as they really are" will be reconstituted in still another shape.

Nowhere is this process more conveniently on display than in literary criticism, where everyone's claim is that his interpretation more perfectly accords with the facts, but where everyone's purpose is to persuade the rest of us to the version of the facts he espouses by persuading us to the interpretive principles in the light of which those facts will seem indisputable. The recent critical fortunes of William Blake's "The Tyger" provide a nice example. In 1954 Kathleen Raine published an influential essay entitled "Who Made the Tyger" in which she argued that because the tiger is for Blake "the beast that sustains its own life at the expense of its fellow-creatures" it is a "symbol of . . . predacious selfhood," and that therefore the answer to the poem's final question—"Did he who made the Lamb make thee"—"is, beyond all possible doubt, No."[1]

In short, the tiger is unambiguously and obviously evil. Raine supports her reading by pointing to two bodies of evidence, certain cabbalistic writings which, she avers, "beyond doubt . . . inspired *The Tyger*," and evidence from the poem itself. She pays particular attention to the word "forests" as it appears in line 2, "In the forests of the night": "Never . . . is the word 'forest' used by Blake in any context in which it does not refer to the natural, 'fallen' world" (p. 48).

The direction of argument here is from the word "forests" to the support it is said to provide for a particular interpretation. Ten years later, however, that same word is being cited in support of a quite different interpretation. While Raine assumes that the lamb is for Blake a symbol of Christ-like self-sacrifice, E. D. Hirsch believes that Blake's intention was "to satirize the singlemindedness of the Lamb:" "There can be no doubt," he declares, "that *The Tyger* is a poem that celebrates the holiness of tigerness."[2] In his reading the "ferocity and destructiveness" of the tiger are transfigured and one of the things they are transfigured by is the word "forests:" " 'Forests' . . . suggests tall straight forms, a world that for all its terror has the orderliness of the tiger's stripes or Blake's perfectly balanced verses" (p. 247).

What we have here then are two critics with opposing interpretations, each of whom claims the same word as internal and confirming evidence. Clearly they cannot both be right, but just as clearly there is no basis for deciding between them. One cannot appeal to the text, because the text has become an extension of the interpretive disagreement that divides them; and, in fact, the text as it is variously characterized is a *consequence* of the interpretation for which it is supposedly evidence. It is not that the meaning of the word "forests" points in the direction of one interpretation or the other; rather, in the light of an already assumed interpretation, the word will be seen to *obviously* have one meaning or another. Nor can the question be settled by turning to the context—say the cabbalistic writings cited by Raine—for that too will only be a context for an already assumed interpretation. If Raine had not already decided that the answer to the poem's final question is "beyond all possible doubt, No," the cabbalistic texts, with their distinction between supreme and inferior deities, would never have suggested themselves to her as Blake's source. The rhetoric of critical argument, as it is usually conducted in our journals, depends upon a distinction between interpretations on the one hand and the textual and contextual facts that will either support or disconfirm them on the other; but as the example of Blake's "Tyger" shows, text, context, and interpretation all emerge together, as a consequence of a gesture (the declaration of belief) that is irreducibly interpretive. It follows, then, that when one interpretation wins out over another, it is not because the first has been shown to be in accordance with the facts but because it is from the perspective of its assumptions that the facts are now being specified. It is these assumptions, and not the facts they make possible, that are at stake in any critical dispute.

Hirsch and Raine seem to be aware of this, at least subliminally; for whenever their respective assumptions surface they are asserted with a vehemence that is finally defensive: "The answer to the question . . . is beyond all possible doubt, No." "There can be no doubt that *The Tyger* is . . . a poem that celebrates the holiness of tigerness." If there were a doubt, if the interpretation with which each critic begins were not firmly in place, the account of the poem that follows from that interpretation could not get under way. One could not cite as an "obvious" fact that "forests" is a fallen word or, alternatively, that it "suggests tall and straight forms." Whenever a critic prefaces an assertion with a phrase like "without doubt" or "there can be no doubt," you can be sure that you are within hailing distance of the interpretive principles which produce the facts that he presents as obvious.

In the years since 1964 other interpretations of the poem have been put forward, and they follow a predictable course. Some echo either Raine or Hirsch by arguing that the tiger is either good or evil; others assert that the tiger is *both* good and evil, or beyond good and evil; still others protest that the questions posed in the poem are rhetorical and are therefore not meant to be answered ("It is quite evident that the critics are not trying to understand the poem at all. If they were, they would not attempt to answer its questions.")[3] It is only a matter of time before the focus turns from the questions to their asker and to the possibility that the speaker of the poem is not Blake but a limited persona ("Surely the point . . . is that Blake sees further or deeper than his *persona*").[4] It then becomes possible to assert that "we don't know who the speaker of 'The Tyger' is," and that therefore the poem "is a maze of questions in which the reader is forced to wander confusedly."[5] In this reading the poem itself becomes rather "tigerish" and one is not at all surprised when the original question— "Who made the Tiger?"—is given its quintessentially new-critical answer: the tiger is the poem itself and Blake, the consummate artist who smiles "his work to see," is its creator.[6] As one obvious and indisputable interpretation supplants another, it brings with it a new set of obvious and indisputable facts. Of course each new reading is elaborated in the name of the poem itself, but the poem itself is always a function of the interpretive perspective from which the critic "discovers" it.

   A committed pluralist might find in the previous paragraph a confirmation of his own position. After all, while "The Tyger" is obviously open to more than one interpretation, it is not open to an infinite number of interpretations. There may be disagreements as to whether the tiger is good or evil, or whether the speaker is Blake or a persona, and so on, but no one is suggesting that the poem is an allegory of the digestive processes or that it predicts the Second World War, and its limited plurality is simply a testimony to the capacity of a great work of art to generate multiple readings. The point is one that Wayne Booth makes when he asks, "Are we *right* to rule out at least some readings?"[7] and then answers his own question with a resounding yes. It would be my answer too; but the real question is what gives us the right so to be right. A pluralist is committed to saying that there is something in the text which rules out some readings and allows others (even though no *one* reading can ever capture the text's "inexhaustible richness and complexity"). His best evidence is that in practice "we all in fact" do reject unacceptable readings and that more often than not we agree on the readings that are to be rejected. Booth tells us, for example, that he has never found a reader of *Pride and Prejudice* "who sees no jokes against Mr. Collins" when he gives his reasons for wanting to marry Elizabeth Bennet and only belatedly, in fifth position, cites the "violence" of his affection.[8] From this and other examples Booth concludes that there are justified limits to what we can legitimately do with a text," for "surely we could not go on disputing at all if a core of agreement did not exist." Again, I agree, but if, as I have argued, the text is always a function of interpretation, then the text cannot be the location of the core of agreement by means of which we reject interpretations. We seem to be at an impasse: on the one hand there would seem to be no basis for labeling an interpretation unacceptable, but on the other we do it all the time.

   This, however, is an impasse only if one assumes that the activity of interpretation is itself unconstrained; but in fact the shape of that activity is determined by the literary institution which at any one time will authorize only a finite number of interpretative strategies. Thus, while there is no core of agreement *in* the text, there is a core of agreement (although one subject to change) concerning the ways of *producing* the text. Nowhere is this set of acceptable ways written down, but it is a part of everyone's knowledge of what it means to be operating within the literary institution as it is now constituted. A student of mine recently demonstrated this knowledge when, with an air of giving away a trade secret, she confided that she could go into any classroom, no matter what the subject of the course, and win approval for running one of a number of well-defined interpretive routines: she could view the assigned text as an instance of the tension between nature and culture; she could look in the text for evidence of large mythological oppositions; she could argue that the true subject of the text was its own composition, or that in the guise of fashioning a narrative the speaker was fragmenting and displacing his own anxieties and fears. She could not, however, at least at Johns Hopkins University today, argue that the text was a prophetic message inspired by the ghost of her Aunt Tilly.

My student's understanding of what she could and could not get away with, of the unwritten rules of the literary game, is shared by everyone who plays that game, by those who write and judge articles for publication in learned journals, by those who read and listen to papers at professional meetings, by those who seek and award tenure in innumerable departments of English and comparative literature, by the armies of graduate students for whom knowledge of the rules is the real mark of professional initiation. This does not mean that these rules and the practices they authorize are either monolithic or stable. Within the literary community there are subcommunities (what will excite the editors of *Diacritics* is likely to distress the editors of *Studies in Philology*), and within any community the boundaries of the acceptable are continually being redrawn. In a classroom whose authority figures include David Bleich and Norman Holland, a student might very well relate a text to her memories of a favorite aunt, while in other classrooms, dominated by the spirit of Brooks and Warren, any such activity would immediately be dismissed as nonliterary, as something that isn't done.

[. . .]

[T]he point is that while there is always a category of things that are not done (it is simply the reverse or flip side of the category of things that *are* done), the membership in that category is continually changing. It changes laterally as one moves from subcommunity to subcommunity, and it changes through time when once interdicted interpretive strategies are admitted into the ranks of the acceptable. Twenty years ago one of the things that literary critics didn't do was talk about the reader, at least in a way that made his experience the focus of the critical act. The prohibition on such talk was largely the result of Wimsatt's and Beardsley's famous essay "The Affective Fallacy," which argued that the variability of readers renders any investigation of their responses ad-hoc and relativistic: "The poem itself," the authors complained, "as an object of specifically critical judgment, tends to disappear."[9] So influential was this essay that it was possible for a reviewer to dismiss a book merely by finding in it evidence that the affective fallacy had been committed. The use of a juridical terminology is not accidental; this was in a very real sense a *legal* finding of activity in violation of understood and institutionalized decorums. Today, however, the affective fallacy, no longer a fallacy but a methodology, is committed all the time, and its practitioners have behind them the full and authorizing weight of a fully articulated institutional apparatus. The "reader in literature" is regularly the subject of forums and workshops at the convention of the Modern Language Association; there is a reader newsletter which reports on the multitudinous labors of a reader industry; any list of currently active schools of literary criticism includes the school of "reader response," and two major university presses have published collections of essays designed both to display the variety of reader-centered criticism (the emergence of factions within a once interdicted activity is a sure sign of its having achieved the status of an orthodoxy) and to detail its history. None of this of course means that a reader-centered criticism is now invulnerable to challenge or attack; merely that it is now recognized as a competing literary strategy that cannot be dismissed simply by being named. It is acceptable not because everyone accepts it but because those who do not are now obliged to argue against it.

The promotion of reader-response criticism to the category of things that are done (even if it is not being done by everyone) brings with it a whole new set of facts to which its practitioners can now refer. These include patterns of expectation and disappointment, reversals of direction, traps, invitations to premature conclusions, textual gaps, delayed revelations, temptations, all of which are related to a corresponding set of authors' intentions, of strategies designed to educate the reader or humiliate him or confound him or, in the more sophisticated versions of the mode, to make him enact in his responses the very subject matter of the poem. These facts and intentions emerge when the text is interrogated by a series of related questions—What is the reader doing? What is being done to him? For what purpose?—questions that follow necessarily from the assumption that the text is not a spatial object but the occasion for a temporal experience. It is in the course of answering such questions that a reader-response critic elaborates "the structure of the reading experience," a structure which is not so much discovered by the interrogation but demanded by it. (If you begin by assuming that readers do something and the something they do has meaning, you will never fail to discover a pattern of reader activities that appears obviously to be meaningful.) As that structure emerges (under the pressure of interrogation) it takes the form of a "reading," and insofar as the procedures which produced it are recognized by the literary community as something that some of its members do, that reading will have the status of a competing interpretation. Of course it is still the case, as Booth insists, that we are "right to rule out at least some readings," but there is now one less reading or kind of reading that can be ruled out, because there is now one more interpretive procedure that has been accorded a place in the literary institution.

The fact that it remains easy to think of a reading that most of us would dismiss out of hand does not mean that the text excludes it but that there is as yet no elaborated interpretive procedure for producing that text. That is why the examples of critics like Wayne Booth seem to have so much force; rather than looking back, as I have, to now familiar strategies that were once alien and strange sounding, they look forward to strategies that have not yet emerged. [. . .]

[T]he point is that while there are always mechanisms for ruling out readings, their source is not the text but the presently recognized interpretive strategies for producing the text. It follows, then, that no reading, however outlandish it might appear, is inherently an impossible one. Consider, for example, Booth's report that he has never found a reader who sees no jokes against Mr. Collins, and his conclusion that the text of *Pride and Prejudice* enforces or signals an ironic reading. First of all, the fact that he hasn't yet found such a reader does not mean that one does not exist, and we can even construct his profile; he would be someone for whom the reasons in Mr. Collins's list correspond to a deeply held set of values, exactly the opposite of the set of values that must be assumed if the passage is to be seen as obviously ironic. Presumably no one who has sat in Professor Booth's classes holds that set of values or is allowed to hold them (students always know what they are expected to believe) and it is unlikely that anyone who is now working in the Austen industry begins with an assumption other than the assumption that the novelist is a master ironist. It is precisely for this reason that the time is ripe for the "discovery" by an enterprising scholar of a nonironic Austen, and one can even predict the course such a discovery would take. It would begin with the uncovering of new evidence (a letter, a lost manuscript, a contemporary response) and proceed to the conclusion that Austen's intentions have been misconstrued by generations of literary critics. She was not in fact satirizing the narrow and circumscribed life of a country gentry; rather, she was celebrating that life and its tireless elaboration of a social fabric, complete with values, rituals, and self-perpetuating goals (marriage, the preservation of great houses, and so on). This view, or something very much like it, is already implicit in much of the criticism, and it would only be a matter of extending it to local matters of interpretation, and specifically to Mr. Collins's list of reasons which might now be seen as reflecting a proper ranking of the values and obligations necessary to the maintenance of a way of life.

Of course any such reading would meet resistance; its opponents could point for example to the narrator's unequivocal condemnation of Mr. Collins; but there are always ways in the literary institution of handling this or any other objection. One need only introduce (if it has not already been introduced) the notion of the fallible narrator in any of its various forms (the dupe, the moral prig, the naif in need of education), and the "unequivocal condemnation" would take its place in a structure designed to glorify Mr. Collins and everything he stands for. Still, no matter how many objections were met and explained away, the basic resistance on the part of many scholars to this revisionist reading would remain, and for a time at least *Pride and Prejudice* would have acquired the status of the fourth book of *Gulliver's Travels*, a work whose very shape changes in the light of two radically opposed interpretive assumptions.

Again, I am aware that this argument is a tour-de-force and will continue to seem so as long as the revolution it projects has not occurred. The reading of *Pride and Prejudice*, however, is not meant to be persuasive. I only wanted to describe the conditions under which it might *become* persuasive and to point out that those conditions are not unimaginable given the procedures within the literary institution by which interpretations are proposed and established. Any interpretation could be elaborated by someone in command of those procedures (someone who knows what "will do" as a literary argument), even my own "absurd" reading of "The Tyger" as an allegory of the digestive processes. Here the task is easy because according to the critical consensus there is no belief so bizarre that Blake could not have been committed to it and it would be no trick at all to find some elaborate system of alimentary significances (Pythagorean? Swedenborgian? Cabbalistic?) which he could be presumed to have known. One might then decide that the poem was the first-person lament of someone who had violated a dietary prohibition against eating tiger meat, and finds that forbidden food burning brightly in his stomach, making its fiery way through the forests of the intestinal tract, beating and hammering like some devil-wielded anvil. In his distress he can do nothing but rail at the tiger and at the mischance that led him to mistake its meat for the meat of some purified animal: "Did he who made the Lamb make thee?" The poem ends as it began, with the speaker still paying the price of his sin and wondering at the inscrutable purposes of a deity who would lead his creatures into digestive temptation. Anyone who thinks that this time I have gone too far might do very well to consult some recent numbers of *Blake Studies*.

In fact, my examples are very serious, and they are serious in part because they are so ridiculous. The fact that they *are* ridiculous, or are at least perceived to be so, is evidence that we are never without canons of acceptability; we are always "right to rule out at least some readings." But the fact that we can imagine conditions under which they would *not* seem ridiculous, and that readings once considered ridiculous are now respectable and even orthodox, is evidence that the canons of acceptability can change. Moreover, that change is not random but orderly and, to some extent, predictable. A new interpretive strategy always makes its way in some relationship of opposition to the old, which has often marked out a negative space (of things that aren't done) from which it can emerge into respectability. Thus, when Wimsatt and Beardsley declare that "the Affective Fallacy is a confusion between the poem and its *results*, what it *is* and what it *does*," the way is open for an affective critic to argue, as I did, that a poem *is* what it does. And when the possibility of a reader-centered criticism seems threatened by the variability of readers, that threat will be countered either by denying the variability (Stephen Booth, Michael Riffaterre) or by controlling it (Wolfgang Iser, Louise Rosenblatt) or by embracing it and making it into a principle of value (David Bleich, Walter Slatoff).

Rhetorically the new position announces itself as a break from the old, but in fact it is radically dependent on the old, because it is only in the context of some differential relationship that it can be perceived as new or, for that matter, perceived at all. No one would bother to assert that Mr. Collins is the hero of *Pride and Prejudice* (even as an example intended to be absurd) were that position not already occupied in the criticism by Elizabeth and Darcy; for then the assertion would have no force; there would be nothing in relation to which it could be surprising. Neither would there be any point in arguing that Blake's tiger is both good and evil if there were not already readings in which he was declared to be one or the other. And if anyone is ever to argue that he is both old and young, someone will first have to argue that he is *either* old or young, for only when his age has become a question will there be any value in a refusal to answer it. Nor is it the case that the moral status of the tiger (as opposed to its age, or nationality, or intelligence) is an issue raised by the poem itself; it becomes an issue because a question is put to the poem (is the tiger good or evil?) and once that question (it could have been another) is answered, the way is open to answering it differently, or declining to answer it, or to declaring that the absence of an answer is the poem's "real point."

The discovery of the "real point" is always what is claimed whenever a new interpretation is advanced, but the claim makes sense only in relation to a point (or points) that had previously been considered the real one. This means that the space in which a critic works has been marked out for him by his predecessors, even though he is obliged by the conventions of the institution to dislodge them. It is only by their prevenience or prepossession that there is something for him to say; that is, it is only because something has already been said that he can now say something different. This dependency, the reverse of the anxiety of influence, is reflected in the unwritten requirement that an interpretation present itself as remedying a deficiency in the interpretations that have come before it. (If it did not do this, what claim would it have on our attention?) Nor can this be just any old deficiency; it will not do, for example, to fault your predecessors for failing to notice that a poem is free of split infinitives or dangling participles. The lack an interpretation supplies must be related to the criteria by which the literary community recognizes and evaluates the objects of its professional attention. As things stand now, text-book grammaticality is not one of those criteria, and therefore the demonstration of its presence in a poem will not reflect credit either on the poem or on the critic who offers it.

Credit *will* accrue to the critic when he bestows the *proper* credit on the poem, when he demonstrates that it possesses one or more of the qualities that are understood to distinguish poems from other verbal productions. In the context of the "new" criticism, under many of whose assumptions we still labor, those qualities include unity, complexity, and universality, and it is the perceived failure of previous commentators to celebrate their presence in a poem that gives a critic the right (or so he will claim) to advance a new interpretation. The unfolding of that interpretation will thus proceed under two constraints: not only must what one says about a work be related to what has already been said (even if the relation is one of reversal) but as a consequence of saying it the work must be shown to possess in a greater degree than had hitherto been recognized the qualities that properly belong to literary productions, whether they be unity and complexity, or unparaphrasability, or metaphoric richness, or indeterminacy and undecidability. In short, the new interpretation must not only claim to tell the truth about the work (in a dependent opposition to the falsehood or partial truths told by its predecessors) but it must claim to make the work better. (The usual phrase is "enhance our appreciation of.") Indeed, these claims are finally inseparable since it is assumed that the truth about a work will be what penetrates to the essence of its literary value.

This assumption, along with several others, is conveniently on display in the opening paragraph of the preface to Stephen Booth's *An Essay on Shakespeare's Sonnets:* [10]

> The history of criticism opens so many possibilities for an essay on Shakespeare's sonnets that I must warn a prospective reader about what this work does and

doesn't do. To begin with the negative, I have not solved or tried to solve any of
the puzzles of Shakespeare's sonnets. I do not attempt to identify Mr. W. H. or
the dark lady. I do not speculate on the occasions that may have evoked particular sonnets. I do not attempt to date them. I offer neither a reorganization of the
sequence, nor a defense of the quarto order. What I have tried to do is find out
what about the sonnets has made them so highly valued by the vast majority of
critics and general readers.

This brief paragraph can serve as an illustration of almost everything I have been saying. First
of all, Booth self-consciously locates and defines his position in a differential opposition to
the positions he would dislodge. He will not, he tells us, do what any of his predecessors
have done; he will do something else, and indeed if it were not something else there would
be no reason for him to be doing it. The reason he gives for doing it is that what his
predecessors have done is misleading or beside the point. The point is the location of the
source of the sonnets' value ("what about the sonnets has made them so highly valued") and
his contention (not stated but strongly implied) is that those who have come before him have
been looking in the wrong places, in the historical identity of the sequence's characters, in
the possibility of recovering the biographical conditions of composition, and in the
determination of an authoritative ordering and organization. He, however, will look in the
right place and thereby produce an account of the sonnets that does them the justice they so
richly deserve.

    Thus, in only a few sentences Booth manages to claim for his interpretation everything
that certifies it as acceptable within the conventions of literary criticism: he locates a
deficiency in previous interpretations and proposes to remedy it; the remedy will take the
form of producing a more satisfactory account of the work; and as a result the literary
credentials of the work—what makes it of enduring value—will be more securely established, as they are when Booth is able to point in the closing paragraph of his book to
Shakespeare's "remarkable achievement." By thus validating Shakespeare's achievement,
Booth also validates his own credentials as a literary critic, as someone who knows what
claims and demonstrations mark him as a competent member of the institution.

    What makes Stephen Booth so interesting (although not at all atypical) is that one of
his claims is to have freed himself and the sonnets from that very institution and its practices.
"I do not," he declares, "intentionally give any interpretations of the sonnets I discuss. I mean
to describe them, not to explain them." The irony is that even as Booth is declaring himself
out of the game, he is performing one of its most familiar moves. The move has several
versions, and Booth is here availing himself of two: (1) the "external-internal," performed
when a critic dismisses his predecessors for being insufficiently literary ("but that has nothing
to do with its qualities as a poem"); and (2) the "back-to-the-text," performed when the
critical history of a work is deplored as so much dross, as an obscuring encrustation ("we are
in danger of substituting the criticism for the poem"). The latter is the more powerful
version of the move because it trades on the assumption, still basic to the profession's sense
of its activities, that the function of literary criticism is to let the text speak for itself. It is
thus a move drenched in humility, although it is often performed with righteousness: those
other fellows may be interested in displaying their ingenuity, but I am simply a servant of the
text and wish only to make it more available to its readers (who happen also to be my
readers).

    The basic gesture, then, is to disavow interpretation in favor of simply presenting the
text; but it is actually a gesture in which one set of interpretive principles is replaced by
another that happens to claim for itself the virtue of not being an interpretation at all. The
claim, however, is an impossible one since in order "simply to present" the text, one must at

the very least describe it ("I mean to describe them") and description can occur only within a stipulative understanding of what there is to be described, an understanding that will produce the object of its attention. Thus, when Booth rejects the assumptions of those who have tried to solve the puzzles of the sonnets in favor of "the assumption that the source of our pleasure in them must be the line by line experience of reading them," he is not avoiding interpretation but proposing a change in the terms within which it will occur. Specifically, he proposes that the focus of attention, and therefore of description, shift from the poem conceived as a spatial object which *contains* meanings to the poem conceived as a temporal experience in the course of which meanings become momentarily available, before disappearing under the pressure of other meanings, which are in their turn superseded, contradicted, qualified, or simply forgotten. It is only if a reader agrees to this change, that is, agrees to accept Booth's revisionary stipulation as to where the value and the significance of a poem are to be located, that the facts to which his subsequent analyses point will be seen to be facts at all. The description which Booth offers in place of an interpretation turns out to be as much of an interpretive construct as the interpretations he rejects.

Nor could it be otherwise. Strictly speaking, getting "back-to-the-text" is not a move one can perform, because the text one gets back to will be the text demanded by some other interpretation and that interpretation will be presiding over its production. This is not to say, however, that the "back-to-the-text" move is ineffectual. The fact that it is not something one can do in no way diminishes the effectiveness of claiming to do it. As a rhetorical ploy, the announcement that one is returning to the text will be powerful so long as the assumption that criticism is secondary to the text and must not be allowed to overwhelm it remains unchallenged. Certainly, Booth does not challenge it; indeed, he relies on it and invokes it even as he relies on and invokes many other assumptions that someone else might want to dispute: the assumption that what distinguishes literary from ordinary language is its invulnerability to paraphrase; the assumption that a poem should not mean, but be; the assumption that the more complex a work is, the more propositions it holds in tension and equilibrium, the better it is. It would not be at all unfair to label these assumptions "conservative" and to point out that in holding to them Booth undermines his radical credentials. But it would also be beside the point, which is not that Booth isn't truly radical but that he *couldn't* be. Nor could anyone else. The challenge he mounts to some of the conventions of literary study (the convention of the poem as artifact, the convention of meaningfulness) would not even be *recognized* as a challenge if others of those conventions were not firmly in place and, for the time being at least, unquestioned. A wholesale challenge would be impossible because there would be no terms in which it could be made; that is, in order to be wholesale, it would have to be made in terms wholly outside the institution; but if that were the case, it would be unintelligible because it is only within the institution that the facts of literary study—texts, authors, periods, genres—become available. In short, the price intelligibility exacts (a price Booth pays here) is implication in the very structure of assumptions and goals from which one desires to be free.

So it would seem, finally, that there are no moves that are not moves in the game, and this includes even the move by which one claims no longer to be a player. Indeed, by a logic peculiar to the institution, one of the standard ways of practicing literary criticism is to announce that you are avoiding it. This is so because at the heart of the institution is the wish to deny that its activities have any consequences. The critic is taught to think of himself as a transmitter of the best that had been thought and said by others, and his greatest fear is that he will stand charged of having substituted his own meanings for the meanings of which he is supposedly the guardian; his greatest fear is that he be found guilty of having interpreted. That is why we have the spectacle of commentators who, like Stephen Booth, adopt a stance of aggressive humility and, in the manner of someone who rises to speak at a temperance meeting, declare that they will never interpret again but will instead do something else ("I mean to describe them"). What I have been saying is that whatever they do, it will only be interpretation in another guise because, like it or not, interpretation is the only game in town.

References

1   Kathleen Raine, "Who Made the Tyger," *Encounter*, June 1954, p. 50.
2   E. D. Hirsch, *Innocence and Experience* (New Haven: Yale University Press, 1964), pp. 245, 248.
3   Philip Hobsbaum, "A Rhetorical Question Answered: Blake's *Tyger* and Its Critics," *Neophilologus*, 48, no. 2 (1964), 154.
4   Warren Stevenson, " 'The Tyger' as Artefact," *Blake Studies*, 2, no. 1 (1969–70), 9.
5   L. J. Swingle, "Answers to Blake's 'Tyger': A Matter of Reason or of Choice," *Concerning Poetry*, 2 (1970), 67.
6   Stevenson, " 'The Tyger' as Artefact," p. 15.
7   Wayne Booth, "Preserving the Exemplar," *Critical Inquiry*, 3, no. 3 (Spring 1977), 413.
8   *Ibid.*, 412.
9   W. K. Wimsatt and Monroe Beardsley, *The Verbal Icon* (Lexington: University of Kentucky Press, 1954), p. 21.
10 Stephen Booth, *An Essay on Shakespeare's Sonnets* (New Haven: Yale University Press, 1969).

Chapter 10

Mikhail Bakhtin

DISCOURSE IN POETRY AND
DISCOURSE IN THE NOVEL

[. . .]

THE WORD IS BORN in a dialogue as a living rejoinder within it; the word is shaped in dialogic interaction with an alien word that is already in the object. A word forms a concept of its own object in a dialogic way.

But this does not exhaust the internal dialogism of the word. It encounters an alien word not only in the object itself: every word is directed toward an *answer* and cannot escape the profound influence of the answering word that it anticipates.

The word in living conversation is directly, blatantly, oriented toward a future answer-word: it provokes an answer, anticipates it and structures itself in the answer's direction. Forming itself in an atmosphere of the already spoken, the word is at the same time determined by that which has not yet been said but which is needed and in fact anticipated by the answering word. Such is the situation in any living dialogue.

All rhetorical forms, monologic in their compositional structure, are oriented toward the listener and his answer. This orientation toward the listener is usually considered the basic constitutive feature of rhetorical discourse.[1]

It is highly significant for rhetoric that this relationship toward the concrete listener, taking him into account, is a relationship that enters into the very internal construction of rhetorical discourse. This orientation toward an answer is open, blatant and concrete.

This open orientation toward the listener and his answer in everyday dialogue and in rhetorical forms has attracted the attention of linguists. But even where this has been the case, linguists have by and large gotten no further than the compositional forms by which the listener is taken into account; they have not sought influence springing from more profound meaning and style. They have taken into consideration only those aspects of style determined by demands for comprehensibility and clarity—that is, precisely those aspects that are deprived of any internal dialogism, that take the listener for a person who passively understands but not for one who actively answers and reacts.

The listener and his response are regularly taken into account when it comes to everyday dialogue and rhetoric, but every other sort of discourse as well is oriented toward an understanding that is "responsive"—although this orientation is not particularized in an independent act and is not compositionally marked. Responsive understanding is a fundamental force, one that participates in the formulation of discourse, and it is moreover an *active* understanding, one that discourse senses as resistance or support enriching the discourse.

Linguistics and the philosophy of language acknowledge only a passive understanding of discourse, and moreover this takes place by and large on the level of common language, that is, it is an understanding of an utterance's *neutral signification* and not its *actual meaning*.

The linguistic significance of a given utterance is understood against the background of language, while its actual meaning is understood against the background of other concrete utterances on the same theme, a background made up of contradictory opinions, points of view and value judgments—that is, precisely that background that, as we see, complicates the path of any word toward its object. Only now this contradictory environment of alien words is present to the speaker not in the object, but rather in the consciousness of the listener, as his apperceptive background, pregnant with responses and objections. And every utterance is oriented toward this apperceptive background of understanding, which is not a linguistic background but rather one composed of specific objects and emotional expressions. There occurs a new encounter between the utterance and an alien word, which makes itself felt as a new and unique influence on its style.

A passive understanding of linguistic meaning is no understanding at all; it is only the abstract aspect of meaning. But even a more concrete *passive* understanding of the meaning of the utterance, an understanding of the speaker's intention insofar as that understanding remains purely passive, purely receptive, contributes nothing new to the word under consideration, only mirroring it, seeking, at its most ambitious, merely the full reproduction of that which is already given in the word—even such an understanding never goes beyond the boundaries of the word's context and in no way enriches the word. Therefore, insofar as the speaker operates with such a passive understanding, nothing new can be introduced into his discourse; there can be no new aspects in his discourse relating to concrete objects and emotional expressions. Indeed the purely negative demands, such as could only emerge from a passive understanding (for instance, a need for greater clarity, more persuasiveness, more vividness and so forth), leave the speaker in his own personal context, within his own boundaries; such negative demands are completely immanent in the speaker's own discourse and do not go beyond his semantic or expressive self-sufficiency.

In the actual life of speech, every concrete act of understanding is active: it assimilates the word to be understood into its own conceptual system filled with specific objects and emotional expressions, and is indissolubly merged with the response, with a motivated agreement or disagreement. To some extent, primacy belongs to the response, as the activating principle: it creates the ground for understanding, it prepares the ground for an active and engaged understanding. Understanding comes to fruition only in the response. Understanding and response are dialectically merged and mutually condition each other; one is impossible without the other.

Thus an active understanding, one that assimilates the word under consideration into a new conceptual system, that of the one striving to understand, establishes a series of complex inter-relationships, consonances and dissonances with the word and enriches it with new elements. It is precisely such an understanding that the speaker counts on. Therefore his orientation toward the listener is an orientation toward a specific conceptual horizon, toward the specific world of the listener; it introduces totally new elements into his discourse; it is in this way, after all, that various points of view, conceptual horizons, systems for providing expressive accents, various social "languages" come to interact with one another. The speaker strives to get a reading on his own word, and on his own conceptual system that determines this word, within the alien conceptual system of the understanding receiver; he enters into dialogical relationships with certain aspects of this system.

The speaker breaks through the alien conceptual horizon of the listener, constructs his own utterance on alien territory, against his, the listener's, apperceptive background.

This new form of internal dialogism of the word is different from that form determined by an encounter with an alien word within the object itself: here it is not the object that serves as the arena for the encounter, but rather the subjective belief system of the listener. Thus this dialogism bears a more subjective, psychological and (frequently) random character, sometimes crassly accommodating, sometimes provocatively polemical. Very often, especially in the rhetorical forms, this orientation toward the listener and the related internal dialogism of the word may simply overshadow the object: the strong point of any concrete listener becomes a self-sufficient focus of attention, and one that interferes with the word's creative work on its referent.

Although they differ in their essentials and give rise to varying stylistic effects in discourse, the dialogic relationship toward an alien word within the object and the relationship toward an alien word in the anticipated answer of the listener can, nevertheless, be very tightly interwoven with each other, becoming almost indistinguishable during stylistic analysis.

Thus, discourse in Tolstoy is characterized by a sharp internal dialogism, and this discourse is moreover dialogized in the belief system of the reader—whose peculiar semantic and expressive characteristics Tolstoy acutely senses—as well as in the object. These two lines of dialogization (having in most cases polemical overtones) are tightly interwoven in his style: even in the most "lyrical" expressions and the most "epic" descriptions, Tolstoy's discourse harmonizes and disharmonizes (more often disharmonizes) with various aspects of the heteroglot socio-verbal consciousness ensnaring the object, while at the same time polemically invading the reader's belief and evaluative system, striving to stun and destroy the apperceptive background of the reader's active understanding. In this respect Tolstoy is an heir of the eighteenth century, especially of Rousseau. This propagandizing impulse sometimes leads to a narrowing-down of heteroglot social consciousness (against which Tolstoy polemicizes) to the consciousness of his immediate contemporary, a contemporary of the day and not of the epoch; what follows from this is a radical concretization of dialogization (almost always undertaken in the service of a polemic). For this reason Tolstoy's dialogization, no matter how acutely we sense it in the expressive profile of his style, sometimes requires special historical or literary commentary: we are not sure with *what* precisely a given tone is in harmony or disharmony, for this dissonance or consonance has entered into the positive project of creating a style.[2] It is true that such extreme concreteness (which approaches at time the feuilleton) is present only in those secondary aspects, the overtones of internal dialogization in Tolstoy's discourse.

In those examples of the internal dialogization of discourse that we have chosen (the internal, as contrasted with the external, compositionally marked, dialogue) the relationship to the alien word, to an alien utterance enters into the positing of the style. Style organically contains within itself indices that reach outside itself, a correspondence of its own elements and the elements of an alien context. The internal politics of style (how the elements are put together) is determined by its external politics (its relationship to alien discourse). The word lives, as it were, on the boundary between its own context and another, alien, context.

In any actual dialogue the rejoinder also leads such a double life: it is structured and conceptualized in the context of the dialogue as a whole, which consists of its own utterances ("own" from the point of view of the speaker) and of alien utterances (those of the partner). One cannot excise the rejoinder from this combined context made up of one's own words and the words of another without losing its sense and tone. It is an organic part of a heteroglot unity.

The phenomenon of internal dialogization, as we have said, is present to a greater or lesser extent in all realms of the life of the word. But if in extra-artistic prose (everyday, rhetorical, scholarly) dialogization usually stands apart, crystallizes into a special kind of act of its own and runs its course in ordinary dialogue or in other, compositionally clearly marked forms for mixing and polemicizing with the discourse of another—then in *artistic* prose, and especially in the novel, this dialogization penetrates from within the very way in which the word conceives its object and its means for expressing itself, reformulating the semantics and syntactical structure of discourse. Here dialogic inter-orientation becomes, as it were, an event of discourse itself, animating from within and dramatizing discourse in all its aspects.

In the majority of poetic genres (poetic in the narrow sense), as we have said, the internal dialogization of discourse is not put to artistic use, it does not enter into the work's "aesthetic object," and is artificially extinguished in poetic discourse. In the novel, however, this internal dialogization becomes one of the most fundamental aspects of prose style and undergoes a specific artistic elaboration.

But internal dialogization can become such a crucial force for creating form only where individual differences and contradictions are enriched by social heteroglossia, where dialogic reverberations do not sound in the semantic heights of discourse (as happens in the rhetorical genres) but penetrate the deep strata of discourse, dialogize language itself and the world view a particular language has (the internal form of discourse)—where the dialogue of voices arises directly out of a social dialogue of "languages," where an alien utterance begins to sound like a socially alien language, where the orientation of the word among alien utterances changes into an orientation of a word among socially alien languages within the boundaries of one and the same national language.

[. . .]

Discourse lives, as it were, beyond itself, in a living impulse [*napravlennost'*] toward the object; if we detach ourselves completely from this impulse all we have left is the naked corpse of the word, from which we can learn nothing at all about the social situation or the fate of a given word in life. *To study the word as such, ignoring the impulse that reaches out beyond it, is just as senseless as to study psychological experience outside the context of that real life toward which it was directed and by which it is determined.*

By stressing the intentional dimension of stratification in literary language, we are able to locate in a single series such methodologically heterogeneous phenomena as professional and social dialects, world views and individual artistic works, for in their intentional dimension one finds that common plane on which they can all be juxtaposed, and juxtaposed dialogically. The whole matter consists in the fact that there may be, between "languages," highly specific dialogic relations; no matter how these languages are conceived, they may all be taken as particular points of view on the world. However varied the social forces doing the work of stratification—a profession, a genre, a particular tendency, an individual personality—the work itself everywhere comes down to the (relatively) protracted and socially meaningful (collective) saturation of language with specific (and consequently limiting) intentions and accents. The longer this stratifying saturation goes on, the broader the social circle encompassed by it and consequently the more substantial the social force bringing about such a stratification of language, then the more sharply focused and stable will be those traces, the linguistic changes in the language markers (linguistic symbols), that are left behind in language as a result of this social force's activity—from stable (and consequently social) semantic nuances to authentic dialectological markers (phonetic, morphological and others), which permit us to speak of particular social dialects.

As a result of the work done by all these stratifying forces in language, there are no "neutral" words and forms—words and forms that can belong to "no one"; language has been completely taken over, shot through with intentions and accents. For any individual consciousness living in it, language is not an abstract system of normative forms but rather a concrete heteroglot conception of the world. All words have the "taste" of a profession, a genre, a tendency, a party, a particular work, a particular person, a generation, an age group, the day and hour. Each word tastes of the context and contexts in which it has lived its socially charged life; all words and forms are populated by intentions. Contextual overtones (generic, tendentious, individualistic) are inevitable in the word.

As a living, socio-ideological concrete thing, as heteroglot opinion, language, for the individual consciousness, lies on the borderline between oneself and the other. The word in language is half someone else's. It becomes "one's own" only when the speaker populates it with his own intention, his own accent, when he appropriates the word, adapting it to his own semantic and expressive intention. Prior to this moment of appropriation, the word does not exist in a neutral and impersonal language (it is not, after all, out of a dictionary that the speaker gets his words!), but rather it exists in other people's mouths, in other people's contexts, serving other people's intentions: it is from there that one must take the word, and make it one's own. And not all words for just anyone submit equally easily to this appropriation, to this seizure and transformation into private property: many words stubbornly resist, others remain alien, sound foreign in the mouth of the one who appropriated them and who now speaks them; they cannot be assimilated into his context and fall out of it; it is as if they put themselves in quotation marks against the will of the speaker. Language is not a neutral medium that passes freely and easily into the private property of the speaker's intentions; it is populated—overpopulated—with the intentions of others. Expropriating it, forcing it to submit to one's own intentions and accents, is a difficult and complicated process.

References

1   C.f. V. Vinogradov's book *On Artistic Prose*, the chapter "Rhetoric and Poetics," pp. 75ff., where definitions taken from the older rhetorics are introduced.
2   C.f. B.M. Eichenbaum's book *Lev Tolstoj*, book 1 (Leningrad, 1928), which contains much relevant material; for example, an explication of the topical context of "Family Happiness."

Chapter 11

Paul Saenger

SILENT READING: ITS IMPACT ON LATE MEDIEVAL SCRIPT AND SOCIETY

ORAL READING AND COMPOSITION in the twelfth century has seemed to many modern scholars to be inconsistent with the monastic ideal of silence set forth by the rule of Saint Benedict. Indeed, a direct and personal relationship with God was a basic tenet of Christianity which even to the early Christians seemed incompatible with the practice of dictating to a scribe. Saint Augustine, in the *Soliloquies*, clearly stated that certain thoughts intended for God were too private to be shared with a secretary.[1] Neither in antiquity nor even less in the early Middle Ages, however, were the techniques of writing and reading conducive to the ideal of private communication with God. For this reason, from the very beginning of monasticism in the sixth century until the time of Saint Bernard in the twelfth century, oral group reading and composition were in practice no more considered a breach of silence than were confession or the recitation of prayers. According to their rule, twelfth-century Cluniac monks were judged to have violated their vows of silence only when a word they spoke was not written in the text.[2] Through oral readings and rote memorization, Benedictine monks retained the biblical and patristic passages they would later use during the hours reserved for silent meditation. Oral composition was similarly not usually construed as a violation of the vow of silence. Thus, treatises on the *ars dictaminis*, which explained the rhythmic rules of the *cursus*, were composed by Cistercian monks, who lived under a rule of silence more strict than that of the Benedictines.[3] Even in the twelfth century, however, the potential conflict between the vow of silence and oral reading and composition did not go completely unnoticed. In recognition of the special silence imposed by Lent, Saint Bernard renounced dictation and literary composition.[4] The general chapter of the Cistercian order carefully determined which monks should have the privilege of orally composing texts.[5] Nevertheless, in the mid-twelfth century it would seem that only monks engaged in book production in the scriptorium consistently applied the rule of silence to reading and writing.

The stimulant to silent reading was not the observance of monastic silence, but the increasingly complex body of thought known as scholasticism that came to dominate education in the twelfth and early thirteenth centuries. Reading aloud, even for the reader, made the comprehension of complex ideas slow and difficult. As early as the seventh century, Isidore of Seville remarked that reading in a loud voice interfered with comprehension, and he recommended that the tongue and lips be moved quietly.[6] This type of quiet reading was similar to the private reading that Saint Benedict had commended in his rule.[7] For Isidore who, like Saint Benedict, wrote before word division, reading could not be entirely visual but only quiet, since it still depended upon gestures of the throat and mouth. The introduction of word separation changed the way children were taught to read. Through the eighth century, they had learned to read in the antique fashion from letters and syllables. In the ninth century, however, the young saint Samson was reported to have learned within a week to recognize *distinctiones* of letters as words.[8] The recognition of words as visible units of letters which word separation made possible must undoubtedly have led to easier and swifter oral reading. True silent reading, that is, reading with the eyes alone, developed only with the evolution of a more rigorous intellectual life in the twelfth and early thirteenth centuries in the *studia* of Cistercian abbeys and at the cathedral schools of the eleventh and twelfth centuries from which universities would emerge. Hugh of Saint Victor described the new mode of reading as *per se inspicientis*.[9] Abbot Richelm of the Cistercian abbey of Schönthal read habitually only with his eyes because this technique deepened his understanding of the text.[10] Robert de Sorbon acknowledged that some would hear and others would read his book.[11] In the fourteenth century *inspixere* and *videre* were employed to denote silent private reading.[12] Their use as a substitute for *legere* has no precedent in Roman usage and is indicative of the change in reading techniques which had transpired since the end of antiquity.

In contrast to the quiet reading recommended by Saint Benedict and Isidore of Seville, silent reading was swift reading. University scholars needed to read faster to master the large and ever-growing corpus of glosses on Scripture and commentaries on canon law which replaced letters and sermons as the preferred literary genre. Because of the greater freedom it afforded to movements of the eye, silent reading favored the perusal and reference consultation of books. Twelfth-century students were advised to read the *glossae*, the basic theological texts, not as narratives but as works to be read selectively and studied.[13] Scholars, therefore, increasingly placed importance on the proper attachment of the gloss to the text. Building on precedents which dated back to the eighth century, they made wide use of intricate symbols, the direct ancestors of modern footnotes, to aid the reader's eye in glancing back and forth between the text and the appropriate gloss. Scribes who copied more extensive biblical commentaries, such as those of Andrew of Saint Victor, developed angular marks, the ancestor of quotation marks, to separate more effectively the biblical text from its exposition.[14]

[. . .]

The transformation of the author from dictator to writer was vividly documented by medieval illuminations. From the ninth to the twelfth century and to a lesser degree in the thirteenth century, authors were customarily shown dictating their works. God as the true author of Holy Scripture was depicted whispering to Old Testament prophets and dictating to the evangelists serving as secretaries taking down the spoken word.[15] The church fathers of antiquity and the early Middle Ages, Saint Augustine, Saint Jerome, Gregory the Great, Sulpicius Severus, and Rabanus Maurus, were drawn either as scribes recording divine dictation or as authors in their own right dictating to secretaries. Secular authors, too, like Horace and the chronicler Marculfus, were similarly presented dictating their works.[16] In the thirteenth century, scenes of literary composition began to change. The evangelists were no longer exclusively shown taking down dictation, but were often portrayed silently copying the divine text from an exemplar usually held by an angel. Saint Paul and Saint John were shown writing and not dictating.[17] In the early fourteenth century, the authors of the lives of Saint Denis were depicted writing their texts.[18] Aristotle, Albertus Magnus, Saint Bonaventure, Vincent of Beauvais, Duns Scotus, Jean Gerson, and many lesser scholastics were presented as scholars reading privately, as teachers, and as writers of their own compositions, but virtually never as dictators or as scribes taking dictation.[19] King David and King Solomon, like other authors, were drawn dictating in the earlier period, but in the fourteenth and fifteenth centuries they were presented writing.[20] Similarly, Saint Jerome, depicted throughout the twelfth century both as a dictator and as a scribe taking dictation, was in the fourteenth and fifteenth centuries regularly painted writing his own works.[21] Authors of antiquity, frequently portrayed in the fourteenth and fifteenth centuries, were also shown writing their own compositions. In the late Middle Ages, both ancient and contemporary authors were typically drawn sitting at a desk surrounded by a complex of lecterns and book shelves designed to hold reference materials and drafts.[22] Such furnishings were not depicted in the manuscripts produced in monasteries of the twelfth century, where authors had composed orally and relied on oral memorization for their citations. The new furnishings were invented to accommodate authors who composed drafts in their own handwriting and compiled citations from easily consulted reference aids.

Before the fourteenth century, writing had been an arduous task.[23] In early illuminations, scribes were drawn writing with a pen in one hand and a knife in the other. In addition to aiding erasure, the knife seems to have served to anchor the specially prepared membrane used for formal books.[24] Writing the bold strokes of Gothic textual script required pressure, which changed in direction with the frequent liftings of the pen. Writing in informal Gothic cursive on casually assembled quires and sheets made the physical act of writing less laborious and more compatible with intellectual activity. In fourteenth-century miniatures, authors composing in the new cursive script were depicted in more relaxed positions. The support, whether parchment or paper, easier to write on than membrane, was usually held in place by the hand in the modern fashion.[25] The author, using Gothic cursive, depicted in miniatures as alone in his study or in an idyllic pastoral setting, was at once freed from the labor of writing and the reliance on scribes. As a result of the new ease in writing, the author achieved a new sense of intimacy and privacy in his work. In solitude, he was personally able to manipulate drafts on separate quires and sheets. He could see his manuscript as a whole, develop internal relationships, and eliminate redundancies common to the dictated literature of the twelfth century. He could also, at his leisure, easily add supplements and revisions to his text at any point before forwarding it to a scriptorium for publication. Initially, composition in written form seems to have been used only for Latin texts, but by the mid-fourteenth century vernacular forms of cursive scripts enabled authors of vernacular texts also to write their works.

The new and more intimate way in which authors silently composed their texts, in turn, affected their expectation of the way people would read them. In the twelfth century, when texts were composed orally, authors expected their works to be read aloud. Guillaume de Saint Thierry had explicitly stated that sacred Scripture should be read exactly as it had been dictated.[26] In the fourteenth century, when texts were composed silently, authors expected them to be read silently. Nicolas de Lyra, the greatest biblical commentator of the fourteenth century, addressed himself to the reader and not to the listener.[27] Jean Gerson advised that the reader place himself in the affective state of the writer.[28] Fourteenth-century scholastic texts composed in cursive script were marked by a new visual vocabulary indicating that both the author and the reader were expected to have the codex before them. Nicolas de Lyra, Denis the Carthusian, and the anonymous author of the *Somnium vidiarii*, when citing references, frequently substituted for the oral form of citation *ut dicit*, favored in the twelfth century, the expressions *ut descripsit* or *ut scripsit*, typically followed by a specific reference to book and chapter.[29] As early as the twelfth century, biblical commentators had made references to portions of their own texts as cited *supra* or *infra*. Scholastic authors used these terms with greater frequency, and in the thirteenth century they began to number their arguments so as to aid the reader in following the complicated structure of responses and objections.[30] New genres of university literature, the *summa* and *tractatus*, were meant primarily for private visual reading and, unlike *lecturae*, they were not read aloud in the university classroom.

[. . .]

Important changes in format of thirteenth- and fourteenth-century manuscripts occurred simultaneously with the spread of silent reading in private and in the classroom. Oral reading had usually consisted of a continuous reading of a text, or of a substantial section of it, from beginning to end. Most Caroline codices, like ancient scrolls, had not been divided into sections shorter than the chapter, and many manuscripts of the Old Testament were not even divided into chapters. From the thirteenth to the fifteenth century, subdivisions were introduced into classical and early medieval texts. In some cases, works which had already been subdivided into chapters in later antiquity were further and more rationally subdivided by university scholars.[31] The new mode of presenting old texts became an integral part of the newly composed texts, which were conceived in terms of chapters and *distinctiones*. Using the points of reference established by the new divisions, tables of chapter headings, alphabetical tables by subject, and running headings became standard features of the scholastic codex.[32] Capitals, used since the ninth century in conjunction with punctuation to indicate breath pauses, were employed in the fourteenth century to help clarify the new sequential argumentation in the fashion *ad primum, ad secundum*, and so on. New forms of punctuation, including the colored paragraph mark, from the early thirteenth century onward came into common use to isolate units of intellectual content.[33] Expanding on the precedent offered by twelfth-century manuscripts of biblical commentary, quotations within a text which had been unmarked in most monastic manuscripts were regularly underlined in red. A system of sequential marginal notes, using letters of the alphabet to denote location in juristic texts, was also established,[34] and by the end of the fourteenth century this system was adapted to gloss literary texts. In the fifteenth century, we find it used for attaching the glosses of Nicolas de Lyra in incunable editions.[35] The intricate diagrams accompanying scholastic texts were understandable only to a reader who held the codex in his own hands. The complex structure of the written page of a fourteenth-century scholastic text presupposed a reader who read only with his eyes, going swiftly from objection to response, from table of contents to the text, from diagram to the text, and from the text to the gloss and its corrections.[36]

[. . .]

The changes in reading effected changes in libraries. The cloister libraries of the twelfth century had been suited to a culture of oral reading. Books had been kept in closed chests and were customarily lent at Easter for a period of one year. The lengthy loan period had reflected the slow pace of reading orally either to oneself or to others in small groups. The carrels of the cloister library, divided by stone walls, had allowed monks to read softly to themselves or to compose by dictating to a secretary without disturbing their confreres. Because monastic authors had retained large amounts of sacred Scripture by rote oral memorization, no formal collection of reference books had been needed. At the end of the thirteenth century, however, library architecture and furnishings began to change dramatically. In thirteenth- and fourteenth-century Oxford and Cambridge colleges and at the Sorbonne and other Paris colleges, libraries were installed in central halls and were furnished with desks, lecterns, and benches where readers sat next to one another.[37] Important reference books were chained to the lecterns so that they could always be consulted in the library. The first such reference collection was established in Merton College, Oxford, in 1289.[38] A similar one was created in the Sorbonne in 1290.[39] Chained reference books typically included dictionaries, the summas of Thomas Aquinas, the biblical commentaries of

Hugh of Saint Cher and Nicolas de Lyra, and other lengthy works frequently cited by scholars. The statutes governing chained libraries emphasized that chained books were provided for consultation by all for the common good.[40] The library was henceforth clearly regarded as a place where professors and students could go to read, write, and study.[41]

It was in the chained libraries of the late thirteenth century that the need for silence was first professed. In the monastery where every reader read aloud, each reader's own voice acted as a screen blocking out the sounds of the adjacent readers.[42] When readers began to read visually, any sound became a source of potential distraction. Even quiet oral reading at the desks of the chained reference collection in the crowded medieval library would have been disturbing and made study difficult. Humbert of Romans, in the *De instructione officialium*, demanded that each Dominican house establish a common reading room in a silent location within the convent.[43] At Oxford, the regulations of 1412 recognized the library as a place for quiet.[44] The statutes of the university library of Angers of 1431 forbade conversation and even murmuring.[45] The statutes of the Sorbonne library, written down in the late fifteenth century but reflecting practices established at an earlier date, proclaimed the chained library of the college to be an august and sacred place where silence should prevail.[46] A similar rule existed in the library of the popes, reestablished in Rome after the Great Schism.[47] Private reading encouraged readers to use the book as an instrument of study by noting passages in the margin with brief phrases, symbols, and doodles. New rules were needed, therefore, to limit such activities in the library in order to preserve collections for common use.[48] Reference tools intended for silent use within the library included aids to the use of the library itself, such as catalogs with alphabetical author indexes and special union catalogs representing the holdings of libraries in a city or region.[49]

Readers who sight read, read faster and used books in greater numbers than their monastic predecessors who had borrowed a volume once a year to read orally. In 1450, a university population which was approximately forty per cent smaller than it had been in 1300 was reading a much larger corpus of scholastic writing than had existed one hundred and fifty years before.[50] In 1476, a layman could read an entire Bible in twenty days.[51] By permitting scholars to read more quickly, silent reading helped to stimulate the creation of larger university libraries and the formation of an increasing number of private libraries. The growing demand for manuscript books at the end of the Middle Ages encouraged university scribes to use Gothic cursive and to employ paper, now more readily available, as a support. Scribes also perfected techniques for the large-scale production of standard manuscript texts. A professional scribe at Angers in the fifteenth century could copy a short work within thirty days, and at Paris a copy of Thomas Aquinas's *Commentary on the Third Book of Sentences* could be prepared within three and one-half months.[52] The pecia system allowed a single exemplar to be simultaneously copied by several scribes, by breaking it up and distributing the sections or *peciae* as exemplars. Imposition, perfected in the fifteenth century, was predicated on visual copying. The intricate manipulations of the sheet which this process required would have been incompatible with dictation.[53] Miniatures and woodcuts depicting late medieval scriptoria showed scribes with sealed lips employing a variety of new mechanically-controlled line markers to guide their eyes in following the text of the exemplar.[54]

The transition to silent reading and composition, by providing a new dimension of privacy, had even more profound ramifications for the culture of the Middle Ages. Psychologically, silent reading emboldened the reader, because it placed the source of his curiosity completely under his personal control. In the oral world of the twelfth century, if one's intellectual speculations were heretical, they were subject to peer correction and control in the very act of their formulation and publication. Dictation and public *lectio*, in effect, buttressed theological and philosophical orthodoxy. Twelfth-century heresy had popular origins and reflected collective spiritual needs rather than individual intellectual curiosity.

The teachings of the heretics such as the Cathars were not based on any corpus of forbidden writings but were communicated orally.[55] Reading with the eyes alone and written composition removed the individual's thoughts from the sanctions of the group and fostered the milieu which the new university heresies of the thirteenth and fourteenth centuries developed. These heresies were spread by the privately read *tractatus*, which increasingly replaced the orally presented *quodlibet* and *lectura* as the preferred vehicle of intellectual expression.[56] Alone in his study, the author, whether a well-known professor or an obscure student, could compose and read heterodox ideas without being overheard. In the classroom, the student, reading silently to himself, could listen to the orthodox opinions of his professor and visually compare them to the views of those who rejected established ecclesiastical authority.[57] Private visual reading and composition thus encouraged individual critical thinking and contributed ultimately to the development of scepticism and intellectual heresy. Joachim of Fiore's *Liber figurarum*, one of the most celebrated heretical treatises of the thirteenth century, contained, as the title suggests, complex diagrams, a certain indication that the work was composed for private visual consultation.[58] In France, Joachim's intellectual heirs, the spiritual Franciscans of the early fourteenth century, composed numerous tracts intended for private consultation. At the University of Paris, students were censured for surreptitiously circulating a vernacular translation of Marsilio of Padua's *Defensor pacis*.[59] Heretical books and pamphlets were often of small format, which made them easier to conceal and to circulate unobtrusively.[60] In England, possession of Lollard writings was legal grounds for formal charges of heresy.[61] At the end of the fourteenth century, the theologian Alphonse de Spina, in the *Fortitudinum fidei*, attributed the origin of heresy to the private and unsupervised reading of Scripture.[62]

[. . .]

The distinction which earlier monastic authors had made between oral reading and silent meditation disappeared in the spirituality of the fourteenth and fifteenth centuries as silent reading became an inseparable prelude to contemplation and divine enlightenment.[63] Vernacular devotional tracts were composed to be read silently in the privacy of an individual monk's chamber and even during the oral performance of the Mass.[64] Books of hours, intended to be read silently, mushroomed in popularity, supplanting the traditional oral liturgical texts: breviaries, missals, and psalters. Since the new prayer books were used by lay men and women for individual reading, copies were needed in far greater numbers than previously when one copy, read aloud, served a group. In the first half of the fifteenth century, scribes produced thousands of Latin books of hours (many with vernacular prayers) and hundreds of manuscript copies of Henry Suso's *Horologium sapientiae*, Gerhard Groote's Netherlandish translations of the *Hours of the Virgin*, and Thomas à Kempis's *De imitatione Christi*.[65]

The new genres of private books of prayer and devotion were illustrated with scenes of silent devotional reading emphasizing the new spiritual role attributed to the book. Before the year 1300, artists typically depicted communication between the Divine and man as exclusively oral. God was shown speaking to his disciples and never by the written word. An early fourteenth-century Anglo-French prayer book portrayed the Virgin communicating visually by pointing to the words in a book.[66] In other fourteenth- and fifteenth-century book illustrations, angels spread the word of God to man by bearing open codices to be read silently, and monks warded off the devil by silently confronting him with the written word of God.[67] In the spiritual writings of the fourteenth and fifteenth centuries, divine communication was described in visual terms. Gerhard Groote recommended that schoolmen read the Bible in the vernacular because its letters would make a fresher visual image on a mind accustomed to reading Latin.[68] Saint Augustine was said to have written prayers which were revealed to him.[69]

[. . .]

The new iconographic importance given to silent reading did not mean that oral reading and dictation vanished completely from illustrated books of the fourteenth and fifteenth centuries. Young children were depicted learning to read aloud,[70] and in books of hours, performances of liturgy were depicted as oral readings.[71] Portraits of the four evangelists, exceedingly common in books of hours, continued to reflect the influence of the early exemplars by showing the evangelists as scribes taking dictation, although subtle changes frequently altered a scene of dictation into one of apparent autograph composition. Scenes of the mortally ill and the aged, too feeble to write, showed them dictating their compositions, usually the preparation of a last testament. Such scenes illustrated the office of the dead in books of hours.[72] Late medieval copies of Italian treatists on the *ars notariae* bore miniatures of their authors dictating and reading aloud model orations to students who took them down in their own books.[73] Poets such as Horace, who were termed dictators in the sense of versifiers, were also depicted dictating their texts to secretary scribes.[74] In miniatures in Italian and French juristic texts, ancient iconographical conventions demanded that emperors and kings be shown dictating ordinances and statutes.[75] Only in exceptional circumstances, however, did artists portray contemporary authors of literary or scholastic texts as dictators, or as scribes taking dictation.

[. . .]

The transformation from an oral monastic culture to a visual scholastic one between the end of the twelfth and the beginning of the fourteenth centuries in the world of Latin letters had at first only a limited effect on lay society, particularly in northern Europe. Until the mid-fourteenth century, French kings and noblemen rarely read themselves but were read to from manuscript books prepared especially for this purpose. When princes such as Saint Louis could read, they read aloud in small groups.[76] In addition to liturgical texts, the literature read to princes consisted of chronicles, *chansons de geste*, romances, and the poetry of troubadours and *trouvères*. Most of these works were in verse and were intended for oral performances. Thirteenth-century prose compilations, such as the *Roman du Lancelot* and the *Histoire ancienne jusqu'à César*, were also composed to be read aloud. The nobleman was expected to *listen* to the feats of his predecessors or ancient worthies.[77]

[. . .]

In the mid-fourteenth century, the French nobility began to accept the same practice of silent reading and composition for vernacular literary texts which had become established for the Latin literature of the universities during the previous century. The reign of John II marked the beginning of a major effort to translate antique literature and scholastic texts into French.[78] After John's death in exile, Charles V continued the royal patronage of translations and was the first king to assemble a true royal library, in one of the towers of the Louvre. The king equipped the library with furnishings identical to those used in contemporary university libraries.[79] In miniatures, he was painted seated in his library reading with sealed lips in silent isolation. Manuscripts also depicted the king attending lectures, visually following a copy of the text in the university fashion as he listened to the lecture.[80] In the fifteenth century, the verb *veoir* was used in aristocratic vernacular texts as a synonym for private silent reading much as in the fourteenth century *videre* and *inspixere* had become to be used in place of *legere*.[81] Authors close to the royal house, including Jean Froissart and Christine de Pisan, were shown as writers in the illuminations decorating their manuscripts.[82] Even princes of the blood were depicted writing their own compositions. Charles V's grandnephew, René d'Anjou, a prolific author, was shown writing out his own texts in the manner of contemporary authors of Latin texts. In the fifteenth century, the word *écrire* became synonymous with composition.[83]

Silent private reading by the king and great princes of the realm, such as Jean de Berry,

Philip the Bold, and René d'Anjou, had a dramatic effect on the number and kinds of books prepared for royal and aristocratic courts. Just as fourteenth- and fifteenth-century university libraries far surpassed the size of earlier monastic collections, royal and aristocratic libraries after 1350 grew to be far larger than their predecessors. Like contemporary schoolmen whose intensity of reading increased because they had adopted the habit of silent reading, laymen also required a greater quantity of reading material, particularly books of hours and works in the vernacular. The new vernacular texts composed for princes were almost exclusively in prose, a contrast to the earlier preference for literature in verse. The new aristocratic books were replete with the tables of contents, alphabetical glossaries, subject indexes, running headings, and intellectual complexities characteristic of fourteenth- and fifteenth-century scholastic codices. Glosses with intricate cross-references accompanied the new vernacular translations of the Bible, Saint Augustine, Aristotle, and Valerius Maximus, forming compound texts awkward and difficult to read aloud by a professional reader but highly suited to visual perusal and study. These were the texts which Jean Gerson specifically recommended for the education of Charles VI.[84] In the first half of the fifteenth century, French authors composed for the nobility new reference books including alphabetical dictionaries of saints and gazetteers.[85] The number of illustrations increased in these vernacular aristocratic books as the role of miniatures evolved from that of mere decoration to aids in the comprehension of the text, serving a didactic function analogous to that of the diagrams accompanying scholastic texts.[86]

[. . .]

The habit of private silent reading among laymen seems to have begun at least a half century earlier in Italy than in northern Europe. Dante's *Inferno* and *Paradiso* were intended to be held under the eyes of the lay reader.[87] The scribes who copied these texts for the libraries of aristocrats and great urban families used either the highly legible Italian Gothic *textualis rotunda formata*, perfected for the deluxe juristic codices of Bologna, or a new variety of Italian *cursiva formata* which seems to have been developed especially for the transcription of lay literature.[88] In the second half of the fourteenth century, the burgeoning lay readership stimulated experimentation with hybrid scripts to achieve even greater legibility in vernacular codices transcribed for lay patrons.[89] Experimental Italian *hybrida* scripts may have inspired the northern *lettre batarde*, but *hybrida* was not adopted in Italy for texts intended for laymen because in the early fifteenth century, under the influence of humanism, scribes and authors turned to Caroline *textualis* as an alternative method of achieving legibility, at least for the increasing number of lay readers who were literate in Latin. Humanistic script was created by taking the writing found in twelfth-century Tuscan codices as a model and incorporating into it elements of letter forms borrowed from Gothic *textualis*. The result was a rejuvenated *littera antiqua* highly suitable for private silent reading.[90]

The punctuation of humanist texts was also influenced by the visual achievements of Gothic manuscripts. Humanist scribes invented the modern quotation marks by borrowing the angular marks used to separate text from commentary in twelfth-century manuscripts and systematically employing them as a consistent substitute for Gothic red underlining.[91] Humanist scribes, building on late medieval and Byzantine precedents, evolved full syntactical sentence punctuation with the characteristically modern usage of the comma and period.[92] They integrated these punctuation markings with the syntactical patterns of late Gothic capitalization in order to achieve optimal conditions for silent reading. The humanist scribe's most original contribution was the use of the parenthesis, a mark specifically employed to give a graphic representation of the aside, a device of ancient oratorical eloquence.[93] The ancients had had no need for such punctuation marks, for when they read Cicero, they read aloud. The parenthesis in fifteenth-century humanist texts permitted the private silent reader to recreate vicariously an oral experience. The parenthesis spread throughout Italy, and at the end of the fifteenth century it was one of the humanistic innovations in graphic language which was most readily received in northern Europe.[94] Used in scholastic texts, it developed nuances which had no direct equivalent in oral rhetoric.

The spread of *lettre de court, lettre batarde*, and humanistic *textualis* in the late fourteenth and fifteenth centuries both reflected and encouraged a dramatic change in the reading habits of the aristocracy and the urban elite of the cities of Italy and the lower Rhine valley. Saint Louis had read aloud surrounded by an entourage. Charles V, Louis XI, Lorenzo de Medici, and Flemish merchants in the paintings of Memling and Van Eyck read to themselves in inner solitude. Vernacular authors of the late fourteenth century began to assume that their audience was composed of readers rather than listeners. Froissart, in the 1370s, expected that young noblemen would *look into* and read his *Chroniques*.[95] Between 1388 and 1392, Philippe de Mezières, anticipating that the young king Charles VI would personally read the *Songe du vieil Pèlerin*, included a special table to guide the secular reader through the complex long histories told in parables and symbols.[96]

[. . .]

The privacy afforded by silent reading and writing may also have increased irony and cynicism. The chronicles of France in the *Rozier de guerre*, which presented itself as the work of Louis XI, was marginally annotated with sarcasms which kings, two centuries before, reading orally with a group would never have permitted themselves to express.[97] Even more important, private reading provided a medium for expressing subversive political thoughts. Charles of France, the rebellious brother of Louis XI, left in his copy of Cicero's *De officiis* underlined passages justifying rebellion and the assassination of tyrants.[98] In the mid-fifteenth century, the privately-read aristocratic manuscript book became the principal medium for disseminating ideas justifying resistance to royal authority, much as the Latin *tractati* of the fourteenth century had provided a medium for those advocating resistance to papal authority.[99]

The new privacy afforded by silent reading had dramatic and not entirely positive effects on lay spirituality. Private reading stimulated a revival of the antique genre of erotic art. In ancient Greece and Rome, material which today might be termed pornographic was read orally and displayed openly in a tolerant pagan society. In fifteenth-century France, where such pornography was forbidden, the practice of private reading encouraged the production of salacious writing, tolerated precisely because it could be disseminated in secret. Miniatures of certain French and Flemish vernacular texts depicted bordello scenes of carnal lust with explicit and seductive realism.[100] Inspired by Boccaccio's *Decameron*, an anonymous Burgundian author prepared for Duke Philip the Good the *Cent nouvelles nouvelles*, an illustrated *summa* of sexual escapades which attributed licentious acts to the same reformed monks and friars who championed poverty and chastity. The author of the *Cent nouvelles nouvelles* anticipated that the prince would read it privately as an "exercise de lecture et d'estude."[101] Like scholastic texts, the *Cent nouvelles nouvelles* was preceded by a table which gave in abbreviated form the high points of each adventure so as to help the reader to browse and choose the story he preferred. The text was circulated in modest format so that it could be discreetly passed from reader to reader much as the forbidden texts of William of Ockam and Marsilio of Padua had been surreptitiously disseminated among university scholars a hundred years earlier.[102] By the end of the fifteenth century, the intimacy of silent reading permitted explicit graphic representations of human sexuality to permeate religious literature. In books of hours, scenes depicting David spying upon the naked Bathsheba in her bath and miniatures showing the embrace of naked male and female figures as representations of the month of May seem to have been intended to excite the reader.[103] In a similar fashion, the new habit of autograph composition allowed laymen to breach matters of erotic intimacy in handwritten notes and letters. Philip the Good, writing in his own hand to his companion John of Cleves, discussed sexual escapades in frank and earthy language.[104]

The freedom of expression which private silent reading gave to hitherto suppressed sexual fantasies also, paradoxically, intensified the depth of lay religious experience. Private silent reading in the vernacular gave laymen the means of pursuing the individual relationship to God which had been the aspiration of erudite Christians since Saint Augustine. *De imitatione Christi*, written by Thomas à Kempis for his fellow monks, was soon after its composition translated into French and circulated at the Burgundian court.[105] Scores of other religious texts including translations and original compositions stressed the importance of reading, vision, and silence in achieving spiritual solace. In the prologue to his *Vie de Christ*, Jean Mansel declared that the spoken word was fleeting while the written word endured, and he called upon knights and princes disposed to devotion for the profit of their souls to *see* the content of his book.[106] Proceeding from the reading of the life of Christ, each person ought to meditate using the "eyes of his contemplation."[107] The vernacular life of Peter of Luxembourg described the scion of an aristocratic family who spent his silent nocturnal hours reading sermons, saints' lives, and patristic texts.[108] In the vernacular literature intended for laymen, separation from the group for the purpose of private reading and prayer was emphasized repeatedly. Peter of Luxembourg himself stressed the need for private prayer and silent study.[109] Ludolf of Saxony's *Life of Christ*, translated for Louis of Bruges, advocated the solitary reading of Scripture as a principal element of the contemplative life.[110] Through the translation, the author now advised pious laymen to place before their eyes the deeds and words of Christ.[111] Books of hours, produced in increasing number for laymen, were tailored to serve the need for individualized spiritual experience.[112] Autograph composition also tended to deepen the lay religious experience. Gaston de Foix composed in written form and did not dictate the book of highly personal prayers which he sent to his friend Philip the Bold.[113]

Isolated private reading and prayer as the pathway to salvation, in turn, may have fostered insecurities about the worthiness of each individual's faith and devotion and thereby stimulated zeal for religious reform. Indeed, the reformed mendicant orders found their strongest supporters among the urban merchant families and the aristocratic families who silently read vernacular religious manuscript books. Three generations later, these same families would become the supporters of John Calvin. On the eve of the Protestant Reformation, the mode of the dissemination of ideas had been so revolutionized that laymen, like university schoolmen, could formulate dissenting views in private and communicate them in secret. The printing press played an important role in the ultimate triumph of Protestantism, but the formulation of reformist religious and political ideas and the receptivity of Europe's elite to making private judgments on matters of conscience owed much to a long evolution, beginning in the twelfth century and culminating in the fifteenth century, in the manner in which men read and wrote.

References

1   "Such things (regarding the knowledge of one's real self) must, then, be written down. But how will you do this? Your health does not admit the labor of writing them. They cannot be dictated, for they demand absolute solitude"; *The Soliloquies of Saint Augustine*, trans. R. E. Cleveland (London 1910) 2.

2   The *Ordo Cluniacensis* of the monk Bernard, cited by Guy de Velous, *Le monachisme clunisien des origines au XVᵉ siècle*, ed. 2 (Paris 1970) 1.80.

3   Noël Valois, "Étude sur le rhythme des bulles pontificales," *Bibliothèque de l'école des chartes* 13 (1881) 168–171.

4   Saint Bernard, *Epistula* 89, in his *Oeuvres complètes* (Paris 1878–1887) 5. 137.

5   *Statuta ord. Cisterciensis* 1134, no. 58; *Statuta capitulorum generalium Cisterciensis*, ed. Josephus-Maria Canivez I (Louvain 1933) 26.

6   Isidore of Seville, *Sententiae* 3. 14.9; PL 83.681.

7   Saint Benedict, *Regulae*, chap. 48.

8   Robert Fawtier, *La Vie de Saint Samson: Essai de critique hagiographique* (Paris 1912) 108. On the ancient mode of learning to read by syllables, see Quintilian (*instituto oratoria*) 1.1.24ff.; Virgil the Grammarian, *Epitomae* 2 and 3; Bede, *Historia ecclesiastica* 5.2, *De arte metrica* 1 and 2. At the end of the Middle Ages, reading by syllables had acquired a distinct stigma; see Nicolas de Clamages, *Le traité de la ruine de l'Église*, ed. A. Coville (Paris 1936) 131.

9   "Trimodum est lectionis genus: docentis, discentis, vel per se inspicientis. Dicimus enim 'lego librum illi,' et 'lego librum ab illo,' et 'lego librum' "; Hugh of Saint Victor, *Didascalicon*, ed. Charles Henry Butimer, Catholic University of America Studies in Medieval and Renaissance Latin 10 (Washington 1939) 57–58.

10   He complained that when devils tormented him, they made him read aloud to interfere with his comprehension of the text: "Saepe cum lego solo codice et cognitione, sicut soleo, faciunt meo verbotenus et ore legere ut tantummodo eo magis auferant mihi internum intellectum et eo mimus vim lectionis intus penetrem, quo magis in verba foris profundor"; Bernard Pez, *Thesaurus novissimus anecdotorum* 1.11 (Augsburg 1721) 390.

11   "Et nota demenciam illorum sacerdotum qui nondum legerunt vel audierunt librum istum . . ."; Robert de Sorbon, *De consciencia et De tribus dietis*, ed. Félix Chambon (Paris 1903) 29.

12   For a list of examples of *ridere* and *inspixere* meaning "to read," see P. Guilhiermoz, *Enquêtes et procès: Étude sur la procédure et le fonctionnement du parlament au XIVe siècle* (Paris 1892) 140. An interesting example of the use of *inspixere* is to be found in rules set forth for the University Library of Oxford: ". . . quod cum ad Universitatis commonem librariam causa studendi accesserint libros quos inspixerint modo honesto pertractabunt, nulli librorum hujusmodi, per rasoras abolitionesve quaternorum seu foliorum, damnum seu praejudicium inferendo"; Henry Anstey, *Munimenta academica* 1, rerum britannicarum medii aevi scriptores 50 (London 1868) 264. For examples of *videre* meaning to read, see Paris, B. N. Ms fr. 24439, fol. 38, and Conradus Heingarter, astrological writings, B. N. MS lat. 7446, fol. 8.

13   Beryl Smalley, *The Study of the Bible in the Middle Ages* (Oxford 1952) 218.

14   Paris, B. N. MSS lat. 356 and 443 are among the numerous manuscripts which contain such marks.

15   A typical example of the dictation of Scripture, Jean Porcher, *Medieval French Miniatures*, trans. Julian Brown (New York, n.d.) pl. 34; Joachim Prochno, *Das Schreiber- und Dedikationsbild in der Deutschen Buchmalerei* (Leipzig 1929) 57*; Paris, B. N. MSS lat. 275 fol. 3v, 818 fol. 2v, 1141 fol. 3.

16   For Saint Jerome as a dictator and scribe, see Bernard Lambert, *Bibliotheca Hieronymiana manuscripta: La tradition manuscrite des oeuvres de saint Jérôme* 4A (The Hague 1972) pls. 3, 4, and 8; Peter Bloch and Hermann Schnitzler, *Die Ottonische Kölner Malerschule* 1 (Düsseldorf 1967) pl. xvi. For Gregory the Great, see *Bibliothèque royale Mémorial 1559–1969* (Brussels 1969) pl. 45; L. M. J. Delaissé, *Medieval Miniatures* (London 1965) 38; Carl Nordenfalk and André Grabar, *Romanesque Painting from the Eleventh to the Thirteenth Century*, trans. Stuart Gilbert (New York 1958). For Sulpicius Severus, Porcher pl. 13; for Rabanus Maurus, Paris, B. N. MS lat. 2430, fol. 1; for Horace, B. N. MS lat. 8123; for Marculfus, B. N. MS lat. 10136, fol. 1.

17   Louis Reau, *Iconographie de l'art chrétien* 3.2 (Paris 1955–1959) pl. 60, example dating from 1260. Other examples: Paris, B. N. MSS lat. 920 fol. 35v, 1170 fol. 4, 10532 fol. 2.

18   Paris, B. N. MS lat. 5286, fol. 3.

19   For representations of Aristotle as a writer, Paris, B. N. MSS fr. 565 fol. 1 and 9136 fol. 1. For Albert the Great as a writer, see Heribert Christian Scheeben, *Iconographia Albertina* (Freiburg i. Br. 1932) 10, 36, and pl. 6. For Saint Bonaventure, see B. N. MS lat. 3046, fol. 1; *British Museum Reproductions from Illuminated Manuscripts* ser. 3 (1925), pl. xlviii; cf. B. N. MS lat. 3841, fol. 1, and J. Bougerol, *Introduction to the Works of Saint Bonaventure* (Patterson, N.J. 1964), frontispiece. For Duns Scotus, *British Museum Reproductions* pl. xxxviii. For Vincent of Beauvais, B. N. MS fr. 6725, fols. 1 and 50. For Jean Gerson, B. N. MS lat. 3024, fol. 2v; cf. Millard Meiss and Elizabeth H. Beatson, *La vie de nostre benoit sauveur Ihesuscrist et la saincte vie de Nostre Dame, translatée à la requeste de très hault et puisant prince Iehan Duc de Berry* (New York 1977) 5.

20   For Solomon as a writer, Paris, B. N. MS lat. 9675, fol. 157; for David as a writer, B. N. MS lat. 727, fol. 50; for Solomon as a dictator, see B. N. MSS fr. 158 fol. 1, 1553 fol. 1. For David as a dictator, Paris, Arsenal MS 1186, fol. 30v.

21   For Saint Jerome as a writer, see Bernard Lambert, *Bibliotheca Hieronymiana manuscripta: La tradition manuscrite des oeuvres de saint Jérôme* 4A (The Hague 1972) pls. 10(?), 12, 14, 15, and 18; Louis Reau, *Iconographie de l'art chretien* 3.2 (Paris 1955–1959) pl. 46; Paris, B. N. MS lat. 13234, fol. 1; Rudolf Beer, "Les principaux manuscrits à peinture de la Bibliothèque impériale de Vienne," *Bulletin de la Société Française de reproduction de manuscrits à peinture* 3 (1913), MS 930, fol. 1.

22   See for example Nicolas de Lyra, Paris, B. N. MS lat. 364; Nicolas Oresme, MS fr. 204, fol. 347; Jean Mielot, B. N. MS fr. 9198, fol. 19; Colard Mansion, Vienna, Austrian National Library MS 2572, fol. 1; Thomas à Kempis, Austrian National Library MS 1576, fol. 7; Pierre le Baud, B. N. MS fr. 8266, fol. 5. For ancient authors including Lucan, Ovid, Josephus, Valerius Maximus, Aristotle, and Livy: B. N. MSS fr. 718 fol. 1, 727 fol. 1, 870 fol. 1, 247 fol. 1, 272 fol. l, 273 fol. 7, 571 fol. 124, 565 fol. l, 6185 fol. 32.

23   Leo Moulin, *La vie quotidienne des religieux au moyen âge X^e–XV^r siècle* (Paris 1978) 287.

24   Pieter F. J. Obbema, "Writing on Uncut Sheets," *Quaerendo* 7 (1978) 353. The frontispiece of the Morgan Library manuscript of the *Bible moralisée* shows a scribe holding the page with his knife as he writes to dictation.

25   Porcher 93. The link between the relaxed writing position and cursive script is revealed in a 1437 miniature depicting the dictation of a royal *ordonnance*, Paris, Arsenal MS 5199, fol. 1. In Paris, B. N. MS fr. 22495, the king's autograph script represented in the miniature appears to be cursive. In fr. 24380, fol. 1, a fifteenth-century artist clearly shows Jean de Beuil composing *Le Jouvencel* in cursive.

26   Guillaume de Saint Thierry, *Epistola ad fratres de Monte Dei* edited in Saint Bernard 5.346. The attribution of the text to Guillaume has been established by André Wilmart, *Auteurs spirituels et textes dévots du moyen âge latin*, rev. ed. (Paris 1971) 258–259.

27   "Ut sic lector eligat expositionem quam tenere volverit vel utranque si volverit . . ."; Nicolas de Lyra, prologue to the *Postillae* on the book of Genesis, *Postilla super totam Bibliam* (Strasbourg 1492; repr. Frankfurt 1971).

28   "Nihilominus testimonium perhibeo vobis quale positum est in epistola mea ad fratres de Monte Dei quod Scripturas, Sacras nullus umquam plane intelliget que non affectus scribentium induerit," Jean Gerson, *Oeuvres complètes*, ed. P. Glorieux (Paris 1960) 5.334.

29   See for example Denis the Carthusian, *Opera omnia* (Montreuil 1896–1908) 36.618 and passim.

30   Saint Thomas made use of such numbering in his *Summa theologiae*. The divisions became increasingly subtle in succeeding centuries; see for example Johannes Capreolus, *Defensiones theologiae Divi Thoma Aquinatis* (Tours 1900–1908).

31   Malcolm Parkes, "The Influence of the Concepts of *Ordinatio* and *Compilatio* on the Development of the Book," in *Medieval Learning and Literature: Essays Presented to R. W. Hunt*, ed. J.J.G. Alexander and M.T. Givson (Oxford 1976) 124–125; Daniel A. Callus, "The 'Tabula super originalia patrum' of Robert Kilwardby O. P.," *Studia medievalia in honorem R. J. Martin* (Bruges 1948) 243–270; Richard W. Hunt, "Chapter Headings of Augustine *De trinitate* ascribed to Adam Marsh," *Bodleian Library Record* 5 (1954) 63.

32   Parkes 118–122; Richard H. Rouse and Mary A. Rouse, *Preachers, Florilegia and Sermons: Studies on the "Manipulus Florum" of Thomas of Ireland* (Toronto 1979) 7–36.

33   Robert Marichal, L'écriture latine et la civilisation occidentale du Ière au XVIe siècle," *L'écriture et la psychologie des peuples* (Paris 1963) 237–240; Parkes 121.

34   Paris, B. N. MSS lat. 4436 and 4523. At an earlier period, the Dominicans used letters to denote a place within a chapter; Rouse and Rouse 9–10.

35   For example, the *Tragedies* of Seneca copied in 1397, Paris, B. N. MS lat. 8824. This system was used to attach Nicolas de Lyra's *Postillae* to the text of the Bible in the Strasbourg edition of 1492.

36   Paul of Burgos, *Additiones ad postillam Nicolai de Lyra* could be used only in this manner. For manuscripts of this text, see Friedrich Stegmüller, *Repertorium Biblicum medii aevi* (Madrid 1940–1961) 4, 197.

37   *Hermanni liber de restauratione S. Martini Tornacensis*, ed. G. Waitz, MGH Scriptores 14 (Hanover 1893) 313, trans, John Willis Clark, *The Care of Books* (Cambridge, 1904) 145–164.

38   H. W. Garrod, "The Library Regulations of a Medieval College," *The Library* ser. 4, 8 (1927) 315. For the growth of reference collections, see the bibliography provided by Richard H. Rouse, "The Early Library of the Sorbonne," *Scriptorium* 21 (1967) 60.

39   Rouse 59.

40   Léopold Delisle, *Le Cabinet des manuscrits de la Bibliothèque nationale* (Paris 1868–1891) 2. 181 n. 6.

41   See the statutes of the library of the University of Angers, Celestin Port, "La bibliothèque de l'Université d'Angers," *Notes et notices angevines* (Angers 1879) 28, and of Oxford, Henry Anstey, *Munimenta academica* 1, Rerum britannicarum medii aevi scriptores (London 1868) 1.263–266. The documents first published by Port have been edited by Marcel Fournier, *Les statuts et privilèges des universités françaises* 1 (1890) 387–389.

42   F. J. McGuigan and W. I. Rodier, "Effects of Auditory Stimulation on Covert Oral Behavior During Silent Reading," *Journal of Experiment & Psychology* 76 (1965) 649–655; Robert M. Weisberg, *Memory, Thought, and Behavior* (New York 1980) 235–236, cf. 159–160. In ancient libraries, oral reading was an accepted practice; see Optatus bishop of Milevi, *De schismate donatistarum advsrsus Parmenianum* 7.1; ed. Karl Ziusa, CSEL 26 (Vienna 1893) 165.

43   Humbert of Romans, *Opera de vita regulari* (Rome 1888) 1.421; K. W. Humphreys, *The Book Provisions of the Medieval Friars* (Amsterdam 1964) 136.

44   Anstey 1.263–264.

45   Port 31.

46   Léopold Delisle, *La Cabinet des manuscrits de la Bibliothèque nationale* (Paris 1868–1891) 2. 201, correctly asserted that the text as given in Zlaude Héméré's manuscript *Sorbonae origines* dated from the establishment of a new building for the library ca. 1483. However, the inference drawn by Delisle that these rules were intended solely for printed books is not supported by fifteenth-century documentary evidence. Precedents for each of the Sorbonne regulations can be found in rules established for the fifteenth century. Moreover, in 1493 the Sorbonne library was still acquiring manuscript books; see Alfred Franklin, *Les anciennes bibliothèques de Paris* (Paris 1867–1873) 1.256 n. 8.

47   Eugène Müntz, *La Bibliothèque du Vatican au XVe siècle d'après des documents inédits* (Paris 1887).

48   At Oxford, Angers, and Paris: Anstey 139–140; Port 32; Delisle 201.

49   Rouse and Rouse; Pieter F. J. Obbema, "The Rooklooster Register Evaluated," *Quaerenda* 7 (1977) 326–353.

50   See Carla Bozzolo and Ezio Ornato, *Pour une histoire du livre manuscrit au moyen âge* (Paris 1980) 90–91, 118–120.

51   F. K. Ingelfi Ider, "Die Religiös-kirchlichen Verhältnisse im heutigen Württemberg am Vorabend der Reformation," Ph.D. Diss. (Univ. of Tübingen 1939) 141, cited by Bernard Moeller, "Piety in Germany around 1500," in *The Reformation in Medieval Perspective*, ed. Steven E. Ozme lt (Chicago 1971) 59.

52   Charles Samaran and Robert Marichal, *Catalogue des manuscrits en écriture latine portant des indications de date, de lieu. ou de copiste* 1 (Paris 1959) 259.

53   In the use of imposition, texts may well have been copied in out-of-sense sequence; see Obbema 337–354.

54   See for example Dorothee Rlein, "Autorenbild," *Reallexikon zur deutschen Kunstgeschichte* 1 (Stuttgart 1937) 1312; Paris, B. N. MS lat. 4.15, fol. 1.

55   M. D. Lambert, *Medieval Heresy: Gopular Movements from Bogomil to Hus* (London 1977) 4, 39, and 43–44.

56   After 1320, the *quodlibet* was no longer an important vehicle for discussing controversial issues. All of Ockham's writings were circulated as private tracts and were not intended for oral delivery to students in the classroom. On the demise of the *quodlibet*, see Gordon Leff, *Paris and Oxford Universities in the Thirteenth and Fourteenth Centuries: An Institutional and Intellectual History* (New York 1968) 249.

57   It was perhaps for this reason that in 1259 the Dominicans forbade bringing to class any book other than the one read by the professor in his lecture; *Chartularium Universitatis Parisiensis* (hereafter CUP), ed. H. Denifle and E. Chatelain, 4 vols. (Paris 1889–1897) 1 386.

58   Lambert, 4 186–189.

59   CUP 3.225ff.

60   M. Esposito, "Sur quelques manuscrits de l'ancienne littérature religieuse du Vaudois du Piemont," *Revue d'histoire ecclésiastique* 46 (1951) 127–159.

61 Anne Hudson, "A Lollard Quaternion," *Review of English Studies*, n.s. 22 (1971) 442.

62 Paris, B. N. MS fr. 20067, fol. 79r–v.

63 In the thirteenth century, oral reading from the breviary had been assumed, even when a single cleric read alone. However, in 1435 the Council of Basel felt it necessary to demand specifically that reading of the breviary be aloud even in solitude. This may be an indication of a liturgical corruption introduced by the growing practice of silent reading. See Fabienne Gégou, "Son, parole, et lecture au moyen âge," *Mélanges de langue et de littérature du moyen âge offertes á Tervo Sato* 37 n. 14. It may be noted that even in manuscript breviaries intended to be read aloud, instructions meant for silent perusal by the priest were written in red so that they would not be confused with the liturgical text written in black. Medieval artists as early as the thirteenth century graphically represented oral liturgical reading in miniatutes illustrating Franciscan breviaries, e.g., Paris B. N. MS lat. 1076, fol. 81v, an indication that late medieval artists could well distinguish between oral and silent reading.

64 See for example Paris, B. N. MS fr. 24439, fol. 38, a vernacular treatise composed to be used for silent meditation while listening to the Mass. An early fifteenth-century English document gives instructions for reading the *Legenda sanctorum* and other Latin devotional texts while listening to the Mass. Significantly, the author used the verb *videre* to denote this kind of reading; William Abel Pantin, "Instructions for a Devout and Literate Layman," in Alexander and Gibson, 399, 404, 421.

65 For the manuscripts of Suso's work see *Heinrich Seuses Harologium sapientiae*, ed. Pius Künzle, Spicilegium Friburgense 23 (Fribourg, Switzerland 1977). Over 800 copies of Groote's translation of the *Hours of the Virgin* survive; Georgette Épiney-Burgard, *Gérard Grote (1340–84) et les débuts de la dévotion moderne*, Veröffentlichungen des Instituts für europäische Geschichte, Mainz 54 (Wiesbaden 1970) 266. Over 500 medieval copies of different versions of the *De imitatione Christi* have been recorded by Stephanus Axters, *De imitatione Christi: Een Handschriften-inventaris*, Schriftenreihe des Kreises Kempen-Krefeld 27 (Kempen-Niederrhein 1971).

66 Paris, B. N. MS fr. 400, fol. 38v.

67 Paris, B. N. MS lat. 10532, fol. 330; Arsenal MS 6329, fol. 145v.

68 Gerhard Groote, *Tractatus de quattuor generibus meditationum sive contemplationum*, ed. A. Hypra in *Archief voor de Geschiedenis van het Aartsbisdom Utrecht* 49 (1924) 314.

69 "Beatus augustinus sequentem orationem scripsit er revelara fuit ei a spiritu sancto . . ."; Book of Hours, Use of Rome copied in Flanders ca. 1460, Newberry Library MS – 53, fol. 230v.

70 See for example Richard Muther, *Die deutsche Buchillustration der Gothik und Frührenaissance* (Leipzig 1884) 2.11.

71 Delaissé 172.

72 Paris, B. N. MS lat. 1176, fol. 140v is an example of such a scene.

73 G. Volpo and L. Volpicelli, *La vita medioevale italiana nella miniatura* (Rome 1960) 64.

74 See illustrations in incunable editions of Horace listed by Anna Cox Brinton, *Quintus Horatius Flaccus, Editions in the United States and Canada as They Appear in the Union Catalogue of the Library of Congress* (Oakland, Calif. 1938) 3–6. Pierre Michaut, who referred to himself as writing, was nevertheless represented in miniatures as a dictator as well as a writer: Paris, B. N. MS fr. 1654, fols. 1 and 7v. Charles d'Orléans appears to be one of the first poets to be represented only as a writer, *British Museum Reproductions from Illuminated Manuscripts* ser. 4 (1928), pl. xlvi. Manuscript evidence confirms that indeed he composed his poetry in written form; Pierre Champion, *Le manuscrit autograph des poésies de Charles d'Orléans* (Paris 1907; repr. Geneva 1975). On the development of written composition of poetry, see Kevin Brownlee, "The Poetic *Oeuvre* of Guillaume de Machaur: The Identity of Discourse and the Discourse of Identity," *Annals of the New York Academy of Sciences* 314.219–233; and P. J. Croft, *Autograph Poetry in the English Language* 1 (London 1973) 1–5.

75 Franz Steffens, *Lateinische Paläographie* (Trier 1909) no. 106 is an example.

76 Geoffroy de Beaulieu, *Sancti Ludovici vita, Recueil des historiens des Gaules et de la France* 20 (Paris 1840) 44; The Confessor of Queen Marguerite, ibid. 79.

77 Bernard Guenée, "La culture historique des nobles: Le succès des *Faits des Romains*, XIIIᵉ–XVᵉ siècles," in *La noblesse au moyen âge XIᵉ–XVᵉ siècles: Essais à la mémoire de Robert Boutruche*, ed. Philippe Contamine (Paris 1976) 268.

78 Pierre Bersuire's translation of Livy's *History of Rome* and Jean de Sy's translation of the Bible with Latin commentary are the principal literary monuments of King John's reign; see Delisle 1 16.

79   Ibid. 1.20; Claire Richter Sherman, *The Portraits of Charles V of France (1338–80)* (New York 1969) 13.

80   Sherman fig. 11. Cf. a miniature depicting King Solomon as a teacher, Rosy Schilling, "The Master of Egerton 1070: Hours of René d'Anjou," *Scriptorium* 8 (1954), pl. 26.

81   For example, Jean Jouvenal des Ursins stared that he had been instructed by Charles VII to go "en vos chambres des comptes, du Tresor de vos chartres et ailleurs pour veoir les lettres et chartres necessaires" for writing the *Traictie compendieux contre les Anglois*; cited by P.S. Lewis, "War Propaganda and Historiography in Fifteenth-Century France and England," *Transactions of the Royal Historical Society* (1965) 16.

82   For Christine de Pisan as a writer, see Paris, B. N. MSS fr. 603 fol. l, 835 fol. 1, and 1176 fol. 1. For Froissart, see B. N. MS fr. 86, fol. 11.

83   Jean Barthelemay used *écrire* in this sense, Paris, B. N. MS fr. 9611, fol. 1. Jean du Chesne, in the prologue to his translation of the *Commentaries* of Julius Caesar, referred to ths "Commentaires que Cesar mesmes escript de sa main," and qualified Caesar as an "escripvain," British Library MS Royal 16 G. viii: Raul Lefèvre, *L'histoire de Jason*, ed. Gert Pinkernell (Frankfurt 1971) 125 referred to Philip the Good of Burgundy as the "pere des escripvains." In the mid-fourteenth century, however Pierre Bersuire had found no ready French translation for the Latin *scriptor*, meaning author; see Jean Rychner, "La traduction de Tite-Live par Pierre Bersuire," in Anthime Fourrier, ed., *L'humanisme médiéval dans les littératures remaines du XII au XIV siècle* (Paris 1964) 170–171.

84   Antoine Thomas, *Jean de Gerson et l'éducation des dauphins de France* (Paris 1930) 50–51.

85   See for example Jean Mansel's *Fleurs des histoires*, in which the saints' lives were arranged "en ordre selon le A. B. C. pour plus legerement trouver ceulx donc len vouldra lire"; Paris, B. N. MS fr. 57, fol. 9. On the early introduction of such tables to vernacular texts, see F. Avril, "Trois manuscrits des collections de Charles V et de Jean de Berty," *Bibliothèque de l'École des chartes* 127 (1969) 293.

86   Sherman 42ff.

87   Erich Auerbach, *Literary Language and Its Public in Late Latin Antiquity and in the Middle Ages*, trans. R. Manheim (London 1965) 299–302.

88   Franz Steffens, *Lateinische Paläographie* (Trier 1909) no. 103.

89   See for example G.I. Lieftinck, "Pour une nomenclature de l'écriture livresque de la période dite gothique," *Nomenclature des écritures livresques du IX au XVI siècle* (Paris 1954) 33.

90   Marichal 231.

91   See for example Chicago, Newberry Library MS f. 101.1.

92   Geoffroy Tory, *Champ fleury*, ed. Gustave Cohen (Paris 1913) fols. 65v–66 cited Byzantine grammarians for this use of punctuation. Cf. Aurelio Roncaglia, "Note sulla punteggiatura medievale e il segno di parentesi," *Lingua nostra* 3 (1941) 6–9.

93   The term and symbol of the parenthesis are known in the fourteenth century, but it is used in the classical sense only in humanistic manuscripts of the fifteenth century.

94   The parenthesis was used in manuscripts in semi-humanistic script in France in the reign of Louis XI. Tardif included it among the signs of punctuation in his treatise on grammar. In about 1500 the Parisian printer Jean Petit used the parenthesis in his editions of scholastic texts. At the end of the fifteenth century, the parenthesis was also used in vernacular texts, e.g., Paris, B. N. MS fr. 15456–15457. The humanistic ideal of written eloquence is reflected by Guillaume Leseur, who wrote of royal historiographer Jean Chartier as a "tres suffisant et elegant orateur" who "a bien sçeu escripre"; Guillaume Leseur, *Histoire de Gaston IV, comte de Foix*, ed. Henri Courteault (Paris 1893–1896) 1.xxiv.

95   Jean Froissart, *Chroniques*, prologue to book 1.

96   Philippe de Mezières, *Le songe du vieil pèlerin* 1. 102.

97   Paulin Paris, *Les manuscrits français de la Bibliothèque du roi* (Paris 1836–1848) 4. 131–135.

98   Paris, B. N. MS lat. 6607.

99   Paul Saenger, "The Earliest French Resistance Theory: The Role of the Burgundian Court," *Journal of Modern History* suppl. 51 (1979) 1225–1249.

100   A typical example illustrates a fifteenth-century copy of the French translation of Valerius Maximus, *Facta et dicta memorabilia*; Robert Melville, *Erotic Art of the West* (London 1973) fig. 116. The miniature is misdated to the sixteenth century in the caption and the text. For other examples, see Edward Lucie Smith, *Eroticism in Western Art* (London 1972). These

manuscripts are the direct antecedents of late fifteenth- and sixteenth-century erotic art, notably that of Hieronymus Bosch; see Anthony Bosman, *Jérôme Bosch* (Paris 1962) 16; Otto Brusendorf and Paul Henningsen, *Love's Picture Book: The History of Pleasure and Moral Indignation from the Days of Classical Greece until the French Revolution* (Copenhagen 1960); Edwards Fuchs, *Geschichte der Erotischen Kunst* (Munich 1912) 175. The bordello was usually represented as a public bath.

101   *Les cent nouvelles nouvelles*, ed. Franklin P. Sweetzer (Geneva 1966) 22.

102   For a description of the surviving manuscript, see Pierre Champion, *Les cent nouvelles nouvelles* (Paris 1928) xcvi–cxvii, and J. Gerber Young and P. Henderson Aitken, *A Catalogue of the Manuscripts in the Library of the Hunterian Museum in the University of Glasgow* (Glasgow 1908) 201–203.

103   Jean Harthan, *The Book of Hours* (New York 1977) 24, 26.

104   A Grunzweig, "Quatre lettres autographes de Philippe le Bon," *Revue belge de philologie et d'histoire* 4 (1925) 431–37.

105   *Thomas à Kempis et la dévotion moderne*, exhibition catalog (Brussels 1971) 34.

106   Paris, Arsenal MS 5205, fol. "F".

107   Paris, Arsenal MS 5206, fol. 174.

108   Paris, B. N. MS fr. 982, fol. 51v. A similar emphasis on private piety existed in England; William Abel Pantin, "Instructions for a Devout and Literate Layman," in Alexander and Gibson 406–407.

109   Paris, B. N. MS fr. 982; fol. 56.

110   Paris, B. N. MS fr. 407, fol. 5.

111   Paris, B. N. MS fr. 407, fol. 7.

112   Jacques Toussaett, *Le sentiment religieux en Flandre à la fin du moyen âge* (Paris 1963) 351–352.

113   Pierre Tucoo-Chala, *Gaston Febus: Un grand prince d'Occident au XIVe siècle* (Pau 1976), text to pl. 9.

Chapter 12

Michel de Certeau

READING AS POACHING

"To arrest the meanings of words once and for all, that is what Terror wants."

Jean-Francois Lyotard, *Rudiments païens*

SOME TIME AGO, ALVIN TOFFLER announced the birth of a "new spe-cies" of humanity, engendered by mass artistic consumption. This species-in-formation, migrating and devouring its way through the pastures of the media, is supposed to be defined by its "self mobility."[1] It returns to the nomadic ways of ancient times, but now hunts in artificial steppes and forests.

This prophetic analysis bears, however, only on the masses that consume "art." An inquiry made in 1974 by a French government agency concerned with cultural activities[2] shows to what extent this production only benefits an elite. Between 1967 (the date of a previous inquiry made by another agency, the INSEE) and 1974, public monies invested in the creation and development of cultural centers reinforced the already existing cultural inequalities among French people. They multiplied the places of expression and symboliza-tion, but, in fact, the same categories profit from this expansion: culture, like money, "goes only to the rich." The masses rarely enter these gardens of art. But they are caught and collected in the nets of the media, by television (capturing 9 out of 10 people in France), by newspapers (8 out of 10), by books (7 out of 10, of whom 2 read a great deal and, according to another survey made in autumn 1978, 5 read more than they used to),[3] etc. Instead of an increasing nomadism, we thus find a "reduction" and a confinement: consumption, organized by this expansionist grid takes on the appearance of something done by sheep progressively immobilized and "handled" as a result of the growing mobility of the media as they conquer space. The consumers settle down, the media keep on the move. The only freedom supposed to be left to the masses is that of grazing on the ration of simulacra the system distributes to each individual.

That is precisely the idea I oppose: such an image of consumers is unacceptable.

The ideology of "informing" through books

This image of the "public" is not usually made explicit. It is nonetheless implicit in the "producers'" claim to inform the population, that is, to "give form" to social practices. Even protests against the vulgarization/vulgarity of the media often depend on an analogous pedagogical claim; inclined to believe that its own cultural models are necessary for the people in order to educate their minds and elevate their hearts, the elite upset about the "low level" of journalism or television always assumes that the public is moulded by the products imposed on it. To assume that is to misunderstand the act of "consumption." This misunderstanding assumes that "assimilating" necessarily means "becoming similar to" what one absorbs, and not "making something similar" to what one is, making it one's own, appropriating or reappropriating it. Between these two possible meanings, a choice must be made, and first of all on the basis of a story whose horizon has to be outlined. "Once upon a time. . . ."

In the eighteenth century, the ideology of the Enlightenment claimed that the book was capable of reforming society, that educational popularization could transform manners and customs, that an elite's products could, if they were sufficiently widespread, remodel a whole nation. This myth of Education[4] inscribed a theory of consumption in the structures of cultural politics. To be sure, by the logic of technical and economic development that it mobilized, this politics has led to the present system that inverts the ideology that formerly sought to spread "Enlightenment." The means of diffusion are now dominating the ideas they diffuse. The medium is replacing the message. The "pedagogical" procedures for which the educational system was the support have developed to the point of abandoning as useless or destroying the professional "body" that perfected them over the span of two centuries: today, they make up the apparatus which, by realizing the ancient dream of enclosing all citizens and each one in particular, gradually destroys the goal, the convictions, and the educational institutions of the Enlightenment. In short, it is as though the form of Education's establishment had been too fully realized, by eliminating the very content that made it possible and which from that point on loses its social utility. But all through this evolution, the idea of producing a society by a "scriptural" system has continued to have as its corollary the conviction that although the public is more or less resistant, it is moulded by (verbal or iconic) writing, that it becomes similar to what it receives, and that it is imprinted by and like the text which is imposed on it.

This text was formerly found at school. Today, the text is society itself. It takes urbanistic, industrial, commercial, or televised forms. But the mutation that caused the transition from educational archeology to the technocracy of the media did not touch the assumption that consumption is essentially passive—an assumption that is precisely what should be examined. On the contrary, this mutation actually reinforced this assumption: the massive installation of standardized teaching has made the intersubjective relationships of traditional apprenticeship impossible; the "informing" technicians have thus been changed, through the systematization of enterprises, into bureaucrats cooped up in their specialities and increasingly ignorant of users; productivist logic itself, by isolating producers, has led them to suppose that there is no creativity among consumers; a reciprocal blindness, generated by this system, has ended up making both technicians and producers believe that initiative takes place only in technical laboratories. Even the analysis of the repression exercised by the mechanisms of this system of disciplinary enclosure continues to assume that the public is passive, "informed," processed, marked, and has no historical role.

The efficiency of production implies the inertia of consumption. It produces the ideology of consumption-as-a-receptacle. The result of class ideology and technical blindness, this legend is necessary for the system that distinguishes and privileges authors, educators, revolutionaries, in a word, "producers," in contrast with those who do not produce. By challenging "consumption" as it is conceived and (of course) confirmed by these "authorial" enterprises, we may be able to discover creative activity where it has been denied that any exists, and to relativize the exorbitant claim that a certain kind of production (real enough, but not the only kind) can set out to produce history by "informing" the whole of a country.

A misunderstood activity: reading

Reading is only one aspect of consumption, but a fundamental one. In a society that is increasingly written, organized by the power of modifying things and of reforming structures on the basis of scriptural models (whether scientific, economic, or political), transformed little by little into combined "texts" (be they administrative, urban, industrial, etc.), the binominal set production-consumption can often be replaced by its general equivalent and indicator, the binominal set writing-reading. The power established by the will to rewrite history (a will that is by turns reformist, scientific, revolutionary, or pedagogical) on the basis of scriptural operations that are at first carried out in a circumscribed field, has as its corollary a major division between reading and writing.

"Modernization, modernity itself, is writing," says François Furet. The generalization of writing has in fact brought about the replacement of custom by abstract law, the substitution of the State for traditional authorities, and the disintegration of the group to the advantage of the individual. This transformation took place under the sign of a "crossbreeding" of two distinct elements, the written and the oral. Furet and Ozouf's recent study has indeed demonstrated the existence, in the less educated parts of France, of a "vast semi-literacy, centered on reading, instigated by the Church and by families, and aimed chiefly at girls."[5] Only the schools have joined, with a link that has often remained extremely fragile, the ability to read and the ability to write. These abilities were long separated, up until late in the nineteenth century, and even today, the adult life of many of those who have been to school very quickly dissociates "just reading" and writing; and we must thus ask ourselves how reading proceeds where it is married with writing.

Research on the psycho-linguistics of comprehension[6] distinguishes between "the lexical act" and the "scriptural act" in reading. It shows that the schoolchild learns to read by a process that parallels his learning to decipher; learning to read is not a result of learning to decipher: reading meaning and deciphering letters correspond to two different activities, even if they intersect. In other words, cultural memory (acquired through listening, through oral tradition) alone makes possible and gradually enriches the strategies of semantic questioning whose expectations the deciphering of a written text refines, clarifies, or corrects. From the child to the scientist, reading is preceded and made possible by oral communication, which constitutes the multifarious "authority" that texts almost never cite. It is as though the construction of meanings, which takes the form of an expectation (waiting for something) or an anticipation (making hypotheses) linked to an oral transmission, was the initial block of stone that the decoding of graphic materials progressively sculpted, invalidated, verified, detailed, in order to make way for acts of reading. The graph only shapes and carves the anticipation.

In spite of the work that has uncovered an autonomy of the practice of reading underneath scriptural imperialism, a de facto situation has been created by more than three centuries of history. The social and technical functioning of contemporary culture hierarchizes these two activities. To write is to produce the text; to read is to receive it from someone else without putting one's own mark on it, without remaking it. In that regard, the reading of the catechism or of the Scriptures that the clergy used to recommend to girls and mothers, by forbidding these Vestals of an untouchable sacred text to write continues today in the "reading" of the television programs offered to "consumers" who cannot trace their own writing on the screen where the production of the Other—of "culture"—appears. "The link existing between reading and the Church"[7] is reproduced in the relation between reading and the church of the media. In this mode, the construction of the social text by professional intellectuals (clercs) still seems to correspond to its "reception" by the faithful who are supposed to be satisfied to reproduce the models elaborated by the manipulators of language.

What has to be put in question is unfortunately not this division of labor (it is only too real), but the assimilation of reading to passivity. In fact, to read is to wander through an imposed system (that of the text, analogous to the constructed order of a city or of a supermarket). Recent analyses show that "every reading modifies its object,"[8] that (as Borges already pointed out) "one literature differs from another less by its text than by the way in which it is read,"[9] and that a system of verbal or iconic signs is a reservoir of forms to which the reader must give a meaning. If then "the book is a result (a construction) produced by the reader,"[10] one must consider the operation of the latter as a sort of lectio, the production proper to the "reader" ("lecteur").[11] The reader takes neither the position of the author nor an author's position. He invents in texts something different from what they "intended." He detaches them from their (lost or accessory) origin. He combines their fragments and creates something un-known in the space organized by their capacity for allowing an indefinite plurality of meanings. Is this "reading" activity reserved for the literary critic (always privileged in studies of reading), that is, once again, for a category of professional intellectuals (clercs), or can it be extended to all cultural consumers? Such is the question to which history, sociology, or educational theory ought to give us the rudiments of an answer.

Unfortunately, the many works on reading provide only partial clarifications on this point or depend on the experience of literary people. Research has been primarily concerned with the teaching of reading.[12] It has not ventured very far into the fields of history and ethnology, because of the lack of traces left behind by a practice that slips through all sorts of "writings" that have yet to be clearly determined (for example, one "reads" a landscape the way one reads a text).[13] Investigations of ordinary reading are more common in sociology, but generally statistical in type: they are more concerned with calculating the correlations between objects read, social groups, and places frequented more than with analyzing the very operation of reading, its modalities and its typology.[14]

There remains the literary domain, which is particularly rich today (from Barthes to Riffaterre or Jauss), once again privileged by writing but highly specialized: "writers" shift the "joy of reading" in a direction where it is articulated on an art of writing and on a pleasure of re-reading. In that domain, however, whether before or after Barthes, deviations and creativities are narrated that play with the expectations, tricks, and normativities of the "work read;" these theoretical models that can account for it are already elaborated.[15] In spite of all this, the story of man's travels through his own texts remains in large measure unknown.

"Literal" meaning, a product of a social elite

From analyses that follow the activity of reading in its detours, drifts across the page, metamorphoses and anamorphoses of the text produced by the travelling eye, imaginary or meditative flights taking off from a few words, overlappings of spaces on the militarily organized surfaces of the text, and ephemeral dances, it is at least clear, as a first result, that one cannot maintain the division separating the readable text (a book, image, etc.) from the act of reading. Whether it is a question of newspapers or Proust, the text has a meaning only through its readers; it changes along with them; it is ordered in accord with codes of perception that it does not control. It becomes a text only in its relation to the exteriority of the reader, by an interplay of implications and ruses between two sorts of "expectation" in combination: the expectation that organizes a readable space (a literality), and one that organizes a procedure necessary for the actualization of the work (a reading).[16]

It is a strange fact that the principle of this reading activity was formulated by Descartes more than three hundred years ago, in discussing contemporary research on combinative systems and on the example of ciphers (*chiffres*) or coded texts: "And if someone, in order to decode a cipher written with ordinary letters, thinks of reading a B everywhere he finds an A, and reading a C where he finds a B, and thus to substitute for each letter the one that follows it in alphabetic order and if, reading in this way, he finds words that have a meaning, he will not doubt that he has discovered the true meaning of this cipher in this way, even though it could very well be that the person who wrote it meant something quite different, giving a different meaning to each letter. . . ."[17] The operation of encoding, which is articulated on signifiers, produces the meaning, which is thus not defined by something deposited in the text, by an "intention," or by an activity on the part of the author.

What is then the origin of the Great Wall of China that circumscribes a "proper" in the text, isolates its semantic autonomy from everything else, and makes it the secret order of a "work?" Who builds this barrier constituting the text as a sort of island that no reader can ever reach? This fiction condemns consumers to subjection because they are always going to be guilty of infidelity or ignorance when confronted by the mute "riches" of the treasury thus set aside. The fiction of the "treasury" hidden in the work, a sort of strong-box full of meaning, is obviously not based on the productivity of the reader, but on the social institution that overdetermines his relation with the text.[18] Reading is as it were overprinted by a relationship of forces (between teachers and pupils, or between producers and consumers) whose instrument it becomes. The use made of the book by privileged readers constitutes it as a secret of which they are the "true" interpreters. It interposes a frontier between the text and its readers that can be crossed only if one has a passport delivered by these official interpreters, who transform their own reading (which is also a legitimate one) into an orthodox "literality" that makes other (equally legitimate) readings either heretical (not "in conformity" with the meaning of the text) or insignificant (to be forgotten). From this point of view, "literal" meaning is the index and the result of a social power, that of an elite. By its very nature available to a plural reading, the text becomes a cultural weapon, a private hunting reserve, the pretext for a law that legitimizes as "literal" the interpretation given by socially authorized professionals and intellectuals (clercs).

Moreover, if the reader's expression of his freedom through the text is tolerated among intellectuals (clercs) (only someone like Barthes can take this liberty), it is on the other hand denied students (who are scornfully driven or cleverly coaxed back to the meaning "accepted" by their teachers) or the public (who are carefully told "what is to be thought" and whose inventions are considered negligible and quickly silenced).

It is thus social hierarchization that conceals the reality of the practice of reading or makes it unrecognizable. Formerly, the Church, which instituted a social division between its intellectual clerks and the "faithful," ensured the Scriptures the status of a "Letter" that was supposed to be independent of its readers and, in fact, possessed by its exegetes: the autonomy of the text was the reproduction of sociocultural relationships within the institution whose officials determined what parts of it should be read. When the institution began to weaken, the reciprocity between the text and its readers (which the institution hid) appeared, as if by withdrawing the Church had opened to view the indefinite plurality of the "writings" produced by readings. The creativity of the reader grows as the institution that controlled it declines. This process, visible from the Reformation onward, already disturbed the pastors of the seventeenth century. Today, it is the socio-political mechanisms of the schools, the press, or television that isolate the text controlled by the teacher or the producer from its readers. But behind the theatrical décor of this new orthodoxy is hidden (as in earlier ages)[19] the silent, transgressive, ironic or poetic activity of readers (or television viewers) who maintain their reserve in private and without the knowledge of the "masters."

Reading is thus situated at the point where social stratification (class relationships) and poetic operations (the practitioner's constructions of a text) intersect: a social hierarchization seeks to make the reader conform to the "information" distributed by an elite (or semi-elite); reading operations manipulate the reader by insinuating their inventiveness into the cracks in a cultural orthodoxy. One of these two stories conceals what is not in conformity with the "masters" and makes it invisible to them; the other disseminates it in the networks of private life. They thus both collaborate in making reading into an unknown out of which emerge, on the one hand, only the experience of the literate readers (theatricalized and dominating), and on the other, rare and partial, like bubbles rising from the depths of the water, the indices of a common poetics.

An "exercise in ubiquity," that "impertinent absence"

The autonomy of the reader depends on a transformation of the social relationships that overdetermine his relation to texts. This transformation is a necessary task. This revolution would be no more than another totalitarianism on the part of an elite claiming for itself the right to conceal different modes of conduct and substituting a new normative education for the previous one, were it not that we can count on the fact that there already exists, though it is surreptitious or even repressed, an experience other than that of passivity. A politics of reading must thus be articulated on an analysis that, describing practices that have long been in effect, makes them politicizable. Even pointing out a few aspects of the operation of reading will already indicate how it eludes the law of information.

"I read and I daydream. . . My reading is thus a sort of impertinent absence. Is reading an exercise in ubiquity?"[20] An initial, indeed initiatory, experience: to read is to be elsewhere, where they are not, in another world;[21] it is to constitute a secret scene, a place one can enter and leave when one wishes; to create dark corners into which no one can see within an existence subjected to technocratic transparency and that implacable light that, in Genet's work, materializes the hell of social alienation. Marguerite Duras has noted: "Perhaps one always reads in the dark. . . . Reading depends on the obscurity of the night. Even if one reads in broad daylight, outside, darkness gathers around the book."[22]

The reader produces gardens that miniaturize and collate a world, like a Robinson Crusoe discovering an island; but he, too, is "possessed" by his own fooling and jesting that introduces plurality and difference into the written system of a society and a text. He is thus a novelist. He deterritorializes himself, oscillating in a nowhere between what he invents and what changes him. Sometimes, in fact, like a hunter in the forest, he spots the written quarry, follows a trail, laughs, plays tricks, or else like a gambler, lets himself be taken in by it. Sometimes he loses the fictive securities of reality when he reads: his escapades exile him from the assurances that give the self its location on the social checkerboard. Who reads, in fact? Is it I, or some part of me? "It isn't I as a truth, but I as uncertainty about myself, reading these texts that lead to perdition. The more I read them, the less I understand them, and everything is going from bad to worse."[23]

This is a common experience, if one believes testimony that cannot be quantified or quoted, and not only that of "learned" readers. This experience is shared by the readers of *True Romances*, *Farm Journal* and *The Butcher and Grocery Clerk's Journal*, no matter how popularized or technical the spaces traversed by the Amazon or Ulysses of everyday life.

Far from being writers—founders of their own place, heirs of the peasants of earlier ages now working on the soil of language, diggers of wells and builders of houses—readers are travellers; they move across lands belonging to someone else, like nomads poaching their way across fields they did not write, despoiling the wealth of Egypt to enjoy it themselves. Writing accumulates, stocks up, resists time by the establishment of a place and multiplies its production through the expansionism of reproduction. Reading takes no measures against the erosion of time (one forgets oneself and also forgets), it does not keep what it acquires, or it does so poorly, and each of the places through which it passes is a repetition of the lost paradise.

Indeed, reading has no place: Barthes reads Proust in Stendhal's text;[24] the television viewer reads the passing away of his childhood in the news reports. One viewer says about the program she saw the previous evening: "It was stupid and yet I sat there all the same." What place captivated her, which was and yet was not that of the image seen? It is the same with the reader: his place is not here or there, one or the other, but neither the one nor the other, simultaneously inside and outside, dissolving both by mixing them together, associating texts like funerary statues that he awakens and hosts, but never owns. In that way, he also escapes from the law of each text in particular, and from that of the social milieu.

Spaces for games and tricks

In order to characterize this activity of reading, one can resort to several models. It can be considered as a form of the bricolage Lévi-Strauss analyzes as a feature of "the savage mind," that is, an arrangement made with "the materials at hand," a production "that has no relationship to a project," and which readjusts "the residues of previous construction and destruction."[25] But unlike Lévi-Strauss's "mythological universes,".if this production also arranges events, it does not compose a unified set: it is another kind of "mythology" dispersed in time, a sequence of temporal fragments not joined together but disseminated through repetitions and different modes of enjoyment, in memories and successive knowledges.

Another model: the subtle art whose theory was elaborated by medieval poets and romancers who insinuate innovation into the text itself, into the terms of a tradition. Highly refined procedures allow countless differences to filter into the authorized writing that serves them as a framework, but whose law does not determine their operation. These poetic ruses, which are not linked to the creation of a proper (written) place of their own, are maintained over the centuries right up to contemporary reading, and the latter is just as agile in practicing diversions and metaphorizations that sometimes are hardly even indicated by a "pooh!" interjected by the reader.

The studies carried out in Bochum elaborating a *Rezeptionsästhetik* (an esthetics of reception) and a *Handlungstheorie* (a theory of action) also provide different models based on the relations between textual tactics and the "expectations" and successive hypotheses of the receiver who considers a drama or a novel as a premeditated action.[26] This play of textual productions in relation to what the reader's expectations make him produce in the course of his progress through the story is presented, to be sure, with a weighty conceptual apparatus; but it introduces dances between readers and texts in a place where, on a depressing stage, an orthodox doctrine had erected the statue of "the work" surrounded by consumers who were either conformers or ignorant people.

Through these investigations and many others, we are directed toward a reading no longer characterized merely by an "impertinent absence," but by advances and retreats, tactics and games played with the text. This process comes and goes, alternately captivated (but by what? what is it which arises both in the reader and in the text?), playful, protesting, fugitive.

We should try to rediscover the movements of this reading within the body itself, which seems to stay docile and silent but mines the reading in its own way: from the nooks of all sorts of "reading rooms" (including lavatories) emerge subconscious gestures, grumblings, tics, stretchings, rustlings, unexpected noises, in short a wild orchestration of the body.[27] But elsewhere, at its most elementary level, reading has become, over the past three centuries, a visual poem. It is no longer accompanied, as it used to be, by the murmur of a vocal articulation nor by the movement of a muscular manducation. To read without utter-ing the words aloud or at least mumbling them is a "modern" experience, unknown for millennia. In earlier times, the reader interiorized the text; he made his voice the body of the other; he was its actor. Today, the text no longer imposes its own rhythm on the subject, it no longer manifests itself through the reader's voice. This withdrawal of the body, which is the condition of its autonomy, is a distancing of the text. It is the reader's habeas corpus.

Because the body withdraws itself from the text in order henceforth to come into contact with it only through the mobility of the eye,[28] the geographical configuration of the text organizes the activity of the reader less and less. Reading frees itself from the soil that determined it. It detaches itself from that soil. The autonomy of the eye suspends the body's complicities with the text; it unmoors it from the scriptural place; it makes the written text an object and it increases the reader's possibilities of moving about. One index of this: the methods of speed reading.[29] Just as the airplane makes possible a growing independence with respect to the constraints imposed by geographical organization, the techniques of speed reading obtain, through the rarefaction of the eye's stopping points, an acceleration of its movements across the page, an autonomy in relation to the determinations of the text and a multiplication of the spaces covered. Emancipated from places, the reading body is freer in its movements. It thus transcribes in its attitudes every subject's ability to convert the text through reading and to "run it" the way one runs traffic lights.

In justifying the reader's impertinence, I have neglected many aspects. Barthes dis-tinguished three types of reading: the one that stops at the pleasure afforded by words, the one that rushes on to the end and "faints with expectation," and the one that cultivates the desire to write:[30] erotic, hunting, and initiatory modes of reading. There are others, in dreams, battle, autodidacticism, etc., that we cannot consider here. In any event, the reader's increased autonomy does not project him, for the media extend their power over his imagination, that is, over everything he lets emerge from himself into the nets of the text—his fears, his dreams, his fantasized and lacking authorities. This is what the powers work on that make out of "facts" and "figures" a rhetoric whose target is precisely this surrendered intimacy.

But whereas the scientific apparatus (ours) is led to share the illusion of the powers it necessarily supports, that is, to assume that the masses are transformed by the conquests and victories of expansionist production, it is always good to remind ourselves that we mustn't take people for fools.

References

1   Alvin Toffler, *The Culture Consumers* (Baltimore: Penguin, 1965), 33–52, on the basis of Emanuel Demby's research.

2   *Pratiques culturelles des Français* (Paris: Secrétariat d'Etat à la Culture, S. E. R., 1974), 2 vols.

3   According to a survey by Louis–Harris (September–October 1978), the number of readers in France grew 17% over the past twenty years: there is the same percentage of people who read

a great deal (22%), but the percentage of people who read a little or a moderate amount has increased. See Janick Jossin, in *L'Express* for 11 November 1978, 151–162.

4   See Jean Ehrard, *L'Idée de nature en France pendant la première moitié du XVIIIe siècle* (Paris: SEPVEN, 1963), 753–767.

5   François Furet and Jacques Ozouf, *Lire et écrire. L'Alphabétisation des Français de Calvin à Jules Ferry* (Paris: Minuit, 1977), I, 349–369, 199–228.

6   See for example J. Mehler and G. Noizet, *Textes pour une psycholinguistique* (La Haye: Mouton, 1974); and also Jean Hébrard, "École et alphabétisation au XIXe siècle," Colloque "Lire et écrire," MSH, Paris, June 1979.

7   Furet and Ozouf, *Lire et écrire*, 213.

8   Michel Charles, *Rhétorique de la lecture* (Paris: Seuil, 1977), 83.

9   Jorge Luis Borges, quoted by Gérard Genette, *Figures* (Paris: Seuil, 1966), 123.

10   Charles, *Rhétorique de la lecture*, 61.

11   As is well known, "lector" (*lecteur*) was, in the Middle Ages, the title of a kind of university professor.

12   See especially *Recherches actuelles sur l'enseignement de la lecture*, ed. Alain Bentolila (Paris: Retz CEPL, 1976); Jean Foucambert and J. André, *La Manière d'être lecteur. Apprentissage et enseignement de la lecture, de la maternelle au CM2* (Paris: SERMAP OCDL, 1976); Laurence Lentin, *Du parler au lire. Interaction entre l'adulte et l'enfant* (Paris: ESF, 1977); etc. To these should be added at least a portion of the abundant American literature: Jeanne Sternlicht Chall, *Learning to Read, the Great Debate . . . 1910–1965* (New York: McGraw-Hill, 1967); Dolores Durkin, *Teaching Them to Read* (Boston: Allyn & Bacon, 1970); Eleanor Jack Gibson and Harry Levin, *The Psychology of Reading* (Cambridge, Mass.: MIT, 1975); Milfred Robeck and John A. R. Wilson, *Psychology of Reading: Foundations of Instruction* (New York: John Wiley, 1973); *Reading Disabilities. An International Perspective*, ed. Lester and Muriel Tarnopol (Baltimore: University Park Press, 1976); etc., along with three important journals: *Journal of Reading*, since 1957 (Purdue University, Department of English), *The Reading Teacher*, since 1953 (Chicago International Reading Association), *Reading Research Quarterly*, since 1965 (Newark, Delaware, International Reading Association).

13   See the bibliography in Furet and Ozouf, *Lire et écrire*, II, 358–372, to which we can add Mitford McLeod Mathews, *Teaching to Read, Historically Considered* (Chicago: University of Chicago Press, 1966). Jack Goody's studies (*Literacy in a Traditional Society* [Cambridge: Cambridge University Press, 1968] and *The Domestication of the Savage Mind* [Cambridge: Cambridge University Press, 1977], etc.) open several paths toward an ethnohistorical analysis.

14   In addition to statistical investigations, see J. Charpentreau et al., *Le Livre et la lecture en France* (Paris: Editions ouvrières, 1968).

15   Roland Barthes, of course: *Le Plaisir du texte* (Paris: Seuil, 1973), *The Pleasure of Text*, trans. R. Miller (New York: Hill and Wang, 1975), and "Sur la lecture," *Le Français aujourd'hui*, No. 32 (January 1976), pp. 11–18. See, somewhat at random, in addition to the works already cited, Tony Duvert, "La Lecture introuvable," *Minuit*, No. 1 (November 1972), 2–21; O. Mannoni, *Clefs pour l'imaginaire* (Paris: Seuil, 1969), 202–217; Michel Mougenot, "Lecture/écriture," *Le Français aujourd'hui*, No. 30 (May 1975); Victor N. Smirnoff, "L'Oeuvre lue," *Nouvelle revue de psychanalyse*, No. 1 (1970), 49–57; Tzvetan Todorov, *Poétique de la prose* (Paris: Seuil, 1971), 241 et seq.; Jean Verrier, "La Ficelle," *Poétique*, No. 30 (April 1977); *Littérature*, No. 7 (October 1972); *Esprit*, December 1974, and January 1976; etc.

16   See, for example, Michel Charles' "propositions" in his *Rhétorique de la lecture*.

17   Descartes, *Principia*, IV, 205.

18   Pierre Kuentz, "Le tête à texte," *Esprit*, December 1974, 946–962, and "L'Envers du texte," *Littérature*, No. 7 (October 1972).

19   Some documents, unfortunately all too rare, shed light on the autonomy of the trajectories, interpretations, and convictions of Catholic readers of the Bible. See, on the subject of his "farmer" father, Rétif de la Bretonne, *La vie de mon père* (1778) (Paris: Garnier, 1970), 29, 131–132, etc.

20   Guy Rosolato, *Essais sur le symbolique* (Paris: Gallimard, 1969), 288.

21   Theresa de Avila considered reading to be a form of prayer, the discovery of another space in which desire could be articulated. Countless other authors of spiritual works think the same, and so do children.

22 Marguerite Duras, *Le Camion* (Paris: Minuit, 1977), and "Entretien à Michèle Porte," quoted in *Sorcières*, No. 11 (January 1978), 47.

23 Jacques Sojcher, "Le professeur de philosophie," *Revue de l'Université de Bruxelles*, No. 3–4 (1976), 428–429.

24 Barthes, *Le plaisir du texte*, 58.

25 Claude Lévi-Strauss, *La pensée sauvage* (Paris: Plon, 1962), 3–47; *The Savage Mind* (Chicago: University of Chicago Press, 1966). In the reader's "*bricolage*," the elements that are re-employed, all being drawn from official and accepted bodies of material, can cause one to believe that there is nothing new in reading.

26 See in particular the works of Hans Ulrich Gumbrecht ("Die Dramenschliessende Sprach-handlung im Aristotelischen Theater und ihre Problematisierung bei Marivaux") and of Karlheinz Stierle ("Das Liebesgeständnis in Racines *Phèdre* und das Verhältnis von (Sprach-)Handlung und Tat"), in *Poetica* (Bochum), 1976; etc.

27 Georges Perec had discussed this very well in "*Lire: Esquisse sociophysiologique*," *Esprit*, January 1976, 9–20.

28 It is nonetheless known that the muscles that contract the vocal cords and constrict the glottis remain active in reading.

29 See François Richaudeau, *La Lisibilité* (Paris: Retz CEPL., 1969); or Georges Rémond, "Apprendre la lecture silencieuse à l'école primaire," in Bentolila, *La manière d'être lecteur*, 147–161.

30 Barthes, "Sur la lecture," 15–16.

Researching and
using literacy

INTRODUCTION

IN THE WESTERN WORLD, mass literacy only came to describe the state of
society at the beginning of the twentieth century. Before that, the spread of the skills of
reading and writing, and participation in 'literary culture', was much more uneven. The
extracts that follow grapple with this state of affairs, charting the growth of literacy in
Western Europe and America from the medieval period onwards, and attempting to uncover
the use of the skills by those who attained them. The story of the achievement of mass literacy
in the West is often considered to be of special importance to contemporary countries with
developing economies because a literate population has been regarded as essential for modern-
isation. But as all these readings demonstrate, the relationship is far more complicated
than often presumed, not least because the benefits of literacy were often uncertain, and the
use of the literary skills are neither controllable nor have always demonstrated social
improvement.

The fundamental question at the foundation of all studies of literacy is how to ascertain
which skills were possessed by whom at what time. The fact that literacy comprises two skills,
the ability to read and the ability to write, which were often taught separately in the past,
presents historians with immediate problems. Because the reading skill was often taught first,
historians have argued that the most standard and direct measure is the ability to sign, which
should indicate some degree of penmanship as well as a level of proficiency in reading. As
the work of Margaret Spufford, Roger Schofield and Carl Kaestle shows, a range of official
documents which required signatures of large numbers of people survive from at least the
Reformation onwards, perhaps the most useful being the marriage registers. These typically
span long periods of time and record an event which the great majority of men, and more
importantly women, experienced at a near common point in their lives.

These measurements and other evidence of the acquisition of the literary skills in the past also shed light on a number of important trends in the distribution of the skills. In many ways, we should not be surprised to learn that for most of the period under study in these extracts more men than women were literate and literacy was higher in urban areas. Its particular prevalence in commercial areas points to a key determinant in the acquisition of the skills: profession or occupation. The spread of literacy in Europe has often been associated with the Reformation, as Protestantism was the religion of the book. However, as Spufford demonstrates, for the merchant classes and many artisans, the need to operate in business seemed to provide the primary motivation for the acquisition of the skills. Occupational need not only often determined who acquired literacy, but also had a decisive impact on who did not, especially at a time when literacy did not generate social mobility. For many, especially those in the labouring classes, the benefits of literacy were uncertain: the acquisition of skills often did not open up employment opportunities, and the time and money spent in educating a child placed great strain on the family budget.

This is not to say that religious societies did not assist in the spread of the skills, or that parents in poor families were not committed to ensuring their children achieved some ability in either or both skills. Children raised in families in which at least one parent was literate were more likely also to achieve literacy. Moreover, religious initiative did boost existing efforts and extend the reach of educational institutions. But the primacy placed on the reading skill again reminds us that these societies were often peopled by many who could read but not write, in other words, partial literates. Although very useful, until the advent of mass literacy, rates of literacy have typically provided an underestimate of the size of the reading public. Sources that measure literacy tend to impose an artificial dividing line between those who were literate and those who were not.

Similarly, the range of skills and their uneven distribution meant that there was never a wholesale replacement of oral culture by literary, or written, culture, as David Vincent so aptly demonstrates. Men and women, particularly those in the artisan and labouring classes, did not have exclusive membership of one group. Instead, there was a long period of overlap between the two cultures. If anything, written culture supported the existence and prosperity of oral culture: folklore provided material for producers of chapbooks and broadsides, and new stories first available in written form were memorised and verbally passed on to others. While the reading skill was not universal, texts were shared among families and communities by reading aloud in groups. Skills were also imparted through the use of the spoken word: classrooms were characterised by noise rather than silent exercises in reading and writing.

The resilience of an oral culture, and thus old forms of knowledge perceived to be backward and unenlightened, within literary culture, highlights the lack of control that structures of authority had over the use of the skills of literacy. As Kaestle points out, literacy can serve many purposes, 'sometimes innovative and liberating', but 'sometimes traditional and constraining'. At a time when the church was intent on imparting skills for the purposes of religion, and instruction centred on the catechism and the memorisation of passages of Scripture, the extent to which these readers were able to make sense of other texts could be limited. Furthermore, while the growth of print culture gave ordinary people new opportunities to practise skills and laid at their feet a wide variety of reading material, Richard Hoggart argues that commercial imperatives could dramatically limit the freedom of men and women in their use of the reading skill. Hoggart composed this reflective piece during the 1950s, when concern about the debilitating effects of popular reading was at its peak, and forecast the emergence of a new caste system or cultural divide based on reading habits. It is interesting to ponder whether such a situation ever actually came about.

Chapter 13

Margaret Spufford

LITERACY, TRADE AND RELIGION IN THE COMMERCIAL CENTRES OF EUROPE

IT SEEMED TO ME that it might well be relevant to the history of the Dutch Republic in a comparative perspective to look at literacy in rather an unusual way. It is well established that urban literacy rates were higher than rural rates,[1] and it is also established that after the Reformation Protestant areas tended to have higher literacy rates than Catholic areas.[2] Historians of literacy tend to focus on Protestantism as an incentive to literacy, since Protestantism is above all a 'religion of the Book'. However, we may be in danger of confusing two quite different motors driving towards higher literacy rates here: there is also an urban need for high literacy, and numeracy skills which are essential for commercial, and indeed, manufacturing development.[3]

This urban need falls into two categories, which should be carefully distinguished from each other. Merchants, bankers, and their factors and office-boys, anyone engaged actively in commerce, had an absolute need for literacy and numeracy to be able to function effectively in the world of national, and international trade, which opened up in Italy in the thirteenth century.[4] As well as this, at certain periods, and in certain trades, literacy and numeracy may have been at least useful, and possibly more than that, amongst the workforce. Artisans, however humble, needed to be literate and numerate: there was a pathetic case of a baker's widow in English Kent who tried to claim the debts due to her husband for his loaves after his death, and had her claim disallowed because the sums were only written up in chalk on the board in his shop. Even in the countryside, the farmer needed to be able at least to read the bond or mortgage which jeopardised his holding.[5] The figures for rural debt in Kent, amongst those for whom probate accounts indicated that the dead men had borrowed on bond, rose from 6 per cent in the decade 1582–92, to 16 per cent in the decade 1602–12, to 34 per cent in the decade 1622–32.[6] I do not think it fanciful to suggest that the written instruments of debt and credit may have provided as powerful an incentive to learn to read in the sixteenth century as the undoubted power of English Protestantism. London's goldsmiths had had a rule in force by 1478, re-issued in the 1490s, forbidding any member of the guild to take an apprentice 'wtout he canne writte and rede'.[7]

Before its 'Golden Age', the fledgling Amsterdam had begun to feel the potential pull of the tide that was to lead to the vast maritime prosperity of the seventeenth-century United Provinces. By 1558, Cornelis Anthonisz' guide to ambitious pilots had already reached its third edition. It advised 'it is above all necessary for an aspiring pilot that he knows how to read and write in order to reckon the tides and to read the rutters of the sea and to understand what has been written in there'.[8]

However, the possible utility of literacy and numeracy to the urban, rural or maritime artisan and the absolutely essential nature of these working tools to his master on the other should be carefully distinguished. Therefore the analysis of the literacy levels of these different urban social groups should be kept strictly apart, where it is possible to do so. Unfortunately, historians of education have rarely produced this sort of meticulous analysis.

The drive for literacy to serve salvation in the Protestant tradition is completely different. However, we must immediately admit its power as a drive: in non-commercial Sweden,[9] our best and earliest example, for which we have evidence on reading, not writing, ability, in the parish of Möklinta, 21 per cent of the total population could read in 1614, but in the 1690s, the examination registers show a level of 89 per cent.[10] But great caution needs to be exercised over assumptions that the Reformation and high literacy levels go together, or ought to go together. In non-commercial Calvinist Scotland there was a myth of the superior effects of 'universal and effective education' born of the Calvinist church's national campaign towards literacy in the seventeenth century. Four Acts of the Scottish Parliament in the seventeenth century to implement this aim were passed.[11] But, as Dr Houston has shown, this myth was nothing but a myth: the communities which had significantly more literate members than any others were Edinburgh and Glasgow, and tradesmen and craftsmen, with professionals, were the groups who were more literate than any other within them. 'Education in eighteenth century Edinburgh was increasingly geared to the needs of a society whose main concern was with commercial activity . . . there was an increasingly secular and utilitarian emphasis on education at the expenses of religion and the classics.'

Edinburgh was the main centre of elite culture in seventeenth- and eighteenth-century Scotland. It was also an important town for publishing and distributing chapbooks, one where access to all forms of oral and literate culture, such as newspapers, plays and sermons, was unusually comprehensive. The capital was also an important centre of new attitudes to business and society.[12]

Comparison of smaller cities, towns and villages elsewhere in Scotland between 1640 and 1770 with those in northern England, show that only small towns in lowland Scotland had substantially superior literacy rates. Those superior rates were found amongst craftsmen and tradesmen.[13] Even in Calvinist Scotland, trade was a greater inducement to literacy than the Kirk.

Elementary investigation of the German situation sounds another forcible note of warning of over-simplification. Despite Luther's own initial enthusiasm to get all children of both sexes and all levels of wealth and poverty reading the Gospels, even in 1529, his *Passional*, aimed specifically at 'children and simple folk' contained a great deal more biblical text in the Latin version than in the German.[14] By 1546 at the latest, he was feeling that the 'common crowd' should be taught through the much safer and clear medium of the catechism, 'where there was nothing to judge, only to learn and recite'. The general education that he and Melanchthon had in mind earlier was one in which the purpose was to 'identify and select able pupils, to skim off the best, and to move them rapidly through the better schools and gymnasia to university and on to their careers'. Able boys were to be trained 'to teach in the church and govern in the world'. In the many new state schools of the German principalities of the second half of the sixteenth century, the Gospel only appeared in Latin or in Greek in the fifth forms, or above. In popular German language schools, the Bible did not appear among assigned books at all. Religious teaching depended on the Catechism. But the pupils did learn to read and to write.[15]

My argument is that of these two motors driving towards literacy, the commercial need was the most imperative or, at least, had most effect.[16] The single exception I have been able to find is the possibly shining example of Lutheran Sweden. But there, religion was enforced by the state, and the minister, who taught reading, could be accompanied by a rural police-man.[17] The example is dubious. Apart from that single possible exception, I suggest that literacy and trade go together primarily, rather than literacy and religion. However, the situation is, of course, much more complex than that. I suggest, too, that after the Reforma-tion, literacy for trading purposes and trade links, also conveyed religion, disputed theo-logical ideas, and polemic. Religious ideas, too, in the form of print, ideas, and religious debate, flowed along the trade routes of Europe, and was bought and sold at inns,[18] along with the other goods already travelling those well-established roads. So trade with an area of Reformed belief communicated Reformed ideas and books, along with cloth, grain, glass or whatever the staple commodities of the area were. So I postulate a post-Reformation fusion of a brisk international commodity market, literacy to handle the trade in these commodities, and belief, or debate about belief, since religion was 'news' of the hottest kind. It was no accident that clothiers, in seventeenth-century England, were notorious purveyors of sub-versive religious ideas and books: they were also trading principally with Reformed Europe.[19]

Yet to pigeonhole is the device of the historian faced with too much data. Oversimplifi-cation must also be avoided. I do not think that in any period, pre- or post-Reformation, the historian can, or should, categorise human motivations and separate them in quite this way. It is likely that men were driven, or tempted, towards literacy not only because their working lives and ability to survive depended on it as a tool, but also because they wished to glorify their God, or avoid damnation. Therefore it is worth illustrating these mixed motives from examples deliberately chosen from both before and after the Reformation.

The great fourteenth-century Italian merchant Francesco Datini, held firmly that 'Messer Domino Deo', the Lord God, was a shareholder in his enterprise, who received 10 per cent of the profits. When Francesco Datini started a new account book, he wrote at the beginning, as many other Italian merchants did: 'In the name of God, and of Profit'.

In 1493, an article appeared in the *Lübecker Postille* which is often quoted as evidence for early North-German literacy,[20] pointing out that books were very cheap now, and scolding 'Be ashamed, greedy man, that you do not seek for books, out of which you might acquire treasure for your soul'. Lübeck's days of commercial glory had passed in the fourteenth century, but there was still worldly treasure to be acquired there at the end of the fifteenth century. But this entry in the *Postille* was concerned to stress the search for God, not Mammon, to a literate audience, which, assuredly, had become highly literate in Lübeck in the first place to serve trade.

A page of accounts for the largest and most prosperous enterprise the world had yet seen, the VOC, has been reproduced for 1681, dealing with the total profits and losses of the trade with India in that year. The 'Profit' section was headed 'God, the Lord, will always provide'. The 'Losses' section was headed: 'God will make them good'.[21] There was no distinction here between VOC thinking, and accounting, and that of Datini three centuries earlier.

The best illustration of all of the seamless garment formed by literacy for trade, and literacy for religion, which is torn apart by the historian only for mental convenience, is provided by the life and work of the Luyken family of Amsterdam.[22] Caspar Luyken, who was a schoolmaster, a specialist in literacy, came to Amsterdam from Essen[23] in 1628. He almost certainly fled to avoid religious persecution, for he was a follower of Jacob Boehme. Twenty years later, he published a religious work arguing for more social justice in industry and trade. He chose the title carefully, to appeal to the maximum contemporary interest in Amsterdam: it was the *Infallible Rule of Profit without Loss*.[24]

His younger son, Christopher, became a bookseller in Amsterdam. He first specialised in Boehmist works, but then adapted to the overriding interests of the city and period that he lived in. He moved his shop to a site near the harbour, and started selling publications for sailors and mariners. Caspar's eldest son, Jan Luyken was a child prodigy, and trained to become a painter. After rebellion against the piety of his family, he adopted it. Despite this piety, his best-known work was inspired by a copy of Hans Sachs and Jost Amman's *Book of Trades*[25] written in Nuremberg back in 1568. Jan Luyken's superb engravings illustrating the tradesmen of Amsterdam, which were the visual equivalent of the descriptions of his predecessor, the equally inspired schoolmaster of fourteenth-century Bruges, came out in his own *Book of Trades* in 1694. But the historian looking for trade alone in seventeenth-century Amsterdam, and indeed, finding it, misses layers of meaning of great importance. The work is full of emblems. The figures are surrounded by scenes, and parables of biblical significance, and the whole book is a set of admonitions directed at his own son, who, in turn, had rebelled against the intense devotion of his home. In turn he, too, became reconciled. A section of the *Book of Trades* is devoted to the international book-trade, and the plate of the 'Bookseller' shows this prodigal son presenting a copy of the German edition of the work to its publisher.

If this fusion of trade, which was naturally principally organised from the cities, and the conveyance of ideas did indeed take place after the Reformation, so that the two drives towards literacy became inextricably intertwined, how can my hypothesis that trade was the original, and remained the most important, motivation towards literacy be tested?

I suggest an examination of literacy figures, where they can be found, or when impressionistic evidence for them exists, of the cities of Europe which in turn dominated European commerce or manufacturing, from the Late Middle Ages onwards,[26] that is, from the south, medieval Italy, to the north, eighteenth-century England.

There are two major difficulties in comparing literacy figures in urban centres from south to north, unfortunately. Modern work on literacy or illiteracy rates depends on the counting of signatures on documents, which are chosen to represent as wide a cross-section of society as possible. It has only been carried out in Amsterdam and England, in our area. Older work proceeds by the number of schools that existed, the proportion of the whole eligible age group in school, or the occupational ownership and diffusion of books in inventories. We will therefore find ourselves comparing the incomparable, the proportion of the school-age group actually attending school in fifteenth-century Florence or sixteenth-century Venice, the number of schools that existed in South Germany, the ownership of books in Strasbourg, with the numbers of elementary schools in the areas of the Southern Netherlands and the numbers and proportions of those who could sign their names in seventeenth-century Amsterdam and in eighteenth-century England. This is very unsatisfactory, but it is simply a by-product of the way scholarship has developed in this field.

Secondly, there is another major difficulty for these primarily interested in the amount of vernacular schooling available. Professor Grendler wrote a helpful definition in a relatively recent paper:

> schools had different purposes, served more than one constituency, and reflected the diversity of society as a whole. The division of schools into Latin and vernacular, apparently a feature of schooling throughout Europe, split society. Latin schools trained the ruling class of leaders, professionals and civil servants; *vernacular schools trained the merchants, artisans and others who inhabited the world of work*'. (my emphasis)[27]

It is, then, the vernacular schools which interest us, since we are asking how far literacy was a necessary tool in the service of either commerce, or religion. But Professor Grendler goes on to say the vernacular schools are more difficult to study because they attracted less 'attention'. And how right he is. I speak from bitter experience of working on English vernacular schools in the sixteenth and seventeenth-century: vernacular schools attracted less attention, in the very practical form in England, of less money. Therefore very few of these schools had endowments: the great Latin grammar schools are easy to trace, whether they are St Paul's in London, or St Anna's Gymnasium in Augsburg. They have endowments, they have records. In England, at least, very few of the vernacular schools had endowments, and they were normally temporary affairs: a young man set up a school after university, as a means to earn a living until he acquired a benefice. So schools usually appeared and disappeared, unless they were, at least, in a market town.[28]

So when I set out to investigate, if I could, the relative power of the two motors to literacy which concerned me, I knew I was also looking for the vernacular schools, which were responsible for teaching in medieval Italy, the skills of reading and writing, and 'abbaco', or commercial arithmetic. In England in the sixteenth and seventeenth century they were likewise responsible for teaching 'reading, writing, and to caste accomptes'. Therefore I knew the investigation was likely to be difficult.

The Italian commercial centres of Genoa and Venice emerged in the twelfth century, and remained important until the seventeenth century. It was no accident that the Aldine Press, established in Venice in the 1490s, was the first press to do long print runs of 1,000 copies. The woollen centre of Florence, the silk city of Lucca, and the metal centre of Milan were commercial centres too, and their time of maximum influence began in the thirteenth century and lasted into the fifteenth. The South German commercial towns, Augsburg, which also manufactured textiles, and Nuremberg, which manufactured metals, became important in the fifteenth century and remained so until the seventeenth. In 1471, the mathematician Johannes Müller, settled in Nuremberg, because, as he explained, 'it is there easiest for me to keep in touch with all the learned of all countries, for Nuremberg, thanks to the perpetual journeyings of her merchants, may be counted the centre of Europe'.[29]

Perhaps it was not accident that Gutenberg had established his first press with moveable metal type in 1439 in Mainz[30] midway on the main trade-route across Germany from Venice to Bruges. In the Southern Netherlands, commercial Bruges and manufacturing mercantile Ghent saw their zenith from the thirteenth to the fifteenth centuries. Antwerp's fortunes rose in the fifteenth century and were brutally destroyed in the 1580s. Despite the post-Reformation establishment of his press, Christopher Plantin told us exactly what his motives were in establishing it in Antwerp. They were just the same as those of Johannes Müller, but commercial dominance had moved northwards since Müller settled in Nuremberg. Plantin wrote: 'No other town in the world could offer me more facilities for carrying on the trade I intended to begin. Antwerp can be easily reached; various nations meet in its market-place; there too can be found the raw materials indispensable for the practice of one's trade; craftsmen for all trades can be easily found and instructed in a short time.'[31]

It is noticeable that amongst them he did not mention religion at all, devout man though he was. Not only could 'craftsmen from all trades be easily found and instructed in a short time' but Plantin knew his printed books could easily be sold to the 'various nations' meeting in its market place.

Assembly of the literacy rates established for these various cities therefore seemed worthwhile. In the case of the Italian cities, there is no Reformation to complicate the issue for us, although there may well be a post-Tridentine movement towards religious education. The Counter-Reformation attitude to literacy also needs investigation.

The success of Augsburg, Nuremberg and Antwerp all straddle the pre- and post-Reformation periods. In all three, it would be interesting to know whether any evidence exists to show a rise in literacy with the rise of their fortunes in the fifteenth century, or conversely, a decline after the demise of their fortunes. In fact, it only appears possible to establish the decline, in numeracy rates at least, in Antwerp. After the fall of Antwerp, we are squarely in the post-Reformation world, and have to deal with the three-fold role of the great cities as commercial centres, centres of literacy, and possibly centres of diffusion of religious debate as well. Literacy has, in the post-Reformation world, a constant dual role as both a commercial, and a theological tool.

[. . .]

Writing this chapter has dispelled many almost subconscious clichés for me. Religion, which I thought so powerful a drive to literacy in both Reformation Germany and Calvinist Scotland, appears relatively ineffectual: only in non-commercial Sweden is it without doubt the most powerful motive, leading by the end of the seventeenth century to the most literate population in Europe. Yet even there, we have a caveat, suggesting state enforcement may have been responsible. The Counter-Reformation vernacular schools in Italy appear at least as effective as Luther's own catechetical schools. Trade, and literacy for trade and work, on the other hand, appear a dynamo without parallel.

The attention paid to secular schooling in medieval Italy was a precedent which may just possibly have been followed in South Germany before Luther, from the number of schools in Württemberg. I bitterly regret that no work was done on the number of artisans able to sign their names in fifteenth-century Frankfurt, before the archives were destroyed. This precedent was certainly followed in the Southern Netherlands, judging both from the number of schools in Brabant, and the extraordinary history of the work of the fourteenth-century scholar of Bruges, teaching both pupils and merchants vocabularies about trades from the *Livre des Mestriers* and its derivatives, above all the history of that copy which came into the hands of Christopher Fugger in Antwerp in 1537. We know the extraordinary number of schoolmasters and mistresses teaching in Antwerp, and their migration north. We also know that only a tiny proportion of women teachers only taught Dutch reading in Antwerp, whereas a quarter of them taught arithmetic. This is a strong contrast with England in the same period, when almost all women teachers only taught beginners to read. They were not only not examined on their capacities like their Dutch counterparts, but, in general, the episcopal authorities did not even bother to license them, like male teachers, despite the importance of their work. But we lack the proportion of the relevant age-group at school in fourteenth- and fifteenth-century Bruges, and then in sixteenth-century Antwerp, to measure against the Italian proportions. The number of those able to sign their names in Antwerp, to compare with later Amsterdam, could be established, too. However, even without these essential pieces of research, the impression remains of a very highly literate society, permeated with commercial values and ability, and purchasing the flood of print coming off the presses from their inception. When we reach Amsterdam we are no longer dealing with an impression, but a fact, established from the unprecedented number of both grooms and brides able to sign their names in the Amsterdam marriage registers, the migration of booksellers northwards, and the reams of print coming off the presses for them to sell. The United Provinces, which ran a volume of trade previously unreached, had a literacy rate which was also previously unreached: judging from the efforts of the Overseers of the Poor to pay school fees, the connection was perceived. In eighteenth-century England of the Industrial Revolution, to which the commercial hegemony passed next, the new prospects were signalled by a wave of commercial publications, and outstanding literacy figures in the towns. The superior literacy figures of Northern Europe have, I suggest, little or nothing to do with Protestantism and religion,[32] and a great deal to do with the shift of the whole commercial axis of Europe in sequence from Northern Italy, to South Germany, to the Southern Netherlands, through the United Provinces, the wonder of their contemporaries, to industrialising England.

Yet we must still not oversimplify. We can strip the work of Jan Luyken of Amsterdam[33] of religious meaning, as we can ignore the fact that one of the most prosperous men in the Bruges school-master's *Book of Trades* of the fourteenth century, the draper, was a man who visited prisoners, orphans and widows in their affliction, according to the directions of the *Letter of St. James*. We can also dismiss as hypocrisy the fact that the scrivener, who 'can well rekene And yelde rekenynges Of all rentes' who in Caxton's addition, practised 'the most noble craft That is in the world' was partly to be esteemed and imitated because the Scriptures were open to him as they should be, to every 'true cristen man' for 'Yf it were not the scripture The law and faith shold perisshe'.[34]

But if we ignore these matters, we lose a dimension. To none of these men, any more than to Datini and the VOC, was there necessarily a conflict between their livelihoods and their faith. Both mattered. Nor should there be a conflict to us. But we do well to remember, so much have we been preoccupied by the importance of literacy to religion, that however much their faith meant to them, pre- or post-Reformation, these men, and the merchants and employees in both the Datini enterprise and the VOC, needed to be literate to stay alive, or in business. In all centuries, the need to earn a living and stay alive, and if possible to make a profit to set up home and raise a family, is the most powerful first motive there is.[35] In the densely populated urbanised 'blue banana' of Europe, the cities, where literacy was a fundamental requirement, acted as poles of attraction.

References

1 R. A. Houston, *Literacy in Early Modern Europe: Culture and Education, 1500–1800* (London, 1988), pp. 140–4.

2 *Ibid.*, pp. 147–50. This proposition is much more complex, not altogether surprisingly in view of, for instance, the thriving Schools of Christian Doctrine established in sixteenth-century Italy.

3 The initial drive towards literacy, which I disregard altogether, is the need of governments of all sorts from early medieval times onwards, for a trained literate bureaucracy to run their administration and taxation systems. This is omitted because it involved a completely different social group, educated in a completely different way, in elite Latin schools.

4 Peter Spufford, *Money and its Use in Medieval Europe* (Cambridge, 1988), pp. 251–63.

5 I first drew attention to the need to consider the relevance of rural literacy as a look to economic survival in *Contrasting Communities: English Villagers in the Sixteenth and Seventeenth Centuries* (Cambridge, 1974), p. 80, n. 40, when I intended a paper on rural moneylending, which was never written.

6 Personal communication from Peter Spufford, who has a grant from the ESRC to work on probate accounts.

7 S.L. Thrupp, *The Merchant Class of Medieval London* (Chicago, 1984), pp. 157–71.

8 Quotation from Cornelis Anthonisz, *Onderwijsinge vander zee om stuermanschap te leeren* (Amsterdam 1558, third impressions), p. 7. I am indebted to Karel Davids for this.

9 Janken Myrdal and Johan Söderberg, *Kontinuitetens dynamik. Agrar ekonomi i 1500 – talets Sverige* (Stockholm, s.a.) Summary.

10 Houston, *Literacy*, p. 151, and Egil Johanssen, *Literary and Society in an Historical Perspective*, A Conference Report, nr. 2(Umeå, 1973). Dr Mark Greengrass suggests, however, that it is misleading to suppose that pure Lutheran fervour drove up the Swedish figures for those able to read. The key to the success, he suggests, lay in the power of the state to enforce the official state religion.

11 Houston, *Scottish Literacy and the Scottish Identity: Illiteracy and Society in Scotland and Northern England, 1600–1800* (Cambridge 1985), pp. 3–9, table 2.6 p. 46, pp. 47–51 and table 2.10 p. 53.

12 *Ibid.*, pp. 46–7.

13 *Ibid.*, p. 53.

14 Ruth B. Bottigheimer, 'Bible reading, "Bibles" and the Bible for children in early modern Germany', *Past and Present*, n.r. 139 (1993), 66–89 (69). Note also p. 68, n. 5, pp. 81, 86–7, which stress the similarity of Catholic and Lutheran Bible-reading habits.

15   This whole paragraph is drawn from R. Gawthrop and G. Strauss, 'Protestantism and literacy in early modern Germany', *Past and Present*, n.r. 104 (1984), 31–55 (33–6, 43 and 47–8). Their work has been refined by Ruth Bottigheimer. The appearance of the Bible in schools had to wait until Brandenburg–Prussia espoused school building and teaching from 1695 onwards, for motives by no means solely religious, but heavily influenced by the Pietist movement.

16   Geoffrey Parker, in his excellent 'Success and failure during the first century of the Reformation', *Past and Present*, n.r. 136 (1992), 43–82 used a great deal of the material I have re-discovered here. What is different is the simple idea of comparing the commercial and religious drives to literacy. I am shaking a well-known kaleidoscope, to see if a quite unfamiliar pattern forms, which has its own integrity.

17   See Wiebe Bergsma, 'Church, State and People', in Karel Davids and Jan Lucassen (eds.), *A Miracle Mirrored: The Dutch Republic in European Perspective* (Cambridge, 1995), pp. 196–228.

18   Alan Everitt, 'The English urban inn', in *Landscape and Community in England* (London, 1985), pp. 155–200 (168–73) on the way in which inns acted as *foci* for trade in different specialities from the mid-sixteenth century onwards. See also my Section II, 'The distribution of dissent, by-employment and communications' in the 'Introduction' on 'The importance of religion in the sixteenth and seventeenth centuries', to Margaret Spufford (ed.), *The World of Rural Dissenters, 1520–1725* (Cambridge 1994).

19   Margaret Spufford, 'The importance'. For the 'subversive' religious works exported from Antwerp, along with Plantin's huge trade in orthodox religious print to Spain, see Spufford, *The World*, pp. 52–4, 56–8.

20   Helga Hajdu, *Lesen und Schreiben im Spätmittelalter* (Fünfkirchen, 1931), p. 51.

21   Femme Gaastra, *Bewind en beleid bij de VOC 1672–1702. De financiële en commerciële politiek van de bewindhebbers, 1672–1702* (Zutphen, 1989), p. 78.

22   This is fully discussed in I.H. van Eeghen, 'Jan Luyken (1649–1712) and Casper Luyken (1672–1708): Dutch illustrators', in C.Berkvens-Stevelinck, H. Bots, P.G. Hoftijzer, and O.S. Lankhorst (eds.), *Le Magasin de L'Univers. The Dutch Republic as the Centre of the European Book Trade* (Leiden, 1992), pp. 129–42.

23   Essen became an Imperial territory of the Abbey of Essen in the Middle Ages, but in the mid-sixteenth century, the municipal council declared the town Protestant: from then on the small town was Reformed, Lutheran *and possibly Catholic*. The Abbey did not give up its government, at least until the 1670s. Neither Catholics nor Protestants in this faction-ridden town would have countenanced Boehmists like Caspar Luyken the elder, who would have been a heretic to all parties. G. Köbler (ed.), *Historisches Lexikon der deutschen Länder* (Munich, 1988), p. 140. I am very grateful to Olaf Mörke for unravelling this for me.

24   Caspar Luyken *Onfeylbare reghel van winste sonder verlies* (Amsterdam, 1648).

25   Jan Luyken, *Het Menselyk Bedryf*, M. Wagner (ed.) (Haarlem, 1987). The Amsterdam copy of Hans Sachs and Jost Amman is mentioned on p. 215.

26   Karel Davids and Jan Lucassen, 'Introduction' in their *A Miracle Mirrored*, pp. 11–12, for the concept of 'Blue Banana'.

27   Paul F. Grendler, 'Schools, seminaries and catechetical instruction', in J.W. O'Malley (ed.), *Catholicism in Early Modern History: A Guide to Research* (St. Louis, 1988), 315–30 (p. 318).

28   Margaret Spufford 'The schooling of the peasantry in Cambridgeshire, 1575–1700' in Joan Thirsk (ed.) *Land, Church and People: Essays Presented to Professor H.R.P. Finberg*, supplement to *Agricultural History Review*, 18 (1970), pp. 112–47. This fluctuating pattern, which makes them so hard to trace, also accounts, in my view, for some of the wild fluctuations in the pattern of literacy rates, measured in terms of ability to sign, found in England in 1642, which is the first data for which we have evidence across the whole country. The results are commented on by David Cressy, *Literacy and the Social Order: Reading and Writing in Tudor and Stuart England* (Cambridge, 1980), pp. 73–4 and Keith Wrightson, *English Society* 1580–1680 (London, 1982), p. 194.

29   Quoted by Benjamin A. Rifkin in his 'Introduction' to Jost Amman and Hans Sachs, *The Book of Trades* (1568, facsimile edn., New York, 1973), p. x.

30   Houston, *Literacy*, p. 156.

31   Christopher Plantin, cited by Houston *Literacy*, p. 142, originally from J. J. Murray, *Antwerp in the Age of Plantin and Brueghel* (Newton Abbot, 1972) pp. 3–4.

32   Grendler, 'Schools', p. 317

33   [. . .] His son actually entered the service of a German publisher in Nuremberg in 1699, so the wheel turned full circle, and the son of the Boemist of Amsterdam sold books, and made them, in the great city where the last famous artisan Meistersinger had had his best-selling *Book of Trades* illustrated.

34   Florens and 'Gilbers li escrivains' *Le livre des mesitiers* ed. H. Michelant (Paris, 1875), pp. 27, 28–9. Caxton's additions, *Dialogies in French and English* (1900), p. 37.

35   There is a certain delightful irony in this author presenting a paper which both stresses the high level of literacy in the cities and towns of Europe, and also suggests that the most powerful drive towards literacy was probably commerce, not religion. Recently I have begun to run the risk of getting typecast as the rural historian who was obsessive in emphasising that English farmers, producing for the market, and even English farm labourers, 10 per cent of whom could sign their names in the seventeenth century, were more literate because more of them possessed *reading* skills, than had been supposed. This has led me on to stress the accessibility of very cheap print to them. The dominence of religion as a subject of this cheap print, together with other evidence, has led me in turn to stress the importance of religion in their lives. So here we have an English farmers' historian, who emphasises the influence of religion in the lives of rural people in the seventeenth century, writing a chapter on the higher literacy rates in towns, and the greater power of commercial motivation, and indeed, simply the basic human need to earn a living, as drives toward literacy. Yet I don't think I have contradicted my own work. Initially I drew attention to the need to consider literacy as a tool to economic survival in rural society in *Contrasting Communities* (p. 80, n. 48) back in 1972, when I mistakenly told the world I was about to write a paper on rural moneylending, which, in the way of such things, never got written. I am not suggesting in this chapter that the countryside was illiterate: only that the literacy rates were lower than in the towns, which we all knew. Nor am I suggesting that religion was unimportant as a drive toward literacy: only that, with the shining exception of Sweden, it was *less* important. But there was no difference in the thinking of a Protestant yeoman like Robert Loder of Berkshire in England, from that of Franceso Datini and the VOC. In his early seventeeth-century account book, he wrote, if the harvest was good 'Praise be to God who giveth the increase'. To countrymen as well as townsmen, there was no necessary conflict between their livelihoods and their faith.

Chapter 14

Roger S. Schofield

DIMENSIONS OF ILLITERACY IN ENGLAND, 1740–1850

RECENTLY AN INCREASING NUMBER of economists have begun to consider education as a process of human capital formation, and to view expenditure on education in terms of private and social investment.[1] This perspective leads naturally to the question of the contribution of education to economic growth, and economists of education have not been slow to appreciate the relevance of the English experience during the eighteenth and early nineteenth centuries.[2]

Unfortunately, the study of education in this period is much less advanced than the study of economic growth. Most accounts rely on inferences drawn from the history of the development of educational institutions and from the history of the popular press, buttressed by a few contemporary and modern studies of the literacy of a limited number of groups. The present consensus is that educational opportunities expanded during the period 1750–1850, so that by 1840 between 67% and 75% of the British working class had achieved rudimentary literacy. Some writers believe that the growth in the middle of the period was not great, and point to a halt in educational advance at the turn of the century,[3] while others have discerned a particularly rapid growth in literacy in the first few decades of the nineteenth century.[4] All agree that there was considerable variation: regionally, between town and countryside, and between different occupational groups.

[. . .]

In this paper [. . .] I shall review the present evidence for the course of literacy in the period 1750–1850, present some fresh evidence, and suggest some implications for the relationship between literacy and economic growth in the period.

I

Arguments from changes in the volume and nature of popular publications to changes in the level of literacy enjoyed by the population at large are particularly insecure. First, there is no necessary relationship between the volume of production and the size of readership, because the number of readers per copy cannot be assumed to have been constant either over time or between publications. Second, changes in both the volume and the nature of publications may have been influenced by many factors other than changes in the level of literacy: for example, technological innovations such as the steam press, or changes in fiscal policy such as the many different rates of stamp duty charged in newspapers in the eighteenth and early nineteenth centuries. But arguments from the increase in educational facilities (the founding of the Charity Schools in the eighteenth century, the Sunday Schools in the 1780s, and the monitorial, industrial, and workhouse schools in the early nineteenth century), although frequently advanced, are also fraught with danger. Some of these schools, notably the Charity and the Sunday schools, were more concerned to impart a moral and religious training, and for them instruction in literacy was a secondary consideration. All schools had great difficulty in securing attendance. Early nineteenth-century surveys showed time and again that the number of children enrolled at school was no guide to the number actually receiving instruction.[5] This was partly because, with the exception of the Sunday schools and some of the institutional schools, fees had to be paid, for despite the large number of ostensibly free schools very few genuinely free places were available. Education was therefore in direct competition with other goods for cash expenditure. It was also in competition with earning capacity, for the early nineteenth-century surveys also show that even in the case of free schools attendance slumped when employment was available.

Thus, the difficulty with indirect measures of literacy, such as the volume of popular publications and the supply of education, lies in the intervention of other variables; but direct measures of literacy also have their drawbacks. The early nineteenth century, particularly the 1830s and 1840s, witnessed a rash of educational, cultural, and moral surveys, made by a wide range of interested parties, many of which investigated the ability of different sections of the population to read and write, often in considerable detail.[6] Unfortunately, the restricted date span precludes their use for a study of literacy over a long period, and their great variety and frequent inexplicitness about the standards of reading and writing being measured make comparisons between them difficult. This is the same problem facing the student of literacy rates in the developing world today, who finds on closer inspection that "able to read" has been defined and measured differently in each country. Indeed, most modern investigations, like most of the early nineteenth-century surveys, rest on answers to questions about literacy rather than on direct tests. Thus, they measure people's beliefs about their literary abilities as expressed to a stranger, not the existence of these abilities. Clearly, if literacy is associated with high status, the dangers of misrepresentation are considerable.[7] For example, in a survey of literacy in East Pakistan in the mid-1960s a sample of rural cultivators was asked whether they could read a newspaper. Fifty-seven percent claimed that they could, but subsequent testing revealed that 15% in fact either could not read at all or could only stumble through the text without comprehension. The level of ability amongst the 42% who really could read also varied widely: about a half of them could only read slowly but with comprehension, while a half (or 22% of the sample) could read fluently.[8] In England in the period 1750–1850, as in East Pakistan in the mid-1960s, there was a wide range of reading ability, and in such a situation the proportion of the population reported as being "able to read" clearly depends on the level of skill taken to comprise reading ability.

Ideally, therefore, measures of literacy should be both standard and direct. For pre-industrial England in the late eighteenth and early nineteenth centuries there is only one measure which satisfies these two conditions: the ability to sign one's name. Although at first sight this is not a particularly meaningful literary skill, it has the advantage of giving a fairly "middle-range" measure of literacy in this period. This is because, ever since the sixteenth century, school curricula had been so phased that reading was taught before writing, and the intermittent nature of school attendance thus ensured that large numbers of children left school having acquired some reading ability, but little or no ability to write. In this period, therefore, the proportion of the population able to sign was less than the proportion able to read and greater than the proportion able to write. Early nineteenth century evidence suggests that the proportion of the population claiming a basic level of reading ability may have been half as much again as the proportion able to sign, and that the proportion able to sign roughly corresponded with the proportion able to read fluently.[9] It also confirms that more people could sign than could write, but this was occasionally denied in the early nineteenth century, for the advocates of state education used the proportion of spouses unable to sign the marriage register as a stick with which to beat the defenders of private education, who consequently made valiant efforts to discredit it as a measure of literacy. Their argument was that many people who could write were inhibited from signing their names by the solemnity of the marriage ceremony or out of feeling for an illiterate spouse. However, such people would presumably have been accustomed to holding a pen and would in consequence have made firm marks. Yet the numbers of such marks in the marriage registers are very small, and are unlikely to have had more than the most marginal effect on literacy rates based on the ability to sign. Another, and contrary, objection which is some-times brought against the use of marriage register signatures as a measure of literacy, is that some people signed who could neither read nor write. Children today may be capable of this trick; but it is *a priori* unlikely in pre-industrial England, given the phasing of instruction in reading and writing, the lack of writing materials in most homes, and the very few occasions in a lifetime in which a signature or mark was required. In practice, such a signature would be ill-formed through inexperience of both pen and letters, but such signatures are rare in this period.

A further advantage of the ability to sign as a measure of literacy is that it is available for a large number of people and thus makes possible comparisons both over time and between residential and occupational groups. The source for this wealth of information is the series of marriage registers kept by the Church of England, for since 1754 the law recognized as valid only those marriages which were registered in the Anglican registers and signed by the parties and two witnesses.[10] The register evidence therefore relates to the 90% or so of the population who were ever married, and measures their ability to sign largely when they were in their mid-20s, some 15 or so years after leaving school.[11] For the period from 1839 to 1914 the Registrar General has published in his *Annual Reports* the numbers and proportions of men and women able and unable to sign their names.[12] Figure 14.1 shows the national annual illiteracy rates (percentages unable to sign) of men and women over this period, plotted on a semi-logarithmic scale to facilitate comparison of rates of change at different periods. The achievement of the second half of the nineteenth century is remarkable: the percentage of men unable to sign fell from just over 30% in 1850 to 1% in 1911, and the percentage of women unable to sign fell from just over 45% in 1850 to 1% in 1913. The fastest rate of improvement was amongst those marrying after about 1885, or leaving school after about 1870. The improvement between about 1850 and 1885 (i.e., school-leavers between about 1835 and 1870) was less rapid, and the rate of improvement between 1840 and 1850 (school-leavers of 1825–1835) was markedly slower still.

[. . .]

One aspect of literacy in this period which is quite clear from the Registrar General's figures based on the marriage registers is a marked geographical variation in the percentage unable to sign. In 1839, the first date for which these figures are available, the metropolitan area of London is the most literate "county," with 12% of males unable to sign, followed closely by three counties near the border with Scotland, all with under 20% unable to sign. The next best group, with 20%–30% unable to sign, comprises a string of counties on the northeast coast, together with Devon and Dorset. The worst two groups, with

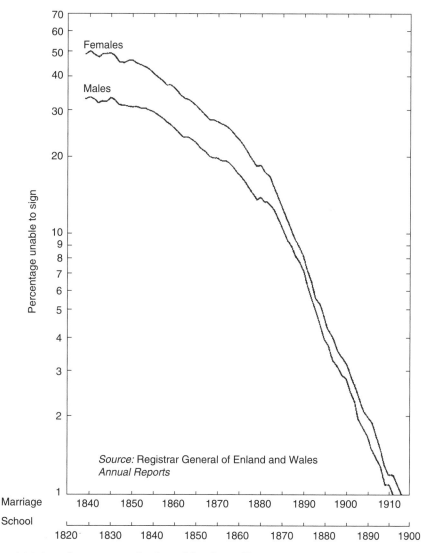

Figure 14.1 Annual percentages of males and females unable to sign at marriage, England and Wales, 1839–1912.

40%–55% unable to sign, are Wales and the West Midlands with Lancashire, and a belt of counties stretching from East Anglia through the Home Counties to Wiltshire. The Midlands and most of the southern coastal counties comprise an intermediate group, with 30%–39% unable to sign. Thus in 1839 the proportion of males who were illiterate at marriage was three times higher in Bedford and Hertfordshire than in Northumberland, Cumberland, and Westmorland. But the Registrar General's figures for Registration Districts, which are available from 1842, show that local variation within a county was even greater than this. Thus, the national estimates of illiteracy for the period before 1838 presented in the current literature, which are based on very small numbers of parishes, are subject to large sampling errors, and accordingly little confidence should be placed in them.

II

The task of obtaining trustworthy figures and of studying this extraordinary variation in illiteracy rates can only be achieved either by making a full enumeration of all marriages registered between 1754 and 1838, or by drawing a properly designed sample. The first alternative is scarcely practicable, if only because the marriages are recorded in 10,000 parish registers, most of which are still lodged in the parish chests. This geographical constraint also makes it sensible to sample marriage registers rather than individual marriage entries. Accordingly, I have drawn a random sample of 274 parishes, a figure which was calculated to produce national estimates with a standard error of about 2%, taking into account a rather strong parish clustering effect. Figure 14.2 shows the national estimates of the percentages of men and women unable to sign in each year during the period 1754–1840. The 274 parishes produced about 1,300 marriages annually in the late 1750s

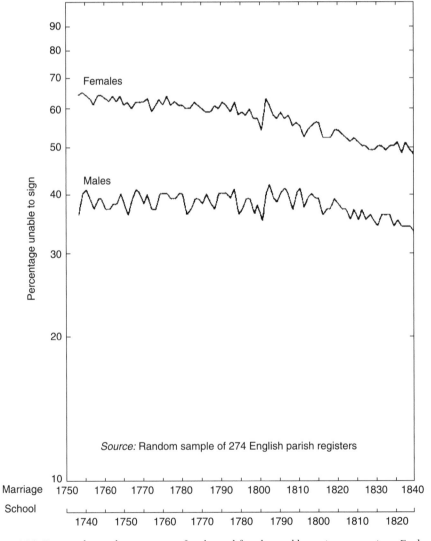

Figure 14.2 Estimated annual percentages of males and females unable to sign at marriage, England, 1754–1840.

rising to about 2,900 in the late 1830s. The effect of clustering on the variance of the sample estimates was greater than expected, and the standard error of the estimates in most years was about 3%. The sampling error lends a tremor to the lines on the graph, but the trends are nonetheless clear.

The percentage of women unable to sign was just over 60% in the mid-eighteenth century, and improved slowly, to fall to just below 50% by 1840. The rate of improvement after 1800 was noticeably faster than before this date, but at no time was it particularly rapid. Allowing for a 15-year lag between schooling and marriage, the quickening of improvement in female illiteracy dates from about the mid-1780s and may possibly be connected with the development of Sunday School education at this time. Male illiteracy, however, followed a somewhat different course. Far from falling throughout this period, as present accounts lead one to expect, it remained more or less stable for 50 years. Just under 40% were unable to sign until about 1795. The percentage then fell toward 1800, but rose toward 1805, and then fell again at a similar rate to that of the women to around 33% in 1840. The turning point is a little less clear for males, but it was probably between 1805 and 1815. If we assume that entry into the labor force may be taken to be the age of leaving school, then some point in the 1790s marks the date around which the literacy of entrants to the labor force may first be said to be increasing since 1740. Despite differences in scale, a comparison of Figures 1 and 2 brings out the marked contrast between the relative stability of both male and female illiteracy in this period, and the dramatic fall in the later nineteenth century.

National figures, however, as we have already observed, summarize and conceal wide variations. Ultimately, the sample results will show how far regional experiences differed from the national trend. But geographical location is only one of many factors which affect illiteracy rates. Others probably included the availability of schooling, and a wide variety of social and economic variables; for example, the concentration of land ownership, the dispersion of settlement, and the occupational structure of the community.

[. . .]

This occupational hierarchy is one of the most consistent features of illiteracy in the past. It is to be found in all regions and at all times, regardless of the level of illiteracy. Naturally the differences between occupations vary, and sometimes categories, particularly some of the trades and crafts, exchange places. The common-sense interpretation of this hierarchy would seem to be that literacy had a different functional value in each of the occupational groups. For example, long before the mid-eighteenth century the sub-culture of the social elite presupposed literacy, and literacy was also essential to the economic functions of men in the professions and official positions. These groups, that is, needed to be literate in order to fulfill their economic and social roles. But others did not, for even in the mid-nineteenth century literacy was by no means indispensible in the social and economic life of large numbers of laborers. In the middle ground of different trades and crafts the superiority of occupations involving commerce and contact with the public (retail food and drink) over occupations involving heavy manual labor (construction and mining) also makes sense in terms of literacy having a different practical value to different occupational groups. Indeed, since schooling in this period involved direct cash expenditure as well as foregoing earnings, the practical utility of literacy would have been a powerful argument either for or against investing in education. For some groups the costs of this investment exceeded perceived benefits. Even in the more literate world of the late nineteenth century the abolition of school fees still left the "costs" of lost earning power to be borne, and universal investment in education was only achieved under the compulsion of the law.

III

In the late eighteenth and early nineteenth centuries a decision to invest in education was a decision to invest in the acquisition of literary skills: the ability to read and, at further cost, the ability to write. For it was primarily these two skills that were taught in the elementary schools; arithmetic and substantive knowledge were offered later, and required a further cash outlay. The acquisition of literary skills, or literacy, might be desirable for three reasons: because it was essential for participation in the life of a particular social group, because it was essential for acquiring skills, or new skills, relevant to a particular occupation, or because it would lead to upward social and economic mobility. It is by and large true that in the late eighteenth and early nineteenth centuries the literate occupations had higher status and were better paid; but the early nineteenth-century educational surveys show that both the subjects children studied and the length of time they stayed at school depended on the occupation and status of their parents, which suggests that the prospect of upward mobility for their children did not lead many working class parents to invest heavily in education.[13] How far literacy was necessary to men and women in order for them to participate fully in different walks of life in the late eighteenth and early nineteenth centuries is a large question. Literacy was clearly widespread: a majority of the population could read, and in the early nineteenth century there is plenty of evidence of a literate culture amongst large sections of the working class. The fall in the illiteracy rate amongst women from 64% in 1750 to 50% in 1850 suggests that literacy became a more important component in the life of women during the period. On the other hand, male illiteracy remained constant until the decade 1805–1815. More remarkably, [. . .] in many occupations illiteracy actually rose during the later eighteenth century and that in the early nineteenth century some occupations were still less literate than they had been in the mid-eighteenth century.

Perhaps no great emphasis should be laid on these figures, for they come from a small number of parishes for which information on occupations is available throughout the period. Yet they at least suggest the possibility that for many males in a variety of occupations literacy did not become more essential as a cultural skill during this period. They might also suggest that, with the conspicuous exception of the clothing and construction trades, literacy may have been no more essential for acquiring economic skills and techniques in the early nineteenth century than it had been in the mid-eighteenth century. Yet technical developments involved thousands of people in learning a multitude of new practical skills. An attempt was made in the eighteenth century to provide practical instruction for the poor in Charity Schools, but although this scheme proved to be greatly to the tastes of the times, it had to be abandoned as uneconomic.[14] For most children in the late eighteenth and early nineteenth centuries, school remained a specialized institution for the instruction of literary skills. Consequently, few children were regular in attendance, and few remained at school for more than 1½ years.[15] Practical economic skills were therefore learned within the context of the household and work-group, as part of a comprehensive process of socialization, of which apprenticeship is a well-known, but formalized example.

Thus, insofar as economic growth in this period entailed the acquisition of a large number of practical skills by a growing proportion of the population, developments in literacy and education were probably largely irrelevant to it. And, insofar as economic growth resulted from the increased productivity of labor brought about by the shift from domestic to factory production, literacy and education were also probably largely irrelevant, for many of the new industrial occupations recruited a mainly illiterate work force, so much so that many industrial communities were markedly more illiterate than their rural neighbors.[16] This contrast has been attributed to a collapse of education in these rapidly growing urban areas, but a large proportion of the work force had moved to these towns after having been educated elsewhere. Thus, urban migration in this period was not only occupation-specific; it was also literacy-specific. This is made clear by the opposite effect, namely, the superior literacy of market and county towns over the surrounding neighborhood. For these communities contained a high proportion of occupations concerned with distribution and exchange, which required the ability to keep the records, and thus presupposed literacy. Indeed, such an intersectoral shift in occupational structure accompanying economic growth may perhaps account for the positive correlation between literacy and economic development in present-day economies.[17] Inferences sometimes drawn from this association are that an illiteracy rate of about 60% is a threshold above which economic growth is unlikely, and that an improvement in literacy is a necessary precondition or concomitant of economic growth. The English experience in the century from 1750 to 1850 may perhaps be taken to cast some doubt on the utility of positing universal relationships between literacy and economic growth. Although it is true that the national male illiteracy rate had crossed the 60% threshold before 1750, the female rate only crossed it definitively around 1795, and female illiteracy was very high in areas of high female industrial employment; for example, it was still 84% in Oldham in 1846.[18] Nor does the static nature of male illiteracy, both nationally until the decade 1805–1815, and in several occupational groups until the mid-nineteenth century, lend much support to the notion that an improvement in literacy necessarily precedes or accompanies economic growth. Indeed, this long period of stability, and the marked contrast between the literacy of commercial classes and the illiteracy of much of the industrial labor force, suggest that for England, at least, the usual causal relationships between literacy and economic growth might profitably be reversed. In this alternative perspective the reduction in illiteracy in nineteenth-century England would appear more as a cultural change brought about by economic growth than as one of the causes of growth.

References

1   For example, *see* M. Blaug, *An Introduction to Economics of Education* (London: Allen Lane, 1970).
2   C. A. Anderson and M. J. Bowman, eds., *Education and Economic Development* (London: F. Cass, 1966), chs. 17, 18, 20.
3   Anderson and Bowman, *Education and Economic Development*, p. 350.
4   L. S. Stone, "Literacy and Education in England 1640–1900," *Past and Present*, 42 (1969), 109.
5   For example, the survey of education in Westminster in 1837–1838 reported that school attendance in winter was down to between a quarter and a half of the number of children enrolled. Second Report of a Committee of the Statistical Society of London, appointed to enquire into the State of Education in Westminster, *Journal of the Statistical Society of London*, 1 (1838): 193–215.
6   These surveys have been well summarized and discussed in R. K. Webb, "Working Class Readers in Early Victorian England," *English Historical Review*, 65 (1950), 333–51; and R. K. Webb, *The British Working Class Reader, 1790–1848* (London: Allen & Unwin, 1955), ch. 1.
7   For example, a survey of education in Newcastle-upon-Tyne in the late 1830s reported, "In making such enquiries our agent was universally regarded as interfering with what they thought he had no concern and they gave answers which he knew in the majority of cases to be false." William Cargill, Esq., and a Committee of the Educational Society of Newcastle, "Educational, Criminal, and Social Statistics of Newcastle-Upon-Tyne," *Journal of the Statistical Society of London*, 1 (1838): 355–61.
8   H. S. Schuman, A. Inkeles and D. H. Smith, "Some Social Psychological Effects and Noneffects of Literacy in a New Nation," *Economic Development and Cultural Change*, 16 (1967), 1–14.
9   Compare the figures cited by Webb, "Working Class Readers," and the figures given in the Registrar General's *Annual Reports. See also* the opinions of an educational inspector of the time: J. F. Fletcher, "Moral and Educational Statistics of England and Wales," *Journal of the Statistical*

Society of London, 10(1847): 212. Signatures as measures of literacy are discussed more fully in R. S. Schofield, "The Measurement of Literacy in Pre-Industrial England," in *Literacy in Traditional Societies*, ed. J. Goody (Cambridge: Cambridge U.P., 1968).

10   Only Jews, Quakers, and members of the royal family were exempt; 26 George II c. 33, usually known as Lord Hardwicke's Marriage Act.

11   A rough idea of the proportion of the population never marrying and thus escaping observation in the marriage registers is given by the proportion of the age group 50–54 that was still unmarried. In 1851 11% of men and 12% of women were unmarried in this age group. These figures do not represent exactly the proportions of men and women never marrying, because although over 99% of all first marriages took place before either partner had reached fifty years of age, it was probably not the case at this period that the mortality of single people below the age of fifty was equal to that of married people. *See* Great Britain, *Parliamentary Papers*, vol. LXXXVIII (1852–1853), "1851 Census of England and Wales," pt. 1, p. cci; and Registrar General of England and Wales, *Annual Report of Births, Deaths and Marriages* (1851–1852), p. viii. Information of sufficient quality on the distribution of ages at marriage is first available in 1851. In this year 73% of all bridegrooms and 70% of all brides were between 20 and 29 years old. A further problem lies in the double-counting of further marriages of widows and widowers, especially if the risk of widowhood and the propensity to remarriage prove to have been social class specific. In 1851, 14% of the bridegrooms and 9% of the brides were widowers and widows respectively (Registrar General, *Annual Report* (1851–1852), p. viii).

12   Registrar General, *Annual Report* (1839–0000).

13   For example, *see* the survey of education in Westminster cited *above, Journal of the Statistical Society of London*, 1: 193–215.

14   "The struggle between the disciplines of labour and literature for the control of the Charity School curriculum ended in the defeat of labour. If success had crowned the efforts of the working Charity Schools the history of elementary education in the British Isles would have followed a different course." M. G. Jones, *The Charity School Movement* (Cambridge, University Press, 1938), p. 95.

15   For example, *see* the survey of education in Westminster cited *above, Journal of the Statistical Society of London*, 1: 193–215.

16   This is visible both in the sample parishes and also in the data printed by the Registrar General in his *Annual Reports*. Since this paper was written, an investigation of the ability to sign in Lancashire has confirmed for a key industrializing area some of the national results presented here. In particular, literacy was found to be *declining* in Lancashire in the later half of the eighteenth century "down to about the 1820s or 1830," and the author concluded that "the English industrial revolution cannot be seen as one nourished by rising educational standards at least at the elementary level." Michael Sanderson, "Literacy and Social Mobility in the Industrial Revolution in England," *Past and Present*, no. 56 (August 1972), pp. 75–104.

17   Bowman and Anderson, "Concerning the Role of Education in Development."

18   Registrar General, *Annual Report* (1846).

Chapter 15

David Vincent

READING AND WRITING

BENJAMIN SHAW'S FORMAL EDUCATION began and ended at Peggy Winn's dame school where he learned to read and to knit. It was not until he was nearing the end of his apprenticeship that he began to become actively literate. The transition from reading to writing was triggered by a crisis in his personal life:

> in the Autum of this year, my Sweethart & I quarreled, & after Sometime she detirmined to leave dolphinholme, so another young women and her set of for Preston, but before she went she promised Voluntearly that she would be true to me &c, this was in October 1792. So when she got work which she did at the factory in moor lane, then belonging to Watson & Co She wrote to me, & let me know where she lived &c and envited me to come to see her at Christmas &c – (This was about the time the french convention tried, & condemned their King Leuis the 16th –) at Christmas I went to Preston, with Samuel Winn my cousin, & staid a few days &c She sent me letters by the waggon from dolphin-holme, & I frequently wrote to hir – this was the begining of my writing, for I never went to any school to write in my life – and wanting to send to her I was ashamed to let anybody know my secrets, I set about writing love letters &c, (it is an ill thing that is good for nothing).[1]

Shaw's halting, makeshift journey between different modes of communicating his heart's secrets constrasted sharply with the polarities which informed much of the contemporary commentary on the spread of reading and writing. To educated outsiders, literacy occupied a world of opposites. The tables of signatures divided populations, the graphs measured change between contrasting conditions. The simple pairing of capacity and incapacity belonged to the later nineteenth century as official bodies began to generate the statistics which justified the investment in elementary education. These indices of progress were a shorthand expression of a more profound dichotomy which had shaped the response of educated society to the unlettered since the invention of printing. An 'oral tradition' had been discovered, embracing a large but rapidly diminishing proportion of the rural populations of Europe. In Protestant societies, the association of a mode of communication with a collective mentality had a history stretching back to the Reformation. Catholicism was stigmatized as a non-literary belief system, deriving its authority from the unverifiable spoken word. 'Romish traditions' were contrasted with the divinely sanctioned message of the Bible, which alone could preserve the Christian message across the millennia. This construction persisted long after the Catholic Church had embraced the objective of a schooled laity, but by the late eighteenth century the notion of an oral tradition was taking on a broader meaning. Now it represented the dividing line not between religions, but between cultures.

The new delineation was driven by the increasingly acute sense of historical change. Communities which relied wholly on speech to record and communicate their collective knowledge were held to be insulated from the corrosive effects of progress. Their songs and stories preserved intact the values and wisdom of long-dead generations. Observers who sought out and recorded such material could not only protect it from the relentless invasion of the printed word but also gain access to a hidden cultural history of immense wealth and longevity. Just as the emerging science of geology could identify aeons of time in a single rock face, so the folklore collector could locate sedimented layers of custom and belief in surviving outcrops of the oral tradition. The Scottish stonemason Hugh Miller taught himself the science of the rocks upon which he worked, and as he travelled away from his native Cromarty in search of employment, discovered his culture's history laid out before him. 'Some three days' journey into the Highlands,' he wrote, 'might be regarded as analogous in some respects to a journey into the past of some three to four centuries.'[2] Thus he became both an internationally renowned geologist, with a fossil named after him, and also one of the relatively few nineteenth-century writers to make a major contribution to the folklore movement from within.[3]

The discoveries had varied significance. The publication of Herder's *Volkslieder* in 1778 set in motion the search for a German national consciousness hidden beneath the artificial political boundaries of the region.[4] Walter Scott's collection of songs for the Minstrelsy of the Scottish Border was integral to his creative revival of Scotland's identity,[5] and elsewhere in Europe both the artefacts of oral communication and the language in which they were conveyed were pressed into the service of nascent nationalist movements. The young Hungarian literati of the 1820s, for instance, saw the uncorrupted peasantry as the major source of the linguistic revival which they sought.[6] By contrast, the host of enthusiastic urban collectors who ventured forth into the neighbouring countryside in ever-increasing numbers during the nineteenth century had a more ambivalent attitude to their source material.[7] Some deployed their findings to attack the spiritual and imaginative bankruptcy of contemporary civilization, but most endorsed the necessity of change.[8] They were alert to the loss threatened by the destruction of the networks of oral transmission, but hostile to the irrational and immoral belief systems which had for too long survived amongst the uneducated. They worked alongside rather than against the new race of trained schoolteachers, celebrating their achievements and often recruiting them to the newly formed folklore societies. The songs and the proverbs were for the museums of disappearing cultures, not for the living world of the modern rural society.

The folklore movement contributed to the rise of the new science of anthropology which in more recent decades has challenged the boundaries of conventional text-based historiography and generated much of the scholarship which informs this study.[9] In the course of disciplinary evolution, the fundamental assumptions of the founding fathers have come under scrutiny. The 'oral tradition' is now regarded more as a by-product of European intellectual history than a substantive category of cultural analysis. The most obvious difficulty is that at least in Western Europe, communities uncontaminated by the written word disappeared at the Reformation and Counter-Reformation – if ever they existed. Although the Protestant churches had varied in their enthusiasm for an actively literate laity in the centuries after Luther, the commitment to vernacular religious literature had ensured that every worshipper was exposed to the written form of their own language. In the most extreme cases, sustained campaigns of disseminating both spiritual texts and the skills required to read them meant that entire populations possessed and used print a century before the oral tradition was discovered. Egil Johansson reported a survey of a Swedish rural parish in the 1720s, whose 600 families owned 'around 400 ABC-books, 650 to 750 Catechisms, more than 1,100 psalters, 29 Bibles, and about 200 other religious books'.[10] Parish records in Iceland revealed that of a thousand households between 1780 and 1800, only seven were without literature.[11] Even in England, where the state and the established church had been far less active in the field, the drive to mass literacy began rather than ended with books in a majority of homes. Studies undertaken in the late 1830s, just as children were emerging from the first officially subsidized church elementary schools, revealed levels of ownership ranging from 52 to 90 per cent in rural areas, and 75 per cent or more in most towns and cities. Only in areas of acute deprivation, such as an Irish slum in London, did the figure fall below a half.[12] Engagement with print in Catholic societies was hampered not so much by the absence of education as by the persistence well into the nineteenth century of Latin in both church services and the school curriculum. Nonetheless, cheaply produced spiritual works in national languages were finding their way into the homes of the rural poor to be read, remembered or at least preserved as visible evidence of piety.

Much of this literature was supplied not by the churches themselves, but by commercial vendors responding to popular demand for both worldly and spiritual reading matter. Pedlars travelled out from urban centres to the surrounding countryside during the early modern period, carrying in their packs devotional texts, tales of wonder and imagination, and practical guides to living, at prices affordable by all but the most destitute peasant families. [. . .] Unlike modern newspapers, which in some respects they represented, these flimsy productions were read and reread for years until they finally disintegrated. At the very least, they ensured that in the villages of Western Europe, and in those of the east within reach of the scattered towns, the populations already knew the meaning of print before the salaried, inspected schoolteachers arrived to tell them in the nineteenth century. Even if they had to borrow both the texts and the skills to read them, they were familiar with the task of decoding the marks on the page and with the consequences for their spiritual, imaginative and practical lives.

Only in exceptional cases would a labourer's household possess a rudimentary library, and even in the precociously literate rural communities of southern Sweden, the bulk of cultural life was conducted through the spoken word and associated forms of ritual behaviour. However, it is now apparent that the characteristic artefacts of the oral tradition, the folk songs and stories which so excited the middle-class collectors, were themselves contaminated by the world of texts. It has been estimated that of the material painstakingly recorded from elderly traditional singers in remote corners of Britain in the late nineteenth and early twentieth centuries, as much as four-fifths had once appeared in printed broadsides.[13] Similar flows from formal to informal reproduction have been traced in Germany and Ireland.[14] Furthermore, the singers themselves were not always as reliant on their capacious memories as educated outsiders liked to suppose. They too were concerned lest they forgot the songs, or failed adequately to convey them to the next generation, and had no compunction about making manuscript copies where they possessed the ability to do so. The assumption that the written tradition stood to the oral much as the railway engine stood to the stagecoach was in some respects the reverse of the truth. Creativity had been a more promiscuous process than the folklorists liked to suppose. Printed songs and stories gradually merged into the oral resources of the community as they were performed and repeated to new audiences, reinvigorating the existing local repertoire and for ever compromising the purity of the folk tradition. By the same measure, transmission over time was by no means as secure a process in pre-industrial settlements as the nineteenth-century rural romantics imagined. Aside from intermittent disasters of war, pestilence and famine, the constant realities of early deaths and short-distance migration continually threatened the chain of communication between generations. The handwritten versions passed from hand to hand, and in countries where print was in short supply, became an important addition to the cultural archive. [. . .] Only when the collections began to appear between hard covers was there a sense of a tradition being embalmed rather than sustained.

Just as the oral forms of communication had depended on the written, so also the reverse was true. Performance was sustained by written forms, and in turn the dissemination of print was assisted by singers and story-tellers. In any community of the labouring poor, both before and during the drive to mass literacy, there were always more people seeking access to the content of books and documents than were able to own or decipher them. The solution was to read them out aloud. Societies where only a small handful of the population were technically literate nonetheless were able to incorporate print and writing into their daily lives through private or public performance. In Hungary, for instance, where literacy rates were in single figures before the nineteenth century, prayer books, passports, contracts and letters were deployed in rural areas by means of borrowing the skills of the handful of neighbours capable [of] reading them.[15] The notion of audience which has become a feature of modern readership studies was literally appropriate to the reception of a large proportion of literature until well into the twentieth century. Most printed words found their way into the minds of most of the populations of the past through their ears rather than their eyes.[16] In this form of consumption, as in all others, deprivation encouraged co-operation. Those who could not afford the cost of an education or reading matter sat at the feet of those who could. In the fireside gatherings known in France as the veillée and in Germany as the Spinnstube, the contents of chap-books were read or recalled by one of the company whilst listeners carried on with household tasks.[17] In Iceland, where the nights were the longest of all, the whole sequence of engaging with the written word, from learning to read to reading aloud to discussing the texts, was conducted on this collective basis.[18]

The rising graph of literacy brought no corresponding decline in the use of the human voice. Children emerged from schools with their ears ringing with the noise of print. The first generation of inspected teachers aspired to harmony rather than silence in their lessons. Only in the more advanced schools of the last quarter of the nineteenth century were pupils permitted to spend part of their lessons quietly reading or writing. Out in the streets, they encountered the vendors of the new forms of cheap literature, who bawled and sang their wares to passers-by.[19] The broadsides and song sheets, which were the transitional forms between the traditional chapbooks and ballads and the later newspapers and cheap periodicals and novels, were sold as they were bought, as vehicles more for performance than for private perusal.[20] The arrival of popular journalism only added to the clamour. 'The penny newspapers, "Daily Telegraph", "Daily News", "Globe", sir?", "Standard, sir?" assail our ears at every hour in all our leading thoroughfares,' wrote an observer of London in the mid-1870s.[21] Every city had its own cries, although contemporary Berlin was held to be quieter than most on account of strict by-laws against street-sellers.[22] The newspapers might be read quietly at home, but the tendency for interest in their contents constantly to outstrip the ability to buy them caused a further extension of the time-honoured means of consumption.

In workplaces where machinery had yet to drown the human voice, artisans took turns to read aloud the contents of a collectively purchased paper. The practice began as political journalism escaped the confines of polite society during the revolutionary crises of the late eighteenth century,[23] and continued until the arrival of cheap mass-circulation daily papers in the years before the First World War. [. . .] Where conditions of labour discouraged such behaviour during the working day, public consumption of the press became a feature of sociability in the evenings, as for instance, in the case of the cafés of Provence: 'A centre-piece of many such gatherings was the reading aloud by one of their number of the newspaper to which the patron or perhaps a prominent (and slightly wealthier) member of the society subscribed. Such readings were often lengthy affairs, whole articles being read out with care, often accompanied by a commentary from the reader, his audience or both.'[24]

The long history of translating the written word into forms which could be used by those without the skills, money or time to read it themselves severely qualified the meaning of the columns of marks and signatures. The simple bifurcation of the literacy tables was not replicated in the realm of cultural practice. Preachers, street-sellers, workplace and fireside readers engaged the illiterate in the world of print.[25] The towns became texts as shop-fronts and vacant walls were covered in increasingly elaborate signs, posters and advertisements.[26] 'At seven I had so far profited by her teaching,' wrote the Coventry ribbon weaver Joseph Gutteridge of his dame school teacher, 'as to be able to make out the contents of the local papers, and I derived much pleasure and knowledge from their perusal. Another means of learning that I made use of was the sign board literature of public-houses and shops.'[27] This material combined print with visual images in ways which drew into the world of codified language the barely literate or those yet to be educated. The various forms of cheap literature themselves made every concession to those who would fail the tests of the schoolmasters. The texts of the chapbooks, broadsides and early cheap novels deployed formulaic repetition or memorizable verses which spoke to the conventions of oral transmission.[28] They were adorned with illustrations ranging from the crude woodcuts on the covers of the wares of the chapmen and colporteurs to the elaborate lithographs on the pages of the newspapers and periodical fiction of the later nineteenth century, which provided points of entry for those unable to cope with the accompanying lines of print, and clues or confirmation for those still uncertain of their abilities. It may indeed be argued that the hybrid forms of popular print provided not only an incentive to learn the alphabet, but far more effective primers for the barely literate than the specialized textbooks which the professional pedagogues were producing for the official elementary schools.[29]

The category of the oral tradition was a means of discriminating between different sectors of the population living in the same chronological moment but belonging to separate eras of development. Those believed to rely exclusively on the spoken word were separated from the literate not just by their specific communication practices but also by the way in which they thought, or rather failed to think. Groups of the European population, particularly those labouring on the land, who still comprised the majority of the total workforce as the mass literacy campaigns commenced, were consigned to the timeless, ancient cultures, in contrast to the temporally conscious, progressive world of readers and writers. The distinction between tradition and modernity was central to how the educated understood their historical identity, and to the way in which they justified the continuing exclusion of the uneducated from political power and economic privilege. The contrast was captured in the catch-all concept of superstition, the joint enemy of the church and the Enlightenment.[30] The term came from without rather than within the language of the uneducated. It referred most frequently to beliefs in magic, but in various contexts embraced a wide range of customary practices which conflicted with the precise and purposeful calendars of contemporary economic and social relations. There was a continuum of outlook and behaviour which stretched from the employment of witches and wisemen to casual drunkenness and violence.[31] Superstition was constituted and preserved by oral transmission and associated ritual forms, and could be attacked most effectively by schoolteachers and the capacity for rational thought and behaviour they instilled in their pupils.

At the heart of the concept was a judgement of what was real. Superstitious beliefs embodied a false sense of time, a false view of the supernatural, and a false estimation of the limits of human agency. As Eugen Weber has written, 'superstition was the religion of others: other credulousness about beliefs we do not share'.[32] Yet as contemporaries were often embarrassed to discover, both the printed word and the agencies which promoted it were deeply implicated in this irrational universe. The church and state educators were motivated by a concern not just with total ignorance but also with the wrong kinds of attempts to instruct the young. The problem was encapsulated by the record left by a Prussian pupil of an unofficial school taught by a working man: 'Once a year, on Shrove Tuesday, it was the custom for the teacher to whip all of his pupils with a fresh birch stick, the local belief being that such beatings had the effect of preventing the farm animals from contracting worms.'[33] This tendency for indigenous instructors to entrench rather than erode traditional belief systems justified the investment in training and inspection, but it remained extremely difficult to control the use made of even the most innocent of books. Everywhere, writing and the written word was interpreted as a physical power.[34] If there was a single core text upon which the European elementary school system was founded it was the anthology of psalms which provided the first and frequently only sustained reading matter for pupils in every denomination and language. However, as a study of the Moscow provinces discovered, 'There are certain superstitions surrounding the psalter, namely that he who reads it from cover to cover forty times is absolved of certain sins, and that it serves as a means of divining, particularly in those cases where the perpetrator of a theft of property is to be found.'[35]

Although such maltreatment of the word of God may have persisted longer in what were held to be the more backward nineteenth-century countries, there was no sense in which the interdependence of magic and print was confined to the European periphery.[36] Joseph Lawson evoked the dense structure of oral and literary authority for the beliefs which permeated his native Yorkshire village in the 1820s:

> Such was the superstition at the time of which we speak, that the whole atmosphere was supposed to be full of good and bad spirits, on errands of mercy or of mischief; the latter mission always preponderating – the evil spirits mostly prevailing over the good. Let us imagine ourselves in Pudsey as it was sixty, or even fifty years ago, on a dark and stormy winter's night, sitting by some fireside, with or without the dim light of a dangle; a few neighbours – men, women, and children – sitting together. The children both dread and like to hear what are called 'boggard tales.' They ask the older people to tell them some tales they have heard before, or a new one. . . . At this time all those who deny the existence of boggards are called infidels and atheists. The Bible even is referred to as a proof of the truth of witchcraft; also the great John Wesley's Journal.[37]

[. . .]

If the notion of an oral tradition tells us more about the prejudices of the educated than the practices of the uneducated, the question remains of how to categorize change in the application of reading and writing during the coming of mass literacy. The written word may have thrust its roots deep into the soil of peasant cultures, and the spoken may have been entwined with the printed as the graphs of signatures rose in the nineteenth century, but transformations did take place in what was read and how it was consumed. A more complex model has to be deployed, which can encompass both the continuing exchange between the two modes of communication, and the diverse layers of meanings and material conditions involved in the rapid increase in the use of literacy. This can be best achieved by identifying a series of transitions which occurred in this period, few of them beginning from nothing, and few if any completed by the time the bulk of the European populations had gained a nominal ability to engage with the world of print. At the heart of the movement was movement itself. Literacy was a means of making connection with other ideas and know-ledge over space and time. Its application altered the user's relationship with the immediate and local discourses sustained by oral modes of communication. Reading and writing pro-moted motionless mobility. The association between education and physical migration was not only inconsistent but also of limited significance. The key journeys were made in the mind. Alexander Somerville, a young farm-worker growing up in the Lammermuir Hills, made his first great journeys without leaving the fields in which he laboured:

> The next book which came in my way, and made an impression so strong as to be still unworn and unwearable, was *Anson's Voyage Round the World*. *Gospel Sonnets*, *Burns' Poems*, old ballads and self-made doggerel, everything gave way to admit the new knowledge of the earth's geography, and the charms of human adventure which I found in those voyages. I had read nothing of the kind before, and knew nothing of foreign countries . . .[38]

He was able to use the fragments of schooling he had received to take his fellow labourers with him on his travels. After a morning's work, he recalled:

> I remained in the fields, and lay on the grass under the shadow of the trees and read about the *Centurion*, and all that befel her. When the afternoon work began, I related to the other workers what I had read; and even the grieve began to take an interest in the story. And this interest increased in him and in every one else until they all brought their dinners afield, so that they might remain under the shadow of the trees and hear me read. In the evenings at home I continued the reading, and next day at work put them in possession of the events which I knew in advance of them.[39]

The nature of change was dramatized by the growth in correspondence. As we have seen, what Chartier properly describes as 'an ordinary kind of writing',[40] had grown rapidly during the course of the nineteenth century. Benjamin Shaw's early attempts at epistolary courtship were increasingly supplemented by mass-produced Valentines, which by the middle of the century were second only to Christmas cards in Britain as a seasonal peak in the annual postal flows.[41] The governments which reformed their postal systems from 1840 onwards were driven by the desire to democratize the practice by making it cheaper and more accessible, and by the intention of transforming the relationship between communica-tion and space. The flat-rate, pre-paid systems were designed to make the state a single cultural entity, and with the formation of the Universal Postal Union in 1875, this ambition was given an international dimension. The first article of the organization stated that there should exist a 'single postal territory',[42] which even at the outset covered 37,000,000 square kilometres and 350,000,000 inhabitants. The concept of a global village was born and given institutional substance almost a century before the phrase was coined. The Universal Postal Union was conceived as both a physical and a moral achievement. It displayed the rationality and power of states in that they could organize complex, large-scale flows of mail within and across their frontiers, and at the same time the ever more elaborate and extensive webs of written exchange would bind together dispersed family members, hostile classes and competing nations into a single, harmonious whole. As the network of contacts became ever more dense, so mutual understanding and dependency would grow, and the ignorance and self-interest which underlay all domestic and international conflict would decline. The UPU was seen by its founders as 'an intimate association of the civilized countries of four parts of the world, upon one of the most important fields of action of the intercourse of nations'.[43] If the more utopian rhetoric was checked by the outbreak of the First World War at a time when the flow of correspondence between and beyond the states of Europe had reached 5,000,000 items a day, the basic features of the organization survived to become the model for the series of international bodies which established after 1918 and again after 1945.[44]

The central issue of movement was highlighted by the close association between the postal and railway networks. Mass correspondence was facilitated by the revolution in physical communication. Britain introduced the first flat-rate postal charges immediately after it had laid down the first mainline railway system in Europe. The speed and security of this new mode of transport encouraged the postal reformers in their ambitions, and in turn the ever-increasing volume of mailbags supplied the fledgling railway companies with an important source of revenue. The uniformed employees of the two services systematically penetrated the remotest corners of their countries, linking the capital to the provinces, the countryside to the towns. The scale of the interdependence is confirmed by the statistics which the communication bureaucracies began to produce. [. . .] [T]here was a close affinity between railway travel and correspondence.[45] Across the nations of Europe, the hierarchy in the per capita usage of the two systems was almost identical, as was the proportional relationship between them. In both modes of communication, the key was use rather than possession. It was not the length of the national rail networks which mattered, but the number of passenger kilometres travelled, just as it was the application rather than the distribution of literacy. Furthermore the relationship was dynamic over time, with both modes of communication expanding at the same speed, country by country, as the era of mass literacy took shape between 1890 and 1913.

Of all the statistical measures of progress which might be connected to the spread of reading and writing, the association between trains and correspondence was the closest. Taking postal flows in 1890 as the standard factor, the correlation with primary school pupils was 0.44, with literacy 0.61, with gross national product 0.93, and with railway passengers 0.94. The near-perfect fit reflected a common enterprise. The figures suggest that the history of mass communication in Europe may have had its own internal dynamic, connected to other material and cultural factors but never reducible to them. By no means every letter was carried by train. The rapidly improving road systems were pressed into service, particularly in countries like France, where broad areas of evenly populated countryside had to be connected to the railway stations; and where geography so dictated, the letters travelled by water, most notably in Norway, where half the mails were carried by boat in 1890.[46] But the *voies ferrées*, as the UPU's tables described them, symbolized, more than any other mode of transport, the speed, the punctuality and the defeat of distance which the postal networks embodied. Contemporaries were convinced that the machinery of communication would do more to encourage the acquisition of literacy and to magnify its consequences than all the exhortations of clerics and politicians.[47] Whilst most children still travelled to school on their feet, the structure of funding and inspection in which their education was now embedded was dependent on regular employment of both correspondence and trains.[48] The interactions between the transfer of people and of information were complex, but both were working to loosen the bonds which tied the mass of the population to the physical and mental surroundings into which they had been born.

References

1   B. Shaw, *The Family Records of Benjamin Shaw Mechanic of Dent, Dolphinholme and Preston, 1772–1841*, ed. A. G. Crosby (Stroud, 1991), pp. 27–8. Shaw was a mill mechanic. He was compelled to marry his sweetheart the following year when she became pregnant.

2   H. Miller, *My Schools and Schoolmasters; or, The Story of my Education* (1854, 13th edn, London, 1869), p. 287.

3   D. Alston, 'The Fallen Meteor: Hugh Miller and Local Tradition', and D. Vincent, 'Miller's Improvement: A Classic Tale of Self-advancement?', in M. Shortland (ed.), *Hugh Miller and the Controversies of Victorian Science* (Oxford, 1996), pp. 206–39.

4   P. Burke, *Popular Culture in Early Modern Europe* (London, 1978), pp. 3–22.

5   On the ambiguities of Scott's work as a collector see, D. Vincent, 'The Decline of the Oral Tradition in Popular Culture', in R. D. Storch (ed.), *Popular Culture and Custom in Nineteenth-Century England* (London, 1982), pp. 20–47.

6   C. A. Macartney, *The Habsburg Empire 1790–1918* (London, 1969), p. 223.

7   See, for instance, R. M. Dorson, *The British Folklorists* (London, 1968); N. Z. Davis, 'The Historian and Popular Culture', in J. Beauroy, M. Bertrand and E. T. Gargan (eds), *The Wolf and the Lamb: Popular Culture in France from the Old Regime to the Twentieth Century* (Saratoga, Calif., 1977).

8   E. Weber, *Peasants into Frenchmen* (London, 1977), p. 471; R. D. Anderson, *Education in France* (Oxford, 1975), p. 148.

9   M. A. Marrus, 'Folklore as an Ethnographic Source: A "Mise au Point" ', in Beauroy, Bertrand and Gargan, *The Wolf and the Lamb* pp. 110–22; J. Boyarin, 'Introduction', in J. Boyarin (ed.), *The Ethnography of Reading* (Berkeley and Los Angeles, 1993), pp. 1–8.

10   E. Johansson, 'Literacy Campaigns in Sweden', *Interchange*, 19, 3/4 (Fall/Winter 1988), p. 94.

11   R. F. Tomasson, 'The Literacy of Icelanders', *Scandinavian Studies*, 57 (1975), p. 69.

12   D. Vincent, 'Reading in the Working Class Home', in J. K. Walton and J. Walvin (eds), *Leisure in Britain, 1780–1939* (Manchester, 1983), pp. 210–11.

13   A. L. Lloyd, *Folk Song in England* (London, 1975), p. 20; R. S. Thompson, 'The Development of the Broadside Ballad Trade and its Influence upon the Transmission of English Folksongs', PhD thesis, Cambridge University, 1974, p. 215.

14   D. O Hogáin, 'Folklore and Literature 1700–1850', in W. Daly and D. Dickenson, *The Origins of Popular Literacy in Ireland: Language, Change and Educational Development, 1700–1920* (Dublin, 1990), p. 2.

15   I. G. Tóth, *Mivelhogy magad írást nem tudsz* (Budapest, 1996), pp. 320–1.

16   J. S. Allen, *In the Public Eye: A History of Reading in Modern France, 1800–1940* (Princeton, 1991), p. 5; J. Brooks, *When Russia Learned to Read* (Princeton, 1985), p. 27; R. Chartier, 'Texts, Printing, Readings', in L. Hunt (ed.), *The New Cultural History* (Berkeley, 1989), p. 153.

17   R. Darnton, 'First Steps toward a History of Reading', *Australian Journal of French Studies*, 23, 1 (1986), p. 14; C. Heywood, *Childhood in Nineteenth-Century France* (Cambridge, 1988), pp. 75–80.

18   Tomasson, 'The Literacy of Icelanders', pp. 71–2.

19   On the street-sellers, see, [H. Mayhew], *London Labour and the London Poor* (London, 1861), vol. I, pp. 234, 297; D. Roche, *The People of Paris* (Leamington Spa, 1987), p. 221.

20   J. R. R. Adams, *The Printed Word and the Common Man* (Belfast, 1987), pp. 34, 121.

21   C. Knight, *London* (London, 1875–7), vol. I, p. 144. Also A. J. Lee, *The Origins of the Popular Press in England 1855–1914* (London, 1976), p. 35.

22   H. Vizetelly, *Berlin under the New Empire* (London, 1879), vol. I, p. 26.

23   I. Markussen, 'The Development of Writing Ability in the Nordic Countries of the Eighteenth and Nineteenth Centuries', *Journal of Scandinavian History*, 15, 1 (1990), p. 50; Roche, *The People of Paris*, p. 220.

24   T. Judt, 'The Impact of the Schools, Provence 1871–1914', in H. J. Graff (ed.), *Literacy and*

Social Development in the West (Cambridge, 1981), p. 267. See also, E. Berenson, *Populist Religion and Left-Wing Politics in France, 1830–1852* (Princeton, 1984), pp. 169–75.

25   R. Chartier, *The Order of Books* (Cambridge, 1994), p. 19.

26   See for instance the impact of the Russian streets in Brooks, *When Russia Learned to Read*, p. 12. On English posters and advertisements see the early contemporary study, [J. D. Burn], *The Language of the Walls* (Manchester, 1855), p. 3.

27   J. Gutteridge, *Lights and Shadows in the Life of an Artisan* (Coventry, 1893), republished in *Master and Artisan in Victorian England*, ed. and intro, V. E. Chancellor (London, 1969), p. 85.

28   Adams, *The Printed Word and the Common Man*, pp. 43–8.

29   D. Vincent, 'Reading Made Strange', in I. Grosvenor et al. (eds), *Silences and Images* (New York, 1999), pp. 181–97.

30   D. Hall, 'Introduction', and R. Chartier, 'Culture as Appropriation: Popular Cultural Uses in Early Modern France', in S. L. Kaplan (ed.), *Understanding Popular Culture: Europe from the Middle Ages to the Nineteenth Century* (Berlin, 1984), pp. 9, 230; J. Devlin, *The Superstitious Mind: French Peasants and the Supernatural in the Nineteenth Century* (New Haven, 1987), p. 218.

31   Anderson, *Education in France*, p. 170.

32   E. Weber, 'Religion and Superstition in Nineteenth-Century France', *Historical Journal*, 31 (June 1988), p. 399.

33   Memoir of J. T. Petzet, a pupil between 1806 and 1812, cited in K. A. Schleunes, *Schooling and Society* (Oxford, 1989), p. 84.

34   B. Holbek, 'What the Illiterate Think of Writing', in K. Schousboe, and M. Trolle Larsen (eds), *Literacy and Society* (Copenhagen, 1989), p. 192.

35   B. Eklof, *Russian Peasant Schools* (Berkeley, 1986), p. 274; Devlin, *The Superstitious Mind*, pp. 37–8.

36   See, for instance, the study of nineteenth-century rural England in M. Pickering, 'The Four Angels of the Earth: Popular Cosmology in a Victorian Village', *Southern Folklore Quarterly*, 45 (1981), pp. 7–12.

37   J. Lawson, *Letters to the Young on Progress in Pudsey during the Last Sixty Years* (Stanningley, 1887), pp. 68–9.

38   A. Somerville, *The Autobiography of a Working Man* (1848; London, 1951), p. 45. Anson's book was first published in 1748.

39   Somerville, *The Autobiography of a Working Man*, p. 47.

40   R. Chartier, 'Introduction: An Ordinary Kind of Writing', in R. Chartier, A. Boureau, and C. Dauphin, *Correspondence: Models of Letter-Writing from the Middle Ages to the Nineteenth Century* (Cambridge, 1997).

41   F. Staff, *'The Valentine' and its Origins* (London, 1969), pp. 25–38; W. H. Cremer, *St. Valentine's Day and Valentines* (London, 1971), pp. 10–13.

42   This phrase appeared at the head of all revisions of the original treaty. See, for instance, Universal Postal Union, *Convention of Paris, as modified by the Additional Act of Lisbon* (London, 1885), p. 1; *Convention of Vienna* (London, 1891), p. 1; *Convention of Washington* (London, 1898), p. 1.

43   *Union Postale*, vol. 1, no. 1 (October, 1875), p. 15.

44   The role of postal co-operation in the development of international co-operation is explored in E. Luard, *International Agencies: The Emerging Framework of Interdependence* (London, 1977), pp. 11–26.

45   Railway data from B. R. Mitchell, *European Historical Statistics* (Cambridge, 1971), pp. 629–40.

46   Union Postale Universelle, *Statistique générale du service postal, année 1890* (Berne, 1892), p. 6.

47   Anderson, *Education in France*, p. 169.

48   R. Thabault, *Education and Change in a Village Community* (London, 1971), pp. 133–5.

Chapter 16

Carl F. Kaestle

STUDYING THE HISTORY OF LITERACY

LITERACY RATES IN COLONIAL BRITISH AMERICA were quite high, and America's rise to nearly universal white literacy was earlier than Europe's. But many of the same research questions are relevant: how to interpret signature rates, whether literacy should be associated with progress, whether there have been declines as well as increases in the history of literacy, how literacy functions as both cause and consequence of social change, and how literacy was related to schooling.

Samuel Eliot Morison noted in the 1930s that American literacy measured by signature counting was high compared to Europe, and that a particularly large percentage of New England immigrants could sign their names.[1] Kenneth Lockridge later made a more extensive study of signatures and marks on more than three thousand New England wills from 1640 to 1800. He confirmed that British America had high signature literacy by European standards and that the rate in New England was higher than in the South and the Middle Atlantic. Still, Lockridge found signature literacy to be lower in seventeenth-century New England than Morison had claimed. Beginning at about 60 percent in 1650 and rising slowly to 70 percent by about 1710, male signature literacy took off in the eighteenth century. By the time the Founding Fathers signed the Constitution, 90 percent of white males who signed documents were signing their names. Female signature literacy paralleled male rates in the seventeenth century, rising slowly from 30 percent in 1650 to 40 percent around 1710, but then tapered off, remaining below 50 percent through the late eighteenth century—"stagnant," to use Lockridge's phrase.[2]

Lockridge argued that Protestantism, and particularly the Puritan version of Calvinism, was the driving force behind New England literacy, that the expansion of literacy was accomplished chiefly through schools, and that its purpose was conservative. Although Calvinism may have "paved the way to modernity," it was intensely traditional in the seventeenth century.[3] Their religious concerns prompted New England Puritans to demand that their towns provide schools, but sparse population during the seventeenth century made the laws difficult to enforce. In the 1700s, however, these laws worked to advance literacy as population became more concentrated, argued Lockridge. His view departed from three other recent interpretations. He contended that the reliance upon schooling was not a result of family breakdown in the face of the wilderness environment, as Bernard Bailyn had argued; that literacy in the eighteenth century was not "liberating," as Lawrence Cremin had argued; and that it was not associated with modern attitudes, as Alex Inkeles and David Smith and other modernization theorists had argued.[4]

As for the first challenge, Bailyn's disruption hypothesis was more subtle than Lockridge allowed. Bailyn was not writing as a simple environmentalist when it came to the transfer of culture in the seventeenth century. Customary English life was disrupted in the New World not only by wild land, sparse population, physical hardship, and contact with native Americans, but also by selective migration, the shift to Puritan religious dominance in New England, new governing arrangements, and the separation from European institutions. The stresses of this situation, coupled with the Puritans' concern about religious decline, produced a public focus on schooling in colonial New England. This focus was reinforced, as Cremin pointed out, by the colonists' traditional reliance on schools, a custom they brought with them from England. Nonetheless, schooling did not have a dramatic effect on expanding literacy in seventeenth-century New England. Although Cremin and Bailyn correctly emphasized the important educational roles of the family, the church, and the workplace, they both acknowledged a growing role for schools as the colonial period progressed. Whatever roles an expanding press and a resurgent evangelical Protestantism may have played in the second half of the eighteenth century, the expansion of literacy also coincided with the establishment of more district schools, closer to people's homes.

As for Cremin's interpretation that eighteenth-century literacy was "liberating" rather than conservative, this reflects his optimistic general conviction that "on balance, the American educational system had contributed significantly to the advancement of liberty, equality and fraternity."[5] There is, of course, evidence on both sides of the issue, which has animated historical debate about American education over the last fifteen years. The enduring contribution of Lockridge's New England study is its warning against an automatic equation of literacy with a liberating modernity. His emphasis on the conservative function of Puritan literacy may be exaggerated, but it serves as a useful reminder that literacy can serve many purposes, sometimes traditional and constraining, sometimes innovative and liberating.

Like their counterparts in England, American historians have tested generalizations with local studies. Alan Tully discovered a nearly constant level of male signature literacy for Chester County (around 72 percent) and Lancaster County (around 63 percent) in southeastern Pennsylvania during the eighteenth century, and he concluded that there had been no educational revolution or expansion of "liberating" literacy in that rural setting.[6] Ross Beales, testing Lockridge's generalizations on rural Grafton, Massachusetts, in the midst of the 1748 religious revival, found levels slightly higher (98 percent males, 46 percent females) than Lockridge's figures would have led one to predict. Beales did not find any relationship between literacy and conversion among women.[7] Attempting to reconcile these contrasting findings, we may speculate that rudimentary literacy rates in eighteenth-century America were lower in some places than Cremin's interpretation would suggest and higher, particularly for women, than in Lockridge's samples. Moreover, the salient influence of revival religion or political ferment cannot be predicted when one focuses on the local level. In any case, one should not expect uniformity.

On the issue of female literacy, however, evidence is mounting to suggest that the eighteenth and early nineteenth centuries were important years of increased rudimentary literacy. Suspicions that some women who could not write could nonetheless read seem well-founded; furthermore, some fragmentary local evidence shows a more dynamic increase in women's signature ability in the eighteenth century than Lockridge found. Tully found a sharp eighteenth-century rise in female signature literacy in his small Pennsylvania samples, and Linda Auwers charted increasing female signature writing in Windsor, an old Connecticut town, from 21 percent in the 1660s birth cohort to 94 percent in the 1740s birth cohort.[8]

Auwers's late-seventeenth-century data for female signing ability correlated not with wealth but with parental literacy and parental church membership; in contrast, the eighteenth-century literacy data correlated with wealth but not with church membership, leading Auwers to remark that Windsor may have been enacting a cultural shift from "Puritan" to "Yankee." Windsor, Auwers admitted, was at the high-literacy end of the spectrum, but it foreshadowed more general eighteenth-century developments. A family's proximity to a school also increased the chances of a daughter's acquiring literacy in Windsor, providing support for Lockridge's emphasis on schools. Literacy was associated with schools, and both were associated with capitalism. William Gilmore, studying more than ten thousand signatures and marks on various documents for a Vermont county from 1760 to 1830, found almost universal male signature literacy throughout the countryside. Female rates, however, ranged from 60 percent to 90 percent, varying with the level of commercial involvement of the community.[9]

Not all literacy was acquired in schools. Gerald Moran and Maris Vinovskis recently redirected attention back to the family, arguing that the changing gender dynamics of instruction within the family generated pressure for more female education in the eighteenth century. In the late seventeenth century, they reasoned, church membership shifted strongly toward females. Thus, the catechizing role within the family fell increasingly to women, who were at a relative disadvantage in terms of literacy. The resolution of this tension was a rhetorical emphasis on pious, educated women in early-eighteenth-century New England and increased female access to schools by the late eighteenth century.[10]

By 1850 the rudimentary literacy rates of white men and women, self-reported to U.S. Census marshals, were nearly equal.[11] The biggest gaps in literacy rates were between native whites, foreign-born whites, and nonwhites, but regional, income, and rural-urban disparities also persisted. Lee Soltow and Edward Stevens, who made the most thorough investigation of these nineteenth-century developments, considered first whether male literacy was "nearly universal" by 1800. Some studies of signatures that report such high rates admit that a significant portion of the population never signed documents, like deeds or wills, and thus perhaps as much as one-fifth of the population is not included in the sample.[12] Soltow and Stevens studied petitions and army enlistment lists and concluded that male literacy as high as 25 percent was common in the early years of the Republic. They also showed that the inability to sign remained widespread among certain groups of white males. Throughout the period 1800 to 1840, 30 percent of merchant seamen could not sign their enlistment papers. Signature illiteracy in the enlistment rolls of the U.S. Army, at 42 percent in 1800 and 35 percent in the 1840s, declined to 25 percent in the 1850s, to 17 percent in the 1870s, and to 7 percent in the 1880s.[13]

In 1840 the U.S. Bureau of the Census added a question on literacy to its survey form. Given the problems inherent in interpreting signature rates, this might be expected to have greatly improved the validity of the available evidence on literacy. Unfortunately, however, the census marshals never administered any literacy test, so the data represent only the self-reported literacy and illiteracy of household residents. Furthermore, the questions differed from decade to decade; over time the census changed the age group questioned, changed the wording of questions on reading and writing, and, finally, added a question on foreign-language literacy. At worst, census illiteracy statistics measure nothing more than people's willingness to admit illiteracy; at best, they indicate a minimal estimate of illiteracy.

Soltow and Stevens analyzed the aggregate rates in this census data and, through samples of individual family schedules, investigated the correlation of literacy with other factors. In general, they concluded that nation building, economic development, and population density all favored the provision of schools and fostered the development of an "ideology of literacy." Literacy rates correlated most strongly with school enrollment rates, with average family wealth in one area, and with the population density of a community. Not surprisingly, high literacy rates were biased toward the North and toward urban areas, but by 1870 the common-school movement, the circulation of print matter, and improved transportation had reduced these biases.[14]

Nonetheless, social-class biases persisted. Like David Cressy's work on seventeenth-century England, Harvey Graff's work on three Ontario cities in 1861 emphasized that social status was highly correlated with literacy, that is, the higher one's social status, the more likely one was to be literate. This is not to suggest the converse, that increased literacy brought improved social status. In fact, Graff concluded that literacy did not affect income and occupational status as much as did ethnicity and family conditions. Although these results were not very surprising, it is useful to be reminded that illiteracy is more a symptom than a cause of disadvantage. The opposite and fallacious view, according to Graff, is what he called the "literacy myth," the belief that literacy by itself improved the careers of nineteenth-century urban dwellers. However, only 10 percent or less of the population were labeled illiterate in his three Ontario cities; he could draw no conclusions about the relative reading abilities of the great majority of people or about the impact literacy had on their lives. Graff's position placed him squarely in the revisionist camp of educational historians but went beyond what can be proved by the census's crude literacy variable.[15]

Although Soltow and Stevens's work is the most detailed study of U.S. Census literacy information for the nineteenth century, the most convenient discussion of the trends in aggregate rates over a longer period is the brief book by John Folger and Charles Nam. According to their analysis, white illiteracy in the census, male and female combined, declined from 10.7 percent in 1850 to 6.2 percent in 1900. Whereas only 4.6 percent of native-born whites admitted illiteracy in 1900, 12.9 percent of foreign-born whites did. Among nonwhites the reported illiteracy rate in 1900 was 44.5 percent.[16] At the turn of the century, concern about illiteracy was focused on black Americans and, to a lesser degree, upon recent European immigrants. The big story in nineteenth-century American literacy is the development of common-school systems and the near elimination of self-reported outright illiteracy among native-born whites.

[. . .]

The early twentieth century witnessed rapid urbanization, black migration northward, pressure for immigration restriction, and a resurgence of racist social theories. Given the white-black and native-foreign gaps in rudimentary literacy, therefore, it is not surprising that census monographs reflected anxieties about illiteracy among black people and European immigrants. Actually, immigrant illiteracy was concentrated among the century's first arrivals and declined rapidly after the restriction of immigration in 1921; black illiteracy decreased dramatically in the late nineteenth and early twentieth centuries, an impressive trend in light of the discrimination, hostility, poor resources, and meager job incentives for black Americans. Higher-order literacy skills are a different matter, of course, and these are not indicated in the census data. Even at the level of rudimentary literacy, gaps remained between native and foreign born, white and nonwhite, North and South, urban and rural, but overall, the twentieth century has been an era of declining illiteracy and convergence of literacy rates across social groups. Today, although the percentage of outright illiterates is small, the absolute number of illiterates remains great. In 1979, only .6 percent of all persons fourteen years of age and older reported that they were illiterate, but this equaled nearly one million people.

As the reported rudimentary illiteracy rates declined among all groups, commentators and analysts turned their attention to higher-order skills. The term "functional literacy" gained popularity in the 1930s. Initially it was applied simply to a level of schooling deemed sufficient to ensure a person's ability to read most everyday print matter, usually the fourth or fifth grade. Later the term came to be associated with performance on actual tests of practical reading tasks encountered outside of schools.

[. . .]

From a long-range perspective one sees not decline but a great expansion of literacy skills in America during the twentieth century, evidenced by increasing educational attainment and increased circulation of print matter. The slight declines of recent years pale by comparison.[17] The problems of today's illiterates, the dearth of writing activity in the schools, the absence of critical reading skills in the workplace, and the negative effect of the electronic media on reading activities are all matters of legitimate concern. They should not lead us to invent a golden age of literacy in some earlier decade.

[. . .]

I return now to the four broad background questions posed in the beginning of the chapter, in the light of the trends, correlations, and interpretations surveyed in the literature review. On the vexed question of whether literacy is a sign of progress and an unquestionable benefit to its possessors, a cautious, critical viewpoint is warranted. The benefits of literacy should be analyzed in specific historical circumstances for various historical actors. Modernization theorists generally argue that literacy is necessarily correlated with modernization and that modernization is a Good Thing. Although literacy has indeed generally proceeded along with other indicators of development used by modernization theorists, literacy also can be used for culturally intolerant or politically repressive purposes.

The uses of literacy are various. As a technology, it gives its possessors potential power; as a stock of cultural knowledge within a given tradition, literacy can constrain or liberate, instruct or entertain, discipline or disaffect people. Princeton historian Lawrence Stone once remarked that if you teach a man to read the Bible, he may also read pornography or seditious literature; put another way, if a man teaches a woman to read so that she may know her place, she may learn that she deserves his. These are the Janus faces of literacy. Although for purposes of public policy, increased literacy is assumed to benefit both individuals and the society as a whole, the association of literacy with progress has been challenged under certain circumstances. Paolo Freire has questioned whether literacy is a good thing for oppressed people if the content and conduct of literacy training are not under their control.[18] From a variety of political viewpoints, American and British culture critics of the 1950s questioned whether mass culture, including popular reading materials, was debilitating to its consumers. Furthermore, throughout history the distribution and maintenance of differential literacy skills have been associated with class, race, ethnicity, and gender. Given these considerations, the answer to the first question—whether literacy is synonymous with progress—must be: It depends upon who is judging, whose literacy is at issue, and whose benefit is being considered.

The answer to the second question—whether literacy is always expanding—is: Usually, but not always. In general, the history of literacy is characterized by expansion, both in the number of people who are literate and in the quality of their literacy skills. But history also provides some examples of declining literacy: in ancient Greece, in medieval Europe, in early industrial towns, possibly among American blacks subjected to harsh slave codes before the Civil War, and allegedly among American schoolchildren in the 1970s. [. . .]

In spite of these examples of decline, the expansion of literacy rates has been the norm since the invention of writing. Historians have found it more difficult to explain the surges and plateaus in this history than to chart them. Our third background issue addressed this difficult causal question: What conditions have fostered the expansion of literacy? The causes of literacy are generally inferred from correlations, and despite much local variation, some correlations persist. Higher literacy rates have generally been associated with people of higher social status, males, Protestants, industrializing regions, and dense population. These generalizations stand up fairly well for the modern West. The correlation of literacy with higher social status, a persistent theme, is hardly surprising, although the correlation can be stronger at some times than at others. The relationship between literacy and industrialization has occasioned heated debate, which can be resolved as follows: Defined as a longterm process in a region or nation, industrialization has been associated with rising literacy; in the short term, at the local level, the onset of factory production often inhibited literacy training—and thus reduced literacy rates—because of child labor and immigration patterns. Among specific urban communities, rising literacy has been more clearly correlated with commerce than with industry. Although it is difficult to disentangle religion from other factors, earlier rises in literacy also correlated with Protestantism. Male rates of estimated rudimentary literacy were consistently higher than those of women until the twentieth century, if we accept signature signing as a proxy for reading ability. However, as we have seen, there is reason to be skeptical about the illiteracy of some who marked with an *X*. Finally, in spite of interesting short-run exceptions, rising literacy has been associated with the expansion of schooling. The most durable patterns in rudimentary literacy, then, are the least surprising.

One of the "causes" of higher literacy rates, in a sense, is higher literacy rates. For example, as more people become literate, the amount of fiction circulating commercially will increase and newspapers will become cheaper; in a society where more reading material is available, there is more motivation for people to learn to read and to use their skills. If schools turn out more highly literate people, this will, in turn, affect the job structure, which can affect the future demands placed on schools. Thus one of the effects of literacy at the societal level is that it fosters more literacy.

But what do we know about the concrete effects of literacy on the lives of individuals? There is only scant empirical evidence on the subject. Educators often have associated literacy with economic advancement, but historians have done little to probe the connection. A few works on industrialization in nineteenth-century America touch upon the subject. Alexander Field argued that skill requirements declined rather than increased during the initial shift to factory labor in the United States, so there would have been little real advantage to the educated industrial laborer sometimes hailed by manufacturers.[19] Stephan Thernstrom documented the importance of child labor in the family economies of Newburyport shoe laborers and concluded that sending children to school would have been counterproductive for workers' families.[20] Thomas Dublin found that literacy correlated with higher wages among Lowell's female textile workers, but not when controlling for ethnicity; he thus concluded that literacy was incidental to higher status in the mills.[21] Harvey Graff, relying on census data, also found that literacy had little weight in overcoming the ethnic bias of the social structure in Ontario cities.[22] Maris Vinovskis, taking as his point of departure Horace Mann's claim that education contributed to greater industrial productivity, pointed out that Mann's evidence was biased, his motives political, and his estimates of the value of education greatly exaggerated.[23] Nonetheless, as Vinovskis has recently reminded us, education was not without economic benefit in nineteenth-century America.[24] It was, however, more valuable to some groups than others. Sketchy evidence suggests that early high schools assisted middling-status white males (sons of both lower white-collar workers and skilled craftsmen) in maintaining or improving intergenerational status.[25] For women, education became an entrée to teaching, and by the late nineteenth century female students predominated in America's public high schools.

The available evidence on the issue of the returns to education may be summarized as follows. First, education paid off better for those in the middle reaches of society than it did for laborers. Second, there was a greater return for education in the twentieth century than in the nineteenth; skill levels were upgraded, education expanded, the clerical and service sectors burgeoned, and a tighter fit developed between an individual's level of schooling and later occupational fate. Third, the benefits to literacy for members of oppressed groups were often more apparent collectively than individually, and in the long run rather than the short run. The Irish shoe worker of 1840 was probably correct in thinking that there would be little benefit in a high-school education for his son, but Irish people as a group have benefited from increased education in the long run. Similarly, expanded education for blacks may have gained them little access to status in white society in the 1890s, but in the long run, education has helped to narrow racial inequalities. The same argument can be made for the history of women. What is implied, of course, is a history of frustration and bitterness for individuals who face a discriminatory world but who recognize the necessity of acquiring literacy, and then higher education, as resources in confronting economic and occupational inequality.

Literacy is discriminatory with regard to both access and content. Problems of discrimination are not resolved just because access is achieved; there is a cultural price tag to literacy. Thus, whether literacy is liberating or constraining depends in part on whether it is used as an instrument of conformity or of creativity. [. . .]

On the fourth background question—the relationship of literacy to schooling—expanding literacy persistently correlates with expanding schooling. This suggests a causal relation, but the history of efforts by outsiders to acquire literacy suggests the relevance of family and group values. For example, white women in America closed the gap in rudimentary literacy between the mid-eighteenth and mid-nineteenth centuries. In a complicated set of realignments, women became more important in organized religion and in the education of children, both at home and in school; they therefore pressed for and received more access to formal schooling themselves. The relative contributions of schooling and of the family are impossible to estimate; increased female literacy resulted from the combined effects of enhanced educational opportunity and higher literacy expectations for girls in the home. The same combination was at work in narrowing the huge literacy gap between white and black Americans. In the 1870 census, shortly after emancipation, 81 percent of black Americans reported themselves to be utterly illiterate, compared with 11 percent of whites. Twenty years later, the black rate was down to 57 percent, compared with 8 percent of whites. Booker T. Washington once described freed slaves as an entire nation wanting to go to school, and they did so, their efforts sustained by family values that were nurtured during the antebellum slavery years, when literacy became associated with power and freedom. Today, the rudimentary literacy rates for all American racial and ethnic groups are very high, above 98 percent, but at higher skill levels gaps persist; both the family and the school remain relevant. The most recent and most thorough study of literacy abilities, the Young Adult Literacy Assessment of the National Assessment of Educational Progress, provided rich background information on gaps in functional literacy among racial, ethnic, and income groups. It reinforced the notion that schools cannot do the job alone. Reading abilities correlated with a wide variety of family factors—not just race, income, and parents' educational level, but also the number of publications that enter the home and how often children read them.[26] Although the policy implications of these findings are problematic, there are ways in which the government can affect the literacy potential of families. This has become one of the themes in the recent campaign against low literacy skills in the United States [. . .]

Our review of the literature revealed a healthy dialogue in which national studies and even larger syntheses have aimed to discover general tendencies over long periods of time, and in which local studies have tested the generalizations, suggesting refinements and new variables, and integrating the story of literacy into the texture of local culture. It takes a certain maturity in a historical subfield to make possible such large-scale syntheses of research as Graff's *Legacies of Literacy* and Houston's *Literacy in Early Modern Europe*. But to suggest new directions and answer new questions we also need studies focused on single communities or more specific topics, studies that address such questions as educational opportunity and the uses of literacy among adults. As more historians become skeptical of the literate-illiterate dichotomy and of the equation of signing ability or census responses with actual reading ability, we will see more studies that deal centrally with the acquisition and uses of literacy and only incidentally with literacy rates. As we move from literacy rates to the uses of literacy, the history of literacy becomes the history of readers. [. . .]

References

1   Samuel E. Morison, *The Intellectual Life of Colonial New England* (Ithaca: Cornell University Press, 1956), 82–85, originally published as *The Puritan Pronaos* (1936).
2   Kenneth A. Lockridge, *Literacy in Colonial New England; an enquiry into the social context of literacy in the early modern west* (New York: Norton, 1974), 38.
3   Ibid., 45.
4   Bernard Bailyn, *Education in the forming of American Society* (Chapel Hill: University of North Carolina Press, 1960), Lawrence A. Cremin, *American Education: the colonial experience, 1607–1783* (New York: Harper & Row, 1970), Alex Inkeles and David H. Smith, *Becoming Modern: individual change in six developing countries* (London: Heinemann Education, 1974).
5   Lawrence A. Cremin, *Traditions of American Education* (New York: Basic Books, 1977), 127.
6   Alan Tully, "Literacy Levels and Education Development in Rural Pennsylvania, 1729–1775," *Pennsylvania History* 39 (1972):302–12.
7   Ross W. Beales, Jr., "Studying Literacy at the Community Level: A Research Note," *Journal of Interdisciplinary History* 9 (1978):93–102.
8   Tully, "Literacy Levels and Education Development;" Linda Auwers, "Reading the Marks of the Past: Exploring Female Literacy in Colonial Windsor, Connecticut," *Historical Methods* 13 (1980):204–14.
9   William J. Gilmore, "Elementary Literacy on the Eve of the Industrial Revolution: Trends in rural New England, 1760–1830", *Proceedings of the American Antiquarian Society*, 92 (1982): 81–178.
10   Gerald F. Moran and Maris A. Vinovskis, "The Great Care of Godly Parents: Early Childhood in Puritan New England," in *History and Research in Child Development*, Serial no. 211, vol. 50, ed. Alice Boardman Smuts and John W. Hagen (Chicago: University of Chicago Monographs of the Society for Research in Child Development, 1986), 24–37. See also E. Jennifer Monaghan, "Literacy Instruction and Gender in Colonial New England," in *Reading in America: Literature and social history*, ed. Cathy N. Davidson (Baltimore: Johns Hopkins University Press, 1989), 53–80.
11   Maris A. Vinovskis and Richard Bernard, "Beyond Catharine Beecher: Female Education in the Antebellum Period," *Signs* 3 (1978):856–69.
12   Gilmore, "Elementary Literacy on the Eve of the Industrial Revolution," 157.
13   Lee Soltow and Edward Stevens, *The Rise of Literacy and the Common School in the United States: a socio-economic analysis to 1870* (Chicago: University of Chicago Press, 1981), 50–52.
14   Ibid., 22–23, 53, 56, 159–60.
15   Harvey J. Graff, *The Literacy Myth: literacy and social structure in the nineteenth-century city* (New York: Academic Press, 1979), ch. 2.
16   John K. Folger and Charles B. Nam, *Education of the American Population* (Washington, D.C.: Government Printing Office, 1967), 113–14.
17   John R. Bormuth, "The Value and Volume of Literacy," *Visible Language* 12 (1978):118–61; Martin Trow, "The Democratization of Higher Education in America," *Archives européennes de sociologie* 3 (1962):231–62; and Trow, "The Second Transformation of American Secondary Education," *International Journal of Comparative Sociology* 2 (1961):144–66.
18   Paolo Friere, *Pedagogy of the Oppressed*, trans. Myra Bergman Ramos (New York: Herder and Herder, 1971), chap. 1.

19   Alexander Field, "Industrialization and Skill Intensity: The Case of Massachusetts," *Journal of Human Resources* 15 (1980):149–75.

20   Stephan Thernstrom, *Poverty and Progress: social mobility in a nineteenth-century city* (Cambridge, MA: Harvard University Press, 1964), 154–57; but see Joel Perlmann, "Working Class Home-owning and Children's Schooling in Providence, R.I., 1880–1925," *History of Education Quarterly* 23 (Summer 1983):175–93.

21   Thomas Dublin, *Women at Work: the transformation of work and community in Lowell, Massachusetts, 1826–1860* (New York: Columbia University Press, 1979), 149–51.

22   Graff, *Literacy Myth*, 190–91.

23   Maris A. Vinovskis, "Horace Mann on the Economic Productivity of Education," *New England Quarterly* 43 (1970): 550–71.

24   Maris A. Vinovskis, "Quantification and the History of Education: Observations on Antebellum Education Expansion, School Attendance and Educational Reform," *Journal of Interdisciplinary History* 14 (1983):856–69.

25   Carl F. Kaestle, *Pillars of the Republic: common schools and American society, 1780–1860* (New York: Hill and Wang, 1983), 121.

26   Irwin S. Kirsch and Ann Jungeblut, *Literacy: profiles of America's young adults: final report* (Princeton, N.J.: National Assessment of Educational Progress, Educational Testing Service, 1986), chap. 7.

Chapter 17

Richard Hoggart

SUMMARY OF PRESENT TENDENCIES IN MASS CULTURE

THE RESILIENCE TO BE FOUND in individuals and local groups is healthy and important. But it can clearly be another form of democratic self-indulgence to over-stress this resilience, to brush aside any suggestion of increasingly dangerous pressures by a reference to the innate right-headedness of man; to point out that people do still persist in living lives by no means as rootless and shallow as the new influences seem to invite, and from that to assume that this will always be so, that 'human nature will always save itself', that 'you can trust in ordinary decency', to save people from the worst effects, that the resilience of human nature will ensure that 'people will always be people'.

It remains to sum up the general lines on which a mass culture seems to be at present developing. As throughout, I shall draw most of the illustrations from publications. But with suitable modifications of detail the conclusions would apply also to the tendencies encouraged by the cinema, sound broadcasting and television (particularly when these are commercially sponsored), and large-scale advertising.

There has been, particularly during the last few decades, a great increase in the consumption of many kinds of material designed to entertain; there has been an absolute increase, not simply one proportionate to the increase in population. Something of this was inevitable, as the technical capacity to provide entertainment on a large scale and as the money available to the majority of people for its purchase both increased.[1] An increase is not in itself necessarily to be deplored; there was room for one. But to some extent the size of the increase appears to have been decided, not so much by the need to satisfy previously unsatisfied appetites, as by the stronger persuasions of those who provide the entertainment.

Thus, within the last hundred years the total number of publications of all types in Great Britain has risen from perhaps one thousand to over five thousand.[2] Undoubtedly, a considerable increase was inevitable during a century in which a large nation became literate and highly industrialised. But the major part of this increase is due to a comparatively recent growth in the number of magazines and periodicals. Or, to take changes over a recent decade: the total circulation of national and provincial dailies increased by one-half between

1937 and 1947.[3] During the same period the total circulation of Sunday newspapers almost doubled itself. Magazines and periodicals had a circulation of about twenty-six millions in 1938, and probably more than forty millions in 1952.[4] Between 1947 and 1952 the total circulation of national morning papers rose by half a million, and that of Sunday papers by nearly two and a half million.[5] Daily newspapers are produced now at a rate of two copies for every household in the country.[6] From the Hulton Survey for 1953 it appears that two out of three in the adult population read more than one Sunday newspaper, and more than one out of four read three or more Sunday papers. The estimated number of copies of daily newspapers issued per one thousand of the population is higher in the United Kingdom than in any other country in the world.[7]

There have been concurrent increases in what I have been calling serious reading, just as there have been increases in the audiences for some more serious pursuits generally. Book production in the United Kingdom is higher than in any other country.[8] A large number are works of fiction, but there has been a substantial increase during recent years in titles of technical and educational books. And we all know of the success since the 1930s of the Penguin and Pelican series. There has been a very great increase in the number of books issued from public libraries, especially during the past twenty-five years.[9] During a Gallup Poll in 1950, 55 per cent of those interviewed said they were currently reading a book; this proportion was higher than that found in, for instance, the U.S.A. or Sweden.[10] There have been increases in the sales of several of the decent periodicals.[11]

These details of more solid reading are encouraging, but need to be qualified. What proportions of the issues from public libraries are of worthless fiction or of that kind of non-fiction which is really only a sort of fiction with the added pleasure of a 'true-life story'? A statistical answer cannot be given, since the question involves distinctions of value. The Derby Survey suggests that fiction of one sort or another accounts for between 75 and 80 per cent of public library issues; and most librarians would say, I think, that much of this fiction is of a very poor kind.[12] There is no virtue in the habit of reading for itself; however unexceptionable its subjects and presentation may be, it can become as much an addiction, as separated from the reality of life, as the reading of some of the more occasional literature I have described earlier. The commercial libraries probably issue between 150 and 200 million volumes per year. Of those issued by the two largest libraries, probably about 90 per cent are fiction; of those issued by the 2d. to 4d. libraries, probably almost 100 per cent are fiction.[13] In the public libraries the issues of the class 'history, biography, travel' from the biggest single non-fiction group, probably accounting now for a quarter to one-third of all non-fiction issues. Again, many librarians would say, I believe, that the books included in that general heading are often of little value. Qualifications of this kind could be raised for a long time. I raise them not to reduce the value of the genuine gains in serious reading, but to make sure that the gains are not assumed to be much greater than they are.

The situation seems to be that a small proportion of keen readers are taking good advantage of their opportunities and that their number is being somewhat increased, but that the great body of people is not only unaffected by such changes, but is affected by quite different tendencies. There seems little likelihood of substantial increases in serious reader-ship, partly because serious reading and popular reading tend to attract different kinds of people (a point to which I shall return), and partly because the great block of popular readers is subject to a different kind of pressure than are the serious readers. There are many movements towards increasing and improving the minority; there are much larger and on the whole more successful movements towards strengthening the hold of a few dominant popular publications on the great majority of people.

*   *   *

I have probably sufficiently shown in earlier chapters that for the really popular publications there must be a constant struggle to expand, to seek very big sales. Thus, it seems as though from year to year the minimum economic circulation of a national newspaper becomes higher, as though each success pushes up the minimum for everyone else. As long ago as 1946 Francis Williams thought it likely that:

> To exist, a modern national paper in Britain must secure a circulation of at the very least close upon a million and a half and preferably one of over two millions (which means that it must regularly be of a kind to appeal to between five and a quarter million and seven million people).[14]

One result of this process appears to have been an increasing centralisation or concentration in popular reading, proceeding at the same time as the considerable increase in the actual reading of popular papers. In short, we seem to be reading fewer different papers, but yet to be reading a greater number; to be reading more often, that is, the same papers as each other. Although the circulation of the daily Press has much increased, the total number of newspapers published in this country has declined during the last thirty years.[15] In most forms of popular publication today a very small number of organs is acquiring very large sales indeed; there is usually a sharp drop thereafter to the circulations of all other organs in that form. In a typical instance, the number of publications in this lower group will be greater than that in the higher group; yet the total sales of the upper few will be greater than those of all in the lower group combined. Thus, in one case two publications have more than half of all sales in their field and six or eight others share the rest. So far as can be seen, this process has not yet exhausted itself; a few organs are progressively acquiring a larger proportion than ever before of the total readers in their fields. This process makes the increases in some 'quality' publications seem hardly relevant to the much bigger problem of increased consumption and increased centralisation of a few huge popular publications.[16] It is occasionally announced, and always seems slightly disingenuous, that a 'quality' publication has increased its circulation by, say, 15 per cent in a year and that no popular publication can show an increase of more than 3 or 4 per cent. But, of course, with a circulation as large as that of the more famous popular journals there is not much room for large percentage increases. The combined increases made by the two best examples of one type of 'quality' publication in a recent year—though they were considerable when expressed as a percentage—amounted to only one-third of the increased sales recorded in the same period by a single popular publication in the same field. The case is typical; the advance by the 'quality' journals is useful, but does not offset the increasing concentration on the mass popular journals.

Indeed, the special difficulties in maintaining circulation are not so much those of the 'quality' papers as those of the popular papers which try to preserve more sober standards in reporting, comment and layout. The General Council of the Press makes this point, but introduces it by placing the onus of responsibility on 'the public'; here, as elsewhere, the General Council of the Press seems readier to indicate the responsibility of readers for the present quantitative and qualitative changes in the Press than to analyse the nature of Press responsibility:

> As an indication of the trend of public taste in a free and highly competitive market, it is significant that for every additional copy gained by the Daily Telegraph during the past year the tabloid newspapers added three. Furthermore, the increased sales of the tabloids were almost exactly counterbalanced by the combined losses of the Daily Mail, Daily Herald and News Chronicle—the Daily Express having remained steady.[17]

As the possibilities of further large expansions in their existing publications become more limited, it is inevitable that the mass-publishing organisations should turn to other publications. The appearance of Junior Editions of some popular dailies in 1954 was a logical next step in the process, though this particular experiment seems to have failed. Presumably it was hoped that they would provide not only a new field for expansion but one in which readers could be cultivated for eventual transference to the versions for adults.

In spite of the increases in the sales of some more serious publications, there appear to be indications that the greater concentration in popular publications makes existence harder for smaller-circulation papers, unless they have a firm audience willing to pay well for them, or are subsidised. The two most recently founded cultural journals, *Encounter* and *London Magazine*, have some financial backing, the latter from the *Daily Mirror* organisation. I suggested above that concentration pushes up the economic minimum at which a paper can be produced. Thus there may be financial problems even though the actual circulation of the paper has not fallen. The death of *John O' London's Weekly* in 1954, when there was said to have been no significant loss in readership, may well be a case in point.

A considerable absolute increase in the amount of material produced, an increasing concentration in the organs supplying the material, consequent greater difficulties for minorities: these seem the main features in the organisational development of popular entertainments and publications. What, in equally brief summary, are likely to be their effects?

The readers of the more popular papers are clearly not only working-class people, though working-class people are likely to form a majority, if only because they are a majority of the total population. No doubt these journals realise that the biggest single group to which they can address themselves is that comprising the three-quarters of the population who today leave school finally at the age of fifteen. In this connection it may be useful to say something more about a matter I hinted at earlier—that is, about one possible effect of the scholarship system. The relation between the intellectual minority in the working classes and those classes as a whole is an immensely complicated subject which I can discuss only tentatively. It is obviously important not to confuse the intellectual minority with the 'earnest' minority: a sense of social purpose does not necessarily accompany the possession of brains. Nor do all those who enjoy advanced education leave their class emotionally or physically. Nevertheless, the intellectual minority, with particular effect during the latter part of the nineteenth century, used to stay within the working classes more than it does today. Its members formed some of the fermenting elements in their groups, and were an important part of that 'working-class movement' which, as I have already noted, help to bring about considerable improvements in the material lot and status of all working-class people. They were able to help to improve conditions partly because they were among the few who were able to meet and engage the managers in other classes with their own weapons, those of the intellect.

Today many of them are selected at the age of eleven and are often translated, by a process of education, into membership of other classes. At present, roughly one in five of the children of all classes go to grammar schools.[18] The home background of some lower middle-class or middle-class children may make it easier for them to win scholarships; and a few working-class children can still not take up scholarships, or they leave the grammar schools early, because of financial pressure.[19] But I was the poorest boy in my class and went to the grammar school along with the next poorest boy and a few others; grants are higher today, working-class people are in general better off, and education is still valued by many working-class people. It therefore seems a large exaggeration to say of 'the best working-class lads', as the Vice-Principal of Ruskin College said recently, 'The majority are still driven by economic pressure to add to the family income as soon as possible.'[20] Of those who go to the grammar schools, not all leave their class, but a substantial proportion do.

The examination at eleven-plus may be in many things clumsy, but it does with a fair measure of success select intellectually agile children. Is it not therefore likely to cause the working classes now to lose many of the critical tentacles which they would have retained years ago? It hardly helps to conclude that this proves only that we must stop speaking or thinking in terms of 'classes', that now each does the work he is best fitted for, and the clever son of poor parents takes up his position in that part of a democratic society where he can be of most value. Few people are likely to regret that clever children in the working classes now have a greater chance of obtaining posts appropriate to their abilities. But even if the title 'working classes' is not used, there exists a great body of people who have to perform the less interesting, the more mechanical jobs. It is a matter of some importance that they are likely to include a smaller proportion of the critically minded than they have hitherto included. For this is happening at a time when many who seek the money and favour of working people approach them constantly along the lines to which they are most receptive and exposed, with material whose effect is likely to be debilitating. By the interaction of these two important factors in contemporary life we might eventually find ourselves moving towards a kind of new caste system, one at least as firm as the old.[21]

I suggested earlier that it would be a mistake to regard the cultural struggle now going on as a straight fight between, say, what *The Times* and the picture-dailies respectively represent. To wish that a majority of the population will ever read *The Times* is to wish that human beings were constitutionally different, and is to fall into an intellectual snobbery. The ability to read the decent weeklies is not a *sine qua non* of the good life. It seems unlikely at any time, and is certainly not likely in any period which those of us now alive are likely to know, that a majority in any class will have strongly intellectual pursuits. There are other ways of being in the truth. The strongest objection to the more trivial popular entertainments is not that they prevent their readers from becoming highbrow, but that they make it harder for people without an intellectual bent to become wise in their own way.

The fact that changes in English society over the last fifty years have greatly increased the opportunities for further education available to the few people who will seek it has, therefore, little direct compensatory bearing on the fact that concurrent changes are bringing about an increased trivialisation in productions for the majority. Most readers of a popular modern newspaper/magazine are unlikely ever to read a 'quality' paper, but they used to read an old-style weekly which was in some respects better than their newspaper/magazine. The new-style popular publications fail not because they are poor substitutes for *The Times* but because they are only bloodless imitations of what they purport to be, because they are pallid but slicked-up extensions even of nineteenth-century sensationalism, and a considerable decline from the sinewy sensationalism of Elizabethan vernacular writers. They can be accused (as can all else for which they stand as examples: the thin *bonhomie* of many television programmes, the popular film, much in commercial radio), not of failing to be highbrow, but of not being truly concrete and personal. The quality of life, the kind of response, the rootedness in a wisdom and maturity which a popular and non-highbrow art can possess may be as valuable in their own ways as those of a highbrow art. These productions do not contribute to a sounder popular art but discourage it. They make their audience less likely to arrive at a wisdom derived from an inner, felt discrimination in their sense of people and their attitude to experience. It is easier to kill the old roots than to replace them with anything comparable. Popular publicists always tell their audience that they need not be ashamed of not being highbrow, that they have their own kinds of maturity. This is true, but it becomes false the moment such people say it, because of the way they say it; that is, because their manner of approach seriously distorts the assumption.

Every tendency I have analysed in popular publications is to be found in some forms of broadcasting—especially in those with commercial connections—and in some ways more strikingly than in publications. There is the appeal to old decencies, as in programmes with titles like, 'For Your Feeling Heart'; there are the new emphases, the stress on the acquisitive and the novel—'For Your Feeling Heart—in this programme You may Make Your Pile'. There is the high-powered modern combination of these two, in programmes where intimate personal problems are exposed before an immense audience and the person afflicted 'wins' some money for his participation. There is the lowbrow gang-spirit of some gramophone-record features in which young men, accompanying their items with a stream of pally patter, offer programmes whose whole composition assumes that whatever the greatest number like most is best and the rest are the aberrations of 'eggheads'. Always the apologists for these programmes make the usual defence—that they are 'in good taste—homely—full of the pathos and joy of ordinary lives'; and that they are also, 'new—arresting—startling—sensational—full of gusto—and handsomely endowed with prizes'.

Most mass-entertainments are in the end what D. H. Lawrence described as 'anti-life'. They are full of a corrupt brightness, of improper appeals and moral evasions. To recall instances: they tend towards a view of the world in which progress is conceived as a seeking of material possessions, equality as a moral levelling and freedom as the ground for endless irresponsible pleasure. These productions belong to a vicarious spectators' world; they offer nothing which can really grip the brain or heart. They assist a gradual drying-up of the more positive, the fuller, the more cooperative kinds of enjoyment, in which one gains much by giving much. They have intolerable pretensions; and pander to the wish to have things both ways, to do as we want and accept no consequences. A handful of such productions reaches daily the great majority of the population: their effect is both widespread and uniform.

They tend towards uniformity rather than towards anonymity. I have suggested that working people are not so much visited by a feeling of anonymity as might appear to those who observe them from outside. Nor do I think that working people have yet a strong *sense* of uniformity: they are nevertheless being presented continually with encouragements towards an unconscious uniformity. This has not yet been found hollow by most people because it is expressed most commonly as an invitation to share in a kind of palliness, even though in a huge and centralised palliness. Most people will respond to such an appeal the more readily because it seems to have much in common with some older working-class attitudes. The result is a high degree of passive acceptance, an acceptance often only apparent and often qualified at present, but which is a ground for more dangerous extensions. From this point of view it sometimes appears that the type of emerging common man will be one who tends, by three simple gestures, a highly complicated machine, and who keeps in a centrally-heated locker a copy of the latest mass-produced sex-and-violence novel—*Some Dames Don't Strip Easy*, to coin a characteristic title—for reading in those parts of the allotted intervals when he is not listening to a radio 'gang' show.

The fact that illiteracy as it is normally measured has been largely removed only points towards the next and probably more difficult problem. A new word is needed to describe the nature of the response invited by the popular material I have discussed, a word indicating a social change which takes advantage of and thrives on basic literacy. All this needs to be considered with special urgency today because it is in continuous and increasingly rapid development. The analysis of changes in some popular publications during the last thirty or forty years should have illustrated the dubious quality of the life such things promote, their greatly increased powers of dissemination and the accelerated speed of their development. The arrival of television is only the latest goad to popular publications; there is not likely to be any halt if matters are left to take their normal commercial course.[22]

[. . .]

I have continually stressed the way in which newer forces are adapting and modifying elements in what was a fairly distinctive working-class culture. No doubt something similar could be demonstrated in the culture of other classes, if only because the newer productions appeal to more than working-class people. This throws further light on the claim to an emerging classlessness which I questioned at the very beginning of this essay. We may now see that in at least one sense we are indeed becoming classless—that is, the great majority of us are being merged into one class. We are becoming culturally classless. The newer women's magazines are in this sense 'classless' whereas the older kind belonged to particular social groups. Mass publications cannot reach an audience of the size they need except by cutting across class boundaries. No doubt many of them have a special warmth for the 'little folk'— the working- and lower middle-classes. This is not because they belong to their audience in the way that older working-class publications often did, nor simply because their producers subscribe to one of the more flattering democratic assumptions, but because that audience forms the majority of their potential readers, because, though they would like to attract many others, they must have this group as the basis of their sales.

From one point of view the old social-class distinction still has some force. It is possible to say that the new mass audience is roughly formed of the total of twenty million or so adults who read the most popular daily newspapers: and then to point out that nevertheless these papers are in some things different, that they can loosely be called either working class or lower middle to middle class. Though this may be true it serves only to underline the general trend. Before the war one could reasonably speak of six or eight popular papers as though they were all more or less level in their effectiveness. If the present trend continues, we shall soon be able to speak only of two or three. Concentration has gone a long way but has had to pause at the rough boundaries of the present most important division in social class, that between the working classes and the middle classes. But from reading these papers it is plain that their differences are largely superficial, that they are chiefly differences of tone and 'properties'. Indisputably, these differences are important to the readers; as to the wider effects which the papers will have, the differences are less important than the similarities, than the fact that the kinds of culture which each paper embodies, the assumptions and appeals, are largely the same. The emerging classless class is likely to be a compound of these two audiences; at present it is held in a separation which is becoming less meaningful from year to year.[23] Many factors are helping to make it less significant. To those already discussed another may be added, a further instance of a possible interplay between material improvement and cultural loss: that it is probably easier to merge working-class people into a larger, culturally characterless class when they no longer have such strong economic pressure as makes them feel the great importance of loyal membership of their known groups. No doubt many of the old barriers of class should be broken down. But at present the older, the more narrow but also more genuine class culture is being eroded in favour of the mass opinion, the mass recreational product and the generalised emotional response. The world of club-singing is being gradually replaced by that of typical radio dance-music and crooning, television cabaret and commercial-radio variety. The uniform national type which the popular papers help to produce is writ even larger in the uniform international type which the film-studios of Hollywood present. The old forms of class culture are in danger of being replaced by a poorer kind of classless, or by what I was led earlier to describe as a 'faceless', culture, and this is to be regretted.

[. . .]

It seems best to end on a note that has occurred throughout, on the peculiarly inner and individual nature of this crisis. This is illustrated most briefly in the recurrent observation that working-class people, though they are being in a sense exploited today, at least have now to be approached for their consent. The force of environment and the powers of persuasion count for a great deal but are not irresistible, and there are many instances of the power of free action. Working people may in much give their consent easily, but that is often because they think themselves assenting to certain key-ideas which they have traditionally known as the informing ideas for social and spiritual improvement. These ideas have a moral origin, and that part of them is still not altogether dead. Democratic egalitarianism has one source in the assumption that all are of equal worth in a much more valuable sense; overweening freedom owes much to the idea that we must try to be responsible for our own fate and decisions; the apparent valuelessness of the permanent open mind rests in part on a refusal to be fanatic, to let the heart ('the feeling heart') become 'enchanted to a stone'. The choice today should therefore be clearer than it was before: it begins from a somewhat freer ground, one less cluttered with material hindrances.

So much is profoundly encouraging. And it may be that a concentration of false lights is unavoidable at this stage of development in a democracy which from year to year becomes more technologically competent and centralised, and yet seeks to remain a free and 'open' society. Yet the problem is acute and pressing—how that freedom may be kept as in any sense a meaningful thing whilst the processes of centralisation and technological development continue. This is a particularly intricate challenge because, even if substantial inner freedom were lost, the great new classless class would be unlikely to know it: its members would still regard themselves as free and be told that they were free.

References

NB: The Derby Survey. This term has been used, in both the text and the notes, to refer to T. Cauter and J.S. Downham, *The Communication of Ideas, a Study of Contemporary Influences on Urban Life* (Chatto and Windus for The Readers' Digest Association, 1954). The Derby Survey divides the population in this way: upper-class 3%; middle-class 25%; working-class 72%.

1   Increase in entertainments: *The cinema*; in this country in 1952 the average number of attendances over the whole population was twenty-seven, which was higher than the U.S.A. average. Expenditure on the cinema in 1952 was nearly 3s per week for every family in the country. There are approximately 4,600 cinemas in Great Britain. The group going most frequently to the cinema is that composed of working-class people aged 16–24 (see Derby Survey, pp. 121–3).

2   Thousand to five thousand publications: Derby Survey, p. 164.

3   Increases between 1937 and 1947:
     Nat. and prov. dailies: 17,800,000 to 28,503,000.
     Sunday newspapers: 15,500,000 to 29,300,000.
     Figures from *Report of the Royal Commission on the Press, 1947–9*, (Cmd. 7700, HMSO, 1949), pp. 5–6 (by permission). A part of these increases might be explained by conditions peculiar to the war-period. But the war has now been over for more than ten years, and total readership has not begun to drop significantly.

4   Magazines and periodicals between 1938 and 1952: P.E.P. *Planning*, xxi, (Balance Sheet of the Press), 384.

5   Increases between 1947 and 1952:
     Nat. morning papers: 15,600,000 to 16,100,000.
     Sunday papers rose to 31,700,000 in 1952.
     Derby Survey, Table 51, p. 168. The authors comment (p. 163),
       'Even when allowance is made for rising prices, we bought more reading material in 1952 than in 1948 (when expenditure was almost exactly double that of ten years earlier)'. It seems as though, in general, the 1937–47 rate of increase did not continue between 1947 and

1955. But, again in general, the new high levels of 1947 were maintained (see P.E.P. *Planning*, xxi (Ownership of the Press), 388).

6   Two daily newspapers per household: Derby Survey, p. 166. Two out of three adults read more than one Sunday newspaper: quoted in Derby Survey, p. 170.

7   Number of daily newspapers per 1,000 people:
Estimated number of copies of daily newspapers per 1000 in the population:

U.K. 611	France 239	Mexico 48
Sweden 490	Italy 107	Turkey 32
U.S.A. 353	Argentina 100	

See UNESCO, *The Daily Press, A Survey of the World Situation in 1952*, No. 7 of Reports and Papers on Mass Communication (HMSO, 1953).

8   Book production in U.K.: During 1953, more than 18,000 titles were issued here as compared with about 12,000 titles for the U.S.A. which has a population three times as large. One should add that we have a large export trade in books, and that not all the titles listed in any year are of new books. Thus, of the titles issued during 1953, roughly 12,750 were of new books (the U.S.A. had 9,000 new books). One in five of the new books published in England was a work of fiction. Figures from the Derby Survey, pp. 182–3, and UNESCO, *Basic Facts and Figures* (HMSO, 1952).

9   Increase in public library issues: During 1952–3 seven books were issued per head of the population as compared with five in 1939. The Derby Survey suggests that, in Derby, 1 person in 6 from the working classes and those with elementary education, and 1 person in 4 from the middle classes and those with secondary and further education, borrow one book a week from the public library (Derby Survey, pp. 165 and 198). As to the buying of books, including the paper-backed series, it is probable that between 125 and 190 million separate volumes are sold in each year (Derby Survey, p. 185).

10   55 per cent reading a book: Quoted in Derby Survey, p. 184. In that survey (p. 190), one-third of those interviewed said they were currently reading a book. A Mass Observation survey in Tottenham, for the British Institute of Public Opinion, gave roughly the same result as the Gallup Poll quoted above.

11   Sales of 'quality' periodicals: In most cases the increase has not been continuous. There was, rather, an increase for a few years after the war and then a slight drop or a steadying. But over pre-war or immediate post-war figures the circulations of most 'quality' periodicals show an increase (see A.P. Wadsworth, *Newspaper Circulations, 1800–1954* (Manchester Statistical Society, 1955)).

The following A.B.C. figures are from the *Newspaper Press Directory* (Benn Brothers, 1955):

Observer	534,752	Sunday Times	577,869
Times	220,834	(audited, not A.B.C.)	
New Statesman	70,598	Spectator	38,353

As examples of recent increases: the *Manchester Guardian* showed 127,083 for 1953, and 146,146 for 1955. The *Listener* has roughly doubled its sales since the war. The *Observer*'s A.B.C. figure for the period January to June 1956 was 601,402.

Literary Reviews:
Encounter had a circulation in mid-1954 of about 15,000, and *London Magazine*, which was started at almost the same time, one of about 18,000 (*Observer*, 18 July 1954). By mid-1956 the circulation of each magazine had dropped considerably, and it was announced that *London Maga-zine* was likely to lose its financial backing.

12   75 to 80 per cent fiction: Derby Survey, pp. 186–7.
13   Commercial library figures: Derby Survey, p. 185.

'a small proportion of keen readers . . .': The Derby Survey lends some support to this view, and speaks more than once of 'a substantial minority of keen book readers'. Were one to omit the number of those whose reading is almost entirely lightweight, one would be left, I think, simply with 'a minority'.

14   Francis Williams, *Press, Parliament and People* (Heinemann, 1946), p. 175.

15   Decline in the total number of newspapers:

We have	122 daily papers for				51 million population		
U.S.A.	1,865	"	"	"	157	"	"
Sweden	160	"	"	"	7	"	"
Switzerland	127	"	"	"	5	"	"
Mexico	162	"	"	"	27	"	"
Argentina	140	"	"	"	18	"	"
Turkey	116	"	"	"	22	"	"
France	151	"	"	"	42½	"	"
Italy	107	"	"	"	47	"	"

(Figures from *The Daily Press*, UNESCO.)

The total number of different newspapers now published here is in most cases proportionately, and in many cases absolutely smaller than that of other literate nations. Syndication will reduce the force of some of the disparities, but not enough to invalidate the general point. A decline in the total number of different newspapers is not, of course, peculiar to the United Kingdom: in the U.S.A. the total dropped by about one-third between 1909 and 1954.

16   Centralization of reading: The centralization on to national, as distinct from regional, papers has taken place most markedly in the morning and Sunday papers. In the evening papers, the provincial press still keeps much of its strength. Most people will have noticed that one result of the present trend is a deterioration in some provincial papers. With syndicated material they try to ape the brightness of Fleet Street, and interlard with that their unconvincing local references. Such papers have the vices of the popular London Press with a drabness wholly their own. Details of centralization may be found in the *Report of the Royal Commission on the Press*, Jacques Kayser's *One Week's News* UNESCO (HMSO, 1953), and Wadsworth's *Newspaper Circulations*.

17   General Council of the Press, *The Press and the People*, (1st Annual Report, 1954), pp. 12–13. The report adds that serious newspapers still represent only about 3 per cent of total Sunday sales.

18   Attendance at secondary grammar schools: See *The Organization of Secondary Education*, W. P. Alexander (Councils and Education Press Ltd), and *Secondary Education Survey*, Joan Thompson, Fabian Research Series (Gollancz, 1952).

19   Scholarships for working-class children: 'In summary, despite the educational and social changes of recent years, the chances of attendance at a grammar-school increase with social level.' From 'Selection for Secondary Education and Achievement in Four Grammar Schools', A. H. Halsey and L. Gardner, *British Journal of Sociology*, vol. IV, No. 1, March 1953, pp. 60–75 (see also *Early Leaving*).

20   Letter to the *Observer*, 6 June 1954.

21   A new caste system: After writing this I was interested to see a somewhat similar point put forward by Prof. Glass in the introduction to *Social Mobility in Britain* (Routledge, 1954), pp. 25–7. He notes that he is there expressing personal views which 'have a value basis'.

22   The popular Press and the arrival of TV: 'Increasing competition from radio and television is affecting the character of the press' (*The Press and the People*, p. 9). Thinking of the popularity of cinema, sound radio, television, and comic strips, one sometimes feels like hazarding the speculation that by the end of the twentieth century the impact of the written word on the majority of the population will be seen to have been a short and almost negligible interlude: that by then the largely oral and local culture dominant until the latter half of the nineteenth century will have been replaced by one that is again oral, but is also visual and massively public.

23   The new classless class: Presumably the large central groups the publicists have in view is roughly what *HRS* calls groups D–E sometimes with C added. Groups D–E account for 71 per cent of the population; with C added, for 88 per cent.

SECTION 4

Reading the masses

INTRODUCTION

IN A GIVEN SOCIETY, the reading public includes those people with the ability to read and/or access reading material. The following extracts capture particular historical moments in a selection of nations when the reading public began to expand beyond the very wealthy, selectively educated or ruling classes to more ordinary people, in part because of a widening distribution of the literary skills, especially the skill of reading, and also as a result of the development of new technologies in printing and accompanying falling costs in production. As a growing number of readers from a variety of social backgrounds joined the reading public, and as authors and publishers attempted to provide for this large and diverse body, mass readerships emerged. To identify the common interests, tastes, habits and values of mass readerships, historians have most often turned to the evidence provided by the actual publications, from production and distribution patterns to textual and paratextual features. These were most often the readers who left no trace behind, though, as the final extract by Martin Lyons and Lucy Taksa demonstrates, where histories of audiences are possible, evidence of reading responses adds valuable texture to existing knowledge of mass readerships.

We begin, however, with Kevin Sharpe's account of reading in post-Reformation England and Anne McLaren's study of the expansion of print in Late-Ming China. In both cases, authors and publishers, although eager to take advantage of expanding markets, expressed concern about the range of unintended responses that could be generated by their texts. Sharpe explains how certain physical attributes of books were developed in order to construct and control the interpretive community of readers. Similarly, in mid-sixteenth century China, while vernacular narratives replaced the classics as reading matter for the 'unlearned', these books contained important commentaries to direct the reader to the moral purpose of the story.

But these Chinese publications still had to appeal to a large number of readers to satisfy publishers' hunger for profits. Thus the readers' desires and abilities had to be taken into account in the production of the books. Illustrations were incorporated to assist those who could not read, the texts were designed to be read aloud, and verses which could be sung or memorised helped to situate these publications within a vibrant oral culture. We find a similar pattern in eighteenth-century England (St. Clair), and in nineteenth-century Bengal (Ghosh) and Russia (Brooks). Readers were, to some extent, the makers of these texts. The great importance of the reader in the production process is perhaps most evident in the case of Russia, where the authors had firm roots in the body of people they were writing for. As they selected folktales for reproduction in the Lubki or even used their own daily experiences to construct stories, we can trace a direct reflection of the world view of their readers.

The extent to which mass readerships were able to exert some influence over their reading material is also evident in the failure of official attempts by the state, churches and social or political pressure groups to control this reading public. The exciting and sometimes crude or even subversive subject matter often presented in the publications for the masses raised concern among the elite. William St. Clair, Anindita Ghosh and Jeffrey Brooks point to the people's rejection of various types of reading material designed to convert and improve readers. In particular, in England, at the turn of the nineteenth century, evangelist Hannah More attempted to seduce common readers by publishing moral tracts which imitated and were distributed along the same lines as those she wished to destroy.

However, even though readers unequivocally rejected More's offerings, their exercise of choice in this matter is not necessarily evidence of their freedom as readers. As St. Clair demonstrates, even though publishers included features designed to appeal to readers, the market largely dictated the reading diet of the masses. The brief window between 1774 and 1842 when copyright laws were relaxed widened the horizons of the common people, as previously unobtainable canonical works were reproduced and sold at cheap prices. The competition meant that the old chapbook trade which had thrived for centuries came to an end. Market conditions, namely the reliance on British publishing giants, thwarted literary independence and dictated the imperial orientation of reading practices in Australia between 1890 and 1930, as Lyons and Taksa show in the final extract. Interviews with surviving common readers from this period highlight the impact of limits to choice: while some remembered titles they read with affection, other grimaced.

Furthermore, through the collection of reader responses to texts, Lyons and Taksa draw attention to the divisions within mass readerships, an element also hinted at in the commentaries included in Late-Ming narratives and in some of the more scattered evidence of readership in Ghosh's account of nineteenth-century Bengal. These reading publics were never homogeneous groups, but contained people with specific class, gender, geographical and age-based identities. The extent to which these identities could establish more specific reading communities who were tied to particular kinds of texts will be examined further in the next section.

Chapter 18

Kevin Sharpe

PURSUING THE READER

THE MOST IMPORTANT MOVE in hermeneutic and critical theory has been to a concern with the reading and consumption of texts. Where 'until recently the reader was perhaps the most neglected element in the framework of literary communication,' the shift from concentration on authors' intentions to the performances of texts led obviously to readers.[1] Any attempt to understand how texts structure and make meaning translates at some point into the question of how meaning arises from the reader's 'encounter with these words on the page'.[2] For, whatever the intentions of authors (or authorisers) of texts, readers bring their experiences (not least of other texts) to any reading. Reading indeed becomes a process in which we translate into our own words, symbols and mental contexts the marks and signs on the page.

If critics have concurred about the importance of the reader in the process of construing and constructing meaning, they have differed greatly about what that place might be and how we might study the reader or the experience of the text. And where for some the reader comes in at the end of a process of authors making meanings which the reader modifies, radical theorists like Roland Barthes posit the reader as the maker of texts, the 'producer of the text',[3] very much in the spirit of Nietzsche's assertion that 'ultimately man finds in things nothing but what he himself has imported into them'.[4] The disputes, of course, about whether texts control readers or readers write texts is inextricably bound up with the discussions of the stability or indeterminacy of meanings that we have seen as the subject of poststructuralist criticisms. And, like all criticism (and history), they are part of large ideological issues about coherence or multiplicity, unity or plurality of meanings and values, in the critics' own culture. Not surprisingly therefore, even in its relatively brief history, the study of readers and reception has manifested itself very differently from critic to critic, and over place and time. Despite their own differences the so-called Konstanz theorists of *Rezeptionsästhetik*, Hans Robert Jauss and Wolfgang Iser, still accord to the text (if not the author) and its formal properties a major role in its own reception.[5] Though Jauss, for instance, argues that 'the oppositions between fiction and reality, between the poetic and practical functions of language' were available as choices to the reader of a work, that 'potential for meaning' was and is 'embedded in a work' and readers came to texts with a 'horizon of expectations'.[6] Such a 'fusion of horizons' connects readers to texts and authors via a set of shared conventions which do not finally determine but which delimit both writing and reading at specific moments in time. Iser places more emphasis on the indeterminacy of the text, but still in his notion of (and title of his major work) *The Implied Reader* suggests a text's foresight and control of the reading process and the guiding devices operative in it. Though critical of earlier Marxist[7] or formalist assumptions that readings were determined by social position or by authors' intentions and texts' formal properties, reception theory tends still to situate reading within the structure of society and literary culture, 'the system of relationships in the literature', as Jauss puts it.[8]

Other critics have approached reading from more personal (liberal humanist, socio-logical, psychoanalytical) perspectives. Norman Holland, expounding his own theory of reading as a 'personal transaction', argues for the extraliterary facts that shape reading by a powerful recalling of his own reading in puberty of Poe's *The Purloined Letter*.[9] Holland questions the notion of a shared response implicit in Jauss and Iser, and insists on the 'unique identity' of the reader in a way that echoes the old emphasis on the individuality of the author – as a coherent self outside of cultural and social relations. Jacques Leenhardt posits a more cultural approach to reading in demonstrating how very different societies, those of France and Hungary, respond to the same novels.[10]

Albeit in less specialised language, everyday experience confirms that the process of reading is something more complex than a simple acceptance or rejection of a unified meaning produced by an author or text, and that reading is a cultural as well as personal action, and indeed that, even in our own lives, it is specific to moments and places. We know that formal novels (even departures from form of the sort practised say by Sterne in *Tristram Shandy*) shape as well as license our imaginative response; that an American reads the irony of an Austen novel rather differently from an English reader; that to read D. H. Lawrence at sixteen and sixty are very different experiences; and that to read in the Library of Congress and on the beach conditions what meaning we take from even the same text – though in this case the place is also likely to influence the text being read. All this is a valuable – and essential – reminder that we read, make meaning of the world, differently in different circumstances. But what it does not do is address the vital question, how. As Robert Darnton recently put it, for all the value of reception theory in turning attention from the authors and texts to the activity of readers, it 'has yet to prove itself because we do not know what reading is even when it takes place under our own noses'.[11] Indeed educational theorists are as divided as critical theorists when it comes to explaining how a child comes to read and whether the one verb accommodates the many (different) practices that are involved in making meaning of signs on the page.[12] Nor, though the subject is understandably now a prominent one, is there any developed understanding of the relationship of the medium of a text – in books, tape, microfilm or computer screen – to the ways we make sense of it for ourselves. Does the poem on the underground train, 'read' as we jostle next to fellow passengers, alert to the pickpocket and our next station, have a meaning different from when read alone in the light of a drawing room fire? Does the scrolled screen render differently from the turned page the unfolding suspense of a thriller novel? How does the removal of the touch on the page affect the pleasures of the text, and is its consequence greater, say, for the reading of erotic fiction than for the economic report?

What such questions do, even when they remain unanswered, is point to the specificity – that is to say to the historicity – of all acts of reading, even if it is the history of the moment of reading this last sentence. Here, as in other respects, theories of reading have not contributed neatly to any history of reading. Theory, however, need not be a rival to history when it comes to understanding how people have read. Jauss and still more Iser urge a diachronic, historical approach to reading as a process of 'successive unfolding' of meanings of a text, 'actualised in the stages of its historical reception', and stress the relationship of literary history to the other histories in which a text is situated and performs.[13] More particularly, the critic Stanley Fish offers a theory of reading or a reader-response criticism that is intrinsically historical. For though he argues that the readers make meanings of texts in the process of reading, Fish delimits the indeterminacy and individuality that implies by arguing that readers (and writers) both act in a context and partake of an 'interpretive community' that determines what is read.[14] 'It is interpretive communities', Fish wrote, 'rather than either the text or the reader that produce meanings. . . . Interpretive communities are made up of those who share interpretive strategies.'[15] Such strategies are historically specific: to write their history is to get to the heart of 'understanding how people construe the symbolic systems made available to them by their culture'.[16]

Along with the New Historicism, many theorists and critics are now calling for a turn to a history of reading as the only means of passing 'beyond the *supposed* experience of a generalised reader' to 'focus on the actual reading experiences and responses of specific individuals to specific works'.[17] As one put it recently, 'literary theorists have debated endlessly whether the reader writes the text or the text manipulates the reader. A history of audiences could lead us out of this deadlock by revealing the interactions of specific readers and texts.'[18] Despite this comforting talk of history and specificity, even Fish's comment (with echoes familiar to seventeenth-century historians) that reading, the structuring of meaning, is 'an event rather than an entity', historians have not for the most part been attracted to the programme of a historicised reception theory or historical reader-response criticism.[19] Indeed the leading historian of print has voiced her scepticism about whether one can recover 'what really went on in the minds of silent, solitary readers'.[20] However, just as since Plato there have been theories of reading, so there have been histories of reading, albeit often written before the questions critical theory has raised. Conventional literary histories, after all, based on ideas of influence and pedigree, chart a history of readings, albeit those enacted by a special category of readers – other writers of 'literature'.[21] And books like Richard Hoggart's classic *The Uses of Literacy* presented some startling findings about what and how working-class readers in the Britain of the 1950s read, showing them extracting what they wanted from books on their own terms.[22] More recent work has unearthed equally striking examples of working-class readers of the *Iliad*, but has also sounded a note of caution to politicising critics in revealing how readers can pass over what the critic identifies as ideological freight, ignoring the 'imperialism' in Kipling's novels for example.[23]

If the reader in our own time confounds assumptions and expectations, what possibility is there for understanding the process of reading in the past? Statistical studies of books published and purchased have plotted large narratives of overall reading patterns: the decline of the classics and religious literature, the rise in the eighteenth century of novels, natural histories and travel literature, the shift to extensive from intensive reading.[24] An early adventurous attempt to pursue *The English Common Reader* over four centuries presented valuable information about the printing, sales, distribution and prices of books.[25] Specialised monographs have debated the degree and extent of literacy in premodern times and researched student notebooks as well as official curricula to determine what was studied at school and university.[26] Such studies throw essential light needed to comprehend reading but somehow do not bring the subject itself under the lamp. As Roger Chartier argues, 'the intellectual use to which readers put their reading is a decisive question that cannot be answered either by thematic analyses of the printed works produced or by an analysis of the social diffusion of the various categories of works' – be it through bookseller or school.[27]

[. . .]

[W]hile there are now signs that English historians – especially of the Middle Ages and the eighteenth century – discern that the history of reading may be central to the understanding of the 'master narratives' of society and politics, English historians of the seventeenth century have largely ignored these developments.[28] This is much more serious than contempt for some modish new field of enquiry, or lack of interest in some exotic or marginal area of study. For the historian of the Renaissance to ignore the theoretical and historical questions about reading, as well as writing, texts is to be guilty of anachronism. For as Darnton acknowledges, 'to be sure the history of the book did not begin yesterday. It stretches back to the Renaissance if not beyond.'[29] Victoria Khan nicely historicises what at times appears to be a new methodology: 'reader response criticism could only be seen as new and fashionable when the assumptions of a humanist rhetorical tradition had been forgotten'.[30] That rhetorical tradition was throughout as concerned with readers and auditors as with orators and writers: rhetoric presumes readers who may be persuaded or not persuaded, able to 'read' as they decided. And, as Erasmus clearly discerned, 'right reading' was as much an ethical practice, an inculcation and practice of virtue and prudence, as learning to write, speak and act. Reading was an action, an activity, through which people learned to be good citizens in a Christian commonweal.[31]

There can be no doubt that Renaissance educational theory placed great emphasis on the arts of reading. What we must also appreciate is the humanist recognition of the independence and power of readers, as well as authors, to construct their own meanings. This recognition stemmed in part from the nature and conditions of Renaissance authorship and writing. Patronage, for example, the tradition not only of dedicating to patrons but writing as if for them primarily, implicitly placed the reader in a position of greater authority (as he or she usually was) than the author. The dedicatee not only provided the livelihood that was the most basic precondition of writing, but also facilitated publication, authorised the work and at times used influence to bypass the censor.[32] The patronage system placed the reader, chronologically and hierarchically, before the author of the text; and arguably the decline of aristocratic patronage was necessary for the emerging prominence of the author by the early eighteenth century. Secondly, since much of humanist writing involved a rewriting of classical texts and arguments, often the Renaissance writer was a reader (in the technical pedagogic sense of exegete, as well as the wider more common meaning) of those texts.[33] In Terence Cave's words, in the Renaissance theory of 'imitatio', 'the activities of reading and writing become virtually identified'.[34] As Nicholas Faret confessed in the aptly titled *The Honest Man* (1632), he had so mingled the views of the ancients with his own that he no longer knew how to unravel them.[35]

As Faret's comment makes clear, this rewriting was never a simple, unmediated rehearsal of classical ideas and texts. Translation was interpretation, an act which translated not only the words from one language to another, but authority over meaning from the original to the new edition and its author/translator.[36] Indeed, the vogue for translations and editions of the classics, far from elevating their authority, appropriated it and opened these texts – as much as the vernacular Bible exposed the scriptures – to interrogation and reinterpretation. 'If venerable texts are to be fragmented and eventually transformed by the process of rewriting, it becomes visibly less necessary to regard them as closed and authoritative wholes.'[37] 'Fragmentation' and 'rewriting' virtually describe the humanist educational programme – especially the practice recommended by Erasmus and all leading educational theorists of keeping a commonplace book in which notes from original texts were reconstituted under subject headings chosen by the note-taker. As we shall see graphically and in detail, the commonplace method made every educated Englishman or woman into a reader who very much made his or her own meaning. From the social system of patronage through to the pedagogic instruction of grammar school education, Renaissance culture foregrounded the reader as a forceful presence in the republic of letters.

Writers themselves were the first to credit the reader's independence and authority.

They knew that certain genres virtually demanded readers to make their own meanings and that the habit and freedom so called up were redeployed as common practice. Bacon, for example, regarded fable, a genre that crossed elite and popular culture, as 'pliant stuff': 'how freely it will follow any way you please to draw it, and how easily with a little dexterity and discourse of wit meanings which it was never meant to have may be plausibly put upon it'.[39] Histories too left space for the interpretation of the reader. In the *Advancement of Learning* Bacon described it as 'the true office of history to represent the events themselves together with the counsels and to leave the observations and conclusions thereupon to the liberty and faculty of every man's judgement'.[39] John Hayward, author of the *Lives of the III Normans*, seemed resigned to the fact that 'men will be not readers only but interpreters, but wresters, but corrupters and depravers of that which they read.'[40] Experience, not least the bitter quarrels over the interpretation of biblical passages during the English Reformation, had instructed that, like it or not, textual meaning was not absolute, that individuals read – and even chose to read – differently.[41] When John Chamberlain sent Dudley Carleton a copy of the controversial preface to Hayward's *Historie . . . of Henry IV* he invited his friend to proffer a different reading to his own: 'I have just got you a transcript of it that you may pick out the offence if you can; for my part I can find no such bug words but that everything is as it is taken.'[42] Writers like Bacon and Montaigne could not but be aware of the potential freedom of the reader, given their own often audaciously independent rereadings of the classical texts they revered. Montaigne boasted that 'I have read in Livy a hundred things that another man has not read in him';[43] and Bacon regarded the practices of commonplacing of most 'profit and use; because they have in turn a kind of observation'.[44]

In a brilliant thesis Terence Cave has suggested that such a recognition of, even some applause for, the openness of texts to variant readings refashioned the act of writing in the Renaissance. In particular he finds in Ronsard, Rabelais and Montaigne a creative tension between a persistent quest for integrity and coherence and a new desire to open their own writings, as well as those they imitated. 'Plural texts like those of Rabelais and Montaigne by drawing the attention to the problem of how they should be read give licence to an interpretative approach.'[45] Annabel Patterson has made a similar argument for Holinshed leaving the interpretation of his multivocal chronicles to 'each man's judgement', so as to foster an independent, critical spirit.[46] It would be fruitful to pursue this thesis for other early modern English texts, though at first reading Jonson's plays suggest a rather different cultural desire to foreclose and control – a difference that invites its own history. Yet whether they welcomed it or not, English writers by the end of the sixteenth century knew that the fate of their texts/selves lay with their readers. In *A Free and Offenceless Justification of Andromeda Liberata*, George Chapman articulated the falsity of any claim to be 'offenceless' by an author, and his fear 'that let the writer mean what he list, his writing notwithstanding must be construed in mentem legentis . . . to the intendment of the Reader'.[47]

In the freedom taken by or permitted to readers in early modern England much was at stake. Fable and history may have been open to interpretation but they were also genres in which political allegories were frequently encoded. Chamberlain was predisposed to expect (in this case subversive) politics in a work of history, and the controversies over Hayward's *First Part of the Life and Reign of Henrie IIII* (1599) encouraged him to do so.[48] And, as Chapman protested, it was not readers but authors who were held responsible for subversive 'meanings': 'If a troublesome meaning is brought to the text by a reader, what blame should the author bear,' he asked, knowing that in practice the force of state power fell upon writers, even when their claims to innocence were genuine.[49] Though proclamations called in books, and made an offence of their possession, quite simply it was – and remains – impossible for censorship to police the way texts are read.[50] Such a realisation may even, it has been argued, have helped to forge an acceptance by authorities of a 'functional ambiguity' in texts, of their capacity for multiple and oppositionist readings provided that, to quote Quintilian, they 'can be understood differently'.[51]

When, however, the state functioned as a reader of texts, and the penalties for libel or sedition were mutilation and even death, authors who desired to open their texts to readers had to tread a careful line. And not all desired or applauded the freedoms taken by the reader, for a number of reasons. In the first place, though Montaigne and Machiavelli struck at its core, many still held to a notion of truth and right that they wished to represent and teach. Hayward, we recall, while admitting that readers would be interpreters, pejoratively spoke of them as potential 'wresters', and 'corrupters' and 'depravers' of what they read.[52] Bacon too felt some readings of a text claimed to discover 'meanings which it was never *meant* to have' and accused Machiavelli of expounding the fable of Achilles 'corruptly'.[53] Ben Jonson famously endeavoured to control the interpretations of his works by extensive marginalia and close supervision of publication.[54] In *Bartholomew Fair* he mocked the judgement of readers and a world in which wealth and status were believed to bequeath understanding and discrimination.[55] Authors therefore developed strategies to contain the hermeneutic liberties of readers. As well as the content and language of their texts they deployed the material features of writing – the size, format and typography of the book – its genre and form, to exercise some measure of control.[56] As readers in turn became more sophisticated in 'reading' and seeing beyond those gestures, so authors adopted different and more sophisticated techniques, in the way they used prefaces, dedications and title pages – ultimately in the way they claimed cultural authority as authors. In some ways the devices (as with the modern dust-jacket with its promises of titillation or scholarly weight – seldom both!) became a game among writers, printers and publishers, and readers – and the state as official reader. But like all games it also had a serious dimension: a desire to win, to gain control of the processes of constructing values. For the historian, observing what Montaigne represented as a tennis match between writers and readers, helps us to grasp the rules of the game and the techniques of play: how meanings circulated between author, text and reader in early modern England.[57]

The ways in which a book is read begin to be determined before the reader has passed beyond a sentence. As one critic reminds us, we know quite a bit about the post we receive before we read it: whether it has a logo, the quality of paper, the nature of the letterhead, whether it is laser-printed, typed or handwritten, and the typography give clues (and directions) to how the missive is to be read and pointers (quite literally with modern graphics) on how it is to be interpreted.[58] Some of the best work in the history of the book has been similarly directed to such issues of its material condition and the material circumstances of its distribution and circulation. We know that when we go to the new history books table in an academic bookshop we are expecting something different from that in a popular chain, and both publishers and booksellers respond to and manipulate our expectations. The size and binding of a book, its publisher, price, jacket (illustration and blurb), the positioning of scholarly apparatus (or its absence), the size of the index, the length of the chapters all predispose us to a view of the book's contents – usually one that is fairly accurate. Moreover such factors all affect where and when we read (one reviewer of my last book indicated that its weight – I think he meant physical – precluded holiday reading), whether in public or, as some academics with more 'popular' works, in private, alone. Books do not just reflect a market, an interpretive community, of readers, but help to construct it: and so help to fashion the way we classify social groups, and concepts like 'serious' and 'popular', that is to say cultural authority.[59]

The history of the book, rescuing the study of bindings, paper, typeface, etc. from the antiquarianism that characterised some earlier studies, has demonstrated beyond question the relation of the material conditions of the book to its 'meanings' in the past, and especially the era of the Renaissance. We would still like to know more about how readers heard about books, since in England catalogues were rare before the second half of the seventeenth century, when advertisements for books as well as other 'commodities' also became more common.[60] It would be interesting too to learn more about how booksellers displayed and categorised their stock, the way in which they began to specialise in types of material. Did the 200 booksellers estimated to be plying their trade in Paul's Yard serve only the capital, or was there an organised informal delivery service through middlemen to the provinces, as well as the established book fairs?[61] Evidently a Cambridge student in the 1620s could hire books he could not afford to buy, and, at least in Kent, there is evidence of a secondhand market, though we know little of how it worked.[62] Was the bookseller's 'hire shop' a place of congress before the Civil War, a place where recommendations about reading and opinions on current issues were offered and exchanged? All such questions relate to the efforts made by readers to acquire books in general and particular titles – efforts which evidence the value placed on reading in early modern England. Darnton also reflects on the importance of other changes – from rag to wood pulp in papermaking, for example – in the reception of books.[63] Whether a book was purchased bound (in what material) or, as commonly, in loose leaf for personal binding – perhaps with one's own stamp or arms – reflected and conditioned the relationship between the book and reader.[64] The many paintings and engravings of Renaissance figures holding books, their fingers marking a page, suggest that what Darnton calls the 'corporeal element in reading' opens into the history of the body and the self as well as of the book.[65] Books in this culture could be treasured personal possessions; they could also be, as John Lyly complained, the fashion of the day: 'we commonly see the book that at Christmas hath appeared bound at the Stationers Hall at Easter to be broken in the Haberdashers Shop.'[66] What determined which books met that fate, or which remained largely fashionable, or cherished by a few, is part of the history of ideology and values.

The size of books, then as today, conveyed messages. Price was of course the obvious one. Given that print runs were usually restricted to 1,250–1,500 copies, whatever the anticipated market, a larger folio book tended to be considerably more expensive, and therefore associated with elites, cultural and social.[67] Ben Jonson's choice of a folio edition for his collected *Works*, coming hard on the heels of James I's own volume (*Workes*, 1616), laid a claim to authority that was not lost on his contemporaries or successors. As D. F. McKenzie showed, the 'unruly Congreve of the early quarto editions settled down into the decorous neo-classicist of the *Works* of 1709' – a stately folio.[68] John Ogilby himself used explicitly political language when he boasted that from his first 'mean octavo' edition of Virgil, 'a royal folio flourished'.[69] Big did not always mean better, nor fit all occasions. The brevity and plainness of the Civil War pamphlets were not just a matter of cheapness, but also of style – a suspicion, as the author of *The Great Assizes Holden at Parnassus* (1645) put it, of 'fine attire'.[70] And the decision to issue the early editions of *Eikon Basilike* as a pocket duodecimo, as well as reflecting the need for secrecy, may have been intended to invoke intimacy and to make of the book a token, the form of which allied the work with chivalric ideals.[71]

References

1   Ian Maclean, 'Reading and Interpretation', in A. Jefferson and D. Robey, eds, *Modern Literary Theory*, 2nd edn (1986), p. 122. For other introductory guides to reader response criticism, see E. Freund, *The Return of the Reader* (1987); S. Suleiman and I. Crosman, eds, *The Reader in the Text: Essays on Audience and Reception* (Princeton, 1980); P. J. Rabinowitz, 'Whirl without End:

Audience Orientated Criticism', in G. D. Atkins and L. Morrow, eds, *Contemporary Literary Theory* (Houndmills, 1989), pp. 81–100; K. M. Newton, *Interpreting the Text: A Critical Introduction to the Theory and Practice of Literary Interpretation* (London, 1990), ch. 7; J. P. Tompkins, ed., *Reader Response Criticism: From Formalism to Post Structuralism* (Baltimore, 1980).

2   Newton, *Interpreting the Text*, p. 85.

3   Ibid., p. 81. See R. Barthes, S/Z (1975).

4   Newton, *Interpreting the Text*, p. 87.

5   H. R. Jauss, *Toward an Aesthetic of Reception* (Minnesota, 1982); W. Iser, *The Act of Reading: A Theory of Aesthetic Response* (1978); Iser, *The Implied Reader: Patterns of Communication in Prose Fiction from Bunyan to Beckett* (Baltimore, 1980).

6   Jauss, *Toward an Aesthetic of Reception*, p. 30; 1. Suleiman, 'Varieties of Audience-Orientated Criticism', in Suleiman and Crosman, *Reader in the Text*, p. 36.

7   Iser, *Implied Reader*, cf. Iser, 'Interaction between Text and Reader', in Suleiman and Crosman, *Reader in the Text*, pp. 106–19.

8   Jauss, *Toward an Aesthetic of Reception*, pp. 12–18, 36.

9   N. Holland, 'Recovering "The Purloined Letter": Reading as a Personal Transaction', in Suleiman and Crosman, *Reader in the Text*, pp. 350–70; cf. Holland, *5 Readers Reading* (New Haven and London, 1975).

10   J. Leenhardt, 'Toward a Sociology of Reading', in Suleiman and Crosman, *Reader in the Text*, pp. 205–24.

11   R. Darnton, 'How to Read a Book', *New York Review of Books*, 6 June 1996, p. 52.

12   See J. A. Langer, ed., *Reader Meets Author: Bridging the Gap* (Newark, Del., 1982).

13   Jauss, *Toward an Aesthetic of Reception*, p. 30.

14   S. Fish, *Is There a Text in this Class? The Authority of Interpretive Communities* (Cambridge, Mass., 1980).

15   S. Fish, *Is There a Text?* p. 14; cf. Fish, 'Is There a Text in this Class?' in D. H. Richter, *Falling into Theory* (New York, 1994), pp. 226–37.

16   Darnton, 'How to Read a Book', p. 52.

17   Suleiman, 'Varieties of Audience-Orientated Criticism', p. 26.

18   J. Rose, 'Re-reading the English Common Reader: A Preface to a History of Audience', *Journal of the History of Ideas* 53 (1992), pp. 47–70, at p. 65.

19   Fish, *Is There a Text in this Class?* p. 3. Conrad Russell spoke of parliaments as events rather than institutions, see his 'The Nature of a Parliament in Early Stuart England', in H. Tomlinson, *Before the English Civil War* (1983), p. 125. Hume writes: 'The paucity of work to date in linking historical particulars with the implications of reader response theory is startling', R. Hulme, 'Texts within Contexts', *Philological Quarterly*, 71 (1992), pp. 69–100, at p. 83.

20   Elizabeth L. Eisenstein, *The Printing Press as an Agent of Change: Communications and Cultural Transformations in Early Modern Europe* (Cambridge, 1979), p. 149.

21   J. Culler, 'Prolegomena to a Theory of Reading', in Suleiman and Crosman, *Reader in the Text*, pp. 50ff.

22   R. Hoggart, *The Uses of Literacy: Aspects of Working Class Life with Special Reference to Publications and Entertainments* (1957).

23   Rose, 'Re-reading the English Common Reader', pp. 49ff., 68.

24   See, for example, H. J. Martin, *Livre, pouvoir et société à Paris au XVII siècle* (2 vols, Geneva, 1969); R. Estivals, *Le Statistique bibliographique de la France sous la monarchie au XVIII siècle* (Paris, 1965); L. Febvre and J. Martin, *The Coming of the Book: The Impact of Printing, 1450–1800* (1958, 1971); F. Furet and J. Ozouf, *Reading and Writing: Literacy in France from Calvin to Jules Ferry* (Cambridge, 1982); R. Chartier, *The Cultural Uses of Print in Early Modern France*, trans. Lydia Cochraine (Princeton, 1987); H. S. Bennet, *English Books and Readers, 1475–1557* (Cambridge, 1952); Bennet, *English Books and Readers, 1603–1640* (Cambridge, 1970).

25   R. Altick, *The English Common Reader* (Chicago, 1957).

26   For example D. Cressy, *Literacy and the Social Order: Reading and Writing in Tudor and Stuart England* (Cambridge, 1980); M. Todd, *Christian Humanism and the Puritan Social Order* (Cambridge, 1987), ch. 3.

27   R. Chartier, *Cultural History: Between Practices and Representations*, trans. Lydia Cochraine (Cambridge, 1988), p. 35.

28   M. B. Parkes, *Scribes, Scripts and Readers: Studies in the Communication, Presentation and Dissemination of Medieval Texts* (1991); M. T. Clanchy, *From Memory to Written Record*, 2nd edn (Oxford, 1993);

J. Raven, *Judging New Wealth: Popular Publishing and Responses to Commerce in England, 1750–1800* (Oxford, 1992); J. Brewer, *The Pleasures of the Imagination* (1997), ch. 4.

29   R. Darnton, 'What is the History of Books?', *Daedalus* 3 (1982), pp. 65–83, at p. 65.

30   V. Khan, *Rhetoric, Prudence and Scepticism in the Renaissance* (Ithaca, N. Y., 1985), p. 19.

31   T. Cave, *The Cornucopian Text: Problems of Writing in the French Renaissance* (Oxford, 1979), ch. 3; Cave, 'The Mimesis of Reading in the Renaissance', in J. D. Lyons and S. G. Nichols, eds, *Mimesis: From Mirror to Method, Augustine to Descartes* (1982), pp. 150–65; A. Grafton and L. Jardine, *From Humanism to the Humanities: Education and the Liberal Arts in Fifteenth and Sixteenth Century Europe* (1986).

32   On the title page of Spenser's *Shepherd's Calendar* it is the name of Sidney as dedicatee that appears, not Spenser. See A. Marotti, *Manuscript, Print and the English Renaissance Lyric* (Ithaca, N.Y., 1995), p. 310.

33   H. O. White, *Plagiarism and Imitation during the English Renaissance* (New York, 1965).

34   Cave, *Cornucopian Text*, p. 35.

35   N. Faret, *The Honest Man or The Art to Please in Court* (1632), pp. 404–5.

36   R. Crosman compares translation and reading in 'Do Readers Make Meaning?' in Suleiman and Crosman, *Reader in the Text*, pp. 152–4.

37   Cave, 'Mimesis of Reading', p. 155.

38   Quoted by J. Wallace, ' "Examples Are Best Precepts": Readers and Meaning in Seventeenth-Century Poetry', *Critical Inquiry* 1 (1974), pp. 273–90, at p. 277.

39   F. Bacon, *The Advancement of Learning and New Atlantis*, ed. A. Johnston (Oxford, 1974), p. 77.

40   Bennet, *English Books and Readers, 1603–1640*, p. 177.

41   For an example, see B. Crockett, *The Play of Paradox: Stage and Sermon in Renaissance England* (Philadelphia, 1995), pp. 97–8.

42   D. Womersley, 'Sir John Hayward's Tacitism', *Renaissance Studies* 6 (1991), pp. 46–59, at p. 46.

43   Khan, *Rhetoric, Prudence and Scepticism*, p. 133.

44   V. F. Snow, 'Francis Bacon's Advice to Fulke Greville on Research Techniques', *Huntingdon Library Quarterly* 23 (1960), p. 372.

45   Cave, *Cornucopian Text*, p. 327. Cf. M. Ferguson, *Trials of Desire: Renaissance Defenses of Poetry* (New Haven, 1983). p. 158.

46   A. Patterson, *Reading Holinshed's Chronicles* (Chicago, 1994). Though the attempt to claim Holinshed as a protoliberal ancient constitutionalist is unpersuasive, the case for the openness of the text is interesting and well made. For a case study in readers' appropriations of a text see A. Beer, *Sir Walter Ralegh and his Readers in the Seventeenth Century* (Houndmills, 1997).

47   J. Kerrigan, 'The Editor as Reader: Constructing Renaissance Texts', in J. Raven, H. Small and N. Tadmor, eds, *The Practice and Representation of Reading in England* (Cambridge, 1996), pp. 102–24, at p. 114.

48   D. R. Woolf, *The Idea of History in Early Stuart England: Erudition, Ideology and 'The Light of Truth' from the Accession of James I to the Civil War* (Toronto, 1990), pp. 107–8.

49   Kerrigan, 'Editor as Reader', p. 114.

50   See in general Annabel M. Patterson, *Censorship and Interpretation: The Conditions of Writing and Reading in Early Modern England* (Madison, 1984). There were attempts to prove treason by imagining the king's death and in the case of Algernon Sydney this was 'proved' from his reading of the classics. See S. Zwicker, 'Reading the Margins: Politics and the Habits of Appropriation', in K. Sharpe and S. Zwicker, eds. *Refining Revolutions: Aesthetics and Politics from the English Revolution to the Romantic Revolution* (Berkley, 1998), pp. 102–3.

51   Patterson, *Censorship and Interpretation*, p. 14.

52   Bennet, *English Books and Readers, 1603–1640*, p. 177.

53   Bacon, *Advancement of Learning*, p. 82.

54   See D. Riggs, *Ben Jonson: A Life* (Cambridge, Mass., 1989), pp. 220–6; R. C. Newton, 'Jonson and the (Re)Invention of the Book', in C. J. Summers and T. L. Pebworth, eds, *Classic and Cavalier: Essays on Jonson and the Sons of Ben* (Pittsburgh, 1982), pp. 31–58.

55   *Bartholomew Fair*, 'The Induction on the Stage'.

56   Jonson's folio works, published the same year as James I's, makes the point. See also the engraved title page, discussed in M. Corbett and R. W. Lightbown, *The Comely Frontispiece: The Emblematic Title Page in England, 1550–1800* (London, 1979), pp. 149–51.

57   C. M. Baushatz, 'Montaigne's Conception of Reading in the Context of Renaissance Poetics and

Modern Criticism', in Suleiman and Crosman, *Reader in the Text*, p. 265. Olson points out that sixteenth-century composers added notations to scores to restrict the performer's freedom of interpretation, D. R. Olson, *The World on Paper: The Conceptual and Cognitive Implications of Writing and Reading* (Cambridge, 1994), p. 88.

58   M. Nystrand, *The Structure of Written Communication: Studies in Reciprocity between Writers and Readers* (Orlando, 1986), pp. 56–7. Nystrand talks of 'pretextual clues' (p. 60). See too A. Manguel, *A History of Reading* (1996), pp. 13–14. Ben Jonson offers a contemporary case, see Epigrams 2, 3 in C. H. Herford and P. Simpson, *Ben Jonson* (Oxford, 1925), VIII, p. 27.

59   Today, of course, one of the most common questions on consumer surveys is which newspapers one reads; and newspapers are categorised according to A-B etc. readership.

60   *A Catalogue of the Most Vendible Books in England* (1658), Thomason E9551/1, with only slight exaggeration, claims in its title 'the like work never yet performed by any'. After the Restoration such catalogues were regular publications. Advertisements in books from the 1640s and 1650s on await study as an aspect of the commodification of print and political culture.

61   Bennet, *English Books and Readers*, 1603–40, p. 1; cf. G. Pollard, 'The English Market for Printed Books', *Publishing History* 4 (1978), pp. 7–48; D. Stoker, 'The Regulation of the Book Trade in Norwich 1500–1800', *Publishing History* 8 (1980), pp. 127–41 and Altick, *English Common Reader*; R. Myers and M. Harris. *Spreading the Word: The Distribution Networks of Print, 1550–1850* (Detroit, 1990).

62   M. Spufford, 'First Steps in Literacy: The Reading and Writing Experience of the Humblest Seventeenth-Century Spiritual Autobiographers', *Social History* 4 (1979), p. 433; P. Clark, 'The Ownership of Books in England, 1560–1640: The Example of Some Kentish Townfolk', in L. Stone, ed., *Schooling and Society: Studies in the History of Education* (Baltimore, 1976), pp. 95–115.

63   Darnton, 'How to Read a Book'; cf. Marotti, *Manuscript, Print*, p. 252.

64   Readers often described their books in terms of physical features: see K. Sharpe, 'Rewriting Sir Robert Cotton', in C. Wright, ed., *Sir Robert Cotton as Collector* (1997), pp. 7–8; cf. Jean Ranson's concern with the 'physical aspects of books', in R. Darnton, 'Readers Respond to Rousseau: The Fabrication of Romantic Sensitivity', in Darnton, *The Great Cat Massacre* (Harmondsworth, 1985), p. 216.

65   Cf. R. Helgerson, 'Soldiers and Enigmatic Girls: The Politics of Dutch Domestic Realism, 1560–1672', *Representations* 58 (1997), pp. 49–87, esp. pp. 77–82. I am also grateful to Richard Helgerson for his presentation on representations of reading at the Folger National Endowment for the Humanities Seminar in July 1997. See A. Johns, *The Nature of the Book: Print and Knowledge in the Making* (Chicago, 1998), ch. 6, Johns, 'The Physiology of Reading', in N. Jardine and M. Frasca-Spada, eds. *Books and the Sciences in History* (Cambridge, 2000), pp. 291–314, and Manguel, *History of Reading*, pp. 151–4.

66   C. Gebert, ed., *An Anthology of Elizabethan Dedications and Prefaces* (New York, 1966), p. 50.

67   Altick, *English Common Reader*, p. 19.

68   Darnton, 'What is the History of Books?' p. 79. See D. F. McKenzie, 'Typography and Meaning: The Case of William Congreve', *Wolfenbütteler Schriften zur Geschichte der Buchwesen*, vol. 4 (Hamburg, 1981), pp. 81–125; R.Chartier, *On the Edge of the Cliff: History Languages and Practices*, trans. Lydia Cochraine (Baltimore, 1997), ch. 6.

69   J. Ogilby, *Africa: Being an Accurate Description of the Regions of Aegypt, Barbary Lybia* . . . (1670), preface.

70   *The Great Assizes Holden at Parnassus* (1645), Thomason E269/11, p. 34; cf. pp. 2, 20–3.

71   S. Achinstein, *Milton and the Revolutionary Reader* (Princeton, 1994), p. 134; L. Potter, *Secret Rites and Secret Writing: Royalist Literature, 1641–1660* (Cambridge, 1989). Marotti compares *Eikon Basilike* to Herbert's duodecimo *The Temple* which, as he says, resembles a prayer-book, Manuscript, Print, p. 289.

Chapter 19

Anne E. McLaren

CONSTRUCTING NEW READING
PUBLICS IN LATE MING CHINA

DURING THE MID-SIXTEENTH CENTURY, authors and publishers
of vernacular texts realized, probably for the first time in the history of Chinese print
culture, that their reading public was no longer restricted to the learned classes. Prefaces
and commentaries of the era show an emerging awareness, which broadened and strengthened during the seventeenth century, that the potential readership for these texts was a
heterogeneous one of officials, literati, collectors among the new class of nouveaux riches,
members of the laity, common people, the relatively unlearned, and even the all-inclusive
"people of the empire" (*tianxia zhi ren*) or "people of the four classes" (*simin*).

This historical shift in perceptions of the constitution of the reading public was a
consequence of the collision of the preexisting manuscript culture, print technology, and
the increasing commercialization of the economy from the mid-Ming period on. The earliest
vernacular narratives belonged to manuscript culture. Vernacular texts circulated in manuscript form for decades within circles of literati and admirers who felt no compunction
about changing the text as it was recopied and passed from hand to hand. But the decision
to publish a text commercially—and the need to recover the expense of engraving it on
woodblocks—compelled editors and publishers to devise strategies to market their texts
to a reading public somewhat broader than the usual coterie of literati and aficionados.
Intrinsic to the marketing process was the emergence of a new discourse that sought both to
legitimize the publication enterprise and to conceptualize the target readership.

In this study my intention is to draw on prefaces and commentarial material from
narrative and dramatic texts dating from the late fifteenth century to the mid-seventeenth
century in order to trace shifting constructions of readers, authors, and editors, the broadening of reading practices during this period, and the emergence of an apologia for vernacular
print.[1] This period, particularly after about 1570, is marked by a dramatic increase in the
volume of books produced by commercial publishers, a surge in the publication of books of a
popular or practical nature, and strong indications of a broadening of readership to include
less learned groups.[2] My concern here is primarily with the "reading public," which I define,
after Natalie Zemon Davis, as the target public addressed by the author or publisher as
distinct from the "audience" or actual historical readers.[3] This study of notional readers
and their reading practices does not give us direct evidence of actual readers or how they

interpreted the works they read, but it does demonstrate the historic specificity of notions of readership, which shifted dramatically during the Ming period (1368–1644), and offers insight into how entrepreneurial writers and publishers actively sought to create a public with particular literacy skills and cultural competencies. Above all this study reminds us, in the words of D. F. McKenzie, of the importance of including the notion of "human agency" in the study of texts, that is, "the human motives and interactions which texts involve at every stage of their production, transmission and consumption."[4]

First I discuss the paradigms underlying notions of readers, authors, and reading practices, beginning with the standards set by the Neo-Confucian thinker Zhu Xi (1130–1200). I argue that the expanding lexicon for authoring and reading texts is based on a set of suppositions seeking to legitimize vernacular print, suppositions that radically extended Zhu Xi's constructions of the (male elite) reader of the Confucian canon. It was from the early sixteenth century that certain publishers put forward the iconoclastic notion that the Classics were archaic and impenetrable but that vernacular texts were capable of imparting the essential moral wisdom of the Confucian Classics in palatable form. Next I trace the lexicon for target readers in sixteenth- and seventeenth-century works, as it developed away from a coterie of literati to broader social groups. Since notions of the reader cannot be discussed in isolation from constructions of authorship, it is also necessary to discuss the contiguous terms for authors, editors, and publishers, with particular focus on that ambiguous group known as the *haoshizhe* (amateur collectors, aficionados) who read, collected, and authored or edited texts. In line with their perceived readership, publishers and authors produced texts with features that suited a variety of reading practices—for example, texts with verse material that could be memorized easily, texts designed to be read aloud or sung, texts with illustrations to assist literacy, typographical features to facilitate reading, and commentaries and glosses to educate the less learned. I focus on the editorial practices of Yu Xiangdou (ca. 1560–after 1637), who was perhaps the first to write commentary aimed specifically at readers with low educational and literacy levels.

Classics for the unlearned

Prefaces to vernacular texts enunciated a set of legitimizing suppositions, which developed into an apologia for fictional writings. Although these were ultimately based on views of the function of literature that dated from antiquity, sixteenth-century preface writers extended these ancient notions in dramatically new ways. One of the oldest literary ideas in Chinese civilization, the notion that literature conveys the Way (*wen yi zai dao*),[5] that is, that literature is a vehicle of moral instruction, forms the fundamental justification for fictional, vernacular texts as well.

The words of Yongyuzi (the pen name of Jiang Daqi), in a preface dated 1494 to the *Narrative of the Three Kingdoms* (*Sanguo tongsu yanyi*), are representative of this axiom: "when you read (*du*) about loyalty it encourages one to be loyal; it is the same with filial piety. If you only read [the text] over and do not observe [its moral] in your own practices, then this amounts to not [really] reading (*dushu*)."[6] The counterpart to this is the concern that some readers may choose to emulate the evil practices portrayed instead of learning to be good by negative example. Zhang Zhupo (1670–98), in his preface to the famous erotic novel *Plum in the Golden Vase* (*Jin Ping Mei*), is particularly concerned about the effect on women as a listening audience:

> The *Plum in the Golden Vase* is a work that women should never be permitted to see. Nowadays there are many men who read passages out loud to their wives

or concubines while taking their pleasure with them inside the bed curtains. They do not realize that, even among men, there are few who recognize the force of exhortation and admonition or respond appropriately to what they read. . . . What would be the consequences if they [women] were to imitate, however slightly, the things they read about?[7]

One could also note here the view of the Qing (1644–1911) commentator Liu Tingji (fl. 1712) on the importance of "reading properly" *(shan du)* the four famous narratives of the Ming era *(si da qishu):* "Those who don't read *Water Margin* [*Shuihu zhuan*] properly, their minds tend to perversity and treachery; those who don't read the *Narrative of the Three Kingdoms* properly, their minds tend to political expediency and deception; those who don't read the *Journey to the West* properly, their minds tend to cunning and deluded imaginings." As for the *Plum in the Golden Vase*, "those who read this book and wish to imitate it are wild beasts."[8]

Increasingly one finds in prefaces an awareness of the difficulty of the Classics, even for some members of the literati class, and the perceived lack of a clear moral message in the official dynastic histories. This awareness was already apparent in the earliest period of print publication in China.[9] For example, the famous Neo-Confucian scholar Zhu Xi, in his work "Dushu fa" (On reading) expresses concern for the inherent difficulties of the Classics and recommends a host of reading practices to overcome these difficulties. Zhu Xi's annotated editions of the Classics constituted the dominant curriculum of education and the examination system until the end of the imperial era, and his ideas about education and reading *(dushu fa)* have influenced Chinese educators for a millennium. It is thus instructive to examine briefly Zhu Xi's ideas on reading—which were clearly directed at aspirants to the literati class—as a benchmark for Neo-Confucian notions of (elite) reading practices during the late imperial period. As I demonstrate, these notions were radically reshaped in the discursive and editorial practices of vernacular publishers three to four centuries later.

Zhu Xi called for intensive, repetitive reading of the Classics to fully comprehend their inner meaning. His admission of his own earlier problems in reading *Mencius* illustrates the sheer effort required for even the best educated to comprehend a text of such antiquity:

> Thereupon he spoke about the method of reading a text *(dushu)*, saying: You should read it ten or more times. Once you've understood 40 to 50 percent of the meaning, look at the annotation. Having understood another 20 to 30 percent, read the classical text again and you'll understand yet another 10 to 20 percent. Previously I didn't comprehend the *Mencius* because its paragraphs were so long. Then I read it in the manner just described, and although at first its paragraphs were long its meaning nevertheless cohered from beginning to end.[10]

Although Zhu Xi notes from time to time the notional clarity of the Classics ("The words of the sages and worthies are luminous, like the sun and the moon"),[11] he is much more aware of the constant risk that students will fail to comprehend the immanent moral principles reflected in the ancient texts: "The multitudinous words of the sages are nothing but natural principles; fearing people would not comprehend them [they] composed them in writing[,]. . . but the problem is that people do not read carefully and seek a way [to comprehend them]. One must reflect on the words of the sages, on what they said and how it can be applied."[12] Elsewhere he notes one must "make a truly fierce effort" to read the Classics.[13]

The metaphors adopted by Zhu Xi repeatedly stress the sheer physical effort required to master the canon. One needs to penetrate beneath the skin of a text,[14] to look for a "crack" (*fengxia*, as if in a clay vessel) with which to pierce the text,[15] to wrest meaning from the text as if leading a massive onslaught through a military siege (*xu da sha yifan*),[16] to interrogate the text like a harsh jailer dealing with prisoners (*ku li zhi yu*)[17] or as if capturing a bandit (*kan wenzi ru zhuo zei*).[18] One must read as if slicing through one's body: "Go down layer by layer, past skin to flesh, past flesh to bones, past bones to marrow. If you read in desultory fashion you'll never attain this."[19] When reading one must sit with one's spine straight[20] and read until one's eyes hurt.[21] Reading for Zhu Xi, as for the ancients,[22] meant recitation: "Generally speaking in reading a text, we must recite it aloud. We can't just think about it. . . . In reading students must compose themselves and sit up straight, look leisurely at the text and hum softly. . . ."[23] The reader is above all an alert and active practitioner who makes the printed page come alive: "[O]n the printed page (*yinban shang*) the speech and patterns appear not to be alive; because they are not alive they cannot be applied. One must savor the flavor and turn it over until it is familiar and only then will the text come alive."[24] The reader is encouraged to become a coauthor, as it were, of the words of the sages: "recite (*shudu*) until its words appear to come from one's own mouth."[25]

Zhu's theory of reading, with its emphasis on recitation and "possession" of the text, seems in many ways to perpetuate the reading and learning practices necessary in a manuscript culture. To one modern observer, his "Dushu fa" appears to be "a nostalgic attempt to convert the print-oriented students of his day to the traditions of pre-print book culture."[26] Yet in his own day he was attacked rather for what were seen as his departures from reading traditions; his use of printed texts and diagrams in pedagogy, for example, was criticized by his contemporary Lu Xiangshan (1139–93).[27] In any event, one suspects that Zhu Xi's idealized model was hardly representative of actual reading practices in the Song (960–1279) or any other period. In the Ming and Qing, the impracticality of his model was implicitly acknowledged in works of household instruction that propagated a vulgarized interpretation of Neo-Confucian intensive reading. In these works, consisting mainly of examples of "laborious study" (*qindu*), the goal of reading was not so much communing with the sages as the more prosaic one of passing the examinations and becoming an official.[28]

A similar process of simplification and vulgarization shaped the institutionalization of Zhu Xi's program of learning in the centuries after his death. In the Yuan (1279–1368), a reduced form of his demanding model curriculum was officially promoted. William Theodore de Bary has shown how this "stripped down" curriculum, based on the Four Books with Zhu Xi's commentaries, was aimed at the "lowest common denominator" of educated Mongols.[29] The first Ming ruler, Taizu (r. 1368–98), a man of peasant origin, settled for an even briefer Neo-Confucian curriculum and sought to extend it throughout the empire.[30] But even in a radically reduced form, this program was still too difficult: the Classics remained abstruse, and Ming Taizu's goal of universal moral education through the Confucian canon was not realized.

Preface writers during the Ming period adopted the by now familiar rhetoric of the perceived difficulty of the Classics and histories and used it to legitimize their own fictional enterprises. For example, the author of an early preface (1522) to the *Narrative of the Three Kingdoms* pointed out the difficulty of official historiography:

> A guest asked me, why is there a need for the *Narrative of the Three Kingdoms*, given that there exists an official history [the *Sanguo zhi*, or Annals of the three kingdoms]. Is not the *yanyi* [elaboration, narrative] superfluous? I answered, "No. The events recorded in the histories are given in detail but the language is archaic, the import is subtle and the inner significance profound. If you are not a highly erudite scholar then once you open up the volume you will most likely fall asleep. So *haoshizhe* [aficionados], using language close to contemporary

idiom, compiled this book by reshaping (*yinkuo chengbian*)[31] [the *Sanguo zhi*] so that it would penetrate the ears of the people of the empire and thus they would comprehend it."[32]

The famed Ming thinker Yuan Hongdao (1568–1610) described the tedium of reading the Classics, contrasting it to the ease with which one could read fictionalized narratives such as *Water Margin*. In a constructed dialogue between a book lover and an interlocutor, he puts forward this view: "People say of *Water Margin* that it is extraordinary and so it is. Whenever I select the Thirteen Classics or Twenty-one Histories, as soon as I open the volume I am overtaken with sleepiness." He adds that stories about heroes of the Han dynasty reach both the educated and the illiterate—"garbed [officials] and women." However, the official *Hanshu* (History of the Han) requires endless explanations to be comprehensible. For this reason a *yanyi* version has been published: "When [classical] compositions cannot get their meaning across, vulgar [works] can; for this reason the [*Dong Xi Han tongsu yanyi* (Narrative of the eastern and western Han)] is termed a popular elaboration (*tongsu yanyi*)." The readership is envisaged as a broad one: "those in the empire who love reading books."[33]

It was during the Ming period that an even more audacious idea was promoted, namely, that fictional writings were not only easier to read than the Classics but also could serve as substitutes for the Classics and impart the same essential moral wisdom. I have located this notion first in a collection of tales in classical Chinese, the *Jiandeng xinhua* (New stories to [read while] trimming the lamp) by Qu You (1341–1427), who held various senior posts as an educator and administrator.[34] In his preface, dated 1378, Qu You explains that he dared not circulate the work because it was "almost an incitement to immorality" and stored the manuscript in his box of books. However, many guests came to request it, and he could not decline them all. Qu then argues that the Classics themselves contain events impinging on "immorality" and "supernatural events." For example, the *Classic of Songs* contains poems about elopement and erotic love, and the *Spring and Autumn Annals* records times of disorder and banditry. In this way, he argues, even fictional tales can be said to have a didactic function akin to that of the canon.[35]

Yongyuzi elaborated the same idea in the earliest extant preface to the *Narrative of the Three Kingdoms* (1494). He notes that "in the composition of the histories, the principle is subtle and the significance profound." Nonetheless, histories lack a broad readership: "[W]hen most people read (*guan*) them they often criticize them and put them aside and pay no further attention because they are not comprehensible to a broad readership (*butong hu zhongren*). Consequently with the passing of time the events of the ages become lost in transmission." In Luo Guanzhong's *yanyi* version of the *Sanguo zhi*, however, "the language is neither too profound nor too vulgar and it is almost equivalent to a history, so if you read and recite (*dusong*) it you can learn a lesson from it."[36]

Fifty years later, Yuan Fengzi, in his 1548 preface to the *Sanguo zhizhuan* (Chronicles of the three kingdoms; another textual system of the *Narrative of the Three Kingdoms*) went one step further than Yongyuzi by declaring that this famous narrative was not just "equivalent to a history" but a substitute for the core Confucian Classics. After all, it contained auguries of good and bad fortune as in the *Classic of Changes*, methods of governance as in the *Classic of History*, human passions as expressed in the *Classic of Songs*, judgments of praise and blame as in the *Spring and Autumn Annals*, and scrupulous observance of the proprieties as found in the *Record of Rites*. According to Yuan, the putative author, Luo Guanzhong (ca. 1330–1400), was concerned about the obscurity of official historiography, which made it difficult for those "of mediocre ability" (*yongchang*) to comprehend. Now that the work was published with illustrations it would be comprehensible to "the people of the empire."[37] Several generations later sentiments of this sort had become commonplace.[38]

In contrast to the Western experience, the sacred texts of Chinese civilization were not translated into the vernacular, although efforts were made to make them more comprehensible.[39] Perhaps the only parallel one could draw here would be the activities of literati during the late imperial period (after ca. 1550) to edit and publish vernacular narratives that sought to draw on the perceived essence of the Confucian Classics for a broader reading public.[40] There was no equivalent of Luther's German Bible in the Chinese experience of vernacular print, but nonetheless literati increasingly promoted the notion that vernacular narratives could serve as Classics for the unlearned, thus developing what could be called an apologia for vernacular print. Around the same time a new lexicon of readership emerged together with a range of reading practices much broader than those prescribed in the Neo-Confucian model of intensive reading.

Constructions of the reader

A number of noted vernacular narratives and plays circulated first in manuscript form to a tiny coterie of aficionados.[41] This was also true for fictional works in the classical language, such as Qu You's *Jiandeng xinhua*. This coterie readership is invariably addressed as members of the literati class or as amateur collectors-aficionados (*haoshizhe*). For example, in his preface of 1494, Yongyuzi refers to "literati collectors" (*shijunzi zhi haoshizhe*) who competed to copy the *Narrative of the Three Kingdoms* in manuscript form.[42] A play based on the popular religious story of Mulian circulated first in manuscript form among "amateur collectors" and then was published so as to meet the strong demand for copies (according to a preface dated 1582).[43] Of the great Ming narratives, the *Plum in the Golden Vase* is known for having a complicated textual history because of its early circulation in manuscript form among a small coterie of appreciative literati readers.[44] To explain the appearance of such manuscripts in print, the author of a preface will frequently construct a dialogue between a publisher and an interested literati reader of the manuscript who acclaims the work and recommends publication. For example, Xiuranzi (the pen name of Zhang Shangde), in his preface dated 1522, praises the readability of the *Narrative of the Three Kingdoms* and refers to what could well be the first published edition of this work through the mouthpiece of a "guest": "The guest looked up and let out a deep sigh, saying 'That is so, do not be offended by my words. One can indeed say it is of assistance in understanding [official] history and does not violate it! Books (*jianzhi*) are as numerous as the sea is vast, but quality editions (*shanben*) are very hard to find. Why not engrave it on woodblocks and publish it to the four quarters to ensure its longevity?' "[45]

Literati, the appreciative readers of vernacular narratives, are referred to in a range of terms: *shizi* (literati), *junzi* (gentlemen), *saoke* (poets), *jinshen* (officials), *shangyinzhe* or *zhiyinzhe* (connoisseurs), *yashi* (men of refinement), and so on. Zhang Xiongfei (fl. 1522–66), in his 1557 preface to a reedition of the Yuan prosimetric narrative *Xixiang ji zhugongdiao* (*Record of the Western Chamber;* in the form of an all-keys-and-modes narrative) by Dong Jieyuan (fl. 1190–1208), spoke of the target reading public as connoisseurs (*zhiyinzhe*) and official gentlemen (*jinshen xiansheng*).[46] The scholar and bibliophile Hu Yinglin (1551–1602) noted that among those who love the *Water Margin* one finds officials and learned men (*jinshen wenshi*).[47]

By the late fifteenth century, preface authors sought to flatter their readers as men of discernment, praising them for preferring the text in question to other less favored works. For example, in a preface dated 1589, Tiandu waichen (believed to be the pen name for Wang Daokun [1525–93]), in exclaiming on the delights of *Water Margin*, its encyclopedic scope and dazzling plot, says, "[O]ne can only speak of this to men of refinement (*yashi*), there is no point discussing it with common men (sushi)." He scorns the *Narrative of the Three Kingdoms*, with its confusing mixture of fact and fiction, as fit only for the appreciation of common men who "sit in the darkness of their ignorance." By contrast, men of refinement will appreciate *Water Margin* as another *Shiji* (Records of the grand historian).[48] Similarly, Xie Zhaozhe (1567–1624) praises a number of fictional works but considers the *Narrative of the Three Kingdoms* and other historical tales boring because they keep too close to historical facts; such texts can delight children in the lanes and alleys but not literati (shijunzi).[49] Preface writers might also apply these distinctions to different versions of the same work, for the great Ming narratives circulated in two textual traditions, one simpler and containing more narrative material than the other. As Zhang Fengyi (1527–1613) noted, in a preface to *Water Margin* written in about 1588–89, connoisseurs (shangyinzhe) would be able to discriminate between the authoritative text produced by Guo Xun (1475–1542) and the commercial product that contained the additional tales of Wang Qing and Tian Hu.[50]

One also finds a wealth of references to social groups of ambiguous or lowly social status. One group is the amateur collectors, who are discussed in the next section on authors and editors. Members of the laity, called "good men and women" (shanren), and congregations addressed by kinship terms (sisters, brothers, etc.) are the designated reading public of chantefables and religious "precious scroll" (baojuan) narratives.[51] Other groups are "people of the empire" (1548, the Escorial edition of the *Sanguo zhizhuan*), "people from the four quarters" (sifang zhi ren) (Xiuranzi, 1522 preface to the *Narrative of the Three Kingdoms*), and "the four categories of people" (simin; specifically, literati, farmers, artisans, and merchants). The four classes of people and the "ordinary people" (fanmin) were also the perceived public for morality books and similar texts.[52] A preface dated 1644 and attributed (probably falsely) to Jin Shengtan (1608–61) declared that the reading public was both "the learned" (xueshi) and "the unlearned" (buxue zhi ren), "heroes and exceptional men" (yingxiong haojie), and "ordinary people and the vulgar herd" (fanfu suzi).[53] Presumably the reader was invited to place himself in one of these categories.

One of the most intriguing terms for designating the reader in Ming times is the category "ignorant [i.e., uneducated] men and women" (yufu yufu). In antiquity the locus classicus of this term referred to the obligation of the ruler to cherish the common people.[54] The leading Ming thinker Wang Yangming (1472–1529) elevated the potential of the yufu yufu in a way unprecedented in previous Confucian thought: "that which corresponds to the mind of the ignorant man and woman may be called 'common virtue.' That which differs from the ignorant man and woman may be called 'heterodox.'"[55] Possibly the earliest use of yufu yufu in vernacular texts is the 1508 preface, attributed to Lin Han (1434–1519), to the *Sui Tang zhizhuan tongsu yanyi* (Popularized elaboration of the *Chronicles of the Sui and Tang dynasties*): "I want to [ensure] this work circulates together with the *Narrative of the Three Kingdoms* so that even ignorant men and women will understand the events of these two dynasties in a glance."[56] Nonetheless, this text is actually designed for "gentlemen coming after" (hou zhi junzi) as a supplement to the official histories.[57] Here the term "ignorant men and women" should be considered a trope used in preface discourse to represent the relative clarity of popularized texts as opposed to the obscurity of official historiography. In other publications the term might well designate a specific reading public, as in the play *Quanshan ji* (Encouragement to do good), based on the Mulian story by Zheng Zhizhen (fl. late sixteenth century). In a preface dated 1582, it is stated that the play was written in order to move the emotions of "ignorant men and women" and thus attain the goal of moral edification.[58]

A related term is *suren* (the common people). Li Danian, in his 1553 preface to the *Tangshu yanyi* (Popularized elaboration of the *History of the Tang*), notes that both the common people and poets (suren saoke) will read and benefit from this work.[59] In another case, Xiong Damu (fl. mid-sixteenth century) declares that he has transformed a work of hagiography about the Song hero Yue Fei (1103–41) into one comprehensible to the less learned. A relative who was also a publisher urged Xiong to rewrite this text in *cihua* form (i.e., prose with some inserted verse) "so that even ignorant men and women will understand [at least] some of it."[60] The rewritten text, which appeared in 1522, was called the *Da Song yanyi zhongxing—Yinglie zhuan* (Popularized elaboration of the restoration of the great Song—a record of heroes). A seventeenth-century edition of the *Narrative of the Three Kingdoms* from Hangzhou contains the following declaration in its preface: "Luo Guanzhong took historical material from the *Sanguo zhi* [i.e., the official history] and from the [*Zizhi tongjian*] *gangmu* [Outline of the *Comprehensive mirror of government*, by Zhu Xi] and made it comprehensible so that ignorant men and commoners (*yufu sushi*) could read and recite it (*jiangdu*)."[61]

It is hard to say how many so-called ignorant men and women actually read historical fiction. Certainly youths acquiring literacy, some of them of humble origin, read vernacular narratives, particularly the simpler commercial versions. Wu Cheng'en (ca. 1506–82), for example, was the son of a clerk in a silk shop. He admitted to hiding from his father and reading unorthodox histories when he was a youth.[62] Chen Jitai (1567–1641), who finally gained the rank of *jinshi* at the age of sixty-eight, came from a poor family in Wuping, Fujian. In his jottings he described how as a child he borrowed a copy of the *Narrative of the Three Kingdoms* from his uncle and became totally engrossed in it, even ignoring entreaties from his mother to come and dine. He was particularly entranced by the illustrations at the top of the text that depicted every stage of the story.[63] The text he read was almost certainly one of the pictorial type, in *shangtu xiawen* format, produced in Jianyang, Fujian. Jin Shengtan, famed for his abridged version of *Water Margin*, has described the tedium of studying the Four Books as a child. When he was eleven years old, he began to enjoy a "vulgar" (*suben*) edition of *Water Margin*.[64]

As far as I can determine, with the exception of *yufu yufu*, women are never addressed as such in prefaces to dramatic and narrative works during this period, but they did nonetheless form an emerging audience for vernacular works.[65] Ye Sheng (1420–74) is commonly cited in this regard. He notes with concern that booksellers promote tales (probably based on dramatic versions) of Cai Bojie and others, tales that commoners such as peasants, artisans, merchants, and peddlers like to copy and store. He notes that "foolish, ignorant women are particularly addicted to them."[66] Most references to women place them as members of a listening audience for chantefables or storytelling.[67] Where one finds references to women reading, it is often associated with auditive reading—that is, reading something out loud to oneself or to an audience. It follows from this that to attract this sort of audience, texts needed to be designed to have an auditive quality. As I discuss below, editors show an awareness of this from the earliest phase of vernacular print. By the mid-Qing period one finds clear signs of the development of a hierarchy of reading. In the late eighteenth century Zhang Zilin noted that women loved reading (*kan*) the vulgar tales of the storyteller, but "if they read books (*dushu*), it just does not penetrate [the ear]."[68] Commentators now distinguished between material based on the oral arts, with an auditory quality, which could be "viewed" (*kan*) by the unlearned, and classical texts, which required considerable effort to study and master, in the Neo-Confucian sense of *dushu*. It appears that the literati reader remains implicitly *male*, whereas the emerging literacy of unlearned groups is often portrayed as *female*.[69]

[. . .]

This issue of gendered reading (and writing) is too complex to be fully treated here. But it is possible to suggest, from a survey of the various types of reading attributed to women, a range of different female literacies: the "auditory literacy" of semiliterate women who read performance-style texts, the more elaborate "courtesan literacy" of high-class courtesans and certain literary heroines, and the simplified Confucian literacy expected of ladies from fine families. Occasionally, too, one finds a member of the literati class noting with astonished admiration the learning of an exceptional woman who has reached male literati standards and can even be deemed a "Woman Metropolitan Graduate."[70] However, although many women could and did read, it would appear that in the fifteenth and sixteenth centuries women were rarely addressed as a target public by editors and publishers of drama and vernacular fiction.

[. . .]

Reading practices and the design of vernacular texts

Publishers and editors (whether "aficionado collectors" or "village pedants") intervened just as actively in the printed transmission of texts as in their manuscript circulation. Print technology and the burgeoning market for publications broadened the range of editorial options considerably, however. Specifically, publishers and editors designed texts to allow for a range of reading practices. Readers brought some of these practices with them from manuscript culture, such as reading, chanting, and singing a text based on the oral or dramatic arts. In other cases, editors took advantage of the potential of the printed page—for example, providing illustrations representing each stage of the narrative so that less literate readers could "read the pictures," or using spacious layout and typography for ease of reading. Other features, such as the use of commentary, were borrowed from elite culture but adapted to the needs of the less learned reader.

One of the most favored reading practices was vocalization, either to oneself or to an audience. The lexicon of vocalization included *songdu* (or *dusong*), *jiangdu*, and *fengsong*.[71] Vocalization was a practice borrowed from Chinese traditional techniques of study; memorization, chanting, and reading out loud were the usual techniques for acquiring an elementary education and, later, mastery of the Classics. Much early educational material was composed in verse, in part to make vocalization and memorization easier. Even before formal education began, parents would teach children to recite classical poems.[72] During the late Ming and Qing periods, potted histories written in parallel prose or verse were in common circulation.[73] Students destined to be shopkeepers, artisans, and merchants were taught to read and chant jingles with a limited number of characters relevant to their specific trades.[74] Formal education began with the rote memorization of primers such as the *Sanzi jing* (Three-character classic) and *Baijia xing* (Myriad family names) before moving on to the Four Books.[75] There was little if any explication. The curriculum emphasized the ability to memorize and recite classical material (much of it in metrical form) and to match rhyming couplets. Gui Youguang (1507–71) complained that local schools focused too much on "reciting the texts and matching lines" to the detriment of moral teaching: "Today people simply teach students to recite and match rhyming lines. If the students recite and match well, then they are thought to be intelligent, but the teachers know not of the nature and sensibilities of their students nor of their character, nor of how they serve their relations and their peers."[76] Zhu Xi sought to make this mindless chanting meaningful by urging that the reader engage his mind actively in the process: "recite until the words appear to come from one's own mouth."[77]

The assumption that a text was to be vocalized or chanted, an integral part of Confucian education, was adopted too in reading practices of texts in general. For example, Zhang Zhupo, in his preface to the *Plum in the Golden Vase*, notes that he was taught to read slowly and savor each syllable: "I would linger over each character as though it were a syllable from an aria of *kunqu* opera."[78] As discussed earlier, women's literacy practices were particularly associated with vocalization. Early editions of the *Narrative of the Three Kingdoms*, including the edition of Xiuranzi, contain a simple jingle before the text proper. This verse prelude, which sums up the main events of the narrative, is commonly found in chantefable texts and served as a useful mnemonic for the reader to chant.

The ability to read a text out loud in meaningful segments (*poju*) was the hallmark of an educated man.[79] Memorization and recitation of favorite texts continued well into the twentieth century. Louis Cha (also known as Chin Yung, 1924–), the popular Hong Kong writer of martial arts novels, has described how his mother and aunts loved to read the *Dream of the Red Chamber:* "Everyone would compete to recite the chapter titles and the poems in the text. If you won you could win a sweet. I used to listen from the side. I felt it was sissy and boring but when my mother put a sweet into my hand I suddenly became interested."[80] Examples could be multiplied endlessly. The common practice of vocalization and memorization, particularly of verse, could well account for the large amount of metrical material in Chinese vernacular narratives, a feature that has long puzzled Western commentators, who tend to regard the verse sections as redundant.[81]

China's earliest vernacular texts took as their model various oral and performance genres that were based on the spoken language of a particular region. Well before the emergence of vernacular print, China had a long-established tradition of what could be called "performance texts" (i.e., texts that record a performance of an oral or religious-liturgical genre or were modeled on these genres). When a performance text (such as a play, chantefable, or melodic narrative) was published, it was essential to make a decision about the spoken language to be recorded as well as the rhyming schemes of its melodies or arias. To succeed in the market, publishers now had to make decisions about the linguistic backgrounds, educational levels, and likely reading practices of their target readership. In Europe, the emergence of a literary reading public was inseparable from the development of new vernacular languages that became a kind of *Hochsprache*, or language held in common by the educated reading public.[82] We still know too little about the choices made by Chinese editors in this regard, but one can point to two contradictory trends, one toward the use of regional languages (*fangyan*) and the other toward a standardized vernacular (*guanhua*, lit. "official language") based mainly on northern speech.

Publishers of some plays and chantefable-type genres sometimes chose to write in dialectal usages or to base rhymed material on the phonological patterns of specific areas. The decision of the (presumably) Beijing-based publishers to rhyme the "Hua Guan Suo" chantefable with the phonology of the northern Wu dialect is one puzzling case.[83] Other examples include lute ballads in Suzhou speech, plays with dialogues in Wu dialect, and plays from Minnan with arias based on local musical and dialect modes.[84] However, apart from the occasional work aimed at wealthy markets in Jiangnan and Fujian, or those designed for the performer, most authors apparently saw themselves as publishing for a national market, or at least a market beyond their immediate areas.

The equivalent in China of the vernaculars shared by educated groups in European countries would perhaps be the "book-reading speech" (*dushu yin*) of the north. "Book-reading speech" was the recitation mode taught in formal education from as early as the seventh century C.E.[85] A key work in establishing the dominance of northern pronunciation was the *Zhongyuan yinyun* (Sounds and rhymes of the central plain, 1324), a manual of rhyming and prosody designed for the composer of dramatic arias and songs. The first Ming emperor, a southerner, commissioned a phonology based on northern *dushu yin*, the *Hongwu zhengyun* (Correct rhymes of the Hongwu era), compiled in 1375, in order to provide a standard for song composition.[86]

Although manuals to assist with the composition of southern arias were also produced, the northern works remained influential even in the south. For example, Wang Jide (ca. 1560–1625) from Shaoxing, south of the Yangzi, noted in his preface to an edition of the *Record of the Western Chamber* (1614), "[T]he writing down of songs is different from that of the Classics and histories. For this reason I have recorded the phonology of the central plain, as in the *Zhongyuan yinyun*."[87] His teacher, Xu Wei (1521–93), also from Shaoxing, wrote an important work on southern drama but declared, "In singing, regional accent is to be avoided more than anything else."[88] Xu Wei's preferred pronunciation standard was probably not the *Zhongyuan yinyun* but a more ancient phonology.[89] Editors recognized that texts based on the performing arts containing a high number of colloquialisms became obscure in succeeding centuries. For example, in his annotated edition of the *Record of the Western Chamber*, Xu Wei explained that his method was not so much to explicate classical allusions as to concentrate on dialect, terms of abuse, the jargon of actors and publishers, examples drawn from glyphomancy, vulgar and refined usages, and so on.[90]

The same basic text might be produced in different versions to meet the linguistic, performative, and literary tastes of varying readerships. For example, Shi Guoqi (Qing) observed that the edition of *Xixiang ji zhugongdiao* in his possession is "a transmitted text for reading" (*liuchuan duben*). It can be distinguished from the songbooks of the same story used by courtesans (*yuanjia changben*). The *duben* version has an abundance of arias, scanty prose, some dialect usages, and no musical notation.[91] Similarly, Ling Mengchu (1580–1644) observed that his edition of the *Record of the Western Chamber* "is really an aid to broad cultivation and can be read as a literary composition; it should not be regarded as a play."[92] According to He Bi, this famous play was in circulation in three types of editions. The "marketplace editions" (*shike ben*), named after the likely sites of performance, included musical annotation and were designed for use by performers. The "commercial editions" (*fangke ben*) included punctuation and commentary; presumably these texts were produced by commercial publishers for aficionados of this famous play. The "old editions" (*jiuben*) contained erroneous phonological annotations done by "village schoolteachers." Nowadays, he notes, the old editions are no longer reprinted.[93] The four great Ming narratives are circulated in two textual traditions, one in simpler pictorial form and the other a more literary text, presumably for differing audiences.[94]

Woodblock publication made possible the replication of endless black-and-white images and the rapid transposition of the same or similar pictures across a number of texts. Vernacular publishers used a range of illustrative modes: pictorial (*shangtu xiawen*, with pictures on the top third of each page and text below), half-folio illustrations, and two-in-one illustrations with one picture on top of the other.[95] By the late Ming illustrations could be grouped at the beginning of a work or even in an independent fascicle instead of interpersed throughout the text.[96] Preface writers believed that illustrations not only attracted readers but also assisted their comprehension of the text. The Yue publishing house (Yuejia) of Beijing, for instance, criticized "marketplace editions" of the *Record of the Western Chamber* because the texts were full of errors, the pictures did not match the progress of the story, and they were not easy to read. They claimed that their edition (1498), in contrast, had a large typeface and pictures that matched each stage of the play for easy comprehension: "Now the songs and pictures match, so people lodged in inns or traveling in boats, whether they be roaming for pleasure or sitting in some distant place, can get a copy of this text, look it over, and sing it correctly from beginning to end and thereby refresh their hearts."[97] Pictures were thought not only to aid the less learned reader but also to help to impart the work's moral wisdom. Yuan Fengzi, in the 1548 preface to the Escorial edition of the *Sanguo zhizhuan*, notes that illustrations (*hua*) were added to the original text: "the illustrations comment on the narrative (*zhuan*) and the narrative speaks of what is in the *Annals* (*zhi*; i.e., the *Sanguo zhi*) and thus the work [achieves its goal of] encouragement to do good and warning against evil."[98]

But, as the Yue publishers pointed out in their self-serving attack on marketplace editions of the *Record of the Western Chamber*, illustrations in "chap-book"-type literature were not always a reliable tool for comprehension.[99] In higher-quality texts, the disjuncture between text and illustration was not a problem, for illustrations were employed largely for aesthetic purposes. As Hegel has noted, the illustrative art of the block print borrowed many techniques and conventions from the fine arts of the elite; and the finest carvers might achieve some degree of fame for their work. In some quality editions of the late Ming, exquisite illustrations are attributed to noted carvers.[100]

Nonetheless, the necessarily representational nature of illustrative art was often viewed as vulgar and merely decorative—the art of mimesis as opposed to the individual, self-referential art of the literati.[101] This would explain the ambivalence some literati publishers felt about the inclusion of illustrations in their own editions. For example, Ling Mengchu considered illustrations a necessary concession to the marketplace. In his literary edition of *Record of the Western Chamber*, he declared, "It should be unnecessary to include illustrations (*tuhua*), but people place importance on 'rouge and powder.' I am concerned that people will complain about the lack of illustrations (*xiang*) and so at each act I have placed titles and plot summaries of four lines (*timu*) together with illustrations (*hui*) in line with the current custom."[102] The same ambivalence is reflected in the lexicon of viewing. Craig Clunas hypothesizes that *guan* (to visualize or contemplate) reflects the aesthete's appreciative viewing of an object of high art, whereas *kan* (look) reflects the gaze of the unlearned at a mimetic depiction.[103]

Commentary was also used to attract readers.[104] Yu Xiangdou was one of the first to use his commentary as a selling point by calling his editions "commentarial editions" (*piping* or *pinglin*). A prolific publisher, he is known for his examination of essay extracts, annotated extracts from classical works, encyclopedias, commercial manuals, almanacs, rhyme guides, and fictional works, many in pictorial form. He produced up to three different editions of the *Narrative of the Three Kingdoms* and one edition of *Water Margin*. Although his works have been scorned by critics, he was one of the first to cater specifically to less learned readers. According to Y. W. Ma, "[W]ith the possible exception of Feng [Menglong, 1574–1646], it is difficult to name another individual in the Ming period who did so much to champion the cause of popular culture in general and vernacular literature in particular."[105]

Yu's commentary to vernacular narratives is quite distinct from the earlier commentarial traditions that concentrated on place-names and the odd phonetic gloss as well as from later commentaries that sought to highlight the aesthetic qualities of a text. In a study of Yu's *Piping Sanguo zhizhuan* (Commentarial edition of the *Chronicles of the Three Kingdoms*), I argued that Yu treated this narrative as a manual on strategy that offered a "watered-down" version of complex historical events, aphorisms dealing with tactics, and simplified didactic lessons.[106] Yu's commentary could be categorized into three types: those making affective points (playing on the readers' emotions and encouraging them to identify with heroes and villains, the victor and the vanquished), those passing judgment on the action (providing moral assessment of tactics), and those pointing up certain social phenomena. His commentary offered contradictory interpretations and, unlike the commentary of later literati on the aesthetics of the novel, did not seek to present a coherent pattern along Confucian lines. It was designed for selective, discontinuous reading by readers interested in the strategic application of the contents to everyday living.[107]

In another edition, this time with the slightly altered title, *Sanguo zhi pinglin* (Annals of the Three Kingdoms, with abundant commentary), held at Waseda University, Yu tried another tactic to attract his reading public. In this edition, likely published after the *Piping* version, Yu has broadened the categories of his commentary to include not just *ping* (evaluations of characters and events in line with the strategy used) but also a battery of other types of commentary, such as *shiyi* (explanations of place-names, allusions, and terms), *buyi* (supplements), *kaozheng* (textual evidence), and *yinshi* (pronunciation). This proliferation of types of commentary was almost certainly a result of the pressure of a highly competitive market for editions of the *Narrative of the Three Kingdoms*. Nanjing editions, from which Yu presumably borrowed, included the above categories of commentary, which imitated the traditional apparatus of the Classics. In spite of the impressive appearance of this "abundant commentary," however, Yu's comments are often quite elementary in nature and were surely directed at a reading public at the foundational stages of literacy. The very first line of commentary in the volume is the elucidation of the term for eunuchs, *huanguan*, as "officials who manage affairs in the palace" (1a). Celebrated historical figures, such as the military strategist Sunzi, are identified; Qin and Xiang are explained as Qin Shihuang and Xiang Yu. One even finds the word *qi* (wife) explained as an alternative term for woman, *fu* (13:5b). As in the *Piping* edition, the *Pinglin* version contains simplified interpretations of events and tactics.

During the Ming period, it was the pictorial editions of editors such as Yu Xiangdou, with their simple commentary and interpretive frameworks, that predominated in the market for less learned readers. Although Yu published these editions for unlearned readers and those in the process of acquiring literacy, he took pains to flatter his target public with the appellation "literati" (*shizi*)[108] and to impress them with the kind of pseudocritical apparatus found in the Classics. The same phenomenon has been noted in the acquisition of curios, antiques, and artworks by nouveaux riches seeking to acquire "cultural capital" in the late Ming period.[109]

References

1   I use the word "vernacular" with some reservations. Some historical novels discussed here, such as the *Narrative of the Three Kingdoms (Sanguozhi tongsu yanyi)*, were composed in simplified classical Chinese. In other narratives, such as *Water Margin (Shuihu zhuan)*, one finds a range of styles from classical to vernacular. Throughout the imperial period, a number of historical popularizations continued to rely on a simplified classical style (Wilt Idema refers to these as "chapbooks"), while literati authors gradually developed a more "inventive" vernacular style in a range of registers (see Wilt L. Idema, *Chinese Vernacular Fiction: The Formative Period* [Leiden: E. J. Brill, 1974], xi–xii, lii–lvii). On the "interpenetration" of both classical and vernacular in so-called vernacular texts, see Patrick Hanan, *The Chinese Vernacular Story* (Cambridge, Mass.: Harvard University Press, 1981), 14.

2   Ōki Yasushi, "Minmatsu Kōnan ni okeru shuppan bunka no kenkyū" (A study of publishing culture in late Ming Jiangnan), *Hiroshima daigagku bungakubu kiyō* (Bulletin of the literature department of Hiroshima University) 50, special issue: 1, 3–5, 15–16. For the economic factors that stimulated the commercialization of the economy and book production during this period, see Timothy Brook, *The Confusions of Pleasure: Commerce and Culture in Ming China* (Berkeley: University of California Press, 1998), 129–33, 167–80.

3   Natalie Zemon Davis, "Printing and the People," in her *Society and Culture in Early Modern France* (rpt. Stanford: Stanford University Press, [1965] 1985), 192–93.

4   D. F. McKenzie, *Bibliography and the Sociology of Texts: The Panizzi Lectures* (London: The British Library, 1986), 6–7.

5   James J. Y. Liu, *Theories of Literature* (Chicago: University of Chicago Press, 1975), 114, 128.

6   Cited in Huang Lin and Han Tongwen, *Zhongguo lidai xiaoshuo lunzhu xuan* (A collection of prefaces from Chinese fiction through the ages) (Jiangxi: Jiangxi renmin chubanshe, 1982), vol. 1, p. 105.

7   Translated by David T. Roy, "Chang Chu-p'o on How to Read the *Chin P'ing Mei* (The Plum in the Golden Vase)," in David Rolston, ed., *How to Read the Chinese Novel* (Princeton: Princeton University Press, 1990), 236.

8   Cited in Huang and Han, *Zhongguo lidai xiaoshuo lunzhu xuan*, vol. 1, p. 383.

9   Chinese commentarial tradition on the classics began in the first century C.E., so one can assume that there were perceived difficulties even at this early stage. See John B. Henderson, *Scripture, Canon, and Commentary: A Comparison of Confucian and Western Exegesis* (Princeton: Princeton University Press, 1991), 43 ff. By Zhu Xi's era, with the emergence of the world's first print culture, the broader circulation of texts made possible by the new technology intensified the issue of how to read and interpret the archaic language of the canon.

10   Translated by Daniel K. Gardner, *Learning to Be a Sage: Selections from the* Conversations of Master Chu, arranged topically (Berkeley: University of California Press, 1990), 154 (5.47). I cite Gardner's lucid translation of excerpts of Zhu Xi's "Dushu fa" where included in his *Learning to be a Sage* but occasionally choose to depart from it to highlight the use of metaphorical terms.

11   Gardner, *Learning to be a Sage*, 151 (5.38). Henderson notes that Chinese exegetes were particularly concerned about the perceived "order and coherence" of the Confucian canon; see *Scripture, Canon, and Commentary*, 113. He notes further the "apparent paradox" in Confucian commentary that the classics are "plain yet obscure" (134).

12   *ZZYL* 11.10a, p. 297. All references below are to the "Dushu fa" in volume 1. For this reference, see 11.10a, p. 297.

13   Lit., *meng shi gongfu lihui*. Translated in Gardner, *Learning to be a Sage*, 132 (4.23); *ZZYL* 10.4b, p. 262.

14   "If you just read the skin (*pifu*) then you will fall into error," *ZZYL* 10.2a, p. 257. See Gardner's more abstract rendition, "If you simply read what appears on the surface, you will misunderstand," in *Learning to Be a Sage*, 129.

15   *ZZYL* 10.2a, p. 257. Cf. Gardner, who refers to the crack as an "opening" in *Learning to be a Sage*, 130.

16   *ZZYL* 10.2b, p. 258.

17   *ZZYL* 10.3a, p. 259.

18   *ZZYL* 10:3a, p. 259.

19   *ZZYL* 10.10a, p. 273.

20   See *shu qi jin gu, ZZYL* 10.2b, p. 258. Cf. Gardner, "keep your body alert," in *Learning to be a Sage*, 130 (4.13).

21   *ZZYL* 10:2a, p. 257.

22   Zhu Xi quotes the locus classicus on reading in the *Xunzi*: "[The superior man] recites texts [*sung shu*; lit. "recites numbers"] in order to penetrate [*guan*] the Way. . . ." Gardner, *Learning to be a Sage*, 136 (4.37).

23   Gardner, *Learning to be a Sage*, 147 (5.16); *ZZYL* 11.3a, p. 283.

24   *ZZYL* 11.2b, p. 282.

25   *ZZYL* 10.6b, p. 266. Cf. Gardner, *Learning to be a Sage*, 135: "in reading we must first become intimately familiar with the text so that its words seem to come from our own mouths."

26   Susan Cherniak, "Book Culture and Textual Transmission in Sung China," *Harvard Journal of Asiatic Studies* 54.1 (1994): 50.

27   According to Robert J. Mahoney, Lu Xiangshan accused Zhu Xi of "neglecting *personal* oral communication" in teaching and relying overmuch on the printed word. See "Lu Hsiang-shan and the Importance of Oral Communication in Confucian Education" (Ph.D. dissertation, Columbia University, 1986), 8.

28   For late Ming examples, see the instructions of noted bibliophile Qi Cheng-ahan (1565–1628), to his sons, *Dushu xun* (Instruction in how to study), and the work of Wu Yingqi (1594–1645), *Dushu zhiguan lu* (Record of reading and meditation). Both can be conveniently consulted together with two examples from the Qing period in Wang Yuguang et al., eds., *Dushu siguan* (Four examples of how to read) (Wuhan: Cishu chubanshe, 1997).

29   Wm. Theodore de Bary, *Neo-Confucian Orthodoxy and the Learning of the Mind-and-Heart* (New York: Columbia University Press, 1981), 49.

30   de Bary, *Neo-Confucian Orthodoxy*, 62. Even examination questions on the Five Classics were dropped during the Ming period.

31   The metaphorical term here comes from the craft of building. A *yinkuo* is a bevel, a tool used to measure angles and ensure that a timber frame is square. In literary studies the term refers to cutting, editing, or reshaping a text.

32   de Bary, *Neo-Confucian Orthodoxy*, 111.

33   A preface to the *Dong Xi Han tongsu yanyi* in Huang and Han, *Zhongguo lidai xiaoshuo*, vol. 1, p. 176.

34   See *DMB*, vol. 2, pp. 405–7.

35   Cited in Huang and Han, *Zhongguo lidai xiaoshuo*, vol. 1, p. 99.

36   Huang and Han, *Zhongguo lidai xiaoshuo*, vol. 1, p. 104.

37   *Sanguo zhizhuan*, held in the Escorial Museum, microfilm at the Harvard-Yenching Library, preface 1b. The idea that the Classics corresponded to a universal moral, historical, or mental order had become commonplace well before this time. See particularly the view of Wang Yangming, which has interesting parallels with the somewhat later preface of Yuan Fengzi (Henderson, *Scripture, Canon, and Commentary*, 48).

38   David Rolston gives several examples, most dating from the seventeenth century and later; see his *Traditional Chinese Fiction and Fiction Commentary: Reading and Writing between the Lines* (Stanford: Stanford University Press, 1997), 108–9, also chap. 5.

39   Discussed in Anne E. McLaren, *Chinese Popular Culture and Ming Chantefables* (Leiden: E.J. Brill, 1998), 4–8.

40   By the seventeenth century the same principle was applied to morality books; see Cynthia J. Brokaw, *The Ledgers of Merit and Demerit: Social Change and Moral Order in Late Imperial China* (Princeton: Princeton University Press, 1991), 168–69.

41   On the importance of hand-copying books long after the invention of printing, see Ōki Yasushi, "Minmatsu Kōnan ni okeru shuppan bunka no kenkyū," 8–10. On the manuscript circulation of fiction and plays, see Robert Hegel, *Reading Illustrated Fiction in Late Imperial China* (Stanford: Stanford University Press, 1998), 158–61. He notes that some manuscript editions became valued collector's items.

42   Cited in Huang and Han, *Zhongguo lidai xiaoshuo*, vol. 1, p. 104.

43   Cai Yi, ed., *Zhongguo gudian xiqu xuba huibian* (Prefaces and colophons on classical Chinese dramas, compiled according to categories), 4 vols. (Jinan: Qi Lu shushe, 1989), vol. 2, p. 620.

44   For a detailed discussion, see Andrew H. Plaks, *The Four Masterworks of the Ming Novel* (Princeton: Princeton University Press, 1987), 55–72.

45   Huang and Han, *Zhongguo lidai xiaoshuo*, vol. 1, p. 111.

46   Cai, *Zhongguo gudian xiqu*, vol. 2, p. 572.

47   Huang and Han, *Zhongguo lidai xiaoshuo*, vol. 1, p. 152.

48   Huang and Han, *Zhongguo lidai xiaoshuo*, vol. 1, p. 125.

49   Huang and Han, *Zhongguo lidai xiaoshuo*, vol. 1, p. 166.

50   Zhu Yixuan and Liu Yuchen, *Shuihuzhuan ziliao huibian* (Collected material on *Water Margin*) (Tianjin: Baihua wenyi chubanshe, 1981), 190. On the early non-extant edition attributed to Guo Xun, see Plaks, *The Four Masterworks*, 283–85.

51   See, for example, the conclusion to the chantefable "Patriarch Kai," which addresses each household member in turn. See McLaren, *Chinese Popular Culture*, 125.

52   Tadao Sakai, "Confucianism and Popular Educational Works," in Wm. Theodore de Bary, ed., *Self and Society in Ming Thought* (New York: Columbia University Press, 1970), 335, 346.

53   Huang and Han, *Zhongguo lidai xiaoshuo*, vol. 1, p. 331.

54   In the *Classic of History*, the following song deals with complaints against the reigning emperor: "It was the lesson of our great ancestor/The people should be cherished;/They should not be downtrodden. . . . When I look throughout the empire/ Of the simple men and simple women (*yufu yufu*),/Anyone may surpass me." James Legge, trans., *The Chinese Classics*, vol. 3: *The Shoo King* (rpt. Taipei: Wenshezhe chubanshe, 1971), 158.

55   Sakai, "Confucian and Popular Educational Works," 339.

56   Huang and Han, *Zhongguo lidai xiaoshuo*, vol. 1, p. 109.

57   Huang and Han, *Zhongguo lidai xiaoshuo*, vol. 1, p. 109.

58   Cai, *Zhongguo gudian xiqu*, vol. 2, p. 615.

59   Huang and Han, *Zhongguo lidai xiaoshuo*, vol. 1, p. 120.

60   Huang and Han, *Zhongguo lidai xiaoshuo*, vol. 1, p. 117.

61   Zhu Yixuan and Liu Yuchen, *Sanguo yanyi ziliao huibian* (Collected materials on the *Narrative of the Three Kingdoms*) (Tianjin: Baihua wenyi chubanshe, 1983), 284.

62   He is attributed with the authorship of the *Journey to the West*. See his preface to the *Yuding zhi*, in Huang and Han, *Zhongguo lidai xiaoshuo*, vol. 1, p. 122.

63   Anne E. McLaren, "Chantefables and the Textual Evolution of the San-kuo-chih yen-i," *T'oung Pao* 71 (1985): 187.

64   This preface, dated 1641, is Jin's third preface and is addressed to his young son. See Huang and Han, *Zhongguo lidai xiaoshuo*, vol. 1, p. 277.

65   The exception would be references to women in chantefables and similar works. There is some evidence that in the seventeenth century women read or made use of various practical texts such as books of model letters. See Ellen Widmer, "The Huanduzhai of Hangzhou and Suzhou: A Study in Seventeenth-Century Publishing," *Harvard Journal of Asiatic Studies* 56.1 (1996): 77–122.

66   Ye sheng, *Shuidong riji* (Daily notes of Ye Sheng) (Beijing: Zhonghua shuju, 1980), j. 21, p. 214.

67   Discussed in McLaren, *Chinese Popular Culture*, 72–76.

68   McLaren, *Chinese Popular Culture*, 73–74.

69   McLaren, *Chinese Popular Culture*, 74.

70   This is the attribute given by the poet Yang Weizhen (1296–1379) to Zhu Guiying, a storyteller who was renowned for her historical tales and learning; see Hu Shiying, *Huaben xiaoshuo gailun* (Survey of short stories and fiction), 2 vols. (Beijing: Zhonghua shuju, 1980), vol. 1, p. 284.

71   All these terms refer to reading or reciting out loud. On the prevalence of vocalization in reading generally, see Wang, *Dushu siguan*, 109.

72   Wang Ermin, "Zhongguo chuantong jisong zhi xue yu shiyun koujue" (Chinese traditional recitation methods and arts of rhyming), *Zhongyang yanjiuyuan Jindai shi yanjiusuo jikan* (Journal of the Institute of Modern History of the Academic Sinica) 23 (1994): 36.

73   Wang Ermin discusses *Longwen bianying* (Spur to easy reading) and *Youxue qionglin* (Jade forest primer) in his "Zhongguo chuantong jisong," 39–41.

74   For example, see the *Siyan zazi* (Miscellaneous words in lines of four syllables), a four-syllable-a-line jingle listing common commodities (Wang, "Zhongguo chuantong jisong," 37). According to Wang, farmers learned jingles about climate, basic astronomy, and the seasons (50); he also reproduces a fishmonger's "seven-syllable-a-line verse about fish names" (55).

75   Wang, "Zhongguo chuantong jisong," 37.

76   Wang Liqi, *Yuan Ming Qing sandai jinhui xiaoshuo xiqu shiliao*, 90.

77   See note 25.

78   Translated by David T. Roy in Rolston, *How to Read the Chinese Novel*, 234.

79   According to the Ming author Wu Yingqi, in *Dushu zhiguan lu*, in the compilation of Wang, *Dushu siguan*, 85.

80   Sun Lichuan, "Zhongguo yanyi: Zhongguo gudian xiaoshuo de dianfan" (The Chinese *yanyi* genre: Models for Chinese traditional fiction), *Ming Bao* 386. 2 (1998): 52.

81   Discussed in McLaren, *Chinese Popular Culture*, 283–84.

82   Erich Auerbach, *Literary Language and Its Public in Late Antiquity and in the Middle Ages*, trans. Ralph Manheim (Princeton: Princeton University Press, 1993), 248.

83   Note the chapter by Furuya Akihiro on phonology in Inoue Taizan, Ōki Yasushi, Kin Bunkyō, Hikami Tadashi, and Furuya Akihiro, *Ka Kan Saku den no kenkyū* (A study of the Hua Guan Suo zhuan) (Tokyo: Kyūko shoin, 1989), 326–46. This text was discovered at a location in the relevant dialect area but was apparently published in faraway Beijing. See McLaren, *Chinese Popular Culture*, 19.

84   For a brief survey of plays and narratives containing dialect, see Zhou Zhenhe and You Rujie, *Fangyan yu Zhongguo wenhua* (Dialect and Chinese culture) (Shanghai: Renmin wenxue chubanshe, 1986).

85   The first known phonological book written to assist students to read texts and scholars to compose literary works is the *Qieyun* of Lu Fayan (ca. 601); see Zhao Cheng, *Zhongguo gudai yunshu* (Ancient Chinese works of phonology) (Beijing: Zhonghua shuju, 1991), 18. The regional languages that formed the basis of *dushuyin* changed over the centuries. On *dushuyin*, see Zhao, *Zhongguo gudai yunshu*, 25–27.

86   Hok-lam Chan notes that because most of the compilers came from the south they were relatively unfamiliar with northern pronunciation; see *DMB*, vol. 2, p. 1642. Zhao argues that the *Hongwu zhengyun* was less influential than the *Zhongyuan yinyun* because the latter reflected actual speech changes in the north (*shuohua yin*) whereas the imperial phonology preserved the "official" phonology of an earlier age; see *Zhongguo gudai yunshu*, 81, 83.

87   Cai, *Zhongguo gudian xiqu*, vol. 2, p. 661.

88   K. C. Leung, *Hsu Wei as Drama Critic: An Annotated Translation of the Nan-tz'u hsü-lu*, Asian Studies Program Publication No. 7 (Eugene: University of Oregon, 1988), 76.

89   Leung, *Hsu Wei as Drama Critic*, 169 n. 163.

90   Cai, *Zhongguo gudian xiqu*, vol. 2, p. 575.

91   Cai, *Zhongguo gudian xiqu*, vol. 2, p. 575.

92   Cai, *Zhongguo gudian xiqu*, vol. 2, p. 678.

93   Cai, *Zhongguo gudian xiqu*, vol. 2, p. 642.

94   On audiences for the two textual streams of the *Narrative of the Three Kingdoms*, see Anne E. McLaren, "Ming Audiences and Vernacular Hermeneutics: The Uses of *The Romance of the Three Kingdoms*," *T'oung Pao* 81.1–3 (1995): 51–80.

95   McLaren, *Chinese Popular Culture*, 59–63; Hegel, *Reading Illustrated Fiction*, 164–289.

96   Hegel, *Reading Illustrated Fiction*, 198. Hegel also notes that illustrations were virtually "ubiquitous" in texts by the late sixteenth century (6).

97   Translation by Stephen H. West and Wilt L. Idema, eds. and trans., *The Story of the Western Wing* (1991; Berkeley: University of California Press, 1995), 287.

98   *Sanguo zhizhuan*, held in the Escorial Museum, microfilm at the Harvard-Yenching Library, preface lab.

99   The same scene could be transposed to other contexts; see McLaren, *Chinese Popular Culture*, 64.

100   Hegel, *Reading Illustrated Fiction*, 96, 142, 151, 193, 290.

101   Craig Clunas, *Pictures and Visuality in Early Modern China* (Princeton: Princeton University Press, 1997), 14–18.

102   Cited in Cai, *Zhongguo gudian xiqu*, vol. 2, p. 678.

103   Clunas, *Pictures and Visuality*, 120.

104   For a detailed study of commentary in "literati" fiction, see Rolston, *Traditional Chinese Fiction*. He outlines three stages in the development of commentarial editions of the Ming narratives. In the earliest stage (late sixteenth century) commentary was "rudimentary" and inspired by commercial motives. The works of Yu Xiang-dou (discussed above) belong to this stage. The second stage was dominated by imitations of Li Zhi commentary; the third stage, by the more inventive commentary of editors who took on an almost authorial role in their revision of the texts (2–4).

105   Y. W. Ma, "Introduction," p. 3, in Hartmut Walravens, ed., *Two Recently Discovered Fragments of the Chinese Novels* San-kuo-chih yen-i *and* Shui-hu chuan (Hamburg: C. Bell Verlag, 1982).

106   McLaren, "Ming Audiences and Vernacular Hermeneutics," 64–80.

107   McLaren, "Ming Audiences and Vernacular Hermeneutics," 67–76.

108   Above the preface to his *Piping* edition, Yu adds some advertising material that refers critically to preexisting editions. One text that does meet with his approval is the one produced by the Liu publishing house of Fujian. Their edition is said to be "free of errors, literati (*shizi*) read it with pleasure," but unfortunately the blocks had worn down so no additional copies of that edition could be printed ("Xu," 2a). Since Yu proclaims that his version is superior to existing texts, he is here flattering his own target readership by implying that they are literati.

109   On the production of printed manuals concerning curios and antiques in the Ming era, see Brook, *The Confusions of Pleasure*, 78–79.

Chapter 20

William St. Clair

AT THE BOUNDARIES OF THE READING NATION

WHEN JOHN CLARE WAS A BOY in Northamptonshire at the beginning of the nineteenth century, the printed texts to which he and his friends had easy access had changed little during the previous 200 years. The King James version of the English-language Bible was read in church and at home, and there were plentiful almanacs, many with astrological and magical prognostications. The ballads and chapbooks sold at fairs and from house to house by chapmen contained many titles which predated the 1600 clamp-down. Other books were occasionally to be found, notably the ancient and misleading guide to sex, *Aristotle's Compleat Masterpiece* and the standard school book, Dyche's *Guide to the English Tongue*. Clare tells how he walked six miles to the nearest town to try to buy a copy of Thomson's *Seasons* which he had heard was for sale cheaply.[1] With agricultural wages around a shilling a day, even Thomson's *Seasons* was beyond the reach of most families.[2]

Nor does Clare's experience appear to have been different from that of many boys. The same ballads and chapbooks were part of the childhood of Edmund Burke, Thomas Holcroft, William Godwin, Francis Place, Samuel Taylor Coleridge, Thomas Carter, George Crabbe, William Hazlitt, William Wordsworth, and Walter Scott.[3] Hugh Miller, who grew up in the far north of Scotland and Samuel Bamford in industrial Manchester knew many of the same titles, and reading in rural Ireland was little different. Two wholesale trade catalogues prepared in 1754 and 1764 at the height of the high monopoly period list the extensive stocks which were then available through the chapman networks of England and America.[4] Although only a few copies of the materials that were advertised have survived, the catalogues enable us to reconstruct the whole culture of print, both literary and visual, that was consistently available to a large constituency of the English-speaking reading nation across many generations.

Chapbooks consisted of twelve or twenty-four pages made from one or two sheets, folded and unstitched. Ballads were printed on one sheet or half a sheet. The length of the texts was, to a large extent, determined by what could be comfortably included in multiples of a half sheet. In many cases there were both chapbook and ballad versions of the same story, and some longer stories were divided into parts which could be bought and read independently or in series. Almost invariably, they were illustrated with at least one wood-cut from a store of blocks, many of which were also very ancient. Manufacturing on the eve of the romantic period had scarcely changed since the sixteenth century. The minimum print run was a ream, or a half ream, equivalent to editions of 1,000 or 2,000 for chapbooks, or 2,000 or 4,000 for ballads, but, when we find that, as early as 1736 a single Irish chapman had more than 2,000 copies of some titles in stock, it seems likely that the normal print run was longer than the minimum.[5] According to Thomas Gent, a printer writing in the early eighteenth century, the apprentices and journeymen who made the ballads worked from five in the morning until midnight.[6]

During most of the eighteenth century, the centre of manufacturing was Aldermary Churchyard in London with stocks held in the Ballad Warehouse nearby. From there the chapbooks and ballads were sold retail to individuals and wholesale to chapmen serving a wide radius round the capital which seems to have been roughly the extreme reach of a man walking. The owners had agents in a nationwide network of English provincial centres, all easily reached by water, where other stocks were held. During the 1720s, newspapers published in provincial towns began to advertise the routes which their chapmen would take round the villages.[7] By the high monopoly period, the popular print sector had become almost completely monopolised in the hands of a single London firm of Dicey, which held the intellectual properties, the unsold stocks, and the manufacturing plant, in all the favourite titles.[8] The Victorian antiquary John Ashton, who made a collection of eighteenth-century chapbooks printed in Newcastle, noticed that many were almost exactly the same as those produced in London, even to the woodcut illustrations. Although these books may have been copied, without permission, from the London originals, as is commonly assumed, they may be evidence of the licensing of manufacturing in the north of England.[9]

The London publishers continued to use the old black-letter fonts for nearly a century after they had ceased to be used in mainstream print. The same woodblocks, some registered as intellectual properties as early as the sixteenth century, were reused again and again until they became so badly worn as to be scarcely recognisable.[10] The same woodcuts were used to illustrate a wide range of texts, that of the Virgin Queen Elizabeth doing equally well for *The Wanton Wife of Bath*. Until the 1580s it had been common for mainstream books, including histories and English-language Bibles, to consist both of printed texts and of engraved illustrations. But suddenly after that date, most newly published books consisted only of print. Some historians have linked the change to an increasing aversion to images as relics of the old Roman Catholic religion. In the popular ballad and chapbook sector, however, illustrations continued to be an intrinsic part of the book all through the whole period of the freeze. This suggests that, as with other sudden shifts in publishing practice, we should be looking for explanations based on changes in the governing structures, perhaps some stricter demarcation between printers and engravers, or some agreement when the popular sector divided from the mainstream, rather than assuming that they reflected changes in readerly taste.[11]

Some editions have silly printing errors even on the title pages, *Tom Stitch the vaylor* (instead of 'taylor') *Sir Bevis, a most nodle* [for 'noble'] *Knight*, signs of haste in manufacturing and the carelessness of a monopolist.[12] Titles were frequently reregistered, and seldom came on the market. Although they looked primitive and provincial, features which have fostered the fallacy that they are emanations of 'the folk', they were actually produced by rich owners who were as much part of the central management of the London book industry as the franchisees of the English-language Bible and the proprietors of Shakespeare.[13] At least one was knighted.[14]

Most chapbooks and ballads, even those abridged from longer works by famous authors, were printed without any author being named, and most were undated. Many had a continuous history back to the age of manuscript, having become private intellectual properties in the earliest days of print.[15] Others were the work of Thomas Deloney, Richard Johnson, and other abridgers, adapters and balladeers of the Elizabethan age. The 1596 anthology of pre-clamp-down ballad versions of longer works, *The Garland of Good Will*, was still available in the romantic period, having apparently been continuously available for over two hundred years. Innumerable thousands read the romance of *Argalus and Parthenia* who had never heard of Sidney's *Arcadia* from which it had long ago been abridged. *Dorastus and Fawnia*, an abridgement of Robert Greene's *Pandosto* (1592) was still being reprinted every few years. And although Shakespeare's plays had long since disappeared from popular reading, the ballads of *Sir Lancelot du Lac* and *The Constancy of Susanna* which Sir John Falstaff and Sir Toby Belch sang in *2 Henry IV*, and *Twelfth Night* respectively, and of which only snatches were given in the printed Shakespearian texts, were still well known across England.[16] According to John Clare the people had heard of Shakespeare but only from playbills.[17]

The stories, verses, and woodcuts were formulaic and predictable, textually as well as materially. Besides their array of kings, queens, and ladies, real and mythical, the residue of mediaeval and renaissance romance, the stories were filled with stock characters, the lusty miller, the shrewish wife, the cheating townsman, the stupid Welshman. The picture of life they offer is harsh and violent, full of unexpected tragedies, murders, seizures of women, tricks, knaveries, and luck. They tell tales of chance encounters with princes, poor men becoming rich – *Fortunatus* has a purse which refills whenever it is empty and a wishing cap which can whisk him to wherever he desires to be. Few of the old stories suggested that a man could raise himself by merit and hard work rather than by drawing a winning ticket in the lottery of life.

The woodcuts, which were sold in black and white but could be coloured in water-colours, had much in common with the printed texts. Hung on walls or pinned to a bench at the work place, many had the same verses as the ballads. Many a cottage and inn at the end of the eighteenth century was decorated with 'a pretty slight drollery, or the story of the Prodigal, or the German hunting in waterwork', the cheap art which Sir John Falstaff recommended to Mistress Quickly.[18] The images appear to have been more strictly religious than the written texts, with innumerable Bible stories from the New as well as the Old Testament, and only a few of the non-canonical biblical myths or the illegitimate supernatural. Although the literary texts of the popular canon are often frozen from pre-Reformation times, the images appear to have been continually added to. It is as if, at some date, ecclesiastical inspectors had brought the popular images into line with the official post-Reformation supernatural while still allowing pre-Reformation popular literary texts to be printed.

Amongst the largest constituencies for chapbooks and ballads during the whole print era were adults in the country areas, and young people in both the town and the country. It would be a mistake, therefore, to regard the ancient popular print as confined to those whose education fitted them for nothing longer or textually more difficult. Many readers, whether adults or children, lived at the boundary between the reading and the non-reading nations. They were the marginal reading constituency whose numbers fell when prices rose and rose when prices fell. Both groups of readers often felt apologetic, or were made to feel guilty, for enjoying this form of reading. Richard Baxter, for example, the seventeenth-century author of religious books which entered the old canon, confessed to reading chapbooks rather as he might have confessed to stealing apples.[19] Samuel Johnson regretted the hours he wasted reading romances in his father's bookshop.[20] To judge from the many warnings against the reading of romance to be found in conduct books, women were among the readerships from the earliest times.

Many of those who read these stories, or who read them aloud to their friends or to their children, had probably heard them from parents, friends, or – a constant worry among the upper-income groups – from house-servants. The printed text and engraved pictures were, we may guess, used more as aids to a performance, with plenty of acting, invention, ritual repetition, and interruptions – just as the chapmen at the fairs told the stories and sang the ballads they had for sale – rather than read, word for word, alone, and in silence.[21] The readership was therefore probably a large multiple of the numbers of copies manufactured and sold, and the tradition was so long lived that it served to set the horizons of expectations of each succeeding cohort of readers and viewers. On the eve of the romantic period, a large constituency of English-speaking readers continued a tradition which went back to the performers, writers, abridgers, and woodcut artists of the English renaissance.

[. . .]

Wordsworth was among the many authors of the romantic period who looked back nostalgically to the reading of their youth that was fast disappearing. As he wrote in *The Prelude* (1850):

> Oh! Give us once again the wishing cap
> Of Fortunatus, and the invisible coat
> Of Jack the Giant Killer, Robin Hood
> And Sabra in the forest with St George!
> The child, whose love is here, at least doth reap
> One precious gain, that he forgets himself.[22]

Other authors too made a conscious attempt to regain something of the spirit of wonderment which they remembered from a world that had been lost. William Godwin at the opposite end of the political spectrum from Wordsworth, praised the power of the ancient chapbooks to stimulate the imagination of children.[23] For Scott, the chapbooks provided a model for the meeting of real historical figures with imagined characters from low life which he exploited in the Waverley novels. The old ballads and chapbooks, many writers believed, had a directness, an absence of cant, a humanity, and a magical quality which had largely disappeared from the classicising mainstream literature of the eighteenth century, and it is easy for readers of the present day to share such feelings. However, the question which the historian of reading needs to address is why an ancient tradition that had seemed secure and timeless less than a generation before should suddenly lose its readerly appeal around 1800. And, for the sudden unfreezing of the tradition, as for the freezing, an intellectual property model provides a more precise and convincing explanation than speculations about changing readerly tastes. What we see, in material terms between 1774 and the end of the romantic period, is the effect on books and reading of the ending of the monopoly in the supply of popular print.

The first effect of the abolition of intellectual property, as we would expect, was the reprinting by newcomers of the old favourites for sale at lower prices, and as with other books, the first breaks occurred in Scotland. It is clear from remarks in Boswell's diary, for example, that the chapbooks which he read in Edinburgh in the 1740s had come from London.[24] By the middle of the century, however, there were thriving chapbook industries in Edinburgh and Glasgow, producing both new titles by modern writers such as Dougal Graham, and reprinting older titles over which the London industry claimed perpetual copyright.[25] As with other books, the commercial contest between the English and Scottish systems appears to have been most keen in the north of England. 'The Wanderer', the hero of the first book of Wordsworth's *The Excursion*, who teaches the poet his sense of natural piety, was a former Scottish chapman who had settled in northern England.

Since the manufacturing costs of popular literature were low relative to the distribution costs, the best way to take advantage of the new economic conditions after 1774 was to manufacture nearer to the final markets. We duly find the presses in the provincial towns that had previously been part of the supply network being used to start local chapbook industries supplying local chapmen. During the romantic period at least seventy-four towns published chapbooks.[26] As with other print, many of these reprinting centres are near the Scottish border. We also find economic competition. In many towns previously supplied from London, too, we suddenly find records of three or four different publishers competing for the chapmen's business, some claiming to offer the lowest prices in the country.[27] In the romantic period in Newcastle, a key distribution centre reached by sea as easily from Edinburgh as from London, there are records of about a dozen publishers producing chapbooks and ballads, and even in a small town like Whitehaven there were half a dozen. By the 1820s many chapbooks and ballads were being printed from stereotypes, sometimes from foundries built in small towns. A stereotype foundry was built in the tiny northern English town of Alnwick as early as 1812, at a time when there was still scarcely any stereotyping in London.[28] Another was in Falkirk, an iron-founding town in the Scottish Lowlands. When the chapbook industry adopted printing by cylinder, enabling chapbooks and ballads to be manufactured and sold in rolls by the yard, prices fell even more drastically than in other sectors.

In much modern writing, it has been assumed that the ballad chapbook industry of the romantic period was a relic of pre-industrial Britain, an older form of print culture lingering in the more rural areas but retreating rapidly towards an inexorable extinction before the forces of modernity. But quantification produces a different picture. During the romantic period there was no decline in chapbook production – on the contrary, more chapbook titles, both old and new, were published, in larger numbers, and in many more towns, than at any previous time. Far from being an industry on the verge of extinction, the chapbook industry of the romantic period formed part of the explosion of reading which began in the late eighteenth century. The boom seems to have continued at least until the 1840s, when the arrival of the railways enabled longer printed texts to reach remoter areas previously supplied by water and by animal power. What happened in the romantic period was not that chapbooks and ballads as such ceased to be produced and sold, but that the traditional titles were replaced by more recently composed texts.

After 1774 the huge corpus of authored literature printed before the middle of the eighteenth century became available not only to be reprinted but to be abridged, excerpted, and adapted. By the end of the century many old-canon novels, books of history, travel, and exploration, had been abridged from texts which were no longer in private ownership. By the 1810s we see the rapid growth of what we might call chapbook gothic, stories of horror, of seduction, of elopements, of Italian castles and German nuns, many of which appear to be abridged adaptations of Minerva Press titles which were coming out of copyright at that time. The children's book industry boomed. We see new versions of *Robinson Crusoe* and *Gulliver's Travels*, some of which take the stories far from the original.[29] We see a proliferation of poetry anthologies for children, of 'Lilliputian Libraries', of abridgements and adaptations of histories and books of travel, of chapbook versions of the beasts, the birds, and the fishes taken from the *Natural History* of Buffon,[30] and much other printed material which would not previously have been permissible.

As with larger books, the ending of monopoly meant a transfer of income from profits to readers. After 1774, furthermore, the prices of old-canon books fell so far that some of those who previously could only have afforded ballads and chapbooks could now buy old canon. The chapmen who had previously taken ballads and chapbooks to the villages now took the old canon, both as small-format books and as parts and numbers.[31] The long separation between modern authored literature and the reading of the economically less well off, that had opened up around 1600, now began to close. From 1798 Cooke's English poets, novels, and classics were circulating across the country at sixpence a part, not far from the price of a traditional chapbook. By 1823, Limberd's *British Novelists* offered old-canon novels at sixpence a title or two pence in numbers of sixteen pages. At these prices, many constituencies of readers whose reading had previously been largely confined to Bible, almanac, and the ballad culture of King James were able to make a leap, not into modernity, but into the less obsolete printed literature of the eighteenth century.

Within a generation of 1774, many titles, such as *Robin Hood*, when adapted, passed into the burgeoning children's book industry. But many dozens of other titles, even although they were for a time offered at a fraction of previous prices, soon ceased to be demanded altogether and were never again reprinted. Some of the ancient stories which we might have expected to survive as children's books, such as *Fortunatus*, quickly died out. With Shakespeare himself now available cheaply, both in full and in adapted, abridged, and children's versions, no one now wanted the ballad versions of *Titus Andronicus* and *King Leir and his Three Daughters*, the nearest to the real thing which had been available to those at the boundaries of the reading nation since the 1590s, and they disappeared without a tear even from Wordsworth. The biggest casualties were the old romances of Christian knights and fighting heroes. In a single generation, *Guy of Warwick* and *Bevis of Hampton*, two of the most famous and most ancient stories of all, which had been read in England by every generation for at least 500 years across the oral, the manuscript, and the print era, died out like the dinosaurs, as part of a sudden mass extinction.

The history of the chapbook and ballad sector of the English book industry offer general lessons about the nature of the links between books, reading, cultural formation and out-comes which go far beyond a particular episode in the long story. If we consider the industry simply as an economic supplier of material goods, we have one of the few examples in economic history where we can trace the effects of an unregulated private monopoly from the first invention of a new product in the sixteenth century, through increasing cartelisa-tion, to near total monopoly. We then see a prolonged period of equilibrium and stagnation, which was followed by an immediate and drastic change as soon as the monopoly was brought to an end. We have, therefore, in this industrial sector, a well-documented historical example of the long-run obsoletising effects of private economic monopoly as such. When, however, we consider the sector as a supplier of literary and visual texts carried by the materiality of print, then another conclusion seems inescapable. It cannot be enough to say that the only or main reason why the ancient print lasted as long as it did is that the texts reflected, in some special way, the mentalities of the readers, or catered for their needs and aspirations.[32] We have to conclude instead that it was only because, in their economic and cultural circumstances, the readers at the boundaries had no alternatives, that they kept the tradition going, and that the moment they had a wider choice, they jettisoned it without regret. In terms of the dynamics of cultural formation, we have an example here of how intellectual property combined with commercial monopoly kept a large constituency of marginal readers in ancient ignorance.

The biggest effect of the breakdown of the monopoly was felt in London. The firm at Aldermary Churchyard was so well established and enjoyed so many advantages that, with some adaptation, it ought to have been able to withstand the abolition of perpetual copyright, or at least to preserve a large part of its business in the south. But in the event it seems quickly to have lost its dominance. Perhaps, like many long-established monopolies, the firm had lost the skills to market and sell its products in conditions of competition, but in any case, in an era of water transport and animal power, London was not a suitable centre from which to run a national chapbook industry. It was in these circumstances, when their business was in decline, that the then owners of the now broken monopoly accepted what was in effect a take-over bid from Hannah More and the Cheap Repository Tract Society, not for the titles or for the plant but for the asset which was now of most value, the chapman distribution network.

If some visitors to popular print, such as Wordsworth, were inclined to nostalgia, others took a different view. Hannah More and her sister were horrified to discover that the actual rural England they found when they set up a school in Somerset was not at all like the picture of harmonious simple life presented in the English georgics of Oliver Goldsmith's *Deserted Village*, James Thomson's *Seasons*, or William Cowper's *The Task*. Literacy levels were low, schools thinly spread and of poor quality, and what they found most disturbing of all, much of England was only in name a Christian country.[33] The mentalities, beliefs, and 'folk' superstitions of the agricultural workers and rural poor, with their astrological pro-gnostications, their fighting champions, their giants, fairies, witches, and enchantments of all kinds were not all that different from the mentalities which had horrified the reformers at the time of the English Reformation. And now, in the 1790s, there was a more frightening prospect. When the news of the French Revolution arrived in the farthest corners of Europe, many of the British elites suddenly realised that if the writings of Voltaire and Rousseau had precipitated such a social and political upset in France, the pamphlets of Tom Paine, and later *Queen Mab, Don Juan*, and the other printed texts of the radical canon, could do the same in England. As Hannah More wrote to Zachary Macaulay in 1796, 'Vulgar and indecent penny books were always common, but speculative infidelity, brought down to the pockets and capacities of the poor, forms a new era in our history.'[34] 'To teach the poor to read without providing them with safe books', she wrote on another occasion, 'has always appeared to me to be an improper measure.'[35] What More and her financial backers hoped to do in taking over the chapman network was to use it to distribute a type of print, mainly newly composed by herself, which would drive out both the old chapbooks and the radical pamphlets. In the struggle to shape the mentalities of the people by controlling their access to print, the tract movement dovetailed neatly into the gap created by tight textual controls and heavy taxes.

At first sight, Hannah More's cheap repository tracts looked almost identical with the print she hoped to displace. But from both an economic and a cultural point of view, they were different. The old ballad and chapbook industry, though a monopoly, was a wholly commercial operation with the final buyers/readers paying for all the costs of production and distribution. The cheap repository tracts were financed not by readers but by subscrip-tions from members of the wealthier classes of society, the same ecclesiastical and political constituency that financed the Society for the Suppression of Vice. Since it was thought that the final customers at whom the tracts were aimed would be less suspicious, maybe more appreciative, if they had to pay at least a nominal amount, the tracts were, according to the initial plan, to be sold at a price which undercut the commercial chapbooks and ballads. The older print was to be driven out by predatory pricing.

As far as the texts were concerned, although they were written as part of a Christian agenda, they contained, like the sermons of Blair, a minimum of formal Christianity. As with Blair, the religion is downplayed in favour of social cohesion and concord between the haves and the have nots. Many of the tracts were essentially conduct books for the poor, infiltrated into the normal reading channels just as Hannah More and her allies also infiltrated conduct novels into the circulating libraries. In the old chapbooks, the local miller was a well-known character. Sometimes he had the luck to meet the king in the street and his fortune was transformed, but usually the miller's role was to seduce the local wives. In Hannah More's adaptation, when winter is harsh, the river freezes, and there is only one mill in the district which is able to operate, the miller invites all the local millers to use his mill without charge, and despite the shortage, not a single one of them puts up his prices during the emergency.[36] In *The Shepherd of Salisbury Plain*, a gentleman is riding across the plain, contemplating the splendour of God in creation, when he meets a poor shepherd, who knows his Bible well, who persuades the gentleman that his lifestyle on a shilling a day is not only morally superior to that of the gentleman but brings greater happiness. Because of his attitude, the shepherd is given money by the gentleman which enables him to buy medicine for his sick wife and move to a new house. On the wall of the shepherd's house, incidentally, where previously there might have been an old ballad, hangs one of the Cheap Repository Tracts.

The key to the success of More's plan was the attitude of the sales force, that is the chapmen. From the start, they agreed to distribute the tracts but only if they were guaranteed their incomes, even if they sold nothing, a condition the promoters accepted. Before long, the promoters turned to completely free distribution. The men and women whose subscriptions paid for tracts to be produced, bought them themselves, usually in bulk batches of a hundred at a time, and sent them to be distributed in hospitals, workhouses, prisons, and among members of the armed forces. The chapmen's insistence from the start that the tracts should be printed on soft paper, rather than the smoother book paper favoured by the promoters, suggests that they were well aware of the ignoble fate to which they would soon be consigned.[37]

Many millions of tracts produced by various societies at the expense of their members were printed during the romantic period, along with many hundreds of thousands of Bibles bought and distributed at heavily subsidised prices. How far the books were actually read, and with what effect, is hard to gauge. The experience of William Cameron, a Scottish chapman in Dunfermline in 1820, may have been typical:

> When I got to the lodgings, I unharnessed myself, and went to a bookseller's named Miller, for ballads or histories, but he had nothing but tracts. These were *a bad fit* but the drink being in the garret I took four dozen of them, went into the street, and began a long story. I soon gathered an audience who relished the story and many bought . . . One of the buyers called me an impostor, saying I had given him John Covy [a tract] in place of what I called.[38]

However, to the American Samuel Goodrich, Hannah More's tracts were the first books he read with enthusiasm, as he recalled later the ecstasy he felt at being able to visit the places where *The Shepherd of Salisbury Plain* was set, and he himself later set up as a producer of improving literature for children.[39] By 1820 some thought that the social benefits of promoting the reading of such 'cheap publications' could be detected in the behaviour of working people. In the past, it was said, it was impossible for a hundred men to gather without turning into a riotous mob, but now crowds of up to 100,000 would assemble, listen to speeches, make petitions, and disperse peaceably.[40]

With popular print, as with the rest of the book industry, the sudden thaw of 1774 was followed by a slow renewal of the freeze, as the brief copyright window was closed. By the 1840s it was possible, using newspaper technology, to produce printed texts of many pages for profitable sale at two pence and the price of access to the cheapest forms of print continued to fall.[41] But the intellectual property regime now again stood in the way of anthologies, abridgements, adaptations, or chapbook versions from mainstream literature. There were no abridgements of the Waverley novels or of Byron.

Denied permission to reprint good modern English literature, the cheap fiction publishers turned to novels first published in the United States, France and Germany which, in the absence of international copyright, could be freely reprinted, translated, abridged, and adapted. As one overseas source after another was closed off, the publishers of cheap fiction increasingly employed hack writers to produce the hack stories needed to fill their columns. As one retail outlet after another was denied them, they were increasingly obliged to bypass the regular bookshops.

By the 1840s, the mechanics institute libraries which had begun as a resource for skilled manual workers had been largely taken over by the middle classes.[43] By the mid nineteenth century the literature and the reading of the working and clerical classes was already largely separated both textually and materially from the literature of the higher-income groups, so reinforcing the other barriers which divided the social classes. We see a continuing proliferation of the illegitimate supernatural, old astrology but now also palmistry, fortune telling from playing cards, and sensationalist 'penny dreadfuls' and 'bloods'. As Wilkie Collins noted in 1858, there was an 'Unknown Public', three million readers 'right out of the pale of literary civilization', a huge constituency of the still-expanding reading nation about which the elites knew little.[43]

The decision of 1774 transferred a huge quantum of purchasing power from book publishers to book buyers, leading to an explosion of reading in the romantic period, a growth in the size of the reading nation, and a sharp rise in the quality of the national literature to which there was now cheaper and more plentiful access. The 1842 Copyright Act produced a reciprocal effect. A wide range of literary texts which were just about to enter the public domain were converted into valuable windfall assets from which the lucky owners could take a rent for many more years. The change kept the prices of the reasonably modern English books higher than would otherwise have been the case, and held back most of the nation's access to recent good literature for another generation. Victorian moralists often complained that their less well-off countrymen read mostly rubbish, and they were right. The intellectual property regime which they established in 1842 was among the main causes.

References

1   Clare's childhood reading can be reconstructed from the many references in 'Sketches of the Life of John Clare, written by Himself . . . March 1821' in Clare's *Autobiographical Writings*. See also *John Clare by Himself* edited by Eric Robinson and David Powell (1996).

2   Hannah More's figure put in the mouth of a character in her tract *The Shepherd of Salisbury Plain* (n.d. 1790s). Reprinted in *The Miscellaneous Works of Hannah More* (1840) i, 130.

3   [. . .] A.S. Collins, *The Profession of Letters. A Study of the Relation of Author to Patron, Publisher, and the Public, 1780–1832*(1928) 32, 51, 53. Burke and others are mentioned in Margaret Spufford *Small Books and Pleasant Histories* (1981) 74. Coleridge's recollections are quoted by Nick Groom, *The Making of Percy's* Reliques (Oxford 1999) 238. Bamford's reading is discussed by David Vincent, *Bread, Knowledge and Freedom. A Study of Nineteenth Century Working Class Autobiography* (1981) 61.

4   *A Catalogue of Maps, Histories, Prints, Old Ballards, Copy-Books, Broad-sheet and other Patters, Drawing-Books, Garlands, & c. Printed and Sold by William and Cluer Dicey, At their Warehouse Opposite the South Door of Bow-Church in Bow-Church-Yard, London* (1754), Bodleian. Another version, 1764, Glasgow, probably a unique souvenir. The title pages of these catalogues, in addition to the royal arms, reproduce the device of a royal patent, affirming the claim to the exclusive rights to print classes of works, such as the ABCS, catechisms, and maps, for which letters patent had been granted in earlier centuries. The Bodleian copy, which belonged to Percy, includes his annotations of other titles he found in the Ballad Warehouse. The whole stock is transcribed by Robert S. Thomson, 'The Development of the Broadside Ballad Trade and its influence upon the Transmission of English Folksong' (unpublished Ph. D thesis, University of Cambridge 1974) 288. The 1764 catalogue was known to Charles Gerring who quoted from it in *Notes on Printers and Booksellers with a Chapter on Chap Books* (1900), but was unsuccessfully searched for by Victor E. Neuburg, 'The Diceys and the Chapbook Trade' in *The Library* (1969). Many of the titles are noted in John Ashton, *Chap-Books of the Eighteenth Century* (1882) 483.

5   Some figures from seventeenth-century inventories are given in Spufford 93. For the 1736 Irish inventory, see Lori Humphrey Newcomb, *Reading Popular Romance in Early Modern England* (New York 2002) 253 and M. Pollard, *Dublin's Trade in Books, 1550–1800* (1989) 219. Other figures in C. R. Cheney, 'Early Banbury Chap-Books and Broadsides' in *The Library*, 1936.

6   Thomson 84, quoting Gent.

7   Robin Myers and Michael Harris, eds., *Spreading the Word: The Distribution Networks of Print, 1550–1850* (1990) 68.

8   [. . .]. Dicey seems to have been the manager and part owner.

9   See Frances M. Thomson, *Newcastle Chapbooks* (1969). The Newcastle list, besides all the old favourites, includes the same handful of modern authored works as are found in Dicey's catalogue and no others. Like the London chapbooks the Newcastle chapbooks are undated, but of the long list of chapbook publishers known to have been in business in Newcastle, there is only one who was undoubtedly operating before 1774.

10 Many examples in the Harvard collection. See Charles Welsh and William H. Tillinghast eds., *Catalogue of English and American Chapbooks and Broadside Ballads in Harvard College Library* (1961).

11 James Knapp, *Illustrating the Past in Early Modern England* (2003) 2.

12 Harvard, no. 1847, Bodleian Douce PP 178, Harvard, no. 569. Some of the Pepys books have obvious errors, e.g. 'Pinted' for 'Printed'. See list in Thompson.

13 The late Victor Neuburg, who did much to advance understanding of English popular culture, seems never to have realised that until 1774 popular print was as much part of the intellectual property regime as other printed texts.

14 Sir James Hodges. See C. H. Timperley, *A Dictionary of Printers and Printing* (1839) 733.

15 For example *The Gospel of Nicodemus*.

16 Both are in the trade catalogues.

17 For Clare's remark see Richard Terry, *Poetry and the Making of the English Literary Past* (Oxford 2001) 177. Both ballads are listed in the 1764 catalogue.

18 *2 Henry IV, ii*, 1, 141.

19 Quoted by Spufford 74.

20 Spufford 75.

21 There are many accounts of story-telling as the main entertainment in the country, some quoted in Collins, *Profession of Letters* 34.

22 In *The Prelude* (1850). St George and Sabra is from Richard Johnson's *Seven Companions* or an abridgement.

23 Writing under the pseudonym William Scolfield, in preface to *Bible Stories* (1802). See William St Clair, 'William Godwin as Children's Bookseller' in Gillian Avery and Julia Briggs, eds., *Children and their Books* (Oxford 1989). The text is reprinted in *Political and Philosophical Writings of William Godwin* (1993), v, 312.

24 *Boswell's London Journal 1762–1763* edited by Frederick A. Pottle (1950) 299. Boswell's collection, with others collected later, is in the Child Memorial, Harvard University.

25 See Dougal Graham, *The Collected Writing of Dougal Graham, 'Skellat' Bellman of Glasgow*, edited by George MacGregor (Glasgow 1883).

26 R.K.Webb, *The British Working Class Reader, 1790–1820* (1955) 30, from the Harvard collection.

27 Shown, for example, by the advertisements on surviving copies: 'These are to give Notice that Chapmen, Travellers, and others may be supply'd with the best sorts of small Histories, Godly Books, Old Ballads, Garlands, Broadsheets & as cheap as at any Place in England' in *David's Repentance*, Wilson of Bristol and Cook of Gloucester, n.d. probably, late eighteenth or early nineteenth century, Lauriston Castle chapbooks, NLS.

28 See Peter Isaac, *William Davison's New Specimen of Cast-Metal Ornaments and Wood Types* (1990).

29 For a text-based discussion see 'Rethinking Folklore, Rethinking Literature: Looking at *Robinson Crusoe* and *Gulliver's Travels* as Folktales, A Chapbook-Inspired Inquiry' in Cathy Lynn Preston and Michael J. Preston eds. *The Other Print Tradition, Essays on Chapbooks, Broadsides, and Related Ephemera* (New York 1995).

30 *Histoire naturelle, générale et particulière* by Georges Louis Leclerc, comte de Buffon (Paris 1769), an English translation of which was published in 1775, for many decades the standard work on natural history and the main source of secondary writings across Europe.

31 'A Catalogue of Chapmen's Books', printed by J. Bew, c. 1800.

32 For a discussion of the mentalities of the population in the rural areas see, among many others, David Vincent, *Literacy and Popular Culture: England, 1750–1914* (Cambridge, 1989), 156.

33 A point Hannah More also made in describing the views of the rest of society in *Thoughts on the Importance of the Manners of the Great to General Society* (1809).

34   G.H. Spinney, 'Cheap Repository Tracts: Hazard abd Marshall Editions' in *The Library* (1939/40) 296, from W. Roberts, *The Bookhunter in London* (1895) ii, 461.

35   Spinney 298.

36   *The Honest Miller of Gloucestershire, A True Ballad* (n.d. 1790s). Reprinted in *The Miscellaneous Works of Hannah More* (1840) ii, 253.

37   For the differing quality of paper see Spinney 303, although he did not realise why soft paper books sold extremely cheaply, or given away gratis, could find takers even if they were never read.

38   John Strathesk, ed., *Hawkie, The Autobiography of a Gangrel* (William Cameron, a Scottish chapman) (1888) 57.

39   S.C. Goodrich, *Recollections of a Lifetime* (New York 1856) 172.

40   *The Black Book or Corruption Unmasked* (1820) 335.

41   For example the *Romancist Library*.

42   John A. Minto, *History of the Public Library Movement in Great Britain and Ireland* (1932) 52, quoting evidence to the *Select Committee on Public Libraries, Reports* (1849–52).

43   Quoted by Martyn Lyons, 'New Readers in the Nineteenth Century' in Guglielmo Cavallo and Roger Chartier, *A History of Reading in the West* (1999) 315.

Chapter 21

Anindita Ghosh

CONTESTING PRINT AUDIENCES

CONTRARY TO COLONIAL AND EDUCATED Bengali expectations, the coming of the printing press in Bengal actually made for an unprecedented democratization of the printed word. Contrasted with the past, when reading was limited largely to the Kayasthas and Brahmins, and the scarcity of manuscripts meant an even more limited diffusion of literary ideas, the arrival of print made for a much broader social initiative and participation in the production of literature. Cheap printing techniques and growing literacy figures among the less privileged sections made for a booming market in the 'small book' trade. Publishing such works was less capital intensive than proper book production, and was pitched at extensive rather than intensive markets. Consequently, these genres were produced primarily for people with little money to spend and little leisure time to read. The demand for such ephemeral works carried with it little regard for literary quality, and thus defined contesting tastes within the world of print. It was the demands and aspirations of these reader groups that guided the commercial book market at Battala and were voiced in its productions.

Cultural theories that emphasize the 'reception' of a text rather than its 'production', and the role of readers in 'constructing' it, have contributed to more sensitive histories of the book in Europe.[1] For some time now, scholars have been highlighting the non-fixity of text, multiple uses of print, and reader's intervention in reconstituting the meaning intended by the author. These works have demonstrated how the coming of print did not sweep away pre-print cultures in medieval Europe. They survived simultaneously with the printed book, often overriding its singular influence.

Such approaches are useful for the Indian situation. They help remind us that when print arrived in India, earlier oral traditions held sway in wider society. Availability of multiple copies of the same work did not inevitably prompt the demise of communal reading and popular performances. Much of the printed literature continued to be read aloud and performed to collective audiences right through into the twentieth century. In fact, in many ways, the printed Bengali book was the direct heir of the manuscript, and preserved on many occasions its formats, genres, and uses. Manuscript compositions not only provided the initial ingredients to the printing industry; they themselves continued to flourish alongside for a long time. Quite typically, most of the writing of the period belongs neither to a residual orality nor to high literacy but to an 'intermediate orality' that successfully evaded the closures of print.[2]

It is also important to recognize that speech, song, and the printed image constituted an integral part of the vernacular print scene in colonial India. Linear narratives, objectively and deductively expositioned, could not feed commercial establishments pitched at wider markets and booming sales. The oral tradition can thus be seen surfacing regularly in the imitations of speech patterns and sung narratives—with liberal use of rustic humour, conversational topical digressions, songs, proverbial usage, elements of magic and fable, didactic reiterations—in Bengali works of the time. Under the circumstances, the message of the printed text could only have been less than totally acculturating.

The study of ways in which various reader groups used print also helps us modify another set of emphases in recent discussion of colonial literature. Gauri Viswanathan and Krishna Kumar argue that school book literature played a unique role in producing and maintaining structures of domination in colonial India.[3] However, neither have explored the reception of these ideologies among Indian readers themselves. Analysing readership and audience for the new print literature, and the ways in which this world understood and used printed texts are important for challenging ideas of passive reception. Shared imagination, collective aspirations, and multiple reading practices mingled in complex ways to encourage differentiated uses and multiple appropriations of the same material objects and ideas. As Roger Chartier comments while discussing the efficacy of the written text vis-à-vis its orally—ritually or otherwise—rendered form: 'Once proposed, these models and messages were accepted by adjusting them, diverting them to other purposes, and even resisting them—all of which demonstrates the singularity of each instance of appropriation'.[4]

New literate communities and reading tastes

Two factors affected the nature of the vernacular print audience in nineteenth-century Bengal—the changed social context of education, as well as new communities entering the folds of print-culture. The period saw the growth of new professional classes, and spread of vernacular education to wider social groups, that made for a significant reading population. With easy access to printed texts, and with tastes that were closer to earthier, pre-print literary cultures, new readers found the cheaper and lighter Battala books very attractive.

The new social context of education is critical here. The traditional connection between landownership and management, and scribal functions of the higher castes in Bengal—the Brahmins, Kayasthas, and Vaidyas—continued into the colonial period. The highly developed system of indigenous schools in Bengal had supplied a community of scribes, officers, and clerks to the administrative departments of pre-colonial regimes, and teachers, priests, and physicians to the community. It was this same scribal population of the higher castes, often with modest interests in land, which crowded the offices of the colonial government in the nineteenth century.[5] These groups, with generations of exposure to the world of letters, were the most obvious constituents of the general reader population.

But apart from this, the colonial administration had also fostered a liberalization of the education system and opened up opportunities for much wider social groups, irrespective of class and caste affiliations, into its vast bureaucratic and commercial framework. This was a distinct change from earlier times when indigenous pathshala education, though technically open to all castes, socialized its learners into an acceptance of their position in the occupational structure.[6] The growing administrative, political, and economic infrastructure in the city of Calcutta exercised a pull on the eligible service population of the surrounding districts. The number of people taking to the opportunities provided by the new education under government initiative grew dramatically from 1860 onwards. A report in the *Calcutta Review* registered an increase in the number of candidates at the Calcutta University Entrance Examination, from 244 in March 1857 to 1327 in December 1863—a fourfold increase within a span of just six years. Of these, 80 to 90 per cent, and sometimes even more, came from the different districts surrounding Calcutta—the most prominent among them being Burdwan, Hooghly, 24 Parganas, Nadia, and Jessore. Six to seven hundred candidates annually presented themselves for these examinations from the above-mentioned areas.[7]

[. . .]

Upward social mobility for groups previously without formal education has been reported in other studies of the period. Thus the tremendous commercial potential of cash crops like jute at this time, Aparna Basu has shown, made many of the cultivating classes prosperous enough to begin sending their sons to school.[8]

The spread of vernacular education had brought the printed word within an easier reach of wider social groups. However, for these first generation learners, the inculcation of tastes and manners of the cultured urban literati remained distant. For most of the readers, education was mostly functional, and although aspiring to more distinguished social status on account of it, they continued to identify in their reading habits with the cheaper, and more sensational productions from Battala. Officials like C.W. Bolton believed that spread of vernacular education had led to the creation of a body of frivolous readers and authors alike. Noting the spurt in production of 'flimsy and silly Bengali dramas', he wrote in 1879:

> It is much to be regretted that the education that so liberal a government as the
> British bestows on the Bengalis, especially at so immense a cost, should be thus
> as it were, frittered away and diverted into a channel other than that for the
> benefit of his [i.e. the Bengali's] poorer and more ignorant countrymen.[9]

Apart from new social groups that came within the folds of vernacular education during this period, age and gender of the newly literate also offered significant pointers to the kind of books preferred. Contemporary observers noted that a lot of the new reader population consisted of boys and girls who were removed from school the moment they had acquired a working knowledge of the language—the boys to assist the head of their family in literate professions like priesthood, accountancy and shopkeeping, and girls to be married.[10] Having missed out on the guidelines to 'essential reading', or 'responsible reading', these new readers took readily to a less formal and more sensational literature. Moreover, it was not just children from respectable middle-class households who attended the new schools. Female education in particular, in the mid-1850s, attracted students from the 'lowly classes', including prostitutes.[11]

By the 1860s and 1870s, antahpur or zenana education had produced a significant body of women with some reading skills.[12]

[. . .]

But a frequent problem for the tutors of the first generation of women readers in Bengal, as elsewhere in India, was the alleged paucity of suitable textbooks for women, especially those from the 'lower classes'.[13] In 1830, a letter from a Bengali gentleman requested the Calcutta Female Juvenile Society to suggest suitable readings for his newly literate wife:

> She [i.e., his wife] is now at a great stand for want of proper books, which to my

infinite regret, are not to be met within the Native presses . . . [the books that are published] are so replete with superstition and irrational ideas of things . . . that I have, therefore, restricted her from touching these.[14]

While public libraries were developing a 'refined' literary taste in reading for significant numbers of educated males, women escaped this influence unless they received individual attention at home or in school. Even a cursory glance at the membership figures of some prominent libraries shows the gendered pattern of public reading.[15]

Library	Males	Females
Burdwan Raj Public Library	5942	nil
Sripore Public Library	1446	357
Uttarpara Hitkari Sabha	150	nil
Baranagar Public Library	68	nil
Burdwan Reading Club	53	nil

Lack of access to such collections for women, very often meant that they read whatever came their way. The vernacular presses churning out romances, traditional legends and ballads, almanacs, and such light literature provided much of their staple fare. As Long commented in 1857, 'if females are not supplied with . . . good books they will be sure to read bad ones', and he went on to report one case in which a native woman had requested her European teacher to procure for her 'the licentious tale of *Vidya Sundar*'. Fortunately, Long noted, she was turned down, and instead given *Sushila*, one of the publications of the Vernacular Literature Society, that related the tale of an 'ideal' girl.[16]

The highly Sanskritized and sombre sadhu style of mainstream Bengali was generally incomprehensible to the average literate woman. Commenting on a Bengali reader meant for females in 1867, the *Someprakash* reviewer alerted the author to the need for a simpler style of writing.[17] While 'high' Bengali became increasingly associated with the educated bhadramahila, the language that still ruled popular imagination amongst a larger literate female audience was the colloquial. Rassundari, recorded her autobiographical account in a simple spoken style.[18] The earthy, uninhibited narrative, with its belief in the supernatural and divine power, makes for a kind of reading far removed from that of middle-class bhadramahila poetesses steeped in Victorian morality and classical Sanskrit literature. It is not a matter of coincidence that a contemporary work instructing women on midwifery, which achieved remarkable success in reaching out to its intended audience, was written in the form of conversation in the colloquial style.[19] Even didactic tracts exclusively meant for a female readership were cast in a pseudo-women's speech style.[20] Pyarichand Mitra and Radhanath Sikdar's monthly journal for women, *Masik Patrika*, was consciously written in a simple language in order to appeal to wider female audiences.[21] Though initially looked down upon, it impressed the Calcutta School Book Society so much that it issued 3600 copies of the journal from its own depository in 1856.[22]

This substantial audience of literate and part-literate women were, therefore, eager consumers of the easily readable ephemeral genres in colloquial Bengali. Sensational novels, romances designed to titillate the senses and bawdy short skits carried tremendous appeal. Advertisements in almanacs testify to an ever increasing and competitive market for such works. Almost invariably reaching the andarmahal of every household, almanacs were an effective medium for Battala publishers to display their latest works. Purporting to impress upon women the need to practise maidenly virtues, many of these works actually made use of the opportunity to render titillating descriptions of female modesty threatened by male lust, the shocking and scandalous lives of prostitutes and wayward women, and sensual romances. Thrillers, murder mysteries, handbooks of black magic, anthologies of sexual riddles and coarse humour were also featured in almanacs. Very often, other publications from the same press or erotic picture prints in the form of chromolithographs were offered free of charge as an incentive for purchase. Thus the *Adarini*, advertised its novel attractions:

Adarini

> This novel shows the rewards of walking on the right path and the vices of a sinful life, the triumph of *dharma* and the defeat of *adharma*, as well as the joys of a virtuous woman and the pains of a public woman. If you want to hear more about the scandalous ways of the Bengali youth of this century, and immoral accounts of the lewd, licentious monsters of the *Kali* Age, the pains of devoted and virtuous Bengali housewives . . . about burning desires of adultery, and more, then keep a copy of the Bengalee's most loved and coveted treasure, *Adarini* at home.[23]

Swarnakumari Debi paints a vivid picture of the reading culture of the Tagore antahpur. Younger children learning to read were often saddled with the task of reciting the Puranas, epics, and even *Hatem Tai* to elderly unlettered women. Reminiscing at a mature age, the litterateur and bhadramahila, recalls with much concern the lack of serious social themes in these readings. Medieval tales like *Annada Mangal, Arobyoponyas, Golebakawali, Laila-Majnun, Prabhashmilan*, and *Rukminiharan*, constituted the typical catalogue. Apparently, while the elder women read Purans and epics, the younger women read novels and poetry. Swarnakumari recalls:

> I remember how a thrill ran through the women's quarters the day *malini* came to sell books. She used to bring all the latest fare of books—poetry, novels, strange tales—and fill up the shelves of my elder sisters' libraries. Chests full of books used to sit comfortably alongside cupboards full of clothes, dolls and toys in our rooms.[24]

The poet and colonial servant Nabin Sen described his dismay when, on return to his native village in 1866 after some years in Calcutta, he realized 'what female education had done to [his] . . . land'. *Path* or communal reading sessions of traditional epics and religious literature had grown out of fashion with women. Novels had taken over the position of traditional manuscripts.[25]

The reading of young educated bhadralok men also went far beyond the confines of the 'respectable'. In reality, while the constructed literary code informed the public sphere of many a 'refined' bhadralok in his mature days, his private youthful world was not always guided by it.[26] The nationalist Bepin Pal recalls in his memoirs how as the lone child of a district Munsif at Jessore and Sylhet, he was brought up under a regime of rigorous discipline befitting his father's social position. His mother's 'one aim and intention' in bringing him up, was to make him 'a gentleman, a bhadralok, as she used to say'.[27] And yet, in recounting the books outside his school curriculum that he read in his boyhood days, he mentions, along with 'pleasant stories from foreign literature' published by the Calcutta School Book Society, cheap popular romances from Battala:

> In those days I used to read a fair number of outside books . . . *Gulevakaolee* . . . and *Kamini Kumar*, both of which were rather prurient publications, . . . caught my boyish fancy.[28]

As a young boy, Rabindranath Tagore was so keen on obtaining a copy of a farce from a lady in the Tagore household, that he had to resort to stealing it from the box where she had kept it under lock and key.[29] The prominent theatre personality and dramatist Amritalal Basu describes having read almost all the Battala books that he could lay his hands on in his school days. He had very easy access to the publications through his classmate, who was the son of a leading Battala publisher.[30] While scholars like Krishna Kumar and Gauri Viswanathan have studied the dominant impact of school textbook literature, the subversion of those very texts through a parallel extra-curricular reading has been underestimated.[31] The success in imposing the school book norms, it may be argued, did not always stretch beyond the walls of the classroom.

Even in the classroom, the 'improving' productions of colonial education found it difficult to attract this youthful audience. A very popular vernacular reader that did a brisk trade at Battala and was used in schools throughout Bengal in the nineteenth century was the *Shishubodh*. It was based on the manuscript version of a traditional text that had been in use in pathshalas in the previous century. The book had some mythological tales and slokas (chants), and the whole of it, with the exception of the alphabets and arithmetic tables, was in verse. The 'improving' textbooks of the nineteenth century were consciously modelled very differently. Scholars like Vidyasagar and Akshay Kumar Dutta provided readers like *Varnaparichay* and *Shishusiksha*, to help school children develop 'elevated' minds. But their efforts were not appreciated by all. Bepin Pal remembered:

> *Shishubodh* was the name of the first printed book placed in my hands . . . though possibly less scientifically arranged and much less nicely got up, I liked this book much better than I did the more modern *Sishusiksha* or *Varna Parichaya* which I had to read later in the school to which I was sent.[32]

Bepin found the attractive stories and simple narrative style of *Shishubodh* far more exciting than the staid academic style of modern primers. Nabin Sen also recounted his teacher compelling him to read works of Vidyasagar, which he did not really enjoy. Instead he turned to whatever he could find of Battala literature.[33]

Young school and college boys were often singled out for attack in newspaper columns for patronizing sensational and puerile Battala novels and dramas, and for attending theatres putting up plays based on these compositions.[34] A reviewer in *Someprakash* expressed his agony over the fact that educated classes in Bengal were actually encouraging their production, instead of scorning away such 'vile' literature. He noted that schoolboys often saved their pocket money to buy Battala books, unknown to their indulgent parents.[35] Educated Bengali youth were often a part of the satirized babu image, despised for their coarse tastes. The following dig must have been intended for the genre of Battala farces that were the staple of such 'nouveau babus':

> The kind of humour that nouveau babus enjoy these days are as intolerable as in disreputable public inns, and certainly not fit for the bhadralok's ears. It is only full of abominable eroticism [*adirasa*] . . . Indeed, not all can create

authentic humour. Above all it needs a learned and thinking brain, and a deep insight into human character . . .[36]

Paul Saenger, while analysing readership in the late Middle Ages in Europe, distinguishes between two kinds of literacy—'phonetic literacy' (that enabled a person to read aloud based on recognition of syllables, similar to oral rote memorization)[37] and 'comprehension literacy' (that enabled the silent reading and full understanding of a text, word by word).[38] Such rudimentary 'phonetically literate' readers can be found in the print world of colonial Bengal.

Formal and institutional education, since the mid-1860s, had widened the scope of the print audience. But there also existed reader groups beyond this, among the products of informal education. Elementary domestic instruction pre-dated print and the new education. It had traditionally featured in many families throughout Bengal. Instruction was imparted by an elder male member in the family, and sometimes by the family priest or gomasta, the village accountant. In his report on vernacular education in 1836, William Adam recorded such instruction prevailing in 238, out of a total of 485 villages in Natore alone.[39] Domestic elementary instruction was mostly functional in nature, and restricted to reading and writing, addition and subtraction, with measurements and accounts being thrown into the curriculum for farmer and trader families. In addition, Adam identified other petty service, artisan, and menial groups that were semi-literate without having undergone any formal training. Groups such as these, which were technically 'literate' but not 'educated', made for a vast unharnessed reading public that was necessarily out of the bounds of a tutored and 'polite' literate world.

As the pioneering vernacular press in Bengal, the early publications of the Serampore Mission Press were instrumental in creating a taste for printed works. Two periodicals in particular, the *Digdarshun* and the *Samachar Darpan*, gained immense popularity when they first appeared. The *Digdarshun*, though mainly intended to be a textbook in native schools, was on many occasions purchased from Serampore by adults to read to their families. The *Samachar Darpan* was a weekly publication featuring mainly news items, aimed at exciting a spirit of reading among mature readers and 'diffusing among them useful information'. Its popularity was so great as to induce the editors to bring down its price to four annas, and bear the cost of postage themselves while mailing the paper to mofussil readers. Early missionary reports noted with great pleasure:

> A copy each [of the *Samachar Darpan*] is sent to the schools for reading out by monitors and elder boys. The master then takes it home and is thereby enabled to indulge his neighbours with a perusal of it. . . . The number of those . . . who flock around a man who has one of them . . . is highly pleasing. . . . There is a reason to suppose that each paper on an average obtains ten readers or attentive hearers.[40]

Although not reliable proof of avid readership, the Christian missionaries who came to Bengal in the early half of the nineteenth century registered tremendous demand for their vernacular tracts. According to the reports of the Baptist Missionary Society, the distribution of Bengali evangelical tracts rose from 60,000 in 1843 to 131,000 in 1847.[41] The general interest in the tracts is evidenced in reports of people coming back to seek explanations for the difficult parts, committing portions to memory, and reading and discussing the works with friends and neighbours. In 1840, Reverend H. Smylie reported from Dinajpur how one person had called together all his village to read a book which one of his neighbours had received, 'to find out, if possible, who this Jesus Christ is'.[42]

People who displayed an interest in the Christian tracts were on many occasions men from the traditionally literate groups. Missionaries at Hatkhola found their places of worship generally filled with respectable Brahmins and babus, who came regularly and took away tracts to read.[43] There is a reference in missionary records to a Brahmin who, not being able to understand some parts of the New Testament, came back with the book, marked by several pieces of paper and straws, where he needed explanations.[44] So much was the eagerness to read, that tracts were often copied out from originals, and circulated in manuscript form among the readers themselves, on their own initiative.[45]

Of course, evidence of circulation figures is not enough to confirm eager readership. Nor is there much currency in the accounts of a group of zealous missionaries wanting to impress their home organizations in England. While gratuitous distribution of the tracts met with great enthusiasm, efforts to carry out sales of scriptural translations in Dacca met with complete failure, despite the abnormally low prices.[46] The alleged popularity of the tracts is further suspect from the fact that not many with just a rudimentary know-ledge of the Bengali language could have followed the highly tortuous and Sanskritized style of the tracts.[47] James Long rightly observed that while it was true that huge numbers of Christian books and tracts had been circulating in Bengal, 'Hindus will receive anything in the shape of *paper*, because it is valuable for domestic or sale pur-poses'.[48] This seems to be supported by the evidence that very often books were pre-ferred to tracts, and larger books were much sought after.[49] Reasonable profits must have ensued from sale of paper received in this way. Shopkeepers, known to have used tracts for wrapping medicine and other practical purposes, were among the purchasers.[50] Others retained the pasterboards for binding their own books.[51] In fact, in squandering away such printed matter as they did, Bengali readers were only conforming to typical models elsewhere.[52]

But the spread of print cultures and the habit of reading were beyond doubt. Even as early as 1821, the *Friend of India* observed:

> . . . the multiplication of printed works has excited a taste for reading hitherto unknown in India, . . . Compared with preceding years when manuscript alone existed, books are now exceedingly common; men of wealth and influence begin already to value themselves on the possession of a library. Even among the inferior gentry, there are few who do not possess some of the works which the press has created.[53]

There is no doubt here that Calcutta, as the nerve centre of the fledgling print industry and vernacular literates, forms the obvious focus for anyone attempting to locate Battala's readership. Nineteenth-century Calcutta had become for the bhadralok, a metropolis in the real sense, providing education, job opportunities, and cultural succour. It is here that the major institutional bases of power lay, and where printed books were in constant circulation. Conversely, the educated middle class or bhadralok was far from being a purely metro-politan phenomenon cut off from the countryside, nor was print restricted to the borders of the city itself. Many were only first generation immigrants who returned to their native villages or towns at least once a year on the occasion of the annual Durga Puja celebrations. Women and family were often left behind at home, which necessitated more frequent returns. Calcutta was still for many a city of opportunity only, a place where they did not feel at home.[54] Besides, job prospects often carried aspiring professionals to the budding suburban towns and administrative headquarters littering the Calcutta hinterland, and eastern Bengal.

These educated bhadralok groups outside the city—in small district headquarters and towns, and even in other provinces such as Bihar and the United Provinces—were responsible for much of the activities that constituted the 'Bengal Renaissance'. The sudden spurt in libraries all over the province of Bengal from the mid-century onwards is a noticeable phenomenon. Some of the earliest public libraries in Bengal had been set up under British patronage. But the Bengali intelligentsia also formed numerous literary societies and libraries. Prominent reading clubs of the period included the Uttarpara Hitakari Sabha, Tamluk Literary Club (1876), Burdwan Reading Club (1875), and the Burdwan Raj Public Library (1881).[55] Public libraries were also set up at Hooghly, Konnagar, Barangar and Sripore between the 1850s and 1870s.[56] Smaller libraries and reading rooms were maintained in the interior towns and villages through public subscription.[57] Enterprising local youth donated books and furniture, marshalled meagre local resources, and solicited patronage of prosperous families to keep these going.[58]

However, readers who patronized these libraries were not simply reading anything that came their way. They had clearly defined preferences. The appeal of the cheaper productions of the vernacular presses was immense. Missionaries were among the earliest to attest to it, in the following words: 'We have but too often seen Hindus in their shops, and elsewhere, poreing [sic] over the vile productions of the Indian press,—books which for the most part ought to be consigned to the flames'.[59] While ostensibly intending to create improved tastes among the reading public of Bengal and disseminate useful information, many of the libraries piled their stocks with the more popular commercial Battala productions. Returning fifteen public libraries in the district in 1909, the *Howrah Gazetteer* deemed no more than four among them worthy of comment, as the others were 'useless', containing 'mainly novels'.[60] Reports in newspapers frequently complained about the low standards of some public collections. A library set up by an amateur dramatics group in Chandernagore was frowned upon for its disreputable collection of books by the editor of *Sadharani*, in 1873.[61] For many of the smaller libraries, novels, dramas, and farces dominated their collections, rather than works in the more serious categories such as history and biography. The inventory of the Jorasanko Library, in 1881, showed 200 dramas, farces, and novels, 125 books on poetry, and only eighteen books on history and geography, seventeen biographies, and twelve books on music.[62] Yet another library returned the following year, 104 works on prose fiction, 132 poetical works and 156 dramas, and another twenty on history, geography, philosophy, religion, and science, out of a sum total of 522 books in its collection.[63] Significantly, 50 out of 165 members of this library were women.

Such energetic reading communities could hardly be circumscribed by the cultural fiat of bhadralok reformers. Cheap print combined with rising literacy created the perfect breeding ground for powerful alternatives in reading and writing. Focusing not on the obvious university and college educated middle-class readers, but rather on the peripheral, partially literate, so far ignored groups in educational-cultural studies, helps unearth a scene of tremendous vibrancy and social comment in vernacular print-cultures.

References

1   Michel de Certeau, *The Practice of Everyday Life*, trans. Steven F. Rendall (Berkeley and Los Angeles, 1984); see also Roger Chartier (ed.), *The Culture of Print: Power and the Uses of Print in Early Modern Europe*, trans. Lydia G. Cochrane (Cambridge, 1989); and *Cultural History: Between Practices and Representations* (Cambridge, 1988); Peter Burke and Roy Porter (eds), *The Social History of Language* (Cambridge, 1987); Jon P. Klancher, *The Making of English Reading Audiences, 1790–1832* (Madison, 1987); Robert Darnton, 'First Steps Towards a History of Reading', *Australian Journal of French Studies*, 23 (1986), pp. 5–32. A more recent and substantial essay is that of Frank Donoghue, 'Colonizing Readers: Review, Criticism and the Formation of a

Reading Public', in Ann Bermingham and John Brewer (eds), *The Consumption of Culture, 1600–1800* (London and New York, 1995).

2   A term used by Kumkum Sangari to characterize small town Indian print-cultures of more recent times. See Kumkum Sangari, *Politics of the Possible: Essays on Gender, History, Narratives, Colonial English* (London, 2002), Introduction, p.xiii.

3   Gauri Viswanathan, *Makes of Conquest: Literary Study and British Rule in India* (London, 1990); Krishna Kumar, 'The Origins of India's "Text Book" Culture', Occasional Papers on History and Society, no. 47, Nehru Memorial Museum and Library or NMML (New Delhi, 1987). See also Krishna Kumar, *Political Agenda for Education* (New Delhi, 1993).

4   Roger Chartier, *Cultural Uses of Print in Early Modern France*, trans. Lydia G. Cochrane (Princeton, 1987) p. 7.

5   This phenomenon has been commented upon by many historians. See for instance, Aparna Basu, *The Growth of Education and Political Development in India, 1898–1920* (New Delhi, 1974), p. 120.

6   Parames Acharya, 'Indigenous Education and Brahminical Hegemony in Bengal', in Nigel Crook (ed.), *The Transmission of Knowledge in South Asia: Essays on Education, Religion, History and Politics* (New Delhi, 1996), p. 111.

7   *Calcutta Review*, vol. xl (1864), p. 143.

8   Aparna Basu, *The Growth of Education*, pp. 114–15.

9   C.W. Bolton, *Report on Publications Issued and Registered in the Several Provinces of British India During the Year 1878*, Selections from Records of the Government, vol. clix (Calcutta, 1879), p. 136.

10   A wide range of reports and memoirs record this observation. See William Adam, 'Second Report on the State of Education in Bengal' (1836), in Anathnath Basu (ed.), *Reports on the State of Education in Bengal, 1835–1838* (Calcutta, 1941); *Calcutta Review*, vol. xxv (July–Dec. 1855), p. 67; and vol. xl (1864), p. 95; Arun Kumar Mitra (ed.), *Amritalal Basur Smriti O Atmasmrti* (Calcutta, 1982), p. 133.

11   *Calcutta Review*, vol. xxv (July–Dec. 1855), p. 68.

12   Even though formal education for women had still a long way to go, home tutoring in enlightened households proved effective. By 1907, 1 in 33 girls of school-going age were attending public schools. See Usha Chakraborty, *Condition of Bengali Women in the Second Half of the Nineteenth Century* (Calcutta, 1963), p. 53; Supplement to the *Calcutta Gazette*, 4 March 1909, no. 29, p. 388.

13   *Third Report of the Calcutta Female Juvenile Society* (1823). For a similar situation facing reformers in contemporary Maharashtra, see Rosalind O'Hanlon, *A Comparison Between Men and Women: Tarabai Shinde and the Critique of Gender Relations in Colonial India* (Madras, 1994), p. 39.

14   *Ninth Report of the Calcutta Female Juvenile Society* (1830), see Appendix.

15   *Annual Report on the Administration of Bengal*, 1876–7, 1886–7. Sripore Library offers an interesting exception.

16   James Long, *Returns Relating to Publications in the Bengali Language, in 1857*, Selections from the Records of the Bengal Government, vol. xxxii (Calcutta, 1859), p. ix.

17   *Someprakash* (2 September 1867).

18   Rassundari Debi, *Amar Jiban* (Calcutta, 1898).

19   See Jadunath Mukherji, *Dhatri Siksha* (Calcutta, 1867).

20   See Kaliprasanna Basu, *Strilokdiger Kathopokathan Natak* (1868).

21   The editorial introduction to the journal defined its audience quite clearly. It was meant for 'women' and 'ordinary people', and written in the colloquial. 'Learned people' were advised to stay away. See *Masik Patrika*, 1855.

22   *Nineteenth Report of the CSBS* (1856).

23   Advertisement in Srirampur Ganguly Press's *Nutan Panjika*, 1896–7, p. 15.

24   Swarnakumari Debi, 'Shekele Kotha', *Bharati* (Chaitra, 1925), reprinted in Abhijit Bhattacharya and Abhijit Sen, *Shekele Kotha*, pp. 63–4. While *malini* translates literally as a female florist, gardener or garland-maker, the woman referred to here must have had a more flexible occupatonal role.

25   Nabin Sen, *Amar Jiban*, 2 vols (Calcutta, 1907), vol. 1, p. 93.

26   Tapati Guha-Thakurta has demonstrated in the context of the Calcutta elite's taste in art, how side by side with the decorating of public spaces like halls, ballrooms, and staircases in their homes with European oils, statues, chandeliers, and Victorian furniture, they had Hindu

religious paintings tucked away in the inner recesses and household altars. Tapati Guha-Thakurta, *The Making of a New 'Indian' Art: Artists, Aesthetics, and Nationalism in Bengal, c. 1850–1920* (Cambridge, 1992).

27   Bepin Chandra Pal, *Memories of My Life and Times, 1857–1884*, 2 vols (Calcutta, 1932), vol. 1, p. 13.
28   Ibid., pp. 35–6.
29   Rabindranath Tagore, *Jibansmriti* (Santiniketan, 1975), pp. 71–2. The book he was referring to was Dinabandhu Mitra's farce *Jamai Barik*.
30   Arun Kumar Mitra (ed.), *Amritalal Basur Smriti O Atma Smriti* (Calcutta, 1982), p. 30.
31   Gauri Viswanathan, *Masks of Conquest*, and Krishna Kumar, 'The Origins of India's "Text Book" Culture'. See also Shibaji Bandyopadhyay, *Gopal Rakhal Dandava Samas: Upanibestibad O Bangla Sishusahitya* (Calcutta, 1991).
32   Bepin Chandra Pal, *Memories of My Life and Times*, vol. 1, p. 17.
33   Nabin Sen, *Amar Jiban*, vol. 1, pp. 123–4.
34   *Sulabh Samachar* (20 September 1879).
35   *Someprakash* (2 October 1882). This is reported again in another less indicting version—one of the speeches during the inaugural meeting of the Society for the Suppression of Obscenity in 1873. Kali Charan Banerjea thus reports how hawkers waylay innocent young children on their way to school and persuade them to part with their pocket money. Alok Ray (ed.), *Society in Dilemma: Nineteenth Century India* (Calcutta, 1979), p. 196.
36   *Sulabh Samachar* (28 June 1879).
37   For 'phonetic' literates among the laity thus it was possible to 'read' texts that were not composed in the language of daily discourse, e.g., Latin prayer books.
38   In fact, the rubrics of the prayer books demonstrated how the most supposedly pious bits, earmarked for silent reading, were in the vernacular so that they could be fully understood and internalized without difficulty, while the communal recitation bits were in Latin. See Paul Saengar 'Books of Hours and the Reading Habits of the Later Middle Ages', in Roger Chartier, *The Culture of Print*, p. 148.
39   'Adam's Second Report' (1836), pp. 192–3.
40   *Second Report of the Institution for the Support and Encouragement of Native Schools*, 1818.
41   *Third Report of Operations in Translating, Printing, and Circulating the Sacred Scriptures in the Languages of India* (1843); *Fourth Report of Operations* (1847).
42   *First Report of Operations* (1840), p. 36.
43   *Second Report of the Calcutta Christian Tract and Book Society* (1828–41), p. 9.
44   *Contributions Towards a History of Biblical Translations in India* (London, 1854), p. 40.
45   *First Report of the Calcutta Christian Tract and Book Society* (1828), p. 16; *Fifth Report of Operations* (1852), p. 58.
46   *Third Report of Operations*, p. 55.
47   In 1867 a publication of the Calcutta Auxiliary Bible Society circulated privately among concerned individuals questioned the efficacy of the difficult language and style of the Serampore translation in popularizing the Christian message. See J. Wenger (ed.), 'Papers Concerning the Bengali Version of the Scriptures' (1867) (BMS).
48   James Long, *Returns*, p. xxii.
49   *First Report of Operations*, pp. 12, 35.
50   Ibid., p. 47; *Third Report of Operations*, p. 62.
51   *First Report of Operations*, p. 30.
52   In seventeenth-century England, for instance, cheap print served the very important secondary function of supplying lavatory paper. Margaret Spufford, *Small Books and Pleasant Histories: Popular Fiction and its Readership in Seventeenth Century England* (London, 1981), pp. 48–9.
53   *Friend of India*, Quarterly Series, 1 (1821), p. 135.
54   There were, in fact, different terms for these urban and rural dwellings—the term *basa* being reserved for the city lodgings, while *bari* meant the ancestral village home. Sumit Sarkar makes this point quite emphatically in 'Calcutta and the Bengal Renaissance', in Sukanta Chaudhuri, *Calcutta: The Living City* (Oxford, 1990), vol. 1, p. 96.
55   *Annual Report on the Administration of Bengal*, 1876–7, 1886–7.
56   Prominent figures instrumental in their founding included Bankim Chandra Chatterjee, Bepin Pal, and Bhudeb Mukhopadhyay. Ananga Bhattacharya (ed.), *Paschimbanger Granthagar*, vol. 1 (Calcutta, 1997), pp. 64, 121.

57   *Howrah District Gazetteer* (Calcutta, 1909), p. 146; *Burdwan District Gazetteer* (Calcutta, 1910), p. 182; *Birbhum District Gazetteer* (Calcutta, 1910), p. 104.

58   Several such enterprises have been recorded in Krishnanagore, Dacca, Midnapore, Burdwan, Darjeeling, Bhadrak, Rungpore, Tamluk, Cuttack, and Calcutta. See Krishnamoy Bhattacharya, *Bangladesher Granthagar*, vol. 1 (Calcutta, 1957); Ananga Bhattacharya, *Paschimbanger Granthagar*, vol. 1.

59   *Fifth Report of Operations* (1852), p. 57.

60   *Howrah District Gazetteer*, p. 142.

61   *Sadharani* (14 Poush, 1280 BS) (1873).

62   Ibid., (21 Chaitra, 1288 BS) (1881).

63   This was the inventory of the Savitri Library. See *Sadharani* (25 Baisakh, 1289 BS) (1882).

Chapter 22

Jeffrey Brooks

THE LITERATURE OF THE LUBOK

THE USE OF LITERACY LED the literate toward involvement in more modern sectors of Russian life, and their thinking changed accordingly. As they developed new values, new ways of looking at themselves and the world around them, and new patterns of thought and imagination, the literate sought to orient themselves by reference to the printed word. The increasing numbers of literate people became a more attractive market for commercial suppliers of popular literature, and the number of books and pamphlets circulating in villages and among lower-class urban residents grew. There was a tremendous upsurge in publishing for the common people in the last half century of the old regime. The expansion came at a time when technological improvements had significantly lowered the costs of printing and distribution, but the electronic media had not yet begun to rival the printed word.

The development of the popular commercial publishing industry in Russia was remarkable in several respects. Expansion took place rapidly, and the educational level of the country as a whole was so low that this industry, like many others in Russia, was staffed by people who were often of peasant or lower-class origins. The popular commercial writers were therefore more familiar with the world of their readers than with the literature and learning of educated Russia. Since they had limited access to literary models from *belles-lettres*, and since there was little existing popular literature appropriate for their readers, they drew largely on folklore and on their own experiences.

The people who succeeded in this industry had entrepreneurial skills of risk taking, organization, and openness to technological change, rather than loyalty to traditional values and time-tested commercial practices. They infused the popular commercial literature that they created and distributed with something of their own values, energy, and initiative. Such a literature was likely to appeal to ordinary people who had hopes, made attempts, and sometimes succeeded to move out of the familiar circle of a traditional agrarian order.

When it became evident that increasing numbers of common people were learning to read, the question of what they would read was of interest not only to the commercial suppliers of popular literature, but to many others as well. Educated Russians who thought about the issue of popular literacy were unanimous in the view that the question of what kind of literature reached the common people was of utmost importance. Representatives of the Church and state and people of more liberal or radical persuasions did not always agree on the choice of material appropriate for the common people. Their ideas on these matters produced another body of books and pamphlets for the common people in addition to the commercial works themselves. The efforts of the commercial publishers, state and Church propagandists, and enlightenment activists to reach "the reader from the people" made popular literacy a major cultural issue of late tsarist Russia as well as a thriving commercial enterprise. The question of what common people should read, and to what extent their own preferences should be respected, reemerged after the October Revolution, when the Bolsheviks formulated Soviet cultural policy.

Thus the expansion of the reading public was paralleled by an equally rapid growth in the quantity and variety of printed materials available. There was a perceptible increase in the number of titles published in the Russian Empire in the first half of the nineteenth century, but the real expansion began after 1850 and continued until war and revolution brought a precipitous decline in publishing, as in much else.

[. . .]

Publications for the common reader were largely of two sorts, the commercial works published for profit and those materials sponsored by educators, propagandists, and others interested in promoting a message among the lower classes. Those who produced the sponsored materials hoped to drive their rivals from the marketplace with a better and cheaper product, but the common people in Russia showed a preference for a variety of commercial publications.

The quantity of commercial publications for the common reader is not easy to determine from the aggregate publishing figures. According to one estimate, commercial publications accounted for roughly 60 percent of all "people's books" in 1892 and 1894.[1] Approximately the same proportion is suggested by the figures available for 1910, when the thirteen major commercial publishers produced 9.8 million copies of people's books out of a total of 14.9 million copies.[2] Official figures for the earlier period suggest that sponsored noncommercial works constituted a higher proportion of the works for the common readers.[3]

The path to the new readers was blazed long before the printed book had a large readership by those who produced and distributed popular prints and manuscript works in the countryside. The popular commercial literature that developed in the nineteenth and early twentieth centuries depended on several generations of facile authors, largely of peasant and petty bourgeois origins. Their talents and energies were channeled by a few entrepreneurial publishers, some of whose lives were rags-to-riches sagas that rivaled anything their authors were able to concoct. The enterprising publishers relied on large numbers of city hawkers and rural colporteurs to carry their goods to remote corners of urban and rural Russia, and to report back on the preferences of customers. Authors, publishers, and distributors were thus all involved in the commercial effort to produce a literature that satisfied the demands of the common reader.

The popular lubok prints

The staple of lower class reading for most of the nineteenth century was the chapbook-like publications distributed by colporteurs and called *lubochnaia literatura*, after the popular prints (*lubki*, sing. *lubok*) that the peddlers also sold. The term "literature of the lubok" was used to describe a wide variety of popular publications, but I use it only to refer to the booklets sold by peddlers, since the peddlers also sold the prints, and the prints and booklets were often on the same subjects.

The lubki were lively illustrations similar to European broadsides. They had short texts, usually at the bottom of the picture, and were often the first printed materials to enter the homes of the common people. Their circulation prepared the way for the book. Explanations of the origins of the term *lubok* are varied. The early student of the question, N. Snegirev, startled educated society in the early 1820s by pronouncing the lubok worthy of intelligent investigation, an opinion shared by Alexander Pushkin but few others.[4] Snegirev suggested that the word was taken from *lub*, the inner bark of the linden tree, which was at one time made into a crude paper, was later used to make the wood blocks for the prints, and from which the itinerant peddlers made the baskets for their wares. The pictures may also have been called lubki because they were at one time cut and printed on Lubianka Street in Moscow. According to D. Rovinskii, the lubok collector and author of the most complete study of the subject, the term did not come into use to describe the prints until the first half of the nineteenth century.[5] The adjective *lubochnyi* was used in the first half of the nineteenth century to describe things that were badly or hastily constructed, and there were *lubochnye* homes, furniture, and goods, as well as illustrations.[6] N. I. Pastukhov, the author of one of the classics of late nineteenth-century popular literature, described the Rogozhskaia district of Moscow in the 1870s as "known for its post houses, with their ramshackle (*lubochnye*) sheds."[7] It was perhaps to avoid this use of the word that Rovinskii, in his classic study, called the prints simply "people's pictures."

At different times, according to I. D. Golyshev, the peasant scholar and lithographer to whom we are indebted for much of our information about the production and distribution of the lubki, the pictures were also called *Suzdalskie*, because at one time the print sellers' villages were located in the district of Suzdal; *friazhskie* and German sheets, because some were of foreign origin; *bogatyri*, because they often showed knights, tsars, and military heroes; *konnitsy*, because many of the knights were on horseback; and *prazdniki*, because many were images of saints or other religious figures.[8]

The lubki were traditionally printed either from wood blocks or copper plates. The earliest paper icons and secular prints date from the beginning of the seventeenth century, soon after the establishment of printing in Russia, when early book illustrators used their art to create single pictures on separate sheets. Originally produced primarily on religious subjects for a largely upper-class audience, the lubki soon began to circulate more widely, and by the eighteenth century they adorned the walls of some of the humbler inhabitants of the cities as well.

The lubki soon lost favor with the upper classes. The rich and well-born developed more refined tastes in illustration during the second half of the eighteenth century as Peter the Great's policy of importing Western culture was taken up by his successors. They learned to scorn the lubki, which began a long descent to lower levels of Russian society, first finding favor among the middle classes of the cities, then with the serving people and tradesmen, and finally, in the early nineteenth century, with the peasantry in the countryside.

As the audience grew more humble, the prints became more simplified and satirical, and the messages cruder and more direct.[9] Parables on daily life, fictional characters familiar from folklore, jokes, and well-known historical scenes became the standard repertoire of the lubok publishers. Snegirev grouped the illustrations around five subjects in the 1870s: religious and moral, philosophical commentaries on the trials of daily life, judicial topics and illustrations of punishments, wars and past events, and symbolic or poetical scenes from legend or folklore.[10] A catalogue of almost all lubki published in 1893 shows that religious pictures comprised about half of the total, and were, for the most part, pictures of the Holy Family, the Savior, and scenes from the history of the church and the lives of saints. Nearly a third of the secular prints were texts of songs and pictures from various literary works. Portraits of the tsar and the imperial family, satirical pictures, hunting scenes (often very bloody), and pictures of various beauties were also important.[11]

The prints were changed to suit the tastes of more sophisticated consumers in the last decade or two of the old regime. Typical of some of the lubki in the last half of the nineteenth century were illustrations of popular fairy tales, examples for moral instruction, and military pictures from the Crimean War, the Russo-Turkish War, and later from the war with Japan and World War I. New subjects touching the lives of the common people, from railroads to city slickers, appeared in the later prints. According to the early twentieth-century art historian A. A. Fedorov-Davydov, the process of secularization of the lubok can be traced back as far as the seventeenth and eighteenth centuries. A comparison of the prints published by the firm of I. D. Sytin in 1889 and twenty years later, in 1909, shows a decline in the number of prints on religious subjects, and an increase in those with secular themes.[12]

Both secular and spiritual authorities looked on the lubok with suspicion at various times during the seventeenth and eighteenth centuries, but their attempts to prohibit the prints were not successful. The Patriarch Ioakim attempted to end the printing and sale of paper icons in 1764, complaining that "any ignoramus cuts on boards and prints on paper corrupt icons of the Savior and the Mother of God, and the saints."[13] Effective censorship was established only in 1839, and in 1851 all hitherto uncensored wood blocks and plates were ordered destroyed by the authorities. "So ended the uncensored people's pictures," recounted Rovinskii.[14]

This destruction was not the end of the lubok, however. Publishers of the prints continued to issue traditional pictures, updated versions of older themes, and new images that captured contemporary interests of the lower-class lubok purchasers. The folkloric, religious, and literary subjects that had characterized the uncensored lubki remained the hallmark of the prints in the second half of the nineteenth century.

The first lubki done on copper plates were the work of typography pupils who used state-owned machines that were at their disposal. In the second half of the eighteenth century, silversmiths who lived in the village of Izmailov, near Moscow, did the engraving, and the pictures were printed at two factories in Moscow. One of the factories was located on Spasskaia Street, a place later associated with lubok literature. At the end of the eighteenth century and the beginning of the nineteenth, small printers who owned their own typographies took over the production of lubki. Some of the printers were located in Moscow, and others were in the neighboring province of Vladimir.

Lithography appeared in Russia in the 1820s, and was rapidly applied with great success to the printing of lubki. The gradual replacement of the old boards and copper plates with lithographic stone improved the quality and increased the quantity of prints that could be produced from a single engraving, but production of the prints still retained a handicraft character.[15] The lithographed pictures were usually hand colored in villages near the presses. According to Golyshev, one thousand self-trained peasant women were employed in the 1860s to hand color the prints in the village of Nikolskoe, eight miles from Moscow.[16] The prints were usually dabbed with a combination of the vegetable dyes the women mixed themselves, and the primitive appearance of many lubki owed much to this process, especially to the rapidity with which the women worked. After coloring, the prints were sold throughout Russia by wandering peddlers or colporteurs known as *ofeni* (singular *ofenia*).

When lithography stones were replaced with zinc plates in the second half of the nineteenth century, the production of people's pictures gradually merged with the manufacture of people's books. The introduction of the cheaper and lighter zinc plates, as well as improvements in ink and varnish and the use of steam presses, made the multicolored chromolithograph an item of mass consumption throughout the industrial world in the last few decades of the nineteenth century.[17] Innovations in the development of photolithography and new types of paper and ink further lowered the costs of printing pictures in the last quarter of the century. Book publishers took over the printing of lubki, and some of them, such as the young entrepreneur I. D. Sytin, who later became the largest publisher in Russia, did away with the crude system of village hand coloring.

The lubki of the late nineteenth century were printed by book publishers, submitted to the censor together with book texts, and often colored at the city presses. They continued to pass through the traditional distribution network of colporteurs, who either came to the city publishing houses to pick up their wares or purchased them at fairs from representatives of the city houses. The lubki retained their place in the daily life of the common people, and many peasant cottages were decorated with a selection of the prints.

The purchasers of lubki in the late nineteenth century could usually find an illustration of a hero or heroine from a favorite story. Alternatively, they could choose a book that elaborated on the adventures and romance suggested by a prized lubok. In order to facilitate the association of the prints and booklets, the pictures on the covers of the books were often brightly colored prints similar to the lubki. The intermingling of the various traditions and images of the lubki with the rapidly changing world of popular book publishing was described graphically in an apparently autobiographical novel, *Bookmen* by M. Chernokov, about the world of the popular publishers, which appeared in 1933:

> Balakan went up to the counter. Reams of pictures in various formats and content lay there smelling of dyes. The first to meet Balakan's eye were the "Saints." "Look Pavel, what beauties! These are the god of the muzhik, and, my heavens, you won't find one muzhik with such a satisfied and full-blooded face. And Tsars? Wonder of nature! They are all shine and sparkle. How can one not love them? Here are 'The Stages of Human Life,' drawn undoubtedly by a janitor. There is some kind of bloody battle—in a word, everything is here. There are the little icons—also a fast-selling item. And now, let's have a look at the books. *Weeping About Sin*, a book for the beginning reader, after which you will not want to read. And here is *How to Get Rich*, a book written by a person who did not have even a kopeck, but wanted to have a lot. There is 'Queen Margo' and 'Ensign Swordbelt,' books of dream interpretation, and all kinds of secrets—everything that the poor mind of the simple person cannot absorb."[18]

The lubki slowly lost their place in the lives of the common people in the early twentieth century, as a different popular imagery became available in illustrated periodicals, photographs, and silent films. At the same time, the lubki themselves lost some of their traditional aspects. The introduction of chromolithography in the 1880s made the process of hand coloring by village craftsmen obsolete. The spread of small rural shops reduced the role of colporteurs, whose sales techniques gave the lubki some of their meaning. As early as 1891 one observer noted, "In many homes where in the past there were abundant colored lubok pictures, they are now replaced by the premiums [pictures given as premiums] of *Niva* (Grainfield), *Nov* (Virgin Soil), *Razvlechenie* (Entertainment), and other illustrated and humorous magazines."[19]

[. . .]

Secular lubok literature

Authors of secular lubok literature treated a wide variety of subjects over the course of the nineteenth and early twentieth centuries, and the changing trends in types of booklets and stories give an indication of changes in popular taste. The number of editions in which a work was published is a relatively accurate guide to popularity, since lubok publishers tended to print editions of a standard size and to reprint popular titles as frequently as every year or two rather than attempting to estimate future demand. Press runs of 6,000 to 12,000 copies were common in the late 1880s and early 1890s, and of 12,000 to 25,000 copies in the early twentieth century.

The majority of secular works were on four main subjects until the 1870s: stories derived from folklore, chivalrous tales, instructive works, and tales about merchants. These can be considered in the traditional subjects of lubok literature. Works in these categories comprised as much as 60 percent of all titles in the 1860s, but their relative popularity declined steadily thereafter, until they comprised about 40 percent of the market in the 1890s and only 20 percent in the 1910s.

A second group of stories maintained a relatively constant market share throughout the century. These included war and travel stories, humorous tales, and nonmilitary historical accounts. Stories of this type constituted about a quarter of all titles throughout the nineteenth and early twentieth centuries.

New subjects that gained popularity in lubok literature in the last decade or two before the Bolshevik Revolution constitute a third grouping of stories about banditry, crime, science, romance, and an admixture of crime and romance. They comprised less than 16 percent of all titles until the 1890s, but by the 1900s their share had risen to 40 percent.

Of the early lubok stories, those based on folklore or on late eighteenth-century archaic tales of chivalry were by far the most numerous. Folkloric subjects alone comprised about 40 percent of all editions in the 1850s, and then gradually declined to only about 10 percent in the decade following 1909. Folkloric subjects are perhaps the most shadowy category of lubok literature. Many of the works were children's stories, intended particularly for the new schoolchildren of lower classes. Sometimes publishers or authors lifted whole texts from scholarly editions of folklore, fairy tales, or the heroic epic poems called *byliny*. At other times they rewrote them to suit their own understanding of what would best appeal to their audience. Among the most popular titles were *Ilia Muromets, The Little Hump-Backed Horse, Ivan the Knight, The Lion Who Raised the Tsar's Son*, and finally *The Story of Ivan the Tsar's Son, the Firebird, and the Grey Wolf*.

Works on subjects from the oral tradition were most closely identified with the lubok prints, and there were many pictures of Ivan the Tsar's son riding the grey wolf, caged firebird in hand, accompanied by Elena the Fair, and of Ilia Muromets battling his fantastic enemy, Solovei the Bandit, who was half bird and half man. Folkloric subjects were often revised for chapbook editions, and lubok authors sought to make the familiar tales more realistic and credible to the contemporary audience.

One example of a folk tale that was radically revised in a lubok edition was the story *Ivan the Knight, His Fair Spouse Svetlana, and the Evil Wizard Karachun*, which was published over fifty-five times during the nineteenth and early twentieth centuries.[20] The version I will discuss here was published in 1900 in Kiev by T. A. Gubanov, one of the major lubok publishers. The subject of the story is almost identical to that of the folk tale of the frog-princess, which appears in the standard late nineteenth-century collection of A. N. Afanasev in three variants.[21]

In each of the three versions of Afanasev's collection, a tsar has three sons of the same age and orders them to shoot arrows to determine who their brides would be. The arrows of the first two sons land beside the beautiful daughters of respectable citizens—in various versions, a general, a prince, a merchant, and a boyar—but Ivan Tsarevich's arrow falls in a swamp and is picked up by a frog. Ivan is distressed. In two versions of the story he wonders, "How can I marry a frog?" but in each case he submits to his "fate": in one version he decides that there is nothing to do but marry the frog, and in the other two the tsar orders him to do so, saying, "Know that such is your fate." He is promptly married at court to the frog in all versions of the tale.

For the chapbook authors, a story about a forced marriage to an unpleasantly disguised princess required a different explanation of motivation and of the rationality of Ivan's action. The anonymous chapbook author confronted difficulties from the first line of the story, not only in the location of the tale, but in explaining how a father might have three sons exactly the same age. The story begins: "In a certain kingdom, not in our state, lived and flourished a certain grandee whose name was Dobromysl. He lived in pagan times when people had several dozen wives." Dobromysl, however, had only three, and on the extraordinary occasion of the simultaneous birth of three sons he had a great celebration. When his sons grew up he ordered them to shoot their arrows "so that you will know your fate." The arrows of the first two fell to daughters of other grandees, but Ivan's arrow disappeared. He hunted far and wide, and eventually found himself lost in a bog. In the middle of the bog was a small hut. He knocked on the door. "For a long time no one answered him, and our knight had already begun to lose patience when suddenly a decrepit old woman appeared on the threshold. Looking at her, Ivan took fright. In her hands the old woman held his arrow."

The fairy tale situation has become a more realistic one, and the wonder of the fairy tale has been replaced by the suspenseful chain of the written narrative, in which the imagination of the reader is prompted and cued by the writer. The more rational and self-conscious Ivan of the chapbook knows that he is in a fix from which he must and can extricate himself. "Is this old mushroom really to be my wife?" he asks. The answer is clearly no. He sits down and suddenly the interior of the hut changes into the parlor of a luxurious residence. He is given a fine dinner and settles into a soft armchair, but when he asks to leave, the old woman tells him to stay because "fate herself has ordered you to have me as your wife." But fate means nothing to the modern Ivan, who suggests she must be joking. "You can count more than two hundred years and are looking into the grave, but I am barely twenty-two," he complains. She is not willing to rely on fate either, and says bluntly, "If you do not marry me you will perish in the marsh." His efforts to outwit her and escape fail, so he agrees to marry her, although the reader knows this is only an expedient. Then she appears in her true beauty as a young woman, but Ivan learns that in order to break the spell she must be presented at court as his bride in the form of the old woman.

When Ivan comes before his father bride in hand, the discussion is the opposite of that in the folk tale. Instead of a father ordering a son to marry an unsuitable bride who turns out to be suitable, the son insists and the father protests. Fate is no longer an adequate justification for unacceptable behavior, and the son knows better than the father. Ivan's father complains that the bride looks like a grandmother, but he agrees to the marriage when he concludes that Ivan has been bewitched.

The lubok and folk versions of the tale are closer together in the subsequent development of the theme. As the rival wives perform tasks for the father, Ivan breaks a prohibition, the enchanted beauty is spirited away, and Ivan then rescues her from a faraway land. Some differences remain, however. The lubok version is more concrete and realistic. More important is the casual way in which the lubok author dispenses with the crucial moral element in the fairy tale. The frog-princess is able to escape from the spell in the fairy tale only when a prince will marry her of his own free will. Good comes of voluntary acceptance of an unpleasant fate. In the chapbook version she is able to gain the necessary promise by force and guile, and the prince agrees to marry her only when the alternative is death in the marsh. Even so, one senses that he kept his promise only because he had learned of her true nature.

Similarly revised versions of familiar folk and fairy tales provoked one of the more perceptive investigators of lubok literature to complain of how "a short, alive, expressive, and dramatic folk story is turned into the wishy-washy rhetoric of the lubok author."[22]

Although the changes the authors made did not win the approbation of the critics, they were important in satisfying the readers and showed the difference in tastes between the audiences for popular fiction and for folklore.

Not all fairy tales in the lubok versions were so meaningfully transformed. The story of Vasilisa the Beautiful, one of the series of tales in which the fantastic witch Baba Iaga appears, turned up as *The Merchant's Daughter* in a 1915 lubok edition published by I. D. Sytin, but the story was not greatly changed. The author of the lubok edition gives more concrete details and clarifies motivations. Although there is even a reference to sending Vasilisa to school, the integrity of the tale is preserved. Vasilisa successfully avoids the machinations of an evil stepmother by being kind and listening to a doll given her by her dying mother. She fulfills the stepmother's request to get fire from the witch Baba Iaga, and the stepmother is burned to a crisp when Vasilisa gives her what she requested. Vasilisa's goodness brings doom to her enemies.[23]

Lubok authors also drew on Russia's epic folk poems, the byliny, and sometimes they used scholarly versions with few modifications. The story of the adventures of Ilia Muromets was published under the name of one of the best-known lubok authors, but it differs little in most respects from the standard texts of the byliny.[24]

The only written materials that rivaled oral culture in the popular milieu before the arrival of lubok literature were the works from the medieval and early modern literary tradition that were primarily available in manuscripts. The compendiums contained laboriously copied selections from the Chronicles, the lives of saints, the Psalter, the Book of Hours, and secular tales widely known and respected among the common people. Among the works of the old tradition still extant in the eighteenth and nineteenth centuries were "The Story of the Kingdom of Kazan" versions of Milton's "Paradise Lost", and satirical tales from the Petrine era, such as "The Story of the Russian Sailor Vasilii Kariotskii".

The secular manuscript works that most captivated the common readers were the chivalric tales, whose popularity became so great and lasting that their names became practically synonymous with lubok literature itself. These stories were known in other variants in many countries. Five of these tales that were particularly popular concerned the adventures of Bova Korolevich, Eruslan Lazarevich, Frantsyl Ventsian, Milord Georg, and Guak. Their names suggest their non-Russian origins—Bova, Frantsyl, Guak, and Milord from the West, and Eruslan from the East. Judging from the textual history of Bova and Eruslan, the stories reached Russia in the seventeenth century in oral and manuscript versions, and dispersed rapidly as folk tales, in handwritten copies, and, since the end of the eighteenth century, in printed editions.[25] Well known among the educated reading public, the stories were circulating in rural Russia by the end of the eighteenth century.[26] With a gloss of Christianity, the addition of the conventions of Russian folk tales, and a dusting with familiar touches from the byliny, the texts were rapidly adapted to suit a Russian audience. The stories were frequently printed in the first half of the nineteenth century, and rewritten after the emancipation, when the new lower-class reading public had taken shape as a well-defined market. In that form they attained wide popularity, and remained a staple of popular reading until the Bolsheviks took power.

The five tales had between six and eight hundred separate printings.[27] Bova and Eruslan appeared each in over two hundred separate editions. The five tales together comprise approximately 15 percent of all lubok editions published from the early nineteenth century through the 1880s, but their share of the popular market declined sharply—to 9 percent in the 1890s and to only 5 percent in the 1910s.

These tales retained their archaic flavor, and their continued success puzzled educated observers. Heroes of the stories were the subjects of folk tales,[28] and the very titles bespoke a link to folklore and to a premodern literary tradition. The heroes' attributes were listed and their consorts identified. Titles such as *The Tale of the Strong and Glorious Champion Eruslan Lazarevich and his Beautiful Wife Anastasia* (1904), and *The Tale of the Glorious, Brave, and Unbeatable Champion Bova Korolevich and About his Beautiful Wife the Princess Druzhevna* (1916) were typical. The stories took place in vague or improbable locations, concretizations of "in a faraway kingdom, in a faraway land" of the fairy tales. Bova wanders from a city called Anton to Armenia. Frantsyl begins in "the Spanish Kingdom," but travels to Turkey and Persia, and Guak proceeds from his home in "the Kingdom of American Florida," to "the Amazonian Kingdom." Most of the action consists of heroic contests between valiant knights and their supernatural opponents, except in the story of Milord Georg, in which the subject is courtly love.

The adventures of Bova set the standard for the chivalric tale. Driven out of his own kingdom of Anton by his mother and her evil lover, the murderer of his father, Bova wanders the world, proves courageous in contests with such fantastic adversaries as the centaur, wins a princess and a new kingdom, and returns to avenge his father's death. Stories of this type were revised to suit more modern tastes and values in much the same way as the fairy tales, and although in eighteenth-century versions Bova repays his mother's treachery by burying her alive, by the late nineteenth century he accepts her sincere repentance, and she lives to a ripe old age.[29]

Educated critics used *The English Milord* as a symbol of all that they found pernicious in the literature of the lubok. The story is about a lord out on a hunt who loses his party and finds himself mysteriously before the Marquise Frederika Louisa Brandenburg. The Marquise is in her palace in the forest, with sixteen lovely handmaidens at her side. As soon as she announces her love for him, Milord forgets his betrothed and swears to be true to the lovely Marquise. The two are then separated, and in the longer versions of the story, Milord has a number of additional amorous adventures before being reunited with the Marquise.[30] In the short versions, Milord's only impropriety is the betrayal of his betrothed.[31] Traces of the early origins of this tale appear even in the short versions, and Milord appeals to Diana, goddess of the hunt, when he gets lost in the forest.

Although these chivalrous tales seemed no more than gibberish to most educated readers, each one contained a simple story, usually about the relations between the sexes. Such tales were passed from generation to generation, and the heroes were familiar to new readers. The theme of courtship and marital strife may have had a special meaning to young readers at a time when families were increasingly disrupted by migration and the search for work outside the village.

[. . .]

The distributors

The publishers of popular printed material retained close contact with their potential customers. Due to the slow development of retailing in the book business, the dearth of small local shops at which books might be sold, and the importance of periodic fairs and markets, publishers had to organize their own retailing to a greater extent than in other industries. The big publishers of books for the common people made arrangements with provincial retailers, who met them in Moscow or St. Petersburg. But more important, they developed close relations with a mass of large-and small-scale peddlers who carried their goods on foot and in horse-drawn carts in cities and in rural areas.

The city trade in lubok-type publications was much older than the rural distribution by colporteurs. Ivan Zabelin dated the sale of manuscripts and printed sheets, some of them Old Believer texts, at the Spasskii Gate as early as the seventeenth century.[32] Despite attempts by the government to prevent the sales, the trade continued, and printed secular and religious works were exchanged at this spot in the nineteenth century. Lubok works were also sold at the city markets. In Moscow, the most important were those at the Sukharevaia Tower and the Smolenskii Market, which, in the words of an observer in 1860, were the two main bazaars for all that was "false, tinted, patched, disguised."[33] The same observer described a display of books ranging from classics to lubok works, and recounted how a cleanly dressed young fellow was tricked into paying a ruble for a copy of the lubok chivalry tale *Guak*.

The sellers at these markets were usually peddlers from city shops or people who accumulated a stock of works in their homes and came out to sell at the Sunday markets. The Sukharevskii Market was the scene of a booming trade in used books and magazines of all sorts in the early twentieth century, and there educated shoppers mingled with the semiliterate, all eagerly engrossed in the perusal of the wares of the many stalls.[34] In St. Petersburg, most of Liteinyi Prospect and some of the streets branching off it were lined with bookshops and stalls of various sorts.[35] Books were also sold in such places at the Tolchevskii Second-Hand Market, at other markets in the city, and on the Field of Mars, where booksellers spread out their wares on bast mats in the appropriate season.[36]

Popular literature appeared not only at markets and bazaars, but also in taverns, on street corners, and on display boxes and baskets of the itinerant peddlers.[37] "Not very long ago," wrote an observer soon after the October Revolution, "it was possible to see in the doorways of large houses improvised bookshops where the little lubok publications were visible in all the colors of the rainbow."[38] In Moscow, itinerant sellers were sometimes called pharisees, a slang expression for people who had neither determined occupation nor place of residence, but lived a transient life selling books and pictures at drinking establishments and post houses.[39] On market days, peasants came into the city to trade, and after they had sold their products, they dispersed to teahouses and taverns. There they were met by the pharisees, who had goods from Sytin or other lubok publishers from Nikolskaia Street, and moved from table to table offering the customers their products. One pharisee told A. A. Bakhtiarov, the prerevolutionary historian of publishing, in the late 1880s that he visited fifty taverns a day, sold mostly almanacs, which he bought for half a kopeck and sold for one, and that he earned 25 kopecks a day and 50 on holidays.[40] Prugavin also described the pharisees gathering outside the shops of the lubok publishers, and, in his estimate, the number of street peddlers ran into the hundreds.[41]

The most numerous rural peddlers were called *ofeni* (sing. *ofenia*), a name that was derived, according to some accounts, from their presumed Greek origins or involvement in Greek trade, after the city of Athens (*Afiny, Afinei, ofeni*). According to other explanations, the traders originally came from the city of Ofena in Hungary.[42] The wandering peddlers who sold books, prints, and other goods were also called *khodebshchiki* (walkers), if they went on foot; *korobeiniki*, after the baskets in which they carried their goods; *kartinshchiki*, if they sold primarily pictures; and *mazyki* or *bogomaskateli*, if icons were their main items of trade.

There were wandering peddlers in Russia long before books and prints were in popular demand. Many of the peddlers who sold books on rural routes came from villages in several districts of Vladimir, Moscow, and Tula provinces.[43] Moscow and Vladimir were provinces in which much of the population was engaged in nonagricultural work, and the peddlers lived in and around trading and industrial settlements, but Tula was largely agricultural. Vladimir was considered the classical province of the peddlers, and there peddlers were concentrated in the vicinity of three large trading villages that were renowned centers of icon painting: Mstera, Kholui, and Palekh. (Palekh is today a center of folk and souvenir illustration.)

[. . .]

The peddlers lent a special character to the rural trade in popular printed material. The kindhearted and wise Uncle Iakov, whose praises were sung by the poet N. A. Nekrasov, may not have been the typical peddler, but these wandering bookmen were likely to have possessed much of his stamina and rambunctiousness. The peddlers were bearers of news in the villages they visited. Some peasants resented their worldliness and their willingness to outsmart the unwary customer, and they were known in some quarters as tricksters and fakers; but they were also sellers of serious religious materials as well as light literature, and this probably earned them some respect. They had to be resourceful and quick-witted to survive in their occupation. They had their own slang and a system of marks, so that the illiterate peddlers could identify prices.

Contemporary descriptions of the peddlers in action point up their importance as promoters of the printed word and as people who brought a bit of excitement into the world of the village. The populist writer A. Engelgart described a lubok peddler selling pictures such as "The Storming of Kars," "The Taking of Plevna," and "The Marvelous Dinner of General Skobelev under Enemy Fire" at the time of the 1877–78 Russo-Turkish War.[44] "This is Skobelev—the general who took Plevna," the peddler said. "Here Skobelev himself sits and points out to the soldiers how they will most rapidly enter the gates of Plevna. There you see the gates; there, our soldiers are running." This particular peddler confused the Russian and Turkish flags, and when Engelgart suggested he was mistaken, the peddler argued that the one with the eagle must be Turkish, because "on the Russian flag there would be a cross."

Rubakin described one peddler near Kiev selling a book with a picture on the cover of a crocodile threatening a girl.[45] "'Yes, you have a look,' the peddler cried, poking the phlegmatic Ukrainian peasant in the nose with the book. 'This is the kind of thing that exists on earth. Start reading and you won't stop.'" In the preface to his fictionalized biography of Sytin, Konstantin Konichev remembered the peddler who regularly visited his village on the banks of the Kubenskoe Lake in Vologda Province before the Revolution, selling not only lubok literature to peasants, but also more serious books to the school teacher. Pronia, "who arrived with his wooden trunk attached to a hand sled," knew which peasants wanted secular tales, and who wanted saints' lives or other religious texts. He also visited the school with "fat" books—that is, thick or serious—purchased with silver rather than with 5-kopeck pieces, and brought Sytin's catalogues for the teachers.[46] After he had done his business and held court, Pronia settled down for the night in the place of honor in one of the peasant cottages on the raised platform over the stove. These traveling bookmen were active agents in widening the frontiers of the printed word in rural Russia, and their arguing and sales pitches helped convince new readers that books were important.

During the mid-1920s, when the peddlers and lubok literature had both vanished from the countryside and printed materials were very scarce, some readers and correspondents of the Soviet newspaper for the peasants, *Krestianskaia gazeta* (The Peasant Newspaper), reminisced fondly about the prerevolutionary peddlers. "These book carriers went through the villages and settlements," recalled one reader, "crying out under the windows of the peasant cottages, 'Books, pictures, don't you need some?'"[47] When the peddler spread out his books in the village or market square, remembered a correspondent from Ivanovo-Voznesensk, "A large crowd of children, older fellows, and even girls surrounded him, hung around beside him for almost the whole day, and bought what was interesting."[48]

The literature of the lubok was the first and most primitive type of Russian popular literature, and it was the material basis for common literacy. In the sacks of the colporteurs could be found the first printed words purchased by semiliterate former schoolchildren, their parents, and other new readers. Parents probably purchased these booklets with literacy in mind, as one Soviet newspaper correspondent recalled in 1922: "Father bought me the tale *About Eruslan Lazerevich*, so that I would not forget how to read, and mother exchanged eggs for *Bova Korolevich*."[49]

[. . .]

References

1   *Ezhegodnik. Obzor knig dlia narodnogo chteniia v 1892* (Moscow, 1893), pp. 36–37; and *Ezhegodnik. Obzor knig dlia narodnogo chteniia v 1894* (Moscow, 1895), pp. 38–39.

2   *Statistika proizvedenii pechati v Rossii v 1910 godu* (St. Petersburg, 1911), p. 72.

3   M. V. Muratov, *Knizhnoe delo v Rossii v XIX i XX v.* (Moscow-Leningrad, 1931), pp. 303–305.

4   N. Snegirev, *Lubochnye kartinki russkogo naroda v moskovskom mire* (Moscow, 1861), pp. 5–6.

5   D. N. Rovinskii, *Russkie narodnye kartinki*, book I, vol. 23, in *Sbornik Otdeleniia russkogo iazyka i slovesnosti Imperatorskoi Akademii nauk* (St. Petersburg, 1881), p. iii.

6   Ibid.

7   N. I. Pastukhov, *Ocherki i rasskazy "starago znakomogo"* (Moscow, 1879), p. 46.

8   I. A. Golyshev, *Sobranie sochinenii*, vol. I, part 1 (St. Petersburg, 1889), p. 11.

9   A. A. Fedorov-Davydov, *K voprosu o sotsiologicheskom izuchenii staro-russkogo lubka*, Institut arkheologii i iskusstvoznaniia (Moscow, 1927), p. 99.

10   F. Iezbery, *Vserossiiskii muzei, ili sobranie predmetov, kasaiushchikhsia poznaniia Russkoi Imperii* (Warsaw, 1879), p. 78.

11   *Ezhegodnik. Obzor knig v 1893* (Moscow, 1895), pp. 252–54.

12   *Tovarishchestvo pechataniia izdatel'stva i knizhnoi torgovli I. D. Sytina* (Moscow, 1910), p. vi.

13   Rovinskii, *Russkie narodnye kartinki*, book 5, vol. 27, pp. 31–35, and Golyshev, *Sobranie sochinenii*, vol. I, pp. 4–5.

14   Rovinskii, *Russkie narodnye kartinki*, book 5, vol. 27, pp. 34–35.

15   E. Gollerbakh, *Istoriia graviury i litografii v Rossii* (Moscow-Petrograd, 1923), p. 32.

16   Golyshev, *Sobranie sochinenii*, vol. I, p. 14.

17   Peter C. Marzio, *The Democratic Art* (Boston: David R. Godine, 1979), pp. 69–88, 176–211.

18   M. Chernokov, *Knizhniki* (Leningrad, 1933).

19   KV, nos. 6–7 (1891), p. 266.

20   *Skazka o Ivan-bogatyre, o prekrasnoi supruge ego Svetlane i o zlom volshebnike Karachune* (Kiev, 1900).

21   *Narodnye russkie skazki A. N. Afanas'eva v trekh tomakh*, ed. V. Ia. Propp (Moscow, 1957), nos. 267–69, vol. 2, pp. 329–37.

22   N. Andreev, "Ischezaiushchaia literatura," *Kazanskii bibliofil*, no. 2 (Kazan', 1921), p. 9.

23   *Kupecheskaia doch' Vasilisa Prekrasnaia* (Sytin: Moscow, 1915), and Afanas'ev, *Narodnye russkie*, vol. 1, pp. 159–65.

24   I. S. Ivin (Kassirov), *Il'ia Muromets, naibol'shii bogatyr' kievskii vo vremena sv. kniazia Vladimira* (Kiev, 1899).

25   V. D. Kuz'mina, *Rytsarskii roman na Rusi* (Moscow, 1964), and L. N. Pushkarev, *Skazka o Eruslane Lazareviche* (Moscow, 1980).

26   Pushkarev, *Skazka*, p. 58.

27   This count is based on Kuz'mina for Bova, Pushkarev for Eruslan, and my count of the other titles.

28   Boris and Iurii Sokolov, *Skazki i pesni Belozerskogo kraia* (Moscow, 1915), pp. 206–209, 213.

29   Kuz'mina, *Rytsarskii roman*, pp. 41, 85.

30   *Povest' o prikliuchenii angliiskogo Milorda Georga* (Moscow, 1901) is a 108-page version and *Povest' o prikliuchenii angliiskogo Milorda Georga* (Moscow, 1890) is 180 pages long.

31   *Povest' o prikliucheniiakh angliiskogo Milorda Georga* (Moscow, 1896) is a 32-page version.

32   Ivan Zabelin, *Istoriia goroda Moskvy*, vol. I (Moscow, 1905), pp. 637–51.

33   *KV*, nos. 3–6 (1860), p. 37.

34   P. Petrov, "Sukharevskii knizhnyi torg v Moskve," *Bibliograficheskie izvestiia*, no. 3–4 (1915), pp. 114–19.

35   *Ocherki istorii Leningrada*, vol. 3, ed. B. M. Kochakov (Moscow-Leningrad, 1956), p. 588.

36   A. A. Bakhtiarov, *Istoriia knigi na Rusi* (St. Petersburg, 1890), p. 263.

37   Andreev, "Ischezaiushchaia literatura," p. 3.

38   Ibid., p. 3.

39   Bakhtiarov, *Istoriia knigi*, p. 263.

40   Ibid., p. 264.

41   A. S. Prugavin, *Zaprosy naroda*, 1st ed. (Moscow, 1890), p. 153. All other references are to the expanded second edition that appeared in 1895.

42   N. Tikhonravov, "Ofeni," in *Vladimirskii sbornik* (Moscow, 1857), pp. 22–23, and N. Trokhimovskii, "Ofeni," *RV*, no. 6 (1866), pp. 560–61.

43   In Vladimir, Shuiskii, Muromskii, Kovrovskii, Viaznikovskii, Gorokhovetskii, and Sudogodskii uezds; in Moscow, Serpukhovskii, and Podol'skii uezds; and in Tula Aleksinskii uezd.

44   A. Engel'gart, "8z derevni", *OZ*, no. 3 (1878), p. 11.

45   *O*, no. 3 (1901), p. 24.

46   Konstantin Konichev, *Russkii samorodok* (Leningrad, 1966), pp. 3–6.

47   M. I. Slukhovskii, *Kniga i derevnia* (Moscow-Leningrad, 1928), p. 152.

48   Ibid., p. 152.

49   G. Gavrilov (a peasant correspondent) in *Bednota*, no. 1241 (June 14, 1922).

Chapter 23

Martyn Lyons with Lucy Taksa

READING AND RECITING

General Fiction

THE CONCLUSIONS OF THIS SURVEY lend support to the notion of the essential continuity of Australian literary culture between the late 19th and early 20th centuries. This culture remained derivative: interviewees' general tastes in fiction appeared very imperial in orientation. Their responses, outlined in this chapter, not only reveal a familiar acquaintance with popular writers such as Ethel M. Dell and Edgar Wallace, but also show persistent respect for the classics of 19th-century English literature. Poetry and children's literature will be discussed in separate chapters; first, readers' experiences of general adult fiction will be presented, suggesting the continuing relevance of the imperial cultural ties, described in rather fatuous terms by Buchan at the head of this chapter.

The economics of Australian book production obstructed Australia's path to literary independence in our period. According to Nile and Walker in *Marketing the Literary Imagination*, Australian book production was a tale of three cities, Sydney, Melbourne, and London, on which the domestic industry heavily depended.[1] In the decade up to 1930, the single largest publisher of Australian novels was Hodder & Stoughton in London. Not until 1930, when our period was coming to a close, did Angus & Robertson loom up to take over the lead in the production of Australian fiction. Buchan's dream, of Britain enriching the Empire from her own cultural traditions, was therefore underpinned by the commercial realities of international publishing.

The readers interviewed were asked to name the authors and novels they remembered best. They did so sometimes with love, at other times with a grimace of anguish. Their responses indicate a degree of acquaintance, but not necessarily of affection. On many occasions, respondents needed to be prompted to provide names of authors they may have come across in their youth. Spontaneous recollections were, as far as possible, registered separately from those memories prompted by the interviewer. Some authors had a strong presence in readers' homes, while others were associated mainly with school reading. Only one author was recalled by over 40 per cent of informants: Charles Dickens, whose various titles were mentioned by 37 (60.7 per cent). The authors most frequently recalled are listed below.

Seven authors were familiar to between 30 per cent and 40 per cent of informants. They are listed in [Table 23.1 below]. A larger group of writers was remembered by between 20 per cent and 30 per cent of informants. These are listed in [Table 23.2 below].

More than 10 per cent of informants were acquainted with Fenimore Cooper, Jules Verne, G. K. Chesterton, Arnold Bennett, Thomas Hardy, the Brontë sisters and Mrs Henry Wood. Other authors recalled included Jane Austen, Anthony Trollope, Edgar Allan Poe, Oscar Wilde and Wilkie Collins among 19th-century classic favourites; Belloc, Conan Doyle, Evelyn Waugh, Edgar Wallace, Compton Mackenzie, W. W. Jacobs and Baroness Orczy among more contemporary authors; Ion Idriess and Nat Gould as Australian representatives; and not forgetting the romances of Ethel M. Dell and the westerns of Zane Grey.

Table 23.1

Writer	Mentions	Percentage of informants
Walter Scott	22	36.1
John Bunyan, *The Pilgrim's Progress*	21	34.4
H. G. Wells	21	34.4
Henry Lawson, short stories	21	34.4
Mrs Aeneas Gunn	20	32.8
Marcus Clarke, *For the Term of His Natural Life*	20	32.8
Rudyard Kipling	19	31.1

Table 23.2

Writer	Mentions	Percentage of informants
Rolf Boldrewood, *Robbery Under Arms*	18	29.5
H. B. Stowe, *Uncle Tom's Cabin*	17	27.9
P. G. Wodehouse	16	26.2
John Galsworthy	15	24.6
Somerset Maugham	15	24.6
John Buchan	15	24.6
'Steele Rudd'	14	23.0
W. M. Thackeray	14	23.0

This list is significant for at least two reasons. First, it demonstrates that the classics of 19th-century English literature continued to frame the reading public's field of vision until well into the 20th century. Second, the absence of any remotely modernist authors is remarkable. Arthur O. did admit to reading James Joyce, 'that mad Irishman', but gave up because his books were 'too hard'. William M. recalled family discussions of Remarque's *All Quiet on the Western Front*, and Bernard F. remembered D. H. Lawrence—but only for the obscenity case surrounding *Lady Chatterley's Lover*. (Lawrence's novel was banned, as was Joyce's *Ulysses*, perhaps the text to which Arthur O. referred.) Otherwise, the avant-garde fiction of the inter-war years did not apparently enter the mainstream experience of the reading public.

The best known authors listed above may be discussed in three main categories: the 19th-century classics, contemporary writers, and Australian fiction. One of the best known works, however, *Pilgrim's Progress*, defies such a categorization. For long one of the key inspirations of English radical thought, Bunyan's book also had a profound influence throughout the 19th century. Many working-class autobiographers used *Pilgrim's Progress* as a reference point in accounts of their own spiritual odysseys. In the 20th century, Bunyan was still relevant for Protestant readers. Almost as many men as women in this survey remembered Bunyan, which was unusual since women generally had a far greater recall of fiction than did male informants. Half of those who recalled *Pilgrim's Progress* had the book at home, also a high ratio. In some homes though, it remained unread. Randolph H., who came from a Methodist background, remembered that it 'accumulated dust' along with the other 19th-century classics which stood untouched in the family bookcase. Two female interviewees disliked its stern morality, and Arthur O. 'struggled through it'.

On the other hand, many readers had a very close relationship with *Pilgrim's Progress*. Kathleen T. exclaimed after being reminded of the title, 'Oh, that's one of my favourite books . . . that was one of my treasures'. It was read aloud to both Nora K. in Inverell and Laura P. in Petersham. Irene A., who became an Anglican missionary, 'was brought up with that . . . we read it from cover to cover . . . more than once'.

These readers had an 'intensive' relationship with *Pilgrim's Progress*, in the sense that it was a stock text inherited from previous generations, often reread, often read aloud in a domestic group, helping thereby to sustain the traditional, religious life of the family. Masie G. had a strong sense of the Protestant work ethic, and *Pilgrim's Progress*, the first title she recalled, reminded her of this. School, she said, was 'work, work, work, the three Rs, morning, noon and night . . . we thought that was the done thing . . . The Bible says if a man will not work . . . did you know that? . . . neither shall he eat; and I think it was Isaac Newton, said "Satan finds some mischief for idle hands to do". Well, Satan's been going overtimes'. These thoughts, prompted by the memory of John Bunyan, placed his pilgrim at the centre of Protestant preferences for the 'edifying' and 'uplifting' literature to which Masie G. frequently referred.

Charles Dickens stood out as by far the best known writer of any form of literature, specifically recalled by 60 per cent of interviewees. He was recalled by informants of both sexes in almost equal proportions. One-third of them remembered having a Dickens at home, sometimes in a complete set of novels; over half also remembered having come across Dickens at school. This was a comparatively high proportion in both cases; Dickens was an author held in high regard both by the school syllabus and by a large number of families. Perhaps most striking of all, however, was the fact that only 11 respondents needed prompting before they recalled the presence of Dickens in their reading. This very low 'prompt ratio', of less than 30 per cent of Dickens readers, was quite exceptional. Dickens, therefore, was usually the object of spontaneous recall, and strongly associated both with the classroom and the family bookcase.

He often formed part of the family inheritance. Daisy B. remembered that her father kept Dickens among the 'good books' in the dining-room bookcase. Four others recalled Dickens displayed with the family's books in the formal area of the house. This could mean that Dickens went completely unread. Rosemary C. had Dickens at home, 'of course', but found him 'boring'.

The Dickens Fellowship, founded in London in 1902, tried to maintain interest in his works. A Sydney branch was established in 1913 under the auspices of Lord Mayor Clarke and soon boasted over 300 members.[2] The Fellowship met in public halls and provided musical occasions, theatricals and recitations from Dickens's works.

The popularity of Dickens is evident, too, throughout Kathleen Fitzpatrick's autobiography, even if the older generation in her family did not fully appreciate him. Fitzpatrick gives this irreverent account of family reading:

> Grandpa was said to have been a great reader of Dickens in his youth, and
> owned the *Works* in a good illustrated edition, on which I feasted before the

morning-room fire, but I never saw him reading them. Aunty Doone read weak, silly novels from a circulating library. Aunty Dot went in for bouts of self-improvement and for years, it seemed to me, she carried Carlyle's *French Revolution* about with her, hoping, I suppose, to take it in by osmosis.[3]

Schools tried to inculcate respect for Victorian literary achievements, but Ronald L. found the small print of his school editions very difficult to read. The tradition was continued by the choice of Dickens for school prizes, or as presents from parents. Laura P.'s Dickens was bought cheaply by her father, and Margaret M. was another who associated Dickens with the gift of *Nicholas Nickleby*.

Ethel Turner's love of Dickens and other 19th-century English novelists is evident from her diary entries for the 1890s. In 1890, she read *The Mill on the Floss* and, the following year, *Ivanhoe*. Between 1892 and 1896 Turner read *Pickwick Papers, David Copperfield, Our Mutual Friend* and *Great Expectations*.[4] Her diary confirms the oral evidence of this survey.

The ability of informants to quote several titles by Dickens was a sign of their familiarity with his works. This was a rare feat; with authors like Jules Verne, or H. G. Wells, hardly any informants could recall more than one title without prompting. Dickens was different. Every major title was evoked in the course of the interviews, with the exceptions of *Hard Times* and *Martin Chuzzlewit*. The most popular were *David Copperfield*, and *A Tale of Two Cities* which had wide romantic appeal. Julia J. won it as a prize, and Letty O. described it as a 'very great favourite', which was read and reread. The Dickens readings most frequently performed by the Dickens Fellowship were scenes from *David Copperfield* and *A Christmas Carol*, together with the death of Sidney Carton in *A Tale of Two Cities*.[5]

For Charlotte C., Dickens was among the 'conventional books' of her youth. Dickens was not alone in this, however, for Walter Scott frequently kept him company in the family bookcase. One-third of informants recalled Scott and, as with Dickens, a large number (exactly one half) remembered coming across Scott at home. The same was true of Thackeray, who completed the triumvirate of 19th-century English novelists preferred by interviewees. Both Daisy B. and Nora K., who came from wealthy Sydney backgrounds, had sets of Scott in the family bookcase. *Ivanhoe* was his best known novel, but some readers understandably complained that he was heavy going. Mabel T. spoke of Scott as if he was an irritating neighbour who would not go away: 'I never got on with him,' she said. Donald W., on the other hand, assured us that he was in the process of reading Scott for the third time.

[. . .]

American works were well-represented in interviewees' recollections, especially by *Uncle Tom's Cabin*, and Cooper's *The Last of the Mohicans*. *Uncle Tom's Cabin* was best-remembered by female readers, and very few of them needed any prompting. It was school prize material for Nora K., and read aloud at home to Laura P. In contrast, Cooper's celebration of warrior virtues in *The Last of the Mohicans* appealed chiefly to male readers. Other American writers, such as Mark Twain, O. Henry and Damon Runyan, were very rarely mentioned by comparison. Ellis's Deerfoot novels are considered later as children's literature.

Bernadette O'C. was nevertheless much aware of the growing influence of modern American fiction in novels and magazines. Her perceptions, which she wrote for us, are worth quoting here. 'The American books', she wrote in a letter:

were new to my parents. American journals were not read where they came from in England – on a/c prejudice probably. It was interesting to have a new slant on things. We had to be careful about spelling. We read the American expressions which became familiar when we got talking pictures – and pronounced them in our own way. We knew the Yanks talked through their noses, but didn't reproduce their manner of speech – we didn't know it. This is amusing to think back on. There was a lot about prohibition, and subterfuges to outflank the government agents who tried to track down stills in the wilds of Kentucky – and stories of bootlegging and how some people wanted to get rich on it. And niggers, of course – good stories about them and their efforts to amuse themselves and better themselves – all sorts of embarrassing situations. Some of the stories were not in straight English, there were unusual expressions which sounded odd to us. All this was in the days before radio and television shows took hold.

American literature presented a society of 'niggers', Indians, boot-leggers and bad language. When Zane Grey had supplied the cowboys, only the gangsters would be missing from the gallery of stock American characters.

Translated writers were rarely recalled by interviewees, except for Jules Verne, remembered principally for *20 000 Leagues Under the Sea*. Henry Lawson's Steelman, it may be recalled, read Verne in *The Geological Spieler*.[6] Two informants read Victor Hugo, two read *Don Quixote*, and two others read works by Thomas Mann. Russian novelists were surprisingly unknown to interviewees, or else had been utterly forgotten by them.

To turn from the giants of the 19th century to writers who were more or less contemporary with interviewees, we must first consider Kipling whose career bridged the centuries. Kipling was one of the very few writers in this survey who was recalled most often by men. His stories dealt with many different aspects of Anglo-Indian society, but his focus on an essentially military world helps to explain his particular appeal to male readers. He was 'a great favourite' for Oliver C., and Amy M. 'thoroughly enjoyed' him. So did Tom H., even if he did find Kipling tame after the excitement evoked by G. A. Henty. A high proportion of Kipling readers (about one in three) associated him with school.

Kipling is now enjoying a minor publishing boom, but he was once a writer unacknowledged by the critics, 'a laureate without laurels' as T. S. Eliot called him.[7] Now he is regarded as one of the greatest, if not *the* greatest English short story writer, but the ordinary readers who made up his huge popular audience perhaps already knew this.

[. . .]

Australian writers such as Jeannie (Mrs Aeneas) Gunn, and Lawson were firmly implanted in the reading memory, but interviewees only recalled a very small range of Australian fiction authors. Twenty informants remembered Mrs Gunn's *We of the Never-Never*, which had sold over 320 000 copies by 1945.[8] Only seven remembered *The Little Black Princess*, which Tom H. pronounced 'not so good' compared to *We of the Never-Never*. In 1929, the Melbourne publishers of *The Little Black Princess* claimed a total print-run of 92 000 for the novel.[9]

These sales were made possible by the adoption of Jeannie Gunn's texts by the school system. Six respondents remembered using her books at school—a relatively high proportion of informants. Agnes B., who was one of them, received *The Little Black Princess* as a school prize. Two out of three who recalled Gunn were women. Daisy B. recalled, '[I] loved that, I read it over and over'. Agatha H. found Mrs Gunn overrated, but she had nevertheless read *We of the Never-Never* twice. Letty O. had gone on a literary pilgrimage to the Northern Territory to find the station where the book was set. It was 'one of my treasures', said Kathleen T. using her favourite phrase, as if opening a literary Aladdin's cave for us.

One must assume that the patriarchal values incorporated in *We of the Never-Never* reflected the aspirations of female readers. 'The Little Missus' is treated with a combination of condescending chivalry and outright misogyny from the very first chapter (entitled 'The Unknown Woman'). The husband, however, is the truly 'unknown' character of the book.

The brevity of Gunn's married life may account for this sketchy treatment by the woman of her husband. The warm glow which infuses her memories was based on a very short acquaintance with the outback. *The Little Black Princess* is similarly unrealistic. In dealing with aboriginal culture through the naive but resourceful child Bett-Bett, Gunn was reducing aboriginality to dimensions which could be easily assimilated by, and were not threatening to, her white readers. As Niall suggests, an adult Bett-Bett would have been too difficult for the author to handle.[10] Perhaps the same is true of her readers.

[. . .]

Henry Lawson was another writer associated with school reading by about 40 per cent of those who remembered him. Readers, however, identified Lawson as a poet rather than a prose author. There was a common tendency to bracket Lawson with Paterson and to compare the two as poets. Lawson's poetic identity had been firmly established in the classroom [. . .]

The Australian author who inspired most enthusiasm was undoubtedly 'Steele Rudd'. He also provoked the most antipathy. Very few informants remained indifferent to *On Our Selection* and its sequels. Oliver C. liked the 'good, clean humour' of 'Rudd's' stories, and Randolph H. liked him 'well and truly'.

On the other hand, Tom H. recognized that 'Steele Rudd' created amusing situations, only to add that he could not be considered a top-class writer. Mabel T. 'never liked' his stories, and Daisy B. said, after prompting, 'I didn't like Steele Rudd, no . . . his humour didn't appeal to me, to me they were silly'. Clearly, he tended to have a more appreciative male readership. Oliver C. remembered that he read him with his brothers, and Rosemary C., who lived in Goondiwindi, asserted: 'in the bush, all the men read it'.

Although several informants recalled the NSW Bookstall series of novels, 'Steele Rudd' was the only individual author they could name. 'Steele Rudd' was sold in 1s paperbacks (the price rose to 1s 3d in the 1920s), printed in linotype on cheap paper. By 1939, a quarter of a million copies of *On Our Selection* had been sold.[11] The Bookstall Company produced 311 titles in all in 885 editions and was in its publishing heyday between the First World War and the death of A. C. Rowlandson, its driving force, in 1922. Except for 'Rudd', however, its productions left no lasting trace on interviewees' memories.

Only a handful recalled Miles Franklin and Ion Idriess, mainly for *The Cattle King*. The Australian fiction writers remembered were therefore few in number; but those mentioned coincided with the results of the popularity poll organized by the *Argus* in 1927.[12] Our respondents had apparently consigned Bridges, Cronin and Collins to oblivion. Turner and Bruce [. . .] were far from forgotten [. . .]. [Marcus] Clarke, who topped the poll, was well known rather than well loved by interviewees.

[. . .]

The thriller and adventure writers of this period promoted imperialistic values and built on their own experience in the Dominions. Rider Haggard, Edgar Wallace and John Buchan, for instance, had all served in South Africa. They had a colossal readership, and their own colonial experience was an important and invisible ingredient of early 20th-century popular fiction.

Buchan was conventionally recalled for his *The 39 Steps*. 'Well', said Tom H., 'everybody had to read *The 39 Steps*.' Richard Hannay was a hero who 'played the game' in the English public school tradition, and he exemplified all its limitations. Buchan was antisemitic, prejudiced against negroes, a Tory and a dour Calvinist.[13] He interpreted Bolshevism as an Asiatic revolt against European culture, and was nauseated by its 'ugly pathological savour, as if a mature society were being assailed by diseased and vicious children'.

Edgar Wallace expressed similar sentiments, but with less ideological conviction. Wallace was more concerned with commercial success than with rooting out moral depravity. Arnold

Bennett wrote of him: 'Edgar Wallace has a very grave defect, and I will not hide it. He is content with society as it is. He parades no subversive opinions. He is "correct".'[14] He was well-read by dedicated mystery and thriller readers in this survey.

Tom H. read Wallace, as well as Conan Doyle, who succeeded, in spite of himself, in establishing a far closer relationship with readers than Wallace ever did. Sherlock Holmes was 'born' a century ago in 1887, but did not come of age until his first appearance in the *Strand Magazine* in 1891. Holmes was a pessimist, a misogynist, a drug addict and an intellectual snob. Even the patient Randolph H. found the man 'rather irritating'.

Three readers recalled Nat Gould's racing stories, but all Pina N. could remember was that she was forbidden to read such 'yellow trash'. Many of Gould's stories have an Australian setting, even some written after his return to England in 1895. Some of his stories were serialized in *The Referee*, which broadened his readership to include a wide range of sporting fans. Two informants recalled reading Gould, and they were both working-class men. They shared another characteristic: neither seems to have read anything else except the sporting pages. This suggests that Nat Gould reached a market of punters that other fiction writers could not penetrate. According to Miller and Macartney, Gould published an average of over three titles per year between 1891 and 1928.[15]

Readers of thrillers rarely identified individual authors in their favourite genre, but they could not by-pass the prolific output of writers such as Wallace or Gould. The western had its own individual master: Zane Grey. With Grey, the western came of age, and according to one American critic, he was the single most popular author of the post-First World War era.[16] His praise of frontier values may have struck a responsive chord in young male readers in Australia. For Grey, the American West had a mythical significance, like the myth of the bush in Australian literary culture. The West was a moral and symbolic landscape, where characters found redemption and recovered their basic human values. Their regeneration, however, could not be complete without a melodramatic shoot-out. Books such as *Riders of the Purple Sage* (1912) ended in a mandatory orgy of blood-letting.

Zane Grey and Nat Gould were men's authors. Women and girls tended to prefer romances by Baroness Orczy and 'heart-throb' merchants such as Ethel M. Dell. Orczy was of Hungarian origin and knew no English until she was 15. She was educated in Brussels and Paris, married an Englishman, and made her enormous reputation with *The Scarlet Pimpernel* in 1905 at the age of 40. Betty S. recalled that her mother passed this book on to her, and she read it in sixth class. 'I was sold', she said, 'I didn't want anything else, ever, except Baroness Orczy.'

[. . .]

In John Buchan's day, therefore, English literature continued to colonize the Australian reading public at every level, from classic fiction of the 19th century to modern humour, thrillers and romances. The American frontier exerted its perennial appeal, while a small group of Australian authors were recalled by informants.

[. . .]

The impression that emerges is that of a public which grew up with the English 19th-century masters in the family bookcase, comprising Dickens, Scott and Thackeray, supplemented perhaps by *Pilgrim's Progress* and *Uncle Tom's Cabin*. This was the core of the fictional baggage of many immigrants from Britain towards the end of the 19th century. Then our readers were introduced to a group of Australian writers, as well as to more Dickens, at school. In later life, they turned to their bookshops and lending libraries for H. G. Wells, P. G. Wodehouse, 'Steele Rudd', or the popular authors we have mentioned. A number of readers associated Jeannie Gunn, Clarke and Boldrewood with the classroom or the school library, which suggests that the educational system was not unreservedly dedicated to the promotion of Anglophile subservience.

[. . .]

Newspapers and magazines

[. . .]

Australia has shared in this staggering expansion of press production. According to Mayer, Australia figured in the top 10 newspaper-reading nations in the world in 1958, estimated by the circulation of daily papers per inhabitant.[17] Australia was then the fifth nation in the world for the consumption of general interest periodicals. This high rate of newspaper consumption was already apparent in 1904 to the government statistician T. A. Coghlan, who smugly reported that:

> Few things show more plainly the social superiority of a civilised people than a heavy correspondence and a large distribution of newspapers. In these respects, all the provinces of Australasia have for many years been remarkable. In proportion to population, it is doubtful whether any country in the world can boast of a larger number or a better class of newspapers than they publish.[18]

Coghlan counted 315 newspapers appearing in New South Wales, of which 107 were published within Sydney and its suburbs.

The general level of prosperity helped to account for this impressive proliferation of newspapers. Before 1914, Australian newspapers were perhaps cheaper than ever, in real terms. Dailies such as the *Telegraph* and the *Sun* sold for only 1d each, and the *Sydney Morning Herald* still cost only 2d in 1920.[19]

The dispersal and density of the population also determined the circulation of such papers. Country areas of new South Wales were served by no fewer than 240 papers in the pre-1914 period.[20] The *Bathurst Times* and the Lismore *Northern Star* had daily circulations of over 7000, and the readers of Orange, whose population was just over 4000, sustained two dailies. These, however, were exceptions. Very few country papers were dailies. The majority appeared once a week, many cost as much as 6d, and had a limited circulation of only a few hundred copies.

By contrast, the daily press flourished in the highly concentrated Sydney market. After 1918, Sydney readers had a choice of two morning and two evening daily papers. The severe-looking *Sydney Morning Herald* led the field with a circulation estimated at 160 000 in 1919, rising to over 200 000 by 1930.[21] The *Herald* had been slow to develop headlines, it did not use cartoons, and photographs appeared in it only after 1911. Yet it outstripped its major competitor, the *Telegraph* (which Jack A. dismissed as a mere 'sausage-wrapper'), in spite of the latter's successful Saturday production, the *World's News*.

The *Sun* was the most popular evening paper mentioned by interviewees, and its circulation reached 148 000 by 1920, only 10 years after it had replaced the *Star*.[22] Like the *Herald*, the *Sun* received cabled news from London, and it became the first Sydney paper to print news on the front page instead of advertisements or announcements.

[. . .]

A paper's content, advertising, prose style, layout, and the nature and location of its sales outlets addressed specific reading communities. The testimony of readers themselves can help us to outline the constituencies of a few popular and recurring titles. The *Sydney Morning Herald* was by far the best remembered daily for interviewees. More than an organ of news and information, the *Herald* was, as now, a local institution with a special claim on our attention. Readers of the *Sun*, the *Bulletin* and *Smith's Weekly* will also be considered in this chapter.

The general level of newspaper consumption recalled by interviewees was high [. . .]. Three-quarters of interviewees read, or came from households that read, at least one regular daily newspaper. Only 10 per cent of them read no regular newspaper at all. This level of regular newspaper readership was higher than that of 60 per cent found by Winchester.[23] It matched the level found by Thiesse amongst urban workers and artisans in France during the *belle époque*, and it far exceeded the newspaper consumption of French peasants in the same period.[24]

Thiesse's study also emphasized differences in consumption habits between city and country, which was certainly true for New South Wales at the beginning of this century. Reliance on a weekly, rather than a daily, newspaper was overwhelmingly a rural practice. Fifteen per cent of readers remembered taking a regular weekly, but no regular daily paper. Twelve out of 14 places of residence given here were in the country. Rosemary C. remembered Brisbane weeklies being delivered by mail to her family's remote station near Goondiwindi. In the First World War, their arrival was awaited with eagerness and, for parents of sons at the front, with trepidation. One house guest shocked Rosemary C. by shouting 'The War News! The War News!' as the weekly paper arrived, and by then turning immediately to the racing page. Arnold R. relied on weekly mail deliveries of the *Gloucester Advocate* for essential information on cattle sales. Irene A. and Nancy B. both remembered the children's sections in the weekly *Cooma Express* and *Temora Mail* respectively.

Weekly papers could be valuable items in the country and were cherished for a variety of useful purposes. At Ariah Park, west of Temora, before 1914, Nancy B. remembered the weekly papers being shredded and then 'hung up in the dunny'. Betty S., in Adelong, told us that papers were sold as wrappers for a penny a pound.

Thirty-seven per cent of rural residents were without a regular daily newspaper, which was almost twice the rate for urban residents. There was no simple dichotomy, however, between rural deprivation and urban plenty. Of those who rarely read a newspaper at all, eight out of 11 were urban residents; of those who read several every day, 14 out of 18 were city-dwellers, and half of them lived in the inner city of Sydney. A wide social spectrum of readers existed in the city, which harboured readers at both extremities of the scale: the avid paper-readers as well as the most marginal members of the newspaper public. In the country, reading patterns were more uniform, but also qualitatively different since rural readers relied more frequently on the weekly press.

Social class had a powerful influence on the level of newspaper consumption [. . .]. All except one interviewee from the business and professional bourgeoisie had at least one regular daily newspaper, and over a third of them recalled several. Eighty-seven per cent of lower middle-class interviewees had at least one regular daily paper, but only 54.5 per cent of working-class respondents did so. The newspaper public of New South Wales was therefore a complex one, with considerable geographical and social variations. Reading practices were different in city and country, and consumption levels suggested strong links between social class and cultural practice in New South Wales society.

Newspaper readers declare their allegiance not only by what they read, but also by how and where they acquire their newspaper. Papers reach their readers by familiar paths, retrodden daily or weekly, each title beckoning its disciples from its own distinctive territory. The daily newspaper, regularly encountered on the doorstep, in a shop, at a street-corner stall, or in a barber's shop, imposes individual habits and private rituals which take their allotted place in the everyday experience of the buyer.

Working-class readers very rarely had newspapers delivered to their home. Kate A. remembered that her father walked from Annandale to the *Herald*'s city offices early in the morning to consult job vacancies advertised in the earliest editions. On train journeys to Katoomba, John H. saw fettlers camped beside the railway line shouting 'Papers! Papers!' to the passengers, asking them to throw newspapers to them from passing trains.

Specialist papers had their own particular collection points, such as the *Catholic Weekly* which Tom H.'s family brought home after Sunday mass. *The Labor Daily* had a unique status in working-class circles. It was 'father's Bible' for Eileen McC., and John P., a labourer at Chullora railway works, also described it as his 'Bible'. Such language, which some readers also used to describe the *Bulletin*, implied the role of the newspaper as a continual work of reference; it also implied a reverential attitude, which embraced the newspaper's symbolic function as a banner of a quasi-religious faith. John Mongan described how important the *Labor Daily* was to him in the 1920s when he was a cleaner on the railway at Clyde. He said:

> I was always interested in politics and my other mate he was a junior with me. On our way to work in the steam train one morning we used to buy two *Labor Dailys* each and read that [instead] of this *Daily Guardian*. You see you could read about what your life was really like and we used to spend a penny each and spread the news trying to get them to read the *Labor Daily* instead of the *Daily Guardian*.[25]

The 'Bible' evidently had a few keen evangelists.

In mid-1925, when it hunted down fascist activities, the *Labor Daily* attained a circulation of over 100 000.[26] A survey of 1926, however, showed that its readers appreciated the paper's sporting coverage more than any other section of news. The *Labor Daily* was often brought home from the workplace itself, or else was encountered in other centres of (predominantly male) working-class leisure. According to Albert P., 'The *Labor Daily* was introduced by the Jack Lang (faction) . . . and recognized working-class people. It was the accepted thing in most homes in those days, wherever you went, in the snooker rooms, barber shops, any sporting venues, the *Labor Daily* was always there'. Working-class reading must therefore be comprehended within the context of urban working-class sociability, in which meeting-places such as the barber's shop might play an important social and cultural role. The working-class experience of daily newspapers could be quite different from that of their social superiors. After all, Henry K., like many others, was a salesboy before he was a reader.

The home delivery of newspapers was a sign of social status. According to Jack A., a wharf labourer who lived in Blacktown in the 1920s, delivery was a luxury. In contrast to the *Herald*, which was often delivered to its middle-class readers, evening papers such as the *Sun* were usually purchased in the city on the way home from work. Albert P., a working-class reader, thought the fact that *Herald* readers had their paper delivered to them was one of its most remarkable characteristics, as he explained: 'the family paper . . . They delivered 'em, they'd fold them up and twist them and throw them into your front garden. It was the most regular paper that came'.

The home delivery of the *Sydney Morning Herald* probably explains why so many female respondents remembered this paper. Two-thirds of respondents who recalled regular *Herald* deliveries were women, whereas regular *Sun* readers were equally divided between men and women. Women were more likely to recall delivered papers, because they did not usually buy daily newspapers personally. This task was carried out by males. Two female interviewees from working-class backgrounds recalled their father buying the *Herald*, and another's father bought the *Sun* regularly for her mother to read. William M.'s mother appreciated the *Sun* for the 'ads for all the latest shopping for ladies', but this did not mean that she bought it herself.

Even methods of obtaining a regular newspaper were determined by social class and by perceptions of sex roles. Albert P.'s comment that the *Herald* was 'a family newspaper' was revealing, since it suggested that the *Herald* did not have the strongly male readership of the *Sun* or the *Labor Daily*. Dependence on the male as the purchaser of the daily newspaper was so marked for three female informants that they identified their marriages as the first time they began to read a regular daily. There was little newspaper reading, either, for Agatha H. in war-time Petersham, after her father had left home.

A portrait of the *Herald* reader can now be attempted. Thirty respondents, or a half of all interviewees, were regular readers or belonged to families which took the *Herald* regularly. The *Herald* was by far the most popular newspaper title recalled by informants. A high proportion were female, and they tended to receive the *Herald* by home delivery.

An exceptionally high proportion (48.5 per cent) were from the business and professional classes who formed our highest social rank. Only 21.2 per cent of regular *Herald* readers in this survey were from the working class. There were, however, four occasional readers of the *Herald* from working-class origins. The *Herald* therefore did have a working-class readership, although often on a casual basis, for instance at weekends or during periods of job-hunting. Most *Herald* readers were from the upper social echelons. John P., for example, who worked for a farmer in Leeton, read the *Labor Daily*, but he knew that his boss took the *Herald*.

No regular *Herald* readers interviewed, however, were farmers, which demonstrated the paper's naturally strong urban readership. The railway network took the *Herald* to William M. and Betty S. in Tamworth and to Maud B. in Lithgow. Over 81 per cent of *Herald* readers in the survey, however, were urban residents, and 13 lived in the inner city.

The *Herald* claimed to have a non-denominational stance, and all the main religious groupings were represented amongst readers interviewed. There were, however, only four Catholic readers and eight non-conformist Protestants. In fact, almost three-quarters of regular *Herald* readers in the survey were Protestants of some kind. This may be explicable simply in class terms, given the extent to which class boundaries and confessional loyalties coincided in New South Wales. The *Herald* emerged from this survey as the daily paper of Sydney's Protestant bourgeoisie, with a part-time working-class public.

The *Herald* was an emblem of Sydney, an urban, and possibly a national monument. It had a symbolic presence, a pedagogic value and, like all national monuments, a commemorative role as well – as seen when readers were recently offered a facsimile edition of the very first edition of the *Sydney Herald* of 1831.

Despite appearances, however, national monuments rarely command unanimous allegiance. The *Herald* was no exception. It provided one particular reading of the life of the city, and was a rallying-point for a certain section of Sydney society. The *Herald* was a familiar and reassuring place where a particular group recognized and identified itself, its tastes and shared ideological assumptions. It may seem perverse to label as a particular group a readership numbered in six figures. Yet the readers saw themselves as members of a distinct family. They hailed each other as the grandchildren of a common matriarch, who appeared stern, sedate, but still deserving of filial affection. The *Herald* aspired to consensus, but its grandmotherly rectitude and Anglophilism could never appeal to all Sydneysiders. The *Herald* has a place in Sydney's collective memory, but it could also inspire a counter-memory among those who rejected or opposed its class basis and symbolic references.

The paper certainly inspired a special kind of loyalty. 'My wife used to say', Cyril S. told us, 'you'll have the *Herald* put in your coffin when you die.' 'Do you remember having a regular newspaper?', we asked Laura P., who replied with great emphasis: 'Absolutely! The *Sydney Morning Herald*! I never remember when we didn't [have it]!'. The *Herald* was so sacrosanct to Daisy B.'s father-in-law that he refused to let it be used as scrap paper. Instead, he preserved piles of back editions which eventually filled an entire room.

The *Herald* was upheld as an exemplary newspaper of great educative value to school-children. At Sydney Technical High School, Ronald L. was taught that it was his daily duty to read the *Herald*'s editorial. Catholic schools apparently shared this respect. Justin S. recalled that the *Herald* was recommended by teachers at De la Salle in Ashfield, and that the editorial was read 'because it was considered of literary benefit'.

The *Herald* was an essential source of reference. Job vacancies were the most important section for Kate A.'s father and Joan P.'s mother. Margaret M. read the share market news; so too did Hilda R., who confided that she had just been on the telephone to her broker as we arrived for the interview.

Four respondents remembered the Births, Deaths and Marriages as a section of the *Herald* very frequently consulted, although deaths seemed more interesting than births or marriages. According to Albert P., a wharf labourer who consistently distanced himself from bourgeois *Herald* readers, 'They always looked for the mortality department'. He remembered a typical exchange with his father over the death notices, which usually provided a great source of caustic amusement:

Albert: I believe so-and-so has passed away, Dad.
Dad: The bastard ought to have been dead years ago.

Respondents remembered the news section of the *Herald* for its reporting of the deaths of the famous. Oliver C. recalled, above all, the announcement of the death of Henry Lawson. Edith M. recalled, 'I can remember my father coming . . . I was in my mother's bedroom . . . and I can remember him coming in and saying "The King is dead", and that must have been King Edward VII . . . and he looked really downcast and sort of if he thought it was a terrible thing for the King to die'. For some readers, then, the *Herald* was a news bulletin with quasi-official status, recording the events in the royal and official year. Its priorities were those of an elite, whose social position was based on imperial connections. Edith M. continued, on the subject of war news: 'Father used to talk about Australian soldiers and say they were very undisciplined. There were stories about how they misbehaved in Egypt . . . and things like that, you know, and he used to become very English and say they were undisciplined'. Here, the *Herald* seemed to present an officer's view of the war effort.

The *Herald* was trusted by its bourgeois readers, who thought themselves very discriminating. Nora K. asserted 'it was thoroughly reliable in those days. It isn't now. It was then'. Charlotte C. said of her parents, who took the *Herald*, 'I don't remember evening papers. I think they probably would have thought they were rubbish.' In such North Shore or Darling Point families, the *Sydney Morning Herald* was a badge of 'good taste' and social superiority.

The *Herald* was not all severity, official news and classified small print. It relaxed at the weekend, and offered entertainment for the young. In Maud B.'s household, children fought for the comic section, and over one in three of regular readers interviewed remembered the weekend comic section and/or the Ginger Meggs cartoon strip. It was just as well that the *Herald* was becoming more diversified and segmented. For Herbert O'N., it was essential to divide the weekend paper into specialized, detachable parts; his family had 11 offspring, and a compartmentalized newspaper with a separate children's section could be shared by several readers at once.

Many informants rose with the *Herald*, but came home with the *Sun*. To some extent, both papers had the same readership. The interviewees included 12 *Sun* readers, comprising 20 per cent of the group. All were urban residents, and half were inner-city residents. In this, they hardly differed from *Herald* readers.

Unlike *Herald* readers, however, *Sun* readers included a substantial number of Catholics (five in all) and no non-conformist Protestant families.

Like *Herald* readers, *Sun* readers tended to come from the upper social strata, but there were a few important differences. Of regular *Sun* readers interviewed, 35.7 per cent were from the commercial and professional bourgeoisie; but the largest group (42.9 per cent) belonged to the lower middle class. This large lower middle-class readership was the most distinctive feature of *Sun* readers to emerge.

Finally, all regular *Sun* readers had at least one parent born in Australia. In comparison to *Herald* readers, the *Sun*'s public seemed to be less predominantly Protestant, more lower middle class, and possibly less Anglophile in origin.

As far as weekly journals were concerned, interviews paid specific attention to the *Bulletin* because of its reputation as a promoter of indigenous literature and national consciousness in the 1890s. At 6d per week and with an annual subscription of £1 in 1912, not everyone could afford the *Bulletin*. The advertisements it carried suggested a comfortably well-off readership. In 1911, for example, the *Bulletin* ran a full-page advertisement for the *Encyclopaedia Britannica*, which was a considerable investment.[27] The complete set of 29 volumes sold for between £23 and £43, depending on paper quality. The *Bulletin* did not aim at the poorer classes.

Twenty interviewees were fairly regular readers of the *Bulletin* or else came from households which were, and another 12 described themselves or relatives as occasional readers. Over half of the interviewed group (32) was therefore able to give us some information on readers' perceptions of the *Bulletin*. They obtained their *Bulletin* from various sources. One was given it via an employer of her mother, who was a domestic servant, and another simply encountered it in 'good barber's shops'. Two read it occasionally on a train journey, another borrowed it from a public library, and another swapped it with fellow itinerants on the road in Queensland, while in search of work on sugar plantations. Like many weekly or monthly journals, the *Bulletin* had a high proportion of casual readers, and a readership considerably wider than the number of purchasers would suggest.

Received notions of the *Bulletin*'s appeal seemed confirmed when Letty O. spoke of its 'bush flavour', but most *Bulletin* readers interviewed were urban residents. Of the regular readers, 53 per cent were urban residents, no doubt reflecting the urban bias of the survey, and over 70 per cent of the occasional readers were urban residents, which probably reflected the greater number of sales outlets in Sydney.

The *Bulletin*'s readership seemed highly gender-specific. No less than 10 informants associated the *Bulletin* with their fathers or step-fathers—in other words, one half of regular readers. 'It was my father's Bible,' asserted Rosemary C. The only two interviewees who expressed an aversion for the *Bulletin* were women. It 'never impressed' either Marian T. or Daisy B. Rosemary C., living 22 miles from Goondiwindi, concluded 'I think it had a way of speaking to the countryman. And to a man's world, too'.

The *Bulletin* appealed most to middle-class informants. Of the regular readers, nine were from business and professional backgrounds and six were from the lower middle class. Many respondents saw it as a journal for a social elite. Joan P., near Walgett, reported that the station managers took it, and Irene A., near Jindabyne, said 'most of the graziers had it'. Albert P., the wharf labourer, felt that the *Bulletin* was 'not the sort' of paper that 'his people would buy'. It was a paper for expensively educated interviewees. Six out of 20 regular readers and three out of 12 occasional readers were privately educated – a high proportion in relation to the educational history of the interviewed group as a whole.

Sixty per cent of regular *Bulletin* readers interviewed were Anglicans; and over three-quarters had both parents born in Australia, but in these aspects they hardly differed from non-readers of the *Bulletin*. Several readers did remark on the Australian content and nationalism of the *Bulletin*. Kathleen T. borrowed copies from her local country library especially for the Australian poetry. 'In those days', recalled Tom H., 'the *Bulletin* was what we might say, a paper encouraging Australian writers and poets.' Bernard F. liked the *Bulletin* because 'it tried to get Australia to have its own reputation, not imported'. These remarks suggest that attempts to nurture a specifically Australian literary culture were appreciated by *Bulletin* readers in the years just before and after the First World War.

A few *Bulletin* readers seemed unlikely flag-bearers of the Australian national consciousness. One was Pina N., from a family of Venetian migrants near Nimbin, who spoke very affectionately of the old *Bulletin*. She had some English neighbours with whom she exchanged magazines. She offered them the *Bulletin* and in return received the *London Magazine*. Perhaps neither Italian farmers nor expatriate Londoners fit accepted patterns of the *Bulletin*'s bush readership.

The political loyalties of the *Bulletin* seemed unclear, or unimportant, to many respondents. Nancy B.'s father read it because 'it was such a general thing, it was non-political'. The *Bulletin*'s racist attitudes, however, certainly made an impact on working-class readers such as Pearl K., who complained about this and its reactionary character. Bernard F., an articulate professional man, made excuses. He thought that the *Bulletin* 'professed attitudes to foreigners, Jews and coloured people [which] were perhaps reprehensible but very much part of the times here then'.

Caricatures, sketches and drawings were among the *Bulletin*'s most successful and memorable features. Four readers enthused about them without prompting, including Merle S., who remembered her father copying *Bulletin* sketches, with great enjoyment. Only two readers recalled the famous Red Page, which one referred to as the 'pink pages', perhaps confusing the *Bulletin* with a well-known business telephone directory. Pina N. also remembered 'Aboriginalities', a series of short stories and jokes with a country setting.

The *Bulletin* invited and received contributions from readers for pages such as these. Two interviewees knew the *Bulletin* either as occasional contributors or as sons of contributors of 'literary, chatty things', as Philip B. put it. This tradition still survives in the *Herald*'s Column 8, but it was a central feature of magazines such as the *Bulletin* and *Smith's Weekly*. This was one means of creating a specific literary community and of colonizing an audience which actively participated in the life of the journal. The possibility of reader participation offered by magazines such as the *Bulletin* prevented their pages from becoming a soap-box from which a monologue was delivered. Instead, the relationship between editor and readers was more democratic and egalitarian, and this was a major factor in the *Bulletin*'s success.

The most convincing candidate for the title of successor of the old *Bulletin* was *Smith's Weekly*, which began publication in 1919, costing 2d. Its price rose to 4d in 1920, but this did not prevent its circulation reaching 150 000 in 1921 and over 200 000 in 1927.[28] Its 24 pages carried a high rate of advertisements (roughly 45 per cent of copy in 1919), over a dozen cartoons, and four regular sports pages. It directed its comic barbs against Aborigines, Jews, Scots and 'pommies', and defended public morality against various racketeers and drug smugglers. It was a populist paper, identifying itself with the grievances of the returned servicemen. Its regular page of Digger Stories was entitled 'The Sailor's and Soldier's Parliament', and the front page carried the emblem of the Australian flag. Its nostalgic historian described *Smith's Weekly* as 'a Public Conscience, a crutch for the fallen, the champion of the underdog, a vehicle of entertainment, a belter of hell out of the mean, the wicked and the pompous, the voice of the Digger . . . *Smith's* regarded only two things as untouchable – the Salvation Army, because it was good beyond criticism, and venereal disease, because it was too dirty'.[29] This view was very sympathetic and indulgent towards the paper's brashness and indisputable racism.

Twenty-four interviewees recalled *Smith's Weekly*, which is in itself a tribute to its popularity, even if one of them said that her parents banned it from the house, and another described it as 'more or less frowned upon' (several others, however, clearly relished its scandalous tone). *Smith's Weekly* had an audience both in Sydney and in the country: one third of respondents who remembered it were rural residents. They came from a broader cross-section of society than *Bulletin* readers. Eight were from the commercial and professional bourgeoisie, another eight from the lower middle class, and 10 from working-class backgrounds (two double entries are included here).

Seven readers nominated the sketches, cartoons and humour as the main reasons why they or their parents read *Smith's Weekly*. Randolph H. liked it for its nationalism, and Arthur O. had contributed paragraphs. But Henry K. resented its offensive racial attitudes towards Aborigines and migrants. 'Of course' he said:

> I never bothered to buy *Smith's Weekly* but of course I read it. I was ideologically opposed to *Smith's Weekly* because it was a racist paper. If one was lying around you'd pick it up. And they invented all these names, for Greeks were 'ox-cheeks', and Italians were 'Dagos' and Aborigines were 'Boongs' and British people were 'Poms' . . . and it was a great instrument in fostering racial divisions among the working class.

Another working-class reader, John Mongan, found it 'entertaining but politically biased'.[30] Once again, Bernard F., on the other side of the class barrier, made excuses for this. He found *Smith's Weekly* 'magnificent . . . a rebel [which] took up many good causes like the welfare of returned servicemen. It carried on the splendid black and white tradition begun by the *Bulletin*. It was a rowdy, disreputable paper, I suppose; it had none of the interests in literature, writers and poetry the *Bulletin* had but yet it was of no little importance in those times in the growth of our country'.

Truth was even more 'rowdy and disreputable', appearing for 3d on Sundays from 1920 onwards. *Truth* called itself 'The People's Paper', but its reputation was made on its sensational reporting of police news and divorce court proceedings. It provided a regular weekend diet of highly dramatized tales of marital infidelity. 'On Sunday afternoon', Herbert O'N. told us, 'most people in Melbourne used to go to bed on Sunday afternoon and read the *Truth*.' Sixteen interviewees recalled the *Truth*, but few were readily prepared to admit that they read it. It was a relief, therefore, to find an uninhibited respondent like Joe S., who declared 'we used to glory in reading the *Truth*. I've always been broad-minded'. Even this remark indicates the depravity commonly associated with the *Truth* [. . .].

If *Truth* was considered a scandalous weekly, *Beckett's Budget* was seen as pornographic or immoral by most of the 10 interviewees who remembered it. Not many would go so far as admit to having read it. 'I never read it', said Agnes B., in typical response, 'but I remember people talking about it.' The paper made an impact which was quite disproportionate to the brevity of its life, but it remained a paper with a semi-clandestine readership.

Beckett's Budget first appeared in 1927 in a guise that gave little hint of its future notoriety. It carried a story by Maupassant, and posed as the defender of small farmers, the advocate of a White Australia policy, and the protector of the sugar industry. It carried sober pages on women's and family issues such as breast-feeding, leisure columns on motoring and radio, and reproduced sports reports from its sister paper, *The Referee*.

Four issues later, Maupassant had disappeared, and exposures of communist activity in the ALP in Queensland now shared space with photographs of chorus girls and bathing beauties. Within six months, the paper had undergone a complete transformation. It appeared on Friday instead of Tuesday to capture the weekend market, and usually carried a front-page portrait of a female model. Its main features were now stories of sex crimes, and extra-marital affairs. The new incarnation of *Beckett's Budget* claimed to be crusading against immorality, hypocrisy and predatory male employers.[31] The paper was 'filthy' for Eileen McC. and 'red-hot' for Flossie P. It was forbidden territory, but, in its short life, it became a publishing phenomenon. Expensive libel damages forced its liquidation, and it was sold to the *Labor Daily* in 1930, eventually becoming the *Australian Budget*.

References

1   Richard Nile and D. Walker, 'Marketing the Literary Imagination: production of Australian literature, 1915–1965', *The Penguin New Literary History of Australia*, gen. ed. L. Hergenhan, Penguin, 1988.

2   The Dickens Fellowship, *Annual Reports, 1914–15*.

3   Kathleen Fitzpatrick, *Solid Bluestone Foundations: memories of an Australian girlhood*, Penguin, 1986, p. 19.

4   Ethel Turner, *The Diaries of Ethel Turner*, ed. Philippa Poole, Ure Smith, 1979.

5   Dickens Fellowship, op. cit.

6   Henry Lawson, *The Bush Undertaker and Other Stories*, Angus & Robertson, 1982, p. 49.

7   Roger Lancelyn Green, *Kipling: the critical heritage*, Routledge & Kegan Paul, 1971.

8   H.M. Green, *A History of Australian Literature*, vol. 1, Angus & Robertson, 1961, p. 644.

9   Marcie Muir, *A Bibliography of Australian Children's Books*, vol. 1, Deutsch, 1970–6, p. 363.

10 Brenda Niall, *Australia Through the Looking-Glass: children's fiction, 1830–1980*, Melbourne University Press, 1984, pp. 208–9.

11 Carol Mills, 'The New South Wales Bookstall Company as Publisher: a brief introduction', in B. Rayward, ed. *Australian Library History in Context. Proceedings of 3rd Forum on Australian Library History*, July 1987, University of NSW, 1988, pp. 115–20.

12 *Argus*, 22 August 1927, p. 15.

13 Gertrude Himmelfarb, 'John Buchan – an untimely appreciation', *Encounter*, vol. 15, September 1960, pp. 46–53.

14 Patrick Howarth, *Play Up and Play the Game: the heroes of popular fiction*, Eyre Methuen, 1973, p. 118. This was admittedly an odd reproach from Bennett, who was hardly a subversive writer either.

15 E.M. Miller and F.T. Macartney, *Australian Literature: a bibliography 1938, extended to 1950*, 2nd ed. Angus & Robertson, 1956, pp. 200–2.

16 John D. Cawelti, *Adventure, Mystery and Romance: formula stories as art and popular culture*, University of Chicago Press, 1976, pp. 230–41.

17 Henry Mayer, *The Press in Australia*, Landsdowne Press, 1964, p. 44.

18 T.A. Coghlan, *A Statistical Account of Australia and New Zealand, 1903–4*, AGPS, 1904, p. 830.

19 R.B. Walker, *The Newspaper Press in New South Wales, 1803–1920*, Sydney University Press, 1976, pp. 105–117; and the same author's *Yesterday's News: a history of the newspaper press in New South Wales from 1920–1945*, Sydney University Press, 1980, ch. 1.

20 Walker, *Newspaper Press*, op. cit., pp. 177–82.

21 Ibid., p. 100; and Walker, *Yesterday's News*, op. cit., p. 12.

22 Walker, *Newspaper Press*, op. cit., p. 100.

23 Lorraine Winchester, 'Popular reading practices in New South Wales, 1900–1930', B. Soc. Sci. honours thesis, University of NSW, 1986.

24 Anne-Marie Thiesse, *Le Roman du Quotidien: lecteurs et lecteurs populaires à la Belle Epoque*, Le Chemin Vert, 1984.

25 Interview recorded by Lucy Taksa on 19 March 1987 for the NSW Bicentennial Oral History Project.

26 Walker, *Yesterday's News*, op. cit., pp. 30–3.

27 *Bulletin*, 29 November 1911, p. 33.

28 Walker, *Yesterday's News*, op. cit., pp. 14–15. In 1922, its circulation was 88,000 in NSW alone.

29 George Blaikie, *Remember Smith's Weekly? A biography of an uninhibited Australian newspaper*, Rigby, 1966, p. 2.

30 Interview recorded by Lucy Taksa on 19 March 1987 for the NSW Bicentennial Oral History Project.

31 *Beckett's Budget*, Friday 20 July 1928, p. 6.

Reading communities

INTRODUCTION

READING IS BOTH A solitary and a communal, participatory activity; it can serve to fashion both an individual and a group identity. Benedict Anderson's influential study of nationalism, *Imagined Communities: Reflections on the Origin and Spread of Nationalism* (1983), argued that the reading material (and readers) fashioned by print capitalism inevitably led to national consciousness. While Anderson offered very little in the way of evidence to support his theory, the four extracts in this section provide compelling substantiation of *how* and *why* discreet, identifiable, reading communities emerged. These four studies of reading communities defined variously by race, class, age, gender, location and occupation across seven centuries and in two continents, also give us detailed information about how these groups accessed and engaged with a diverse range of reading material, from annotated manuscripts to children's literature, and from the English classics to American popular fiction. Armando Petrucci's examination of the change in reading practice from the twelfth to the fifteenth century in Italy argues that the increasing literacy of lay people and the production of books in the vernacular Italian (rather than in Latin) created both a new reading community, and a new reading practice. Through his example of Niccolò Niccoli, Petrucci demonstrates the shift in early Renaissance Florence from structured, scholastic, heavily annotated, guided group reading (*lectio*) used in the universities, to a more intensive, individual, freely negotiated humanist engagement with unglossed texts. Petrucci's exposition indicates how the reading practice of a particular group demanded books to meet its needs (you may want to compare Petrucci's approach to that of Grafton and Jardine in Section 6, *Individual Readers*, extract 28).

While Petrucci explores an emergent though nebulous bourgeois reading community, Jonathan Rose closely examines a much more precisely defined group in his a detailed study of a self-selecting reading community, that of miners in the valleys of South Wales in the early twentieth century. Rose uncovers the catalogues and borrowing records of the Welsh miners' libraries (subscription institutions founded solely to cater for the reading needs of these communities) and he combines this with the detailed close analysis of the autodidactic accounts of reading left by former miners who rose through the ranks of the newly formed Labour Party. Rose's reading community is defined by class, occupation, gender, income, access to reading material, and location; he finds that discreetly identifiable groups do not always read what we might expect them to read. Miners did not read books about mining, Rose discovers, nor despite the prevalence of socialist politics in the coal mines, were they particularly interested in Marx, preferring to read popular fiction and cheaply reissued English classics instead.

Two contrasting and complementary American studies of specific reading communities in the nineteenth-century, both in environments of relatively book scarcity, round off this section, and remind us again of the social nature of reading. Christine Pawley provides a micro-analytical study of the customers of the Sage Library in the mid-west frontier settlement of Osage, Iowa from 1890 to 1895. She notes that Osage readers overwhelmingly preferred fiction to other types of material, that they often systematically borrowed works by the same author, that women borrowed more heavily than men, and that family reading was the single most important cultural activity in the community. While Pawley's reading community is defined by location and access rights, and its reading took place at home, Elizabeth McHenry's exploration of African-American readers in the mid-nineteenth century rediscovers the reading rooms and libraries established by freed slaves to promote literacy and reading for self-improvement for their own community in the period before emancipation. McHenry's study, unlike the previous three extracts, focuses not only on how a particular reading community got hold of and read books, but also on a collective claim to a particular space for reading and self-improvement.

Two further recent studies not included in this reader are worthy of your attention and demonstrate how reading communities have been diversely constituted and examined. In *Provincial Readers in Eighteenth-Century England* (2006), Jan Fergus combines the book sale records (1744–1784) of the provincial firm of Samuel Clay with the register of Rugby School. Drawing upon accounts left by individual old boys, Fergus identifies a close relationship between the reading tastes of this schoolboy community, and the often sadistic institutional culture imposed upon it. Fergus' self-defined reading community is determined by age (schoolboys), location (Rugby was a boarding school), class (it was fee paying), literacy (all students could read on entry), gender (single-sex institution) and access to books (Clay). While Fergus studies a very precisely defined and geographically restricted reading community, Priya Joshi's *In Another Country: Colonialism, Culture and the English Novel in India* (New York, 2002) takes on a far bigger task in assessing the consumption of English fiction by Indians in the Victorian age. Her approach is necessarily macro-analytical; she provides a detailed statistical survey of the library catalogues, genre categories, and borrowing records of two particular Indian established libraries in Bengal. Joshi's analysis indicates that Anglophone Indian readers strongly preferred fiction, especially bestselling British authors, such as Bulwer-Lytton, Scott, Dickens and Disraeli, over all other types of books (fiction was two and half times more requested by readers than other books). Joshi's reading community is defined by language and income, and her investigation restricts itself explicitly to the consumption of English language fiction by the Anglophone Indian elite; you might want to compare her approach to Ghosh's study of the relationship between orality and print in Bengal in the same period (see Section 4, *Reading the Masses*, extract 21).

Studying the access to and engagement with books of a particular group of readers alerts us again to the construction and self-definition of community identity through the vital act of social reading, mediated by many other filters: politics, race, nationalism, gender, class, location, and occupation. Reading communities, unlike mass audiences, as these studies show, did not merely passively consume whatever material came there way; instead, they strove actively to meet their own particular need for books, and in the process, redefined their collective identity through the act of reading.

Chapter 24

Armando Petrucci

READING IN THE MIDDLE AGES[1]

T HE THOUSAND YEARS INCLUDED in the Middle Ages constitute a
particularly important period for a study of reading conceived as the techniques and
behaviors, both individual and collective, comprised in an act of reading that itself must be
seen as having psychological-physical, cultural, and social aspects. Indeed, the models and
conditions of reading usual in late antiquity were radically transformed during the Middle
Ages. This period also saw the formation and diffusion of modes of reading that would
be those of the modern age and of the cultural universe distinguished by printing with
movable type.[2]

[. . .]

The situation concerning the Middle Ages, moreover, is far more complex than it
appears at first glance. One can distinguish three reading techniques that were broadly
diffused and used deliberately for different purposes: silent reading, "in silentio;" reading at
a low voice, called murmuring or rumination, which assisted meditation and served as an
aid to memorization; and, last, reading aloud, which required, as in antiquity, a particular
technique and was very similar to the practice of liturgical recitation and chant. Each of
these techniques corresponded to a precise function and was used in specific circumstances
and milieus—the first and probably the second occurring in the solitude of the cell, and the
third in public, in the presence of the community. In the world of Christian culture, all three
were broadly influenced by the techniques and practices of liturgy and prayer.

In reality, it would seem that the most important phenomenon in the domain of early
medieval written culture had less to do with the contrast between silent and vocalized
reading than with the obvious gap—although one that has been little stressed until now—
between practices of writing and practices of reading. Everyone who has a direct acquaintance with early medieval manuscripts knows how defective these were as instruments to
facilitate the average reader's reading and comprehension of the text. The widespread use of
continuous writing, without spaces to separate the words; the indiscriminate use of capitals,
which often give neither guidance nor orientation; punctuation that was rare, arbitrary, and
with little or no differentiation, or that was simply absent: all these made reading difficult,
even for well-educated readers. The overall impression is that there was no effort to shorten
the time required for reading, for indeed everything contributed to keep reading extremely

slow, attentive, almost stumbling. Thus, one of the fundamental characteristics of the activity of reading in the early Middle Ages lay in the slow mechanism of spelling out words.

[. . .]

Paul Saenger has recently argued a different thesis in this connection. Claiming that word separation was "the contribution of the early Middle Ages to the evolution of Western written communication," he ascribes its first appearance in a partial fashion to manuscripts executed in the eighth century in the British Isles.[3] A summary inquiry applied to a number of facsimile collections, however, shows that in reality the situation in the early Middle Ages was more confused and complex than Saenger's suggestive but brief observations would suggest. There were, in effect, two widely used practices at that time: that of continuous writing and that, to which recourse was had especially by scribes of limited talent, of introducing separations into groups of letters in a fashion that was irregular and arbitrary. Often, indeed, the break came in the very middle of a word, at great harm to the reader.

It is true that a regular separation of words does appear in certain manuscripts of the eighth and ninth centuries. But this was not an exclusively insular practice; it occurs as well in German manuscripts, some from centers founded by the Irish but also some from centers of autochthonous origin. The practice also appears in some Swiss Rhenish manuscripts and in a certain number of manuscripts from northern Italy. These were probably zones where, as in the British Isles, limited knowledge of Latin had hastened the invention of instruments permitting easier reading of the text. In the Carolingian period the two practices were in use simultaneously. In southern Italy, the separation of words appears between the ninth and tenth centuries but became widely diffused and obligatory only in the first half of the eleventh.

On the whole, then, one has the impression that the scribe of the early Middle Ages was scarcely sensible to the problems and practice of reading. This indifference can only come from the limited experience he himself had with the practice. In fact, the scribe of the early Middle Ages was destined and trained (if he received any training at all) for writing rather than for reading, which explains the high number of raw, unskilled, and uneducated scribes that characterize the production of books in the early Middle Ages.[4] It is thus not surprising that the chronicler Ekkhard IV of San Gall tells us that in the second half of the tenth century his homonymous predecessor Ekkhard I assigned to copy books those young brothers whom he judged to be less intelligent and less adapted to study: "et quos ad literarum studia tardiores vidisset, ad scribendum occupaverat et lineandum" (and those whom he saw came later to the study of letters, he employed in writing or lining).[5] The fact that this occurred in a monastery like San Gall, which at that time was a very active center for producing books, renders this practice still more significant.

The subscriptions that some scribes affixed to their manuscripts when their work was done confirm that during their work the copyists of the early Middle Ages paid little attention to the needs of reading—or of readers. In fact, they rarely address their natural interlocutor, the reader. When they do, moreover, they never join the reader in dialogue, never evoke the reasons and sense of their work, and especially never show the least interest in the use for which it was done. The only clearly expressed intention is to obtain prayers for the good of their soul in exchange for the pains that they have taken.

More generally, the early Middle Ages appear as a period in which the minimal need to read corresponded to and was paralleled by a marked illiteracy in reading. One has the overall impression that there was an important category of semi-illiterates, lay and ecclesiastic, who in one fashion or another were capable of writing something—the subscription to a brief text—without having any familiarity with reading and books: thus, the number of readers was still more restricted than the number of persons able to write. This conclusion only confirms, from a different angle, the characteristic divide between reading and writing practices just discussed.

Having said this, one must add that circumstances in the early Middle Ages scarcely provided much incentive to read. Books were kept in places that usually were poorly adapted to reading, nor did there generally exist spaces specially equipped for that purpose: one read in the places reserved principally for other activities, such as the cell, the refectory, and the cloister. As an arduous activity, reading was consequently rather rare and even, surprising as it may seem, a marginal activity in the context of early medieval civilization. One does witness an increase in the production and circulation of books during the Carolingian period; the ninth and tenth centuries also must have seen more reading, as witnessed by the frequency with which books were borrowed. But these shifts were not sufficiently radical to alter the general conditions of reading, which remained quite laborious despite the adoption of the new unified script, caroline minuscule, that permitted an objective improvement in the model of reading. Other modifications occurred in the course of the eleventh century that manifestly aimed at facilitating the reading and comprehension of the text: a progressive and expanding use of separated writing; the use of the hyphen for words not ending on a line; the use of the double apex when two i's came in succession; the use of the majuscule form of the *s* when the letter was found at the end of a word.[6] These mark the arrival of new cultural times, when new roles and new functions would be created for books and writing in a society that itself was being transformed.

In the twelfth and thirteenth centuries, the framework of written culture underwent profound changes due to a variety of well-known factors that can be listed rapidly as including: the general increase in the diffusion of reading and writing; the progressive increase in the production of written documents and private acts of writing;[7] the marked (although difficult to measure) increase in the production and circulation of books; and the creation of new cultural structures and institutions (advanced schools, universities). The more intense circulation of written products that resulted from these trends in turn provoked in society a need for reading that was considerably stronger than previously. In its wake there also appeared a specific demand for written products that were organized in a way to facilitate rather than impede reading itself, a tendency that was also furthered by the emergence among the most educated readers of a new relationship with the text and the progressive affirmation of new modes of reading. As Malcolm Parkes notes, "During the course of the twelfth century the monastic culture gave way to the culture of the schools. There were new kinds of books—a more technical literature—and new kinds of readers. The monastic *lectio* was a spiritual exercise which involved steady reading to oneself, interspersed by prayer, and pausing for rumination on the text as a basis for *meditatio*. The scholastic *lectio* was a process of study which involved more ratiocinative scrutiny of the text and consultation for reference purposes."[8] It was precisely to answer this type of need that concepts such as *ordinatio* and *divisio* of the text were introduced into the program of the new model of reading. Although these had been quite foreign to the text/book relationship in the early Middle Ages, Jordan of Saxony in 1220 placed them at the basis of what he called the *forma tractatus*: the text/book of scholastic/university culture.

The twelfth and thirteenth centuries, therefore, saw a radical transformation of the model, techniques, and general conditions of reading. The scholastic/university book differed from its early medieval predecessor at several points. It was generally of large format and thus heavy, hard to manage, and difficult to transport; it also needed solid, fixed support when being read. Writing was laid out in two relatively narrow columns, with more compressed text, so that one line of text corresponded closely with the visual field of recognition or fixation:[9] the quantity of text that could be taken in at a single glance. The text was carefully articulated in a series of divisions and subdivisions (chapters, paragraphs, subparagraphs) more detailed than in the past, all for the purpose of rendering comprehension and especially consultation easier: according to Vincent of Beauvais, the "capitulatio" was made so that "operis partes singule lectori facilius elucescant" (the parts of the work would be manifest to the individual reader).[10] The articulation of the text was placed in relief and emphasized by a rich series of graphic interventions and tools including rubrics, paragraph marks, initials and majuscules of different size, running titles, reminders, indices, and alphabetical tables, all of which enclosed, delimited, and cut up the text, rendering it thus accessible in small portions that could easily be found again. Thanks to numerous abbreviations, reading became incomparably more rapid than before and often was transformed into a practice—consultation—specifically belonging to the professional researcher.

[. . .]

Reading thus became a practice that one could organize and determine in advance, having as its objective the cultural preparation and the didactic and scientific activities of the new professional intellectual, whether lay or religious: professor, jurist, physician, theologian, notary.

No longer separated from writing, reading became instead still more closely bound to it. People read *to* write: this is the sense of the *compilatio*. They read and wrote together when commenting and annotating.[11] They wrote while reading when composing, because every text was—necessarily—based on the *auctoritas* of its predecessors and on the permanent use of citation.[12] Thus, at the beginning of the twelfth century, archivist and chronicler Guibert de Nogent linked *perpetuitas legendi* and *continuatio scribendi* in the same process, as complementary and necessary stages of an intellectual's activity.[13]

In practice, these changes went beyond techniques of reading, touching as well its mechanical conditions, its places and spaces, the material means used, the behaviors and attitudes of readers. Libraries, as we know, were transformed. In the course of the thirteenth century there appears a completely new kind of place dedicated to reading and study in common that indeed becomes essential: one room, of variable length on a basilical plan, equipped with benches disposed horizontally in parallel rows, and the books arranged in rows and attached by a chain. This is the typical library of the mendicant orders, the new model for reading in common. Laymen could also enjoy these novelties because the orders' libraries often functioned as libraries for universities of higher culture, welcoming visitors who came from outside the orders.[14]

The existence of such places meant that all intellectuals saw their modes of private reading change, because it was precisely the reunification of writing and reading into a single practice that permitted intellectuals to express their claims and obtain more space for their work than they had had before—spaces that were also better organized and better equipped. The Esdra who, in the Amiatina Bible of the beginning of the eighth century was represented, in conformance with "ancient" models, sitting on a stool, knees resting on a little bench, carrying a manuscript on his knees, gave way to the image of a clerk wearing eyeglasses, installed in a solid chair before a vast writing bench which protected and isolated him. He was surrounded by desks intended for activities of reading and writing, shelves, open and closed books, notebooks, foolscap, and all other writing materials.[15]

In reality, the very ideology of reading, which in the early Middle Ages had been linked to the religious practice of *ruminatio* of the divine word, underwent a total transformation in the new universe of official culture, henceforth dominated by the image of public teaching. John of Salisbury contrasted private reading, which he defined as an "*occupatio per se scrutantis scripturas*," to magisterial reading, which generally took place in public and joined teacher and student: "*docentis et discentis exercitium*."[16] This latter style of reading, the *lectio*, was fundamentally the same as university scholarly research. It was a reading that, while dividing and commenting on texts, fixed them in an authoritative manner and imposed on them a hierarchy. One read to others actively, but one read through someone passively. Reading was given and it was received. The *lectio*, with its fixed rules and unequal exchange, became the predominant European model of individual and common reading of the thirteenth and fourteenth centuries.

It was not the only model, however, for in the thirteenth and fourteenth centuries, in all of Europe but most especially in the towns and communes of Italy, the increasing literacy of lay people gave birth to literary works in vernacular languages for them to read. The production of books in vernacular languages grew steadily, spreading into more and more regions.

The production of books in vernacular languages demonstrates that a demand existed. And if a demand existed, that was because there was a reading public. But on the whole this was not the public of official culture in Latin. Certainly there were judges, notaries, and clerks who owned and read books in vernacular languages: Petrarca himself did so, even if he felt he had to defend himself for it. But they were a minority. The great mass of those who read works in vernacular languages were essentially monolingual literates who did not know Latin but had nevertheless learned to read and write: they were merchants, artisans, shop-keepers, artists, accountants, shop or banking employees, as well as some workers and some women. In their reading, these people could not refer to any traditional model susceptible of being transmitted by repetition or other formal instruction. They could not adopt the learned model, which was too difficult, complex, and costly for them. By force of circumstances, they thus had to invent new modes of reading that, in ideology and practice, were different from those of learned people, modes that were independent of any institution, rule, norm, and ritual and—in a word—free.

Different readers do not in themselves account for the different styles of lay/bourgeois reading in comparison with those of official culture. There were differences as well in the means by which books were produced. The book in a vernacular language was most often written in the milieu where it was read, by readers themselves who recopied texts for their own use and that of their children or their friends. There was still more difference in the physical appearance of the reading matter, which generally took the form of books written on paper, with a medium format, in nontypical cursive scripts preferably laid out on the whole page. The text was presented without commentary, with simple illustrations or ornamentation drawn by pen and colored with inks or inexpensive colors. Finally, there was a difference in the places where books were kept and read. According to customary usage, although recurring by analogy rather than a direct inheritance from the early Middle Ages, books in vernacular languages—always rare—were kept in the family chest with important documents, account books, and all the papers of the household. As for the act of reading, it was done at home, the shop, the counter, wherever it was possible. Belonging to the sphere of leisure and free time rather than work, this activity had no special place.[17]

There was also another mode of existence for books and the practice of reading that, although transmitted from generation to generation, stood apart as the exclusive preserve of a particular social class: the aristocracy. Courtly reading in the later Middle Ages differed markedly in practice from scholastic or bourgeois reading for many reasons linked to both physical book models and personal behavior patterns. Physically, the books that fulfilled courtly commissions and usages were made of parchment, of medium or small format, written in formal script laid out in two columns, illuminated or ornamented more or less richly depending on the particular case but, like the bourgeois model, lacking commentary. Moreover, the practice of courtly reading, again like the bourgeois model, was never restricted to particular places or locations. Indeed, it had available to it the broad social spaces of courtly life: salons and large bedchambers and, outside, the open spaces of the courtyards, gardens, and parks. [. . .] [I]t was often accompanied by physical exercises such as walking, games, dancing, and fencing, or it could alternate with such activities, being then followed by music. Finally, while the reading of the clerk or the merchant remained almost invariably a purely masculine activity, courtly reading engaged women as well as men, as we recall from the common reading of Paolo and Francesca immortalized by Dante (*Inferno* 5, ll. 127–38).

In Florence at the turn of the fourteenth and fifteenth centuries, "a band of arrogant youths"[18] headed by Niccolò Niccoli effected a radical return to antiquity in the domain of studying classical texts and producing books. The promoters of this movement were all bourgeois or petits-bourgeois. But they resolutely rejected models of books current in contemporary mercantile vernacular culture to seek out a model three or four centuries earlier: the books from the Romanesque period, still written in caroline minuscule, that were totally different from the books of the scholastic/university period. This effort had some precedents in the late fourteenth-century activities due to certain humanists, most notably Petrarca; but it had never before been pushed to its fullest consequences. What resulted was a complete renewal of a kind of book that displays the following characteristics: reduced (small or medium) format, sometimes almost square; an absence of commentary that liberated the texts from stifling interpretations; disappearance of the fixed and visible system of dividing and organizing the text; and a revolution in graphics resulting from the substitution for gothic textura of a minuscule imitated from the caroline while a capital of roman type replaced the uppercase letters of gothic style. Finally, the abbreviations that had been so abundant in university tradition practically disappeared.[19]

The consequences of these changes for modes of reading were very important. Reading, deprived of the devices that had been installed to make it faster, had to return to a slow and reflective rhythm, concentrating on the text that was now the sole master of the page. Consultation of books, deprived of the subsidiary instruments that university culture had furnished, had to modify its rhythms and functioning. But the most important innovation, and that most weighted with consequences, was the replacement of a compact graphic system whose elements were closely knit together along the line by a ventilated system in which words, but especially letters, seen and fixed as independent signs, were henceforth separated from each other. Later this phenomenon would become one of the characteristic modes of reading specific to printing. But at the beginning of the fifteenth century it apparently sprang rather from this new, more rational form of visual perception, one that, according to Walter Ong, constituted one of the innovations of humanism, a perception that was also expressed by a better balance of black and white on the page, on the lines and between the lines of the new model of reading.[20]

These changes did not entail comparably radical modifications in the conditions of reading which, in contrast, remained bound to the model of the preceding period. In practice, modes of reading in the fifteenth century continued to obey the rules elaborated in the preceding period in the milieu of scholastic/university culture, at least as regards the physical conditions of reading: furniture, equipment, the disposition of places for reading, etc. The respect for tradition in this aspect of intellectual life is apparently explained by the fact that the humanist, in his role as intellectual, renounced neither the prestigious model of the university professor nor the static, authoritarian, and hierarchical reading that was its corollary. From this point of view, the decisive break with the past was produced only in the third quarter of the fifteenth century when the consequences were felt of three innovations that had taken place in the domain of written culture: the creation of state libraries, founded on the humanistic model by some of the greatest princes and sovereigns of Europe and Italy; the coexistence of manuscript and printed books in the system of reading; and, finally, the birth of the new lay book of small format: the *enchiridion* or the "pocket" book of the new generations of readers.

In such a context, the experience that an Angelo Poliziano must have had of reading seems particularly significant.[21] This intellectual, modern in so many ways and clearly different from most of his contemporaries, treated the world of books as an open and inexhaustible reservoir, diachronic and plurilingual in its immense possibilities of development. But at the same time he maintained a relationship with books that was freer, more supple, and less concerned with ownership; it was often realized outside of any institutional framework or any fixed rituals. This reading sometimes was accompanied by other physical and intellectual activities, as we see in two extracts from his letters written in vernacular:

> "Ieri sera cominciamo a leggere un poco di s. Agostino. E questa lezione risolvessi alfine nel musicare e in iscorgere e dirozare certo modello di ballerino che è qua." (Yesterday evening we begin to read a little Saint Augustine. And at the end this reading turned into playing music and jumping up and polishing a certain model of dancing practiced here.)[22]

> "Visitiamo questi orti, che ne è piena la città Pistoia e qualche volta la libreria di maestro Zambino, che ci ho trovato parecchi buone cosette, et in greco et in latino." (We visit these gardens, in the very heart of the city of Pistoia, and sometimes the bookstore of master Zambino, where I found several good items in both Greek and Latin.)[23]

Poliziano was a professor; he was also the greatest textual philologist of his time. And yet in his fashion of reading, in the suppleness of the relationship he maintained with books and texts, one easily recognizes the hedonistic ambitions that were traditionally part of aristocratic education and that one finds in lay and bourgeois reading in the printing epoch. In a word, it is the reading of a cultivated person of the modern epoch.

What has just been said shows clearly how new tendencies and practices dawned in the world of written culture of the Middle Ages, both among the cultural avant-garde and in recently literate classes who for the first time had wholesale access to books. In the beginning, these tendencies and practices were adopted employing old models of reading whose links to preceding cultural systems made them impractical for the new usages. This is why the promoters of new practices soon sought to modify the model of reading then in use, and thus to imagine, produce, and impose a new type of book. It was only in a second stage that the diffusion of the new model of reading produced, little by little, a modification of the instruments and places of reading.

The history of the slow and progressive formation and propagation of the humanistic mode of reading supports this interpretation. In 1366, Petrarca, in a letter to Boccaccio, extolled the virtues of the ancient caroline minuscule that, by its complete simplicity, represented for him the ideal of writing. It was, he wrote, "castigata et clara seque ultro oculis ingerens" (plain and clear and offering itself to the eyes) (*Fam.*, XXIII, 19, 8). The objectives were thus clear and the tendencies evident from the beginning. Yet another thirty years were needed before a group of avant-garde intellectuals brought to realization the new model of book to which Petrarca aspired, and it was still longer before, under the influence of different circumstances, there were changes in the places and, by extension, the very ideology of reading. Thus liberated from the comfortable but rigid schema of the scholastic *lectio*, reading was finally transformed into a freer (and more problematic) relationship with the printed text.

References

1   Originally published as "Lire au moyen âge," in *Mélanges de l'École Française de Rome* 96, no. 2 (1984): 603–16.

2   On reading in the Middle Ages, see H. J. Martin, "Pour une histoire de la lecture," *Revue française d'histoire du livre* 46 (1977): 583–609; G. Severino-Polica, "Libro, lettura, 'lezione' negli Studia degli ordini mendicanti (sec. XIII)," in *Le scuole degli ordini mendicanti* (Todi, 1978), pp. 375–413; P. Saenger, "Silent Reading: Its Impact on Late Medieval Script and Society," *Viator* 13 (1982): 367–414 and "Manières de lire médiévales," in *Histoire de l'édition française*, vol. 1: *Le livre conquérant. Du Moyen Age au milieu du XVIIe siècle* (Paris, 1982), pp. 131–41.

3   "Silent Reading," p. 377; see also the paper of M. B. Parkes, "The Contribution of Insular Scribes of the Seventh and Eighth Centuries to the 'Grammar of Legibility,'" in *Grafia e interpunzione del latino nel medioevo* (Rome, 1987), pp. 15–30.

4   See Armando Petrucci, *Writers and Readers in Medieval Italy*, Charles M. Radding (trans) (New Haven, 1995), Chapter 5.

5   *Casuum Sancti Galli Continuatio I auctore Ekkehardo IV* in *MGH, SS II* (Hannover, 1829), p. 122.

6   See A. Petrucci, "Istruzioni per la datazione," in "Censimento dei codici dei secoli X–XII," *Studi medievali* 3d ser. 9 (1968): 1115–26.

7   See M. T. Clanchy, *From Memory to Written Record: England, 1066–1307* 2d ed. (Oxford, 1993), pp. 44–80.

8   "Influence of the Concepts of Ordinatio and Compilatio in the Development of the Book," in *Medieval Learning and Literature: Essays Presented to R. W. Hunt* (Oxford, 1976), p. 115.

9   J. Taylor, *Insegnare a leggere a scrivere* (Milan, 1976), p. 25.

10   Cited by Parkes, "Contribution," p. 133.

11   For the reader "legens et rescribens," see Severino-Polica, "Libro, lettura," pp. 394–95.

12   For the four ways "faciendi libros," of the scribe who "scribit aliena, nihil addendo, vel mutando," the "compilator" who "scribit aliena, addendo, sed non de suo," the "commentator" who "scribit et aliena et sua," and finally, of the "auctor" who "scribit et sua et aliena, sed sua tamquam principalia," see Bonaventure, *Commentarium in I librum Sententiarum*, in *Opera Omnia*, vol. 1 (Ad claras aquas, 1882), pp. 14–15.

13   M. C. Garand, "Le scriptorium de Guibert de Nogent," *Scriptorium* 31 (1977): 3.

14   See Armando Petrucci, *Writers and Readers in Medieval Italy*, Charles M. Radding (trans) (New Haven, 1995), Chapter 10.

15   See A. Petrucci, "Gli strumenti del letterato," in *Letteratura italiana*, vol. 1: *Il letterato e le istituzione* (Turin, 1982), pp. 2, 3, 6, 7.

16   See the reference in Severino-Polica, "Libro, lettura," pp. 377–78.

17   See Petrucci, "Biblioteche antiche," pp. 543–46.

18   Felicitously expressed by E. H. Gombrich, "From the Revival of Letters to the Reform of Arts: Nicolò Niccoli and Filippo Brunelleschi," in *Essays in the History of Art . . . to R. Wittkower* (London, 1967), p. 82.

19   See the synthesis in A. Petrucci, " 'Anticamente moderni e modernamente antichi,' " in Petrucci, *Libri, scrittura e pubblico nel Rinascimento. Guida storica e critica* (Bari, 1979), pp. 21–36.

20   W. J. Ong, "System, Space and Intellect in Renaissance Symbolism," in *Bibliothèque d'humanisme et renaissance* 18 (1956): 228.

21   Petrucci, "Biblioteche antiche," pp. 551–54 (below, pp. 231–35).

22   Letter of 8 April 1476 to Clarice Orsini, in A. Poliziano, *Prose volgari inedite e poesie latine e greche edite e inedite* (Florence, 1867), p. 47.

23   Letter of 31 Aug. 1478, p. 61.

Chapter 25

Jonathan Rose

THE WELSH MINERS' LIBRARIES

THE MINERS' INSTITUTES OF SOUTH WALES were one of the greatest networks of cultural institutions created by working people anywhere in the world. One would have to look to the Social Democratic libraries of Wilhelmine Germany or the Jewish workers' libraries of interwar Poland to find anything comparable.[1] Many of the Welsh miners' libraries began in the nineteenth century as mechanics' institutes, temperance halls, or literary societies, at first under middle-class patronage. Victorian colliers commonly authorized deductions from their wages to pay for their children's education, but when school fees were abolished in 1891, this flow of money (usually 1d. or 2d. per pound) was redirected toward the miners' institutes. They also received contributions from coal companies and other benefactors, but as the miners themselves usually covered the ongoing expenses, they controlled acquisitions. In 1920 Parliament set up the Miners' Welfare Fund, which taxed coal production and royalties and directed the revenue to fund pit baths, welfare halls, scholarships, and libraries. By 1934 there were more than a hundred miners' libraries in the Welsh coalfields, with an average stock of about three thousand volumes. In smaller villages the collection might consist of only a few hundred books, and the librarian was usually a miner who volunteered to mind the shop one evening a week.[2] The larger institutes were well-equipped cultural centers offering evening classes, lecture series, gymnasia, wireless rooms and photography labs for amateurs, and theaters as well as libraries.[3] They hosted concerts, amateur drama, traveling theatrical troupes, opera, dances, trade union and political meetings, choirs, debating societies, and eisteddfodau (Welsh cultural festivals), and about thirty of the Welsh workmen's halls were equipped with cinemas.[4] The pride of the movement was the Tredegar Workmen's Institute: by the Second World War its library was circulating 100,000 volumes a year. It boasted an 800-seat cinema, a film society, and a popular series of celebrity concerts, where the highest-priced tickets went for 3s.[5]

An underground university

There were similar institutions in all the coal regions, many of them established by mine owners with the frank intention of making their workers sober, pious, and productive. Around 1850, nineteen out of fifty-four collieries in Northumberland and Durham had some kind of library or reading room.[6] Yet there was a special ferment in the South Wales coalfields, rooted in the peculiar cultural environment of the region. Wales had a tradition of weaver-poets, artisan balladeers, and autodidact shepherds going back to the seventeenth century.[7] Welsh Nonconformity, Sunday schools, choral societies, temperance movements, and eisteddfodau all championed education and especially self-education. Penny readings had been especially popular in Wales, sponsored by chapels of all denominations, with a high level of participation by working-class members.[8] In 1907, thirteen out of fifty-three residential students at Ruskin College were South Wales miners.[9] Wales could also boast high concentrations of WEA students in 1938–39: 2.90 per 1,000 population in South Wales, and 6.25 (highest in the nation) in North Wales.[10] But in 1914 public libraries served only 46 percent of the Welsh population (compared with 62 percent in England), and most of the neglected areas were small towns and rural regions.[11] According to a 1918 parliamentary enquiry, "not a single municipally maintained public library is to be found in the central Glamorgan block of the coalfield."[12] Miners' libraries filled that vacuum: they were rarely established where public libraries already existed.[13]

Though affluent intellectuals denigrated the "Little Bethels" of the mining regions, collier-intellectuals recognized that they provided an enormous stimulus for debate and literary analysis, not unlike the yeshivas of Eastern Europe. Durham miner Jack Lawson conceded that "there were tendencies to narrowness and hypocrisy" in the chapels[.]

[. . .]

[I]t was at a Methodist society that Lawson first found working people who shared his intellectual passions. One had been well into his thirties before his wife taught him to read: in his old age he was successfully tackling the New Testament in Greek, and Nietzsche. Others ultimately became teachers, ministers, musicians, social workers, and even professors. Their houses were open to each other and they visited on impulse:

> We talked pit-work, ideals, the Bible, literature, or union business. The piano rattled, the choir was in action, and we sang with more abandon than any gang who has just learned to murder the latest film song. . . . I was encouraged to express myself; to preach and to speak. I was given their warm, helpful friendship, and the hospitality of their homes. No longer was I "queer" or "alone." My thoughts and dreams were given direction. Even when they did not understand or agree they encouraged, and ignorant and intelligent alike combined to set my feet firmly on the road I had haphazardly been looking for.[14]

The parents of D. R. Davies (b. 1889) had no formal education and could not read English until fairly late in life, but his father (a collier) composed Welsh poetry and hymns, as well as a cantata performed by the chapel choir. Their home was often filled with neighbors discussing religion:

> Conversation was invariably about things that mattered, and ideas were the staple of intercourse. Without knowing it, I breathed a strong, stimulating intellectual atmosphere. In later years I realized what a great advantage I had enjoyed. It has been my lot to know at different times wealthy, polished and educated families amongst whom argument about great ideas was bad form. An

entirely different and better start was mine. In my homelife, it was ideas that mattered. By their intellectual intensity my parents created in me a zest for ideas which gave direction to my life. . . . My home did for me as a boy what the University is supposed to do, according to Newman, for youth—it awoke and encouraged a love of ideas for their own sake. And that advantage outweighed most of the handicaps under which I lived, handicaps neither few nor light.

All the children had music lessons and were singers, one with the Moody Manners Opera Company. "I was constantly listening to Bach, Handel, Mozart, Mendelssohn and Schubert—oratorios, cantatas and masses," Davies recalled. There was one schoolteacher who, in a class of sixty, "create[d] in his pupils an independent passion for knowledge," and inspired Davies to read Macaulay's *History of England* before his twelfth birthday. Because it was leavened with that spacious enthusiasm for music, literature, history, and theological debate:

> the Welsh Nonconformity in which I was reared did not make for narrowness and fanaticism of mind as so many of the frustrated, embittered critics of my generation have maintained. Today [mid-1950s] we are living upon the capital of those same "tin Bethels", and when that gives out (as it is now doing) the futility and leanness of our contemporary life will become more obvious and disastrous. It is true that our fathers, in Wales, taught us a religion of cast-iron dogma, which, according to all the theories, should have made us obscurantists, inhabiting a very small world. But it did not. In some mysterious way we became freemen of a spacious world. Along beside the narrow dogma went a broad culture. What happened to me demonstrates that fact clearly. Can anything promote a wider interest than history? And history led to politics, which, in turn, opened the door on many intellectual horizons. And music. It fed the spirit as an instrument of perception, as an organ of knowledge. It made for inner refinement. We had few of the graces and polish of manners, characteristic of an affluent society, but music gave us something better. It created in us a fastidiousness of moral as well as literary taste. It gave us a sense of the necessary relation between content and form. I very much doubt whether, fundamentally, Eton or Harrow would have given me a better start, educationally, than the "tin Bethel", the elementary council school, and my home.

Even the perpetual Bible reading, in English and Welsh, stimulated an appetite for secular literature. "I defy any child of ordinary intelligence to read the Bible constantly (in the Authorized Version) without acquiring a genuine literary taste, a sense of style, and at least a feeling for the beauty of words. Before I was twelve I had developed an appreciation of good prose, and the Bible created in me a zest for literature," propelling him directly to Lamb, Hazlitt's essays, and Ruskin's *The Crown of Wild Olives*. Later, after a day of exhausting mine work, he would attend union meetings, chapel meetings, literary and debating societies, lectures, and eisteddfodau, and then do some fairly heavy reading. He joined the library committee of the Miners' Institute in Maesteg, made friends with the librarian, and advised him on acquisitions. Thus he could read all the books he wanted: Marx, Smith, Ricardo, Mill, Marshall, economic and trade union history, *Fabian Essays*, Thomas Hardy, Meredith, Kipling, and Dickens.[15]

[. . .]

Marx, Jane Eyre, Tarzan

Except for the occasional schoolteacher, shopkeeper, or clergyman, the miners' libraries served a working-class clientele; and miners determined acquisitions. The book selection committee at Tredegar was headed by that stalwart of the Labour Party's left wing, Aneurin Bevan. The borrowing records of these libraries—unlike those of public libraries—can therefore offer a profile of working-class reading preferences uncontaminated by middle-class cultural hegemony. Only three usable registers out of the hundred-odd South Wales miners' libraries have survived, but they are the best source we have to address the question that every study of reader response must begin with: Who read what?

Historians of the Welsh coalfields have offered three possible answers: *Das Kapital, Jane Eyre*, or *Tarzan of the Apes*. South Wales was a hotbed of labor militancy where, according to historians of the left, many workers were well-versed in the Marxist classics. Then there is *The Corn is Green* school of novels and memoirs, which describe a thriving autodidact culture in the coalfields, where colliers fervently studied the classics in adult education classes. The third answer was proposed in 1932 by Q. D. Leavis in *Fiction and the Reading Public*. Mrs. Leavis was nostalgic for a prelapsarian Elizabethan age, when the masses enjoyed Shakespeare and Marlowe. In the Victorian period, however, the reading public began to divide between high and low literature, and after the First World War the two audiences were irreconcilably divorced. The masses now consumed rubbishy crime fiction and romances, while the great modernists—Lawrence, Joyce, Woolf, Eliot—were read only by small educated coteries.

Frankly, Mrs. Leavis's methods of literary sociology were crude. She dismissed out of hand the notion that you might ask people what they were reading and why they were reading it. Instead, she stationed herself in Boot's Circulating Libraries with a notebook: since Boot's specialized in light best-sellers, she got the results she was looking for. She also seized on the statistic that three out of every four books borrowed from public libraries were fiction, which she took as prima facie evidence of low literary tastes. (It proves more conclusively that Mrs. Leavis retained the Victorian literary prejudice against fiction.)[16]

We can test all these theories against three miners' libraries, beginning with the Tylorstown Workmen's Institute. We have the complete borrowing record for the year 1941, when there was a total of 7,783 loans.[17] Most of them fit Mrs. Leavis's definition of trash literature—books with titles such as *Corpses Never Argue* (13 loans), *Lumberjack Jill* (19), *A Murder of Some Importance* (24), *The Mysterious Chinaman* (18), *Anything But Love* (31), *The Flying Cowboys* (31), and P. G. Wodehouse's deathless *Right-Ho Jeeves* (17). The standard adventure novels also had their fair share of readers—Jack London's *White Fang* (17), Conan Doyle's *His Last Bow* (6) and *The Lost World* (15), Victor Hugo's *The Hunchback of Notre Dame* (12), Alexandre Dumas's *The Man in the Iron Mask* (4) and *The Three Musketeers* (11), John Buchan's *The Thirty-Nine Steps* (5), James Fenimore Cooper's *The Last of the Mohicans* (2), *Robinson Crusoe* (1), and *The Swiss Family Robinson* (5). There was considerable demand for such children's classics as *Little Women* (20), *The Prince and the Pauper* (8), and a remarkable Victorian survival, Hesba Stretton's *Jessica's First Prayer* (13).

On the whole, the greats and near-greats among the Victorians and Edwardians did not fare well. John Galsworthy's *A Modern Comedy* (4) and *The Forsyte Saga* (1), H. G. Wells's *Kipps* (1) and *The Island of Dr. Moreau* (3), Arnold Bennett's *Hilda Lessways* (2) and *Anna of the Five Towns* (2), Charles Reade's *Peg Woffington* (2) and *The Cloister and the Hearth* (1), Wilkie Collins's *The Woman in White* (5), Elizabeth Gaskell's *North and South* (1) and *Mary Barton* (2), and Rudyard Kipling's *Plain Tales from the Hills* (2) were all outpaced by A. J. Cronin's *The Citadel* (6) and Stella Gibbons's spoof *Cold Comfort Farm* (16). Bernard Shaw had a large number of readers, but they were spread thinly across his various works: *Man and Superman* (2), *Heartbreak House* (3), *Misalliance* (1), *Back to Methuselah* (1), *The Doctor's Dilemma* (4),

Androcles and the Lion (2), *Pygmalion* (1), *John Bull's Other Island* (2), *Major Barbara* (1), *Plays for Puritans* (2), *Plays Pleasant* (4), *Plays Unpleasant* (1), and his novel *Cashel Byron's Profession* (1). Only one classic could compete with the best-sellers: *Pride and Prejudice* was loaned no less than 25 times, but that was in the wake of the 1940 film version starring Greer Garson and Laurence Olivier, and Austen's popularity did not carry over to *Mansfield Park* (2). The only Dickens novel much in demand was *A Tale of Two Cities* (7), followed by *David Copperfield* (3), *Barnaby Rudge* (1), and *Oliver Twist* (1). Shakespeare's plays and a volume on Shakespeare's characters were borrowed a total of six times, *Gulliver's Travels* seven, *Anna Karenina* only three, Bacon's essays once, Longfellow's poems once. It may seem remarkable that Willa Cather's *Death Comes for the Archbishop* was checked out eight times, but a 1930 poll of readers of the *Sunday Dispatch* placed it among the postwar novels most likely to be read a generation hence.[18]

Mrs. Leavis bemoaned the indifference of the reading public to modernist literature, and Tylorstown confirms her pessimism. *A Passage to India* was borrowed once, Eugene O'Neill's *Strange Interlude* once, Robert Graves's *Goodbye to All That* twice. It seems extraordinary that all of five readers took out Virginia Woolf's *The Years*, but even including those, the fact remains that literary modernism accounted for barely one in a thousand loans.

Though Tylorstown was in what was supposed to be Britain's Red Belt, there was scarcely more interest in politics. The collection included biographies of Labour Party leaders George Lansbury (2 loans), Keir Hardie (1), and James Maxton (2). There were a few readers of foreign affairs, as represented by John Gunther's *Inside Europe* (5) and Michael Oakeshott's *Social and Political Doctrines of Contemporary Europe* (2). Beyond Reuben Osborn's *Freud and Marx* (2), there was hardly any demand for either these thinkers. Books by or about Lenin were taken out by six readers, Hewlett Johnson's *The Socialist Sixth of the World* by five, but the invasion of Russia on 22 June did not increase interest in the Soviet Union. Politics were more palatable if cast in the form of a dystopian thriller: there were eleven borrowers of Jack London's *The Iron Heel*, a prophesy of fascism that inspired Orwell's *Nineteen Eighty-Four*.

Closer to home, there were only two borrowers each for Walter Hannington's *The Problem of the Distressed Areas*, E. Wight Bakke's *The Unemployed Man*, and H. A. Marquand's *South Wales Needs a Plan*; and just one for Orwell's *The Road to Wigan Pier*. Miners were not much interested in reading about miners: only one of them checked out Richard Llewellyn's *How Green Was My Valley*, and two read *These Poor Hands*, a memoir by Welsh collier Bert Coombes. In contrast, there were ten borrowers for a more romantic kind of proletarian literature, W.H. Davies's *The Autobiography of a Supertramp*. The difference was that Davies took his readers away from the coalfields, recounting his wanderings through England, Canada, and America. "Yer writing about the pits?" a workmate asked J. G. Glenwright, a Durham mineworker with aspirations to authorship. "Nothing much to write about, is there? Just the muck and the dirt and that. An' perhaps a nasty accident, now and then."[19] The daughter (b. 1924) of an unemployed Rainton miner borrowed novels of social realism from the Carnegie Library, but her mother objected: "There's enough misery in the world without dwelling on it. Next time fetch a nice historical novel back."[20] As a WEA lecturer in the early 1930s, Roger Dataller found that emigrés from Staffordshire preferred that he did not discuss *The Old Wives' Tale*: "Having left the Five Towns they did not in the least wish to be reminded of the district again." *Sons and Lovers* provoked a more positive reponse among miners: one recalled vividly that he too, as a child, had listened cowering in his bedroom while his parents quarrelled.[21]

Fortunately, the catalogue to the Tylorstown library has survived, so we can compile a list of books the miners did not borrow but probably could have.[22] In 1941 they checked out nothing by Walter Scott, John Ruskin, or Thomas Hardy. They had no interest in the poetry of Keats, Shelley, or Siegfried Sassoon. They ignored *Women in Love, Testament of Youth*, and *A*

Portrait of the Artist as a Young Man. The political writings of G. D. H. Cole, John Strachey, Bertrand Russell, and Ness Edwards's *History of the South Wales Miners* were left undisturbed on the shelves. And no one touched *Das Kapital*, Marx's *Critique of the Gotha Program*, or Engels's *Origin of the Family*.

Of course, there is a bias involved in any short-term study of library records. It can exaggerate the impact of a best-seller, which may enjoy a brief supernova of popularity and then, a year or two later, be forgotten. If a classic is borrowed at a slow but steady rate over the decades, it may eventually surpass the readership of the most popular light fiction. We can test that hypothesis against the Cynon and Duffryn Welfare Hall Library register, which records reading habits over a generation, from 1927 to the early 1950s. These records confirm the popularity of the authors Q. D. Leavis loved to hate: Edgar Rice Burroughs, Warwick Deeping, Jeffery Farnol, E. Phillips Oppenheim, Gene Stratton Porter, Edgar Wallace. But there was also some interest in the standard English classics. Demand for *Pride and Prejudice* (9 loans), *Wuthering Heights* (16), *Robinson Crusoe* (9), *Oliver Twist* (7), *Westward Ho!* (7), and *Vanity Fair* (10) was modest but sustained over many years. Even *Culture and Anarchy* had four borrowers, and there was a striking and continuing demand for some Victorian sensation novels and bestsellers—Grant Allen's *Dumaresq's Daughter* (18), R. D. Blackmore's *Lorna Doone* (13), Bulwer-Lytton's *The Disowned* (11), Florence Marryat's *Facing the Footlights* (20), and Mrs. Henry Wood's *East Lynne* (16). The last had nearly a million copies in print by 1909. In Welsh miners' libraries, Mrs. Wood was the fourth most frequently stocked novelist, behind only Dickens, Scott, and H. Rider Haggard.[23] She was also the most popular author among working people in Middlesbrough, as Florence Bell discovered in 1901.[24] In the Cornish working-class town of Megavissey in the early 1920s, *East Lynne* and *The Channings* "occupied half the population all the time," wrote a fisherman's daughter.[25]

There was not a trace of interest in modernist fiction at the Cynon and Duffryn Library. For these readers, the art of the novel culminated with Bennett, Galsworthy, and Wells. As for books on politics and social issues, only five can be located in the entire collection. Understandably, no one read what Lloyd George had to say about *The People's Will* in 1910, or a clergyman's report on *Ten Years in a London Slum*. What is more remarkable is that these miners, like those at Tylorstown, cared little for books about themselves: only five borrowed James Hanley's *Grey Children*, a report on unemployed Welsh colliers. Wales was a pacifist stronghold, and the only political tracts that really engaged this community dealt with the horrors of war: H. L. Gates's *The Auction of Souls* (13 loans), an account of the Armenian massacres, and *Disarm! Disarm!* (15), a novel by pacifist Bertha von Suttner. Following that pattern, perhaps the most popular political book in Tylorstown was *The Bloody Traffic*, Fenner Brockway's 1933 exposé of the munitions industry. It had eight borrowers in 1941, when Britain's survival depended on her arms factories.

This neglect of politics was entirely typical. A survey of nineteen miners' libraries catalogues between 1903 and 1931 found that all the social sciences accounted for only 5.3 percent of book stock; at only one library did the proportion rise above 10 percent. There was nothing by Marx on the shelves at Treharris in 1925, Tredegar in 1917, or the Cwmaman Institute in 1911; and only 1.6 percent of stock at Cwmaman was in the "Politics, Economics and Socialism" section. Granted, many libraries built up their socialist collections over time, especially during the "Red Thirties," but though Tredegar eventually acquired the complete works of Lenin, he remained unread. At Cwmaman, as at other miners' libraries, readers mainly demanded fiction, which rose from 52.6 percent of loans in 1918 to 81.7 percent in 1939: politics never accounted for more than 0.5 percent. At the Senghenydd Institute library in 1925, on the eve of the General Strike, the proportions were 93.4 percent fiction, 0.4 percent economics.[26] Any historian of working-class culture in early twentieth-century Britain must deal with this inescapable fact: the readers of Marx and Lenin were infinitesimal compared with the fans of Mrs. Henry Wood.

Very revealing, in this context, is a 1937 survey of 484 unemployed men aged eighteen to twenty-five in Cardiff, Newport, and Pontypridd. Only 3 percent were involved in any kind of political organization, compared with 16 percent in religious groups, 11 percent in sports clubs, and 6 percent in adult education classes. One might expect these young men to be the shock troops of discontent, but none of them completely rejected Christianity. Though only 8 percent were active church members, 35 percent attended church or chapel at least once a month. Only seven of these men were politically active—either Labour, Communist, or Conservative. Fifty-seven percent identified reading as a major leisure activity, but it was usually the daily paper (if their family took in one), mainly for sports, news headlines, and the horoscope. They read books for escape (Westerns, aviation, crime and detective stories), purchasing cheap paperbacks, then exchanging them among friends, family, and comrades in the Employment Exchange queue. Hardly anyone was aware that such books were available at the public library—only 20 percent ever visited the libraries, and just 6 percent were regular borrowers. Another escape was the cinema: nearly everyone went at least once a month, 22 percent at least twice a week. Only 8 percent listened to anything on the radio but dance bands and variety: everything else was dismissed as "highbrow."[27]

Where, then, were the Marxist miners of South Wales? The most plausible answer is that the literary and political interests of Welsh working people could vary enormously from town to town. As an adult education bulletin noted in 1929, the Welsh valleys were remarkable for their isolation:

> The miner or his wife may pay a visit to Cardiff once or twice a year, or spend Bank Holiday on Barry Island, but it is quite likely that he has never been into the next valley, while the one beyond that may be entirely *terra incognita* to him. Communications are bad, and the geographical isolation has led to a corresponding mental isolation. This is aggravated by the fact that the whole population of the valley is dependent on the coal industry. There is no variety in industrial life, and there is almost no differentiation into social grades such as may be found in any ordinary town. This makes for an extraordinarily friendly spirit; there is little shyness and much hospitality. But it has tended to make also for a narrowness of outlook. The miner may never have met an agriculturalist, a factory worker, or a docker, nor mixed with any society but that found in his own immediate surroundings. He never sees either the inside or the outside of a really fine building, be it church or office, public building or home. His horizon is formed by the tops of the bare hills which for so long have shut him away from the rest of the world. His middle distance is furnished with the seemingly endless rows of slate-roofed cottages, each as cramped and ugly as the one which he and his family occupy, and his foreground is the tiny kitchen, the untidy street, or the narrow seam of coal at which he expects to spend 47 hours every week between the ages of 14 and 70. Death is an ever-present possibility down the pit; life seems anyhow precarious when the chance of employment is, at the best, dependent on unknown forces and incomprehensible world move-ments, or, at the worst, dependent on the word of an unpopular manager, himself the tool of some remoter authority distrusted and disliked.

This cultural environment was hospitable to sectarian dogmas of various kinds: Welsh Nonconformity, miners' syndicalism, and the Marxism preached by the National Council of Labour Colleges (itself subsidized by the South Wales Miners' Federation). Steeped in the

Welsh tradition of theological debate, miners plunged quite readily into adult classes in philosophy and history, though instructors often found them wedded to a simplistic economic determinism: "Any superstructure of Church or State, institutions or art, was disregarded as being irrelevant." A class that included some non-miners was likely to be receptive to a more complex view of historical causation.[28] The village of Mardy was a "little Moscow," where in 1933 ninety colliers were studying the proletarian philosopher Joseph Dietzgen at the Miners' Institute,[29] but reading tastes were very different in Tylorstown, just a few miles down the valley. Miners in the anthracite region to the west, around Llanelli, Swansea, and Port Talbot, were not so Marxist as those farther east;[30] and Aneurin Bevan's Tredegar was a moderate Labour town with hardly any Communists.[31] The intellectual climate could vary dramatically from mineshaft to mineshaft: as one collier explained, "The conveyor face down the Number 2 Pit was a university," where Darwin, Marx, Paine, and modernist theology were debated, while "the surface of Number 1 Pit a den of grossness."[32]

These extreme cultural variations can also be attributed partly to the fact that literary activities in a given community usually depended on the initiative of a few energetic individuals. Whatever their class, whether they patronized miners' institutes or Boot's Circulating Libraries, readers relied heavily on the advice of librarians in choosing books. A miner with a passion for the English classics was a likely candidate for institute librarian: in that capacity he could acquire the books he wanted to read himself and recommend them to his neighbors. In Penrhiwceiber the collier who supervised the Miners' Library three evenings a week steered a fellow pit worker toward Jack London, Gorky, A. E. Coppard, Chekhov, Maupassant, and Flaubert's *Madame Bovary* and *A Simple Heart*.[33] If Marxists were in charge of acquisitions (and they often were) they could do the same for leftist literature.[34] And if no one in town provided intellectual guidance, there was always *Tarzan of the Apes*.

Library acquisitions policies could shape reading habits, especially in isolated villages where there were few other sources of books. This pattern becomes apparent in the borrowing ledger of our third miners' library, maintained by the Markham Welfare Association. Here at last we find a coal town with classic literary tastes. In the first period covered by the ledger (September 1923 to December 1925), Jane Austen, the Brontës, Dickens, and George Eliot are the most popular authors. In Markham as in Cynon and Duffryn, no one borrowed Marx, but there was a continuing demand for Mrs. Henry Wood. Even in the depressed interwar years, there were still a few readers of Victorian self-help tracts: Samuel Smiles, James Hogg's *Men Who Have Risen*, and W. M. Thayer's *From Log Cabin to White House*.

Then there is a gap in the ledger. In September 1928 a new Markham Village Institute was opened, paid for mainly by the Miners' Welfare Fund.[35] The record resumes in March 1932, revealing that reading habits had hardly changed at all over nearly a decade. Indeed, judging from the borrowings, it appears that the Markham Library acquired very few if any new volumes. The probable cause was the prolonged and deep depression that crippled the coal industry from the early 1920s. After the boom years of the First World War and the immediate postwar period, demand for coal collapsed. French and German mines resumed full production, more efficient American mines captured markets, oil was becoming an increasingly important energy source. Daily wages, which averaged as much as 21s. 6¾d. in February 1921, were down to 9s. 5½d. by October 1922. Between 1920 and 1937, 241 pits closed in South Wales, the employed workforce shrank from 271,161 to 126,233, and total annual wages plummeted from £65 million to £14 million.[36] The Welsh unemployment rate was 13.4 percent in December 1925, 27.2 percent in July 1930, and in the Merthyr area as high as 47.5 percent by June 1935.[37]

The miners' institutes had been funded by deductions from miners' wages, the Miners' Welfare Fund, and by local governments. Now all these sources dried up. Between 1920 and 1928 the Cwmaman Workmen's Institute and Library saw its income cut from more than

£2,500 to just over £450. At the same time, circulation more than doubled, from 14,966 to 31,054. That was a common pattern throughout South Wales, where armies of unemployed miners had plenty of time on their hands and few other distractions. If their libraries did not close down completely, librarians' wages were slashed, central heating was done without, and acquisitions of new books came to a dead stop. (Even in good times the Miners' Welfare Fund rarely subsidized the purchase of books.) The book budget for the Ferndale Workmen's Institute went from more than £315 in 1920 to zero in 1929. Under those conditions, the old stock would be borrowed over and over again until it was reduced to waste paper. By 1929, investigators for the Carnegie Foundation were reporting that, in the typical miners' library, 50 to 100 percent of the collection was unfit for circulation. By 1937, many libraries had bought no new books in the past decade.

A few miners of this era remembered reading every book in their library. Though the borrowing ledgers show that some volumes were never touched, these claims may not be much exaggerated. One library in Ynyshir was patronized by 300 out-of-work miners who borrowed a total of 500 books a week, an average of eighty-six books per miner per year.[38] Enduring prolonged structural unemployment, any one of them could have exhausted a collection of several hundred volumes. Out-of-work men commonly and quite plausibly claimed to read three or four books a week.[39] In a collective memoir of twenty-five unemployed people, eleven testified that the Great Depression gave them more time for reading (including a London fitter who went through a novel a day), four took up adult classes, and a colliery banksman used the opportunity to write a novel.[40] "It brought a bubbling sense of freedom at first," wrote dole-queue veteran Walter Greenwood, "a secret elation in being at liberty to indulge in a feast of uninterrupted reading at home, the public library or in those Manchester bookshops where, by tacit consent, the kindly proprietors permitted young men and students to browse among the new books."[41] "Thousands used the Public Library for the first time," recalled itinerant laborer John Brown, who read Shaw, Marx, Engels, and classic literature until he exhausted his South Shields library. "It was nothing uncommon to come across men in very shabby clothes kneeling in front of the philosophy or economics shelves."[42] If the library stocked Jane Austen (or Mrs. Henry Wood, for that matter) she would have been read, simply because she was on the shelves. "I just went through the catalogue," recalled Jack Lawson, and without any more guidance than that he was introduced to Dickens, Scott, Charles Reade, George Eliot, the Brontës, Hardy, Hugo, Dumas, Shakespeare, and Milton.[43]

The lack of new books only encouraged literary conservatism among the miners, who continued to read Victorian best-sellers into the 1930s. Even in prosperous times their libraries had relied partly on purchases and donations of used books, and they always tended to preserve their old stock. Of 1,433 volumes in the Treharris Institute library catalog in 1894, about 900 were still there 31 years later; and all but thirty of the 953 volumes in the 1896 Cymmer Institute catalog were in the 1913 catalog as well.[44]

Availability, according to Q. D. Leavis, explains why the masses attended Shakespeare in 1600: "Happily they had no choice." Except for bearbaiting and a few chapbooks, what else competed for their attention?[45] In the twentieth century, she argued, capitalism produced an ever-increasing flood of trash novels—and by virtue of their sheer volume, these diverted readers from the great books. In an isolated mining village, where there was nothing much to read but some tattered copies of Victorian classics, the corruption of reading tastes might be delayed, but inevitably *The Bowery Murder* and *The Slave Junk* would penetrate the remotest Welsh valleys. As if to confirm Mrs. Leavis, the Markham library acquired, by March 1935, a new batch of books by lowbrow authors: Warwick Deeping, Jeffery Farnol, E. Phillips Oppenheim, Edgar Wallace. The borrowing record up to October 1936 does indeed manifest a literary Gresham's Law, with bad books forcing out the good. In the rush to read *Anna* the *Adventuress, Captain Crash, The Sloane Square Mystery*, and *Pretty Sinister*, borrowings of the English classics drop precipitously.

The next phase in the ledger, from April 1937 to March 1940, reveals an even more striking shift in quite another direction, produced by a world in crisis. Ethiopia had been conquered, the Japanese had invaded China, a civil war was raging in Spain, a European war was on the horizon. In Markham, the escapist fiction that was so popular a few years before had dramatically given way to the literature of political commitment: Zola's *Germinal* (18 loans), Henri Barbusse's antiwar novel *Under Fire* (7), Walter Brierley's *Means Test Man* (11), Upton Sinclair's *Oil!* (22), Ralph Bates's *Lean Men* (on the Spanish Revolution of 1931, 13 loans), Mulk-Raj Anand's *The Coolie* (9), and Robert Tressell's bitter proletarian novel *The Ragged Trousered Philanthropists* (20). Markham miners read *Quiet Flows the Don* (10) and the socialist realism of Feodor Gladkov's *Cement* (22). *Salka Valka*, a portrait of Icelandic fishermen by Halldór Laxness, won a large following (18 loans) with its Christian communist message. The same readers still found Marx hard to tackle, but ten of them borrowed Engels's *The Origin of the Family*. Proletarian intellectuals like T. A. Jackson, Bert Coombes, W. H. Davies, Willie Gallacher, and Joseph Dietzgen had a few borrowers each. But even in this politically conscious phase, readers in all three communities were more interested in conflicts abroad than in issues closer to home. Ellen Wilkinson's polemic on unemployment in Jarrow, *The Town That Was Murdered*, had only one borrower. There was more interest in Agnes Smedley's *China Fights Back* (7), John Langdon-Davies's *Behind the Spanish Barricades* (3), and *Mein Kampf* (6). Hywel Francis may have exaggerated the proletarian internationalism of the Welsh coalfields, but it certainly existed here, where the banner of the Markham Miners' Lodge proclaimed "The World is Our Country: Mankind are Our Brethren."[46]

The final section of the register covers July to December 1940—the Battle of Britain—and once again there is a marked change in borrowing habits. Now politics gives way to *Outlaws of Badger Hollow, Murder Must Advertise*, Sherlock Holmes, Edgar Wallace, and Marie Corelli. Perhaps the Nazi–Soviet Pact had dampened interest in Russia. The war had created new jobs, but not necessarily in the mines: many former colliers now made long and tiring commutes to munitions factories.[47] That might explain why the people of Markham now sought relief in easy reading. Only two of them borrowed anything as challenging as *Point Counter Point*—the only appearance of modernist literature in the entire ledger.

References

1   For an account of the latter, see David Shavit, *Hunger for the Printed Word: Books and Libraries in the Jewish Ghettos of Nazi-Occupied Europe* (Jefferson, NC: McFarland, 1997), ch. 1.

2   Christopher M. Baggs, "The miners' libraries of South Wales from the 1860s to 1939", unpublished PhD thesis, University of Wales, Aberystwyth (1995) is the definitive history of the movement. See particularly ch. 8 for the tricky calculations involved in estimating the number of libraries and the size of their collections. See also his " 'Well Done, Cymmer Workmen!': The Cymmer Collieries Workmen's Library, 1893–1920," *Llafur* 5 (1990), no. 3: 20–27.

3   James Hanley, *Grey Children* (London: Methuen, 1937), 32–37.

4   Peter Stead, "Wales and Film," in *Wales Between the Wars*, ed. Trevor Herbert and Gareth Elwyn Jones (Cardiff: University of Wales Press, 1988), 166.

5   D. J. Davies, *The Tredegar Workmen's Hall 1861–1951* (n.p., 1952), 80–93.

6   John Benson, *British Coalminers in the Nineteenth Century* (London: Longman, 1989), 152–54. J. Ginswick, ed., *Labour and the Poor in England and Wales 1849–1851* (London: Frank Cass, 1983), 2:57–60.

7   Geraint H. Jenkins, *Literature, Religion and Society in Wales, 1660–1730* (Cardiff: University of Wales Press, 1978), 24, 129–30, 198–99, 209–10, 254, 288–90, 293–99, 303–304.

8   Walter Haydn Davies, *The Right Place, the Right Time: Memories of Boyhood Days in a Welsh Mining Community* (Llandybie: Llyfrau'r Dryw, 1972), 206–10.

9   Richard Lewis, *Leaders and Teachers: Adult Education and the Challenge of Labour in South Wales, 1906–1940* (Cardiff: University of Wales Press, 1993), 62.

10   Harold Marks, "Some WEA Statistics: How Efficient are the Districts?" *Highway* 32 (March 1940): 64.

11   Alec Ellis, "Rural Library Services in England and Wales before 1919," *Library History* 4 (Spring 1977): 69.

12   Commission of Enquiry into Industrial Unrest, No. 7 Division, *Report of the Commissioners for Wales, including Monmouthshire*, Parl. Sess. Papers, 1917–18, vol. XV, Cd. 8688, pp. 12, 19, 28, 30.

13   Baggs, "Miners' Libraries," pp. 141, 148–50.

14   John James Lawson, *A Man's Life* (London: Hodder & Stoughton, 1932), 109–15.

15   David Richard Davies, *In Search of Myself: the Autobiography of D.R. Davies* (London: Geoffrey Bles, 1961), 18–19, 27–31, 36, 51–52.

16   Q.D. Leavis, *Fiction and the Reading Public* (London: Chatto & Windus, 1932), 4–7, 43.

17   The complete borrowing record for Tylorstown, the nearly complete record for the Markham Welfare Association Library, and a discussion of the methodological problems involved in using such documents, are in Jonathan Rose, "Marx, Jane Eyre, Tarzan: Miners' Libraries in South Wales, 1923–52," *Leipziger Jahrbuch zur Buchgeschichte* 4 (1994): 187–207. The borrowing records for all three miners' libraries are held by the library of the University of Wales, Swansea.

18   Leavis, *Fiction and the Reading Public*, 36.

19   J.G. Glenwright, *Bright Shines the Morning* (London: Martini Publications, 1949), 82–3.

20   Mary Craddock, *A North Country Maid* (London: Hutchinson, 1960), 151.

21   Roger Dataller, *Oxford into Coal-field* (London: J.M. Dent, 1934), 130, 180.

22   I write "probably" because not every book listed in a library catalog is actually on the shelves. Also, the catalog was apparently compiled in 1945, and some of these books might have been acquired in the interim.

23   Baggs, "Miners' Libraries," 510.

24   Lady Florence Bell, *At the Works: A Study of a Manufacturing Town* (London: Edward Arnold, 1907), 165–6.

25   Mary Lakeman, *Early Tide: A Megavissey Childhood* (London: William Kimber, 1978), 172.

26   Baggs, "Miners Libraries," 386–92, 403, 423–30.

27   A. J. Lush, *The Young Adult* (Cardiff: University of Wales Press Board, 1941), 47, 50, 72, 79–82.

28   "Adult Education in the Rhondda Valley," *Bulletin of the World Association for Adult Education* 40 (May 1929): 19–21.

29   Hymie Fagan, "An Autobiography", Brunel University Library, p. 93.

30   T. Brennan, E. W. Cooney, and H. Pollins, *Social Change in South-West Wales* (London: Watts, 1954), 69–70.

31   Dai Smith, *Aneurin Bevan and the World of South Wales* (Cardiff: University of Wales Press, 1993), 209.

32   Davies, *Right Place*, 102–104.

33   Robert Morgan, *My Lamp Still Burns* (Llandysul: Gomer, 1981), 116.

34   The activity of Marxists on miners' library committees is charted in Hywel Francis, "The Origins of the South Wales Miners' Library," *History Workshop* 2 (Autumn 1976): 183–205, esp. Appendix 6.

35   Miners' Welfare Fund, Annual Report, 1929, pp. 38–39.

36   Hywel Francis and David Smith, *The Fed: A History of the South Wales Miners in the Twentieth Century* (London: Lawrence & Wishart, 1980), 33, 48.

37   Kenneth O. Morgan, *Rebirth of a Nation: Wales 1880–1980* (New York: Oxford University Press, 1981), 211–12.

38   Baggs, "Miners' Libraries," 178. David E. Evans, "Report on the Condition of Libraries in the Aberdare Urban District Council, and County Borough of Merthyr Tydfil," 17 May 1929; and Brinley Thomas, "Report on the Condition of Workmen's Libraries in the Rhondda Urban District," in South Wales Miners' Library, Swansea.

39   B. L. Coombes, *These Poor Hands: The Autobiography of a Miner Working in South Wales* (London: Victor Gollancz, 1939), 221–22. Jimmy O'Connor, *Memories of a Market Trader* (Peterborough: Minimax, 1984), 20. Alexander Baron recalled a sergeant in a Wessex battalion who spent his unemployed years in the public library reading Dickens, Thackeray, and Jane Austen: "Four

books a week was nothin' to me in those days." Alexander Baron, *From the City, From the Plough* (New York: Ives Washburn, 1949), 160–62.

40   H. L. Beales and R. S. Lambert, eds., *Memoirs of the Unemployed* (London: Victor Gollancz, 1934), 79, 95–96, 105, 119, 127–28, 133–34, 145–46, 154, 170, 176–77, 208–209, 234, 239–40, 262.

41   Walter Greenwood, *There Was a Time* (London: Cape, 1967), 184–5.

42   John Brown, *I Was a Tramp* (London: Selwyn & Blount, 1934), 201, 208, 215.

43   Lawson, *Man's Life*, 77–80.

44   Baggs, "Miners' Libraries," 167–68, 268–71, 330.

45   Leavis, *Fiction and the Reading Public*, 83–85.

46   Hywel Francis, *Miners Against Fascism: Wales and the Spanish Civil War* (London: Lawrence & Wishart, 1984), 29–39.

47   E. D. Lewis, *The Rhondda Valleys* (London: Phoenix House, 1959), 260–61.

Chapter 26

Christine Pawley

"A BENEFIT AND A BLESSING": THE SAGE LIBRARY

ONE WAY TO SUPPORT the theory that the local selection process reflected the reading tastes of Osage's inhabitants is to investigate the actual choices of individual library patrons. While accession records provide valuable information about reading matter that the public library made available to the community, circulation records give an even more detailed picture. Circulation records can show, for example, how the choices of anomalous patrons compare with those of patrons who fit the majority profile, as well as test assumptions about reading choices of older as opposed to younger library users or about the choices of men versus women.

Broadly speaking, the choices of Sage Library patrons confirmed cultural authorities' suspicions that, if left to their own devices, the reading public would largely choose a reading diet of fiction. Almost without exception, Osage users charged out novels. Some also read history, biography, and inspirational writings, but fiction was the main choice for most men and women, girls and boys, irrespective of age and class, most of the time.[1] Table 26.1 presents the top twenty choices of title by Osage library patrons over the period 1890–95, not counting duplicates or renewals.[2] Seventy borrowed one or more of four volumes of Thomas Talmage's *Series of Sermons*. The remaining titles are all single volumes and all fiction. Whether or not a title appeared in the ALA's *Catalog* stands as a rough indicator of acceptance by cultural authorities.[3]

Several titles on this list had been best-sellers or near best-sellers but by 1890 were far from recent publications.[4] *Airy, Fairy, Lilian* was a "better-seller" in 1879, as was *Ben-Hur* in 1880. *Faith Gartney's Girlhood* had been a best-seller in 1863, and Susan Warner's *Queechy*, as long ago as 1852, but these titles were still read frequently in Osage twenty, thirty, and even forty years later. Some titles were by authors who had attained best- or better-seller status for other books, such as E. P. Roe (*Barriers Burned Away* [1872] and *Driven Back to Eden* [1885]). Leading journals of the time categorized many of these popular titles as "sensational" or "sentimental." Leading librarians of the time agreed. Of the top ten titles checked out, ALA's *Catalog* recommended only three, and of the top twenty titles, only nine.[5] Major figures in the library world roundly condemned many authors that Sage Library patrons favored. "Perhaps we cannot altogether banish this wretched stuff from our catalogues," complained an 1883 *Library Journal* report, "but can we not make some beginning

Table 26.1 Most popular titles, 1890–1895

Ranking	Title	Author	Recommended in ALA Catalog	Borrowers
1	*History of England*	James A. Froude	Yes	77
2	*An Original Belle*	E. P. Roe	No	71
3	*Series of Sermons*	Thomas Talmage	No	70*
4	*A Brave Lady*	Miss Mulock	Yes	69
5	*For Another's Sin*	Bertha M. Clay	No	68
6	*Airy, Fairy, Lilian*	The Duchess	No	67
7	*Young Mrs. Jardine*	Miss Mulock	No	64
8	*A Broken Wedding Ring*	Bertha M. Clay	No	60
9	*His Own Master*	J. T. Trowbridge	No	56
10	*Daniel Deronda*	George Eliot	Yes	54
11	*Sights and Insights*	A. D. T. Whitney	No	53
12	*Armadale*	Wilkie Collins	Yes	50
12	*The Virginians*	W. Thackeray	Yes	50
14	*Ben-Hur*	Lew Wallace	Yes	48
14	*Faith Gartney's Girlhood*	A. D. T. Whitney	Yes	48
16	*Diana*	Susan Warner	No	46
16	*Odd or Even*	A. D. T. Whitney	No	46
18	*The Colonel's Daughter*	Charles King	Yes	44
18	*The Letter of Credit*	Susan Warner	No	44
18	*Little Lord Fauntleroy*	F. H. Burnett	Yes	44
18	*Queechy*	Susan Warner	No	44

* Probably an underestimate, because titles affected by book number problems have been excluded from the analysis.

toward that end by refusing place any longer to the works of such writers, for example, as . . . Bertha Clay . . . Gaboriau, Mayne Reid, Ballantyne, Alger, Oliver Optic . . . and their like?" "Weak and flabby and silly books tend to make weak and flabby and silly brains," contended Librarian of Congress Ainsworth Spofford. "Why should library guides put in circulation such stuff as the dime novels or 'Old Sleuth' stories, or the slip-slop novels of 'The Duchess,' when the great masters of romantic fiction have endowed us with so many books replete with intellectual and moral power?"[6]

Cultural authorities thus condemned dime novels on the grounds of both intellectual and moral deficiency. Stories by Bertha M. Clay and "The Duchess" (the pseudonym of Margaret Wolfe Hungerford) were often targeted by critics as examples of working-class reading and therefore inferior.[7] In many ways, however, these books were deeply conventional, even by the moral standards of the middle classes. Despite its sensational title, *For Another's Sin* (in Osage, the more popular of the two Clay books) had an impeccably moral tone. The story tells of angelic and martyred Adelaide Carew's efforts to save her husband, Lord Carew, from the wiles of a "temptress"—a Spanish-born duchess. The worst the duchess contemplates is divorce from her rich and elderly husband; at the climax of the book she urges Lord Carew to leave Adelaide and marry her instead. While divorce was uncommon in the late nineteenth century, it was not unknown. Osage was home to several divorced men and women, including a number in public life (for example, lawyer L. M. Ryce and successful milliner Lizzie Ryce). Because divorced citizens played prominent roles in the local establishment, many Osage readers may not have seen the threat of divorce as the terrible moral danger that the book portrays. Moreover, the religious rhetoric and the racist portrayal of the duchess as foreign, dark, passionate, and unscrupulous may have touched a familiar chord. The condemnation of divorce in *For Another's Sin* may have seemed old-fashioned, but its message fit very well the evangelical nativism that characterized Osage's dominant culture.

Airy, Fairy, Lilian's popularity also endured. This story tells of young, beautiful Lilian, an orphan whose stormy relationship with her handsome and titled guardian unsurprisingly ends with marriage and the rout of Lilian's unpleasant older rival. As in other works by The Duchess, the British upper-class characters live in surroundings of splendor and good taste. Their ethical attitudes are basically sound: conflict occurs over trifles, and the story moves quickly, if predictably, from one irreproachably virtuous scene to another. Yet the characters are not stuffy or pompous (unlike those of clergyman E. P. Roe, for instance); on the contrary, they are often witty and self-deprecating. It is easy to see why the book had such appeal.

The working classes may have suffered middle-class criticism for reading Duchess and Bertha M. Clay stories, but they were not the only "guilty" ones. In Osage, about 64 percent of Bertha M. Clay readers were business, professional, and other white-collar workers, and another 17 percent came from the skilled craftworker class. Only 6 percent of the readers were working class, while 12 percent came from farm families. The readers of the Duchess show a roughly similar class distribution: 61 percent were middle class; about 20 percent, from skilled craftworker families; 12 percent, from working-class families; and 5 percent from farm families. The numbers are too small to draw general conclusions, but they do suggest a substantial middle-class readership for cheap fiction that was simultaneously denigrated by the proponents of "self-improvement." Readers of both authors were predominantly female—82 percent for the Duchess, 72 percent for Bertha M. Clay, but male readers of Bertha M. Clay included the octogenarian Artemus S. Hubbard, John D. Wing (an insurance agent in his late fifties), the blacksmith and sometime councilman John C. Davis, and Frank Bronson (in his forties and clerk of the court). Neither were the readers entirely from younger age groups: 23 percent of Bertha M. Clay readers were over forty by 1890, and about half of those were over fifty.

At what was, at first sight, the other end of the cultural spectrum, seventy-seven library patrons checked out one of the twelve volumes of James A. Froude's *History of England*.[8] The first charge was not until February 1894, which suggests that the library had only just acquired the set at that time. Thus this large number of charges took place in a relatively short period of time—just over a year. Readers were mostly women (66 percent) and middle class (72 percent). Thirteen readers (16 percent) were from skilled craftworker families, four (5 percent) from laboring families, and five (6 percent) from the farming group; 66 percent of the readers were older teenagers (born after 1875). Thirteen-year-old Max Katz (teenaged son of Ben and Jeannette Katz) was the youngest; he charged out two volumes in March 1894 and a further three in March 1895, once renewing one volume. Very possibly the young people were using the books for schoolwork, except that ten (29 percent) of the thirty-five charges by young people that took place in 1894 occurred during the summer months of July and August, when school was closed. Thus general interest likely played a part in the work's popularity. Among the older readers were Norwegian-born Mrs. Hovelson, Catholic Anne Sheehan, fifty-five-year-old farmer Byron Benedict, and women's leader Clarinda Hitchcock (whose daughter Augusta also read Froude's work).

The popularity of Froude's *History* may seem misplaced when compared with library patrons' other favorite choices, at least until one examines the books. Froude's was a highly popularized version of the history of sixteenth-century England, retold with plenty of action and adventure. Froude leaves his own sympathies in no doubt, and his view of the Reformation would have reinforced his Osage readers' Protestant allegiance. Similarly,

Thomas Talmage's sermons (also serialized in Osage newspapers) were far from learned and scholarly; rather, they maintained a rhetorical style designed to capture the casual reader's interest. These two choices may have counted technically as nonfiction, yet in style and even content, they were not far removed from the fiction that otherwise dominated readers' selections.

Although Froude's and Talmage's works were popular with the predominantly Protestant library users, they would have been books to avoid for Catholics. Talmage, a Protestant preacher, was clearly a danger to Catholic sensibilities, but Froude's history, too, with its undisguised Protestant leanings, was also heavily condemned by Catholic critics. In a detailed eighteen-page review, a *Catholic World* writer accused Froude of "violent partisanship, tortured criticism, paltering with the sense while tampering with the text of authorities, attribution of false motives and a scandalous wealth of abusive epithets."[9] With such books as these circulating so frequently from the public library, it is small wonder that Osage's Catholics gave the library a wide berth.

Analyzing the popularity of authors as opposed to single titles provides another view of what people chose to read. Some authors had written several books, but no single title ranked high in popularity. The library held few duplicate copies of any particular title, so patrons were probably accustomed to substituting titles by their favorite authors if they found that their first choice was already charged out. Table 26.2 presents the ranking of the top twenty authors for all borrowers. The Sage Library's most popular author, Pansy, wrote stories with a Christian message for young people. The library collection contained thirty-five titles by Pansy. Of the twenty-eight without book number problems, two women read thirteen: Ruby Hoag (Methodist, later thirties, married but without children) and Kittie

Table 26.2 Most popular authors, 1890–1895

Ranking	Author	Borrowers
1	Pansy	456*
2	Miss Mulock	431*
3	E. P. Roe	331*
4	Wilkie Collins	323
5	A. D. T. Whitney	306*
6	Susan Warner	290*
7	Sophie May	237*
8	Harriet Beecher Stowe	233*
9	Oliver Optic	222*
10	Elijah Kellogg	216*
11	William Dean Howells	197*
12	George Eliot	161*
13	Clara Burnham	153
14	Charles Dickens	141*
15	Edward Eggleston	135
16	J. G. Holland	133
17	Bertha M. Clay	128
18	Charles Reade	121*
18	C. A. Stephens	121
18	Walter Scott	121*

* Probably an underestimate, because titles affected by book number problems have been excluded from the analysis.

Kathan (Congregationalist, early twenties, unmarried, daughter of a successful horse trainer, and the most voracious reader among library users). Charles H. Bacon (Baptist, early fifties, member of the City Council) read eleven, and Ella G. Benedict (Baptist, early forties, unmarried CVS matron) read ten. More than books of any other author, Pansy's titles were read systematically by patrons, who often returned week after week to exchange one title for another. For example, Mamie Aldrich charged out *Divers Women* on 22 October 1892 and *Grandpa's Darlings* on 5 November 1892.[10] Then she took a break from Pansy. But the following spring, in eight successive weeks from 4 March 1893 to 13 May, she charged out six more (*The Pocket Measure, Links in Rebecca's Life, Ester Ried Yet Speaking, Cunning Workmen, Our Commonplace Day*, and *Miss Priscilla Hunter*). She renewed *Ester Ried* once and charged out *Links in Rebecca's Life* on two separate weeks.

Patrons frequently had "runs" on favorite authors, systematically checking out titles by particular authors week after week until they exhausted the supply or their own interest, before shifting to a new author.[11] For example, in February 1893 John Goodbrand (aged thirteen, son of a Scottish-born farmer) checked out two titles by Walter Scott, followed by Eugene Sue's *Mysteries of Paris*, which he renewed once. He then checked out four more titles by Scott in four weeks. His next use of the library took place in December 1893, when he checked out three titles by William Thackeray, renewing two, in the space of five weeks. In eleven weeks between the end of February 1892 and the end of May 1892, Mary Starr (widow, aged fifty-nine, a Methodist born in Germany, living with one son) checked out eleven titles by William Black. In June and July 1892 she checked out only books by the three Brontë sisters—first Anne, then Emily, followed by three titles by Charlotte. In November and December she checked out three titles by Charles Dickens. Between mid-August 1892 and the end of October 1892, Clara Whitley (aged twelve, physician's daughter, Congregationalist) checked out eight titles by Pansy, renewing two. This pattern of behavior seems to reflect a well-organized choice based on experience and enjoyment. While critics of the public library may have deplored some of these choices and especially the speed at which library borrowers moved from one book to another, they would surely at least have approved of this planned, systematic approach to use of the library collection.

Books by Pansy enjoyed a wide readership despite the author's stated aim of targeting her messages at the young. Although 31 percent of the readers were in the twenty-and-under age bracket, 29 percent were over forty, and 5 percent were over sixty. Women were the great majority of readers—over 81 percent. Most readers were also middle class (25 percent from the business and professional group, 48 percent from the white-collar group). However, many with relatively diverse characteristics read one or more titles, including Max Katz, Dr. W. H. H. Gable, Alvin B. Bisbee (Methodist farmer in his sixties), Dr. Lelia O. Goldsworthy (Baptist physician in her thirties), and Erika Anderson (Lutheran, late thirties, Swedish-born wife of a laborer). This diversity vanishes when one concentrates only on the overall picture of Pansy readers as young, female, and middle class. Although largely accurate, such a picture still lacks the detail that brings to life the reading practices of Osage library users.

Another Osage favorite, Miss Mulock, authored such best-sellers as *John Halifax, Gentleman* (1856), and *The Ogilvies* (1849). Born in 1826, Dinah Mulock had a precarious childhood, an experience she drew on again and again in her novels. Her Irish evangelist father was undependable and improvident, and while still a teenager, the now motherless Dinah found herself eking out an impecunious existence in London with her brothers when her father deserted his children. Dinah's writing helped pay the bills, and eventually, with the publication of *John Halifax, Gentleman*, she became well enough known that she could put poverty behind her. Remaining childless after her marriage, throughout her life she was appreciated for her generosity to the poor. Her experiences of a feckless father, a mother's death, and the movement from poverty to comfort were themes that recurred in her novels.[12] In exploring these themes, she did not shrink from confronting issues of class, ethnicity, and the value of conventional Christianity. Her novels *Young Mrs. Jardine* (1879) and *A Brave Lady* (1870) were two of the Sage Library's most frequently charged books, popular with male and female readers of all ages.

Although the central character in *Young Mrs. Jardine* is a man (Roderick Jardine), this is a book about womanhood and the central event in a Victorian woman's life: marriage. Leaving behind a life of fashionable gaiety, the young Roderick (heir to his nouveau riche mother's fortune) travels from his native Scotland to Switzerland in search of a long-lost cousin on his father's side. Having located her with astonishingly little difficulty, he promptly falls in love with her. Significantly, her name is Silence. Miss Mulock invests Silence with all the qualities of a paragon: she has "calm, blue, almost English eyes" and "short, curly fair hair"; she has stolen into Roderick's life like "sunshine or any other blessed silent thing"; not only is she well educated (speaks three languages) but she also sings in "pure high soprano"—in short, she is a "priceless treasure."[13] Moreover, in addition to these conventional attributes of a well-bred, middle-class young woman, she has learned from a life of genteel poverty how to manage on a minuscule income—a quality that proves invaluable to them both when Roderick's mother cuts off his allowance in revenge for his unsuitable match.

In the end, of course, both halves of the family are reconciled, his mother, sister, and Roderick himself transformed by Silence's love and forgiveness. In the meantime, however, Miss Mulock expands on the contrast between these women: on the one hand, the calm, competent, and spiritual Silence and, on the other, Roderick's parvenue, fun-loving, ignorant, and *noisy* mother (who yet has a heart of gold). It is Silence, living her undemanding, unsophisticated life, who focuses on hearth and home, who is the more fulfilled, maintains the author. Her education is valuable in that it enables her to converse with the "old" families of the country and to bring understanding and insight to the problems that beset her husband. Silence models the perfect ancillary.

In *A Brave Lady*, Miss Mulock also focuses on the conflicting demands of marriage and motherhood. The story's main plot concerns a wife's struggle to support her vain and irresponsible husband while trying to feed her children and help the family stay honorably out of debt. The characters are more strongly drawn than in the later work: Edward Scanlon (not coincidentally an Irish clergyman) is a far less worthy character than Roderick Jardine, while his wife, Josephine, questions her marriage and the social position of women in much more radical terms than does the young Silence Jardine. Driven by her husband's embezzlement of the school building fund to plan a permanent separation, Josephine Scanlon consults a book on the question of her legal rights and is appalled to discover that "according as the law of England then stood, and with little modification, now stands, a married woman has no rights at all."[14] Saved from resorting to this disgraceful expedient by an inheritance and her husband's premature descent into dementia, Josephine finds no relief in riches. Her children all die from accident and illness, and eventually she finds herself titled and mistress of a stately home, but alone. But never one to lack resources, in old age she rescues herself from this loveless existence by winning the affection of the local curate's young daughter, Winifred Weston. When after much doubt Winnie finally marries an Irishman—another Edward but, despite his ethnic origin and descent from tradespeople, a kind and honorable man—Miss Mulock not only redeems the Irish male but reconciles class difference and strongly states her vision of marriage as an equal partnership.

Readers of Miss Mulock came from all age groups: 37 percent were over forty, another 41 percent were teenagers. Moreover, 37 percent of the latter group (15 percent of the total) were boys. Louie Davis, for instance, read six of her books. Miss Mulock was much less popular with young men in their twenties, however. Of the one hundred readers between twenty-one and thirty in 1895 (28 percent of the total), only 15 percent were male. The Sage Library possessed nineteen titles by Miss Mulock.[15] Ella M. Johnson (Catholic, in her twenties, married to a clothing merchant, with no children) read the largest number—eight. Several other young women read six or seven. Two men—Frank O. Bronson and William F. Hunt (in his twenties, student son of a stone mason)—both read five. The charges made by Jennie Gutches (the teenage daughter of a "dealer") show a fairly typical pattern of preference for a particular author (see Table 26.3). Jennie interspersed these choices with charges of many of the Sage Library's other most popular authors—A. D. T. Whitney, E. P. Roe, Bertha M. Clay, and Wilkie Collins, for instance. Her charges of Miss Mulock's books show not only that she read several titles by this author but also that she sometimes "revisited" titles. Apparently, patrons quite often reread the same book. Frank Bronson, for example, seems to have read *Young Mrs. Jardine* on three separate occasions. He first charged it out on 27 September 1890 and renewed it the following week. Nearly a year later, however, on 13 June 1891, he charged it out again, renewing it on 20 June. On 29 April 1893, he chose the book yet again, this time keeping it for only one week. Blanche McLaughlin (the teenaged daughter of a carpenter) also chose *A Brave Lady* at three separate times: in September 1890, December 1891, and April 1892.

Many other popular titles were charged out more than once—and sometimes several titles—by the same borrower. *Airy, Fairy, Lilian* was actually charged out ninety times, although by only sixty-seven library users. Lorena Bath checked it out for a week in March 1891 and then again in November of that year. She checked it out for a third time in December 1893 and renewed it the following week. Thirteen-year-old John L. Creelman (son of a harness-maker) checked out *A Broken Wedding Ring* in July 1893 as well as in September of the same year, renewing it again in September. The titles most often charged out more than once were *Airy, Fairy, Lilian, For Another's Sin, Young Mrs. Jardine*, and *An Original Belle*.

Several explanations are possible for repetitious charges. The most straightforward is that the patron needed more than one week to finish the book and therefore renewed it for an additional week. But this seems an inadequate explanation for repetitions several months

Table 26.3 Charges made by Jennie Gutches of books by Miss Mulock

Title	Date
A Brave Lady	07/26/90
John Halifax, Gentleman	10/25/90
Young Mrs. Jardine	11/22/90
Young Mrs. Jardine	11/29/90
Agatha's Husband	12/13/90
Agatha's Husband	12/20/90
My Mother and I	01/17/91
Two Marriages	04/22/93
John Halifax, Gentleman	09/23/93
John Halifax, Gentleman	09/30/93
Mistress and Maid	12/02/93
Mistress and Maid	12/09/93
My Mother and I	12/16/93
Mistress and Maid	02/17/94

or years apart. Most likely is that patrons liked to reread favorite books. The predominant mode of reading seems to have been extensive, in that most patrons changed books every week, reading rapidly a large number of different titles—the typical "library habit of reading." But some readers may have shifted to a somewhat more intensive mode for certain old favorites. The fact that such authors as Miss Mulock relied on a stock of themes and characters that rendered different titles essentially similar supports the view that her readers were perhaps not reading so extensively as might first appear. Both the systematic reading of several titles by the same author and the revisiting of the same title perhaps constituted a sort of intensive mode of reading.[16]

Yet another strong possibility is that books were being passed around among family members. It might be hard for more than one (or at most two) readers to finish a book in a single week, hence the need for multiple charges of the same title. Users may even have been charging out books on a regular basis on behalf of a family member. A library rule may have encouraged cooperative borrowing of this nature. Although I can find no direct evidence that the library limited use to two members of the same house, a 1903 report points strongly to that conclusion. "The Sage Library Board have just revised the regulations of the library and reading room," announced the *Mitchell County Press*. "Under the new rules any resident of Osage not under ten years of age may obtain cards and draw books from the library, except that but three cards can be issued to one family."[17] This announcement implies that before the new rules came into effect, at most only two cardholders were allowed from the same household.[18] Thus in families of more than two, library use was something that had to be shared in a conscious fashion.

While Miss Mulock provides an example of one genre of fiction—the sentimental, domestic novel—another genre was typified by the books of Horatio Alger. Although the most favorite author group does not include Alger, his books nonetheless enjoyed a constant and steady demand. The Sage Library held seven of his titles, three of which are affected by book number problems. Alger books often appeared in series bearing such titles as Frank and Fearless, Luck and Pluck, and Brave and Bold. They formed part of a late-nineteenth-century publishing trend toward boys' stories that glorified masculine ideals of rationality, strength, enterprise, and courage.[19] Alger's books have often been held to symbolize the meteoric rise to success—supposedly the hallmark of the Gilded Age. But his stories also represented nostalgia for a middle-class rural lifestyle that ran contrary to most Americans' experience at the end of the nineteenth century.[20] Alger's fiction reflects a mistrust of industrialization; he casts factory owners in villainous roles and depicts farm and family as the moral order's salvation. In contrast to his distaste for the industrial, Alger affirmed the Protestant virtues of hard work and frugality. However, Alger's heroes often benefited from an element alien to the Protestant ethic: they were frequently lucky. They might, for instance, receive a rich man's benevolence, having saved his daughter from a dire fate. But even luck was a reward for the virtuous. Although in the 1920s Alger's books would be criticized and even derided, in the 1890s they still reflected a middle-class reform mentality that resonated in the rhetoric of Osage newspapers and pulpits.[21]

Perhaps the most popular author among Sage Library patrons was Protestant clergyman E. P. Roe, who turned to writing inspirational stories with considerable financial success and who wrote in a vein similar to Horatio Alger. In 1872 he published his first best-seller, *Barriers Burned Away*, which told a story in the Alger mode. Denis Fleet, a young man from a poor rural background, "rises" to "success" by dint of hard work, honesty, and an act of heroism in the great Chicago fire of 1871. He saves a wealthy young woman who previously considered herself "above" him and thus wins both love and fortune. Denis's background may have lacked material advantages, but Roe is careful to give him educational and spiritual qualifications; these, he implies, have greater value than wealth. Early in the novel, Denis's father, influenced by his pious wife, undergoes a death-bed conversion and so assures himself of eternal salvation. As Denis and his mother stand by the dying man's bedside, they hear, "in faint, far away tones, like an echo from the other side, 'Forgiven!' " At the end of the book, Christine (the wealthy heroine who becomes Denis's wife) is similarly "saved" through espousal of Denis's faith: "She has lost sight of the transient laurel wreath which she sought to grasp at such cost to herself and others, in view of the 'crown of glory that fadeth not away,' and to this already, as an earnest Christian, she has added starry jewels."[22] Roe's language and sentiments followed conventions familiar to his Osage readers. These included the elderly Artemus Hubbard, Lorenzo Rice, and Mary Warburton, as well as younger readers such as Bruce and Guy Sweney. Grace E. Smith was another teenage reader; she checked out the book three times, a few months later using language similar to Roe's to write her classmate's obituary for the *Seminarian*.[23]

E. P. Roe sets *An Original Belle*—perhaps the Sage Library's most popular novel—in the Civil War. The "belle" of the title is Marian Vosburgh, only child of well-to-do parents and courted by any number of eligible young men. By chance she overhears a conversation between the Vosburghs' Irish maid and her working-class suitor. When the Irishman accuses the maid of "flirtin' wid that was an' spakin' swate to the t'other," the young woman defends herself: "Faix, an' I'm no wourse than me young mistress."[24] Appalled, Marian reconsiders her own lifestyle, and decides that being a "conventional" belle is not for her—it is too shallow. As one after another of Marian's admirers depart for the Union army, she makes bravery in the Union cause her touchstone. One who fails to achieve her standard of a "gentleman" is Willard Merwyn, recently returned from Europe, the rich son of a southern mother and a (dead) northern father. In a careless moment Merwyn solemnly promises his mother never to take arms against the South but to keep this oath a secret. When he falls in love with Marian, he can neither pass her bravery test nor explain himself. During the course of the story, Marian's father learns to trust the young Merwyn, though he cannot persuade his "headstrong" daughter to do likewise. When a former suitor sends two "colored" slaves to the Vosburghs' New York house, Marian and her father become the objects of murderous Irish rage during the New York race riots. Merwyn, now the honorable upholder of law and order, comes to their rescue. Though outnumbered (though not outarmed) he takes a stand against the terrifying "mob" and saves Marian's father from assassination, almost at the cost of his own life.

The story is an amalgam of sensation and sermon, mixed with ethnic, racial, and gender prejudice. Long moralizing passages issue from the mouths of Roe's more worthy characters. But Roe alleviates this turgidity by the drama of his battle and mob scenes and via the comic relief provided by the African American and Irish characters. Both speak in a caricature of their native accents; while the Irish let loose plenty of supposedly Catholic-inspired oaths—"Faix" and "By the holy poker"—the African Americans talk in reverent tones about "de Linkum ossifers" and "de gallant sogers and gemlin." In the end, Marian has to agree with her father; she begs Merwyn's forgiveness for misunderstanding him, and after Merwyn's southern mother recognizes the errors of *her* ways, the two young people are united. Thus is the natural order of things reestablished: the (Irish, Catholic) working class is firmly put in its place by the police, the African American servants are grateful but passive recipients of upper-class, white goodwill, and the "ladies" come to realize that the "gentlemen" were right all along.

Although seventy-two different library patrons chose to read *An Original Belle*, the novel failed to attract the same sort of devotion as the books of Miss Mulock. Several patrons found it necessary to renew the title, but none revisited it in the same way that Jennie Gutches, Frank Bronson, and Blanche McLaughlin revisited *Young Mrs. Jardine* or *A Brave Lady*. Perhaps Roe's characters did not elicit the same sort of sympathy as did Silence Jardine and

Josephine Scanlon, or perhaps Osage readers found Roe's continual moralizing less than compelling. The same lack of attachment holds for Roe's other books, including *Barriers Burned Away* and his best-selling *Driven Back to Eden* (with one exception—Grace Smith charged this book out on two separate occasions, a year apart).

Driven Back to Eden was the only novel E.P. Roe wrote explicitly for young people. Echoing a common sentiment of the day, Roe uses the book to condemn the vices and impurities of city life and extol, by contrast, the idylls of the countryside. In his story, the narrator is husband and father in the Durhams, a family that Mr. Durham believes to be suffering from the dangers of the city in which they live. His sons and daughters are up to no good on the streets, while his wife is driven to distraction by anxiety. In particular, his daughter Winnie is led astray by "evil" story-papers loaned her by a neighbor's daughter. To his horror, Durham finds her reading "a cheap vile journal, full of the flashy pictures that so often offend the eye on news-stands." However, he consoles himself, "thank heavens Winnie is only a child and can't understand these pictures." The father tears up the paper and consigns it to "its proper place, the gutter." After seeking the necessary information in books on gardening and the rural life, Mr. Durham moves his family to the country—"Eden"—where "outdoor life and pure air, instead of that breathed over and over," would bring quiet to his wife's nerves and roses back to her cheeks. The rest of the story is a vindication of this decision, and ends with a New Year's celebration at which the father expresses the value of their move to the country: "By pulling all together, there is almost a certainty of our earning more than a bare living and of laying something up for a rainy day. The chief item of profit from our farm, however, is not down in my account-book, but we see it in your sturdier frames and Minnie's red cheeks. . . . Now for the New Year. Let us make the best and most of it, and ask God to help us."[25]

Forty-five patrons checked out this polemic lauding rural life and the Protestant virtues of hard work, thrift, and saving. Of the thirty readers whose religious affiliation is known, twelve were Methodist and thirteen Congregationalist. They were not all young people, however. Of the total forty-five readers, information on age is available for thirty-seven. Fifteen were born before 1870, only two after 1880. And females did not predominate; readers included twenty-four women and twenty-one men. While no one "revisited" this book, its charges demonstrate an interesting pattern of family borrowing. Grace Smith, then in her midteens, checked the book out at the end of 1890, renewing it once. Her eighteen-year-old brother Raymond also borrowed the book at the end of 1890. He first checked it out a week before Grace and then again in the new year, after she had returned it. Similarly, Joseph Billmeyer (aged twenty) and Estella Billmeyer (aged sixteen) monopolized the volume between them for five not-quite-consecutive weeks. First Joseph checked it out on 21 February 1891. The records show that both Joseph and Estella checked the same volume (book number 893) out again two weeks later on 7 March—presumably a clerical error, but an instructive one (it is not hard to imagine the librarian becoming confused or flustered as brother and sister competed for her attention). In any case, on 14 March, Joseph renewed it. And on 21 March, Estella checked it out yet again. One renewal was the limit without incurring a fine, according to the library rule. Did Joseph ask his sister to check out the book for him, since he still had not finished it? Did Estella want the book for herself? Or was the book making the rounds of other family members? Again, a pattern of family borrowing supports the view that books were indeed passed around within families and that close relatives cooperated in the borrowing of books. It also suggests, however, that family members took some responsibility for their own reading and did not simply rely on one member to provide reading for the whole group.

Despite their unimpeachable messages, the works of E. P. Roe failed to meet universal favor either in Osage or the world beyond. Frederick Beecher Perkins gave *Barriers Burned*

Away a "b" in his selection guide, thus ranking it above the works of E. D. E. N. Southworth but below the works of Charles Reade, Walter Scott, or Wilkie Collins.[26] Reviewers were critical of Roe on literary grounds, but his defenders pointed to the moral good produced by his writings. In Lyman Abbott's opinion, "No man, woman, or child ever read through one of Mr. Roe's books and arose without being bettered by the reading." E. P. Roe was one of an informal coalition of middle-class social gospelers, writers of successful literature, and Christian novelists who saw the preservation of Christian values as a bulwark against urbanization and large-scale enterprise.[27] In many ways, Sage Public Library users were the ideal audience for Christian success genre writings, directed as these were to middle-class, American-born Protestants. Christian success authors, with their nativist leanings, held up as an ideal by the independent farmers, merchants, and craftworkers who formed the bulk of Osage's population. This literature was anachronistic, but from the perspective of Osage's Protestant middle class, it had real meaning. These people encountered Protestant evangelical language combined with exhortations to self-improvement on a daily basis in the booster press and churches, and when they had the chance they themselves wrote in a similar vein.[28]

In the 1890s, Osage inhabitants probably sensed that problems of urbanization and industrialization were far from their own daily lives, but in their reading choices—as well as through their local newspapers—they chose to confront them by proxy. Perhaps they felt a sense of satisfaction at the proposed remedy, however unrealistic. After all, realist authors such as Hamlin Garland, who had firsthand knowledge of the hardships and deprivations of rural life, were already criticizing the rural idyll represented in E. P. Roe's works and in school textbooks. In 1893 the Sage collection contained no books by Garland, and although in the early 1890s townspeople were aware of him and proud of his writing success, it is unclear how many had read his work. By 1890 several short stories had appeared in the *Arena* and the *Century* (both available in the Sage Library), and his first published book, *Main-Travelled Roads*, came out in 1891. That summer, Garland gave a talk at the Osage Baptist Church titled "The New American Novel," in which he acquainted Osage inhabitants with the unfamiliar genre.[29]

As town dwellers, the majority may have supported the "rural idyll" view, turning their backs on the "reality" beyond the city boundaries. Some criticized the realist view Garland and other authors espoused for contradicting the prevailing booster ethos peddled by the local newspapers. "Any one who imagines the farmer in Iowa is in straightened circumstances should take a drive in the country and note the existence of prosperity to be seen everywhere," admonished the *Mitchell County Press* in 1892. "New houses, substantial barns and other improvements denote quite plainly that the farmers of Mitchell County at least are enjoying deserved prosperity." In 1895 the *Sun* quoted an address by Congregational pastor William Gist to the New Haven Congregational Club in which he, too, tried to refute Garland's negative picture: "Hamlin Garland, however great a writer he may be, in so far as he attempts to picture farm life in Iowa is wrong. I happen to live in the same town where Hamlin Garland grew to manhood."[30]

[. . .]

Family reading records suggest that for many inhabitants library use was a cooperative affair, as different family members rotated library cards and shared books. And reading must have taken on a communal aspect in homes where warm, well-lit space was limited. Electric light reached some Osage streets and businesses by the early 1890s, but it was many years before electricity was common in the homes of any but the most affluent. During the long, cold winter evenings, many families read by the light of one or two lamps in the only well-heated room in the house (in middle-class homes, probably the parlor). Neither could individual family members expect much privacy at home. Census data show that nuclear families tended to be large; in addition, the household often included extended family members, boarders, or employees. Thus a solitary reader in Osage was a remarkably privileged one. Although the Sage Library users generally were more affluent than most of the community, their affluence was relative: it did not include electric light and central heating in more than a handful of homes until after the turn of the century. And few Sage Library patrons inhabited mansions.

Clerk of the Court Frank Bronson and daughters Birdie and Blanche (aged fourteen and twelve years old, respectively, in 1890) charged out 377 books during the borrowing period 1890–95. Frank's wife, Ella, did not then hold a library card. Of the three, Birdie was the most prolific reader (180 charges), but her father was responsible for 114, while Blanche charged out 83. Between 1890 and 1891 Frank and Birdie visited the library together virtually every week (Birdie missed only one week, Frank missed four). During the following year, Birdie maintained her rate of reading, but Frank's fell off sharply. Blanche started to use the library in July 1892, Frank evidently having relinquished his card to her, for the two girls were in the library practically every week. During the fourth year (1893–94), however, Birdie checked out no books, and father and sister Blanche resumed their old reading pattern, checking out books weekly. Blanche was responsible for fifty-two charges during this fourth year, while Frank missed only two weeks. In the fifth year Frank was absent from the circulation records, but Birdie was back and again charging out many books. She and Blanche missed only five weeks between them.

If the Bronsons were making reading choices mainly for themselves, all three shared a taste in reading. Birdie's and Frank's favorite authors included Wilkie Collins and Miss Mulock. Birdie charged out books by Wilkie Collins thirteen times, and Frank, four times. Frank charged out ten volumes of Miss Mulock, including five charges of *Young Mrs. Jardine* at three separate times (the five charges include two renewals). Birdie made six charges of Miss Mulock. They both also liked Bertha M. Clay: Frank and Birdie checked out *For Another's Sin* three times each and *A Broken Wedding Ring* three times between them (Birdie was responsible for two charges). Blanche's favorite author was Oliver Optic (six charges), although Birdie checked out even more books by Oliver Optic than her younger sister—seven charges. All three Bronsons favored A. D. T. Whitney; Birdie made four charges, including one renewal, and Blanche and Frank made three each (including one renewal each). However, a strong possibility exists that library cardholders took the preferences of others into consideration when choosing their weekly book. The Bronsons may have been choosing books on behalf of Ella or at least bearing her tastes in mind. Whether they were picking books for themselves or for general family reading, it seems likely that they were doing so on the basis of a taste they held in common, not one strongly differentiated on the basis of age or gender.

This pattern of apparent rotation of library cards also shows up in the reading records of other families. In physician John L. Whitney's household, younger members usually visited the library in the company of their mother, Ada. Four Whitneys made a total of 322 charges between 1890 and 1895. In the first year, Ada accompanied her twelve-year-old son, Roy. The following year (1891 to 1892), however, Ada checked out no books, and Roy went with older brother Ralph, then in his late teens. The two boys' record shows an identical charge pattern; both charged out a book a week for the entire year, except for the same three weeks in July and August and two weeks in the New Year. In 1892 to 1893, Ralph was probably away at college (he studied at Grinnell in the early 1890s and by 1895 was at medical school in Chicago). Early in the year Roy made library trips with his sister, Clara, three years younger. After the summer, however, Roy's visits stopped. By this time he was sixteen or seventeen, and perhaps he too went away to school in the fall. In 1893 to 1894, Roy hardly used the library, although Clara was a frequent visitor. From 1894 to 1895 Ada started to use the library again; she and Clara charged out books mostly on the same dates, and on the whole their absences also coincided.

Despite their age difference, Roy's and Ralph's reading was not dissimilar. In March 1892 Ralph started reading Elijah Kellogg's books by checking out *The Young Ship Builders*. The following week he exchanged this for *The Hardscrabble*. The following two weeks Roy checked out *The Young Deliverers* and *Child of the Island Glen*, while in the two weeks after that first Ralph and then Roy checked out *Wolf Run*. It is hardly plausible the two brothers acted independently. Probably they both read the books that came home, no matter who was "responsible" for them. The fact that they checked out the same book in successive weeks suggests they were cooperating in their borrowing. But it also indicates that each was acting primarily on his own behalf. Such a borrowing pattern, as well as the sheer number of books borrowed, strongly suggests that borrowers actually read what they checked out. It is implausible to think people would go to the trouble of visiting the library on a weekly basis throughout the year to check out a single title they then failed to read.

Bert Sides and his nephew George Stillman (only four years his junior) provide the most poignant example of a family reading pattern. The Sides family was extraordinarily unfortunate even in those times of early and unexpected death. Of nine children, seven had died by the mid-1890s, including three library users. Twenty-two-year-old Minnie died unexpectedly in a matter of days; Joe also died suddenly while attending Cornell College, and sister Mrs. A. Stillman died of tuberculosis, leaving grandparents to raise her young sons, of whom George was the first. Of all the members of the family, Bert was the most active reader. From 1890 to 1895 he checked out 186 volumes. Particularly noteworthy, however, is the way his reading pattern intertwined with George's. For the period April 1893 through the end of March 1895, the two teenage boys visited the library almost weekly. Much of their reading consisted of popular novels, but some charges were quite idiosyncratic. For example, they were the only two teenagers to charge out J. S. C. Abbott's *Life of Napoleon Bonaparte*, between them accounting for twenty charges.[31] They must have been fond of history, for in August 1894 George checked out William Napier's *Peninsula War*, volume 1, while Bert checked out volume 2. Both boys read Froude's popular *History of England*, but they also read de Tocqueville, Disraeli, and Macaulay, all far from popular—at least in Osage. The two clearly collaborated in their reading: Bert probably influenced his nephew.

These family reading patterns suggest that library readers were often influenced in their selection of books by relatives. Household members (including boarders and employees) likely passed books around in a sort of informal circulation system. Although family influence cannot entirely account for fuzziness in age and gender demarcation in reading patterns (some patrons lived alone or lived only with others of the same age or sex), analysis of family use suggests a social context for reading and cautions against interpreting reading solely in terms of individual preference. Reading was—and is—a social activity; people derive meaning from this activity at least in part through such social practices as sharing books with others, sharing opinions and recommendations of books with others, and following social trends expressed through the phenomenon of the best-seller.

References

1   Some notable exceptions existed. Ariel K. Eaton, Laura Eaton's octogenarian father-in-law, made thirty-one charges between July 1892 and March 1894. Of these, all but two consisted of volumes 3, 4, and 5 of Hildreth's *History of the United States*. Eaton was writing a local history, parts of which were published in area newspapers, and his public library use contributed to this research.

2   Thus, for example, seventy-seven different individuals borrowed one or more volumes of James A. Froude's twelve-volume *History of England* during the five one-year borrowing periods. Because of "ties," twenty-one different titles are listed in the table. The next title in the table would be ranked number 21.

3   Some inconsistencies limit the *Catalog*'s usefulness in this respect. The *Catalog* includes Miss Mulock's *Brave Lady* but not *Young Mrs. Jardine*. Similarly, it includes A. D. T. Whitney's *Faith Gartney's Girlhood* but not *Sights and Insights* or *Odd or Even*. The ALA selectors limited themselves to a total of about five thousand titles. They probably made a choice to exclude some titles of "acceptable" but prolific authors in the interest of diversity. Thus, inclusion in the *Catalog* is only a rough guide as to cultural acceptability.

4   Frank Luther Mott has set out criteria for judging whether a book qualified as a "best" or "better"-seller. A best-seller was a book that likely had a total sale "equal to one per cent of the population of continental United States for the decade in which it was published." He excludes certain classes: "Bibles, hymnals, journals, text-books, almanacs, cookbooks, doctor-books, manuals and reference works." Better-sellers were "runners-up believed not to have reached the total sales required for the over-all best sellers" (Mott, *Golden Multitudes: The Story of Best Sellers in the United States* [New York: Macmillan, 1947], 303, 315).

5   *Catalog of "A.L.A." Library*. Several works of J. T. Trowbridge were included in the *Catalog*, though not *His Own Master*.

6   "Report of the Young Men's Association of Buffalo," in *Library Journal*, 7 (July–August 1882): 175–76, quoted in Carrier, *Fiction in Public Libraries*, 119–20, 121.

7   Denning, *Mechanic Accents*, 23–24. See also Mary Noel, *Villains Galore: The Heyday of the Popular Story Weekly* (New York: Macmillan, 1954), 186–90.

8   James Anthony Froude, *History of England from the Fall of Wolsey to the Death of Elizabeth* (New York: Charles Scribner, 1870).

9   "Mr. Froude's History of England," *Catholic World* 11, no. 63 (1870): 289–306.

10   No census information is available on this patron.

11   Emily B. Todd has tentatively dubbed this type of systematic reading "binge reading" in " 'Binge Reading' and Historical Fiction: A Study of the Richmond Library Company's Borrowing Records (1839–1860)" (paper presented at the annual meeting of the Society for the History of Authorship, Reading, and Publishing, Madison, Wisconsin, July 1999). Todd's research supports the belief that library patrons did actually read what they charged out and that patrons charged books mostly to read silently to themselves. Although Sage Library patrons were restricted to one book a week, the library users in Todd's study were permitted to return on consecutive days to exchange books. Such speedy "consumption" suggests that readers were reading to themselves rather than reading out loud to others.

12   Elaine Showalter, "Dinah Mulock Craik and the Tactics of Sentiment: A Case Study in Victorian Female Authorship," *Feminist Studies* 2, nos. 2/3 (1975): 5–23.

13   Miss Mulock, *Young Mrs. Jardine*, 3 vols. (London: Hurst and Blackett, 1879), 1:95, 138, 84, 126.

14   Miss Mulock, *A Brave Lady* (New York: Harper and Brothers, 1870), 100.

15   One title, affected by the multiple book number problem, cannot be considered here.

16   Wayne Wiegand, private discussion, 1999.

17   *Mitchell County Press*, 4 January 1903.

18   Further implications of this rule for family borrowing patterns are further discussed below.

19   Kimberley Reynolds, *Girls Only? Gender and Popular Children's Fiction in Britain, 1880–1910* (Philadelphia: Temple University Press, 1990), 51.

20   Jackson Lears records that late-nineteenth-century advertising images similarly reflected "sentimental agrarianism," thus reassuring the newly urbanized: "The same incipient media culture that popularized the rhetoric of domesticity in ladies' magazines also represented the visual embodiments of the domestic ideal; the old homeplace, the vine-covered cottage, the still point of the turning world" (*Fables of Abundance: A Cultural History of Advertising in America* [New York: Basic, 1994], 102–3).

21   See the discussion in Richard Weiss, *The American Myth of Success* (New York: Basic, 1969), esp. 53–56.

22   E. P. Roe, *Barriers Burned Away*, Warne's Star Series no. 59, 12, 341.

23   See Christine Pawley, *Reading on the Middle Border: The Culture of Print in Late-Nineteenth-Century Osage, Iowa* (Amherst: University of Massachusetts Press, 2001), chapter 2, pp. 39–60.

24   E. P. Roe, *An Original Belle* (New York: P. F. Collier and Son, 1902), 23.

25   E. P. Roe, *Driven Back to Eden* (London: Ward, Lock, 1885), 3–4, 13, 275.

26   Perkins also gave a "b" to the works of Herman Melville, Anthony Trollope, and Emily and Anne Brontë, so the classification cannot be read as corresponding entirely to modern canonical judgments of literary taste.

27   Lyman Abbott, quoted in Weiss, *American Myth of Success*, 69.

28   Ibid., 116.

29   *Osage News*, 21 July 1891.

30   *Mitchell County Press*, 4 August 1892; *Osage Sun*, 20 October 1895.

31   Although little evidence exists for a general interest in Napoleon among Osage library users, Matthew Schneirov points out that nationwide, Napoleon approached the status of a cult figure: "Accounts of Napoleon's life and anyone remotely related to him appeared frequently in popular and genteel magazines during the 1890s. In addition to the magazine articles, there were twenty-eight books about Napoleon published between 1894 and 1896." Schneirov links this interest with a common popular magazine focus on the "masculine" virtues of strength and action, expressed in biographies of military heroes (Schneirov, *Dream of a New Social Order*, 155).

Chapter 27

Elizabeth McHenry

"AN ASSOCIATION OF KINDRED SPIRITS": BLACK READERS AND THEIR READING ROOMS

THAT FREE BLACKS FELT IT a priority to circulate printed texts in part by forming and sustaining reading rooms and libraries suggests the extent to which they believed in the power of the written word and the importance of literary study. Like their enslaved brethren in the South, antebellum free blacks in the urban North recognized that reading was a potentially transforming activity, not only for individuals but also for society as a whole. Literary and intellectual contributions, they believed, would disprove the discourse of black intellectual inferiority, altering the standing of African Americans in American society. Taking part in educational programs and exhibiting publicly voices that were "learned," free blacks believed, would enable them to make economic gains and move into trades from which their people were largely excluded. In the first decades of the nineteenth century black leaders increasingly expressed concern that "we have not produced any to excel in arts and sciences." "What station above the common employment of craftsmen and labourers would we fill," they wondered, "did we possess both learning and abilities?"[1] In the midst of a dominant society for whom knowledge of the arts, sciences, and literature was highly valued, free blacks became increasingly aware that they needed to read widely and produce documents that were sophisticated in their presentation as well as their content. At the beginning of the nineteenth century they began establishing independent societies to promote literary skills and to ensure that, as a group, they would not be excluded from the benefits associated with reading and literary study.

The literary societies they formed between 1828 and 1860 were at the heart of a political agenda for promoting opportunities and equality for the nation's free black population that was grounded in African American literary practice. Literary societies were both large and small; they planned reading lists and provided regular opportunities for black writers to publish original creations, both orally and in print. Members ensured the development of their literary skills by supporting one another while also maintaining an environment where ideas could be openly discussed and critiqued. The libraries and reading rooms established by these institutions were central to their activities and to the fulfillment of their objectives. They were locations where books and other printed texts and materials were housed; but more important, they were social locations where reading led to conversation and printed texts of all varieties could be enjoyed, discussed, and debated in the company of others.

So central was the library to the objectives of one of the earliest African American literary societies, the Colored Reading Society, formed in 1828 for "Men of Colour, who are citizens of the City and the Liberties of Philadelphia," that the rules and regulations surrounding its establishment and use dominated the society's constitution.[2] Members were to pay an initiation fee and monthly dues; "with the exception of light [and] rent," this income was to be spent entirely on books. "All monies received by this Society," reads the constitution, were "to be expended in useful books, such as the Society may from time to time appropriate." The constitution went on to specify that "all books initiated into this Society, shall be placed in the care of the Librarian belonging to said institution," whose duty it was "to deliver to said members alternatively, such books as they shall demand." The librarian was also to pay "strict regard that no member shall keep said book out of the library longer than one week, without paying the fine prescribed in the constitution, unless an apology for sickness or absence." Members were reminded more than once that "those shall be the only excuses received."[3] They agreed to "meet once a week to return and receive books, to read, and express whatever sentiments they may have conceived if they think proper, and transact the necessary business relative to this institution. . . . It shall be our whole duty," they resolved, "to instruct and assist each other in the improvement of our minds, as we wish to see the flame of improvement spreading amongst our brethren and friends" (Whipper, *Address*, 108).

The guiding principle of Philadelphia's Colored Reading Society was that "the station of a scholar highly versed in classic lore . . . is indeed higher than any other occupied by man." Members looked to fill their library with texts that would allow them to cultivate both intellectual competence and artistic sensibility. They subscribed to the belief that the "acquisition of knowledge is not the only design of a liberal arts education;" in addition to amassing knowledge, a goal of their reading and their selection of texts was to "discipline the mind itself, to strengthen and enlarge its powers, to form habits of close and accurate thinking, and to acquire a facility of classifying and arranging, analyzing and comparing our ideas on different subjects" (Whipper, *Address*, 110). The "cultivation of taste" required attention to "the study of belle lettres, to criticism, to composition, pronunciation, style, and to everything included in the name of eloquence" (Whipper, *Address*, 113). They believed that classical texts would facilitate the fulfillment of their ambition. From these texts, "a fund of ideas is acquired on a variety of subjects; the taste is greatly improved by conversing with the best models; the imagination is enriched by the fine scenery with which the classics abound; and an acquaintance is formed with human nature, together with the history, customs, and manners of antiquity" (Whipper, *Address*, 111). In addition to the classics and works by "our best English writers," the society filled its library with "books treating . . . the subject of Ancient Modern and Ecclesiastical History, [and] the Laws of Pennsylvania." It also subscribed to two of the most important journals of the time, the abolitionist publication the *Genius of Universal Emancipation* and the first African American newspaper, *Freedom's Journal*.[4] The founders of the Colored Reading Society believed that exposure to all of these texts and the conversations they inspired would allow the society's membership to "contribut[e] something to the advancement of science [and literature] generally amongst our brethren," while also providing opportunities to "become acquainted with the transacting of public affairs" (Whipper, *Address*, 118, 110).

Like that of most early African American literary associations and their libraries, the fate of the Colored Reading Society is uncertain.[5] One of its founding members, William Whipper, was a part of a group that began the Philadelphia Library Company of Colored Persons in 1833, which suggests that the Library Company of Colored Persons may have absorbed the membership of the Colored Reading Society. Modeled after the Library Company of Philadelphia, begun by Benjamin Franklin in 1731 for "literary and scientific discussion, the reading of original essays, poems, and so forth," the membership of the Library Company of Colored Persons was composed of free black men.[6] From its first announcement, the Library Company of Colored Persons boasted that it was neither "sectarian" nor "a mere fractional effort, the design of any single society among us." Rather, the Library Company was formed in recognition of the "necessity of promoting among our rising youth, a proper cultivation for literary pursuits and improvements of the faculties and powers of their minds," and designed "to embrace the entire population of the City of Philadelphia."[7] A request for "such books and other donations as will facilitate the object of this institution" accompanied the public announcement of the organization. Books and other printed texts were to be made accessible at minimal cost. Members could read on their own or participate in a reading schedule. In addition, in order to promote research, discussion, and debate, the Library Company sponsored a weekly lecture series, which ran from October through May. The Library Company of Colored Persons was still a strong institution in 1837, when James Forten, Jr., at a meeting of the Moral Reform Society, cited it as an example of the state of learning among the colored population in Philadelphia. "Our Library Association is gaining strength every day," he reported. "We have a well supplied stock of books collected from the most useful and varied productions of the age."[8] By 1838 the Library Company had more than 600 volumes in its collection and at least 150 members.[9]

Although the Library Company of Colored Persons was organized by Philadelphia's black elite, the impact of its activities, like readings and lectures that were open to the public, reverberated throughout a larger segment of the black population. It shared with societies composed of less distinguished individuals the common understanding that the "condition" of African Americans could "only be meliorated by their being improved in morals, literature, and the mechanic arts."[10] The founders of New York's Phoenix Society, organized in 1833, called on "every person of color to unite himself, or herself, to [the Phoenix Society], and faithfully endeavor to promote its objects" (Phoenix 141). To facilitate this, the society had a unique policy on fees: its constitution stipulated that membership would be open to "all persons who contributed to its funds quarterly, any sum of money they may think proper." The ultimate goal of the Phoenix Society was to transform New York City's entire black population into a "useful portion of the community" (Phoenix 141). To do this they planned to "establish circulating libraries in each ward for the use of people of color on very moderate pay—to establish mental feasts, and also lyceums for speaking and for lectures on sciences" (Phoenix 144).

It took only eight months for the Phoenix Society to begin fulfilling its goals. In a letter dated December 7, 1833, and printed in the *Colonizationist and Journal of Freedom*, Samuel Cornish, a coeditor of *Freedom's Journal*, and one of the founders of the Phoenix Society, outlined the goals and activities of the "library and Reading Room lately opened by the executive committee of the Phœnix Society." "The objects of the institution are generally improvement and the training of our youth to habits of reading and reflection," he explained.[11] Cornish's letter to the *Colonizationist and Journal of Freedom* includes an appeal for "donations from the favored people of New York, in books, maps, papers, money, etc., for the benefit of our feeble institution." The variety of printed materials Cornish lists—all considered worthy of a place in the newly formed library—offers some indication of the broad definition of what were considered valuable texts by black leaders in their attempt to establish literary culture in antebellum black communities. The acknowledgment of a number of donations in a February 1834 issue of the *Emancipator* indicates that his appeal was well received.[12] The Phoenix Society's library was reported to be a "good collection of valuable books" that included "much that is rare and choice in English Literature [and] a considerable amount of History and Science."[13] This was the library in which the anonymous member of the Phoenixonian Literary Society expressed interest after hearing of the Phoenix Society's demise; there is no record of any response to his query, and the fate of the Phoenix Society's library remains unknown.

It bears drawing attention to the Phoenix Society's emphasis on training African Americans in "habits of reading and reflection," for the distinction between this and more basic lessons in literacy offers important insight into the multiple purposes of the earliest African American literary societies and their libraries. In addition to "courses of lectures . . . on morals, economy, and the arts and sciences generally," the society offered three "class[es] of readers," each consisting of "25 or 30 or more." Each class was to have "selected its course of reading and appointed the readers, whose duty it shall be to read for one hour. All classes shall note prominent parts, and then retire into the adjacent room to converse on the subjects, together with occurrences of the day, calculated to cultivate the mind and improve the heart."[14] Rather than the acquisition of basic literacy, the emphasis in this description of the Phoenix Society's offerings is on the sharing of texts and the discussions that might then subsequently take place. Because the text was read aloud by an appointed "reader," it was possible to form a "class" that included those with various levels of literacy; indeed, it is likely that there were people in the Phoenix Society's "classes of readers" who were themselves technically illiterate. Because the silent reading of the text was not privileged over its oral performance, literate, semiliterate, and even illiterate members of the Phoenix Society could appreciate a text, and the discussions that followed its reading could involve those who listened to the text's performance as well as those with the ability to read it for themselves. The objectives of some of the earliest African American literary societies, libraries, and reading rooms had less to do with the development of basic literary skills than they did with cultivating the mind by fostering basic literary skills, that is, those skills that derive from exposure to texts and the rigorous critical analysis and discussions that they prompt.

Rather than a means of training individuals in basic literacy, the pursuit of literary culture that culminated in the development of African American literary societies, libraries, and reading rooms in the antebellum United States was geared toward helping their members prove, through their literary activities, the capacity of the black mind by demonstrating a propensity for developing what one early contributor to the black press called "a literary character."[15] Simply put, association with literature and literary study offered free black Americans in the urban North a way to refute widespread claims of their innate inferiority. Displays of literary character would mark black Americans as public and refined figures, giving them the positive reputation that would, in the words of one black leader, "arrest the progress of prejudice, and . . . shield [the free black community] against the consequent evils."[16] Literary study would provide free blacks with the tools needed to represent themselves more fairly and accurately and lead to the "[g]ood principles [that] will soon break down the barriers between [the black] and the white population."[17]

Additionally, reading, library use, and organized literary study were promoted as positive alternatives to the host of negative and "immoral" distractions that faced the free black community daily. Particular concern was expressed again and again for what one anonymous contributor to the *Colored American* described as "the rising generation," by which was meant those "young men whose evenings are unemployed, and who now spend their leisure hours in the theatre or porter house (which leads to the brothel and gaming tables)." In an article titled "Literary Societies," this writer called these institutions "of more importance than any others in the present age of Societies and Associations." With more of them in the black community, susceptible young men "might be induced to make the reading room their place of resort, and thus instead of injuring their health, wasting their money, and acquiring immoral habits, they might be storing their minds with useful knowledge, and erecting a reputation which would be far superior to the ephemeral renown which pleasure confers on their votaries, and they might also establish for themselves a character which time itself could not destroy."[18] Developing literary character, the components of which included morality, self-discipline, intellectual curiosity, civic responsibility, and eloquence, was cast as both a private virtue and a civic duty; it benefited the individual, but it was essential for the common good as well. In developing literary talents, individual black people contributed not only to their own improvement, but also to the advancement of their race.

Announcements of new opportunities for literary study and interaction that expressed similar concern for the many obstacles to the development of literary character in the black community appeared regularly in African American newspapers in the 1830s. Like the one placed by antislavery activist and journalist David Ruggles in the 16 June 1838 issue of the *Colored American* (see figure 27.1), most made reference both to the distractions of urban life and to the difficulties of finding access to literary texts or appropriate environments for their

--▸▸▸●◗●◂◂◂--
CIRCULAR.

Reading Room at the office of the New York Committee of Vigilance, at the corner of Lispenard and Church Streets, New York city.

As moral virtue is the standard of good society, it is evident that no society can possess it without intelligence; that intelligence can only be acquired by observation, reading and reflection, and as the present and future prosperity of young men in this community,— (whose characters are forming for good or evil) whose complexion furnish an apology for our fairer and more favored citizens to exclude them from Reading Rooms, popular lectures, and all places of literary attractions and general improvement, and as the prosperity and the existence of good society depends upon our intelligence and virtue;—the subscriber is impressed with the fact that without some centre of literary attraction for all young men whose mental appetites thirst for food, many are in danger of being led into idle and licentious habits by the allurements of vice which surround them on every side, Therefore, deprecating the condition of our youth, and from a sense of duty which is due from every friend of intelligenee and good society, I have opened a *READING ROOM*, where those who wish to avail themselves of the opportunity, can have access to the principal daily and leading anti-slavery papers, and other popular periodicals of the day. We hope that the friends of literary improvement, among all classes of our citizens, in this part of the city, will encourage our enterprise.

Terms of Subscription, payable in advance.—$2,75 per annum; $1,37½ per six months; 25 cents per month; 6¼ cents per week.

☞ Strangers visiting this city can have access to the Reading Room, free of charge.

N. York, May 1st, 1838.   DAVID RUGGLES.

☞Editors of newspapers, friendly to human improvement, will please copy the above.   D. R.

--▸▸▸●◗●◂◂◂--

Figure 27.1 David Ruggles announces the opening of his Reading Room. From the *Colored American*, 16 June 1838, 69. Reproduced by permission of the American Antiquarian Society.

appreciation. Observing that "intelligence can only be acquired by observation, reading and reflection," Ruggles condemned the exclusion of African Americans "from Reading Rooms, popular lectures, and all places of literary attractions and general improvement" by those he termed "our fairer and more favored citizens." He expressed the commonly held fear that "without some centre of literary attraction for all young men whose mental appetites thirst for food, many are in danger of being led into idle and licentious habits by the allurements of vice which surround them on every side." Ruggles's effort to remedy this situation centered on the opening of a "READING ROOM, where those who wish to avail themselves of the opportunity, can have access to the principal daily and leading anti-slavery papers, and other popular periodicals of the day." The conclusion of his announcement served as an invitation to participate in the activities of the reading room: "We hope that the friends of literary improvement, among all classes of our citizens, in this part of the city, will encourage our enterprise."[19] Inherent in this and similar announcements that appeared in the newspapers of the time is the insistence that literary texts and the institutions that would provide access to them were vital to the "present and future prosperity of young men in this community."[20]

It is notable that almost every antebellum African American library or reading room for which there are extant records included in its holdings products of the African American press, and it is this source that shows precisely what free blacks were reading. Despite the apparent success of public appeals by newly formed African American literary organizations for the donation of bound books, the very fact that these were sought in this manner points to the fact that books were expensive and thus relatively difficult to procure. It is also notable that most of the bound books included in the library were publications by European and primarily English authors, a fact that supports the idea that one aim of African American libraries and reading rooms was to help their users enter the literary mainstream. But after 1827, when *Freedom's Journal* made its inaugural appearance, African American newspapers were in almost constant production, and the very diversity of their content made them desirable components of local libraries and reading rooms. By including productions of the African American press, libraries and reading rooms affirmed their dedication to serving specifically African American interests and concerns as well as the more general needs of the community. Stories that appeared in two of the most prominent early African American newspapers, *Freedom's Journal*, which ceased publication in 1829, and the *Colored American*, published between 1837 and 1841, provided the free black community with narratives and reports that were educational tools in themselves, supplying their readers with a steady stream of interesting reading material that was consumable by a readership of various ages and literacy levels. The vignettes included in the newspaper were interesting and compelling, if often sensational. Brief enough to be consumed in short periods of time, they were also convenient to read aloud. Stories included in *Freedom's Journal* were written for sharing, in a format that lent itself to their being read aloud. In addition to their informational value, these features made the newspapers important resources for newly literate and semiliterate readers. The newspapers were perhaps most valuable for their adult readers, for whom the acquisition of education was a more independent endeavor. But they were also important tools in formal educational institutions that served free black youth. Although by 1830, New York's African Free School on Mulberry Street claimed that its library included over 450 volumes, the school also received *Freedom's Journal* and recognized it as an invaluable part of the collection.[21] When Charles C. Andrews, a teacher at the school, wrote to the editors of *Freedom's Journal* to thank them for "furnishing gratuitously, the regular weekly numbers of the 'Freedom's Journal,' for the benefit of the Library in the School" (see figure 27.2), he assured them that the newspaper was being put to use: "much good," he reported, "may be calculated to result from such a journal being perused by *such readers*, as will have access to its pages."[22]

NEW-YORK AFRICAN FREE SCHOOL

MR. JOHN B. RUSSWURM.

DEAR SIR—It becomes my pleasing duty, at the request of the Board of Trustees of the *"New-York African Free School,"* to acknowledge, in their behalf, your generosity in furnishing gratuitously, the regular weekly numbers of the *"Freedom's Journal,"* for the benefit of the Library in the School in Mulberry-street.

I do this with great satisfaction, first, because the act which merits it bespeaks a liberal heart; and, secondly, because much good may be calculated to result from *such a journal* being perused by *such readers*, as will have access to its pages.

It cannot but be acceptable to you, Sir, to be informed, that our Library now consists of about three hundred well selected volumes. Allow me, in this place, to relate the following pleasing fact.

One of our little scholars, aged about ten years, was questioned on some astronomical and other scientific subjects a few months ago, by a celebrated and learned doctor of this city; the boy answered so readily and so accurately to the queries, was at last asked, how it was that he was so well acquainted with such subjects? His reply was, that he remembered to have read of them in the books of the School Library.

Very respectfully,

CHARLES C. ANDREWS,

Teacher of African Free School, No. 2.

Figure 27.2 A letter of thanks to John Brown Russwurm for donating copies of his newspaper to a school. *Freedom's Journal*, 9 November 1827. Reproduced by permission of the American Antiquarian Society.

In many ways, both *Freedom's Journal* and the *Colored American* were designed to serve as libraries unto themselves, supplying their weekly readers with the variety of texts that replicated on a smaller scale what might have been found in a well-stocked European-American reading room. Like curators or librarians, whose acquisition and control of material give shape to a collection, the editors of the earliest African American newspapers acted as stewards of literary culture, considering themselves responsible for shaping the reading choices and influencing the practices of black readers. The editors of *Freedom's Journal* promised readers that a central function of their publication would be to assist their readers in selecting "such authors as will not only enlarge their stock of useful knowledge, but such as will also serve to stimulate them to higher attainments in science." This service would help readers avoid "time . . . lost, and wrong principles instilled, by the perusal of works of trivial importance."[23] Evident in this promise is the extent to which *Freedom's Journal* sought to guide its readers in their selection of texts. Articles included in the newspaper were exemplary of the ways a written text might serve as a manual to self-improvement and the standards of good character and "respectable" behavior. Titles such as "Formation of Character," "Duty of Wives," "Duties of Children," "Accurate Judgment," and "Economy" suggest that the editors of the newspaper believed they should seek to strengthen the moral condition of the individual, the race, and the nation.[24]

Freedom's Journal promoted literary study as an alternative to idleness and moral decay; the *Colored American* also did this, but was more self-conscious in its presentation of itself as a substitute for those without access to other sources of reading material. "Our people must be supplied with mental resources," insisted the writer of an introductory editorial to the newspaper. Editors of the *Colored American* agreed, offering the weekly publication to the free black population as a means of access to these needed resources. In addition to exposure to literary texts, one form of needed knowledge among the *Colored American's* target population was perceived to be a certain level of cultural literacy, not only about their own expanding and prosperous democracy but about the distant regions increasingly within the national consciousness. The first three issues of the paper included a series of articles written for the *New York Weekly Advocate* on various historical and organizational aspects of the United States. After recounting the general history of the country from its "discovery," these articles outlined the origins and relevant statistics of each state. Included in the information communicated in this series as "useful for present and future reference" was the structure of local and federal government, anticipated population figures for the various states in 1837 based on the population in 1830, and a listing of the "Vessels of War, in the United States Navy, 1836." Subsequent issues of the *Colored American* feature an extensive article titled "Principal Features of the Various Nations on Earth," compiled specifically for the newspaper, as well as a biographical sketch of Benjamin Franklin. By offering its readers a kind of advanced course of study on national history, state statistics, and eminent American lives, the *Colored American* was implicitly demonstrating the kind of cultural literacy its editors believed necessary for creating an informed African American citizenry.[25]

Like the material libraries and reading rooms that existed in black communities, the *Colored American* aspired to supply its readers with lasting access to texts that would be central to their acquisition of "useful knowledge" while also providing a basis for engagement with others in productive conversation. Singlehandedly, it fulfilled the role of a reading room by distributing texts on a diverse range of subjects to an audience that could then come together to discuss and debate what they had read. In this, the *Colored American* considered itself a valuable resource that should be preserved for future rereading and later reference. Beginning with the first issue, the editors regularly published this reminder to "File Your Papers:" "As the advocate will not only be devoted to the passing events of the day, but also in a great measure to useful and entertaining general matter, which may be perused at any future time with as much interest as at the present, we would suggest to our readers the importance of preserving a file of the journal. By doing this, they will, at the end of a year, have a neat little volume, and also have at hand the means of amusing and improving their minds during leisure hours."[26] This advice is telling, especially when contrasted with the anxiety expressed over the modest size of the publication by the paper's editor in its first issue: "Our paper, though somewhat small in size, will be found valuable in contents."[27] Taken together, a year's worth of individual issues of the newspaper would form a "neat little volume"—practically a book. In the same way that the *Colored American* presented reading as an imperative activity, it presented books as items to be treasured: they were promoted as the agents and, increasingly, the emblems of an appropriately cultivated intellect. Later issues of the newspaper carried advertisements for "whole libraries" containing "the most valuable Standard Religious and Scientific Works," which were available for purchase for only "twelve dollars" (see figure 27.3).[28] A library was advertised as something "every family ought to have," and the *Colored American* offered itself as an affordable collection that would, like a library of bound books, testify to the social, civic, and moral standing of its owner.[29] For the sum of $1.50 per year, it provided free blacks with both an encyclopedia of "useful information" and a source of appropriate entertainment. Even if the issues would remain unbound, possession of a full year's run of the *Colored American* was something of which to be proud.

What I have outlined here is a sort of virtual library or reading room; throughout the antebellum period, editors of African American newspapers considered the durability of their publications a prime aspect of their appeal and distanced the publications from the ephemeral qualities of a newspaper by representing them as book-like. "People seldom preserve newspapers," these editors understood, "but almost always preserve their books."[30] Their belief that "books preserve themselves" motivated them to promote their newspapers as enduring records of African American accomplishments and cultural production.[31] Founders of the *Christian Recorder*, for instance, emphasized in the prospectus of the newspaper that it would be produced "in a form so as to be folded as a book or pamphlet, that families and individuals may have books made of it and preserved for future reference."[32] Bound or unbound, their editors insisted, issues of the *Christian Recorder* must be considered lasting texts, as good as books. This emphasis serves as a reminder that, for early black readers, printed texts were first and foremost functional. The creation of long-lasting sources of literature was considered crucial to "develop the talents of our young people, and to furnish data for future comparison."[33] The support of black authors and the development of an African American literary tradition depended on the creation of lasting libraries, for literary texts would not serve to educate or inspire black people if they did not survive to reach multiple generations.

In their newspapers African Americans found what one reader of the *Weekly Anglo-African* called "a library . . . of no small value."[34] In the case of the *Weekly Anglo-African*, one particular focus of its "collection" was material that would allow its readers to appreciate and preserve the literary arts of black people. In addition to letters, essays, and extended book reviews, a regular feature of the *Weekly Anglo-African* was a "poems, Anecdotes, and Sketches" column. The content of this column was entirely explained in its title. In one issue, Frances Ellen Watkins's poem "Be Active" was followed by an anonymously authored poem called

---

ADVERTISEMENTS.

Cheapest Publications in the World!

☞ A WHOLE LIBRARY FOR TWELVE DOLLARS. ☜

The Library has been published under the supervision of the following Clergymen:

Rev. Jonathan Going, of the Baptist Church.
Rev. J. F. Schroeder, of the Protestant Epis. Church.
Rev. John M. Krebs, of the Presbyterian Church.
Rev. John Tackaberry, of the Meth. Epis, Church.

Figure 27.3 Advertisement for "A whole library for twelve dollars," from the *Colored American*, 9 June 1838, 64. Reproduced by permission of the American Antiquarian Society.

"He's None the Worse for That" and two works of short fiction, "The Negro of Brazil" by "An Old Tar" and "The Lost Diamond" by Mrs. F. D. Gage.[35] Short, moralistic vignettes appeared alongside excerpts from recently published works of fiction and nonfiction. Even the extended book reviews that were included in the *Weekly Anglo-African* offered readers significant literary texts that enhanced their critical perspective as they suggested further reading. Reviews and advertisements for Frederick Douglass's *My Bondage and My Freedom*, a biography of the Reverend Jermain W. Loguen, and William C. Nell's *The Colored Patriots of the American Revolution* shared space with recommendations for Lydia Maria Child's *The Right Way, The Safe Way*.[36] The number as well as the diversity of texts supplied on a weekly basis by the *Weekly Anglo-African* was appreciated by readers, who recognized the advantages that would accompany such literary exposure. In the words of one of the newspaper's patrons, through active interaction with the literary texts included in the *Weekly Anglo-African*, "readers are taught to think for themselves, and are stimulated to express their thoughts in appropriate language. By this means," this reader recognized, "they will make rapid advances in literature."[37] Evidently, the newspaper audience's eagerness to consume its literary offerings sometimes came at the expense of their reading another text commonly associated with African American readers: the Bible. A small item included in a February 1860 issue of the newspaper and titled "Popularity of the 'Anglo-African'" reported that one New York City preacher had complained to his congregation that "he knew Christians who could be found sitting up late at night reading the 'African Paper,' while their Bibles were totally neglected."[38]

In the fall of 1859, on the eve of the Civil War, the *Weekly Anglo-African* capitalized on its own successful standing as a virtual library for black readers by opening a reading room in New York City. Located at 178 Prince Street, the Anglo-African Reading Room opened with much fanfare. To publicize the existence of the reading room and ensure its immediate popularity, the committee responsible for its organization instigated "a course of popular lectures" to be held periodically at the reading room. Although they chose to promote the lectures rather than the reading room itself in their initial announcement, the text of it makes clear that the "object of the course [of lectures]" was to "aid in the establishment of a reading-room." By providing ready access to literary material and promoting attention to literary character in the black community, the reading room, this group recognized, would constitute an essential and lasting addition to the black community. Organizers hoped that the reading room would be inviting to "the masses," a space "where the barriers of complexion, sect, or party shall have no existence whatever—a place where young and old may resort to inform themselves upon the current events of the age, and enjoy the various and piquant pleasures produced by the learned review or well stored magazine." Intergenerational as well as interracial, the Anglo-American Reading Room was envisioned as a "place . . . not for the *colored man*, and not for the *white man*, but for the PEOPLE."[39]

To this end, the "list of lecturers" was to "comprehend the representatives of color and those who are not." Speakers were to encompass a wide range of subject matters and perspectives, representing "the pulpit, the bar, the bench, the editorial chair—the Presbyterian, the Congregationalist, the Methodist, the Baptist, the Universalist—learning, eloquence, and enthusiasm."[40] Reports of lectures and meetings held in the Anglo-African Reading Room suggest that these events, serious or playful, were dominated by a spirit of interaction rather than opposition. Speakers assembled could be contentious, their addresses challenging, but they were thought-provoking as well. Exposure to this sort of environment and the intellectually challenging climate it encouraged seems to have been precisely the type of exercise the reading room hoped to provide. Surely, gatherings advertised as "A little lemonade—a few declamations and doughnuts!" were entertaining, but they were serious and academic too. As had traditionally been the case, the success of the reading room lay in its combination of intellectual exercise and society. "To sit alone and gorge one's self with venison and wine, is not our taste," wrote one correspondent for the *Weekly Anglo-African* in praise of the reading room's activities. "An association of kindred spirits can sometimes find profitable conversation over a cup of coffee, refreshing our minds as well as bodies, and sharpening the ideas by social interchange of sentiment."[41] This understanding was shared by readers of the *Weekly Anglo-African* who did not live near the Anglo-African Reading Room. Writing from Hartford, Connecticut, "Sigma" used these words to express her belief in the advantages of the social aspect of literary study afforded by reading rooms, for both men and women: "We feel glad to know that a reading room has been started in your city, and although we cannot enjoy its benefits yet we console ourselves with the idea that it will be productive of good, especially if the ladies patronize it and enter into discussions upon the merits of the different periodicals on file. Nothing calls into action and better strengthens one's judgment as this habit of conversing on what we read."[42]

That African American libraries and reading rooms were initially focused not only on housing and preserving texts but also on situating conversations around them illustrates the extent to which the literary habits of black readers were oriented toward far more than the acquisition of basic literacy skills. By reading (whether independently or as part of a group) and, most important, by participating in the conversations inspired by the texts they read in the context of a literary society library or reading room, free blacks in the urban North found ways of exposing themselves to the literary environments that would contribute to their presenting themselves as "fit for society, [and] better neighbors in any community."[43] Although African American readers would develop a taste for solitary, individual reading in the years following the Civil War, their initial understanding of reading as it developed in the antebellum period was tied to the specific context of the literary society, library, and reading room for good reason. In an atmosphere rife with political setbacks, the confusion of various antislavery efforts, and complex questions about emigration, never had there been greater need for free blacks to assert in strong public voices their commitment to liberty and equality. These voices developed and found maturity through collective reading and literary activities such as those sponsored and sustained by the texts included in the early black press as well as those collected by early African American libraries and reading rooms. These institutions' orientation toward communal reading and their focus on the discussions promoted by the various texts they included in their collections allowed free blacks to forcefully enter into public debates about the future of black Americans in the United States and to raise the voice of conscience in a society seemingly deaf to its own ideals.

References

1   William Hamilton, *An Address to the New York African Society, for Mutual Relief, Delivered in the Universalist Church, January 2, 1809*, reprinted in *Early Negro Writing, 1760–1837*, ed. Dorothy Porter (Boston: Beacon, 1971), 36.
2   William Whipper, "Original Communications," *Freedom's Journal*, 20 June 1828, 98.
3   William Whipper, *An Address Delivered in Wesley Church on the Evening of June 12, Before the Colored Reading Society of Philadelphia, for Mental Improvement* (1828), reprinted in *Early Negro Writing*, 108. Subsequent references to this text will be cited parenthetically as Whipper, *Address*.
4   Whipper, "Original Communications," 98. This announcement makes clear that the Reading Room Society forbade the inclusion of "every book that is chimerical or visionary" from its library.
5   When Joseph Willson outlined the most prominent of the active literary societies of Philadelphia in 1841, the Colored Reading Society was not mentioned. See Joseph Willson, *Sketches of the Higher Classes of Colored Society* (Philadelphia: Merrihew and Thompson, 1841), 27.

6   George Maurice Abbot, *A Short History of the Library Company of Philadelphia* (Philadelphia: n.p., 1913), 3.

7   "Philadelphia Library Company of Colored Persons," *Hazard's Register of Pennsylvania*, 16 March 1833, 186 (page is numbered incorrectly in original; it should be 176).

8   *Minutes and Proceedings of the First Annual Meeting of the American Moral Reform Society, Held at Philadelphia* (1837); reprinted in *Early Negro Writing*, 238.

9   Pennsylvania Abolitionist Society, *The Present State and Condition of the Free People of Color in the City of Philadelphia* (Philadelphia, 1838), 30.

10   *Address and Constitution of the Phœnix Society of New York, and of the Auxiliary Ward Associations* (1833); reprinted in *Early Negro Writing*, 141. References will be cited as "Phoenix."

11   Samuel Cornish, "A Library for the People of Color," *Colonizationist and Journal of Freedom*, February 1834, 306–7.

12   Samuel Cornish, "Phœnix Library—Donations," *The Emancipator*," 4 February 1834. This letter was first published in the *New York Observer*.

13   "A Phœnixonian," "To the Editors of the Colored American," *Colored American*, 16 February 1839, unpaginated.

14   Cornish, "A Library for the People of Color."

15   "Examiner," "Characteristics of the People of Color—No. 3: Literary Character," *Colored American*, 16 May 1840, unpaginated.

16   "To Our Patrons," *Freedom's Journal*, 16 March 1827.

17   Samuel E. Cornish, "Original Communications," *Freedom's Journal*, 13 July 1827, 70.

18   "Literary Societies," *Colored American*, 5 October 1839, unpaginated.

19   "Circular," *Colored American*, 16 June 1838, 69. Charges for the use of the facilities underscore Ruggles's commitment to making it accessible to all. "Strangers" were welcomed free of charge. All others were to pay according to how long they wished to use the library: yearly rates were $2.75; monthly the charge was $0.25, and the library could be used for a week for 6½ cents.

20   Ibid.

21   Charles C. Andrews, *The History of the New-York African Free-Schools* (1830; rpt. New York: Negro University Press, 1969), 103.

22   Charles C. Andrews, "New York African Free School," *Freedom's Journal*, 9 November 1827, 138. In his letter, Andrews calls it a "pleasing fact" that *Freedom's Journal* joined "three hundred well selected volumes" in the school's library. His pride in the collection is evident in the anecdote he relayed to readers of the newspaper: "One of our little scholars, aged about ten years, was questioned on some astronomical and other scientific subjects a few months ago, by a celebrated and learned doctor of this city; the boy answered so readily and so accurately to the queries, [and] was at last asked, how it was that he was so well acquainted with such subjects? His reply was, that he remembered to have read of them in the books of the School Library."

23   "To Our Patrons," *Freedom's Journal*, 16 March 1827, 1.

24   See *Freedom's Journal*, 14, 21, 28 February and 21 March 1828.

25   Table: "Vessels of War, in the U.S. Navy, 1836," *Weekly Advocate*, 7 January 1837, unpaginated. For subsequent installations of the same series, "A Brief Description of the United States," see the issues of 14 and 21 January 1837.

26   "File Your Papers," *Weekly Advocate*, 7 January 1837, unpaginated.

27   "Our Undertaking," ibid.

28   "Cheapest Publications in the World! A Whole Library for Twelve Dollars," *Colored American*, 9 June 1838, 64.

29   "Household Libraries," *Colored American*, 7 July 1838, 80.

30   "Reasons why the Repository should be Continued and Patronized," *Repository of Religion and Literature, and of Science and Art*. This announcement is reprinted on the inside back cover of virtually every issue of the *Repository*; see, for instance, January 1862.

31   Ibid.

32   M. M. Clark, "Prospectus of the Christian Recorder of the African Methodist Episcopal Church," in Daniel Payne, *History of the African Methodist Episcopal Church* (Nashville: Publishing House of the A.M.E. Sunday School Union, 1891), 278–79.

33   "Reasons why the Repository should be Continued and Patronized," *Repository of Religion and Literature, and of Science and Art*, inside back cover (see, for instance, January 1862).

34   Letter from Rev. Amos Gerry Beman, *Weekly Anglo-African*, 29 October 1859, 1.

35   "Poems, Anecdotes, and Sketches," *Weekly Anglo-African*, 30 July 1859, 1.

36   "A New and Exciting Book [review of *Life of Rev. J. W. Longuen*]," *Weekly Anglo-African*, 1 October 1859, 1; a review of William C. Nell's *Colored Patriots of the American Revolution* was published in the 30 July 1859 issue of the *Weekly Anglo-African*, 3; Child's work was reviewed in "New Books," *Weekly Anglo-African*, 2 June 1860, 2.

37   "Should the 'Anglo-African' Be Sustained?" *Weekly Anglo-African*, 9 June 1860, 2.

38   "Popularity of the 'Anglo-African,' " *Weekly Anglo-African*, 4 February 1860, 3.

39   "Anglo-African Lectures," *Weekly Anglo-African*, 15 October 1859, 2.

40   Ibid.

41   "Amusements." *Weekly Anglo-African*, 31 March 1860, 1.

42   Sigma, "Letter from Hartford," *Weekly Anglo-African*, 3 December 1859, 1.

43   E[lisha] W[eaver], "To Our Subscribers," *Repository of Religion and Literature, and of Science and Art* 4 (October 1859): 192.

SECTION 6

Individual readers

INTRODUCTION

THE INDIVIDUAL CASE STUDY is at the heart of the history of reading, and is a distinctive feature of the discipline. Simon Eliot observes that 'any reading recorded in an historically recoverable way is, almost by definition, an exceptional recording of an uncharacteristic event by an untypical person' (Eliot, 1994). But the value of the case study to the historian of reading is that this type of study allows the scholar to penetrate deeply into the habits and practices of the individual reader in question, and to reconstruct to some degree the social, cultural and personal contexts in which the acts of reading took place. This kind of micro-history is useful not only for what it tells us about the extraordinary reader who is being studied, but also for the information it provides about the ordinary social practices with which he or she is surrounded.

The extracts in this section range across a variety of historical periods, from the sixteenth century to the nineteenth, and include studies of male readers from relatively diverse cultural and geographical backgrounds. For the purposes of comparison, those interested in female historical readers should consult John Brewer's case study of Anna Larpent, 'Reconstructing the Reader: Prescriptions, Texts and Strategies in Anna Larpent's Reading' (in Raven, Small and Tadmor (eds), *The Practice and Representation of Reading in England* (1996)), Kate Flint's *The Woman Reader, 1837–1914* (1993) and Jacqueline Pearson's *Women's Reading in Britain, 1750–1835: A Dangerous Recreation* (1999). At first sight, the readers introduced in this section seem to have little in common beyond the serendipitous survival of evidence that in some way records their reading experiences, but some patterns and continuities do emerge when these case studies are considered together. The active nature of the disparate reading experiences is immediately clear in all of the extracts, for example, as is the part played by reading in the formation and/or understanding of identity and selfhood.

In ' "Studied for Action": How Gabriel Harvey read his Livy', Anthony Grafton and Lisa Jardine take as their case study the Elizabethan scholar, poet and pamphleteer, Gabriel Harvey, looking in detail at Harvey's successive readings of his copy of Livy's *Roman History*

(Basle, 1555) with different companions. Their primary evidence is Harvey's marginalia in this book. Grafton and Jardine argue that, for early modern scholarly readers, as exemplified by Gabriel Harvey, reading was actively 'goal-orientated', intended to have a practical, often political or military, purpose. They show that the activity of reading, at least in the scholarly and political circles frequented by Harvey, was envisaged as having a purpose and an outcome beyond the acquisition of information or the pursuit of pleasure. In Grafton and Jardine's model, the Elizabethan reader reads in different ways for different purposes (professional advancement, political intrigue, military strategy, for example), but the reading is always directed towards a specific goal, and the reading practices employed vary according to the goal. Reading to facilitate action is conceived of as a professional activity, involving specific equipment, and a particular kind of attention, and as a public performance, rather than an individual experience.

Arianne Baggerman focuses on a different kind of reader in her study of the eighteenth-century Dutch child Otto van Eck, using his diary as her evidence. Baggerman points out the many difficulties of studying Otto's reading through his diary, suggesting that both his choice of reading matter and his responses to the books he read were dictated, or at least directed, by his parents, who read his diary as a means to understanding his spiritual and intellectual development. The diary is therefore neither a transparent nor spontaneous account of Otto's own thoughts; rather, like so many diaries and journals, it is a document that is mediated and controlled, in this case by parental supervision. Nonetheless, this gives us valuable information about societal and cultural expectations about children's reading, as well as the way in which reading was conceived of as a means of promoting spiritual reflection and meditation in late-eighteenth-century Dutch culture. The diary also provides information about what was read (it includes a list of some thirty-five texts) and about reading practices.

In his account of the excise officer John Dawson as reader and annotator, Stephen Colclough focuses on the relationship between Dawson's annotations and his way of reading. Like Gabriel Harvey, Dawson utilised a kind of annotating code that helped him to highlight the most important or useful parts of any book he read. For Dawson, as for Harvey and Otto van Eck, reading was directed actively towards a particular goal; in Dawson's case, the goal was the accumulation of (primarily historical) knowledge. Through marginal annotations, abstracts of texts, textual corrections, cross-references, handwritten indexes and a catalogue of his library, Dawson sought to organise and codify his knowledge, and to make the retrieval of salient information from his books easier. He is thus characterised by Colclough as 'a close reader determined to put his texts to work', but Colclough also makes the point that Dawson needed to turn the contents of his volumes into his own writing in order to make sense of them and put them to work for him.

The last extract in this section, James Secord's account of Thomas Archer Hirst's reading of *Vestiges of the Natural History of Creation* in the late 1840s, presents a reader who was deeply immersed in the latest publications. Secord's evidence comes from Hirst's detailed journals. Like Otto van Eck's diary, Hirst's journal charts his reading and the journey of his spiritual progress as well as his daily activities. For Hirst, reading was a way 'to assert his independence of judgement'. His responses to his scientific reading were also a way for him 'to distance himself from the faith in which he had been raised'. In Secord's discussion of the journal, we are once again reminded of the public and social nature of reading; in 1848, Hirst and his circle of friends and fellow-workers gather in pubs, in their rooms, and at work to read *Vestiges* and discuss their reading.

In all of these extracts, we are introduced to readers for whom active, purposive reading was a central part of life. It is frequently portrayed as having been vital to their understanding of their very identities and selves, as well as to their roles as social beings. These case studies record and analyse, of course, only the reading experiences of specific individuals. But in so doing, they provide some insight into the specific reading practices, as well as, more broadly, the cultural importance of reading to those individuals, and to the cultures to which they belonged.

Chapter 28

Anthony Grafton and Lisa Jardine

"STUDIED FOR ACTION": HOW GABRIEL HARVEY READ HIS LIVY

ALL HISTORIANS OF EARLY MODERN culture now acknowledge that early modern readers did not passively receive but rather actively reinterpreted their texts, and so do we. But we intend to take that notion of *activity* in a strong sense: not just the energy which must be acknowledged as accompanying the intervention of the scholar/reader with his text, nor the cerebral effort involved in making the text the reader's own, but reading as intended to *give rise to something else*. We argue that scholarly reading (the kind of reading we are concerned with here) was always goal-orientated — an active, rather than a passive pursuit. It was conducted under conditions of strenuous attentiveness; it employed job-related equipment (both machinery and techniques) designed for efficient absorption and processing of the matter read; it was normally carried out in the company of a colleague or student; and was a public performance, rather than a private meditation, in its aims and character.[1]

Above all, as we shall see, this "activity of reading" characteristically envisaged some other outcome of reading beyond accumulation of information; and that envisaged outcome then shaped the relationship between reader and text. In consequence, a single text could give rise to a variety of goal-directed readings, depending on the initial brief.[2] Inevitably this has consequences for specific readings of given texts by a reader briefed (by himself or others) in particular ways, which mean that the modern historian cannot afford to prejudge what will constitute its focus or central theme. Indeed, we would argue that, if we use our own understanding of the salient features of the text of Livy (say) to identify the points of crucial importance to an Elizabethan reader, we are very likely to miss or to confuse the methods and objects at which reading was directed.

[. . .]

What we attempt here is to show one kind of purposeful reading in process. We have chosen to focus on directed reading conducted in the circle (and under the auspices) of prominent Elizabethan political figures, because we ourselves find the interaction between politics and scholarship here particularly exciting for the light it can cast *both* on political affiliation (who shared what political beliefs) *and* on the activity of the scholars these figures retained more or less formally in their service. At one level, of course, the discovery of close connections between political theory as contained in classical texts and Tudor political practice is not unexpected; it is the *nature* of the connection which is surprising (its method-ical character, its persistence as an emphasis in scholarly reading, the seriousness with which "reading" was treated by those active in the political arena). Elsewhere, in work we are currently engaged in on other readings in other contexts (medical, astronomical, philosophical and dialectical), where the modern reader is less prepared for it, we are finding equally unexpected, related conjunctions of reading practice and application to specified goals.

[. . .]

"A word will suffice for the wise": scholars and martialists

On 18 February 1601 Sir Thomas Arundel wrote a letter to Sir Robert Cecil, defending himself against any implication in the Essex rising, and urging clemency for the earl of Southampton.[3] With this letter was enclosed an unsigned paper in the same hand, which contains the following passage:

> I can not but wrighte what I think may avayle you so dothe my love manyfest my follye. Theare is one Cuff a certayne purytane skoller one of the whottest heades of my lo: of Essex his followers. This Cuff was sente by my lo: of Essex to reade to my lo: of Southampton in Paris where hee redd Aristotles polyticks to hym wth sutch exposytions as, I doubt, did hym but lyttle good: afterwards hee redd to my lo: of Rutlande. I protest I owe hym no mallyce, but yf hee showd [?] faultye heerein, w[ch] I greatelye doubte, I can not but wish his punish-ment. [In Latin] A word will suffice for the wise (*verbum sapienti*).[4]

Henry Cuffe, one-time professor of Greek at Oxford, and secretary to the earl of Essex, had as one of his duties (according to Arundel) that of professional reader: "to reade to my lo: of Southampton", and to provide his own expositions of the text (Aristotle's *Politics*).[5] The note suggests that there was a specific category of employee in a noble household such as Essex's: the scholar, retained to "read" with his employer and his employer's associates. And there is a strong suggestion that this reading is politically aware, that it serves a political purpose, of which the scholar/secretary is apprised, and in which he is actively involved ("hee redd Aristotles polyticks to hym wth sutch exposytions as, I doubt, did hym [Southampton] but lyttle good"). This might lead us to reassess the accusation levelled at Cuffe by Essex after his arrest (according to Camden; proof, according to Mervyn James, of Essex's violation of "all the canons of honour"): "you were the principal man that moved me to this perfidiousness".[6] Was it to Cuffe's line in "exposytions" that Essex was attributing blame, on the grounds that these had led him to believe that his political activities were sanctioned by the authority of classical political texts?[7]

A second letter from the Essex circle further supports the idea of scholar-secretaries employed for "reading" — providing interpretations of textual material on pragmatic political themes. An undated letter to Fulke Greville, attributed to Essex, advises Greville as follows:

> Cosin Foulke: you tell me you are going to Cambridge and that the Ends of yo[r] going are, to get a Scholar to yo[r] liking, to liue wth you, and some 2, or 3 others to remain in the Uniuersitie, and gather for you; and you require my Opinion, what Instruction, you shall giue those Gatherers. to w[ch] I will, more out of Affection for yo[r] Satisfaction, to do what I can, then out of Confidence that I can

doo any thing: and though you get nothing ells by this idle discourse; yet you shall learn this, that, if you will haue yo[r] Friend pe[r]form what you require, you must require nothing aboue his Strength. Hee that shall out of his own Reading gather for the use of another, must (as I think) do it by Epitome, or Abridgment, or under Heads, and common places.[8]

In our earlier work on humanist education we noted, tentatively, that some humanist teachers suggested that a nobleman or prince might employ a poor but gifted young man to read and excerpt the classics for him. Here we suggest that some Elizabethan great houses supported a recognizable class of scholar who performed exactly this function, acting less as advisers in the modern sense than as facilitators easing the difficult negotiations between modern needs and ancient texts. Such readers read, either alone or in company, on their employers' rather than on their own behalf, for purposes and with methods that varied dramatically from occasion to occasion. We propose to show how one such individual actually used his skills to derive counsel from the texts. Our facilitator is Gabriel Harvey; his employment was in the household of the earl of Leicester.[9]

[. . .]

Reading "in the trade of our lives": the Philip Sidney reading

Gabriel Harvey was born in 1550 of a prominent Saffron Walden burgher family, and died there a highly respected local public figure in 1630. He took his B.A. at Christ's College, Cambridge, in 1569–70, was a fellow of first Pembroke Hall (where he took his M.A., against some internal college opposition), and then Trinity Hall (of which he made an unsuccessful attempt to become master). He occupied a number of university posts, including university praelector of rhetoric (1573–5) and university proctor (1583). He obtained his LL.B. in 1584, and was incepted Doctor of Civil Law at Oxford in 1585. In the late 1580s he practised in the Court of Arches in London. He held a secretarial post with the earl of Leicester briefly in 1580, and appears to have had other official connections with members of the court circle (in particular members of the so-called "war party" — Low Church opponents of Elizabeth's policy of political appeasement in Europe). He published both "high" educational works, and popular works (including several exchanges of letters with his friend Edmund Spenser, and some "low" pamphlet material). His publishing career was terminated after a rancorous series of pamphlet exchanges with Thomas Nashe, at the end of which, in 1599, both men's works were banned from publication.[10]

Harvey's Livy is a grand and heavy folio in sixes, printed in Basle in 1555.[11] In this edition, the text of Livy appears flanked by both critics and supporters. Two elaborate commentaries, one by Ioannes Velcurio and one by Henricus Glareanus, follow the text and explicate it, often phrase by phrase. Instructions for reading history, by Simon Grynaeus, precede it. Lorenzo Valla's iconoclastic demonstration that Livy had committed a genealogical error also appears, lest the reader feel more reverence than a Roman classic properly demands. The entire book is densely annotated by Harvey, indicating successive readings over a period of more than twenty years.[12]

At the end of book three of the first decade of Harvey's Livy there is the following note:

> The courtier Philip Sidney and I had privately discussed these three books of Livy, scrutinizing them so far as we could from all points of view, applying a political analysis, just before his embassy to the emperor Rudolf II. He went to offer him congratulations in the queen's name just after he had been made

emperor. Our consideration was chiefly directed at the forms of states, the conditions of persons, and the qualities of actions. We paid little attention to the annotations of Glareanus and others.[13]

Here is an extremely precise reference. Just these three books, read through by Harvey and Sidney, tête-à-tête, with an eye to political analysis, and "shortly before his embassy to Emperor Rudolph II". They were particularly interested in types of republic, in the protagonists' character and circumstances, and in the types of action. They deliberately ignored — as men of action perhaps should — the humanist commentaries.

In October 1576 Sidney returned from Ireland, probably escorting the body of the earl of Essex, who had died there on 22 September.[14] While in Ireland he had accompanied his father, Sir Henry Sidney (governor-general in Ireland), with the task of dealing (apparently pretty unsuccessfully) with bands of rebels.

This was Sidney's first active service. He set out on his embassy to Rudolph in February 1577. Between Ireland and this first diplomatic service Sidney was in England; he visited John Dee on 16 January 1577 and sent a letter from Leicester House on 8 February.[15] It seems reasonable to infer that he and Harvey read Livy at Leicester House between October 1576 and February 1577.[16]

In book one of the third decade Harvey once again links a "reading" of Livy with members of Sidney's circle or associates:[17]

> Each decade is fine, but this one should be studied by the best actors. The quality of the content, and its great power; where the virtue of the Romans suffers so much. Certainly some light can be shed by Louis le Roy's Commentaries on Aristotle's Politics; Bodin's Republic and Methodus; du Poncet's Turkish Secrets in the Gallic Court; Sansovino's Political Maxims; the recent works on politics by Althusius and Lipsius; a few others. And it is fitting for prudent men to make strenuous efforts to use whatever sheds light on politics: and to increase it as much as they can. Two outstanding courtiers thanked me for this political and historical inquiry: Sir Edward Dyer and Sir Edward Denny. But let the project itself — once fully tried — be my reward. All I want is a lively and effective political analysis of the chief histories: especially when Hannibal and Scipio, Marius and Sylla, Pompey and Caesar flourished.[18]

Other evidence complements these notes, enabling us to reconstruct Harvey's role in full. In Harvey's Sacrobosco (now in the British Library), which carries the inscription "Arte, et virtute, 1580" on its title-page,[19] a note on sig. aii[r] reads: "Sacrobosco & Valerius, Sir Philip Sidneis two bookes for the Spheare. Bie him specially commended to the Earl of Essex, Sir Edward Dennie, & divers gentlemen of the Court. To be read with diligent studie, but sportingly, as he termed it".[20]

So Sidney, by 1580, apparently had his own views on "reading" for those in the political arena. Or did he? Osborn prints a letter from Sidney to Edward Denny which came to light in a "near-contemporary transcript" in 1971. It is dated 22 May 1580, on the eve of Denny's departure (like Spenser) in the train of Lord Grey, the new governor of Ireland, appointed to put down Irish disturbances more single-mindedly than had Henry Sidney.[21] It apparently answers an inquiry from Denny as to what he should read to improve his mind (and presumably his prospects), and is something of a set piece. It also makes clear, as Sidney does elsewhere in his letters, that in the face of Elizabeth's determined resistance to military engagement aspiring men of action like himself and Denny have a good deal of time on their hands, and that "reading" and "study" are the approved, character-forming way of relieving boredom:

You will me to tell you my minde of the directinge your studyes. I will doe it as well as the hast of your boy [the waiting messenger], and my little judgement will hable me. But first let me reioyse with you, th[t] since the vnnoble constitution of our tyme, doth keepe vs from fitte imployments, you doe yet keepe your selfe awake, w[t] the delight of knowledge.[22]

For the foundation of study Sidney naturally prescribes scriptural reading. But when he comes to "the trade of our lives", he specifies reading which is (we would argue) quite clearly based on that "reading" with Gabriel Harvey three years earlier:

The second parte consists as it were in the trade of our lives. For a physician must studdy one thinge, and a Lawyer an other, but to you th[t] with good reason bend your selfe to souldiery, what bookes can deliver, stands in the books th[t] profess the arte, & in historyes. The first shewes what should be done, and the other what hath bene done. Of the first sorte is Langeai in french, and Machiavell in Italian, and many other wherof I will not take vpon me to iudge, but this I thinke if you will studdy them, it shall be necessary for you to exercise your hande in setting downe what you reed, as in descriptions of battaillons, camps, and marches, with some practise of Arithmetike, which sportingly you may exercise. Of them I will say noe further, for I am witness of myne owne ignoraunce. For historicall maters, I would wish you before you began to reed a little of Sacroboscus Sphaere, & the Geography of some moderne writer, wherof there are many & is a very easy and delightful studdy. You have allready very good iudgement of the Sea mappes, which will make the other much easier; and provide your selfe of an Ortelius, th[t] when you reed of any place, you may finde it out, & have it, as it were before your eyes.[23]

"Some practise of Arithmetike, which sportingly you may exercise" — echoed in Harvey's "To be read with diligent studie, but sportingly, as [Sidney] termed it" in his copy of Sacrobosco — indicates that Harvey saw this letter (it is even possible he wrote it).[24] It seems clear to us that we do indeed have here an agreed "reading" of history, for the "trade of our lives" — politics and "souldiery". And the source of that reading, since, as we shall see, the copiousness and consistency of Harvey's annotations must establish him as its originating influence, is that "armchair" politician (as he used to be characterized) Gabriel Harvey.

We begin here because the Denny letter/Harvey marginalia connection establishes at the outset some real-life events and outcomes for Harvey's reading of Livy. It will be an important part of our argument to maintain that Renaissance readers (and annotators) persistently envisage action as the *outcome* of reading — not simply reading as active, but reading as trigger for action. Here we may note how the chance opportunity to collate the marginal notes of an individual known only as a reader (and thus labelled politically non-participant by later scholars) with a "letter of advice" from an individual known to be politically and diplomatically active seems to sharpen up "reading" into potential "advice", and provide a link between the absorption of information (as we would tend to judge reading) and public practice.

[. . .]

"I ran over this decade on Hannibal in a week": the Colonel Thomas Smith reading

At the bottom of page 428 of the Livy Harvey records a debate he participated in at Hill House, Theydon Mount, home of his patron Sir Thomas Smith, in which Livy's historical commentary stimulated a lively topical discussion of Elizabethan military strategy:

> Thomas Smith junior and Sir Humphrey Gilbert [debated] for Marcellus, Thomas Smith senior and Doctor Walter Haddon for Fabius Maximus, before an audience at Hill Hall consisting at that very time of myself, John Wood, and several others of gentle birth. At length the son and Sir Humphrey yielded to the distinguished secretary: perhaps Marcellus yielded to Fabius. Both of them worthy men, and judicious. Marcellus the more powerful; Fabius the more cunning. Neither was the latter unprepared [weak], nor the former imprudent: each as indispensible as the other in his place. There are times when I would rather be Marcellus, times when Fabius.

We can date the event to which this note refers with some accuracy. Between 1566 and 1570 Sir Humphrey Gilbert was on active service in Ireland.[25] He was knighted for his services on 1 January 1570, and returned to England at the end of that month, remaining there until July 1572, when he was sent to the Netherlands against the Spanish.[26] From summer 1571 he was certainly involved with Sir Thomas Smith in a speculative project to obtain a monopoly on a supposed procedure for transmuting iron into copper.[27] Sir Thomas Smith was in France from December 1571. Harvey knew John Wood in 1569, when he noted in his copy of Smith's *De recta et emendata linguae anglicae scriptione dialogus* (London, 1567), that the book was a gift from Smith's nephew, his "special friend".[28] The Hill House debate, then, took place some time in 1570, or early 1571.

In 1571 three of the four participants in the debate were actively involved in military and diplomatic affairs. Specifically, Sir Thomas Smith, his son and Sir Humphrey Gilbert were all actively engaged in the Elizabethan conquest and settlement of Ireland. Gilbert (the ruthless suppressor by force of the Fitzmaurice rebellion) and Smith junior (shortly to head the military campaign for the Smith family settlement venture in the Ards) argue the case for Marcellus, whose unscrupulousness and ruthlessness Livy contrasts with Fabius' measured strategy. Sir Thomas Smith and the elderly diplomat Haddon win the debate with their case for the rule of law and policy.[29] These distinguished Elizabethans used Livy — and Harvey — to work out anew in debate the Roman relationship between morals and action — law and military engagement.

At the bottom of page 518 Harvey writes in the margin:

> I ran over this decade on Hannibal in a week, no less speedily than eagerly and sharply, with Thomas Smith, son of Thomas Smith the royal secretary, who was [Smith junior] shortly afterwards royal deputy in the Irish Ards — a young man as prudent as spirited and vigorous. We were freer and sometimes sharper critics of the Carthaginians and the Romans than was fitting for men of our fortune, virtue or even learning, and at least we learnt not to trust any of the ancients or the moderns sycophantically, and to examine the deeds of others, if not with solid judgement, at least with our whole attention. We put much trust in Aristotle's and Xenophon's politics, in Vegetius' book Of Military Affairs and Frontinus' Stratagems. And we chose not always to agree with either Hannibal, or Marcellus, or Fabius Maximus; nor even with Scipio himself.

Evidently the Hill House debate emerged from or accompanied a full-scale reading of the text. This can be dated: the letters patent authorizing the Smiths to embark on a private venture to colonize the Ards region of Ireland were issued on 16 November 1571; Sir Thomas Smith was appointed principal secretary in July 1572, but "long before that" (any time after spring 1571) Burghley and others were referring to him as "secretary"; he left for France on an ambassadorial assignment on 15 December 1571.[30] Thomas Smith junior, Sir Thomas's natural and only son, was recruiting volunteers in Liverpool early in 1572, and was killed in Ireland, during the unsuccessful first attempt to establish the Smith venture, in October 1573.[31] So the reading referred to also took place some time early in 1571. This date is corroborated by a remark in Harvey's *Foure Letters* (London, 1592), in which he records that the earl of Oxford "bestowed Angels upon mee in Christes Colledge in Cambridge, and otherwise voutsafed me many gratious favours at the affectionate commendation of my Cosen, M. Thomas Smith, the sonne of Sir Thomas, shortly after Colonel of the Ards in Ireland".[32] Harvey was elected to a fellowship at Pembroke Hall at the end of 1570, and presumably left Christ's (the college at which he took his B.A.) shortly thereafter — that is, early in 1571.

So while Thomas Smith prepared himself for his crucial military expedition to Ireland (the expedition which was supposed to make his career politically, as well as his own and his father's fortunes), he read Livy with his intellectual companion and close friend ("cosen") Gabriel Harvey.

[. . .]

Positioning the reading: choosing your occasion

The Sidney, Smith junior, Preston and "Arches" readings by Harvey of his Livy (to which we can assign fairly precise dates) give us distinctive contexts for reading (and therefore, we shall argue, distinctive "ways of reading", which need have little in common with one another). The first (chronologically, with Smith junior) we, like Harvey, might term "pragmatic" — or "militarie, stratagematical". This reading is addressed by the prior agreement of the readers to a specific Elizabethan political context, and in particular, to the demands of impending military campaigns. The version of strategy which it yielded turned out in the event to be of limited relevance to the task in hand, and we might want to argue that this is intrinsic to the sources: Livy was never very strong on campaigns.[33] This was also, one might add, Harvey's earliest engagement with "politics" via history, and therefore arguably the most ambitious in terms of the pay-off he hoped for.

The second reading (with Sidney) we might term "moral, politique". This, we would argue, is a careerist reading — one designed to promote the career of a courtier, and at the same time to bring the hopeful facilitator to the notice of a court circle. This side of Harvey (and of his reading) has been repeatedly invoked by those who have encountered his marginalia, but needs to be looked at again, as we shall do here. The appropriate context is provided by the closing passages of a familiar letter from Harvey to John Wood.[34]

The salient point is that Harvey treats the relationship between university political theory and court political practice as reciprocal: "you must needes acknowledge us your Masters in all generall poyntes of Gouernment, and ye greate Archepollycyes of all aoulde, and newe Commo[n] welthes". "Particular matters of counsell, and pollicye, besides daylye freshe newes, and A thousande both ordinary, and extraordinary occurrents, and accidents in ye worlde" are provided by those actively engaged in law and politics: but these nevertheless must be assessed against the general theory that only university men can provide.[35]

[. . .]

At the end of the Livy are two Harvey notes which we may take as our own "positioning". Both relate the reading of history to Harvey's own mentors and patrons, and thus to the immediate social and political context of his study of Livy. The first (after the "Finis") relates to Sir Thomas Smith, Harvey's hero on at least three grounds: for his personal support of Harvey's own university studies and encouragement of his political career aspirations; for his own exemplary progress via political theory and university office to the diplomatic service and high government office; and for his uncompromising intellectual and publishing career:

> Sir Thomas Smyth, the Queenes principal secretarie; in his trauails in Fraunce, Italie, Spaine, & Germanie; but especially in his ambassages in Scotland, Fraunce, & Netherlande; found no such use of anie autours, as I heard himself say, as of Liuie, Plutarch, & Iustinian. He much commended Sallust, Suetonius, Tacitus, & sum other of the best: but his classical and statarie historians were Liuie, Plutarch, Halicarnasseus; & verie fewe other. Of the new, Cominaeus, Guicciardine, Jouius, Paulus AEmilius, Egnatius, & but fewe other. Not the most, but the Best; was his rule. And I am for Geometrical, not Arithmetical Proportion. An other of owre cunningest, & shrewdest ambassadours in Fraunce, Sir Nicholas Throgmarton, was altogither for Cesar, & Liuie; Liuie & Cesar. Not a more resolute man in Ingland: & few deeper heds: as Mie Lord Burgley will still saye.[36]

The second note, at the end of the *elenchus* of Glareanus, sets up the relationship between the various reading contexts just described, and the Livy:

> The notablest men, that first commended the often & aduised reading of Liuie into mee, were these fiue, Doctor Henrie Haruey, M. Roger Ascham, Sir Thomas Smyth, Sir Walter Mildmay, Sir Philip Sidney: all learned, expert, & verie iudicious in the greatest matters of priuate, or publique qualitie. Once I heard M. Secretarie Wilson, & Doctor Binge preferr the Romane historie before the Greek, or other: and Liuie before anie other Romane historie. But of all other Sir Philip Sidney, Colonel Smyth [i.e. Smith junior], and Monsieur Bodin wunne mie hart to Liuie. Sir Philip Sidney esteemes no general Historie, like Iustines abridgment of Trogus: nor anie special Roman historie like Liuie: nor anie particular historie, Roman, or other, like the singular life, & actions of Cesar: Whome he values aboue all other, & reputes the greatest actour, that euer the World did afforde. And therefore makes exceeding account of Sallust, Velleius, Suetonius in Latin; Plutarch, Dion, Iulian in Greek: Who as effectually, as briefly display him in his liuelie colours. But of none makes so high reckoning as of Cesars owne Commentaries, peerles & inaualuable works. Where his friends, & enimies beholde a most worthie man; modest in profession; pithie in discourse; discreet in iudgment; sound in resolution; quiet in expedition; constant in industrie; most uigorous in most daunger; surmounting the wisest in pollicie, the brauest in valour, the terriblest in execution, the cunningest in huge artificial works; allwaies inuincible, often incomparable, sumtime admirable in the accomplishment of the weightiest affaires, dowtiest exploits, & finest designes, that could be plotted bie himself in the profunditie of his surprising conceit. The onlie Mirrour of most excellent valour, & more excellent Witt: to this day vnmatchable, in so manie reuolutions of high, & deepe spirits; aspiring to the greatest things vpon Earth; & leauing no possibilities vnextended. Yet amongst so manie valorous minds, & euen amongst so many

puissant Cesars, still but one Cesar. He, that brauely gaue it owt for his resolute word, Aut Caesar, aut nihil: howsoeuer exceedingly beholden to Machiauel, was indeed nihil in comparison of Cesar.[37]

On the one hand we have Henry Harvey, Roger Ascham, Sir Thomas Smith and Sir Walter Mildmay, "all learned, expert, & verie iudicious in the greatest matters of priuate, or publique qualitie" — significant men with one foot in the university world, the other in diplomacy. On the other we have Smith junior and Bodin (of whom more shortly), distinctively in the world of politics, strategy and opportunity. In the middle we have Sir Philip Sidney, symbol, even before his death, of both camps — the man of cultivation and learning, court figure and literary darling, but whose achievements were cemented by his exemplary performances in active military engagement (and in the first place, in Ireland).[38]

[. . .]

If this is reading, what was political thought?

There seems no reason not to take seriously Harvey's aspiration to read Roman history in a way directly applicable to contemporary affairs of state. We take Bodin, Machiavelli, Daneau and Hotman seriously because they published (thus demonstrating a persisting academic preference for the treatise as "authentic" intellectual history). It might, however, be argued that Harvey is a better source for understanding of Elizabethan political thought, precisely because his observations are juxtaposed with the text of Livy itself, and because, as he indicates, contemporary politicians valued the readings he gave. As to whether Harvey's claims to have the ear of the politically influential are genuine: the claims of individuals are often, in intellectual history, our only guide to contact and influence. And although the pamphleteering Nashe has seen to it that posterity disparages Gabriel Harvey's achievements, it is interesting to note how often Nashe's jibes may equally be read as *confirming* Harvey's own claims.[39]

Harvey's methods and concerns were clearly shared with those members of the political elite with whom he claimed connections. Thomas Smith, his patron — and an eminently respectable figure in modern histories of political thought — lived in a world as steeped in classical texts and modern technical writers as Harvey's own. Smith's friend Walter Haddon once wrote to ask his opinion of a recent dinner-table conversation where the French ambassador had denied that Cicero was a competent lawyer (an argument that "became so heated that it was very hard to find a way to end it"). Smith replied at length from Paris, where he was serving as English ambassador, with appropriate diplomatic tact, that Cicero had been a splendid lawyer, *given the condition of the law of his day*. The scholar-diplomat's mature grasp on such issues, which enabled him to reply so deftly to a difficult question, came from the circle of "facilitators" he frequented in Paris. He had been discussing such issues — though less frequently than he would have liked — with Petrus Ramus and Louis le Roy, as he had discussed them years before with their predecessor at the Collège Royal, Jean Strazel.[40] And he would soon produce a spectacularly successful adaptation of his own of an ancient model for political writing: a brilliant account of England's institutions, modelled on his "conjectural reconstruction of the form used by Aristotle in his lost books on many of the Greek states".[41] Very likely it was Smith who introduced Harvey to the thought of Bodin — whose innovative ideas on inflation Smith accepted.[42]

In at least one case we can watch Harvey and the Smiths, father and son, responding to a single supplementary reading of a sharply "political" kind. Harvey remarks on his reading of the third decade that:

> M. Thomas Smith, & I reading this decade of Liuie togither, found verie good
> vse of M. Antonie Copes Inglish historie of the two most noble Captaines of the
> World, Annibal, & Scipio. Which sumtime giues a notable light to Liuie; & was
> worthie to be dedicated to King Henrie the VIII. in the opinion of Sir Thomas
> Smith, who much commended it to his sonne. [In Latin] However, it is sweeter
> to drink the waters from the very source. And I am one of those who will never
> have had their fill of Livy's wise and lively style.[43]

The introduction to Cope's *Historye of the Two Most Noble Captaynes of the World, Anniball and
Scipio* (London, 1548), specifies in an introductory letter (to which Harvey here refers) that
Cope writes as a scholar (he was chamberlain to Queen Katherine Parr), to make his own
scholarly contribution to knowledge useful for warfare and conquest. Among the military
achievements which Cope maintains contribute to Henry VIII's international political
standing he includes "the wyse and woorthy conquest of the realme of Irelande, wher of at
this present your maiestee weareth the Diademe".[44] An appropriate volume for Sir Thomas
Smith to draw to the attention of his son as part of his "political" preparation for the
Ards campaign. Harvey's racily pragmatic annotations in English to this decade do indeed
appear to take their tone from the Cope. For example, at the top of the page following the
inscription above: "Annibal, a laborious & hardie; a valiant & a terrible Youth. A ventrous
& redowted Captain in the Prime of his age. [In Latin] He acted accordingly".[45] And at the
top of the next: "The Romanes neuer so matched & tamed, as bie Annibal a long time.
And therefore his Historie the more notable in manie weightie respects".[46] In his copy of
Frontinus — which we have on our book-wheel; and which elsewhere in the Livy Harvey
notes he and Smith included in their reading — Harvey heads the discussion of Hannibal's
tactics "in Aphrike agaynste Scipio": "Yᵉ order of Annibal, & Scipio, in that most famous
battel betwene them. These orders, more particularly analyzed in yᵉ Inglish History of
Annibal, & Scipio: owt of Liuy, &c".[47]

Observations such as these (which in Harvey's Livy form a series of running heads
to the third decade) represent Hannibal as a freebooting buccaneer. They culminate in a
marginal note to the speech of Hannibal's which closes the decade. In this speech Hannibal,
who has been recalled to Carthage after sixteen years' sustained combat against the Romans,
philosophically comes to terms with his situation, sues for peace as instructed, and warns
Scipio not to trust in fortune, but only in reason. At the top of the page Harvey records
Thomas Smith's enthusiasm for such lofty thoughts from the great captain of the world:

> M. Smith, Colonel of the Ardes in Ireland, did maruell at nothing more in all
> Liuie, then at this discreete, & respectiue oration of Annibal, after so manie
> braue resolutions, impetuous aduentures, & maine battels.

> [In Latin] A wise oration of Hannibal's.
> Full of sagacity, tried and tested, and maturely reflected upon.[48]

These last two sentences are from an earlier reading, possibly actually contemporary with
the Smith reading, as opposed to retrospective (the first note). At the bottom of the page
Harvey writes:

> Here at last we see Hannibal as more a cautious counsellor than a fierce general.
> It is not surprising that Hannibal made Fabius a politician and a pragmatic:[49] for
> Scipio makes Hannibal himself orator and philosopher. The spirit of youthful
> courage is one thing; that of mature prudence, another; that of old age's

temperance, yet another. Each has its own diction, its own style, more or less temperate and, as it were, bridled.[50]

[. . .]

Affective style: an effective force for action

There seems to be an interesting tension here, between the *aspiration* to find advice on tactics and strategems in such episodes, and Harvey's very evident attraction to the stylistic and affective in such a speech. Once again, this contributes to our sense of the reader, Harvey, as intermediary between text and its effect in practice: style and affectiveness are textual catalysts; the occasions for their recall may be those on which oratory does indeed provoke, and alters the course of events. There is clearly a strong sense in which Harvey sees the cut and thrust of political debate — particularly in the pointed exchange between military adversaries — as a serious and important part of "gaining the upper hand" in political and military affairs. Near the beginning of the Livy he has a long note on Livy's style and its importance:

> Livy's style, especially in the speeches. No Latin or Greek speeches deserve more careful reading or meticulous selection than Livy's; Périon assembled them into a sort of technical order. Hence, when I have time to read, or to imitate, or even to emulate speeches, I prefer no others to these, or others of Livy's, which are both sharp in sense and polished in expression. Nothing, in general, is either more toughly concise, or more vividly expressed. Atticism itself seems to be outdone here. [Later] The style is meticulously polished here: now splendidly ample, now brilliantly concise, now expertly modulated, often adamantine. It is always budding or flowering. Had he not known Caesar, Sallust, Virgil intimately, I would find his method of composition amazing. It is at once so brilliant and so solid; no more brilliant than grave, no less subtle than ornate. [Later] Certain well-rounded and clever sayings — like Spartan apophthegms — are also most delightful. His variety almost never fails, and his strength almost never flags. This judgement is still mine; nor could I be easily induced or desperately coerced to adopt another view.[51]

When we turn to Harvey's copy of Livy's *Conciones* we do indeed find them annotated confidently as politically effective (not simply exercises in speech-making):

> Anyone must be delighted by that vividly varied style. Relevant here are the political letters of Mehmet II to popes, emperors, kings, princes, states, with the answers. Also some very prudent and sharp opinions in the letters of the rulers of the world. What is more spirited, more skilful, more concise, more penetrating than either of these? What is more appropriate to a judicious orator, especially an ambassador or a royal counsellor? Every excellent pragmatic must become thoroughly conversant with them.[52]

These notes give a vivid sense of how Harvey treats virtuoso oratory as an integral part of strategy, comparable with military tactics in its ability to influence the outcome of political confrontation (even though elsewhere, as we shall see, he made serious efforts to master Roman writings on warfare tactics and battle formation). We should not find this surprising. Livy and Machiavelli had both stressed the vital importance of effective rhetoric to generals as well as to statesmen; and Harvey had given much of his career to the study of oratory.

Between these two extremes, Harvey appears ultimately to settle for *aphoristic* history, as crucially policy-forming for the politician; and this is consistent with his commitment to Bodin, Daneau, Hotman and others, associated with contemporary moves to reform the legal systems and political structures of modern states using ancient models. It is in a book of aphoristic sayings from Demosthenes that Harvey quotes Bodin on history; and it is at the end of that work that he cross-refers (evidently for something like the first time) to "Daneau's very new aphorisms", as appropriate reading at this point.[53] Annotating the introductory letter (addressed to Henry VIII) in his copy of Morysine's translation of Frontinus' *Stratagems*, Harvey writes: "Aphorisms and examples will speedily make you great and admirable. Of longer discourses and histories there is no end. They tire the body and confuse the intellect and the memory".[54] The passage against which this is written is also marked with Harvey's "martial" sign (δ ma), and the "aphorisms" in question are pointedly triggering to action (and peculiarly appropriate as usual to the "war party" among whom Harvey sought his patrons):

> Whan tyme byddeth spende, sparynge is great waste. Loue is lewdenesse, whan tyme biddeth hate. Peace is to be refused, wha[n] tyme forceth men to warre. Wherefore, I haue besydes this my tra[n]slation [of Frontinus], in an other tryfle of myn, exhorted al my contrey me[n], peace laid aside, to prepare for warre.

At the bottom of page 271 of the Livy, on a page which Harvey heads in his "military" vein, "The Romanes neuer so matched & tamed, as bie Annibal a long time", we find a marginal note in his diplomatic mode: "No repose or delay here. No notes can equal the author himself, not even the sharpest discourses or aphorisms. He is still sharper himself, and deeper".

[. . .]

Harvey's view of Livy's style — and his belief in its peculiar transparency as narrative — emerges most clearly from his note on the commentator Velcurio's effort to define the historical style. Velcurio writes for students learning to imitate. He explains Livy's style as "copious" and "grave", and emphasizes Livy's trick of weaving a special form of "period" "from several clauses or members, in such a way that it both expresses a given matter copiously and embraces and connects several matters in the same sentence".[55] This quality sets Livy off from other historians like Sallust and Caesar. Velcurio advises the student to cut Livy's "periods into their constituent parts" to see the historical style in detail, and gives rules for producing it in one's own prose (for example, "Very often in the historical period several nominatives and other cases are referred to a single verb, as if predicated"). And he makes clear that Livy's periodic prose makes him second only to Cicero as a teacher and model of eloquent Latin.[56]

Harvey disagrees. His comment reads:

> Second to Cicero. Yet he is often ahead of him in the force of his aphorisms. Often, too, he describes persons, places, actions and things of great beauty more vividly. I have often found Quintilian a sort of composite of Cicero and Livy. Nor did any later Roman have a more florid style, more splendid aphorisms, or a more profound intellect, or a freer judgment, or finally more faith in his own intellect. Had there been no Livy there would have been no Fabius [Quintilian]; and had there been no Fabius, there would have been no Lorenzo Valla, whom I have felt to be the leader of so many modern critics.[57]

Harvey sees Livy as a master in a different sense than Velcurio does. Livy's prose presents people and events concretely, in three dimensions, offering an experience more cinematic than literary in our terms. Yet at the same time he offers exactly the sort of tuition one would expect to find in a master of rhetoric: invention, judgement and elocution, the basic parts of rhetoric, appear in the less explicit categories Harvey applies.[58] Livy offers both explicit and implicit lessons: both the immediate vision of war *in actu* and the considered formulations needed by the statesman *in potentia*.

[. . .]

How well did Harvey read?

Harvey's reading of Livy would not earn the admiration of most modern classicists. He accepts Livy's accounts even when they are certainly erroneous — as in the case of Hannibal's disastrous delay at Capua, which the parallel account in Polybius shows to be Livy's own moralizing invention. But he also read Livy as Livy meant to be read — as a master rhetorician offering the history Cicero had called for in *De oratore*, a "work for orators" — and in doing so he praised exactly those qualities in Livy that had impressed his own classical model of the good rhetorician, Quintilian. Often he did pick up and work with small but important clues in Livy's text, clues that reveal Livy's own ambivalent assumptions. At one point, for example, reading Velcurio's comment on Romulus' and Numa's efforts to establish a religion at Rome, Harvey remarks that "There are many things that I think in passing as I read, which I hardly dare to write down".[59] Surely he referred here to Livy's own sense that the ancient Roman religion was literally false but socially useful, a tool to create social discipline — a sense that conflicts clearly, most modern readers would think, with Livy's efforts to proclaim his piety. Here and elsewhere Harvey's sheer skill and penetration are impressive.[60]

Was Harvey deluded to think that flexible reading could take him to the top? Not necessarily. Another surviving piece of political "ephemera" suggests how much a part of a contemporary agenda his aspirations to annotate the margins of contemporary political practice may have been. A memorandum prepared by Robert Beale in 1592 for the private use of Edward Wotton, it explains in severely practical terms "The Office of a Councellor and Principall Secretarie to Her Majestie". It offers sage advice about how to define the privy council's agenda, avoid cabinet council "which does but cause iealousie and envie", and abbreviate the letters submitted to the council so that its members will at least have read a summary of the matters they must decide on. It also offers readings of many ancient historians: "Remember what Arrian saith in the life of Alexander . . . So likewise towards your fellow councellors behave yourself as Maecenas counselled Augustus . . . Be diligent. Remember the saying of Salust". Beale is quite unapologetic in his provision of these humanist axioms. Indeed he stresses in his conclusion that a good principal secretary must be a good reader of the classics: "By the readinge of histories you may observe the examples of times past, judging of their successe."[61]

In his copy of *The Arte of Warre* Harvey summarizes the authors he would wish to have to hand in designing his own spurs to action in the field of war, including contemporary advisers after the manner of Beale's to Wotton:

> Mie principal Autors for Warr, after much reading, & long consideration:
> Caesar, & Vegetius: Machiauel, & Gandino: Ranzouius, & Tetti: with owr Sutcliff,
> Sir Roger Williams, & Digges Stratioticos: all sharp, & sound masters of
> Warr. For yᵉ Art, Vegetius, Machiauel, & Sutcliff: for Stratagems, Gandino,

> & Ranzouius: for Fortification, Pyrotechnie, & engins, Tetti, & Digges: for y^e
> old Roman most worthie Discipline & Action, Caesar: for ye new Spanish, &
> Inglish excellent Discipline & Action, Sir Ro: Williams. Autors enough; with
> ye most cunning, & valorous practis in Esse. [Another time] Owr Inglish
> militar Discipline, vnder General Norris, in ye Dialogue, intitulid, The Castle of
> Pollicy: Vnder ye Earle of Leicester, In his owne Lawes, & Ordinances. The Spanish
> Discipline, vnder ye Duke d'Alua, & ye Prince of Parma, ye best Discipline now
> in Esse, newly discoouerid by Sir Roger Williams.[62]

We suggest that Harvey hoped his skills could win him a position exactly like Beale's, as a valued political adviser who combined practical experience and legal expertise with detailed study of the ancients. Harvey's mode of reading, in fact, was precisely the sort of serious political discourse that his authoritative contemporaries esteemed (and employed university men for). And we suggest that though Harvey did not succeed as completely as he hoped, his humanism was not at fault.[63] Harvey's ability to read was perhaps his one uncontested asset; it took him far and yielded fascinating and contradictory visions of the Roman past.[64]

If Harvey was ultimately proved wrong, and the fashion for employing this type of erudite facilitator in policy-making was short-lived, this may have more to do with political events than with the individual practitioners. Isaac Casaubon came to England in 1610. Although he shared Harvey's intense interest in reading history, and even his belief that the lessons of history could be reduced usefully to succinct axioms, he had no patience with learned advisors in the political arena.

> Note [he wrote in one miscellany] that just as the "book-trained doctor" whom
> we read about in Galen and Aristotle and the "book-trained ship's pilot" are very
> dangerous, so absolutely is the "book-trained politician" (*politicus e libro*). The
> count of Essex's case is a tragic example of this. When this man, noble in other
> respects, was at a loss, a scholar who was later hanged gave him advice in Lucan's
> words. The tag was to this effect: you who have found no friends as a private
> individual will find many once you take arms. That verse doomed Essex.[65]

So much for Henry Cuffe, one of the learned readers with whom we began. To Casaubon — who translated and commented on Polybius, but nourished no personal hope of advancement in court and political circles — the world of the late Elizabethan facilitator already belonged to a lost past which seemed alien and a little absurd, as well as tragic.

[. . .]

"Read what you can then rightly call your own": Harvey's programme

Harvey's Livy and its companions on the wheel seem to show, when considered together, a coherent programme to master the whole world of learning and make it readily usable in political action. This is no coincidence or aberration; Harvey's intellectual ambitions in fact embraced the mapping of the whole intellectual landscape of his time. No single book offered more data between two covers than that great information-retrieval tool of the sixteenth century, Simler's epitome of Conrad Gesner's *Bibliotheca*. This vast, alphabetically ordered compendium gave brief notices, bibliographies and judgements of the writings of all serious authors, ancient and modern alike, from Aaron Batalaeus to Zyzymus. Harvey read it with care, marking the margins continuously with *signes de renvoi* and occasionally calling attention to his special favourites among the authors listed: notably Rudolph Agricola and Lorenzo Valla. After the preface he entered a programmatic note that reveals as explicitly as anything he ever wrote the contours of his intellectual enterprise as a whole:

> One needs Gesner's great Bibliotheca, especially for summaries and critiques of different authors. These are most important in reading classic and many other authors thoroughly and with the proper attentiveness and utility. Certainly any philologist must find it helpful to have at hand succinct summaries and intelligent critiques of all outstanding writers, and especially those who are classics or of outstanding importance in their field. This is the most important skill of modern criticism, and the highest vocation of the knowledgeable discourser. This is how important it is to be a suggestive summarizer and a sharp critic. But note, I use Hesiod's distinction: "half is more than the whole". One must select the best material from the best writers; the most appropriate material from individuals; the most active, from the best and most appropriate writers . . . Read what you can then rightly call your own. The sum of Socrates's wisdom is this: "Think and act". "Experience outdoes inexperience". Everything rests on art and virtue.
>
> Gabriel Harvey. 1584.[66]

Thus critical reading, skilful annotation and active appropriation emerge as the central skills, not just of the student of history, but of the intellectual *tout court*. Reading always leads to action — but only proper reading, methodical reading — reading in the manner of a Gabriel Harvey.

And here we must emphasize again that Harvey's ideals and methods were not idiosyncratic or whimsical. No text by Philip Sidney has provoked more debate than his letter to his brother of 15 October 1580 on the reading of history. Some have seen this as a manifesto of Sidney's commitment to the modern, continental style of reading history — a reasonable inference given his praise of Tacitus and emphasis on the technical study of chronology. Others have taken it as a criticism of contemporary over-emphasis on the theory of historiography — also a reasonable inference given his remark that "For the method of writing Historie, Bodin hath written at large, yow may reade him and gather out of many wordes some matter". In fact, however, a comparison between this document and Harvey's Livy makes clear that Sidney was purveying, not his own wit, but Harvey's method, to his brother. As Harvey had insisted in practice, Sidney insisted in theory on the variety of roles each historian plays — and in which he must be appreciated by the competent reader: "An Orator in making excellent orations *out of the substance of the matter* [e re nata] which are to be marked, but marked with the note of rhetoricall remembrances; a Poet in painting forth the effects, the motions, the whisperings of the people". Like Harvey, Sidney saw the chief task of the intellectual, ancient or modern, as serving as "a Discourser, which name I give to who soever speakes *not just concerning what happened, but about the qualities and circumstances of what happened* [non simpliciter de facto, sed de qualitatibus et circumstantiis facti]"[67]— a definition that embraces both what Harvey saw in Livy and what he hoped himself to become. And even in taking an independent attitude towards Bodin, Sidney did not deviate from, but continued, Harvey's brand of humanist scholarship. Harvey's tactics as a reader, in short, yield us a general insight into the ways in which some late sixteenth-century intellectuals tried to cope with the flood of information that the presses poured over them.

Just occasionally, the carefully-weighed political inferences in which Harvey took such pride are interrupted by a more emotional response of the kind we tend to like now — though even then the emotion was directed not at the book he read, but at the act of reading it. "Why am I delaying so?" he exclaims at the beginning of book six, where he thought that Livy's detailed account of antiquities left off and a more strictly political narrative began. He urged himself simply to read, and not to write anything down:

> This vulgar bad habit of writing often makes readers dilatory and usually makes actors cowardly. The followers of Socrates were wiser: they preferred teachings that were unwritten, spoken, preserved by memorization. "Take your hand from the picture", runs the old saying. "Take the pen from your hand", so runs my saying now.[68]

Here, for once, Harvey, as reader, offers a response of the intensity the modern reader hopes for. Our challenge in the present exploration of Renaissance reading has been to find a position which will allow us not to prefer such occasional exclamations to Harvey's self-consciously measured aphorisms, but to make both together a part of the reconstruction of an entirely unfamiliar brand of engagement with experience and intellectual history.[69]

References

1 See, for example, a suggestive passage in Henry Wotton's commonplace-book: "In reading of history, a soldier should draw the platform of battles he meets with, plant the squadrons and order the whole frame as he finds it written, so he shall print it firmly in his mind and apt his mind for actions. A politique should find the characters of personages and apply them to some of the Court he lives in, which will likewise confirm his memory and give scope and matter for conjecture and invention. A friend to confer readings together most necessary": L. P. Smith, *The Life and Letters of Sir Henry Wotton*, 2 vols. (Oxford, 1907), ii, p. 494.

2 A fine example of this is the reading which John Dee offered Sir Edward Dyer, in 1597, of Dee's own *General and Rare Memorials Pertayning to the Perfect Arte of Navigation* of twenty years earlier (1577). Dyer had written requesting Dee's advice on "Her Ma.ties Title Royall and Sea Soveraigntie in St Georges Chanell; and in all the Brytish Ocean; any man[er] of way next envyroninge, or next adioyning vnto, England, Ireland and Scotland, or any of the lesser Iles to them apperteyning": British Lib., London (hereafter Brit. Lib.), Harleian MS. 249, fos. 95–105, at fo. 95. What Dee gives Dyer is a route through *General and Rare Memorials* which will yield a "reading" which answers his question, and he does this with great textual precision: "In the 20th page of that boke, (against the figure, 9 in the margent) begynneth matter, inducing the consideration of her Ma.ties Royall Sealimits, and her peculiar Iurisdiction, in all the Seas, next, vnto her Maties kingdomes, dominions and Territories. {Note this worde, NEXT for it will haue diuerse vses in the Consideration, *De Confinio in Mari statuendo, vt in Terra*} And here vppon, in the 21 page, both in the Text, and allso in the Margent, is pregnant matter conteyned: and the same confirmed by the lawes Ciuile: and the great Ciuilien doctors Iudgm[en]t, there alledged" etc. (*ibid.*). William Sherman is currently working in the Cambridge University English Faculty on this and other of Dee's manuscript writings, in the context of Dee's own role as a political facilitator (or "intelligencer", as Sherman prefers to term him). This work will form part of our collaborative book, *Reading in the Renaissance*.

3 Bodleian Lib., Oxford, Ashmolean MS. 1729, fo. 189, Sir Thomas Arundel to Sir Robert Cecil, 18 Feb. 1601. We are extremely grateful to Paul Hammer for bringing this letter and its enclosure to our attention, and for his unerring ability, in the course of his own work, to pick up from the political correspondence of the 1590s items which confirm our intuitions about the relationship in that period between "arms and letters".

4 *Ibid.*, fo. 190. In a personal communication, 21 July 1989, Paul Hammer comments: "In enclosing this note on a separate piece of paper and unsigned, it seems very probable Arundel was following a common procedure for dealing with sensitive information".

5 Henry Cuffe was in the end hanged for his part in the abortive rebellion (Southampton got life imprisonment). Here, however, we set on one side the emotive "conspiracy" testimonies of the

state papers and Camden's *Annales*, and concentrate on Cuffe's *profession*. The state papers (but not Camden) contain a version of Cuffe's scaffold speech which is entirely appropriate to the profession of scholar in service to the man of arms: "Scholars and Martiallists (thoughe learning and vallour should have the p[re]hemynence yet) in England must dye like dogges and be hanged: To mislike this, were but folly; to dispute of it, but tyme lost; to alter it impossible; but to endure it manlye, and to scorne it magnanimitye": Public Record Office, London (hereafter P.R.O.), SP12/279, no. 26. See also the document containing Cuffe's final confession, in which he tried to maintain a distinction between the guidance he gave on policy (which he admitted) and the use to which that advice was put (for which, he tried to maintain, he could not be held responsible). The document records, "My Lord Graye saide, this is no time for Logicke": P.R.O., SP12/279, no. 25.

6   William Camden, *Historie of Elizabeth Queene of England* (London, 1630), p. 187; cited in Mervyn James, *Society, Politics and Culture: Studies in Early Modern England* (Cambridge, 1986), p. 458: "Particularly discreditable was his betrayal of a dependant, his secretary Henry Cuffe, and his ascription to him of such a high politic act as his revolt, which his status required him to take upon himself. When the earl taxed Cuffe that 'you were the principal man that moved me to this perfidiousness', the latter in his turn 'taxed briefly and sharply the earl's inconstancy, in that he betrayed those most devoted to him' ".

7   See also Henry Wotton, *Of Robert Devereux, Earl of Essex: And George Villiers, Duke of Buckingham: Some Observations by Way of Parallel, in the Time of their Estates of Favour*, ed. Sir Egerton Brydges (priv. pr., Lee Priory, Kent, 1816), pp. 32–4.

8   Bodleian Lib., Tanner MS. 79, fos. 29^r–30^v. We are grateful to Paul Hammer for this reference also, and to William Sherman for making a preliminary transcription for us. The remainder of the letter details methods for making epitomes and commonplace collections, and the kinds of work usefully to be epitomized.

9   We owe the term "facilitator" here to Rachel Weil of the University of Georgia.

10 This summary is based on V. F. Stern, *Gabriel Harvey: His Life, Marginalia and Library* (Oxford, 1979); G. C. Moore Smith, *Gabriel Harvey's Marginalia* (Stratford-upon-Avon, 1913). For some recent remarks on Harvey's relationship with Andrew Perne at Cambridge, see Patrick Collinson, "Andrew Perne and his Times" (unpublished paper).

11 Princeton University Lib., Deposit of Lucius Wilmerding Jr., *T. Livii Patavini, Romanae historiae principis, decades tres, cum dimidia* (Basle, 1555) (hereafter Harvey's Livy). The volume is inscribed "ex dono D^{ris} Henrici Harveij. A. 1568", and contains notes made during the period 1568–90. We are extremely grateful to the owner and to Princeton University Library for allowing us access to this volume.

12 On Harvey's habits of annotating, see Moore Smith, *Gabriel Harvey's Marginalia*; C. Brown Bourland, "Gabriel Harvey and the Modern Languages", *Huntington Lib. Quart.*, iv (1940–1), pp. 85–106; H. S. Wilson, "Gabriel Harvey's Method of Annotating his Books", *Huntington Lib. Bull.*, ii (1948), pp. 344–61; J.-C. Margolin, "Gabriel Harvey, lecteur d'Erasme", *Arquivos do Centro Cultural Portugues*, iv (1972), pp. 37–92; Stern, *Gabriel Harvey* (and her bibliography, *ibid.*, pp. 272–3).

13 Harvey's Livy, p. 93. In all instances where excerpts from Harvey's marginalia are given in modern English this indicates that the original annotation was in Latin.

14 See H. Hore, "Sir Henry Sidney's Memoir of his Government", *Ulster Jl. Archaeol.*, v (1857), pp. 299–323: "Here [Galway] heard we first of the extreame and hopelesse sickness of the earl of Essex, by whom Sir Philip being often most lovingly and earnestly wished and written for, he with all the speed he could make went to him, but found him dead before his coming, in the castle at Dublin" (p. 314). We are grateful to William Maley for this reference.

15 The Dee visit included Leicester, Philip Sidney and "the latter's close friend, Edward Dyer": J. M. Osborn, *Young Philip Sidney, 1572–1577* (New Haven and London, 1972), pp. 449, 451.

16 An additional clue is that on sig. Fii^r of Gabriel Harvey, *Gratulationes Valdinenses* (London, 1578), "a poem is described as having been presented to Leicester in 1576": Stern, *Gabriel Harvey*, p. 39. There is one further piece of tantalizing circumstantial evidence suggesting that Harvey may have been in some way associated with Sidney even earlier. In Osborn, *Young Philip Sidney*, pp. 402–3, there is a series of three letters from the biographer of Ramus, Theophile de Banos, concerning his edition of Ramus's *Commentaries*, preceded by a biography of Ramus, which the printer Wechel (also a friend of Sidney's) had just produced. The first letter promises that:

"if I cannot find a friend to take them [Ramus's *Commentaries*], I will send a man specially to Master Harvey in Antwerp, so that you will safely receive them". "Master Harvey" must have been returning to England, thus a carrier for the book. In the event, de Banos sends two further anxious letters, because the book has apparently not arrived, and in March he receives word from Sidney that he has still not received it: *ibid.*, pp. 408–9, 416–17. From January until the beginning of the Cambridge Easter term (April?), Harvey was inexplicably out of Cambridge, and nothing is known of his whereabouts: Stern, *Gabriel Harvey*, pp. 30–1. Harvey was a dedicated Ramist, and in any case the Sidney/Ramus/Wechel connection — Sidney exchanges letters with Wechel authorizing him to buy him the latest books at the Frankfurt book fair, for which he will reimburse him — is intriguing.

17   On fo. 53^r of Brit. Lib., Sloane MS. 93 (the so-called Harvey letter-book), somewhat cryptically inserted in the narrative, is a fragment of a letter from "Immerito" (Spenser) at court which reads: "The twoe worthy gentlemen, Mr. Sidney and Mr. Dyer, have me, I thanke them, in sum use of familiaritye; of whom and to whome what speache passith for your creddite and estimation, I leave yourselfe to conceyve, havinge allwayes so well conceyvid of my unfainid affection and good will towardes yow. And nowe they have proclaymid in there αφειωπαγω". Stern mistakenly makes this a letter *from* Harvey. Stern, *Gabriel Harvey*, p. 39.

18   Harvey's Livy, p. 277.

19   Stern, *Gabriel Harvey*, pp. 233–4.

20   Transcribed *ibid.*, p. 79.

21   See L. Jardine, " 'Mastering the Uncouth': Gabriel Harvey, Edmund Spenser and the English Experience in Ireland", in J. Henry and S. Hutton (eds.), *New Perspectives on Renaissance Thought: Essays in the History of Science, Education and Philosophy in Memory of C. B. Schmitt* (London, 1990), pp. 68–82.

22   Osborn, *Young Philip Sidney*, appendix 5, pp. 535–40, at p. 537.

23   *Ibid.*, p. 539.

24   Or Spenser, with Denny in Ireland, saw it. At any rate, there is a direct connection between Harvey and the letter.

25   D. B. Quinn, *The Voyages and Colonising Enterprises of Sir Humphrey Gilbert*, 2 vols. (London, 1940), i, p. 12.

26   *Ibid.*, i, pp. 17–18, 22–3.

27   M. Dewar, *Sir Thomas Smith: A Tudor Intellectual in Office* (London, 1964), pp. 149–55; Quinn, *Voyages and Colonising Enterprises of Sir Humphrey Gilbert*, i, pp. 20–1.

28   Stern, *Gabriel Harvey*, pp. 14–15. The book is now in the Wilmerding deposit, Princeton; another inscription identifies it as "John Wood's book, a gift from the author himself" (Johannis Woddi liber ex ipso Authoris dono).

29   Haddon (1516–72) wrote Elizabeth's answer to Osorius in 1563, published in Paris "through the agency of Sir Thomas Smith, the English ambassador": *s.v.* Walter Haddon, *Dictionary of National Biography* (hereafter *D.N.B.*). In 1567 Thomas Hatcher published a collection of Haddon's works, *Lucubrationes passim collectae et editae: studio et labore Thomae Hatcheri Cantabrigiensis*; Hatcher also published *In Commendation of Carr and Wilson's Demonsthenes* (*s.v.* Hatcher, *D.N.B.*). Hatcher and Harvey were apparently friends, and Harvey's copy of Demonsthenes' *Gnomologiae* had previously belonged to Hatcher; Harvey acquired it in 1570.

30   Dewar, *Sir Thomas Smith*, pp. 123, 131.

31   D. B. Quinn, "Sir Thomas Smith (1513–1577) and the Beginnings of English Colonial Theory", *Proc. Amer. Philos. Soc.*, lxxxix (1945), pp. 543–60, at pp. 548–9.

32   Cited in Stern, *Gabriel Harvey*, pp.65–6.

33   See Jardine, "Mastering the Uncouth".

34   We have used Walter Colman's transcription, which we gratefully acknowledge.

35   One might want to observe that the somewhat insistent note in Harvey's remarks about the usefulness of university men has less to do with pushiness than with the need to earn a living. There are a number of points in Harvey's biography, starting with the Pembroke quarrel with Neville, where it is obvious that Harvey's career is suffering from his not being a man of means, and therefore financially self-sufficient *before* any earnings from the various posts he sought. See, for example, the letter to the master of Pembroke, John Young, on the disputed Greek lecture-ship in 1574: "For the bestowing of the lecture, do in it as you shal think best for the behoof of the Collidg. For mi part I am the more desirus of it, I must needs confes, bicaus of the stipend,

which notwithstanding is not great": Brit. Lib., Sloane MS. 93, fos. 27^r–34^v, cited in Stern, *Gabriel Harvey*, pp. 26–7. Contrast Sir Thomas Smith's earnings, as itemized in the *Dictionary of National Biography*.

36   Harvey's Livy, p. 829. This seems to be the only reference to Throckmorton in the marginalia. Throckmorton and Smith were ambassadors together in France in 1562–4: according to the *DNB* (*s.v.* Sir Thomas Smith), Smith juinor – aged fifteen – was in France with his father on this embassy. Throckmorton died in February 1571.

37   Harvey's Livy, sig. P 1^r. This note can be dated before 1586, since Sidney's views are recorded in the present tense.

38   See the verses written by Harvey for the Cambridge volume *Academiae Cantabrigiensis lachrymae tumulo nobilissini equities: d. Philippi Sidneij* (1587). The second poem is headed, "De subito & praematuro interitu nobilis viri, Philippi Sydneji, utiusque militiae, tam armatae, quam togate, clarissimi equitis." (Concerning the sudden and premature death of that noble man, Philip Sidney, the most celebrated knight of both kinds of office, as much of arms as of civil affairs).

39   See, for example, Nashe's remarks about Harvey's legal practice in the Court Articles, as cited by Stern, *Gabriel Harvey*, pp. 81–2. Or we may choose to accept Harvey's own word (as set out in a 1598 letter to Sir Robert Cecil) that given the opportunity, in the form of reliable financial support and secure employment, he would have publisehd: "manie other mie Taicts & Discourses, sum in Latin, sum in Inglish, sum in Humanitie, Historie, Pollicy, Lawe, & the sowle of the whole Boddie of Law, Reason; sum in Mathematiques, in Cosmographie, in the Art of Navigation, in the Art of War, in the tru Chymique without imposture (which I learned of your most learned predecessor, Sir Thomas Smith, not to contemne) & other effectual practible knowlage, in part hetherto unrevealed, in part unskilfully handeled for the matter, or obscurely for the forme; with no more speculatve conceit, then industruous practis, or Method, the two discovering eies of this age". For, says Harvey: "I had ever an earnest & curious care of sound knowledg, & esteemed no reading, or writing without manner of effectual use in esse: as I hope shoold soone appeare, if I were setled in a place of competent maintenance, or had but a foundation to build upon": *ibid.*, p. 125.

40   W. Haddon, *Lucubrationes* (London, 1597), pp. 280–1, 284–7.

41   Haddon, *Lucubrationes*, p. 306.

42   See Thomas Smith, *A Discourse of the Commonweal of this Realm of England*, ed. M. Dewar (Charlottesville, 1969), pp. xv n. 14, xxvi.

43   Harvey's Livy, p. 269.

44   A. Cope, *Historye of the Two Most Noble Captaynes of the World, Anniball and Scipio* (London, 1548), sig. aiv^r.

45   Harvey's Livy, p. 270.

46   *Ibid*, p. 271.

47   Harvey's copy of *The Strategemes, Sleyghtes, and Policies Of Warre, Gathered Togyther, by S. Julius Frontinus, and Translated into Englyshe, by Richard Morysine* (London, 1539), sig. E iv^v–E v^r. Hereafter Harvey's Frontinus.

48   Harvey's Livy, p. 511.

49   We translate Harvey's *"pragmaticus"* as "pragmatic" throughout, for want of a more appropriate word. Harvey takes the term directly from Cicero, *De oratore*, where Antonius advises the orator not to fill his head with legal detail, but to employ someone to get it up for him: "This is why, in the lawcourts, those who are the most accomplished practitioners retain advisors who are expert in the law (even though they are very expert themselves), and who are called 'pragmatics' " (Itaque illi disertissimi homines ministros habent in causis iuris peritos, cum ipsi sint peritissimi, et qui pragmatici vocantur). See also Quintilian, *Institutiones oratoriae*, xii.3.4.

50   Harvey's Livy, p. 511.

51   *Ibid.*, leaf facing p. 1, recto.

52   Transcription by Walter Colman. Copy in Worcester College, Oxford. See also Sir. Thomas Smith's library list, Queen's College, Cambridge: R. Simpson, *Sir Thomas Smith's Booklists, 1566 and 1576* (Warburg Institute Surveys and Texts, xv, forthcoming). This copy of Livy's *Conciones* has Thomas Smith's signature on its title-page ("Thomas Smyth"), that is, Smith junior. Which suggests that the two might well have had the two Livy texts together (on the book-wheel!) during their reading.

53   Transcription by Walter Coleman; Harvey's copy of Demosthenes, *Gnomologiae*, sig. o3^r (now in the Brit. Lib.).

54   Harvey's Frontinus, at present in the Houghton Lib., sig. a vi^r. Another marginal note here refers the reader to Aphthonius' *Progymnasmata* for similar aphorisms.

55   Harvey's Livy, sig. H 6^v.

56   *Ibid.*, sig. I^r.

57   *Ibid.*

58   See Harvey's annotations in his copy of *T. Livii Patavini conciones, cum argumentis et annotationibus Ioachimi Perionij* . . . (Paris, 1532). Hereafter Livy's Conciones.

59   Harvey's Livy, sig. I 3^r.

60   For Livy's intentions and reception in antiquity, see P. Walsh, *Livy* (Cambridge, 1970).

61   Conyers Read, *Mr Secretary Walsingham and the Policy of Queen Elizabeth*, 3 vols. (Cambridge, Mass. and Oxford, 1925), i, appendix, pp. 423–43. Wotton also failed to achieve the office he expected either in 1592 or three years later, when the matter was broached again: *ibid.*, i., p. 423.

62   *The Arte of Warre: Written in Italian by Nicholas Machiuel: And Set Foorth in English by Peter Withorne* . . . (London, 1573), fo. Cix^r. The "newly discoouerid by Sir Roger Williams" dates this to 1590–1.

63   In spite of Nashe's exuberant fantasies about Harvey's being chased back to Cambridge after an ignominiously brief employment with Leicester, these marginalia suggest a much more continuous toing –and-froing on Harvey's part between Cambridge and London, and constant contact with the political circle he claimed to advise in London. Spenser praises Harvey as a "looker-on" who "Ne fawnest for the fauour of the great . . . But freely doest", in a 1586 sonnet, written from his own minor-official post in Dublin: Moore Smith, *Gabriel Harvey's Marginalia*, p. 57, which confirms that Harvey held no official post, but nevertheless suggests that Harvey is intellectually active, in a desirably unconstrained fashion, in the circles of "onlookers" outside the immediate court circle.

64   Possibly by 1590 the more "topical" works on the technology of war and military tactics were making Harvey's humanistic approach appear a little dated. See G. Parker's citation of Sir Roger Williams, also writing in 1590, saying that Alexander, Caesar, Scipio and Hannibal were doubtless "the worthiest and famoust warriors that ever were", but that their escape had little relevance to the modern age: G. Parker, *The Military Revolution: Military Innovation in the Rise of the West, 1500–1800* (Cambridge, 1988).

65   Bodleian Lib., Casaubon 28, fo. 127^r. For Casaubon's instructions on deriving axioms from classical historians (specifically Tacitus), see MS. Casaubon 24, fo. 125^{r-v}. For Casaubon and Polybius, see A. Momigliano, "Polybius' Reappearance in Western Europe", in his *Essays in Ancient and Modern Historiography* (Oxford, 1977), pp. 79–98.

66   Moore Smith, *Gabriel Harvey's Marginalia*, pp. 125–6; our thanks to the Houghton Library, for letting us inspect the Gesner (now in that collection).

67   See above, p. 330, for Harvey's record of precisely such a concern on Sidney's part when reading Livy's third decade. "[In reading,] our consideration was chiefly directed at the forms of states, the conditions of persons, and the qualities of actions". On Sidney's letter, see E. Story Donno, "Old Mouse-Eaten Records: History in Sidney's *Apology*", *Studies in Philology*, lxxii (1975), pp. 275–98.

68   Harvey's Livy, p. 149.

69   Here as in other areas the methods used by early modern historians are more primitive than those that have long been used by students of earlier periods. The need to study literature, reading, the making of books and the interpretation of texts in conjunction was understood by biblical and classical scholars of the eighteenth century; see F.A. Wolf, *Prolegomena to Homer [1795]*, trans. A. Grafton *et al.* (Princeton, 1985). Medievalists have assimilated the same lesson without undue difficulty or resistance; see, for example, B. Stock, *The Implications of Literacy* with its significant subtitle: *Written Language and Models of Interpretation in the Eleventh and Twelfth Centuries*. Even the best-informed historians of the book in the early modern period have taken a narrower view of their task; see R. Chartier, "Intellectual History or Sociocultural History? The French Trajectories", in D. LaCapra and S.L. Kaplan (eds.), *Modern European Intellectual History: Reappraisals and New Perspectives* (Ithaca and London, 1982), pp. 38–9 for a programmatic statement exemplary in both its strengths and its limitations.

Chapter 29

Arianne Baggerman

THE CULTURAL UNIVERSE OF A DUTCH CHILD[1]

At present I am somewhat slow to rise, since early on it is rather cold. Yet we have a perfectly green May. If I weren't deaf, I'd rise early to hear the nightingale.[2]

THESE WORDS ARE THOSE of Otto van Eck, a ten-year-old boy from the Dutch urban gentry, and the green month of May he rejoices in, is that of 1791. His diary runs until November 17th, 1797. By then the weather has worsened considerably. The bulky document of 1560 pages ends thus: "Yesterday bad weather and snow. Today better with frost, wind east." This is the most comprehensive diary by a child hitherto found in Europe. Its often exhaustive descriptions of everyday life render it a source of information for a variety of historians. Detailed recordings of the boy's arguments with his sisters are interspersed with religious contemplations. We read about rides on horseback or in the goat-cart, but also get lengthy reports on the progress of Otto's illnesses, when he has to rub himself with pitch and bathe in fresh supplies of seawater brought in by the fishmonger every day. The diary is full of fine anecdotes, for instance about Otto's argument with his "collegue" Tomas: "Today I have spoken rashly again, for which I needlessly earned Tomas' dislike; that one does not correct people by scolding them is best learned by experience."[3]

But the diary also has aspects which are attractive to students of reading culture. In most cases we have to put up with indirect sources, taciturn characters such as intended readers in prologues,[4] dead readers in inventories,[5] or the hasty ones one meets in booksellers' files.[6] None of these readers informs us as to their motives: Why did they own this or that book? For the purpose of conversation, or as a guide for everyday life? And did they actually read these books, or did they merely purchase them to fill their bookshelves? They also keep a profound silence as to their reading habits: were the books read aloud in company, or did the readers ensconce themselves *cum libello in angello*, with a booklet in a corner? And how did they interpret texts—to the letter? Or did they give them new meanings?

Such questions can only be answered directly through personal evidence: letters, diaries and autobiographies, sources which are not only rare, but also insufficiently investigated. A more fundamental knowledge of reading habits in past centuries is provided by no more than a few famous readers, scattered through time and space. The sixteenth-century Italian miller, for example, whose bizarre interpretation of the Creation Story is described by Carlo Ginzburg[7] or the much-quoted seventeenth-century Englishman Samuel Pepys, with his secret consumption of scandalous booklets that "did hazer my prick para stand all the while."[8] Another famous example is Darnton's French silk-merchant Jean Ranson, who read and reread the work of his hero Rousseau as if it were the Bible.[9] Ranson's English counterpart is Anna Larpent, whose highly extensive reading habits have been exhaustively documented by John Brewer.[10] And this short tour of our historical readers' pantheon ends with two American celebrities: the nineteenth-century publishers Joseph T. Buckingham and Samuel Goodrich, who play a central part in David Hall's *The uses of literacy in New England*.[11] Otto van Eck's diary may therefore be considered a find, if only because his talkativeness would enable us to brighten up the international company of chiefly adult historical readers with a Dutch child, a youthful reader who would spontaneously answer all the questions we are so eager to ask. But upon closer consideration, this private document turns out to be far from spontaneous. So before anything can be said about Otto's reception of literature, the specific function of his diary has to be dealt with.

As it turned out we are not the only ones to read Otto's daily outpourings. Otto's parents, too, thought this diary would gain them a clear insight into the mental and emotional development of the child.[12] This "wish for knowledge" presumably resulted from their own reading: the educational treatises of the Enlightenment. Like their foreign colleagues, Dutch educators assumed that a child was born as a tabula rasa. Children were thought to be controlled by positive impulses which were generated by sensory perceptions. However, these positive impulses could be reversed. Therefore parents were advised to watch keenly over their children's passions and to intervene whenever the wrong impulses threatened to prevail. This might very well be the reason why Otto's parents encouraged their child to keep a diary and supervised its contents. That they did so becomes apparent after a few pages. Otto's firm resolve henceforth to finish his homework on time, leads to the following comment, written in a different hand: "Now keep this in mind, and act accordingly, for it is better not to make promises than not to keep them. Promise less often; rather do."[13] Another of Otto's notes makes clear that he has more readers than just his parents: on July 13th, 1793, Otto describes his unwillingness to let the family's acquaintances read his diary, allegedly having "feared to do so out of false shame . . . of which Father disapproved, saying that by acting thus I gave people a much worse image of myself than a straightforward confession of a few lapses ever could have done."[14]

In other words, Otto's diary was a medium under control. Nor was it the boy himself who took the initiative to keep a diary. He was prompted to do so in gentle and sometimes less than gentle ways. Especially when he grows older Otto begins to resist this duty and sometimes manages to neglect his diary for days on end. To the great exasperation of his readership: "The reason why I haven't kept journal for such a long time is that I purposely desisted from doing it, hoping it would be entirely forgotten and I could wholly leave it off."[15] Otto wasn't free to choose his subject either. His readers were mainly interested in his innermost feelings. Not in the daily course of events. This is made clear by the following quotation: "This morning, when Mother saw my journals of last week, she said that my way of keeping them was not to her liking, and that instead of filling them with my lessons and games, these being almost the same every day, I should rather refer to my rational behavior and the passions that guide me and the lapses of which I make myself guilty. This, I must confess, is useful as well."[16]

Whenever Otto lacks the inspiration to make confessions or do some serious thinking he is advised to seek refuge in literature and "to read a letter by Charles Grandisson, who was of great use to me, since he taught me it is no great merit to obey one's parents under constraint; however children should find pleasure in doing everything their parents command."[17] But the behavior of elephants, too, provides inspiration for moralistic contemplations: "I went to Father, complaining I knew of nothing to put down, wherefore he advised me to read something. . . . I did so at once, and marvelled about the sensibility, tolerance and prudence of elephants."[18] Sometimes Otto cannot get himself to add a personal touch to his reading and resorts to summarizing it point by point: "1. An honest man should always keep his word. 2. One must converse with the pious and avoid bad company."[19]

Not surprisingly Otto's true passions turn out to be of a non-literary kind. He reserves his enthusiasm mainly for outdoor activities. The diary contains quite a few exuberant descriptions of murmuring brooks, rides on horseback or in the goat-cart, successful fishing expeditions, and summer afternoons when, lying in the grass, he stares up at the clouds drifting by. His perfunctory notes on literature contrast sharply with this. Basedow's *Manuel*,[20] for instance, is handled with lively reluctance. Otto has asked his father for permission to go for a ride before doing some reading. His request is turned down: "No time like the present," as his father flatly comments.[21] On a rainy afternoon Otto is forced to seek entertainment in books, but this has "given him little joy."[22] And so his father's complaint seems well-founded: Otto, apparently, does "not go about his business with fitting diligence, but makes light of it, favoring rides on horseback, fishing, carpentry, or idleness, whereas little is thought of pleasurable reading."[23] Obligatory reading for entertainment clearly wasn't considered a contradiction in terms.

The nature of the source, the controlling and disciplining character of the diary, in combination with its author's lack of enthusiasm for his daily reading, is not without problems. These also confront the researcher who wants to know more about Otto's reading habits, literary preferences, and personal interpretations of the texts. The diary contains no less than thirty-five titles of books read by Otto. Most of these fit seamlessly into our picture of what the perfect enlightened citizen to be should read. The list includes works by Mrs. Cambon van der Werken, Madame de Genlis, Buffon, Pluche, and last but not least Rollin's famous *Histoire Romaine*. Yet we'd be ever so delighted to know what book it was that Otto borrowed from his friend, little Keesje Reepmakers. It seems he got quite carried away by it, for he claims to have been so engrossed in it that he became completely oblivious to his surroundings, even forgot to do his homework and clearly forgot to mention the title as well.[24] As a rule the books Otto reads because he wants to, not because he has to, are precisely the ones that tend to be just hinted at. It was a "nice little book" he'll say. So perhaps the titles encountered in the diary tell us more about Otto's parents' preferences than about his own predilections.

To return to the problems concerning the interpretation of this journal. The status of this diary as a medium under control not only hampers the reconstruction of Otto's literary consumption but also troubles our view of Otto's reception of the texts. Someone whose diary is supervised by his parents and who therefore out of duty fills it with literary contents can't be expected to interpret his books too freely. In addition, Otto's parents also monitor his reception during reading. For Otto seldom reads alone. In the mornings we see him bent over religious works together with his father. Several passages in the diary make clear that this reading is by definition a joint activity. So for instance when his father is called away: "This morning during breakfast I was prevented from reading aloud to Father because again a farmer came to see him, so I couldn't help it."[25] At noon during dessert he often reads the Philantropine Basedow's *Manuel elementaire*. And his reading of Rollin's *Histoire Romaine* appears to have been mostly reserved for supper. At The Van Eck's the nourishment for mind and body was consumed in close conjunction, it seems. With regard to the rest of Otto's books a less regular pattern of eating and reading can be discerned. But even here it is often noted that he has read the work with a parent, or else their involvement is shown by their comments. The biblical Samson and Delilah story for instance leads his mother to remark that "children who marry against their parents' wishes seldom prosper."[26] Even when Otto reads a fable from the *Manuel* that, "proved one must heed the counsel of the elderly, or regret it when it is too late," the parental comment doesn't fail to come: "Mother says I will henceforth experience this myself, since I've been walking through the muck wearing my shoes, instead of (as my mother so often told me) putting on my clogs."[27]

Perhaps this active involvement of Otto's parents is the reason why his abstracts of the books he has read lack in self-will. His summaries hardly deviate from the original text or the intentions of the author. And if an alternative interpretation turns up, one can never be quite certain who is actually responsible for it. Two examples illustrate this. First there is Otto's peculiar addition to a story from Martinet's *Catechism of Nature*, comparable to Pope's *Essay on Man*. In this book Otto read a passage about the effects of sunlight. The sun is said to rise for both good people and notorious villains. This injustice is to be righted in the hereafter, "though God at times allows the wicked to prosper in this world, yet he is just, and surely after death they will suffer the fate they deserve."[28] In the original work an exposition on sunlight does indeed occur, but it is a rather technical one. Martinet does not say a single word about good and bad people or about retribution in the next world.[29] This addition seems to be entirely Otto's idea—or that of his parents. An intermediate form is possible as well: cooperation between both parties. Normally speaking Otto's books, the Enlightened children's books of the eighteenth century, abound with moralism. Pride always goes before a fall, evil is punished all the time, and good will ever prevail. It is not inconceivable that Otto, suddenly noticing the absence of such a moral in Martinet, alerted his parents to the injustice of an even distribution of sunlight among good and bad people. After which his parents may have soothed the child with the remark that this injustice would yet be righted in the world to come. Likewise at variance with the original message is Otto's reception of an illustration in the *Manuel*.[30] He claims to have seen a picture there of a dying man who contentedly bids his obedient son farewell. This appears to have impressed Otto deeply, for he notes: "This idea of my father rejoicing in me on his death-bed will, hopefully, restrain me from doing anything that might sadden my parents."[31] The *Manuel* actually contains two illustrations of dying men.[32] But the captions are of a totally different nature. It is likely that Otto's parents used these pictures to illustrate a message of their own, in which case we are dealing with a manipulated reception. There are more cases in which Otto's parents play off their own mortality against him. The well-known parental trick to stimulate good behavior in children: Once I'm dead you'll be sorry![33] Which leads us to the epilogue of this story. How did it all end with Otto and his parents?

Eventually Otto's concern that his parents would lay down their weary heads in discontent proved to be unjustified. When he is seventeen years old, in fact the roles are reversed: it is Otto himself who lies on his death-bed, succored by his sorrowing parents. His father, Lambert van Eck, gives an account of this death scene in the family book.[34] In his description several elements familiar from the diary converge. To begin with, Otto makes a last confession. He hadn't always honestly owned up everything to his parents, so they "had a much better opinion of him than he deserved." Otto then proceeds to make a naïve confession "of his flaws and omissions," and his parents are deeply moved. Also, Otto continues to read till the day of his death. As his father writes: "Until the very last he glanced over the periodicals and newspapers, but with the discords of this world he wanted to have nothing to do." But even now he is far more enthusiastic about nature than about culture: "he welcomed every display of nature's loveliness—and for this reason the flowering little trees he was sent, and the little birds and fishes he kept in his room, gave him much joy. And whenever the spring sun illuminated all this he found dying much harder, he declared, than when the weather was dark and dreary."

To a book historian Otto's diary is a gold mine, and no doubt much more communicative than the sources generally used by book historians. One learns a great deal about Otto's literary consumption, his reading habits and his reception of the texts, much more than I've been able to say in this paper.[35] But it has to be interpreted with due caution. As should be clear by now, as a source this diary is not uncomplicated. Besides being hard to interpret at times, Otto's diary also makes for a disenchanting experience for those book historians who naïvely assume that books always have been a blessing to mankind. In the field of book-historical research many questions spring from the desire to know more about the social distribution of books, for "the more readers, the merrier," as it is supposed. Otto's participation in book culture is guaranteed. The contents of his bookcase suffice to equip a fully-grown exhibition on the whole range of juvenile literature in the second half of the eighteenth century. But Otto by no means fits the image of a reader, eager to use this medium. When we've finally found a reader of flesh and blood ready to tell us much more about his literature than those dumbfounded types in booksellers' files or inventories, books turn out to be a burden. Otto prefers to go out and play.

References

1   This article is based on a lecture at the ASECS-conference 5–9 April 1995 in Tucson, Arizona. The diary of Otto van Eck will be published by Arianne Baggerman and Rudolf Dekker by Uitgeverij Verloren (Hilversum) in the series *Egodocumenten*. The editors are also preparing a book-length English study on Otto van Eck and his diary.

2   Rijksarchief Gelderland (RAG), FA van Eck, 1041, 82; 3–4–1791. Hereafter we will cite Otto's diary with reference to the date of the entry.

3   23–8–1791.

4   For an example of such an analysis, see: A. Baggerman, *Een drukkend gewicht. Leven en werk van de zeventiende-eeuwse veelschrijver Simon de Vries* (Amsterdam: Rodopi, 1993), 202–226.

5   J. de Kruif, "En nog enige boeken van weinig waarde." Boeken in Haagse boedelinventarissen halverwege de 18e eeuw, *Historisch Tijdschrift Holland* 26 (1994): 314–28.

6   J. J. Kloek, W. W. Mijnhardt, "In andermans boeken is het duister lezen. Reconstructie van de vroeg negentiende-eeuwse leescultuur in Middelburg op basis van een boekhandelsadministratie," *Forum der Letteren* 29 (1988): 15–29. More recently: H. Brouwer, *Lezen en schrijven in de provincie. De boeken van Zwolse boekverkopers 1777–1849* Primavera Pers, Leiden, 1995 (diss.).

7   C. Ginzburg, *The Cheese and the Worms. The Cosmos of a Sixteenth-century Miller* (London: Routledge & Kegan Paul, 1981).

8   R. Chartier, "De praktijk van het geschreven woord" in: R. Chartier, ed. *Geschiedenis van het persoonlijk leven*. DI. III. (Amsterdam: Agon, 1989), 95–139, 122. (Translation of *L'histoire de la vie privée*. Parijs/Seuil 1987, T.3).

9   R. Darnton, "Readers Respond to Rousseau" in: Idem, *The Great Cat Massacre and Other Episodes in French Cultural History* (New York: Basic Books, 1984).

10   J. Brewer, "Cultural Consumption in Eighteenth-century England: The View of the Reader," in: R. Vierhaus e.a. (Hrsg.). *Frühe Neuzeit—Frühe Moderne? Forschungen zur Vielschichtigkeit von Übergangsprozessen* (Göttingen: Vandenhoeck & Ruprecht, 1992) (*Veröffentlichungen des Max-Planck-Instituts für Geschichte*), 366–91.

11   D. D. Hall, "The Uses of Literacy in New England, 1600–1850" in: W. L. Joyce e.a., eds., *Printing and Society in Early America* (Worcester: American Antiquarian Society, 1983).

12   See for an analysis of the pedagogical methods of Otto's parents: R. Dekker, *Uit de schaduw in 't grote licht. Kinderen in egodocumenten van de Gouden Eeuw tot de Romantiek* (Amsterdam: Wereldbibliotheek, 1995), 73–87.

13   6–5–1791.

14   13–7–1793.

15   12–11–1794.

16   16–5–1795.

17   14–6–1791.
18   25–8–1791.
19   26–9–1791.
20   [J. B. Basedow], *Manuel élémentaire d'éducation* 4 dln. (Berlin: Dessau, 1774).
21   1–11–1793.
22   18–11–1795.
23   12–8–1794.
24   12–1–1795.
25   23–1–1794.
26   19–2–1792.
27   2–12–1792.
28   27–11–1792.
29   J. F. Martinet, *Katechismus der natuur* I, 4 dln., (Amsterdam: Johannes Allart, 1777–1778), 34–40.
30   J. B. Basedow.
31   4–5–1791.
32   Basedow, *Manuel élémentaire* deel III, Tab. XI en Tab. XLVII.
33   For example on 5–7–1796.
34   RAG, FA van Eck, 1041, 41.
35   See for a more elaborate analysis: A. Baggerman, "Lezen tot de laatste snik. Otto van Eck en zijn dagelijkse literatuur (1780–1798)," *Jaarboek voor Nederlandse boekgeschiedenis* I (Leiden: Nederlandse Boekhistorische Vereniging 1994) 57–89.

Chapter 30

Stephen Colclough

"R R, A REMARKABLE THING OR ACTION": JOHN DAWSON AS A READER AND ANNOTATOR

MUCH OF THE MOST COMPELLING evidence for the history of reading has come from studies of the ways in which readers annotated the texts that they owned or borrowed. For example, the close examination of Gabriel Harvey's annotated Livy by Lisa Jardine and Anthony Grafton, and the work of William Sherman on John Dee, has led to the identification of a class of professional readers who were paid to transform reading as "public performance" into political action during the late sixteenth century.[1] Jardine and Grafton make no claims for this form of reading as a normative practice, but their methodology suggests that a history of reading that accounts for the varied and active practices of individual readers will be quite different from that constructed using the text itself as evidence: "If we use *our own* understanding of the salient features of the text of Livy (say) to identify the points of crucial importance to an *Elizabethan reader*," they argue, "we are very likely to miss or to confuse the methods and objects at which reading was directed."[2] Traditionally, historians of reading have been concerned with the kinds of texts consumed by a particular audience at a given historical moment, recoverable, at least in theory, from production figures and ownership records, but the work of the above scholars, and others involved in recovering the history of the book, has led a new wave of historians to focus upon the nature of consumption, upon "how" texts were read, and the rules that governed access to them.[3] For example, recent work on seventeenth-century readers by Kevin Sharpe and Steven Zwicker has concentrated upon what Zwicker calls "the ways in which readers reshaped books", and H.J. Jackson's book-length study, *Marginalia: Readers Writing in Books*, incorporates examples of discursive annotations recorded between 1700 and the present day.[4]

Much recent work on the history of reading thus suggests that it is "a marginal enterprise," but some scholars remain sceptical about the ability of marginalia to produce evidence of either typical readers or "the mental process accompanying reading".[5] "Typical" readers are difficult to recover from any source, of course, and Jackson's work on marginalia takes issue with those who use autobiographies, surveys and bestseller lists as evidence of the "common reader."[6] Indeed, the concept of the "common" or typical reader appears increasingly anachronistic to scholars who are concerned with issues of difference, and historians of print culture now recognise the need to grapple with both the "sheer variety of experiences of reading in the age of print", as well as "the obstinate, irreducible individualism" of a reader who can resist or misread, and as both Grafton and Jackson have acknowledged, it is the production of case studies of individual readers that will allow such theories to be tested.[7] The issue of "mental process" is perhaps more difficult to deal with. Some historians of reading claim that the marks left by the reader on the page may be the best evidence that we have of this process, but I think that such an assumption comes dangerously close to making reading with pen in hand a normal, everyday practice, rather than a distinct mode of reading that was utilised when readers thought it necessary.[8] Those who read with the pen chose to engage with the text on a particular level and the examination of books that contain marginalia and other forms of annotation will help us to recover an important material dimension of reading practice that historians concerned with mental process tend to ignore. Most of the studies of marginalia that have been undertaken so far have tended to concentrate on either authors, academics or the reception of canonical texts because this material is most accessible, but it is the aim of this paper to shed more light on reading outside the academy by concentrating on one reader, the excise officer John Dawson (1692–1765), who did not have the privileged access to texts enjoyed by many intellectuals.

What we know about Dawson's life is mainly derived from his own autobiographical writings, and these often make him sound like a character from a novel by Defoe. Born in Leeds in 1692, the eldest child of a textile worker, he moved with his family to Ireland in 1695 when his father joined the excise, and remained there until his father's death in 1709. After returning to England he spent time in the navy before becoming an excise officer in London in January 1714, but gave up his commission in the same year after inheriting his grandmother's estate, and subsequently married the daughter of his London landlord. By the end of 1715 Dawson had returned to the excise, but after selling his inheritance, took a series of jobs, including publican, soldier, and merchant sailor, before being press-ganged into the Navy in 1719. He rejoined the excise in Penshurst, Kent in 1722, and remained there until the death of his estranged wife in 1727, when he returned to London to become an excise officer in the "London Brewery". In January 1729 he married Phillecia Andrews, a widowed staymaker, and they set up house together in Hoxton, a new suburb north of the city of London, where he continued to live and work until his death in 1765.[9]

In 1765 Dawson bequeathed his collection of books to the Church of St. Leonard, Shoreditch, for use as a parish library, and 635 of the original 879 volumes are now held by the Hackney Archives Department in London.[10] The contents of the library were recorded when the books were given to the Church, but an earlier catalogue compiled by Dawson in 1739 allows us to view the library as it evolved and it is with the books bought before 1740 that I am concerned in this paper.[11] The 1739 catalogue contains details of 104 volumes (seventy-one titles) and is divided into five sections that organize its contents according to size. These sections, which range from "books in folio" to "small twelves", are then subdivided into columns that record a shortened version of the title, the month and the year in which each book was acquired ('when first had') and either its "price" or its "value".[12]

The most expensive purchase listed in this catalogue is the folio edition of Stow's *Survey of the Cities of London and Westminster* bought for £4 in 1733, but most of the values recorded range from 1s to 10s per item, for books either in octavo or duodecimo.[13] Both the size of Dawson's household, which included an apprentice, and the fact that he recorded purchasing other luxury goods, such as silverware, suggests that he was a fairly typical member of the middling ranks of urban society. As Lorna Weatherill's study of British probate inventories has demonstrated, book ownership was increasing amongst this section of the population from the late seventeenth century, and its expansion was most rapid in London, which had the highest incidence of book ownership in the country by 1705.[14] The 1739 catalogue thus provides an unusually detailed record of the texts owned by a member of the urban,

"middling" sort, whose access to texts was not uniquely privileged by a University education, or a position in the Church, and we can tell a great deal about the way in which he
made meaning from these texts from annotations in the surviving volumes.

If we compare Dawson's catalogue with the list of books belonging to a Cambridge
student, John Gibson, whose 216 volumes were valued as part of a distraint for debt in
1722, some differences are immediately apparent. The student's collection included a core
of theology and a significant number of texts in French, Greek, Hebrew and Latin. Dawson's
library, by contrast, was almost exclusively vernacular and contained only one Classic in
translation.[15] As David McKitterick has argued, "Latinity" could be almost as important as
literacy in determining the ways in which readers deployed their skills during this period,
and the absence from his collection of books in languages other than English confirms that
we are dealing with a reader from outside the scholarly tradition.[16] The libraries of British
scholars also usually included texts printed outside the British Isles, but all of the surviving
books bought before 1740, and those titles that can be identified from the 1739 catalogue,
were printed in London.

Most of the books that Dawson bought during the 1730s were octavo in format, and he
had a particular passion for both history and practical texts, such as dictionaries and gazetteers. For example, the octavos section of the 1739 catalogue includes eleven volumes of
Abel Boyer's *History of the Reign of Queen Anne* (1703–13), as well as dictionaries and volumes
of instructions such as the "Practical Surveyor". Fortunately, many of these texts have
survived as part of the 1765 bequest and Dawson's copy of John Holwell's *A Sure Guide to the
Practical Surveyor* (1678) displays many of the features that are typical of his annotated
books.[17] This text was one of a number of books that he inherited from his father and the
title page includes the ownership marks of the older man. On the verso, Dawson added his
own signature and the date "February 14*th* 1709/10". All of Dawson's books include such
marks of ownership and he also often recorded their position within his library, on, or near
to, the title page.[18] Like most of his books the *Sure Guide* does not include discursive
marginalia, but Dawson added page numbers to the headings in the list of "contents" in order
to make it easier to use and corrected some mistakes in pagination in the appendix, as well as
creating two manuscript indexes, which are now bound into the book's end pages. Such
indexes occur frequently in his books and in this instance they provide page numbers for
"The Tables" and "The Plates in this Book". Similar examples of texts being worked over in
order to make information retrieval easier can be found throughout the collection. Dawson
often included similar tables to store supplementary information and the *Sure Guide* also
contains an incomplete manuscript table that has been used to record additions to the text.[19]
Such practical texts, used regularly to retrieve and store information, are a major feature of
his library, and we need to recognise the significance of such books to the history of reading.

This evidence suggests that Dawson's annotation system was devised in order to allow
him to retrieve information more easily than the printed apparatus allowed, and his books
reveal a close reader determined to put his texts to work. Of course, many texts printed in
the early eighteenth century were less than perfect: the printed word "had merely reached
the most textually advanced stage that was practical under a certain set of circumstances,"
and consequently either the print-shop or the reader would have needed to make final
adjustments by annotating the printed page.[20] Dawson's texts include several corrections of
this type, and a survey of annotations from the British Library's collections reveals that he
shared many of his annotation strategies with other early eighteenth-century readers.[21]
These annotations expose the varied and active practices of readers in this period, but they
also show some common patterns, which suggest that the individualism of the reader was
usually expressed within certain codes, and that readers frequently responded to the physical
structure of the printed object by mimicking its language, or by exposing its faults. However,

Dawson differs from these readers in applying manuscript tables, indexes and other forms of addition so extensively, and I now want to examine the ways in which he used these additions to make sense of the volumes of history that he owned.

Daniel Woolf's work on British probate inventories and private catalogues from this period reveals that by the early eighteenth century "history had established a place for itself in the private libraries of persons well below the level of either noblemen [. . .] or [. . .] the *nouveau riche*."[22] Dawson's library was thus part of a growing trend amongst the "middling sort" for the collection of secular books, but Woolf's findings suggest that the sheer number of histories that he owned was unusual. Of the thirty-nine octavo volumes recorded in the 1739 catalogue, twenty-nine (seventy-four percent) were histories, and the fact that he also owned a number of expensive folios, such as Isaacson's *Historica Chronologica* (1633), Echard's *History of England* (1707), and Camden's *Britannia* (1722) that were valued together at over £5 in the catalogue, suggests that he was prepared to invest heavily in one of his favourite subject areas.[23] Woolf's survey suggests that by 1700, many small private libraries included significant numbers of historical works, but that ten to fifteen percent was typical, and that more than forty percent was very unusual indeed.[24]

Dawson's collection is also particularly notable because he favoured annals and chronologies that included near contemporary events, such as Abel Boyer's *History of King William III* (1702–03) and Thomas Salmon's *Chronological Historian* (1733), and his surviving books provide important evidence about the ways in which he understood and made use of their contents.[25] Marginalia occurs more often in Dawson's volumes of history than in any of the other genres that he owned, and his copy of *The Peerage of England . . . Volume II* (1711) includes a number of features that are typical. This volume contains corrections to errors in dating and cross-references to passages on the same subject in *Volume I*, but it does not include scholarly cross-references to other competing accounts of events of the kind often deployed by scholarly readers.[26] Dawson preferred to add additional pages of manuscript to his books rather than annotate their margins, and these additions provide important evidence about the way in which he interpreted history. Dawson also added additional subject headings to the printed index of *The Peerage*, but it is the two additional manuscript indexes, listing each peerage by place and each peer by name, that are the most striking feature of this book.[27]

Dawson appears to have created these indexes in order to make it easier to consult the book on a regular basis, but they were also the product of a close reading. Indeed, they suggest that Dawson needed to engage with history on this level, to turn the contents of his volumes into annals, or other forms of his own writing, if he was to make sense of them and put them to work. For example, his copy of the *Atlas Geographus* (1711), a history despite its title, is one of the most thoroughly worked over texts in the collection and contains a large number of tables bound into the beginning of each new section. "A Perticular Table No 3" precedes the section on France and contains a "contents" list constructed by copying each side heading from this section of the volume. In the text itself, the corresponding side headings have been underlined to make finding these sections easier. This extension of the volume's printed apparatus is followed by a series of headings and references that are part personal index, part commonplace book. Notes under headings such as "Batles [sic] in France" make reference to unusual events such as "a batle fought by women in men's cloaths" and provide rare evidence of Dawson as a curious reader, picking over his histories for interesting narratives.[28] Such notes are a striking contrast to the carefully constructed annals that we find elsewhere, and they suggest something of the range of practices and methodologies that Dawson brought to bear on his books, but his annotation practices are dominated by the construction of "tables" and "indexes" such as those found in *The Peerage of England*.

[. . .]

This evidence suggests that one of the ways in which Dawson created meaning out of the histories that he owned was through abstraction, but further clues to the way in which he constructed abstracts from Salmon can be found within that volume's extensive coded marginalia and the table of "The Signification of the Marks in this Book" that he added to the book's front matter. By using the marginal codes, PM, PP, Pa and PD for "Parliament meet", "prorogued", "adjourn'd", and "Dissolved", Dawson was able to locate the information that he needed to construct his list of parliaments, but these marginal codes also help us to understand the ways in which he read certain passages and episodes from this volume. Of course, by using a code, Dawson was drawing upon a technique for reading history that had been available since the Renaissance. Gabriel Harvey used astrological symbols to call attention to interesting historical lessons in his books, and Dawson's use of capital letters mimics the form, if not the purpose, of Bodin's *Methodus* (1566), in which the author encouraged readers to place the letters "CH" in the margin next to an example of the "*consilium honestum*" of a government.[29] Dawson's, "R R" for "a Remarkable Thing or Action", and "R R R" for "an Extraordinary Remarkable Thing or Action", are direct descendents of this method, and although there is something slightly comic about this terminology—how does one distinguish between the merely "remarkable" and the "extra-ordinary remarkable"?—, both the structure of this code, and its distribution in the margins, tells us something about the active nature of Dawson's reading practice.

For example, after Salmon's final entry for the year 1647, Dawson ruled a line across the page and then continued to add to the margins as the "remarkable" events of the English Civil War unfolded. Next to the passage for 30 January, "The king being ordered to be put to Death this Day," he left a sign that indicated that this was a "remarkable" event ("R R"), but he does not appear to have responded to Salmon's obvious sympathy for the monarch, or to his opposition to Cromwell, and after the words "he submitted to the block and his head was severed" he wrote "Ex" in the margin—code for the "execution of a malefactor". This is perhaps the closest that Dawson gets in his marginalia to challenging the author or question-ing the authority of the text, and it provides a rare insight into his reading at an ideological, or political level.

Dawson began work on a series of autobiographical writings in 1720, and the folio volume "My Own Life", deposited as part of the library in 1765, contains a sequence of annual summaries that include a mixture of personal reminiscence and notes on significant historical events.[30] Dawson stored information for this project in the volumes of history that he owned, including Boyer's *History of the Reign of Queen Anne Digested into Annals*, which contains autobiographical notes on the end pages corresponding to the years covered by each volume. The margins of his copy of *The Chronological Historian* are even more densely covered with markings from the year of his birth (1692) onwards and Dawson obviously used this text to supply much of the historical framework for the "Life", but he also noted national events that were of autobiographical significance by marking them with a "R.R.R" in the margin. For example, in the 1714/15 section of the text, he added this "mark" to a passage that recorded the issuing of a reward of £1,000 "to any Person who should discover the Author [. . .] of a Libel, intitled *English Advice to the Freeholders of England*".[31] Why should this event be more remarkable than the execution of the English monarch? This event was "extraordinary remarkable" because as he recorded in the January 1714/15 section of the "Life":

> [January]
>   13: I set out for Hull in order to go to London to get into the excise againe, and call'd at the Lord Downs's where I got the Advice to the Freeholders of England[.]

29: I was committed to Hull Gaol about the advice to the Freeholders of England Where I continued till apr.29.[32]

That he was imprisoned for three months for possessing a copy of this text suggests that reading could be a dangerous act in 1715, and it is hardly surprising, therefore, that Dawson should have used his marginalia to draw attention to an event that was of such importance in his own life. This evidence suggests that when Dawson read contemporary history he tended to take it personally, searching out evidence of events in which he had been involved and reconstructing the accounts of these, and other contemporary events, as part of his auto-biographical project, his own "Life". Dawson's annotated histories were thus part of a purposive reading strategy that aimed to construct a complex autobiography that would place the individual "life" within the context of contemporary European history, but they cannot simply be reduced to that purpose. As the chronological list of the "Kings of England" from 828–1727, constructed from the same volume demonstrates, for Dawson, to "read" history was to engage in the processes of abstraction and marginal annotation.

As David McKitterick recently noted, the autobiographical records that would help us to make sense of annotated books rarely survive. The Dawson collection is remark-able because it contains a diverse range of sources including catalogues, a miscellany, diaries, and an autobiography, as well as notebooks and accounts, which help us to see the role played by annotations in his reading life. Dawson's annotation strategies were obviously an important part of his reading experience but his diaries and miscellany reveal other ways of reading, and the importance of both ephemeral texts and transcription to his reading life; Dawson frequently read with the pen in hand, but this was not his only mode of reading.[33]

References

1   William Sherman, *John Dee: the Politics of Reading and Writing in the English Renaissance* (Amherst: University of Massachusetts Press, 1995); Lisa Jardine and Anthony Grafton, " 'Studied for Action': How Gabriel Harvey Read his Livy," *Past and Present*, 129 (1990): 30–78.

2   Jardine and Grafton, 31 (my italics).

3   The best example of this early approach is Richard Altick, *The English Common Reader; a Social History of the Mass Reading Public, 1800–1900* (Cambridge: Cambridge University Press, 1957). For a critique of trends in writing the history of reading, see Roger Chartier, *The Order of Books*, trans. by Lydia Cochrane (Cambridge: Polity Press, 1994), 1–24.

4   Kevin Sharpe, *Reading Revolutions: the Politics of Reading in Early Modern England* (London: Yale University Press, 2000); Steven N. Zwicker, "The Reader Revealed," in *The Reader Revealed*, edited by Sabrina Alcorn Baron, Elizabeth Walsh and Susan Scola (Washington: Folger Shakespeare Library, 2001), 11–17 (15); H.J. Jackson, *Marginalia: Readers Writing in Books* (London: Yale University Press, 2001).

5   This phrase is taken from Anthony Grafton's, "Is the History of Reading a Marginal Enter-prise?: Guillaume Bude and His Books", *Papers of the Bibliographical Society of America*, 91 (1997): 139–57; Jackson, *Marginalia*, 254. The collection *Readers in History: Nineteenth-century American Literature and the Contexts of Response*, edited by James L. Machor (Baltimore: Johns Hopkins University Press, 1993) is typical of a school of thought that argues against using records of individual reading experience as evidence of "typical" reading practices.

6   Jackson, *Marginalia*, 253.

7   Grafton, "Is the History of Reading a Marginal Enterprise", 141, Jackson, *Marginalia*, 256.

8   Grafton's assertion that the Renaissance scholar read with pen in hand because he "set out not only to converse with the ancients, using the classical tradition, but to document the progress that he made in doing so" suggests that the creation of marginalia often occurs in unique cultural and intellectual circumstances. "A Marginal Enterprise", 155.

9   John Dawson, "The Life of John Dawson; Officer of Excise," West Yorkshire Archive Service, Manuscript MS: KC688, Kirklees District Archives, Huddersfield.

10   For details of the Dawson collection, which also includes diaries and notebooks, see *A Directory of Rare Book and Special Collections in the United Kingdom and the Republic of Ireland*, 2nd edition, edited by R. C. Bloomfield (London: Library Association, 1997), 230–31; Tony Brown, "John Dawson: His Life and Library", 3 vols, unpublished FLA thesis, London, Library Association, 1973. I would like to acknowledge the kind assistance of the staff at both the Hackney and Huddersfield archives. All references to the manuscripts are reproduced with their permission.

11   "A Catalogue of the Books of Mr John Dawson of Hoxton Deceased, Left by Will to the Vicars of S. Leonard in Shoreditch, 1765," Dawson Collection, D/F/Daw-/1, Hackney Archives Department, London. The 1739 catalogue is contained in a notebook compiled between 1730 and 1759, D/F/Daw-/2, 155–63.

12   For a transcript of the 1739 catalogue, see Stephen Colclough, " 'A Catalogue of My Books': The Library of John Dawson (1692–1765), 'Exciseman and Staymaker', c.1739," *Publishing History* 47 (2000): 45–66.

13   Evidence from the catalogue suggests that this was probably John Stow's, *A Survey of the Cities of London and Westminster . . . Corrected, Improved and Very Much Enlarged . . . by John Strype*, 2 vols (London: Churchill, Knapton [and others], 1720).

14   By 1725, 52% of the London inventories sampled included books. Lorna Weatherill, *Consumer Behaviour and Material Culture in Britain, 1660–1760*, 2nd edition (London: Routledge, 1996), 49.

15   E.S. Leedham-Green, *Books in Cambridge Inventories: Book Lists from Vice-Chancellor's Court Probate Inventories in the Tudor and Stuart Periods*, 2 vols, (Cambridge: Cambridge University Press, 1986), Vol. I, 588–92; John Dryden, *Fables Ancient and Modern; Translated from Homer, Ovid, Bocace, and Chaucer* (London: Jacob Tonson, 1713).

16   David McKitterick, "Book Catalogues: Their Varieties and Uses," in *The Book Encompassed: Studies in Twentieth-Century Bibliography*, edited by Peter Davison (Cambridge: Cambridge University Press, 1992), 161–75.

17   Abel Boyer, *The History of the Reign of Queen Anne, Digested Into Annals*, 11 vols (London: A Roper, F. Cogan, 1703–13); John Holwell, *A Sure Guide to the Practical Surveyor, in Two Parts. The First Shewing How to Plot All Manner of Grounds . . . The Second Shewing How to Take the Ground Plot of any City or Corporation* (London: Christopher Hussey, 1678).

18   For example, his copy of [Arthur Collins], *The Peerage of England Or, A Genealogical and Historical Account of All the Flourishing Families of this Kingdom . . . Volume II. Part II* (London: Sanger and Collins, 1711) contains the note: "John Dawson's Book Oct: 1730, No. 52: Case 1. app: 8; No. in app: 6" on the end pages. There are no shelf details in his copy of Holwell, but these may have been lost when this volume was rebound in the 1950s.

19   His copy of Laurence Echard, *The Gazetter's: or Newsman's Interpreter* (London: John Nicholson, 1704), for example, has additional entries that list towns not included by the editor.

20   David McKitterick, *A History of Cambridge University Press: Printing and the Book Trade in Cambridge, 1534–1698* (Cambridge: Cambridge University Press, 1992), xiii.

21   The Reading Experience Database (RED) includes details of over 100 annotated books printed between 1690 and 1740, now in the British Library's collections. For details of the RED project, see Stephen Colclough, "Recording the Revolution: Reading Experience and the History of the Book," *Siegener Periodicum zur Internationalen Empirischen Literaturwissenschaft* 19 (2000): 36–55.

22   D. R. Woolf, *Reading History in Early Modern England* (Cambridge: Cambridge University Press, 2000), 156.

23   Henry Isaacson, *Saturni Ephemerides Sive Tabula Historica Chronologica* (London: Henry Siele & Humphry Robinson, 1633) valued at 12s; Laurence Echard, *The History of England* (London: Jacob Tonson, 1707) valued at £2 2s; William Camden, *Britannia or a Chronological Description of Great Britain and Ireland* (London: J. & J. Knapton, 1722), valued at £3.

24   "Even in 1700 when the titles available had expanded enormously, most catalogs would contain no more than a fifth-part historical matter, and generally somewhere in the range of 10–15 percent," Woolf, *Reading History*, 157. Of the 107 volumes that Dawson owned in 1739, 43 can be classified as history.

25   Abel Boyer, *The History of King William the Third*, 3 vols (London: A. Roper and F. Coggan,

1702–03); Thomas Salmon, *The Chronological Historian. . . . From the Invasion of the Romans, to the Death of King George First*, 2nd edition (London: Mears, 1733).

26   *The Peerage of England: Or, A Genealogical and Historical Account of All the Flourishing Families of this Kingdom . . . Volume II. Part I* (London: Sangar and Collins, 1711). A good example of a contemporary volume annotated by an anonymous scholarly reader is the British Library's copy of Thomas Salmon, *A Review of the History of England in Two Volumes*, 2nd edition (London, 1724), which includes references to alternative and competing sources in the margins (BL: 598.e.16). This volume was later owned by the scholar-collector Francis Hargrave (1741?–1821).

27   This annotation system is continued in *The Peerage of England: or, an Historical Account of the Present Nobility*, fourth edition, 2 vols (London: W. Taylor, 1717), which contains ten pages of "tables" listing dukes, earls, viscounts and barons.

28   *Atlas Geographus: Or a Compleat System of Geography Ancient and Modern*, 2 vols (London: John Nutt, 1711). The passage on "women in men's apparel" is found on p. 1054 of volume II, Dawson's notes follow p. 1336.

29   For a discussion of the symbols used by Harvey, see William Sherman, *John Dee: the Politics of Reading*; Jean Bodin, *Methodus, ad Facilem Historiarum Cognitionem* (Paris, 1566); Bodin is discussed in Anthony Grafton, "Discitur ut Agatur: How Gabriel Harvey Read His Livy," in *Annotation and Its Texts* edited by Stephen A. Barney (Oxford: Oxford University Press, 1991), 108–29 (117–18).

30   "The Life of John Dawson; Officer of Excise", West Yorkshire Archive Service MA: KC688, Kirklees District Archives, Huddersfield.

31   *Chronological Historian*, 336.

32   "The Life of John Dawson," f.15v.

33   David McKitterick, "Women and their Books in Seventeenth-Century England: The Case of Elizabeth Puckering," *The Library*, Vol. I (2000): 359–380 (380).

Chapter 31

James A. Secord

SELF-DEVELOPMENT

I must, however, remind my reader that the "I" who speaks in this book is not the author himself, but it is his earnest wish that the reader should himself assume this character, and that he should . . . hold converse with himself, deliberate, draw conclusions and form resolutions, like his representative in the book . . . and build up within himself that mode of thought the mere picture of which is laid before him in the work.

Johann Gottlieb Fichte, *The Vocation of Man* (first English translation, 1848)

MOST READINGS LEAVE LITTLE or no trace—an ownership signature or a few pencil marks. Only certain types of reading, such as academic study and reviewing, produce more substantial records. Recovering the voices of readers who are not literary producers and who do not have established reputations is more difficult. Even so, the nineteenth-century material—thanks to increased readerships, the popularity of diary keeping, and the evangelical revival—is more extensive than anything available before or since. It is surprising that there are no analyses of nineteenth-century readers comparable to those available for earlier periods, such as John Brewer's study of the educated Englishwoman Anna Margaretta Larpent and Robert Darnton's account of the Rousseau-reading French merchant Jean Ranson.[1] The difficulty is not to find detailed records of reading, it is locating them for a specified title.

For *Vestiges* there is an exceptional source in the journals of the eighteen-year-old Thomas Archer Hirst of Halifax in West Yorkshire.[2] Born in 1830, Hirst was the youngest son of Thomas Hirst, a merchant who bought wool from producers, graded it, and sold it to manufacturers. Hirst's father was a liberal Congregationalist and supporter of the Whig Lord Morpeth in the 1835 elections; his mother, Hannah, came from a wealthy Anglican family. The elder Hirst had died in a drinking accident in 1842, and although there was some money (through his mother) the three boys needed to find work suitable to their middle-class status.

Halifax was a bustling place with a population of twenty thousand, mostly manual laborers engaged in the textile, engineering, and machine tool industries. The steep and narrow streets lent "a touch of antiquity," but worsted mills and mill workers' dwellings circled the center. Working conditions were bad in the mills; sanitation throughout the city was appalling. As one reporter complained, Halifax was "a marvel of dirt."[3] The railway mania was at its height, so when Hirst left school in 1845 at fifteen he was apprenticed for five years to a civil engineer, Richard Carter, to train as a surveyor. This was thought to offer a good route toward a secure future as a professional man. Probably following the example of Carter's chief surveyor, the Irish Orangeman John Tyndall, Hirst began recording details of his reading in novels, periodicals, poetry, theology, and especially science. Because Hirst was so young, his journal is explicit about activities that most readers took for granted.

Hirst read *Vestiges* when he was defining his personal faith, his sense of himself, and his vocation in life. Tyndall described him as "our junior apprentice, a youth upwards of 6 feet high, and about 16 years of age—an immense development of brain which is in true keeping with his extraordinary powers of thinking."[4] Hirst explored the book in the same way as many other young working- and middle-class autodidacts in cities: through discussions with friends at home, in taverns, at work, and at the Mechanics' Institution and his local Mutual Improvement Society. He studied it closely for nearly a month, copying out long passages from it in his journal. He read reviews and Miller's *Footprints*, noting his own reactions and those of his friends. In its combination of diary, commonplace book, and conversational record, the journal reflects Hirst's immersion in contemporary periodicals, social problem fictions and the writings of Thomas Carlyle. Hirst was precisely the kind of reader addressed by the YMCA, the useful knowledge publishers, the infidel mission, and by *Vestiges*.

Alternatively, Hirst could be (and usually has been) taken as a type of reader who later assumed a position on the national stage. In the 1860s and 1870s, he became known as a mathematician and for his membership of the X-Club, the inner circle of science "pure and free, untrammelled by religious dogmas."[5] Like others of his generation, Hirst emerged from a spiritual crisis to become one of the leaders of a new faith in science. Many came from backgrounds in provincial Dissent, notably the evolutionary philosopher Herbert Spencer; Tyndall shared Hirst's training as a surveyor, as did Alfred Russel Wallace. There is, however, a crushing familiarity about this way of telling the story. Only in retrospect can Hirst's case be seen as typical of the leaders of mid-Victorian science; and this view gives little idea of the struggles that were involved. Each experience of reading becomes more generally revealing the more locally it can be situated. Hirst read *Vestiges* not as a future X-Club member, but as a participant in Halifax's lively local culture of self-improvement.

Reading *Vestiges*

[. . .]

Vestiges served as a talking point for Halifax's young men in pubs, on walks, in their rooms, and at work. Soon after its appearance, it had been fiercely opposed in the conservative *Halifax Guardian*, the only locally published newspaper:

> If the writer is prepared to admit that these "vestiges" as narrated by geologists prove that creation was *not* effected in six days, and that death was *not* a new feature brought into the world by man's fall, he might as well admit the more consistent view of the work reviewed, and declare that all nature is progressive, that rolling stones begat lobsters; leaping lobsters, frogs; wind-inflated frogs, oxen; and that man is but a more perfect kind of monkey, beginning with the Carib and ending (at present) with the Caucasian, but capable of still further development, perhaps, into the angel![6]

Admit the findings of geology, the review argued, and the whole godless scheme followed as a matter of course. Opinion in the town on such issues ranged from the God-denying materialism of Owenite infidels to those who anticipated the imminent reign of Christ on earth.

The first mention of *Vestiges* by Hirst in his journal is in the record of a conversation with his close friend Francis Booth in July 1847. [. . .] Booth, whose mother lived in a cottage on the edge of the moors, had begun as an errand boy in a printer's office but had risen to a responsible position in a local wool mill. Their talk brought up the issue of divine mystery, which they agreed was essential to reverence for the Creator. However, Booth was more skeptical in suggesting that scientific progress undercut this mystery, and hence our reverence. In reply, Hirst argued that science could only enhance devotion as it discovered general laws, perhaps even "one great natural law." Booth responded by pointing up the relevance of geology, and especially of *Vestiges*, to this debate.[7]

The enthusiasm of his friends spurred Hirst to read for himself. He borrowed the sixth edition or (more probably) its cheap reprint[8] on 1 August 1848 from the library of the local Mutual Improvement Society. His decision to read it grew out of his earlier conversations. For nearly a month the library copy accompanied Hirst wherever he went, both as a physical object and as an intellectual interlocutor. The small size of the book was convenient, but Hirst said nothing about this nor about any other aspect of the work's physical form. For him, unlike some other contemporary readers, the book was the text. He read at home, after chapel, in the evenings, in public reading rooms, and in the Mutual Improvement Society library. Sometimes he read for hours; sometimes in moments snatched from other activities. But wherever he was and whatever the time, "reading *Vestiges*"—a recurrent phrase—was an identifiable activity, to be taken up where left off. Most of Hirst's reading was done silently and by himself; and through the writing in his journal, it became part of the record of his life.

The pages of summary and reflection in Hirst's journal are the best evidence for his deep immersion in an approach to reading that he would have learned through the kind of study recommended in the learned traditions of Congregational Dissent.[9] At a basic level, Hirst was concerned to report—as neutrally as possible—the plain meaning of what *Vestiges* said. Many entries in the journal are long chapter summaries and quotations, written out like the documents he copied for his master, with his own views clearly distinguished. He made few notes on the geological chapters, being already familiar with Mantell, Lyell, and the "beautiful digest of the science" in Chambers's Information for the People.[10] After a week's relatively slow reading, he noted that the author "begins to announce his hypothesis, and that in a masterly manner," and from this point onward the book is abstracted at great length. By the thirteenth of August, a Sunday, he had reached the chapter on "the history of mankind, their peculiar forms, languages and colour." Here again, "all facts [were] in accordance with his theory" of a common origin.[11] The following day, he read the chapter on the "purpose of the animated creation" and summed up its discussions of the origins of evil. *Vestiges*, through its reliance on law, had a profound answer to the problem that had puzzled philosophers for centuries and one that Paley's *Natural Theology* had not solved. "The virtuous man is as liable to such misfortune as the wicked—a fact that would be difficult to reconcile under any other view of the purpose of creation."[12]

Although Hirst had read to the end after the first two weeks in August, he had the book reentered in his name at the Mutual Improvement Society, to abstract what he had identified as its novel argument about organic development. Several pages reported the text without comment and often verbatim, but in closing his discussion of the chapters on transmutation Hirst summed up his own view:

Such is a general outline of this most extraordinary of theories, a theory evidently the result of a calm, impartial, honest, as well as scientific investigation, divulged with a manly spirit and sustained, in spite of the prejudice and ridicule of the world. Such is ever the fate of one who steps forward so much in advance of his fellow beings. But although believing this theory as likely to be modified in many particulars according to the further discoveries of science, I must say it is the most plausible attempt that ever I heard or saw, to explain the creation and development of the world and its organic inhabitants, by natural law. And at the same time I feel certain that it will have given an impulse to investigation—set it in a proper track, as it were—from which impulse may be anticipated a greatly advanced state of science, together with its attendant blessings.[13]

Hirst had read with devouring attention, more closely in fact than any book up to this point in his life other than the Bible.

Hirst by no means agreed with everything *Vestiges* said. One evening his friend Booth came over to play the flute and piano, and they discussed the book. Booth accepted that the further development of new species probably occurred without divine intervention, according to the *Vestiges* scheme, but doubted whether life could originate from nonliving matter. In contrast, Hirst maintained that if natural law explained species it was likely to do the same for life itself.[14] A few days later Hirst and his friend Roby Pridie, son of the local Congregational minister, read together a "very cleverly written" analysis of the book in an old number of the *British Quarterly Review*.[15] In discussing this review, and another in the same number, Hirst drew the line at the natural origin of human reason and free will. Having just read the chapter on animal intelligence twice, he became convinced that the author "is evidently a materialist or something approaching it—he believes that mind is a function of the brain, governed by as fixed laws as any other part of nature." On this principle, the human soul ought to be explicable as a development from the lower animals, yet the book also stated that man alone might have been "endowed with an immortal spirit."[16] This seemed inconsistent, and Hirst doubted whether man could have developed from the apes.

At the end of August 1848, having finished with *Vestiges*, Hirst borrowed *Explanations*, presumably from the Mutual Improvement Society's library, and completed it four days later. On the evidence of entries in the journal, he had seen only one review of the original work (in the *British Quarterly*), so the sequel gave an opportunity to judge both the criticisms and the author's response. Hirst was impressed: "he certainly sets to rights many of his reviewers' objections." At the same time, though, Hirst thought the new work shifted its ground more than its author was willing to say. What had been widely seen as the principal claim of *Vestiges*, its "particular theory" of development was now being acknowledged as subsidiary to the larger issue of natural law. This backtracking and "toning down," at least from Hirst's perspective, made the argument "less startling" but also more probable, "capable of directing enquiry into a channel nearer the true one."[17] References to *Vestiges* continue to crop up in the journal over the next year, culminating in an intensive debate among Hirst's friends about Miller's *Footprints*.

Independent reading

The first thing that strikes a modern reader about Hirst's engagement with *Vestiges*—and the many other books he read—is its extraordinary intensity. Almost no one reads like this any more. It is the reading practice of a self-improving autodidact, shaped by traditions of Bible-reading among Congregationalists, Presbyterians, and the other denominations of learned, liberal Dissent. Yet what would, a few decades earlier, have been written out as the journey of a soul to Christ has here become a quest for self-identity through an understanding of nature.[18]

Hirst had learned to read at the town school in Heckmondwick. Built in 1809 by subscription, this offered a grounding in basic literacy and arithmetic. When Hirst attended, the school had about 150 scholars, both boys and girls, who paid a small weekly sum for their lessons. A library of several hundred works was housed in the same building, supported by twenty-four subscribers.[19] In the Dissenting traditions that dominated practical education in Yorkshire and Lancashire, the Bible provided a template for how all books should be read: slowly, line-by-line, and with utmost attention to the nuances of the reader's relationship (or lack thereof) with God. Hirst's experience of *Vestiges* embodied ideals at the heart of the exegetical practice of old Dissent: close reading, the consultation of parallel texts, and the need for private judgment. The roots of these techniques are to be found in the Reformation, although they were not distant memories, nor simply the reflections of pious conduct manuals. This is the way Hirst and his friends had learned to read.

These exalted ideals of reading may have their origins in a broadly evangelical tradition, but one book that Hirst hardly ever read was the Bible, even on Sundays. This was most unusual for someone of his background and serious intellectual interests, and he blamed his early schooling, which had made reading the Bible anything but a transcendent experience. The failure of faith was a failure of education in reading:

> To-day I have read my Bible, rather an unusual thing for me—and why? Because my teachers have taught me to profane it. I have been made [to] repeat it when its living passages were meaningless to me; instead of impressing me with its sacredness and making it a sealed book to me until I was by training worthy to open it, I have gabbled it like a parrot, and attached to its living oracles an unworthy, conventional meaning.[20]

This criticism of the dangers of rote learning was itself characteristic of the Dissenting literature on education, which warned of the dangers of introducing biblical instruction at too early an age. The spiritual development of the individual could proceed only through close engagement with the inspired word.

[. . .]

Hirst's quest for a sense of identity was especially acute, as his formal education had ended at the age of fifteen, three years after his father's death. Hirst was apprenticed to Carter and moved with his mother and sister to Halifax. It was at this time that he had begun to keep a journal of his spiritual progress and everyday activities. He played music, fished, skated, drank, played chess and cards, hunted for fossils, went to church, chapel, and theater, and talked with friends in taverns and local societies.

[. . .]

With his employer's encouragement, Hirst began to follow an eclectic program of self-education. Most unusually (and probably through an arrangement with the family), Carter allowed his apprentice to read during working hours, although most of the young man's time was occupied with copying documents, surveying, and carrying transits, chains, and theodolites from field to field. Hirst enjoyed the companionship the job provided, but found the work dull, scarcely reflecting his interest in abstract geometry and trigonometry. As early as September 1846 his answer to a mathematical conundrum appeared in the *Family Herald*, a London-based weekly with stories, useful knowledge, and correspondence columns.

Hirst put reading at the heart of self-improvement: "My studies during the past year may be seen from the books I have read."[21] Every evening he wrote long entries in his journal, which show him as a keen and knowledgeable reader of science. By the time he checked *Vestiges* out of the library, he had already read Lyell's *Principles of Geology*, Humboldt's *Cosmos*, Mantell's *Wonders of Geology* ("the first book of really useful information I ever read through"),[22] Combe's *Constitution of Man*, Jeremiah Joyce's *Natural Philosophy*, Cuvier's *Theory of the Earth*, and numerous other works. He also paid serious attention to theology, though the number of titles was smaller, and he rarely studied his Bible. Books that discussed the theological implications of science were of special interest, including John Pye Smith's *On the Relation between the Holy Scriptures and Some Parts of Geological Science* (1839), Combe's *On the Relation between Religion and Science* (1847), and several of the Bridgewater Treatises.

Hirst read almost no poetry, as he noted when examining Alexander Pope's *Essay on Man* (a work in any case related to his philosophical concerns), and few novels. These included Dickens's *David Copperfield* and *Dombey and Son*, Goldsmith's *Vicar of Wakefield*, as well as Bulwer-Lytton's *The Caxtons*, read in *Blackwood's*, and Kingsley's *Yeast*, which appeared anonymously in *Fraser's*.[23] The story of *Yeast*, which concerned the struggles of a young man to find a creed, was peculiarly appropriate to his own situation, and he approached each new serial in *Fraser's* in keen anticipation that it might be by the same author.

Novel reading was not sinful—nor was dancing or the theater—but its value was debatable. One of Hirst's friends, Haley, gave a paper on it at the Franklin Society, which they later discussed.[24] Hirst rarely commented in any detail on novels in his journal, reserving his close attention for "serious" reading. Different books needed to be read in different ways. At best, as he reflected when in bed with a cold, "stirring fiction" could serve as a medicine by harmonizing with the state of his mind.[25] The right kind of reading was central to self-improvement.

Hirst owned only a handful of the titles he read, and his journals do not mention buying secondhand books or clubbing together with others to make purchases. These were often the only options for workingmen who could not afford regular library subscriptions. Even on his limited income as an apprentice, Hirst could afford three or four pounds each year to gain access to collections from which he could borrow. The Mutual Improvement Society had been founded in 1846 by a group of workingmen (known as the "Old Muffs") for self-improvement and elementary education.[26] Hirst, with his superior upbringing and education, served as one of their teachers and was a keen supporter and user of the library in their rooms in Waterhouse Street. Besides this collection, he also used the Mechanics' Institution library (with over twenty-seven hundred volumes, founded in 1825) and the circulating library run by John MacCarthur on Jail Lane.[27] Hirst did not seek to join the local Literary and Philosophical Society, as this would have been both expensive and inappropriate for someone of his age and status. There were many other sources of books in Halifax, including two "public" subscription libraries (one for Anglicans, with ten thousand volumes, the other for Dissenters).[28] However, nothing compared with the riches available to Liverpool and Manchester gentlemen, nor to genteel readers in Oxford, Cambridge, Edinburgh, and London; Sedgwick and Whewell each had more books in their college rooms than did the Halifax Mechanics' Institution or Mutual Improvement Society in their respective libraries.

Newspapers and magazines played an important part in the process of close, comparative reading. In local reading rooms and his master's office, Hirst regularly scanned Edward Miall's weekly *Nonconformist*, whose Dissenting outlook and political liberalism he broadly shared; the local conservative weekly, the *Halifax Guardian*; and occasional copies of the liberal weeklies such as *Chambers's Journal*, the *Family Herald, Howitt's Journal*, and the *People's Journal*. He did not read much in the quarterlies, which were expensive and not easily available, although he knew the importance of the *Edinburgh*'s review of *Vestiges* from the discussion in *Explanations*. The sole exception was old numbers of the *British Quarterly Review*, which Hirst's friend Pridie is likely to have obtained from his father, a Congregational minister. Among the monthlies, he read *Fraser's* if it had a good serial. Hirst recognized that all this was what might be expected for someone of his religious and political background— and so, unwilling to limit his horizons to a particular party, he also read the Tory *Blackwood's*. Hirst had nothing but scorn for the radical Chartist and Owenite press, condemning the views taken in the latter as "preposterous."[29]

Hirst's experience shows the dramatic expansion of the range of books available to young men in the middle class and the highest reaches of the artisan class. Nothing like this would have been available to an eighteen-year-old apprentice at the start of the century. Even those lower in the social scale could gain access to a wider range of texts than ever before. *Vestiges* was a common book in the kind of collections young men like Hirst used throughout the country; a survey of catalogues shows it was found in the mechanics' institute libraries of Evesham, Keighley, Liverpool, Manchester, and Warrington, among many others.[30] For working-class autodidacts lower in the social scale, obtaining up-to-date books was a continual struggle, as in the cases of the ribbon weaver Joseph Gutteridge, the compositor William Chilton, and the schoolteacher Mary Smith.

Access placed important constraints on how books were read. Mary Smith, who also read Carlyle and Fichte, had raced through *Vestiges* in a single night as though it were a novel; but this was at least in part because the book was secretly borrowed from her employer, and had to be back on the drawing room table in the morning. Smith's employer, in turn, had borrowed the volume from a circulating library, which gave him more time for reading but meant that any reactions would have to be recorded in a separate journal. Wealthier readers who owned their own copies could record their reactions directly in marginal annotations. Hirst, in contrast, had to write out large parts of the text in his journal; but this became a form of "mental ownership" that he preferred, even after he could afford to buy more books. In copying huge chunks into the journals, he effectively wrote his own *Vestiges*, making his journal into a commonplace book, a private anthology of the kind recommended by John Locke and many authors of advice manuals.[31] The copying of prose did for Hirst what the memorization of poetry did for other readers: it made books more closely part of himself.

Comparative reading

Such an eclectic program of reading meant that Hirst did not experience books as continuous narratives, but as texts broken up through juxtaposition with other texts. "Reading *Vestiges*" had thus both an internal coherence of its own—partly through the physical experience of turning the pages of a particular volume—but was also open-ended. Close reading is often discussed as if it were an improbably self-contained process, in which the narrative structure of a work shapes the reader's experience. Hirst, like most readers, moved between writings by many different authors in the course of each day—many of them, such as advertisements, placards, and written instructions on medicines—not recorded in his journal. Through the process of juxtaposition, he could structure his own horizon of expectations.[32]

The journal is a record of how Hirst did this. He moved, often as part of a clear plan, between *Vestiges* and other books. These included Paley's *Natural Theology*, Chambers's *Information for the People*, John Phillips's *Geology of Yorkshire*, Forster's *Life of Goldsmith*, and other works, which he examined in the summer of 1848. He was very explicit about the process, especially in the case of Paley's *Natural Theology*, which became a way of extending the discussion between Paley's grandson and Tyndall. After reading the chapters on astronomy side by side, Hirst concluded that the theory of nebular condensation in *Vestiges* offered a superior explanation, although Paley could be used to show that problems still remained—not least that under the development theory, the sun would at some point cease to emit light. Hirst also noted Paley's caution against evading the need for a Creator by substituting the term "natural law"; but was pleased to see that *Vestiges* "particularly alludes" to this point.[33]

The one comparative reading Hirst resolutely refused to make was between *Vestiges* and the biblical story of creation. This was an explicit decision, a boundary drawing that recognized the troubled relations between scientific and religious writing. After spending a Sunday morning at church, hearing a "very good sermon" by the archdeacon on divine omnipotence, and the evening at home in a close reading of *Explanations*, Hirst wrote that true science and true religion would never contradict one another. Correlation between the books of natural and revealed truth would eventually occur, but should not be undertaken prematurely. As with geology, "so with the 'Vestiges'—any contradiction that may occur between its theories and our religious opinions ought only to act as an incentive for testing that theory on its own or scientific merits."[34]

This "testing" became a form of dialogue, so that the arguments of one text were set off against others. Reading one chapter in one work and comparing it with another allowed Hirst to insert fragments of books into a continuous narrative of his own experience, communicated in his letters and conversations and best embodied in his journal. Seen from a wider perspective, Hirst's practice can be understood in the context of the increasing dominance of periodical publication during the 1840s.[35] Hirst's experience of reading complete books like *Vestiges* was structured by his immersion in monthly magazines like *Fraser's* and *Blackwood's*, monthly part works (such as the novels of Dickens), and the secular literary weeklies. Reading was thus a fragmented process, focused more on chapters than on long arguments, and more on comparison and contrast than on single narratives. The whole process, Hirst believed, could be kept under control through a well-regulated critical mind exercising independent judgment.

Periodicals were vital to the process of juxtaposition. Hirst read newspapers and magazines not to agree with them, but to think with them. The literary weeklies offered a very different context for debate than the quarterlies or newspapers, but shared their commitment to intellectual liberality. The *People's Journal* had been one of the strongest supporters of *Vestiges*, complaining of "bullying" tactics and "grossest misrepresentation" by its opponents, whose only interest was in maintaining their own power. "Freedom of speculation in theory," the *People's Journal* noted, "is the natural ally of the advance of useful discoveries in human science, and it becomes us to cherish carefully the one if we regard the other."[36] The *Nonconformist*, on the other hand, condemned *Vestiges* as "erroneous and pernicious."[37] Yet Hirst was soon reading the newspaper's reformist political editorials in terms taken directly from the book. Reflecting on events during the revolution of 1848, he thought France was attempting to advance too quickly up the progressive scale of civilization. Hirst's comparison was with a growing infant: just as a child needed "the governing care of a father" at certain stages of its development, so did a limited monarchy best suit the French nation. Such an image resonated with many parts of *Vestiges*, especially its quotations from Herschel about the nebular hypothesis. In this way, the journal brought politics and science together in the day-to-day work of writing and reading.[38]

Intensive reading did not just involve assimilating facts or memorizing other people's opinions. Hirst despised those who parroted platitudes or what they had read in reviews. The best periodicals, he thought, offered a range of opinions on different issues, as close adherence to a particular line became repetitive and predictable. Opinions in the different journals to which Hirst had access could scarcely be more different. Within a single period-ical, even within a single review, there could be different perspectives to be compared and contrasted. In May 1845 the *British Quarterly* had calmly demolished the development hypothesis as an unsupported generalization, but stressed the need to do this "not in the spirit of bigotry, but in the spirit of men earnest for truth." Yet a note added as an afterthought took a much stronger line, praising John Sheppard's anti-Vestigian tract (which many thought a model of bigotry) for its "learning and acuteness."[39]

Hirst read such articles to sharpen his own opinions and gain unexpected perspectives. Two days after reading the *British Quarterly*'s review, Hirst consulted the essay on James Cowles Pritchard's *Physical History of Man* in the same number. He found the reviewer's reliance on divine intervention unconvincing:

> Now, this appears to me to be a very imperfect solution of the question. He does not believe external circumstances have exerted such changes (in contra-diction to known facts), because he considers them accidental, and thus not consistent with the idea of Deity, forgetting or denying that Science is continu-ally tracing such effects to natural laws, and why may not natural laws have produced the differences in the races of men?

Judging by what the reviewer said, Hirst agreed more with Pritchard, that racial types were the products of nature and circumstance, and thought this "in accordance with Divine Writ."[40] The next day, after working at the office, Hirst reread the parallel chapter in *Vestiges* on human origins, finding it "a striking contrast" to the review, "and after all, a much more plausible theory."[41] He remained equally unshaken after reading an attack on spontaneous generation and evolution in the *Ethnographical Journal*, which Francis Booth loaned him in March 1849 in connection with their continuing conversations. In opposing transmutation, Hirst noted, the author of this article appealed to the "good principle" that the expertise of men like Lamarck and Geoffroy Saint-Hilaire "ought not to bias our minds with regard to its correctness."[42] Authority should not overrule independent judgment.

The range of printed materials newly available to men in Hirst's situation posed what much of the advice literature saw as a potential threat to independent judgment. Critical comparison and juxtaposition of views could easily become superficial, pandering to light conversation—what Tyndall had condemned as "the goose-cackle of society"—rather than serious study. Hirst was particularly impressed by a long letter from Tyndall to a common friend, warning against trying to digest books in too many different subjects, without sufficient critical attention:

> I know one or two most extensive readers who could talk for half a century about various systems of Philosophy, and can tell you the opinions of this and that great man upon such and such subjects; and yet the intellectual power of these readers is truly contemptible. They are merely so many conduit pipes through which information from some other spring finds a passage—throw them into circumstances which demand the exercise of original power, and they get instantly tangled and helpless. This comes from their having contented themselves with driving a retail trade in the opinions of other men, without enquiring into the reasons of these opinions.[43]

Such a system, although calculated to impress, was mechanical and deadening: the reader's mind lost its integrity, becoming part of the machinery of public discussion condemned by

Carlyle. Promiscuous readers became "a kind of hamper basket for stowing away the products of braver minds," followers rather than leaders. The remedy, Tyndall suggested, was to gain a general idea of a book on first perusal, and then to focus on novelties and problems, *"noting down your observations in writing"*—something that Hirst already did, but aspired to do more thoroughly. It was also crucial to read on a definite plan. Hirst agreed. He copied Tyndall's letter into his journal, and looking back on the year's reading on the last day of 1848, he noted that "[i]n science I have hovered about the whole field. It is time I should settle on one."[44]

[. . .]

The end of reading

Hirst's reaction to *Vestiges* was so strong that he might seem to embody the ideal reader projected in the text. Hirst not only agreed with much of what he had read, but did so as part of a process of self-realization, so that his journal records his own development through the successive chapters. By copying long passages into his private journal, he incorporated the text directly into his sense of who he was and what he was to become. If Jean Ranson is a "Rousseauist" reader of Rousseau in Darnton's classic study, Hirst could be portrayed as precisely the kind of Vestigian reader the *Vestiges* author had had in mind. This, however, involves taking too limited a view of the opportunities afforded by a book.[45]

In the first place, Hirst transformed *Vestiges* by reading it in juxtaposition with other works and in the context of intense discussion with friends. He made books his own, or to put it another way, he pulled them apart to combine them with other works and make them more useful for his own purposes. Like the compiler of a commonplace book or anthology, he looked for "beauties" and passages of particular interest in relation to other works he was reading at the same time. Hirst thereby experienced the book more like the monthly serials and review essays he enjoyed and less as a completed, self-contained narrative to be taken in at a single sitting. The dominance of periodicals was reshaping the fundamental practices of reading.

As a reader, Hirst's needs contrasted with those anticipated by the author. True, Hirst was young and in search of a creed, and came out of religious traditions not all that different from those experienced by Chambers himself. But he resisted the extension of the development theory to man, for that would undermine the notion of free will that was at the heart of his faith. As Hirst came increasingly to adopt perspectives drawn from transcendental philosophy, he conceived of the relations between his individual will, his body, and the external world in a new and very different way from that projected in *Vestiges*, which defined free will as merely a result of the interplay of the phrenological faculties.[46] Hirst's encounter with *Vestiges* and the replies to it thus became part of the process of redefining his own perspective as a reader, the "I" of which *Sartor Resartus* and the *Vocation of Man* spoke so powerfully. Like many young men in Britain and America, particularly those with backgrounds in Congregationalism, Hirst found in these works a way of thinking through who he was.

The issue of free will came to define Hirst's quest for a role in changing the society around him. Halifax in the 1840s presented the liberal middle classes with overwhelming problems in practical political economy. Although built on a steeply sloping hill, the town was badly drained and filthy, with unemployment, destitution, and hunger rife even among the "respectable" poor in the mid-1840s. The population increased dramatically in the middle decades of the century, and over four-fifths of the people were engaged in manual labor. Working on tithe surveys in the surrounding countryside, Hirst became acutely aware of the class divisions and social inequality enforced by the rates, which many found almost impossible to pay in times of destitution.[47] His experience of these conditions encouraged his search for a higher calling.

No single book—and certainly not *Vestiges*—had a transforming effect on Hirst's life. Even his radical self-absorption in Carlyle, Emerson, and Fichte was not a surrender to favorite authors, but a way for Hirst to assert his independence of judgment and to distance himself from the faith in which he had been raised. He could not agree that scientific progress destroyed wonder and mystery; and *Vestiges*, which would have fallen into *Sartor's* category of mechanized cosmological "Dream Theorems," pointed a way forward for Hirst. Early in 1850 he made the great decision of his life. Following Tyndall's example, and assured of a modest financial independence after his mother's death, he gave up surveying and left England for the Continent to study mathematics, physics, and chemistry at Marburg. Eventually he would obtain a doctoral degree in mathematics, teach at University College, and join the X-Club.

References

1   John Brewer, "Reconstructing the Reader: Prescriptions, Texts and Strategies in Anna Larpent's Reading," in *The Practice and Representation of Reading in England*, ed. James Raven, Helen Small, and Naomi Tadmor, 226–45 (Cambridge: Cambridge University Press, 1996); R. Darnton, "Readers Respond to Rousseau," in Robert Darnton, *The Great Cat Massacre and Other Episodes in French Cultural History* (New York: Vintage 1984) pp. 209–49. For analogous examples, see William H. Sherman, *John Dee: The Politics of Reading and Writing in the Eglish Renaissance* (Amherst: University of Massachusetts Press, 1994); Kevin Sharpe, *Reading Revolutions: The Politics of Reading in Early Modern England* (New Haven: Yale University Press 2000) (on Sir William Drake); Lisa Jardine and Anthony Grafton, " 'Studied for Action': How Gabriel Harvey Read his Livy." *Past and Present*, no. 129 (1990): 30–78. For a review, see Stephen Colclough, "Recovering the Reader: Commonplace Books and Diaries as Sources of Reading Experience," *Publishing History*, 44 (1998): 5–37.
2   William H. Brock and Roy M. MacLeod, eds., *Natural Knowledge in Social Context: The Journals of Thomas Archer Hirst FRS* (London: Mansell, 1980), "Introduction: The Life of Thomas Hirst," pp. 5–37 gives the best account of Hirst's life; see also Helen J. Gardner and Robin J. Wilson, "Thomas Archer Hirst: Mathematician Xtravagant", *American Mathematical* Monthly, 100 (1993): 435–41, 531–38, 723–31, 827–34, 907–15. Brock and MacLeod (microfiche) is a microfiche edition; with an index of the typescript version of Hirst's entire journal. The original of this transcription is in the archives of the Royal Institution.
3   J. Ginswick, *Labour and the Poor in England and Wales 1849–1851*, 8 vols (London: Frank Cass, 1983), 1:170. For miscellaneous details about Halifax I have relied on the local newspapers and the principal contemporary street directory, J. U. Walker, *Walker's Directory of the Parish of Halifax; to which is Appended, a Variety of Useful Statistical Information* (Halifax: J.U. Walker, 1845).
4   Brock and McLeod, microfiche, 7 June 1846, f. 24 n. 38, quoting from Tyndall's *Journal*, vol. 1, f. 129.
5   Quoted in Ruth Barton, " 'An Influential Set of Chaps': The X-Club and Royal Society Politics 1864–85." *BJHS* 23 (1990), 53–81, (57).
6   "Literary Notices," *Halifax Guardian*, 12 Apr. 1845, 6.
7   Brock and MacLeod, microfiche, 13 July 1847, ff. 89–90; for Booth, see J[ohn] T[yndall], "Memoranda Concerning Dr. Hirst," *Proceedings of the Royal Society of London* 1893, 52:xiv–xviii.
8   Hirst does not identify the edition, but this can be determined from passages quoted in the diary; compare Brock and Macleod, microfiche, f. 271 with *Vestiges* 6, 238 and *Vestiges* 7, 137–38. *Vestiges* is listed in the *Alphabetical and Classified Catalogue of the Library of the Halifax Mechanics' Institution and Mutual Improvement Society* (Halifax: printed by N. Burrows, 1851), 36. The earliest surviving catalogue, this was compiled after the amalgamation of the two institutions.
9   This tradition of learning has been more fully discussed in the American context; see Cathy N. Davidson, *Revolution and the Word: The Rise of the Novel in America* (New York: Oxford University

372 JAMES A. SECORD

Press, 1988), pp. 69–79, and Leon Jackson, "The Reader Retailored: Thomas Carlyle, His American Audiences, and the Politics of Evidence," *Book History* 2 (1999), 146–72, (161–62).

10   Brock and MacLeod, microfiche, 1 Aug, 1848, f. 257.

11   *Ibid.*, 13 Aug. 1848, ff. 266–67.

12   *Ibid.*, 14 Aug. 1848, f. 267.

13   *Ibid.*, 17 Aug. 1848, f. 272.

14   *Ibid.*, 9 Aug. 1848, f. 264.

15   *Ibid.*, 19 Aug. 1848, f.273.

16   *Ibid.*, 23 Aug. 1848, f.278.

17   *Ibid.*, 3 Sept. 1848, f. 285.

18   For the importance of religious models in the institutions of self-improvement in Halifax, and other West Riding towns, see S.J.D. Green, "Religion and the Rise of the Common Man: Mutual Improvement Societies, Religious Associations and Popular Education in Three Industrial Towns in the West Riding of Yorkshire c. 1850–1900," in *Cities, Class and Communication: Essays in Homour of Asa Briggs*, ed. Derek Fraser (New York: Harvester Wheatsheaf, 1990), pp. 25–43.

19   Personal communication, 16 June 1998, from Elizabeth Briggs of the Kirklees District Archives, West Yorkshire Archive Service.

20   Brock and MacLeod, microfiche, 6 Oct. 1849, f. 525. *Ibid.*, 12 June 1847, f. 64.

21   *Ibid.*, 31 Dec. 1848, f. 338.

22   *Ibid.*, 12 June 1847, f. 64.

23   See *ibid.*, passim; these titles and many others can be retrieved from the index to this microfiche edition.

24   *Ibid.*, 3 Sept. 1848, f. 285.

25   *Ibid.*, 2 June 1849, f. 414; early examples of this idea (and its converse, that the wrong kind of reading could cause disease) are discussed in Adrian Johns, *The Nature of the Book: Print and Knowledge in the Making* (Chicago: Chicago University Press, 1998), pp. 580–81, and "The Physiology of Reading in Restoration England", in Raven, Small and Tadmor, 158–61. For its later history, Kelly J. Mays, "The Disease of Reading in the Victorian Periodicals," in *Literature in the Marketplace*, ed. John O. Jordan and Robert L. Patten (Cambridge: Cambridge University Press, 1995), pp. 165–94 and Alison Winter, *Mesmerised: Powers of Mind in Victorian Britain* (Chicago: University of Chicago Press, 1998), pp. 329–30.

26   "A Meeting of 'Old Muffs,'" Horsfall Turner Collection, Newspaper Cuttings Book, vol. 4, f. 91, Calderdale Central Library, Halifax.

27   Brock and MacLeod, microfiche, 12 Oct. 1848, f. 300. The Mechanics' Institution's proceedings and minute books (HMI: 1–7) are preserved in the Calderdale District Archives in the Calderdale Central Library, Halifax. The number of books in its library is taken from a loose circular of 1847 in HMI: 2. For the institute's history, see Mabel Tylecote, *The Mechanics Institute of Lancashire and Yorkshire before 1851* (Manchester: Manchester University Press, 1957), pp. 224–40, and "Opening of the New Hall of the Mechanics Institute," *Halifax Courier*, 17 Jan. 1857, with an illustration.

28   The combined catalogue of the amalgamated Halifax Subscription Library and Halifax Literary and Philosophical Society (Halifax: T. and W. Birtwhistle, 1874) shows a copy of the sixth edition of *Vestiges*, as well as *Footprints* and other related works.

29   Brock and MacLeod, microfiche, 13 June 1847, f.65.

30   D.A. Hinton, "Popular Science in England, 1830–1870" Ph.D. diss., Bath University (1979), 256 n. 117.

31   On anthologies and narrative form, see Richard Price, *British Society, 1680–1880: Dynamism, Containment, and Change* (Cambridge: Cambridge University Press, 1997).

32   "Intensive," reading of a single book is usually contrasted with "extensive" reading of many. In the present case, the two practices coexist; the intensive reading of a few works occurs against the backdrop of exposure to a much larger number.

33   Brock and MacLeod, microfiche, 2 Aug. 1848, f. 258.

34   *Ibid.*, 2 Sept. 1848, ff. 285–86.

35   On this issue, see N.N. Feltes, *Modes of Production of Victorian Novels* (Chicago: University of Chicago Press, 1986), Linda K. Hughes and Michael Lund, *The Victorian Serial* (Charlottesville: University Press of Virginia, 1991), Mary Poovey, *The Proper Lady and the Woman Writer: Ideology*

as *Style in the Works of Mary Wollstonecraft, Mary Shelley, and Jane Austen* (Chicago: Chicago University Press, 1988), and several of the essays in John O. Jordan and R. L. Patten, eds, *Literature in the Marketplace: Nineteenth Century British Publishing and Reading Practises* (Cambridge: Cambridge University Press, 1995). Margaret Beetham, "Toward a Theory of the Periodical as a Publishing Genre," in *Investigating Victorian Journalism* ed. Laurel Brake, Aled Jones, and Lionel Madden (Basingstoke: Macmillan, 1990), pp. 19–32 and Lyn Pykett, "Reading the Periodical Press: Texts and Context," in Brake et al 1990 offer the best overviews. For Hirst, as (one suspects) for most readers, practical problems of time and access were crucial in structuring the text into the discrete units associated with "serialized" reading.

36   W.J. Fox, "On the Progress of Science in its Influence upon the Condition of the People," *People's Journal*, 10 Jan. 1846, 30–35, at 34.

37   *Nonconformist*, 9 July 1845, 490; *Nonconformist*, 13 Aug. 1845, 569.

38   Brock and MacLeod, microfiche, 12 Aug. 1848, f. 266.

39   "Vestiges of the Natural History of Creation," *British Quarterly Review* 1 (May 1845): 490–513, at 513.

40   Brock and MacLeod, microfiche, 21 Aug. 1848, ff. 274–76.

41   *Ibid.*, 22 Aug. 1848, ff. 276–78, at f. 276.

42   *Ibid.*, 29 Mar. 1849, f. 375.

43   J. Tyndall to James Hayran, [1848], Brock and MacLeod, microfiche, 4 Sept. 1848, ff. 286–87.

44   *Ibid.*, 31 Dec. 1848, f. 338; for similar recommendations in the Congregational advice literature, see Pye Smith 1839, 327.

45   R. Darnton, "Readers Respond to Rousseau: The Fabrication of Romantic Sensibility," in Darnton 1984, 209–49. Ranson is perhaps too perfect a reader of Rousseau to be an entirely satisfactory example of the disturbing, disrupting effects that reading can have.

46   *Vestiges* 1, 349.

47   James R. Moore, "Wallace's Malthusian Moment: The Common Context Revisited," in *Victorian Science in Context*, ed. Bernard Lightman (Chicago: University of Chicago Press, 1997), pp. 290–311 (300–303).

SECTION 7

New directions and methods in the history of reading

INTRODUCTION

AS THE RANGE OF extracts featured in this reader demonstrates, the history of reading is a methodologically and intellectually diverse field of study. Not only has scholarship in the history of reading traditionally utilised a very wide range of material (from readers' marginalia to library borrowing records, and from paratextual commentary to diaries) in order to recover reading practices, but it has also engaged with many different methodological and theoretical perspectives. This final section of the reader brings together five extracts representative of some of the more important recent developments in the field (1998–2010), each one opening up a new methodology or technology, or indicating a new direction for research in the history of reading.

The first two extracts both utilise the evidence offered by readers' responses, though from radically different perspectives and historical periods. Noting the interpretive gap between macro- and micro-analytical approaches to the recovery of the 'common reader' in the nineteenth-century, Teresa Gerrard chooses to examine the 'Answers to Correspondents' section of a particular popular British Sunday newspaper, *The Family Herald*, from 1860–1900. The *Herald*'s widespread circulation (print runs of over 125,000 copies per week), the volume of its readers' responses (some 200 letters per week), the demography of its readership (the newly literate working class and lower middle classes) and the fact that a substantial proportion (30% in 1900) of the 'answers to correspondents' directed readers to reading matter not contained in the pages of the *Herald* indicates the importance of this approach to mapping out the reading lives of ordinary people in the period. In a similar vein, but examining reading practices a century later in the USA, Paul Gutjahr analyses the reader reviews of the Evangelical-Protestant and explicitly millenarian and apocalyptic *Left Behind* fiction series submitted to and published on the world's largest internet book retailer, www.amazon.com.

No fewer than 1700 readers had left their unsolicited comments between the publication of the first bestseller in this series in 1995, and the end of Gutjahr's survey in September 1999. Gutjahr's analysis demonstrates that readers of the *Left Behind* series were as likely to be seduced by the apparent readability of the fiction as they were by their explicitly Evangelical content, and more compellingly, that some 15% of the reviewers were by their own admission, bringing their reading of the novels to their understanding of the Bible (especially the Book of Revelation) – in effect, as a form of intertextual commentary. Gutjahr's examination of a particular contemporary publishing and reading phenomenon reminds us that Amazon's extraordinarily large repository of readers' reviews, as well as the sophisticated contextual information gathered through the act of customers' browsing and previous purchasing history, offers scholarship perhaps the largest single unexploited resource for understanding con-temporary reading practices.

While Gerrard and Gutjahr collate and analyse the archived responses of readers, Isabel Hofmeyr examines the extraordinary afterlife of one book, Bunyan's *The Pilgrim's Progress*, through its multiple vernacular translations and receptions across sub-Saharan Africa over the course of a century. In this extract, Hofmeyr reconstructs the engagement with *The Pilgrim's Progress* of Mata, head porter of the Baptist Missionary Society at San Salvador in the Kongo Kingdom (today M'Banza Kongo in Angola), not through his own written record of reading (should such a thing have existed), but through his self-identification with the character of Pliable, reported in the account of the missionary Thomas Lewis. Hofmeyr recovers a particularly Africanized form of engagement with the printed book, for *The Pilgrim's Progress* was popularised through public readings, magic lantern shows, choir ser-vices, and performances where Africans were encouraged to identify with and act out the parts of the allegorical characters of Bunyan's narrative. Straddling the fields of cultural studies, postcolonial theory, and the history of reading, Hofmeyr's approach reminds us that the interdependency of oral and literate culture has continued despite the rise of the printed book, and even more pertinently, that readers have an almost inexhaustible capacity to refashion texts and their meanings in unexpected ways through the act of reading itself – nor should we only look for evidence of this in written records alone. Hofmeyr's compelling analysis situates the reading of a text within the wider non-literate culture of nineteenth-century Sub-Saharan Africa, highlighting the fact that the evidence of reading often lies beyond the physical site of the reading act itself, but this is not a practice only prevalent in a predominantly oral culture.

Danielle Fuller's study of the Canadian Broadcasting Corporation's recent 'Canada Reads' radio and television series reminds us that if anything, contemporary readers are even more indebted to the non-textual apparatus mediating reading than their pre- or semi-literate forebears. Fuller notes the extent to which 'Canada Reads' carefully mimics the conventions of reading groups, while advocating a broader agenda for a unified Canadian reading community, an implication often resisted by its participants. Fuller's study admirably demonstrates the extent to which contemporary reading practice is co-extensive with, and in many senses, inseparable from, other media and forms of cultural consumption: radio broadcasts, television interviews, film adaptations, mass reading events, celebrity endorsement, weblogs, podcasts, and commercial marketing. Contemporary studies of reading must consider the evidence offered up by the whole range of broadcast and narrowcast media, as well as the increasing use of social networking and collaborative knowledge construction (such as the wiki model), in order to assess how readers engage with and respond to reading matter.

If Fuller shows how the proliferation of new media and technology has disaggregated public engagement with reading, Rosalind Crone, Mary Hammond, Katie Halsey and Shafquat

Towheed in their exposition of *The Reading Experience Database* (www.open.ac.uk/Arts/
reading/, RED) show how new, web-based developments in the digital humanities can afford
considerable new insights into the historical practice of reading: in this case, of British readers
from 1450 to 1945. RED catalogues the recorded engagement of readers with reading matter
of all kinds (from epitaphs to unpublished manuscripts, and ephemera to the Bible) in the form
of a multiply-indexed and searchable open access database with nearly 30,000 entries. This
developing internet resource would have been impossible to achieve in the era before contextual digital databases, strongly indicating the extent to which technological developments
can support both new methodologies and interpretation in the history of reading. As this last
extract makes clear, the considerable effort to recover the evidence of readers and their particular reading practices through the centuries has only just begun. Much work still remains to
be done, on both a micro- and macro-analytical level, before broader historical and cultural
trends in reading practice can be substantiated with both qualitative and quantitative evidence.
Recent developments in psychology, physiology and neurology offer the tantalising prospect of
being able to exactly chart each individual interaction with text in the near future. And perhaps
most pertinently, this section of the reader reminds us that the history of reading is not only a
past practice that we need to excavate, but a contemporary, ongoing process of reading and
constructing meaning from texts, in which we all participate.

Chapter 32

Teresa Gerrard

NEW METHODS IN THE HISTORY OF READING: "ANSWERS TO CORRESPONDENTS" IN *THE FAMILY HERALD*, 1860–1900

T HE HISTORY OF READING, defined as the study of the consumption of the printed word, has attracted an increased amount of attention in recent years, not only as a new topic within the history of the book, but as its very corollary. Furthermore, this renewed interest comes not only from book historians but from literary critics and cultural theorists alike.[1] The question of who in the past was reading what, and indeed that of who was believed to be reading what, are now seen as crucial to the understanding of production and marketing strategies, from the author to the bookseller, and to the formation and validity of cultural theories regarding the dissemination of ideas. Of equal import are questions dealing with how and where these texts were intended to be read – aloud or silently, in company or alone, in public or in private – and how and where these texts actually were read – passively or interrogatively. The effects of changing attitudes towards reading and of changing reading practices are of importance to both the cultural theorist and the book historian, while the effect of particular texts upon historical readers, the way they interpreted and used them, is of significance to the reader-response critic and the cultural historian.

This shared interest has resulted in a number of studies specifically devoted to one or more of the above topics and has thus greatly extended our knowledge of the history of reading. At the same time, however, the diversity of approaches and the limitations of the available sources have left us somewhat bewildered as this growth in scholarship has been accompanied by a corresponding growth in complexity. The main problem, where to uncover evidence, is joined by a further one – how to bring this very often disparate evidence together when it is actually found.[2] Macro-analytical studies, based on changes in the *English Short Title Catalogue* and publication figures, over-generalize changes in reading tastes, while thematic surveys aimed at evaluating reading habits focus upon the theoretical views of contemporary reformers, educationalists or other observers, rather than the readers themselves. Through the use of wills, subscription lists, autobiographies, the inventories of private and the borrowing records of public libraries, micro-analytical studies necessarily focus upon the particular or the individual, upon the recoverable (and hence exceptional) reading experiences of the readers of certain texts or certain genres, or upon the reading histories of a small number of historical readers.[3] Thus, while macro-analytical studies and thematic surveys attempt to set the general picture of changing attitudes towards reading matter, micro-analytical studies of actual readers rely upon exceptions for the main body of their evidence. Combining these two approaches is very difficult.

The problem is particularly acute when we come to study the British common reader of the nineteenth century. Most historians concerned with this reader tend to focus on the working-class autobiographers whose reading habits are more accessible, rather than upon the masses.[4] Or, when they do attempt to examine the 'ordinary' working-class reader, they tend to rely upon the testimonies of outside observers, an analysis of the literature itself, or upon more circumstantial evidence such as library borrowing records, sales and publication figures.[5] Autobiography gives us insight into the highlighted reading experiences of an exceptional minority only (those who felt compelled to write their life story), while outside testimonies and bare figures provide us with general quantitative evidence and deductions which are divorced from the readers themselves. Thus while both types of study are interesting in themselves, it is very hard to bring them together since the 'whos' and the 'whats' of the former source cannot be aligned with the 'whos' and the 'whats' of the latter.

Thematic studies based on the outside observations of social commentators, such as the readership surveys of the middle-class social investigators, tend to deal with educational, religious or fictional works and with imagined, theoretical or politically-constructed readers.[6] Likewise, macro-analytical studies based on publication and sales figures indicate the relative popularity of certain books and genres, but deal with an undefined reading audience. On the other hand, micro-analytical studies tend to fall into two broad categories. Those based on autobiography or diaries deal with works of literary status and with exceptional groups of readers – generally the autodidacts of the working class.[7] Alternatively, those which focus upon library borrowing records deal with a restricted supply of books to a group of readers defined by geographical location, or, in the case of the South Wales miners, as the politically active minority.[8] Thus, the more a so-called group of 'common readers' is defined for further study, the more they and their reading experience become an exception.[9] The incompatibility of studies focusing on individual reading instances with those dealing with very general reading habits is, it seems, an unavoidable limitation, given the available sources.

[. . .]

One hitherto unexplored area of documentary evidence of reading does, however, offer a way out of this dilemma. The coming of the penny weekly journal and the popular Sunday newspaper, and the introduction of the penny post in the 1840s, brought with them a new publishing phenomenon – namely, the 'Answers to Correspondents'. These sections of the popular weeklies, devoted to answering or discussing any query or topic raised by readers' letters, enable the limitations of the over-generalized and the over-specialized studies to be redressed in three ways. Firstly, they allow a manageable group of common (as opposed to exceptional) readers to be defined for close examination. Secondly, they combine the specific reading experiences with insights into the general reading habits of the common reader. Thirdly, they make possible a history of reading that is neither limited by genre nor restricted to books of literary merit. In comparison to other sources, 'Answers to Correspondents' enable us to reach further down the reading scale in terms of audience and further across it in terms of the reading matter which is being discussed – from J.W.J., the pupil teacher who is struggling with the geometrical works of Euclid, to J.D.W. of Crewe, who wishes to know what the inscription 'Warranted, 14 F.K., 25 years' on a Waltham lever watch signifies.[10] Using this source, it is therefore possible to construct a reading history that focuses more firmly on the common reader, that consolidates the techniques of micro- and macro-analytical studies and can redress their limitations.

In this case study I focus on the 'Answers to Correspondents' within the *Family Herald* for the period 1860–1900, in order to show how this source can be used to explore both the specific and the general reading experiences of common readers. The nature of the 'Answers to Correspondents' and of the reading experience brought about by them is firstly considered. The topics which are being discussed within these 'Answers' are then analysed in order to ascertain how many refer to reading matter, and those which do are examined in greater detail. A statistical analysis reveals general changes in reading tastes and habits, while a final study of the specific reading experiences shows that the evidence provided differs widely from that of other sources. The unusual nature of the reading experiences revealed through the 'Answers to Correspondents' makes this source a particularly valuable one.

Sales figures, contemporary observation and internal evidence indicate that the popular penny Sunday newspapers and magazines, such as the *Family Herald*, drew their readership from the expanding lower-middle and working classes during the latter half of the nineteenth century. Founded in December 1842, the *Family Herald* was published for almost a century, until April 1940. Although it is difficult to establish exact sales figures, it is evident that the *Family Herald* enjoyed a wide circulation for most of this period. According to Amy Cruse, an estimated 125,000 copies were sold per week within the first few years of publication, and this level of distribution appears to have been sustained throughout the remainder of the nineteenth century.[11] For example, an article of 1894 states that: 'Such papers as the *Family Herald*, depending entirely on fiction . . . seem to have greatly extended their circulation', while an advertisement of 1901 contains the following quotation from the *Illustrated London News* – 'The *Family Herald*, that joy of tens of thousands of innocent English households'.[12] The publishers' own claim, that:

> The combined circulation of the *Family Herald, Family Herald Supplement, Happy Hour* and *One-Story Magazine*, as certified by an eminent firm of Chartered Accountants, amounts to an average of 300,000 copies weekly.

does not therefore appear to be a great exaggeration.[13] Contemporary observation, that the *Family Herald* was read by members of the 'Unknown Public', is confirmed by such figures and by internal evidence. According to information taken from the 'Answers to Correspondents', readers of the *Family Herald* were not autodidacts, autobiographers or future political activists but small shopkeepers, domestic servants, factory workers, clerks and members of the armed forces, female as well as male readers. As a result, additional information contained within 'Answers to Correspondents' can be used to ascertain the interests of a significant group of common readers.

The overwhelming popularity of 'Answers to Correspondents' in the second half of the nineteenth century is shown by the sheer number of communications received each week by various journals and newspapers. For example, Virginia Berridge has estimated that the *Weekly Times* alone was receiving an average of 167 questions per week in 1886, while in 1870 the editor of the *Family Herald* stated that he was in receipt of roughly 200 letters per week.[14] Indeed the launch of *Answers* in 1888 by Northcliffe, a weekly devoted entirely to 'Answers to Correspondents on Every Subject Under the Sun', also testifies to this.

Despite their evident popularity, 'Answers to Correspondents' have never been the subject of serious research. This may be due to the fact that they are belittled within contemporary surveys of popular periodicals as containing useless information, thus deterring the researcher.[15] It is, however, more likely that they have been overlooked because of their very nature. They are not only a unique publishing phenomenon, but a rather curious one. Unlike the 'Letters to the Editor', this section was made up entirely of the editor's answers, preceded by the correspondent's signature or pseudonym, while the letters which had prompted these replies remained unpublished. The replies themselves varied in length and in clarity. Generally, a handful were answered with a small paragraph, a larger number by one or two sentences, and even more by short phrases or a few words. As a result, many of the replies do not make much sense to the casual reader.

The most logical explanation for the format of these pages, that the intended audience of each answer was the enquiring correspondent only, does not hold true upon closer inspection. Certain topics within these seemingly personalized answers were thrown open to the knowledge or opinions of other readers.

[. . .]

[B]y means of an answer to their query, many were referred not only to previous articles, but to previous answers in earlier issues – a somewhat cumbersome way of gaining information.

The editors of these pages, it appears, were essentially making two assumptions about the reading habits of their journal's audience. Firstly, they believed that the majority would actually read the published answers. In fact, in an advertisement for the *Family Herald* which ran in *Mitchell's Newspaper Press Directory* from 1867 until 1900, the *Saturday Review* is quoted as saying that, within the *Family Herald*, 'The Answers to Correspondents cannot be fictitious, a romance and a life history being embodied in almost every one of them'.[16] The fact that these pages warrant a mention within an article examining the magazine's general character, and that this quotation is then used by the proprietors in an advertisement for the magazine, implies that these pages were seen as attractive reading matter, or as a main component of the journal itself. The second assumption is that readers kept old issues and could thus easily refer back to previous 'Answers' as well as to articles.[17]

These assumptions do not appear to be unfounded. Within these pages we find readers corresponding via the editor with one another, debating the occasional running theme, advising each other, or commenting upon previous answers. For example, one person signing herself 'A SAUCY MINX' was told, 'We are sure A.B.C. will be glad you liked and thoroughly agreed with her letter' regarding suitors, whilst 'THOMAS KING writes in with regard to a reference to the "unpardonable sin" in our Correspondence columns in No. 1947'.[18] As the above suggests, the answers were not the personalized reading matter they appeared to be upon first glance. Rather they were open to and indeed intended for mass consumption.

There is some evidence to suggest that the second assumption, that readers kept their old issues, is also true. For example, in January 1900 the following answer appeared:

> JAMIE HILL – sends us an extract from the *Family Herald* written in 1850, prospectively on the last half of the century, and particularly on its end, when the writer imagines "some of the grey-headed men and women of that epoch remembering these words." Our Correspondent does remember the words . . .

and had, it appeared, recently re-read them.[19] Other 'Answers' also indicate that old issues were kept and referred to for common as well as commemorative reasons. In Issue No. 1171 Ronald of the Bath and Spa Waters was informed that it was No. 526 which contained recipes for the skin, while a substantial number of other readers were directed towards issues containing articles on subjects as diverse as photography, deafness and marriage proposals.[20] A number of the very short 'Answers' simply state 'see number *n*', also suggesting that many of these replies were to straightforward questions asking in which issue particular articles might be found. One other reason why back issues may have been kept, sold and bought after their initial publication date is, of course, because they contained serialized fiction. For example, on the same page as the aforementioned Ronald we find

Nelly being advised that 'Twice Married' commenced in No. 1122 and that she therefore 'requires eleven Numbers, and they will cost . . . 1s 3d post free'.[21] The proprietors of the *Family Herald* claimed not only that 'All the numbers of the *Family Herald* are constantly kept in print', in order to meet this demand for back issues, but that:

> Wherever there is a bookseller or newsman to be found the *Family Herald* can be obtained, no matter in what part of the world.[22]

When there was no bookseller or newsagent, personal overseas subscriptions were also catered for; Inquirer in Burma being informed in 1860 that 'monthly parts of the *Family Herald* are sent free to India by post for 14s per annum'.[23]

Overseas readership of the *Family Herald* appears to have been limited mainly to expatriates, such as E.B.S.'s South African friend, referred to in the following quotation:

> We are much obliged to you for forwarding the quotation from your South African friend's letter, with its very gratifying compliment about the readableness of the *F.H.* from the beginning to end. We hope the copies you have sent out have done ten fold duty. Papers forwarded to friends abroad are often a great delight, and as you say, "keep old memories green".[24]

The publishers of the *Family Herald* were, of course, well placed to capitalize upon the demands and interests of their readers. Not only were they keen to hear their views on the *Family Herald* in general, but they also appear to have responded to reader queries by meeting, or possibly even pre-empting, the demand for specific cheap books. Having a complete run of a story in serialized form was bettered only by having the same in book form. A handful of readers were advised that stories such as 'Wilful Doreen' had 'now been published in book form', or regrettably that there were no book publication plans. Serialized stories were not the only things to be treated to publication in book form. The '*Family Herald*'s useful series of *Handy Books*', most of which could be procured for seven half-penny stamps, included titles such as *Domestic Cookery, Economic Cookery, Hints on the Toilette* and *Health and Happiness*.

Thus these 'Answers' are able to tell us something about the business acumen of the publishers and the general reading habits of these nineteenth-century journal readers. If we now look more closely at the topics being discussed within these answers, the results are even more interesting. A statistical analysis of roughly 450 answers for each of the years 1860, 1880 and 1900 (the discrepancy in the actual number of queries looked at each year being due to the fact that only full pages were used) reveals that in 1860 about 13% of the answers, or roughly one in every eight, make reference to reading matter not contained within the *Family Herald* itself (i.e., this figure excludes the aforementioned references to previous articles or 'Answers'). By 1880 the figure had risen to roughly 25% or just under one in every four, and by 1900 to just over 30%, or roughly one in every three. Whilst these figures are exploratory, based on a small sample, they do indicate that an increasingly substantial percentage of correspondents were requesting information on written works, or were being directed towards them by the editor. Unlike other sources, these references are not limited either by genre, supply or literary merit, but range quite widely from titles such as *A Dictionary of Cant and Vulgar Words* to *The Art of Perfumery*, from the 'wants' columns of daily newspapers to catalogues of books on the Russian language. They included information on the best dictionary to buy or use, discussions on classical literature, and the dishonesty of advertisements which had duped readers.

The quantity and quality of these replies allow a crude statistical analysis of changing reading patterns and uses to be made. A comparative analysis by genre of 120 titles taken from the *Family Herald* for each of the three years provides the following information. As a genre, references to newspapers and magazines remain fairly static throughout: at fifteen in the 1860 sample, seventeen and a half in 1880, and nineteen in 1900.[25] However, it should be noted that the number of titles being recommended to readers, or to which they are directed for information, increases over the period. Where 'see local paper' would have sufficed for the two earlier sample years, we find references to the '*Stamford Mercury, Yorkshire Post* and the *Preston Guardian*' in 1900. There is also a greater diversity of magazine titles for the later date – ranging from *The Lady's Pictorial* to *The Animals Friend* – in accordance with the growth in the number of available titles.

Unsurprisingly, an increase in secular reading, especially of works of fiction, is balanced by an overall decrease in the reading of religious literature. References to the Bible and discussions about religion in general fall from seventeen instances in 1860, fourteen in 1880, to only four in 1900. This decrease is countered by an overall increase in information on and discussion about works of fiction which occurs between 1880 and 1900. From very small totals of only seven and six in 1860 and 1880 respectively, this figure then increases to a total of twenty-two in 1900. If references to poetry (both in prose and verse) are then added to this category, the increase is even more striking, making the total twelve for 1860, eight for 1880, and jumping to thirty-seven and a half for 1900. Thus, by 1900 works of a fictional character account for almost one-third of all the enquiries, recommendations or discussions about reading material (compared to less than one-tenth for the two earlier periods), while references to religious literature are negligible.

The single largest group for the entire period is made up of dictionaries, directories (such as the *London Directory*, and various trade directories) and general reference books (such as the *Penny Cyclopedia*, medical dictionaries, various catalogues and almanacs); items which would not have been read in their entirely. The comparative figures for this genre are twenty-two and a half for 1860, twenty-four for 1880 and eighteen and a half for 1900. The fact that they figure quite largely within the correspondence pages implies that, as early as 1860, people were using the print media in order to gain specific facts and even addresses.

[. . .]

The overall drop in referrals to dictionaries, reference books and directories in 1900 may indicate an increased familiarity with this genre and the methods for obtaining specific facts from printed sources.

This same familiarity with the genre may also explain the changes in the totals of the 'how to' book or guide, a category made up of titles such as *Etiquette of the Ballroom, Etiquette of Courtship and Marriage, The Secret of a Good Memory, Ventriloquism Made Easy* or *Fancy Dress Described*. This rises from thirteen in 1860, to a peak of twenty-eight and a half in 1880 (representing almost a quarter of the titles mentioned that year) and then falls to fifteen in 1900. Indeed, the fact that three titles were being given per answer in 1900, where one would have sufficed in 1860 or 1880, certainly implies this and confirms the earlier findings on the number of newspapers referred to. For example, in 1900 a correspondent was supplied with the titles of three different books, all of which explained the games of draughts and backgammon – Berkeley's *Draughts and Backgammon*, Sturge's *Guide to the Game of Draughts* and Chambers's *Handbook on the Game of Draughts and Backgammon &c*. If, as appears to be the case, more titles were being published by 1900, then the drop in the number of queries regarding such reading material may well be explained by an increased familiarity with the genre as a whole. In fact, of the fifteen who wrote in for information on 'how to' books in 1900, five were told that no such book existed, or that practical experience was preferable to book knowledge. For example, An Uneducated Lady was told: 'there are no books that can teach any one to write in the same way that a few manuals will help a scholar to pass an examination . . .', whilst Nicotiana, who wanted information on how to grow tobacco for commercial purposes, was told: 'The only possible method of learning how to cultivate any plant, or cereal, or fruit is to go through a course of actual training. Reading a book will not serve the purpose'.[26] Such 'Answers' imply that the correspondents had great faith in the printed word and were making demands of the print media in accordance with this.

Indeed, the same attitude is also reflected by the correspondents' opinions regarding reading itself. For instance, Conversazione was told: 'It is not much reading, but careful reading, that makes the man of information', whilst Ignoramus wished to be furnished with a 'list of books or scheme of study' which would enable him to 'give an enlightened opinion on any subject'.[27] Such requests for reading lists imply that these common readers wanted to read in order to better themselves mentally and intellectually. At the same time, however, they imply that this interest in the print media was directed by a desire to appear more knowledgeable in dealing with others. Desire and reality, however, did not always match up. For example, in 1900, Forlorn of Kansas City was asked:

> Have you read *David Copperfield*? Your verbal floridness reminds us of Mr. Micawber, but he used his big words correctly . . . you say that "the rapture occasioned me language would retreat at the attempt to depict" when the "principle (?) of a high school, who had the kindness to survey my small library, and was simply amazed at my high opinion of literature and proficiency in the various branches politely alighted his hand on my shoulder and said, 'Your attitude is simply egregious' ".[28]

Having ridiculed this correspondent, the editor of the *Family Herald* continued to state that, in his opinion, this correspondent is 'misled by extreme egotism'.

Fortunately, the editor did not hold such a low opinion of all his readers. Unlike many of the social commentators of the period, he did not bemoan their lack of intellect nor assume that they would only be interested in reading popular fiction of the type contained with the *Family Herald* itself – titles such as 'How Dulcie Loved', 'Sister or Wife?', 'Married in Black'. In fact, the reading lists which he recommended (to both male and female correspondents), and the authors whom he quoted or referred to, could not be further removed. They included classic fiction writers such as Defoe, Fielding and Swift, contemporary novelists such as Twain and Dickens, poets such as Coleridge, Byron, Pope, Shelley and Wordsworth, and the philosophy of Burke, Emerson and Francis Bacon – to name but a few. Such lists and citations indicate that the editor did not think it implausible that some readers of the *Family Herald* would also read works of a higher literary merit (while continuing to read the *Family Herald*, of course). As far as fiction is concerned, this belief that some correspondents would read and enjoy both popular and canonical texts in tandem is somewhat surprising. Such a view was not shared by the contemporary literary surveyors, nor is it commonly accepted by present-day historians or cultural theorists – the contemporary view being that readers would progress from popular fiction to works of higher literary merit; the present-day view being that the reading of one form of literature tends to preclude reading of the other.

Therefore we must ask whether the editor's view of his readers was a realistic one – is there actually any evidence to suggest that the readers of the *Family Herald*, either on their own initiative or on the advice of the editor, actually read any of the works of higher literary status? The evidence contained within these pages suggests that a limited number did. For example, we find the editor agreeing with R.S. that:

> the genius of the past age, of Richardson, Fielding, Smollett, Gibbon, Addison,

Steele, and others, was of much more vivid as well as solid a nature than the ephemeral and over-lauded authors of the present day . . .[29]

Elsewhere we find a correspondent relaying his own and his friend's views on Carlyle to the editor, and another who had apparently sent in his or her opinion on the literary merits of Gray's *Elegy*.[30]

This implies that reading one form of literature (i.e. popular fiction) certainly did not preclude reading others. However, many of the 'Answers' also imply that readers were having problems with the more difficult works. While some enjoyed poetry, stating that it helped to fill an otherwise monotonous life, other readers [. . .] read it too literally.

[. . .]

There were certain skills or ways of reading which these common readers simply had not acquired, while the manner in which such reading matter was approached implies that there existed a certain amount of confusion when it came to dealing with canonical works. For example, Erin wished to know if Milton was a suitable author to be chosen as one's favourite. Similarly, many were keen to hear the editor's opinion on certain authors.

Such evidence suggests two things. Firstly, that these common readers were aware and somewhat in awe of the canon, and, secondly, that they were driven as much by deference towards this canon and by their own egos as they were by general enthusiasm to read or attempt to read such works. These two suggestions have further ramifications for the way in which other sources are used.

In his 1992 article, 'Rereading the Common Reader', Jonathan Rose states that:

> Throughout the Victorian period and well into the twentieth century, the British working class maintained a vital autodidact culture that, quite independ-ently of ruling-class cultural hegemony, found inspiration in the canonical works of Western culture.[31]

[. . .]

Rose accepts that both popular and canonical, or 'high' and 'low', literature might be read by the same reader, but nevertheless argues that the British working-class autobio-graphers and autodidacts tended to draw a clear distinction between these different forms of fiction, concluding that 'working people can recognise great literature when they see it'.[32] While the 'Answers' also suggest that a number of common readers were making these distinctions, they imply that they were doing so in a deliberate attempt to acknowledge cultural hegemony, rather than in spite of it. This, and the fact that many seem to have attached a certain kudos to the reading of canonical literature, must therefore be considered as a reason for the distinction being made so clearly within autobiography.

The 'Answers to Correspondents' thus provide documentary evidence of very different reading experiences to those contained within other sources, along with insights into the otherwise obscured practical questions which occupied the minds of common readers as they encountered the written word in all of its forms. Compared to autobiographical recorded reading experiences, those contained within the 'Answers' are more spontaneous, and as a result (although not intentionally) they are less self-promoting. Compared to library reports, they enable us to examine a wider supply of titles and, compared to sales and publication figures, to define a manageable group of common readers and trace the changes in their particular reading tastes.

Fortunately, this fruitful source is also an abundant one, since most of the penny publications containing 'Answers to Correspondents' can be used to examine further the reading habits of common readers. According to Mitchell's *Newspaper Press Directory*, there existed a total of seventeen penny weekly magazines in 1860, ten of which (including the *Family Herald*) are described as 'popular' fiction journals.[33] By 1880 the number of penny weeklies had risen to a total of eighty-three, and seventeen of these are similarly described as fiction journals.[34] By 1900, 304 penny weeklies are recorded in the *Press Directory*, forty-seven of which are described as fiction journals. A comparative analysis of the 'Answers to Correspondents' within such publications, and of those within the popular penny Sunday newspapers, may help to establish the validity of findings. For example, by examining the 'Answers to Correspondents' within the *London Journal* (the only other penny weekly fiction magazine to be published continuously throughout 1860–1900) and *Reynolds's Newspaper*, I hope to determine whether or not they support some of the broader theories suggested by the above case study.[35] Did the percentage of correspondents enquiring about or being directed towards reading matter actually increase over the period as a whole? Do the other 'Answers to Correspondents' reveal similar changes in taste with regards to the reading matter which is under discussion? Were common readers likely to attempt to read the classics out of deference, or was this practice peculiar to the readers of the *Family Herald*? The 'Answers to Correspondents' within the *Family Herald* raise new questions within the history of reading which other 'Answers' may help us to solve.

Unlike other sources, 'Answers to Correspondents' can be used to explore various aspects within the history of reading – they enable us to examine the relation of the common reader to the text; to establish who in the past was interested in reading what and why; to ascertain how texts were interpreted and how they were approached; to determine how the printed word was used and how it was regarded. Their utility is not limited to one area of investigation and they thus represent a source which is of use to the book historian, the cultural theorist and the literary critic. If used in conjunction with other sources, it may be possible to build up a more rounded view of the reading experience of the nineteenth-century common reader.[36]

References

1   A collaboration between literary theory and the history of reading is urged by Robert Darnton in 'First Steps Towards a History of Reading', *Australian Journal of French Studies*, Vol. XXIII, No. 1, 1986, pp. 5–30, reprinted from Robert Darnton, *The Kiss of Lamourette: Reflections in Cultural History*, London 1990. For such an analysis of readers for early American novels see Cathy N. Davidson, *Revolution and the Word: The Rise of the Novel in America*, Oxford 1986. For an historical approach which is more in line with classic reader-response criticism see James L. Machor (ed.), *Nineteenth-Century American Literature and the Contexts of Response*, Baltimore 1993.

2   See Darnton, 'First Steps Towards a History of Reading', pp. 7–10, on this problem.

3   For example, Carlo Ginzburg examines the reading history of a sixteenth-century individual common reader from Friulia in *The Cheese and the Worms: The Cosmos of a Sixteenth-century Miller*, trans. by Anne and John Tedeschi, Baltimore 1980.

4   See David Vincent, *Bread, Knowledge and Freedom: A Study of Nineteenth-century Working Class Autobiography*, London 1982; Jonathan Rose, 'How Historians Study Reader Response: Or What Did Jo Think of *Bleak House*?', in John O. Jordan and Robert L. Patten (eds), *Literature in the Market Place: Nineteenth-century British Publishing and Reading Practices*, Cambridge 1995, pp. 205–8; Jonathan Rose, 'Rereading the English Common Reader: A Preface to a History of Audiences', *Journal of the the History of Ideas*, Vol. LIII, No. 1, pp. 50–68; and Richard Altick, *The English Common Reader*, Chicago, repr. 1983, pp. 245–59, for drawing attention to this source.

5   See Amy Cruse, *The Victorians and Their Reading*, London 1935, pp. 120–5; Louis James, *Fiction For the Working Man, 1830–1850*, Oxford 1963; Paul Kaufman, *Libraries and Their Users: Collected Papers in Library History*, London 1969; Hywel Francis, 'The Origins of the South Wales Miners' Library', *History Workshop*, Autumn 1976; and Jonathan Rose, 'Marx, Jane Eyre, Tarzan: Miners' Libraries in South Wales, 1923–52', *Leipziger Jahrbuch zur Buchgeschichte*, 4, 1994, pp. 187–208.

6   In this instance, 'political' refers to the utilization of particular images of working-class readers
        in order to urge the passing or barring of certain reforms, or the promotion of certain ideals.

7   Altick, *The English Common Reader*; Vincent, *Bread, Knowledge and Freedom*; Rose, 'Rereading the
        English Common Reader'.

8   Kaufman, *Libraries and Their Users*; Francis, 'The Origins of the South Wales Miners' Library';
        Rose, 'Marx, Jane Eyre, Tarzan'.

9   To the extent that certain texts are taken as indicative of the readers themselves; see especially
        James, *Fiction For the Working Man*.

10   *Family Herald*, Vol. XVIII, No. 921, 22 Dec. 1860, p. 540 and Vol. LXXXV, No. 2977, 12 May
        1900, p. 28.

11   Cruse, *The Victorians and Their Reading*, p. 124.

12   Joseph Ackland, 'Elementary Education and the Decay of Literature', *The Nineteenth Century*,
        No. 35, Mar. 1894, p.421, and *The Newspaper Press Directory*, No. 56, London 1901, p. 341.

13   *The Newspaper Press Directory*, No. 60, London 1905, p. 553.

14   Virginia Berridge, 'Popular Sunday Papers and Mid-Victorian Society', *Newspaper History From the
        Seventeenth Century to the Present Day*, ed. George Boyce, James Curran and Pauline Wingate,
        London 1978, p. 252; *Family Herald*, Vol. XXVIII, No. 1433, 8 Oct. 1870, p. 364.

15   For example, see 'The Byways of Literature', *Blackwood's Magazine*, Vol. LXXXIV, 1858,
        pp. 210–11; and Wilkie Collins, 'The Unknown Public', *Household Words*, No. 439, 21 Aug.
        1858, pp. 219–20.

16   This quotation first appeared in *The Newspaper Press Directory*, No. 22, London 1867, p. 174.

17   Whilst this is also a present-day assumption, especially when magazines contain serialized
        articles, the idea that readers would reread previous 'Answers' is a more curious one.

18   *Family Herald*, Vol. LXXXIV, No. 2971, 31 Mar. 1900, p. 348, and Vol. XLV, No. 1951, 11 Sept.
        1880, p. 316.

19   Ibid., Vol. LXXXIV, No. 2961, 20 Jan. 1900, p. 188.

20   Ibid., Vol. XXIII, No. 1171, 7 Oct. 1865, p. 364.

21   Ibid.

22   Ibid., Vol. XVII, No. 873, 21 Jan. 1860, p. 604.

23   Ibid., Vol. XVIII, No. 889, 12 May 1860, p. 28.

24   Ibid., Vol. LXXXIV, No. 2970, 24 Mar. 1900, p. 332.

25   The half figure indicates that one answer referred to two genres.

26   *Family Herald*, LXXXV, No. 2981, 9 June 1900, p. 92, and Vol. LXXXIV, No. 2973, 14 April
        1900, p. 380.

27   Ibid., Vol. XVIII, No. 899, 21 July 1860, p. 188, and Vol. LXXXIV, No. 2970, 24 Mar. 1900,
        p.332.

28   Ibid., Vol. LXXXV, No. 2977, 12 May 1900, p. 28.

29   Ibid., Vol. XVIII, No. 905, 1 Sept. 1860, p. 284.

30   Ibid., Vol. XLV, No. 1947, 14 Aug. 1880, p. 252, and Vol. LXXXIV, No. 2965, 17 Feb. 1900,
        p. 252.

31   Rose, 'Rereading the Common Reader', p. 54.

32   Ibid., p. 63.

33   The other nine are *Cassell's Illustrated, Home Magazine, The Lamp, Leisure Hour, London Journal,
        Parlour Journal, Reynolds's Miscellany, Sunday at Home* and the *Weekly Magazine*.

34   The other sixteen being *Ben Brierly's Journal, Bow Bells, Every Week, Family Reader, Fireside Companion,
        Half-Hour, Hull Miscellany, Leisure Hour, Ladies' Sunday Reader, Ladies' World, London Journal, People's
        Friend, Quiver, Shamrock, Sunday at Home* and the *Weekly Welcome*.

35   See Teresa Gerrard, ' "Answers to Correspondents" in *Reynolds's Newspaper* and the *Family
        Herald*', for a comparative analysis.

36   The specific reading experiences revealed within the 'Answers to Correspondents' will be
        recorded in the Reading Experience Database (RED). For further information, see Simon Eliot,
        'The Reading Experience Database: Problems and Possibilities', *Publishing History*, 39, 1996,
        pp. 87–97.

Chapter 33

Paul C. Gutjahr

NO LONGER LEFT BEHIND: AMAZON.COM, READER-RESPONSE, AND THE CHANGING FORTUNES OF THE CHRISTIAN NOVEL IN AMERICA[1]

ONLY IN THE LAST TWO DECADES have American Evangelicals—an umbrella category for certain more conservative American Protestants and 38 percent of the United States' general population in 1990—begun to warm to the presence of Christian novels.[2] Although this fact is striking in itself, it is made all the more intriguing by the reasons that lie behind this acceptance. By examining the history of twentieth-century Protestant book publishing in the United States in general, and the reasons behind the astounding success of the Left Behind novel series by Tim LaHaye and Jerry Jenkins in particular, I will argue in this essay that the last significant vestiges of opposition to the Christian novel receded from American Protestantism because the fictional form of the novel became an important, and largely untapped, resource for explicating the non-fictional content of the Bible. Further, the ability of fiction to explain scripture has not only helped pave the way for American Evangelicals more readily embracing the Christian novel, but has also led to blurring the line between the categories of sacred and fictional literature.

[. . .]

Religious and nonreligious antinovel writers most often grounded their arguments in two lines of deeply intertwined reasoning. Preeminent among these was a Scottish Common Sense philosophical notion of the importance of basing one's life on the truth. As one critic preached in 1807, novels removed one from the truth through their tendency to "give false notions of things, to pervert the consequences of human actions, and to misrepresent the ways of divine providence."[3] Virtuous action, and thus the ability to lead a worthwhile life, depended on embracing what was true and avoiding even the slightest hint of dissimulation or falseness. A second line of reasoning argued that novels with their romantic and adventur-ous tales inflamed the imagination, and thus the passions. Awakening uncontrollable animal instincts once again worked at cross purposes with ideals of virtue, which were heavily dependent on notions of hard work, discipline, and perseverance.[4]

Finally, Protestants added a third line of reasoning to these antinovel polemics. They protested that novels were dangerous because they took time away from more worthy activities, principal among these being Bible reading and other devotional practices. Further, they feared that novels, even more dangerously, might so influence American reading tastes that the Bible would come to seem nothing more than "a wearisome book."[5]

In the end, it was this concern with the Bible that fueled much of the Protestant hesitancy to accept the novel form. A concern with truth (as most explicitly revealed in the Bible) was the cornerstone of American Protestantism in the late eighteenth and early nineteenth centuries. It is not surprising, then, to note that various theological camps that held more tightly to the importance of Bible reading and a biblical hermeneutic propounding of the absolute historicity of the Bible played a key role in the development of the acceptance of fiction among American Protestants. Examining these camps as they manifested themselves under the auspices of different denominations is one of the best ways to trace the changing attitudes among American Protestants toward the novel in general, and the Christian novel in particular.

[. . .]

Near the end of the nineteenth century, as what would become known as American Christian Fundamentalism began to gather strength, a different kind of Protestant publishing was emerging. Denominations had long had their own publishing enterprises to facilitate their efforts in religious education, governance, and missions, but the new breed of Protestant publishers was not linked to particular denominations. These publishers sought to work with broader constituencies, which shared core theological beliefs rather than denominational labels. Such common commitment could be traced back to the interdenominational publishing efforts of the American Bible Society, American Tract Society and American Sunday School Union, but by the end of the nineteenth century cross-denominational publishing would begin to move away from the nonprofit realm of these earlier publishers.[6]

The advent of this new type of Protestant publishing came with the founding of Revell Publishing by Fleming H. Revell in 1870.[7] The brother-in-law of the renowned evangelist Dwight L. Moody, Revell quickly built a publishing house that eclipsed all other firms in its annual production of Christian titles. For more than a century, Revell would maintain its spot as the preeminent nondenominational publisher of Christian titles, only to be challenged in terms of its power and prestige by the aggressive houses of Zondervan and Thomas Nelson in the 1950s and 1960s.[8]

Although Revell would maintain its immense influence and importance in nondenominational publishing circles well into the 1970s, by the mid-twentieth century a host of other American nondenominational houses had also been established. To name only a few, these houses included David C. Cook (1875), Broadman (1891), Moody (1894), Kregel Books (1909), Eerdmans Publishing (1910), Zondervan Publishing (1931), Crossway Books (1938), and Baker Book House (1939). These firms gained greater and greater popularity by focusing on "Evangelical Christians" or "Evangelicals," a group composed of a wide spectrum of differing denominations and backgrounds who share a commitment to the historicity and trustworthiness of the biblical text, as well as a belief that salvation comes through living a spiritually transformed life based on the redemptive work of Christ alone.[9] While membership in mainline denominations has declined since World War II, Evangelicalism has experienced consistent growth. Denominations with the highest percentage of Evangelicals, such as Southern Baptists and Assemblies of God, have grown substantially in the postwar years, while denominations with a lower percentage, such as the Congregationalists and Episcopalians, have suffered serious declines in membership.[10]

Because of its focus on Evangelical Christians, this kind of for-profit nondenominational publishing has come to be called Evangelical-Christian publishing.[11] These publishing houses also became the most active and successful segment of American religious book production in the second half of the twentieth century. The publishers were so successful that by the

1970s major media companies were taking notice of these houses and moving in to acquire them. ABC acquired Word Publishing in 1974, while Rupert Murdoch's Harper bought Zondervan.[12]

Crucial to our concern here, however, is the fact that even as Evangelical-Christian publishing expanded both in titles and volume of sales throughout the twentieth century, with the notable exception of historical romances there continued to be a strong reserve against Christian novel titles. Novels had been largely accepted by American Protestants by the early twentieth century, but more conservative Christians still withheld their approval and support from novels that explicitly commingled Christian teaching and the novel format.

[. . .]

Although American Protestants had a history of meeting fiction with wary skepticism, they nevertheless did read novels in ever increasing numbers as the nineteenth century wore on. The reluctance to read novels, however, remained more pronounced in the fundamentalist wings of American Protestantism well into the twentieth century, showing itself most virulently in the area of Christian fiction. This is most clearly seen in how Evangelical-Christian publishing did not engage in the production of novels on any large scale until the closing decades of the twentieth century.[13] Instead, the most powerful segments of the more conservatively bent Christian-Evangelical publishing world focused on producing self-help books, biblical commentaries, and devotional guides, rather than Christian fiction.

In fact, most of the bestselling Christian novels of the first three quarters of the twentieth century were not produced by Christian publishing firms, but trade houses such as Harper and Brothers, Grosset and Dunlap, Macmillan, and Houghton Mifflin. Such bestsellers included Bruce Barton's *The Man Nobody Knows* (1925), William Lyon Phelps's *The Carpenter of Nazareth* (1926), and Lloyd Douglas's *The Robe* (1942). It should be noted that in the first half of the twentieth century, trade houses had a clear advantage over their Evangelical-Christian counterparts in the areas of marketing and distribution. Far superior resources in advertising and a far greater number of sales venues made them better able to produce best-selling fiction. Yet seeing successful religious fiction titles appear from trade presses did little to move Evangelical-Christian publishers toward producing their own fiction titles. Even when Evangelical-Christian publishers did produce these titles, they usually did not promote them as aggressively as their other books. A noticeable, large-scale commitment on the part of Evangelical-Christian publishing houses to adding Christian fiction titles did not appear until the 1980s.

This shift in the 1980s toward a pronounced interest in fiction titles appeared in two genres that Evangelical-Christian publishing houses showed themselves increasingly eager to produce.[14] The first of these was the Christian romance, the one genre in which Christian novels had appeared in significant numbers throughout the early twentieth century. The all-important distribution link for Christian publishers, the local Christian bookstore, has long had as its main clientele homemakers in their twenties and thirties.[15] Christian publishers began to discover that in adopting the romance formulas of such successful series as Harlequin, they could sell a great number of fiction titles to their customers.

Perhaps more than any other single author, Janette Oke would rock the Christian publishing world, with her first romance, *Love Comes Softly* (1979). Over the next decade, Oke would sell more than eight million copies of her novels, starting a fiction boom among Christians that would only gain speed throughout the 1980s and 1990s.[16] Oke's success did much to open the door to a host of new Christian romances, which would appear in series such as Zondervan Publisher's romance lines, Serenade Serenata and Serenade Saga.[17]

The other genre is more singularly Christian and of more recent inception. It centers on issues of supernatural intervention and warfare, as God and Satan battle for human souls.[18] While romances have clear precedents in American Protestant and trade publishing, spiritual warfare novels do not. These novels are a more unique genre, almost totally monopolized by Evangelical-Christian publishing. This kind of fiction saw its first breakaway bestseller with Frank Peretti's *This Present Darkness* (1986). Peretti would follow up the vast success of this novel with others in the same genre, but a host of imitators would also join the market. The most successful of those to follow in Peretti's wake would be Jerry B. Jenkins and Tim LaHaye's novel series on the end times, *Left Behind*.

[. . .]

In the early 1990s, author and theologian Tim LaHaye approached Frank Peretti about co-authoring a book about the end of the world and the return of Christ.[19] Peretti turned down LaHayes's offer because he wished to continue working on his own projects, but LaHaye did not give up on his idea and eventually enlisted the help of another established Christian author, Jerry B. Jenkins. Out of this collaboration, *Left Behind*, the first book of the series, appeared from Tyndale Publishing House in 1995.

Any doubt about the rising importance and popularity of Protestant fiction disappeared in the face of the absolutely astonishing sales of this book and the series it spawned. A one-book contract turned into a six-book series as hundreds of thousands of copies of *Left Behind* flew off the bookstore shelves. Eventually, Tyndale Publishing House would expand the series deal to an expected twelve books as sales for the sixth volume, *Assassins*, topped 1.4 million copies in the first five months of its release. During the summer of 1999, many of the titles from this series climbed up and down the bestseller lists of Amazon.com and the *New York Times*. The rise of Protestant fiction had found a new champion, as seven million copies of the series were in circulation by the end of 1999.

The reasons for the popularity of the series are complex and enigmatic. The series itself is based on a premillennial dispensational theological view of the end of the world. This view espouses that all those who have acknowledged Jesus Christ as their savior will be taken to be with Christ in Heaven before the world is given over to the horrendously destructive reign of Satan's most evil henchman, the Antichrist. The reign of the Antichrist will last for seven years and is commonly known as the Tribulation. The Tribulation only ends with the second coming of Jesus Christ, who takes dominion over the earth and establishes his millennial (one-thousand-year) reign of peace. Christ's millennial rule will be ended by yet another battle, which Christ wins, followed by the creation of a new Heaven on Earth. In this premillennial view, believers are saved from having to experience the Tribulation, but nonbelievers are not. They are forced to live in a world ruled not by God's grace but by the diabolical and deadly will of the Antichrist.

There is little doubt that one of the appeals of these books is that they comfort Christians with a view of the end times that allows them to forego the torturous pain of the Tribulation. LaHaye and Jenkins go beyond this conclusion, however, and broaden their explanation of the series's success by saying that the books meet Americans' immense spiritual hunger. Other factors almost certainly come into play when one considers the immense success of this series at the close of the twentieth century. The approach of the end of a millennium, fears over Y2K computer problems, and how these events might fit into biblical prophecy have clearly helped the series sell.[20]

It is also important to note that the Left Behind series grows out of a firmly established tradition of books on biblical prophecy long popular in the United States; this popularity was only enhanced by the approach of the year 2000. It is estimated that in 1999 alone more than one hundred apocalyptic titles appeared in the United States.[21] Many of the prominent books in this genre have sold extraordinary numbers of copies. Paul Billheimer's *Destined for the Throne* has sold more than 750,000 copies since it was first published in 1975, and David Wilkerson's *Set the Trumpet to Thy Mouth* (1985) has sold more than a million copies.[22] Clearly the most prominent book in the category of prophetic bestsellers is Hal Lindsey's

The Late Great Planet Earth. First published in 1970, Lindsay's work, presenting his view of the end of the world, became the bestselling nonfiction title of the entire decade.[23] By 1999, *The Late Great Planet Earth* had sold thirty-five million copies, leading one scholar to comment that "only the Bible itself has outsold Hal's" book.[24]

[. . .]

From a literary point of view, the Left Behind series seems to have little to offer. Of the first six books in the series, the first, *Left Behind: A Novel of the Earth's Last Days*, is clearly the most carefully crafted. This makes sense given how tight the production schedule became for Jenkins and LaHaye once the series became popular. Jenkins and LaHaye increased their production speed to release two books a year by 1999, as they were at the same time becoming increasingly involved in a number of projects connected to the series, such as a movie version, graphic renditions of the novels in a comic-book format, and a Left Behind series for teenagers.

[. . .]

As is clearly evident in this case, what may appeal to the professional scholar or literary sophisticate is not always a good indication of public taste or overall popularity. While scholars of the Left Behind phenomenon often find it hard to get through the books in order to analyze them, the books themselves continue to sell in the millions. Any understanding of such popularity is usually left to the realm of conjecture and anecdotal evidence, but there does exist another source of information on what has moved readers—particularly Christian readers—to embrace these books. This source is Amazon.com's Web site, home of the world's largest Internet bookseller. Information made available on this Web site enables one to gain a much fuller picture of what reasons lie behind the colossal sales statistics of this book series.

Amazon.com and the Left Behind Series

On the simplest of levels, the popularity of a book depends not only on its content, but also on the power of its publisher to accomplish certain tasks. Critical among these tasks is an ability to produce and distribute the book in sufficient volume, along with getting the book placed in sales venues that will make it widely available to the reading public. The family-owned Evangelical-Christian publishing firm of Tyndale, which is small compared to most trade publishing enterprises, has done a magnificent job in accomplishing these basic tasks. Once the popularity of the Left Behind series had been established through their more traditional sales outlets such as Christian bookstores, mail-order catalogues, and bookselling Web sites, Tyndale found itself able to place the book series in key sales outlets that do a high-volume business and carry only a limited number of titles. Such outlets include grocery stores; retail chains such as Wal-Mart, Target, and K-Mart; airports; and hotel shops. By 1999, it was easy to buy any one of the series titles because of their wide availability.

Contributing to this increased availability was the Internet's largest bookselling Web site, Amazon. Aside from its absolutely massive inventory, Amazon.com has also made itself famous in terms of its commitment to excellent customer service.[25] Among the many services it offers its customers is an opportunity to write reviews of various books. Thus, thousands of short book reviews are posted on this Internet site, making it a wonderfully rich resource for reader response explorations. Amazon.com puts but one restriction on these reviews: they must not contain offensive language or hateful content. The reviews may be of any length and are not edited by the powers-that-be at the Web site. As of 9 September 1999, seventeen hundred readers had chosen to post reviews of the Left Behind series on the Amazon.com Web site.[26]

As mouth-watering a possibility as having seventeen hundred responses to a literary series is, there are a host of caveats that need to be kept in mind in approaching this kind of information, some of which will be mentioned briefly here. First, Amazon.com appeals to a specific, computer-literate, creditable clientele. It is impossible to say just how accurate a representation this clientele is of the nation's reading public as a whole, as it is also impossible to say how representative these readers are of those who read this particular series.

Second, it is impossible to tell much about the readers themselves. Aside from offering the content of their reviews and an occasional note on geographical location, the reviewers remain largely anonymous. There is no way to confirm either the content or the identity of those who write these reviews.

Finally, those who write the reviews tend to have strong opinions about the book upon which they are commenting. They need to be motivated to get back online to key in their thoughts, and the majority of the Left Behind reviews are unabashedly positive. Amazon.com has a five-star rating system whereby readers can give five stars to their favorite books and one star to books they hate. The majority of those writing in, an impressive 73 percent, gave the books five stars. The average number of stars for the seventeen hundred reviews posted was 4.25. Reading these reviews is much like going to a mutual affirmation society meeting, where only those with positive things to say make it a priority to contribute. Reviewers are also almost entirely self-professed Christians, making the pages that hold these reviews take on the air of a virtual religious tent meeting where theological quibbles, pleas for the conversion of nonbelievers, and testimonies to the power of the series are freely exchanged.

These pitfalls having been acknowledged, there is still a wealth of information offered by the reviewers on why the Left Behind series has experienced such popularity. A two-step approach has been used to cull through the data of these seventeen hundred reviews. First, the reviews were analyzed as they appeared on the Web site and categorized by common characteristics. Second, those who posted their reviews in the late 1990s on Amazon.com were also given the opportunity to give their e-mail accounts, a practice that Amazon.com has since curtailed. Three hundred of the reviewers were then contacted via e-mail with the follow-up survey that appears in Appendix B (not included here).[27] Out of these three hundred surveys, sixty-eight were automatically returned due to incorrect address information. Of the 232 surveys that were successfully sent out, there was a 36 percent response rate, with 83 completed surveys returned. As Appendix C shows (not reproduced here), these 83 completed surveys break down almost equally in terms of male and female respondents. The respondents represent eighteen denominations from twenty-eight states.

To take these seventeen hundred reviews as a whole, a number of characteristics stand out as giving clues to the vast popularity of the series among Christian readers. These characteristics can be broken down into roughly six categories, which include the sex of the readers, the age of readers, the denominational affiliation of the readers, thoughts on how exciting the books are to read, how these books promise to be useful tools for evangelism, and finally how these books serve to illuminate certain biblical passages.

In looking over both the seventeen hundred reviews posted on the Web site and the follow-up survey material, it is immediately striking that this series has attracted male as well as female readers. Because names are not always used among the seventeen hundred posted reviews, exact figures are impossible to obtain, but the information that is available from the seventeen-hundred review sample affirms the almost perfect fifty/fifty split noted among the eighty-three follow-up surveys. Such a ratio is particularly noteworthy because Evangelical-Christian publishers have long acknowledged women readers as their most important market segment.[28] In this case, however, men as well as women are reading these books. It is also clear from the follow-up surveys that once a male reader has read one book, he is likely to go on and read the rest of the series. Seventy-six percent of the readers in the follow-up survey had read five of the six books released by the end of 1999.

A number of reasons might account for the high percentage of male readership. First, the books are written by men, and the male characters are clearly better developed in the course of the narrative. This fact is underlined by the follow-up survey material that points to Cameron "Buck" Williams, the younger hero of the series, as clearly the most well liked of the series's major characters. Forty percent of those surveyed pointed to Buck as their favorite character. The next favorite character was the older male hero of the series, Rayford Steele, with 14 percent of the respondents pointing to him as their favorite character. The presence of Buck Williams, a recent convert with a lot of heart, and maybe not too much sense had a wide appeal for male readers in particular in this survey. Buck is a character, as one male respondent phrased it, who is "active and daring."[29] Another respondent underlined this sentiment by stating that he liked Buck's "sense of adventure" (no. 7). To a man, courage in the face of tremendous opposition marks the heroes of these stories.

This courage brings us to a second issue, which has distinct and wide appeal among male readers who responded to the follow-up survey, namely, an emphasis on action over relational issues in the plot. These readers constantly gave clues that they were attracted to the strong male characters in the books because of how these characters dealt with the adventures and challenges they faced in the clearly action-oriented plots. The degree to which fast-paced action makes these books appealing is captured in how one male reader stated he had a hard time picking a favourite character because "my favourites tend to be the ones that get killed off!" (no. 15). Relational issues are downplayed as world events, harrowing escapes, rescue missions, and various murder plots are foregrounded.

Not only have these books sold well because they have appealed to both men *and* women readers, but they have also attracted readers from a broad spectrum of ages. According to the follow-up sample, once again there is almost a perfect split between readers over the age of thirty and those who are younger than thirty. The books' reliance on simple vocabulary and a heavy emphasis on a straightforward narrative with few flashbacks and a clear focus on telling what are supposed to be factual events strikes one as reminiscent of a journalistic style. These books are not likely to scare off those intimidated by more sophisticated literary works. The style of fact-filled newspaper articles is strongly echoed in this series, and the familiarity that readers have with more common pieces of printed material such as newspapers and magazines may be one of the reasons that these books have been able to attract readers of such a wide range of ages.

Along with revealing the books' wide-ranging demographic appeal, the follow-up surveys show that readers associated with certain denominations also favor these books. Perhaps not surprisingly, because Tim LaHaye describes himself as a Baptist, most of the follow-up surveys came from Baptists. Although not every self-identified Baptist surveyed was specific about his or her particular brand of Baptist, there were several in the sample who noted an affiliation with either Southern Baptist or Independent Baptist churches. The more liberal American Baptist wing is mentioned only once in the denominational answers in the survey, and one wonders if the majority of Baptists surveyed are from more conservative theological wings of this broadly defined denominational title. Southern and Independent Baptists have a strong history of being identified with a literal interpretation of the Holy Scriptures, a view that LaHaye and Jenkins both clearly espouse and that is reflected throughout the Left Behind series. It makes perfect sense that those trained in a certain kind of theological thinking (in this case often favoring traditions rooted in premillennial dispensational theology) would find these books particularly appealing because they would reinforce one's already present theological view and perhaps enhance that view with even more insights. As one reader stated, these books have "served as a confirmation for beliefs I already had, and therefore strengthened my faith" (no. 5).

Aside from this demographic information on the series's readership, many of the clues to the popularity of these books are found most directly in how readers interpret the books' content. Chief among the attractive aspects of these books are their thrilling plots. Just how exciting the books are to read is mentioned by a noticeable 41 percent of Amazon.com reviewers. Reviewers use variations of the phrase "I could not put the book down" no fewer than 224 times when commenting on this series. Other representative comments include "It was breath taking from the first to last page";[30] "I found myself reading in the car, at home, at work, anywhere I could" (1 June 1999); "I stayed up until 2am and read the entire book in 1 day" (19 August 1999); and (the rather painful) "I literally inhaled this book from cover to cover" (1 August 1999). One reviewer even wrote, "i could not put it down my family would come by the door and think i was crazy, because i was so into the book that i was shouting, 'Go go,'! And all this crazy stuff" (15 August 1999). Clearly, the most cited reason for enjoying the book Left Behind was just how engaging and fast-moving the plot was. Readers often coupled this excitement with its spiritual message, but even when they did so, they usually first mentioned the absolutely thrilling nature of the narrative.

Reviewers were so enamored with these books that they wanted to tell friends about them. In this case, however, their recommendations centered on the fact that these books were not just another novel to enjoy. They hold the books up as a gripping way to talk about spiritual issues. One in ten reviewers pointed to the books as great evangelistic tools, which could be used to make non-Christians aware of central spiritual truths. One reader captured the evangelistic promise of the series in writing: "I pray that all who believe or want to believe will read this book and pass it on to someone they love, so that none may be left behind" (11 August 1999); while another wrote, "[M]y best friend read 'Left Behind' last night and was saved."[31]

The combination of these first two characteristics—fiction as an engaging, evangelistic tool—has long been recorded as explanations for the gradual acceptance of fiction among American Protestants. In 1854, Joseph Holt Ingraham specifically dedicated his book to the Christian women of the nation, writing in his introduction that he hoped that the work would be a means of tempting people to consider the truth of Christianity.[32] The exciting story of Lew Wallace's Ben-Hur was not only read by millions of Americans, but sections of it became staples in Sunday school classes across the country, and Charles Sheldon used cliff-hanger sermon stories such as In His Steps to attract people, whether they belonged to his congregation or not, to his Church's Sunday evening services.[33]

So, it comes as little surprise that readers are attracted to the Left Behind series because of its engaging story lines and evangelistic promise. What is of particular interest, however, is just how many of the readers of this series point to these books as interpretive aids in their study of scripture. The series clearly served as a kind of modern-day midrash on the Bible. As one reader succinctly put it, "I'm pleased the writers led me through a Bible study course in this exciting novel."[34]

[. . .]

[The] last category that dominates the Amazon.com reviews is especially interesting. This category reveals a strong connection between reading these novels and reading the Bible. Fifteen percent of the seventeen hundred Amazon.com reviewers made a point of stating that the Left Behind series stood as a biblical interpretative asset. More specifically in this sample, 12 percent of reviewers drew a connection between these novels and the Book of Revelation. Repeatedly, readers of the Left Behind series commented on how the novels moved them to "spend more time reading the book of Revelation"[35] and how the series "cleared up a lot of confusing Revelation" for them.[36] Such significant numbers point to the fact that the days when biblical fact and novelistic fiction should never mix are gone.

Just how readers of this series used these volumes in relation to their understanding of scripture was the chief concern of the eighty-three follow-up interviews. From a desire to gain greater insight into how these novels might interact with biblical interpretation, the follow-up interviews were designed with the first two questions focusing on how these books influenced a reader's biblical interpretation and his or her theology.

A remarkable 70 percent of those surveyed pointed to these books as having influenced their interpretation of various Bible passages. The majority of changes mentioned by these readers in regard to their Bible reading also implied theological shifts, most often identified with the reality and imminence of God's coming judgment. Representative of this interpretative influence are comments such as "I did not know what they [Bible passages] were refuring [sic] to or what it meant that I was left behind[;] it all started making sense to me"; while another reader commented, "I GAINED A DEEPER UNDERSTANDING OF THE END TIMES AND THE BOOK OF REVELATION."[37]

Those who felt that the series had influenced the way in which they interpreted scripture pointed largely to the clarifying nature of the novels when it came to the more obscure narrative of the Bible. While 20 percent of those answering the follow-up survey pointed to the series as an influence on their general interpretation of the Bible, well more than half of those surveyed pointed to this series as an aid in their reading of the Book of Revelation. Typical of the help offered by this series when it came to the Book of Revelation is a comment by a reader who wrote that she could now "comprehend exactly all that it has to say about the end times" (no. 1).

[. . .] Left Behind tells a narrative closely bound to a certain premillennial textual interpretation of the Book of Revelation, but rather than telling it in a dry-as-dust exegetical commentary, it gives biblical interpretation to its readers in the midst of a plot full of romance, violence, revenge and intrigue. These elements certainly are not lacking from the Bible itself, but they are used by LaHaye and Jenkins in a forceful way to make sense of an obscure text.

The clarifying nature of the Left Behind series seemed to take three dominant forms in regard to the Book of Revelation. First, the nature and importance of biblical prophecy was strengthened through reading the series. Many readers of books in the Left Behind series seemed to become more thoughtful about the role of prophecy in their own religious beliefs. One writer summed up a common sentiment in writing, "I treat the prophesy passages with more reverence and importance than I once did" (no. 58).

The second concerned the interpretation of biblical symbolism. A large number of readers were convinced to take the book's symbolism more seriously, with such telling confessions as "I have learned to take verses in Revelations literally" (no. 64). Several readers commented on the ability to open new interpretative possibilities when it came to the biblical text. One reader commented that the way the Antichrist was portrayed in the novel made her realize that he is going to "appear just like you and I to win over those necessary to get him into the position he's prophesied to be in" (no. 38). Another reader stated that the series had "shown me how symbolism in the Bible could possibly mean something more modern" (no. 76). In this instance, the reader pointed to how the word *sword* in Revelation 13:14 could refer to a weapon's nickname, such as the "saber," a high-powered handgun used to shoot the Antichrist in *Assassins*.

The third regarded a new appreciation for the scope and importance of God's return and judgment. One reader wrote, "In particular, their [LaHaye and Jenkins's] portrayal of the seal and trumpet judgments (Rev. 6, 8:6–9:21) has helped me to evaluate more closely the intense physical nature of the judgments as opposed to them being just explicit symbolism of the wrath of God" (no. 18). Another reader wrote: "The depictions in the book have provided colorful descriptions of events described in revelations that have helped me to better visualize and teach on the subject myself. For example, the series describes many of the tribulations (earthquakes, natural disasters, etc.) that are described cryptically in scripture" (no. 59). What the Bible seems all too often to describe in tantalizing and cryptic brevity is fleshed out and made more understandable by the Left Behind series.

What makes this connection between Left Behind and the Bible all the more intriguing is the fact that many of those in the follow-up survey spoke in a way that gave life-changing power to these novels in terms that are traditionally reserved for the Bible alone. Significantly, 11 percent of those completing follow-up surveys pointed to these novels' quasi-sacred quality. One reader captured this quality in writing: "I found salvation where as before I was only a believer. I feel that this is the most profound works I have ever read. I now know the meaning of being 'saved' . . . I had never read very much of the Bible previous" (no. 10). Another reader wrote, "This is sad but I have never been a bible reader. . . . Reading these books made me understand that I need to do more in trying to serve and glorify our Lord" (no. 31). Such comments show a blurring between the Bible and the Left Behind series as the series showed a tremendous ability to influence the religious sentiments of its readers.

Conclusion

Perhaps the most significant finding of this study is how the reader response information located on Amazon.com challenges neat categories about what may or may not be considered a sacred text. It is clear from the responses that in many cases the readers of the Left Behind series were influenced by these novels in a markedly biblical way. For example, the novels were a constant source of self-examination and spiritual introspection and a catalyst for evangelistic endeavors. Nearly one in three reviewers, an impressive 30 percent, said that these books had caused them to reflect on their own spiritual convictions.

The truthfulness of the books, along with the way this truth could catalyze religious belief, is clearly seen in comments such as, "This series has had a profound impact on my life. It has made me make SURE that I am ready, as I believe that these books are not just great fiction, but PROPHETIC fiction. This stuff WILL happen!" (no. 6); "I just hope that this series isn't seen as totally fictional, and I cringe when it is labelled so" (no. 13); and "I can't say I was a Christian before reading book [Left Behind], but I am a believer because of this book."[38] For many of the series's readers, the divine truth and power once reserved only for the Bible could be found in the words of LaHaye and Jenkins, collapsing the long-standing Protestant distinction between biblical fact and novelistic fiction.

Although one might anticipate some connection between the Left Behind series and the study of the Bible, that so many readers closely associated the content of the series and of the Bible is noteworthy. As one reader put it, "Left Behind is probably as close as the real thing gets next to the Bible."[39] In reflecting upon such comments, one is forced to consider whether readers of the Left Behind series are so saturated with biblical and inspirational literature that every book they read is inevitably compared to those they regularly consume as a part of their religious reading diet. Although such a connection is clearly possible, it should be noted that it may not fully explain why readers are so quick to elide books in the Left Behind series with the Bible. In a broad-based 1999 study of American Christians and the arts, Robert Wuthnow—a sociologist of American religion—reported that 45 percent of self-identified American Christian Fundamentalists had read at least one novel in the past year.[40] Thus, evidence exists to support a view that more conservative Christian readers have reading habits that reach beyond the Bible, potentially giving them a greater ability to make distinctions between various forms of sacred and fictional literature.

Readers of the Left Behind series may so quickly connect books in the series with the Bible simply because the books themselves so clearly position themselves as an almost step-by-step guide through the Book of Revelation. As has been noted, readers constantly commented on how the series helped them understand the Book of Revelation. With the added knowledge given to them by these books, readers found themselves moved to embrace doctrinal positions and affirm religious allegiances in ways once only attributed to the influence exercised by the Holy Scriptures and the most venerated religious works. In the Left Behind series, we have an example of just how important fictional works can be when connected to sacred texts. By virtue of readers mentioning time and again that these novels had contained a divinely inspired truth that redirected or reaffirmed their theological stances and religious allegiances, these books move from the realm of simple fiction to sacred texts.

No longer does there seem to exist Timothy Dwight's great "gulph" between the Bible and novels, even for the most theologically conservative American Protestants. Not only are such Protestants reading Christian novels, but we now have convincing evidence that their novel reading and Bible reading are not hermetically sealed activities. In the complex interplay between different sources of information that constantly inpinge on readers, listeners, and viewers, a clear and influential connection exists between the reading of sacred and nonsacred works. Such a connection forces one to reconsider how best to define the term *sacred text*.

References

1   The author would like to gratefully acknowledge two fellowship grants that helped bring this article to completion. These grants were awarded by the Center for the Study of Religion at Princeton University under the directorship of Robert Wuthnow and Marie Griffith and the Christian Scholars Foundation under the directorship of Bernard Draper.

2   This figure was cited in a 1990 Gallup poll. See Barbara A. Stedman, "The Word Become Fiction: Textual Violence from the Evangelical Subculture" (Ph.D. diss., Ball State University, July 1994), 39. For thoughtful treatments of American Evangelicalism, see George Maarsden, ed. *Evangelicalism and Modern America* (Grand Rapids, Mich.: William B. Eerdmans, 1984); and James Davison Hunter, *Evangelicalism: The Coming Generation* (Chicago: Chicago University Press, 1987). An excellent treatment of the more conservative wings of American Evangelicalism is Joel A. Carpenter, *Revive Us Again: The Reawakening of American Fundamentalism* (New York: Oxford University Press, 1997). For figures on the size of American Evangelicalism, see George Gallup, Jr., *Religion in America 1982* (Princeton: Princeton Religion Research Center, 1982), 31.

3   Samuel F. Jarvis before the society of Phi Beta Kappa in 1807 as quoted in Terence Martin, *The Instructed Vision: Scottish Common Sense Philosophy and the Origins of American fiction*, (Bloomington Ind: Indiana University Press, 1961) 61. Martin offers a wonderful overview of Scottish Common Sense's view of the novel in his work, at 57–103.

4   Herbert Ross Brown gives a good overview of this line of argumentation in his book, *The Sentimental Novel in America 1789–1860* (Durham: Duke University Press, 1940), 3–51.

5   "Beware of Bad Books," tract no. 493 (New York: American Tract Society, n.d.) 2. For a treatment of fiction's relationship to Bible reading, see Paul C. Gutjahr, *An American Bible: A History of the Good Book in the United States, 1777–1880* (Stanford: Stanford University Press, 1999), 143–73.

6   Rewarding treatments of the massive, nonprofit publishing enterprises of nineteenth-century American Protestantism include David Paul Nord, "The Evangelical Origins of Mass Media in America, 1815–1835," *Journalism Monographs* 88 (May 1984); and Peter J. Wosh, *Spreading*

the Word: The Bible Business in Nineteenth-Century America (Ithaca, N.Y.: Cornell University Press, 1994).

7   Jan Blodgett, *Protestant Evangelical Literary Culture and Contemporary Society* (Westport, Conn.: Greenwood Press, 1997) 25.

8   Allan Fisher, "Evangelical-Christian Publishing," *Publishing Research Quarterly* 14, no. 3 (Fall 1998): 4.

9   George Marsden, ed., *Evangelicalism and Modern America* (Grand Rapids, Mich.: William B. Eerdmans, 1984), viii; and George Marden, *Understanding Fundamentalism and Evangelicalism* (Grand Rapids, Mich.: William B. Eerdmans, 1991), 4–5. See also Jamse Davison Hunter, *Evangelicalism: The Coming Generation* (Chicago: University of Chicago Press, 1987).

10 Roger Finke and Rodney Stark, *The Churching of America, 1776–1990: Winners and Losers in Our Religious Economy* (New Brunswick: Rutgers University Press, 1992), 248.

11 This categorization was coined by Allan Fisher in his groundbreaking overview of recent developments in this area of publishing: "Evangelical-Christian Publishing."

12 Fisher, "Evangelical-Christian Publishing," 4.

13 Blodgett, *Protestant Evangelical Literary Culture*, 45–46.

14 A helpful taxonomy for Christian fiction titles can be found in Blodgett, *Protestant Evangelical Literary Culture*, 65–113.

15 Fisher, "Evangelical-Christian Publishing," 6.

16 Blodgett, *Protestant Evangelical Literary Culture*, 47.

17 A thought-provoking treatment of Oke's work is found in Barbara A. Stedman, "The Word Become Fiction: Textual Voices from the Evangelical Subculture" (Ph.D. diss., Ball State University, 1994). Stedman does a survey and analysis of 218 readers of evangelical fiction in Muncie, Indiana; the results of this survey underscore her countless insights into contemporary Evangelical-Christian publishing.

18 Blodgett, *Protestant Evangelical Literary Culture*, 98–102.

19 Steve Maynard, "Christian Fiction Charts Leader Will Visit Area: Frank Peretti's 'Visitation,' "*Tacoma News Tribune*, 14 August 1999, B7.

20 Maynard, "Christian Fiction," B7. See also Kenneth L. Woodward, "The Way the World Ends," *Newsweek*, 1 November 1999, 67+; and Boyer, *When Time Shall Be No More*. It should be noted that the Amazon.com reviews and the follow-up surveys compose data all collected between September and December 1999, the final few months before the advent of a new millennium.

21 Kelly Ettenborough, "Readers Snapping Up Revelation Series," *Arizona Republic*, 4 August 1999, B7.

22 Paul Boyer, *When Time Shall Be No More*, 6.

23 Cheryl A. Forbes, "Unlisted Bestsellers," *Christianity Today*, 23 June 1972, 40.

24 Hall, "What Hal Lindsey Taught Me," 84.

25 Joshua Quittner, "An Eye on the Future," *Time*, 27 December 1999, 60.

26 The breakdown by title for these reviews is *Left Behind*, 726; *Tribulation Force*, 136; *Nicolae*, 178; *Soul Harvest*, 204; *Apollyon*, 336; *Assassins*, 120.

27 These follow-up surveys were sent out to the most recent reviewers who had listed their e-mail addresses on their Amazon.com reviews. No attempt was made to determine who might get these follow-up surveys other than the date of their posted review. The most current reviewers were targeted in the hopes that their e-mail addresses were still current. The eighty-three responses to this follow-up survey were numbered 1 through 83 and the responses are referenced to this numbering system in the following notes.

28 Fisher, "Evangelical-Christian Publishing," 6.

29 Follow-up survey no. 6. Further citations of follow-up surveys appear in the text.

30 Amazon.com reader review for *Left Behind*, 30 August 1999. Dates of further *Left Behind* reader reviews are cited in the text.

31 Amazon.com reader review for *Apollyon*, 29 April 1999.

32 Joseph Holt Ingraham, *The Prince of the House of David* (New York: Pudney & Russell, 1855), V–vi.

33 "The Head of Medusa, and Other Novels," *Atlantic Monthly*, May 1881, 711. The story of the success of *In His Steps* is retold in Timothy Miller's *Following in His Steps: A Biography of Charles M. Sheldon* (Knoxville: University of Tennessee Press, 1987), 71–95.

34 Amazon.com reader review for *Soul Harvest*, 19 July 1999.

35 Follow-up survey no. 7.

36   Follow-up survey no. 60.
37   Follow-up surveys nos. 40 and 50. (Further citations of follow-up surverys appear in the text.)
38   Amazon.com review for *Left Behind*, 10 August 1998.
39   Amazon.com reader review for *Left Behind*. 11 January 1999.
40   Robert Wuthnow, "Arts and Religion Survey" (unpublished results from a national survey, Princeton University, Department of Sociology, 1999).

Chapter 34

Isabel Hofmeyr

MATA'S HERMENEUTIC: INTERNATIONALLY MADE WAYS OF READING BUNYAN

IN THE DAYS LEADING up to her death in 1923, Emily Lewis (third wife of Thomas Lewis) spoke often of *The Pilgrim's Progress*. Her funeral was held at the Camden Road Chapel and, in the oration, Rev. George Hawker told the congregation how, on her deathbed, Emily alluded to her favorite portion of the story—Christiana in the Land of Beulah. She spoke of "how the allegory . . . accorded with her own experience."[1]

This section invoked by Emily comes toward the end of the second part of the book. Beulah Land borders on heaven and acts as a celestial waiting room. Here faithful pilgrims at the end of their journeys recuperate before being summoned by a heavenly postal service to cross the River of Death. We receive detailed reports of how eight pilgrims in turn are called, we hear their last words and wishes, and then we witness each person crossing the River in their own trademark style: some pause midstream to issue last instructions, some cross over in a flash, some wade through singing, some require a helping hand, and some discover stepping stones that see them to the other side.

In invoking Beulah Land on her deathbed, Emily Lewis was practicing the well-developed art of Nonconformist dying. As the moment around which Protestant belief is arranged, Nonconformists not only invested time preparing themselves for death but also choreographed the details of their own departure. Believers were urged to think about which books they would have by their deathbed and which people they would summon.[2] *The Pilgrim's Progress* was recommended as "a book to live and die upon."[3] One nineteenth-century commentary observed: "the descriptions of the pilgrims' crossing the river are full of instruction and comfort for dying believers, and have been helpful to many in looking forward to a dying day."[4] The language of the final scene—"receiving a summons from Beulah Land"—had also entrenched itself as a euphemistic discourse for dying.'[5]

Like many Nonconformist women, Emily chose to invoke the second half of the book and so to compare herself and her life to the pilgrimage of Christiana. There has, of course, been much debate on the gender meaning of Bunyan's text.[6] Much contemporary opinion maintains that the story of Christiana offers women only circumscribed forms of spiritual authority. The first half of the story concerns Christian and narrates his epic struggle for religious truth and interpretive authority, defined as men's business. The second half tells a story of community and church within which women must take their obedient places. This view is quite possibly one that Emily Lewis (a good Baptist woman) endorsed. But she might simultaneously have entertained other readings of the story as well. Perhaps Christiana's travels became a way of summarizing Emily's time as a missionary along with husband Thomas in northern Angola. Perhaps, like other Nonconformist women, she also identified strongly with Christiana's companion, the knight Great-heart, who defends the party against dragons, giants, and hobgoblins. Like some of her later Nonconformist female colleagues, she may have dreamed of herself becoming "Woman Greatheart" (the name of a Methodist pageant).[7] Similarly, she might have admired Great-heart and Christiana for their platonic yet intimate relationship and, like others, construed it as a model of marriage in which women commanded chivalrous respect.

Whatever Emily Lewis thought of these matters, it is clear that the story—both in life and death—offered her a way of talking about the delicate and unspoken dimensions of her life. Many other Protestants applied the text to their lives in similar ways, and throughout the nineteenth century, as we have seen, Nonconformists used the book's allegorical dimension to put their personal spiritual feelings into words. A Scottish pastor reported that his congregants conscripted the language of Bunyan to "give expression to their personal Christian experience." One man, suffering from doubt and despair declared, "*I am the man in the iron cage.*" He refers to the well-known tableau that Christian observes in the Interpreter's House. Here Christian sees a sighing figure, eyes downcast, sitting in an iron cage. Christian engages the man in conversation and learns that he is a "man of despair," unable to flee his cage. He once had faith and was a devout believer. However, he turned to a licentious life and was then rejected by God. In comparing himself to this image, the Scottish congregant taps into an accessible field of reference and finds a way of talking about his depression and doubt, while possibly hinting at some unsavory episodes in his past life. Another of the Scottish minister's flock underwent a dangerous operation that might have robbed her of her speech. After the operation, the pastor visited her in hospital. Turning to him, she whispered, "The jewels are all safe!" Her phrase refers to a scene in which the character Little Faith is robbed. The assailants make off with his spending money but fail to find his jewels—his belief in Christ. The woman in hospital uses the image to signal that both her voice and her faith have survived the operation.[8]

Like this woman, many readers wove the text into the inner recesses of their lives. They were able to do this by summoning up a widely shared and deep knowledge of the text. This implicit understanding hung like a backdrop to much Nonconformist discourse and could easily be activated through a phrase or name from the text. Such words could in turn ignite a moment of becoming a Bunyan character like Christiana in Beulah Land, or the Man in the Iron Cage.

This method of reading in which one likened oneself to a character was not only found on Camden Road. The case of Mata, a Kongo-speaker and head porter for the BMS at San Salvador, provides an instructive example. His association with the mission society dated back to the earliest arrival of the BMS in the Kongo Kingdom in the 1870s and Mata accompanied Baptist notables on their initial itinerations. He also led many of the "pioneering" BMS explorations into the interior, including the dash to "discover" the Stanley Pools in 1881, where they earned second prize (the French explorer, de Brazza came in first; the BMS, second; and the much ballyhooed Stanley—ultimately the eponymous winner—traipsed in third).[9] In July 1899, Thomas Lewis asked Mata to act as head porter for an expedition to Zombo, a highland region seventy miles east of the Kongo Kingdom. During the journey, the party encountered difficult terrain. Thomas Lewis explains:

> Our troubles increased considerably when we got into a swamp . . . all of us
> made many slips and disappeared over our heads in the muddy water. There
> were plenty of papyrus to cling to, so we were all able to draw ourselves in
> eel-like fashion to a place of safety. At one point, just as I was reappearing

after a slip into the mud, I saw Mata, who was supposed to help me, standing on a tuft of papyrus laughing as if it were great fun. He wanted to know from me if this was Christian's 'Slough of Despond'! He had only just emerged from a dip himself, and his face was all slime, and he named himself 'Pliable,' which was far from being true. After about two and a half hours we got out of the mire 'on that side which was farther from our own house,' and looked in vain for the man who carried our dry clothes.[10]

In this passage, Mata interprets Bunyan's text by comparing himself to one of its characters, Pliable, a neighbor of Christian. With his associate Obstinate, Pliable initially tries to dissuade Christian from setting out on his journey. Pliable, is however, won over by Christian's determination and, along with Obstinate, accompanies the protagonist briefly on his journey until they both stumble into the Slough of Despond. A disgusted Pliable berates Christian for misleading him, scrambles out of the bog, and heads for home leaving Christian to press on to the bank "on that side of the Slough that was still farther from his own house."[11]

Emily and Mata, then, both employ similar textual strategies that involve likening themselves to characters in the story. How might we figure the relationship between their two reading methods? Are they the same thing in that Emily's is the "original" practice and Mata's the "belated" copy (despite being chronologically prior)? Or, to put it in more contemporary terms, does Mata "subvert" or "rewrite" Emily's original? Indeed, are these terms even useful? Might the relationship between these two reading strategies not be more interesting than these tired scenarios suggest? Might these two intellectual strategies not be more unpredictably wrought in the tangled web of the Congo and Camden Road?

One may argue that the Baptist missionaries were the most powerful players, and it is consequently their methods of reading that prevail. This sense of mission prerogative, for example, is apparent in Lewis's extract about Mata as Pliable, an ancedote that exemplifies a set of standard mission conceits for portraying the "gauche" convert. The reader back home is provided with a familiar point of reference—The Pilgrim's Progress—and shown a naive but sincere convert striving to use the text. Thomas Lewis—as knowing missionary—winks at his metropolitan audience who chuckle indulgently at Mata's childish comparisons while admiring Lewis's level-headedness. The clownish convert plays foil to the missionary's sturdy good sense.

One response to such episodes is to dismiss them as so much mission ballyhoo. Indeed, how do we even know that Mata in fact said what Lewis claimed? Lewis, it seems, scripts the scene on his own terms. He has "voice" and Mata has none. Lewis writes the story. Mata, the head porter, carries the burden. There is little more to say on the matter.

Yet, if we look beyond this immediate extract, the picture becomes more intricate. Comparing oneself to Bunyan characters was something of a pastime among porters on such trips. Elsewhere in this text, Lewis tells us of a guide who led the party miles out of the way.[12] The porters on the expedition named him Mr. Talkative, no doubt because like his counterpart in The Pilgrim's Progress, he too misled people. The porters and Mata, then, were not averse to entertaining themselves by "trying on" different characters.

It was a game of deceptive simplicity. Take, for instance, Mata's self-comparison with the character Pliable. On one level, the comment could be quite straightforward. Pliable is the character who, along with Christian, sinks into the Slough of Despond. Likewise, Lewis and Mata stumble into a swamp and Mata may simply have been trying to make light of a tense moment. Yet, the original episode in The Pilgrim's Progress presents a number of complications. Pliable, as we mentioned earlier, is someone who has been persuaded against his better judgment to undertake a difficult journey. The expedition to Zombo—to establish a new mission—was exceedingly dangerous. Zombo had for centuries been a slave-raiding zone for the Kongo Kingdom. A party coming from that kingdom would not be well received. If it included men in trousers, who would be taken as Portuguese or Arab, fears of slave-raiding would only increase and the party would be unlikely to survive. Indeed, the first time Lewis set off for Zombo in June 1898, Mata flatly refused to go. Only after Lewis threatened to replace him as head porter did he reluctantly agree. As matters turned out, everyone survived the first expedition. A second was undertaken in July 1899 and it is from this journey that Lewis's swamp episode comes.[13] Both journeys were exploratory trips with a view to establishing a new mission at Quibocolo that Lewis ultimately headed. The mission proved to be less than a success and by 1912 had enrolled only ten converts.[14]

Mata's comparison can be read, then, on various levels. Most obviously, it diffuses a number of tensions by acknowledging everyone's folly—beginning with his own. Like Pliable in the text, he tries to persuade the protagonist not to undertake an apparently suicidal mission. However, as matters turn out in *The Pilgrim's Progress*, Christian is, of course, right and achieves his goal. Like Pliable, Mata thought Lewis would not succeed in his expedition and, like Pliable, he was wrong. But at the same time, by taking on the role of someone who warned against over-hasty ventures, Mata comments on Lewis's pigheaded-ness in pursuing a mission venture that could never work. Anticipating many twentieth-century critics, Mata's comparisons raise questions around who the hero of the text really is. Christian is nominally the "hero" in so far as he is the main character. But as critics have suggested, he is a "wobbly" protagonist.[15] Right up until the very end, he is prone to being led astray and could backslide at any moment. He needs constant guidance and propping up from stronger and more experienced characters like Evangelist and Interpreter. Like other African Christians, Mata uses *The Pilgrim's Progress* to question the distribution of spiritual authority in mission stations. Is Lewis really the hero? Does he really know where he is going? Also, if Lewis is Christian, then who is Evangelist? Who, in the mission venture, is guiding whom? This question became ever more pressing on the Zombo expedition, where, from existing accounts, it is clear that Mata did much of the negotiating and proselytizing.[16]

So far, of course, Mata's reading strategy is indistinguishable from Emily's or Fuller's, which we examined in the previous chapter. In all instances, the text becomes a kind of checker-board. On it, one could "try on" different characters and take up different positions. This method of teaching Bunyan—and indeed other texts—was widely used in Protestant mission stations. Although not set in Africa, this description of using Bunyan slides in Palestine/Lebanon in 1899 gives an insight into how converts or would-be converts were encouraged to think of themselves as characters in Bunyan's story:

> the schoolroom was packed full of people, men, women and children. . . . Our catechist . . . explained the pictures and brought out the story of redemption very well. A few days later we went to Zaneb [a Druze girl of twelve] and she was full of the pictures. Those of Christian seem specially to have struck her. His burden, the losing of it at the cross and his crossing the river were her chief favourites. . . . It was now quite easy to tell her to put herself in Christian's place and her burden would fall off too, and so on. [After a second showing] the impress of the first night was deepened and in subsequent visits she often alluded to Christian's experience.[17]

Closely allied to illustration was the role of pageant, tableau, and performance, a form routinely used on missions. Productions of *The Pilgrim's Progress* were common and, in these, students acted out the story and thus briefly became the characters.[18] These tableau-like forms often functioned like living illustrations and possibly furnished a forum where partici-pants began to think of creating Africanized illustrations for the text. [. . .] [I]n two cases these illustrations took the form of photographs in which prominent members of the mission took the parts of the characters in the text. To a local audience, these individuals had quite literally "become" the characters in the text. [. . .] [S]uch conjunctures opened up new possibilities for reading the text as a "biography" of those appearing in its illustration.

A further factor promoting this method of reading was the ways in which the text was fractally reproduced, as we have seen, in media like magic lantern slides, wallcharts (figure 8), postcards (figure 7), and pageants,[19] a method in turn made possible by the episodic and hence friable nature of the text. Like many allegories, the relationship between scenes in *The Pilgrim's Progress* is not strongly causal or driven by "normal" rules of plausibility.[20] There is, of course, the overarching framework of the journey, but this simply acts as a backdrop to a series of episodes, many of which could be extracted, as mission forms of teaching the text showed, and disseminated as freestanding items. Part of the missionaries' strategy was no doubt to reassemble these units at some later point, and they were clear on how the scenes related to each other. For them, the "string" on which these various "beads" could be threaded was the stages of Christian spiritual experience and growth. This point is illustrated by an account from an LMS missionary, David Carnegie, who describes how he taught the text to a class of Ndebele enquirers in present-day Zimbabwe:

> Some fourteen anxious inquirers came forward of their own accord asking me to explain to them the way of salvation. I formed them into a class, which, with one or two exceptions, has been going on ever since. . . . *The Pilgrim's Progress* has been my text book, and a more suitable one I think could not be found for giving these people a clear conception of what the Christian life really means. The whole outline of the book, with its simple illustrations, has been more or less explained to my class, and we hope the words of wisdom and power have touched some of their hearts. We have had over four months at this work weekly, and it does my heart good to see how one or two of them appreciate and understand my explanations of the various stages of progress in the Christian life.[21]

From this description, it is clear that Carnegie taught the book in weekly "rehearsals" using illustrations to "summarize" the various episodes in the story. (These classes were done in Ndebele at the time Carnegie was completing a translation of the text with his wife and assistant. These class discussions no doubt helped to suggest at least some phrases and forms of discourse for the final version.) Carnegie is very clear on how these various episodes hang together: they are to be collated as "the various stages of progress in the Christian life." However, there is no guarantee that this is how the enquirers saw them. They could have extracted individual episodes that interested them, particularly since the story was related orally. In local oral narrative traditions, episodes can be shifted from one story to another or added and subtracted (rather, in fact, as Bunyan himself did in his various versions of the text).[22] Given that, in this case, *The Pilgrim's Progress* appears to be the very first Christian text they encounter in the mission, they might have regarded it as important enough to preserve the original sequence that Carnegie set out. Yet, whatever the case, Carnegie's method of teaching encouraged his inquirers to see themselves as characters, either in the whole story or in its parts.

This mode of "being someone else" was an interpretive technique that characterized much teaching on evangelical mission stations. That Mata derived his reading techniques from such mission teaching is beyond doubt. Mata had had contact with missionaries since the late 1870s and, although the Kongo *Pilgrim's Progress* only appeared in print in April 1897 (two years before the expedition), parts of the book were disseminated verbally and "rehearsed" by means of magic lantern slides, sermons, Sunday school classes, choir services, and the like.[23] The Kongo Protestant community was small and close knit, so Mata would undoubtedly have encountered the story.

Yet, at the same time, there were other sources of interpretation on which Mata drew. His primary interpretive community would have been other Kongo Protestants, who, as the scholar Mpiku has shown, evolved their own reading strategies.[24] These, as Mpiku argues, entailed formulating novel ways of reading on the back of traditional literary techniques. One strategy was to "embezzle" (détourner) the oral story or "folktale" (nsamu or kimpa) by "extorting" or "extracting" (tirer) a new Christian message or meaning from the tale.[25] Mpiku cites the following story as an example of this method. A father sends his four sons to hunt and demands that they bring back many birds. The first two sons construct their traps badly and return empty handed to the village. The third son works diligently and shrewdly and catches many birds while the fourth son whistles away his time. The father rewards the third son and punishes the rest. Traditionally, the story was taken to underline the need for filial obedience and reward for personal attainment. Pauli Dikoko, a member of the Swedish Mission (on the north bank of the Congo River and about sixty miles from San Salvador), reworked this story for the mission station periodical *Minsamu Miayenga* by attaching new meanings to the anecdote. In his view, the father stands for God; the forest where the sons hunt represents the assembly of nations that have already been evangelized; the third son is the evangelist who accomplishes his task by following God's commandments; the other brothers are those who reject their pastoral calling.[26]

Another Protestant convert, Davidi Malangidila similarly "embezzled" a story, "The Slaves who Became Apes." In this tale, a group of slaves, seeking to escape their perpetual suffering transpose themselves from a human to an animal species and become apes. In terms of the story's traditional moral economy, this switch is seen to be cowardly since the slaves run away from, rather than face up to, their difficulties. For Malangidila, however, the story carries a different meaning. In his view, the slaves represent Christians who have fled Satan's world in order to seek shelter in God's kingdom.[27]

Mission periodicals printed such traditional stories but with their new Christian exegeses appended. A well-known proverb separated the story from its explanation: "If you use a proverb, you must be able to explain it."[28] With this proverb, the Kongo Protestants proclaim the superiority of their new Christian analogical method. The interpretation that follows after the proverb is a demonstration that those who have "spoken" or written the story can explain it properly. The proverb, relying on indirection, can also politely imply that non-Protestant practitioners tell stories but cannot explain them properly or systematically.

In using such methods of "the Congo parable" (as such stories became known in English mission discourse),[29] these early evangelists weave together the "folktale" and the proverb and redirect their value and power toward a new enterprise. They also did much the same with the dream. Dreams had always been popular and were interpreted as predictions of future events. Kongo catechists began collecting, writing down, and publishing records of dreams in mission periodicals. These were then explicated as Christian allegorical visions in which each element in the dream was linked analogically to some aspect of Christian belief.[30]

The new Kongo Protestant interpretive matrix is made from grafting together the "folktale," the parable, the dream, and the proverb. In so doing, several intellectual fields are aligned in new ways and generic boundaries are redrawn. The "folktale" and the Bible, for example, become intellectual neighbors, both sources of hidden meaning that can be revealed by using the same method of interpretation in which stories are extrapolated in a parable-like fashion. Both sets of texts ("folktale" and Bible) are applied in the same way and their shared methods of interpretation confer on them a kinship. This idea of approaching the Bible through "folktale" is, of course, very Bunyanesque. As much criticism has shown, Bunyan, prior to his conversion, was an ardent consumer of ballad, popular narrative, and folktale. *The Pilgrim's Progress* is consequently a mixture of romance and biblical form in which the latter "disciplines" the former. Harold Golder has demonstrated this point in relation to the episode of Giant Despair in which Christian and Hopeful trespass on the Giant's land and are imprisoned.[31] In this episode, Bunyan takes several folktale elements (namely the outline of the well-known story Jack the Giant Killer, and the folktale formula of the two brothers) and freights these with doctrinal "ballast." This doctrine is introduced by means of a series of metaphors associated with religious melancholy. For example, the by-way that leads Christian and Hopeful from the narrow way and into Giant Despair's land betokens a turning aside from the true road into a side road of indulgence. Christian and Hopeful are prevented from returning to the true road by driving rain that mounts into a small flood, a symbol of doubt and despair that at times threaten to overwhelm believers.[32] Through this doctrinal "ballast," Bunyan is able to contain the worldliness of the folktale and turn it toward more spiritually edifying ends.

However, at times, the attempt to import doctrinal issues is not so subtle and, in many instances, Bunyan inserts his "theology" insistently and "raw" into the text. For example, in his discussion with Mr. Talkative, Faithful delivers himself of an extensive lecture on the relationship of faith and works and the conviction of sin as a necessary precondition to salvation.[33] But Kele readers circumvented these dollops of theology and foregrounded the narrative "skeleton" of the story. Under such treatment, the story loses its ideological padding and the narrative bones of the story stand out.

In seeking to expunge the theology, African readers were not necessarily attempting to make Bunyan less religious. Indeed, they could have been doing the opposite. By taking out the theology, they could in fact have been making the book more amenable to religious exegesis. As we have seen for Kongo Protestants, a precondition for religious analysis was a "clean" story with the interpretation happening outside the boundary of the narrative. Attempts, then, to "abridge" the theology, could in fact have originated in this form of exegesis that presupposed an uncluttered story as a necessary prerequisite for hermeneutic investigation. This strategy of interpretation also serves to make the story more allegorical. As Kaufmann has pointed out, The Pilgrim's Progress is not consistently allegorical and often breaks out in lengthy "literal-didactic" excursions.[34] It was precisely these sections that the Kele and Kongo Protestants weeded out.

Such interpretive techniques proved to be enduringly and tenaciously popular among Kongo and Kele Protestants. William Millman, who worked at the mission station Yakusu, reported in the early 1900s that he had translated forty of Aesop's fables, but burnt the lot after being questioned by a young man if they were God's word.[35] Millman interpreted the comment as ignorance on the questioner's part, which it could well have been. But it might also have been an interesting generic classification at work in which a fable and the Bible belong together because they both use similar literary and explanatory techniques.

By burning his translations, Millman attempted to withstand popular opinion and taste. Many missionaries of necessity gave in and attempted their own forms of "embezzlement" by colonizing existing African forms. Particularly from the post–First World War period when ideas of "de-Westernizing" Christianity became more widespread, mission thinking and practice produced a rich stream of "mimicry." Jesus, for example, became an "African storyteller."[36] Missionaries became "Christ's medicine men," while Charles Wesley found himself described as an "ancestor in the tribe of Christ."[37] Missionaries received advice on how to make their forms look "old and familiar," or, as another mission commentator said, "There are other ways in which we can be NATIVE. We can learn their proverbs and love their ancient history and bring it into our talks with them."[38] This mimicry came full circle when in the 1950s, BMS missionaries indicated that there was an urgent need for a book of "African Fables with Christian Applications."[39] What they were requesting was "the Congo parable," a genre originally pioneered by Kongo catechists in the nineteenth century. It was a form that Mata had clearly mastered. Just prior to the departure of the second Zombo trip in July 1899, the new church at San Salvador was inaugurated. There were extensive celebrations with many sermons, speeches, eulogies, and prayers. Mata was one of the speakers. After telling a travel story of a previous expedition, he concluded with a number of "Congo parables," which Gwen Lewis found "entirely incomprehensible to Europeans."[40]

Mata, then, practiced different Kongo Protestant reading strategies. One of these involves the "Congo parable" technique in which a folk story is taken (or extracted from other texts) and then subject to Christian exegesis. It is, of course, very similar to the exegesis applied to parables, but its distinctiveness is to subject non-Christian material to this form of interpretation. British Baptists at San Salvador likewise brought with them a range of reading strategies. With regard to *The Pilgrim's Progress*, one of these was an inherently dramatic technique of reading in which one imagines oneself as a character. From the report of the Zombo trip, we know that Mata added this method to his hermeneutic repertoire. We also know that British Baptists were aware of the "Congo parable." Gwen Lewis might initially have found them incomprehensible, but from the early 1900s, the form was being reflected in the *Missionary Herald* and in BMS publications.[41] It was presumably one of the Congo forms that Camden Roaders likewise followed with interest. The Baptist call in the 1950s for a book of "African Fables with Christian Applications" was a belated recognition of the importance and durability of the form. Baptists had finally adopted Mata's hermeneutic as their own.

References

1   George Hawker, "Funeral Address for Emily Margaret Lewis," 1923, Camden Road Church Papers in *An Englishwomans's Twenty-Five Years in Tropical Africa* (London: Hodder and Stoughton, n.d.).

2   Alexander White, *Bunyan Characters in the Pilgrim's Progress*, (Edinburgh: Olliphant Anderson and Ferrier, n.d.) 301, 302.

3   White, *Bunyan Characters*, 299–300.

4   J.H.W., introductory notice to *The Pilgrim's Progress* (Edinburgh: Andrew Stevenson, n.d.) xvi.

5   Phrase from *The Free Church of Scotland Monthly*, April 1899, 88.

6   Margaret Olofson Thickstun, "From Christiana to Stand-fast: Subsuming the Feminine in *The Pilgrim's Progress*." *Studies in English Literature, 1500–1900* 26 (1986): 439–53; Kathleen M. Swaim "Mercy and the Feminine Heroic in the Second Part of *Pilgrim's Progress*." *Studies in English Literature, 1500–1900* 30 (1990): 387–409; Margaret Soenser Breen, "Christiana's Rudeness: Spiritual Authority in *The Pilgrim's Progress*."*Bunyan Studies* 7 (1997): 96–111.

7   Hugh A. Davison, *The Pageant of Woman Greatheart* (Leeds: James Broadbent, 1937).

8   Quotations from J.H.W., introductory notice to *The Pilgrim's Progress*, x, xi.

9   Information on Mata drawn from Thomas Lewis, *These Seventy Years: An Autobiography* (London: The Carey Press, 1930) 168, 174, 182–83, 185–86, 219; Hawker, *An Englishwoman's Twenty-Five Years*, 202–204, 220–21. Information on Stanley Pools from Brian Stanley, *The History of the Baptist Missionary Society, 1792–1992* (Edinburgh: T. And T. Clark, 1992) 122–24.

10   Lewis, *These Seventy Years*, 184–85.

11   Bunyan, *The Pilgrim's Progress* (London: Penguin, 1987) 57.

12   Lewis, *These Seventy Years*, 184.

13   Information on the Zombo expeditions from Lewis, *These Seventy Years*, 171–82; Hawker, *An Englishwoman's Twenty-Five Years*, 198–226.

14   Hawker, *An Englishwoman's Twenty-Five Years*, 192–93; Stanley, *The History*, 134.

15   Stanley Fish, *Self-Consuming Artifacts: The Experience of Seventeeth-Century Literature* (Berkeley: University of California Press, 1972) 230–60.

16   Hawker, *An Englishwoman's Twenty-Five Years*, 202–204.

17   "Report," *The Female Missionary Intelligencer*, January 1899. My thanks to Terry Barringer for this reference.

18   " 'Interpreter's House,' " 252 (report of a school production of the play in Mbereshi, Northern Rhodesia); Ennals, "Last Christmas at Yakusu," *Missionary Herald*, December 1931, 281 (report of pageant presentation of parts of the story at Yakusu, Upper Congo).

19   For sermons, see Jennings, sermon on Bunyan, A/38, Jennings Papers, BMS Archives; for classroom and Sunday School, see "The Month's Mail: South Africa", *The Chronicle of the London Missionary Society* 11 (1902), 41–42; for debating and literary society, see Lovedale Missionary Institution (LMI), "Literary Society: Syllabus – First Session 1874", *Report for 1874*; for school plays, see LMI, *Report for 1948*, 35. For magic lantern, see *Seed Time and Harvest*, December 1919, 2; Austin, "The Pilgrim's Progress in a Congo Setting," 151; on magic lantern slides in southern Africa, see Paul Landau, "The Illumination of Christ in the Kalahari Desert", *Representations* 45 (1994), 26–40; for Bunyan extracts in school readers, see Stewart Xhosa Reader, Std V, extracts in ts. Version, MS 16,340 (d) (1); MS 16,343 (g); and MS 16,399 (g) (i) & (h) (ii), Lovedale Papers, Cory Library, Rhodes University, Grahamstown (hereafter Lovedale Papers); Whitehead, report of Work undertaken by Whitehead in *Missionary Herald*, June 1916, included in A/53, Whitehead Papers, BMS Archives; for drama, see Ennals, "Last Christmas at Yakusu", *Missionary Herald*, December 1931, 281; for hymns see Subcommittee of the Uganda Diocesan Literature Committee, 15 February 1954, S39/36 —which mentions that, in keeping with the English model, a poem in *The Pilgrim's Progress* ("He who would valiant be. . .") had been a Ganda hymn for some time—ICCLA Papers, Conference of British Missionary Societies/International Council for Mission Archives, SOAS, University of London (hereafter referred to as the ICCLA Papers).

20   Angus Fletcher, *Allegory: The Theory of a Symbolic Mode* (Ithaca: Cornell University Press, 1964) 181–83.

21   "South Africa," *The Chronicle of the LMS* 11 (1902): 41.

22   Sharrock, "A Note on the Text," in *The Pilgrim's Progress*, 29. On a model of oral storytelling that suggests this procedure, see Harold Scheub, *The Xhosa Ntsomi* (Oxford: The Clarendon Press, 1975).

23   See note 19 above.

24   Mbelolo ya Mpiku, "Introduction à la littérature Kikongo" *Research in African Literatures* 3, no. 2 91972): 117–61.

25   Mpiku, "Introduction," 128.

26   Mpiku, "Introduction," 128.

27   Mpiku, "Introduction," 128–29.

28   Mpiku, "Introduction," 129.

29   Pugh, "By Way of Illustration," *Missionary Herald*, March 1907, 63–64; Pugh, "In Parables," *Missionary Herald*, March 1911, 71–72; Hawker, *An Englishwoman's Twenty-Five Years*, 192–93; R.H. Carson Graham, *Under Seven Kongo Kings* (London: Carey Press, n.d) 30.

30   Mpiku, "Introduction," 129.

31   Harold Golder, "Bunyan's Giant Despair." *The Journal of English and Germanic Philosophy* 30, no. 3 (1931): 361–78.

32   Golder, "Bunyan's Giant Despair," 365, 366.

33   Bunyan, *The Pilgrim's Progress*, 130–32.

34   U. Milo Kaufmann, *The Pilgrim's Progress and Traditions in Puritan Meditation* (New Haven: Yale University Press, 1966) 19.

35   Section entitled "Discussion" in Herbert Smith, "The Need for Union Literature in Congo." In *The Congo Missionary Conference of Protestant Missionaries* (Baptist Missionary Societies: Bolobo, n.d.) 78.

36   Jesse E. Gwynne Daniell, *The Religion of the Hearth* (London: The Sheldon Press, 1928) 16–17. Book included in 543/30, ICCLA Papers.

37   *Missionary Herald*, January 1929, 23; Senior, "John Wesley," 544/14, ICCLA Papers.

38   Mackenzie, "Talking Women," 543/40, ICCLA Papers; *Congo Mission News*, July 1940, 12.

39   Bangala Committee, Area Priority List for 1959, 544/14, ICCLA Papers.

40   Hawker, *An Englishwoman's Twenty-Five Years*, 192–93.

41   See note 29.

Chapter 35

Danielle Fuller

LISTENING TO THE READERS OF
"CANADA READS"

MASS READING EVENTS SUCH as "Canada Reads" and "One Book, One Community" programs have certainly attracted criticism for their vulgarization of a cultural practice (literary interpretation) and their pandering to "the prizes and showbiz mentality" that has "infiltrated" Canadian literary culture (Henighan 66).[1] Former editor and publisher Roy MacSkimming describes "the One book craze" as "the reductio ad absurdum" of a "blockbuster culture" that generates a "fixation with competition and success" (373). Writer and critic Aritha Van Herk accuses the series of "reducing the whole rainbow of Canadian Literature to Michael Ondaatje's *In the Skin of a Lion*" (140). In one of only two published academic essays to engage with "Canada Reads," Smaro Kamboureli offers a trenchant critique of "the tropes that inform the culture of celebrity" (47). She illustrates how "Canada Reads," through its championing of Ondaatje's novel in series one (2002), inevitably enacts the logic of the "imperium of affect" (45). Meanwhile, Laura Moss implicitly recognizes the show's position within a global market economy and various institutional and ideological structures when she notes that the series "showcases Canadian writing, promotes Canadian writers, encourages literacy, and supports the publishing industry in Canada." Her unease lies in the framing and interpreting of Canadian writing with "depoliticized discussions" that "reinforce certain popular notions of Canadianness," such as global peacekeeping and an idealized multiculturalism. As she points out, this inclination alone is a good enough reason for Canadian literature critics to take the "Canada Reads" "game" seriously. But in her preoccupation with the celebrities, Guy Vanderhaeghe's "thinly-veiled dig at academic discourse,"[2] and "the watered-down aestheticism" of the show's book discussions, Moss pinpoints the anxiety that some of us may feel about our own role as so-called "expert" or "professional" readers when Canadian literature is conveyed in so many popular cultural formations – book groups, radio "games," "One book, One Community" programs. Nonacademic readers are missing from Moss' ruminations on "Canada Reads" and from most other commentaries on the state and status of Canadian literature.

[. . .]

"Canada Reads" is a "game": it is a radio show (and, less successfully, a television show) that adapts a popular reality TV format ("Survivor"). It is not a university seminar, nor a literary journal, nor an academic conference. These obvious differences in media and in intended audience among these events are worth signposting. The producers of "Canada Reads" are neither academics nor literary reviewers: they are experienced mass media professionals who make radio programs for Canada's public broadcaster. When, as literary academics, we cast our critical gaze upon a radio show, it is important to consider not only the implicit agenda of the producers and the discursive effect of the broadcasts, but also the context and materiality of the show's production. I have commented elsewhere upon the production history of the show, its mixed success at constructing a media spectacle in an age of techno-capitalism, and the CBC's historical involvement with the publication and promotion of Canadian literature (Fuller and Rehberg Sedo). Here, I want to begin my discussion of reading practices by briefly examining the production team's selection of the on-air panellists.

"Canada Reads" was formulated during a period of upheaval at the CBC by an interdisciplinary production team drawn from a number of different production units (Fuller and Rehberg Sedo 6–7; 15–17). Senior producer, Talin Vartanian, describes herself as a "keen reader" of Canadian literature, although not "a literary maven," and nominates other CBC colleagues, including Ann Jansen, Jackie Carlos, and David Barnard – all of whom were involved in the first two series of "Canada Reads" – as more "widely read" (Vartanian and Barnard). When I asked Vartanian and Barnard about the format of the show, they linked both their choice of a balloon debate and their selection of panelists with their objective of increasing the size and demographic range of the audience for CBC Radio One:

TV: There are plenty of programs that deal with books in a serious fashion. . . . You have to come up with something that is unique and different. So, [we had] the idea of turning it into a little bit of a game. But also picking people to be the panelists who are not at all earnest. Who are playful. Who are unexpected. DB: Yeah, it's surprising that they're [the panelists] talking about books because, "wait a minute, that person, I've never heard that person talk about books before."

DF: That was a deliberate choice then?

TV: Oh yeah, like deciding to pick people who we know to be readers but who are known primarily as politicians or musicians or in some other cases, actors. And putting them into the role of a reader and getting them to talk about it in a way that is compelling to a listener because they think, "oh, I get to listen to Justin Trudeau talk about something other than his dad." And so that, the curiosity factor, draws people to the radio. It's not to hear another book show (Vartanian and Barnard).

Making radio that sounded lively, and that might generate some dramatic surprises (like Trudeau voting against his own book choice) were paramount concerns in the producers' minds. The choice of "non-professional" readers was deliberate, and so was the engagement with celebrity culture which, the producers hoped, would bring some new (and hopefully younger) listeners to the show precisely because it was not like a "serious" book review program.

In year one (2002), Vartanian brainstormed with her colleague Jan Wong, in order to select panelists who would work well together to produce "magic," "chemistry," and "good radio" in a studio discussion game (Vartanian and Carlos 2003). In subsequent years, other production team members were involved in these discussions. They consulted their contact diaries, thus drawing upon their own social and cultural networks. Some panelists in years two through five (2003–2006) were likely chosen as a result of being contacted in a previous year for the "Canadians Recommend" website feature. While this description of process suggests some of the limitations involved in selecting panelists (many of them were likely names and people already known to CBC insiders; each panelist had already to have some degree of media visibility), it also demonstrates the pragmatics of producing a radio show with a limited (and temporary) staff and restricted economic resources. Thus, selecting Olivia Chow as a panelist (2005) does not necessarily indicate the producers' endorsement of her political position (and, after all, Kim Campbell was a panelist in 2002), any more than choosing Jim Cuddy (2004) indicates the producers' preference for a particular type of popular music. What the selections may suggest is the Toronto-centric content of the average Front-Street-based CBC insider's Rolodex, and their sporadic efforts to find panelists from other regions.

"Canada Reads" was conceived for the medium of radio; its popular format was intentional, and it explicitly promotes the reading of Canadian literature. Via the show, the CBC is able to extend its role as a "literacy sponsor." According to Deborah Brandt's formulation, "literacy sponsors" "are any agents, local or distant, concrete or abstract, who enable, support, teach, model, as well as recruit, regulate, suppress, or withhold literacy and gain advantage by it in some way." (166, quoted in Hall 651). The tension articulated by Brandt between facilitating literacy and limiting it to a particular ideological formation is illustrated by R. Mark Hall's compelling analysis of Oprah Winfrey's career as a literacy sponsor. Hall argues that, "valuing literacy for transformation, as Winfrey does, means that other ways of reading – and consequences of literacy – don't register on "Oprah's Book Club" (661). By contrast, although the "Canada Reads" broadcasts have represented the view that reading is valuable because it can transform the individual, such literacy is not the primary or only type advocated. Implicit in the project and the original question, "What is the book that the whole of Canada should read?" (CBC 2002), and the amended version which omits the moral imperative implied by "should," is another model of transformation that marries the reading of Canadian literature to the development of a collective cultural literacy via the creation of an imagined community of readers (Fuller and Rehberg Sedo 13–21). Informed by the liberal nationalist ideology driving the CBC's foundational mandate to "enlighten, reflect and connect Canadians," the model of cultural literacy imbricated in the content and format of "Canada Reads" is about producing "better," more culturally competent and socially aware, citizens. Of course, it is precisely this project of social improvement, and the exercising of the CBC's cultural authority that underwrites it, that irritates many critics of "Canada Reads" (Bethune 52; Gordon Ai8; Niedzviecki 16). In sum, reading to learn about Canada and Canadians was an explicit, if secondary, theme of several broadcast discussions over the program's first four years. Since I have discussed the cultural work of national imagining that "Canada Reads" performs via its book selections and on-air discussions elsewhere (Fuller and Rehberg Sedo), my focus here is the series' representation and evaluation of scholarly and colloquial reading practices.

Although none of the "Canada Reads" panels has to date featured an academic, "the scholar's position of authority within the world of reading," or, at least, the scholar's way of reading ("privileging the cognitive, ideational, and analytic mode," [Long, "Textual" 192]), seems irrepressible.[3] At times this approach is satirized by the panelists: "Can I use the "P[ostmodern]" word?" wondered writer Will Ferguson discussing Sarah Sinks in year two (2003). Three others disavowed any academic reading: "I had to switch off my university head," declared rock musician Jim Cuddy in year three (2004).' Notions of literary value associated with scholarly reading practices trigger anxiety about levels of cultural competency: "I'm just feeling intimidated now!" declared the then-Mayor of Winnipeg Glen Murray after the initial discussion in year three about the criteria panel members used to select their books. For the show's on-air readers, an academic mode of reading is associated with formal literary features, knowledge of stylistics, and a specialist vocabulary: these elements insistently return in nearly every radio discussion. Given that each year at least one panelist has taken literature at an undergraduate and/or graduate level, the employment of interpretative and evaluative models for considering literature that are common within the academy is not in the least surprising. What is more significant is the airtime that they are afforded, and the ways that editing the show for drama and pace, and to enhance the personality dynamics among the on-air panelists, references the authority, and even upholds the value, of scholarly reading practices.

Although no academic critic has been an on-air panelist, a few scholars of Canadian literature have acted as consultants, providing sound-bites about specific texts and/or producing materials for the show's website. Janet Paterson wrote the readers' guide for *Next Episode/Prochain Episode* (winner of the 2003 series); Terry Riegelhof prepared the guides for *Beautiful Losers* (2005) and *Cocksure* (2006) (at the behest of their publisher McClelland & Stewart), and Gwen Davies prepared the time-line website feature for the 2005 winner, *Rockbound*. All three scholars were excited that these books and their writers were gaining a wider audience through their exposure on the radio show (Davies, Paterson, Riegelhof). By deferring to these "expert" scholarly readers for interpretations of literary texts and their contexts, the producers of "Canada Reads" are acknowledging the value that they place upon "academic" reading practices – practices that are, in fact, given airtime, even when the panelists adopt some of the social behaviors more commonly found in many (non-institutional) book groups.[4] Asking "professional" readers (as opposed to the "celebrity" readers) to produce the supporting website materials also reinforces the pedagogical imperative embedded within the CBCs mandate to "enlighten Canadians" – an obligation that neatly meshes with the rhetoric of on-air readers who frequently describe what they have "learned" from the selected books.

Are "less schooled" ways of reading that are not so "text-intensive, ideational, and analytical" represented and legitimated on-air (McGinley and Conley 219)? The short answer is "yes" they are represented, but they are not always legitimated. A variety of "nonaesthetic systems of value" (Long, *Book Clubs* 150) have been articulated on air by some panelists and on-line through the discussion boards and the celebrity recommendations web feature. Practices include reading as a politically transformative practice and valuing books for their "ability to create moral empathy" (Long, *Book Clubs* 150). Reading in order to understand and empathize with different worlds is also represented (Long Book Clubs; Rehberg Sedo "Badges"), as well as reading as a form of subjective identification (as when readers seek connections to their personal experience). Non-aesthetic or vernacular reading practices are not necessarily apolitical or devoid of aesthetic appreciation, although they are often so perceived. On-air reader Glen Murray proved to be a skilled and politically engaged vernacular reader, for example. In 2004 he claimed that, "I like novels that move me outside my comfort zone . . . I want to get annoyed and angry when I read." His advocacy of Thomas King's novel *Green Grass, Running Water* supported a reading practice oriented toward political transformation: it required questioning his own values as well as seeking to understand the novel's "non-European framework," King's "satire of Christian values," and his use of indigenous oral tradition. During a verbal battle with the other panelists who variously described and downgraded the novel as "too didactic [and] slight," (Jim Cuddy) "NativeLite-humour without the danger" (Zsuzsi Gärtner), and "a little cute" (Franchie Pelletier), Murray found an ally in Measha Brueggergosman. In her declaration that *Green Grass* was "the book that Canadians should challenge themselves with," Brueggergosman echoed Murray's notion of reading as potentially politically transformative.

Similarly, in series four (2005), Toronto City Hall politician Olivia Chow framed Margaret Atwood's *Oryx and Crake* as an environmentally engaged and politically topical book that provokes reflection upon and engagement with scientific advances and contemporary social issues. Chow also presented the novel as a useful tool in the project of increasing literacy among young men: the sector of the population whom librarians in all northern industrialized countries are most actively attempting to involve in reading (Bans and

Pidgeon; Carnell; Jones). On a number of occasions, she explicitly sought the support of fellow panelist Roch Carrier, former National Librarian of Canada, for this project. The "game" format of the show meant that Carrier was initially reluctant to back Chow on this point, since his role was to promote Volkswagen Blues, but there was also an implicit clash of reading practices at play in their encounters. Carrier's eloquent advocacy of Poulin's novel centered on aesthetics, while Chow's interpretations of all five novels were directed by a highly mimetic reading practice. Subsequently, *Beautiful Losers* with its non-linear narrative and ludic engagement with genre codes was a "difficult" read for Chow, whereas for Carrier, Cohen's novel "still smack[ed] . . . of the new, and the outrageous and the revolutionary." While Glen Murray's political advocacy of King's novel was upheld by at least one panel member, Chow's political reading of Atwood's novel lost ground as the other panelists devalued her other contributions to the discussions. Chow was gradually made to appear less intellectual and astute than the other panelists. Donna Morrissey corrected her "mis-reading" of Cohen's representation of women, and the novel's champion, Molly Johnson, cited the various "experts" whom she had consulted about the historical literary value of the novel (including, ironically enough, Margaret Atwood). The comments of Carrier and host Bill Richardson about the "ground-breaking" form, content and literary brilliance of *Beautiful Losers* were given considerable air-time.[5] *Beautiful Losers* thus became the test-case through which the 2005 panelists proved their critical mettle and Chow failed the test.

Panelists who read and interpret through non-academic frames tend to get side-lined, especially if they are women. In 2003, actor Mag Ruffman's vernacular reading practice was predicated on the desire for immersion in, rather than analysis of, the text. Compared to the other panelists, Ruffman came across as distinctly un-schooled in literary criticism and the art of debate. Her comments frequently seemed banal and unengaged – and I admit that I found this irritating and unsatisfactory, particularly in regards to her "failure" to make a compelling case for Helen Humphrey's *The Lost Garden*. The journalist Brian Bethune inter-preted Ruffman's stance (ironically?) as a comic performance: "From early on Ruffman decides to play the ditz, a part she takes on with shrewdness and comic timing" (Bethune 52). On closer examination, however, Ruffman's performance as a reader hints at a col-loquial reading practice that is given time and credence within many face-to-face book groups (Long, *Book Clubs* 152). Her introductory comments to *The Lost Garden* emphasize the necessity of accessibility and a compelling plot that enable a reader's immersion in a fictional world, and she hints at the importance of believable characters to reader identification with that imagined reality: "My book is very easy to read – you go through it quite fast. . . . It's a great book because you can't put it down. . . . It's a book that I've lent to five or six people and they've read it in one sitting. . . . It's a lovely book and the characters are great and the story is great." Note too, that Ruffman has shared this book with other readers – maybe with what scholars of book dubs term her "trusted others" (Rehberg Sedo "Badges") in an act of "social exchange" (Hartley 91).

Unfortunately for Ruffman (and Humphrey's novel), the "Canada Reads" panelists do not recognize her commentary as the beginnings of a non-aesthetic evaluation and, furthermore, the Survivor-style competition militated against them reading "with" her in the collaborative and collective style of book group book talk (Hartley 137; Long *Book Clubs*; Rehberg Sedo "Badges"). Instead, presenter and chair Bill Richardson cut into Ruffman's introduction to add information about the book's setting, as if to correct her style of commentary. In a later broadcast, writer Nancy Lee mounted an eloquent literary defense of the novel that brought its presentation into line with the promotion of the other novels. Colloquial reading practices are present in the radio shows but the demands of the show's contest format, editing, and the need to produce a dramatic "spectacle" frequently conspire with the cultural authority of aesthetic interpretation to contain them (Fuller and Rehberg Sedo 13–4).

Despite these examples, I would like to suggest that, with each series, "Canada Reads" has given increasingly more on-air time to vernacular reading practices, including shared reading practices that mimic the form and function of face-to-face reading groups. In 2005 (series four), for example, a range of reading practices (as well as diverse interpretations) were undertaken, tested out and, in some cases, rejected by the five panelists in favor of alternative interpretive modes. These included both passionate, personalized and identificatory readings, such as writer Donna Morrissey's vivid anecdote about her father's experience in the Newfoundland fishery as part of her promotion of Frank Parker Day's *Rockbound*. Singer Molly Johnson commented upon the failure of identification as a sustained form of reader engagement in relation to Mairuth Sarsfield's *No Crystal Stair*. "I wish there had been books around about being black in Canada when I was 17. My mother knows Mairuth. . . . I had lots of points of entry into this book but I didn't think the story was that great." In both cases, Johnson and Morrissey offered other ways of reading the same texts. Morrissey's advocacy of *Rockbound* involved the invocation of humanist values (she refers to the "age-old questions of humanity" that Parker Day explores, for example); a political and environmental reading of the text in terms of the contemporary destruction of the Atlantic fishery; and an interpretation of the novel informed by western generic conventions of "fable," "myth," and "romance." Johnson referenced a series of approaches to *No Crystal Stair*, the consideration of narrative form; a socio-political reading that established the book as an important articulation of "Black community and disappeared history," and the socially valuable capacity of the novel to generate "book talk" among friends even if, as an individual reader, Johnson was not particularly engaged by either the characters or the story: "I had really great conversations with the women in my world," she enthused.

There were other ways in which "Canada Reads" series four sounded more like a book group discussion than a "knock-out" contest. Although the Survivor format of the show demands that individuals champion a specific book and vote off another each day, the panelists in 2005 were far more reluctant than those in previous programs to dismiss or condemn each other's books, despite Bill Richardson's prompting. Richardson made repeated references to book debate as boxing but, rather than taking each other on, the 2005 "Canada Reads" panelists occasionally ditched the rules of the game. In broadcast four, Roch Carrier underlined his view that all the books were "good books" that listeners could enjoy, while in the final broadcast, Olympian fencer Sherraine MacKay added, "they're only rejected because we're playing this silly game." She then proceeded to initiate what might be described as a "Peggy Atwood love-in" among the discussants. The "Canada Reads" panelists adopted other book group-type behaviors that were given extended air-time. Notable was Olivia Chow's presentation of her research into the origins and images of "Oryx." Instead of allowing the pace and drama of a debate to drive editorial decisions, in this instance the producers retained Chow's discourse on *Oryx*, which became somewhat disconnected from her analysis of the novel. Whereas Chow's comments on *Beautiful Losers* were dismissed by the other panelists, her contextual research on Atwood's novel was not. Her diversion away from the text would have been familiar territory to any listener-reader who belongs to a book club: the ways that books can prompt members to research both relevant and tangential material and then share it with the group is a common component of "book talk" (Long, *Book Clubs*; Rehberg Sedo "Badges"). Equally striking in this regard was Chow's description of a "Canada Reads" "feast" that she had held with friends (themed dinners being a staple of many book groups [Hartley 16–7]); Johnson's narration of her reading history of Cohen's *Beautiful Losers* and her seeking out of "expert" opinion on it as part of her preparation for the show (note that she asks writers rather than academics); and the exchange of familial stories of physical work and rural communities that occurs between Morrissey and Carrier in a discussion about *Rockbound*. While this group of panelists did not consistently exhibit book group behaviors, they were more accommodating of vernacular reading practices than previous on-air readers.

[. . .]

Through its online presence and the local activities it inspires, "Canada Reads" offers scholars of Canadian literature an opportunity to investigate the uses that readers make of the show and its book selections.[6] Specific demographic data for "Canada Reads" is not available, but data relating to the audience for CBC radio as a whole suggests that the majority of listeners are over 35 with age groups of 50 years and over recording the highest weekly listening hours (between 20 and 25) (Friends). Feedback received by the producers of "Canada Reads" has included e-mails from teachers, high school students, and other readers under 35, suggesting that the show has to date attracted a small number of younger readers/listeners (Vartanian and Barnard). While it is difficult to determine whether or not the show creates new readers for Canadian literature and, if so, how many, sales figures for selected titles suggest that the series is successful in creating a wider readership for the featured books (Fuller and Rehberg Sedo 28). More significantly for my purposes in this essay, postings on the show's website in the second, third and fourth series of "Canada Reads" (2003–2005) offer evidence for a range of reading practices, not all of which are determined by the on-air discussions or by the medium of expression.

The material examined includes comments posted on the CBC's on-line discussion boards, which were active for approximately six weeks during the 2003 and 2004 series of "Canada Reads." In 2005 the discussion boards were replaced by a new version of the "People's Choice" award. For two months, readers were invited to post short commentaries about the book they would recommend to Canadians, rather than simply entering a title on a ballot (as in 2002) or voting for one of the five featured books (2003 and 2004). The 2005 People's Choice feature produced an interesting series of reading narratives, many of which were highly autobiographical in content. Taking part in a written form of exchange may be one factor that encouraged participants to borrow from the textual genres of memoir and autobiography, and to respond to each other's contributions by mimicking the content, semi-formal register, and narrative structure of previous postings. A majority of the commentaries articulate the emotional and/or intellectual role that a particularly beloved book has played in the reader's life, for example. Nearly all readers chose books that had not yet been featured on "Canada Reads," and several took issue with the show for failing to highlight a particular author (such as David Adams Richards) or genre of writing (notably fantasy and children's fiction, genres that are often marginalized by academic critics).

The postings suggest that the "Canada Reads" producers are neither responding to nor particularly paying attention to what Canadians really read and want to read "together." Readers' nominations of books, genres, and authors can also be interpreted as offering some resistance to the canonical approach that underwrites at least half of the "Canada Reads" book choices. A sizeable number of readers make no reference at all in their postings to the show or its literary selections. It is tempting to interpret these commentaries as a rejection of the CBC "nannyism" cited by Hal Niedzviecki in his disparaging remarks about "Canada Reads" and "One Book, One Community" programs (16). Further, the articulation of alternative Canadian literature lists within a medium provided by the CBC could be interpreted as a meaningful form of public engagement with (and negotiations of) hierarchies of literary value.

The format of the "People's Choice" forum mediates the reading practices recorded there and the language used to describe "value." Many postings expressing opinions about the post-ers' reading histories and preferences adopted the style of a reading diary or, more appropriate to the medium, a reader's blog. The reader/blogger both notes and reflects critically upon their reading habits, while seeking to influence those of other readers who may use the web as a resource in selecting books to read (Rehberg Sedo "Convergence").[7] Several readers of this type employ the language of avid, voracious book readers to articulate the pleasure they gain by consuming Canadian fiction: "the chapters I had devoured" (Crystal Walsh, St John's); "I was consumed by the story" (Karen, St John's); "I would recommend [this book] to anyone seeking a taste of Canadian literature" (Alison Lennie, Edmonton). This discourse of consumption not only reflects the pervasive consumer-oriented organization of contemporary Western societies; it also expresses a visceral reading experience that "feeds" both imaginative and bodily needs. Perhaps this pleasure is replayed for readers who share their reading experiences with others through online postings or blogging?

Discussion boards mediate reading practices differently from the People's Choice format. By inviting post-ers to debate directly with each other, albeit in a written rather than an oral form, the "Canada Reads" discussion boards elicit more overt examples of readers negotiating with notions of literary value, and reflecting on the role that reading plays in their everyday lives. In the two years that the "Canada Reads" team ran the on-line discussion boards (2003 and 2004), the moderator was also kept busy refereeing the eloquent outbursts of outrage and support for the show's format, the quality (or not) of the book chat on-air, and the various conspiracy theories about the "political agenda" of those running the show. Additionally, readers used the boards to explain the value that specific books held for them. There were overt expressions of the "identity work" that readers were undertaking with and through reading, sometimes alone, but also within groups (Turner 102). These ranged from the feel-good affirmation of an un-problematized Canadian identity, to critical reflections upon notions of national and regional identities. A reader in Waterford, Ontario exemplifies the celebratory, affirmative reading experience, one apparently shared by members of their book group:

> Our group has read a number of the Canada Reads selections and our choice is
> *The Colony of Unrequited Dreams* by Wayne Johnston. This tale embraces the spirit
> of "Canadianism." We felt Canadian reading it and believe this to be the ultim-
> ate compliment to a Canadian book and its author. We are enjoying the lively
> panel discussions taking place on the CBC this week and believe Canada Reads
> is a great way to celebrate Canada Book Week and the wonderful Canadian
> Literature that is available. We look forward to next year's list. Kudos to the
> CBCI (23 April 2003).

The irony of adopting Johnston's anti-colonial historical fiction of Newfoundland, a book that laments the province's lost chance of becoming a sovereign state, is invisible here, just as it was on-air when, championed by Justin Trudeau, it was held up as a great example of Canadian federalism (Sugars 169 n.1) I am particularly struck by the willingness of readers in Ontario to "embrace" a Newfoundland story as the epitome of all things Canadian, thereby neatly inverting the usual cultural function of Newfoundland as central Canada's marginalized "other" – the "handout province" – requiring too much taxpayer's money. A reversal of this sort may well be inflected by nostalgia for the lost world of small rural townships that Johnston represents in *Colony* as well as his evocative passages of lyrical landscape description that fulfill an urban longing for apparently cohesive communities (Fuller "Strange" 22).

This particular group of readers, in common with a number of other post-ers, employ the "Canada Reads" selections as a resource through which to build their shared reading list. They also use the books to celebrate being "Canadian" through a literature that they regard as high in quality if and when it affirms their sense of a collective identity. While these uses of

Canadian literature may not coincide with the motivations of many of the "professional readers" who teach and research it, they should not all be dismissed out of hand as "un-politicized" (Moss). At times, as noted in the Waterford example, on-line readers perform readings that uphold dominant nationalist ideology, but these readings can offer scholars insights into the relation between mainstream representation of Canadian literary culture and the perpetuation of normative values. Further, from the perspective of cultural politics at least, the state funding of Canadian literary culture post-Massey-Lévesque Commission to the early 1990s appears to have paid off. The post-ers on the "Canada Reads" website demonstrate an awareness of Canadian writing in various genres, and most readers celebrate the fun involved in reading these books. Indeed, the various pleasures derived by these Canadians in their reading of Canadian literature suggest another area for critical investigation that has been under-researched by literary scholars.

The other reading practice which dominated the "Canada Reads" discussion boards was more critically self-reflexive:

> I read to be a little unsettled, to have my perspectives called into question, so that I am reminded to tread carefully in my interactions with others. The world is not simple, issues are not black and white. The energy and creativity in life lie in the grey areas, the realm of the ambiguous – the uncomfortable domain of *Next Episode* (Mark, March 2003).

The textual, written medium of the discussion board (less "instant" than online chat, for example) combined with the ability of the commentator to reread and reflect upon previous postings carefully, can lead to more developed analyses than are sometimes given space on-air. Another post-er wrote a more extended analysis of self-transformation, perhaps encouraged by the example of earlier contributors such as Mark:

> I believe it was a brave move of the panel to select *Next Episode* [as the winner] not only because it was a French Canadian novel, but because terrorism and separatism is something that effects us all [sic] . . . and no matter where we are in Canada – it is better to try to understand each other through the perspectives of our regionality than to dismiss the value of our diverse Canadian experience. I myself was sure *Colony of Unrequited Dreams* would win – but I am glad *Next Episode* came out on top because it is important to understand the many different perspectives Aquin gives in this novel – the insane, the desperate, the separatist, the Quebecois, and, ultimately the Canadian. The decision was not about politics, it was about having an open mind – trying something new and different and uncomfortable because you might enjoy it anyway (Angela, April 2003).

While Angela's commentary veers between a liberal discourse of diversity and a more ideologically radical stance that seeks to recognize and value differences within the Canadian polity, she is certain about the value that Canadian literature has for her.

Mark's and Angela's notion of reading books in order to have your identity and assumptions "unsettled" was echoed by many readers on the discussion boards in both 2003 and 2004. By contrast, only one on-air example from those two years adopts a similar stance: the occasion in 2004 when Glen Murray and Measha Brueggergosman mounted their passionate defense of Thomas King's novel. This example shows that the reader-listeners of "Canada Reads," empowered in part by the more reflective, written mode of communication available to them on-line, sometimes read against the grain of the show's tendency to default to a reading practice structured by canonical aesthetics. Although postings on discussion

boards can be a frustrating source for investigating reading practices since post-ers frequently do not provide their location, gender, age, or other detail about their lives, the
"Canada Reads" postings demonstrate readers "at work" negotiating with literary texts, with
the cultural authority of the CBC, with the on-air discussions, with different constructions
of "Canadian" identity, and with each other's opinions.

Meanwhile, academic readers have also responded to "Canada Reads" through various
media. Some scholars of Canadian literature posted brief critical comments on-line via the
CANLIT-L listserv, or, via personal blogs (e.g. "scribbling woman"). Many of the CANLIT-L
postings echoed the content and concerns of the "non-academic" readers who posted on the
"Canada Reads" discussion boards. Issues featured on CANLIT-L included the negative
criticism of selected books necessitated by the "Survivor" format of the show; the "dullness"
of conversation during year one (2002), the sensationalist mis-representation on-air of
Prochain Episode as a novel "whose hero is a terrorist" in year two (2003) (Forsyth), and, most
provocatively, whether or not the series showcases Canadian literature in a way that is
laudable. The latter theme elicited a small handful of largely positive responses from post-ers
in February/March 2005 who felt that "any show that promotes literature and gets people
curious and reading" (Lesk) or "that gets Frank Parker Day read" (Dean) had some cultural
value. Perhaps not surprisingly, post-ers identifying themselves as librarians also shared this
view, and were particularly quick to express their support for the show during the first year
(2002). Academic dis-ease with "Canada Reads" has, to date, focussed on its perpetuation of
the culture of celebrity and global commodity capitalism (e.g. Kamboureli; Lynch). Via the
CANLIT-L listserv, Gerald Lynch has twice expressed his dissatisfaction with "Canada Reads"
and literary awards as vehicles of consumer capitalism focussed on "selling one thing a lot"
(2003). In other words, academic readers have been preoccupied with the wider cultural,
ideological significance and structural situation of "Canada Reads," and, perhaps surprisingly
for people whose training privileges textual criticism, they have been rather less concerned
with the actual content of the show, the on-air discussions, and the books selected.

Finally, a small but growing band of academic readers wish to "use" or respond to
"Canada Reads" by engaging with the show more directly and inter-actively. English and
library faculty members at UBC, UNBC and the University of Winnipeg, among others,
have been involved with tie-in events such as panel discussions or book displays on- and off-
campus during the radio series. Other academics have incorporated critical readings of the
show, its book selections and its construction of a reading public into their undergraduate
teaching of Canadian literature (Moss "correspondence"; Rifkind). The former "hands-on"
responses to "Canada Reads" might be described as a particular vernacular reading practice:
they are certainly socially oriented in their direct engagement with non-academic readers,
and in their possible contribution to better "town/gown" relations. The pedagogical
responses, meanwhile, are clearly influenced by cultural studies approaches to literary-
cultural production and reception. They also represent dynamic pedagogical strategies
through which to engage the interest of students whose reading competencies have been
developed on-line as much as they may have been learned through reading print texts.

Undergraduate students in a Canadian literature classroom or posting in a Virtual
Learning Environment can, of course, be considered to form a reading group, albeit one that
is framed and structured by institutional educational imperatives. The final reading practices
that I want to consider are those of people who also demonstrably and regularly read
together and who, arguably, do not require a series such as "Canada Reads" to recommend
Canadian writing that they might enjoy. Established book groups have their own rules of
selection and modes of discussion and evaluation which, while not as "free" or "anarchical"
as one scholar of reading has suggested (Petrucci 367), are by no means enslaved to the
hierarchies of value consecrated by universities and literary review editors (Hartley 45–71;

Long, *Book Clubs* 116–30). Take two different book groups located in the same part of Nova Scotia.[8] Both groups decided to read one of the 2005 "Canada Reads" books, *Rockbound*, before it won the on-air competition. Members of the "Red Tent group" were motivated to read Frank Parker Day's 1928 novel by a local CBC Radio-Halifax competition in which book groups in Nova Scotia were invited to demonstrate why their discussion of *Rockbound* should be selected for broadcast. The Red Tent group won the competition and their discussion of the novel was aired on Maritime Noon, with extracts broadcast nationally on Sounds Like Canada. The other book group, "Judith's Book Club," had no direct involvement in the production of either local or national "Canada Reads" programs. Their "act" of reading *Rockbound* had a different context, although both groups share the same geographic "place" (Cavallo and Chartier 2), and are composed primarily of women ranging in age from 30 to 60. Listening to the groups discussing both *Rockbound* and "Canada Reads" offers some fascinating insights into the ways in which readers interpret texts in a face-to-face group discussion. Members are aware of the conventions that frame how literary fiction is represented not only by a national broadcaster but also by academic "experts"; they understand the exigencies of radio as a phatic medium that must engage and hold the attention of the (often-distracted) listener, and they employ and value their local and experiential knowledge as an interpretative resource. It would, therefore, be incorrect and overly simplistic to label their shared reading practice as an example of the "trend" for "personalized" criticism (Taylor R1).

One of the most compelling aspects of the Red Tent discussion is their analysis of how their regular reading practices were changed and mediated by the editing strategies and agendas of the local CBC radio show producers. The group rehearsed; they created a stage-set; they turned the meeting into something of a celebratory ritual featuring food and wine. Their regular social practice as a reading group was transformed into an event. Several non-members were present at the taping, including the writer Donna Morrissey who championed *Rockbound* on "Canada Reads." Another one-off participant was local CBC Halifax radio host, Don Connelly, who turned out to have some pre-conceived notions of book groups that inflected the questions that he asked, the editing that took place after the recording, and the point at which he stopped the taping. Connelly had asked them, for example, whether they belonged to the book group for primarily social reasons – which they energetically refuted. Here are members of the group recalling how they performed a book group discussion of *Rockbound* for the radio:

> Pam: We did *Rockbound*! We did it two nights before [the taping of the radio show]! To rehearse amongst ourselves, just to chat about the book – so that we didn't sound completely stupid.

> Pat: We don't usually have a meal. We did a meal – we thought, "we'll roll up the carpet." It was at Gail's – we went into Gail's living room and there was all these huge honking microphones and all the air was just sucked right out of the room. Like there was this gas! And it wasn't like a normal discussion.

> Mariene: Although we'd had lots of normal discussion around the table while we ate. I thought that we had great discussion in the kitchen and we had good talk in the kitchen.

> Hilary: We had good wine too!

> [laughter]

Pat: And I thought that Don Connelly cut us off just as we were starting to get going. I was ready to go and he said, "that's a wrap!" We were just starting . . .

(Red Tent)

Not only did the Red Tent feel that their "normal discussion" was cut short and restricted to what they regarded as preliminaries, they also articulated how they allowed the radio-friendly controversy about the reception of *Rockbound* by the inhabitants of Ironbound (the community that Parker Day visited while researching his novel) and Connelly's directorial agenda to hi-jack their usual textual pre-occupations:

Marlene: [The discussion] was fascinating and we've had lots of conversations when we've really diverged and gone off on a tangent and we've still gotten something out of it at the end of the night. But I remember there was one point when [Don Connelly] said, because we'd been talking about the Ironbounders and this and that and we were very wrapped up in [the controversy] and people's connections to this, and then he said, "Let's talk about setting." And we went "huh?"

[laughter] (Red Tent)

Rather than debate characterization, setting, language, and the historical contexts for the book as they normally do, the Red Tent's "Canada Reads"-mediated discussion focussed largely on the dramatic controversy surrounding Frank Parker Day's fictional representation of actual people and events. Admittedly, this is a controversy that still has some force on the South Shore of Nova Scotia 80 years later, and hence knowledge about the local reception of Day's novel could be referenced by book group members from family and community memories. Talk about the Ironbounders' upset over Day's novel in the 1930s thus served the dual purpose of providing engaging radio, and allowing the group members to exchange their local knowledge (drawn not only from local gossip but also from meeting Donna Fink, former Ironbound resident).

Although the context and act of reading *Rockbound* was different for Judith's Book group, their shared reading practices as a group are well established and not dissimilar to those of the Red Tent group. While Judith's Book group gave some space to the discussion of the *Rockbound* controversy, its treatment on radio, and their envy of the Red Tent group's brush with media stardom, they spent most of their time discussing plot, characterization, and the dialect Parker Day employs in the novel. In common with the Red Tent, many members of Judith's Book group used the "Afterword" (written by Gwen Davies, University of New Brunswick) in order to connect fictional place-names and family names with their local knowledge of the South Shore. They did so as part of their examination of Maritime mores and values, which was prompted by the book's depiction of a small rural community in which privacy is impossible, the work ethic is predominant, and moral rule-breaking is punished. They recognized this world from their own experiences, and members of this group exchanged stories about their family history, demonstrating not only a staple of book group talk, but also the trust they have placed in each other (Rehberg Sedo "Badges"). Unlike the Red Tent, some members of Judith's group appeared to desire a truthful representation, and they pointed out what they see as moral inconsistencies in the fictional world of the novel, by referring to their familial and local knowledge. The readers in this group have confidence in their reading practices. One participant's comment captured the group's belief in their interpretive agency as readers – and as possessors of local knowledge:

P8: But this is Frank Parker Day's gaze on a place, right? This is not necessarily the way it was, this is the way he saw it, but we're reading the book right? (Judith's Book group)

This comment helps to contextualize members' assessment of the use-value that the "Canada Reads" series has for them. They reported that it generates discussion for their meetings, but does not necessarily influence what they select to read together:

P2: I think we have to say our involvement with "Canada Reads" is that we discuss it. Like when "Canada Reads" is going on we have incredible discussions around it.

P1: But only because we're doing Rockbound are we here [laughter and overtalk]. Has "Canada Reads" ever influenced our book group? And, so far, the answer is no. (Judith's Book group)

However, some members had bought books selected by "Canada Reads" to read outside the group, such as Whylah Falls (attracted by the Nova Scotian connection), and Next Episode (because it won in 2003). Here, they were relying on the CBC's well-established cultural authority and its long history as a promoter of Canadian writing (Fuller and Rehberg Sedo 18–9). They were, in fact, using "Canada Reads" and the CBC as a "trusted other" – that is, a resource for finding pleasurable and intellectually stimulating books that they would enjoy (Rehberg Sedo "Badges"). The on-line readers I have discussed often used the show and its website in a similar way, perceiving the CBC to be a trustworthy, although not perfect, cultural authority. As book group members, the Red Tent and Judith's Book Group also used the "Canada Reads" radio debates to stimulate discussion, but did not necessarily allow themselves to be directed by either the interpretations or reading practices that they heard on-air.

What lessons are to be learned from listening to the on-air, on-line, and book group readers of "Canada Reads"? With respect to the radio series, the vernacular practices favored by book groups seem to be combined with selected elements of a more "academic" mode of reading. This mix suggests to me the importance of developing nuanced analyses of non-academic reading practices and theories capable of explaining the pleasures, politics, and social relations that reading practices both shape and resist. Some off-air readers are clearly looking to CanLit for "a kind of mimetic account of national experience" (Hulan 38), and yes, some of them are reading in the "un-politicized" and "personalized" ways that mirror the practices of some on-air celebrity readers (Moss; Taylor). However, not all readers use "Canada Reads" or Canadian Literature in the same way. As my brief consideration of on-line readers suggests, some readers are not simply imagining a unified Canadian community; they are, in many cases, questioning that nationalist construction. Others, like the book group readers, re-embed the series and the books within their established selection procedures and interpretive practices. For the two groups I considered, reading Rockbound can involve drawing upon familial and local knowledge as well as familiarity with literary genres and narrative strategies. Gender also appears to be significant: the on-air readers of "Canada Reads" who employed affective reading practices were usually women, as were the majority of members of the two Nova Scotian book groups.

Reading Canadian literature as a shared social practice requires our attention as literary critics. The social dynamics and social rituals of shared reading were briefly illuminated when the Red Tent book group became radio stars. We could also profitably interrogate how far the media of radio, television, and the Internet shape and legitimate the various reading practices demonstrated by the readers of "Canada Reads." Smaro Kamboureli is right when she argues that the culture of celebrity "remains loudly mute about the ideology of the knowledge it transmits" (46). Rather than laughing anxiously (or dismissively) about celebrities undertaking literary interpretation, scholars need to identify and critique the ideological work that is being performed in the name of reading Canadian literature. More generally, we should examine what "happens" to the interpretation of literary fiction when it moves through the communicative strategies that structure and characterize mass media and the Internet. When we undertake any of the investigations I have suggested, we also need to be self-reflexive about our own position, power, and responsibility within processes of knowledge production and consumption. We need to be prepared to shift our ground outside our disciplinary training, and in our relations with and attitude to "non-academic" readers. Investigating and reaching a better understanding of contemporary book cultures and events like "Canada Reads" may enable us as "professional" readers to participate more directly, more provocatively, and more creatively in popular readings of Canadian literature.

References

1   The research informing this essay forms part of a collaborative interdisciplinary project, "Beyond the Book: Mass Reading Events and Contemporary Cultures of Reading in the UK, USA and Canada," funded by the Arts and Humanities Research Council (UK; grant number 112166). For more information about the project, visit <www.beyondthebookproject.org>. I wish to acknowledge the invaluable contributions of my research collaborator, DeNel Rehberg Sedo (Mount Saint Vincent University).

2   I believe that Moss is referring to Vanderhaeghe's comment quoted in a CBC press release announcing the winner of the 3rd series, 'Canada Reads *The Last Crossing* (February 20, 2004): "For me, it was a great pleasure to have the books debated in such a passionate, intelligent, and decidedly not sombre fashion."

3   It is helpful to remember that, in the academy, the "scholar's position of authority within the world of reading" nominated by Long is confirmed and practiced through both oral and written media. With regards to the attainment of prestige, advancing scholarly claims through written discourse is, however, privileged over oral communication within most Euro-American institutions. Scholarly written texts adopt a very different mode of communication from the type of conversational radio discourse we hear on "Canada Reads." While the on-air panelists do not, of course, reproduce the rhetorical strategies of scholarly written discourse in their broadcast conversations, they employ elements of academic literary discourse in order to demonstrate their own cultural capital and ability to judge literary texts.

4   I am not claiming that all book groups which meet outside the classroom adopt identical modes of social interaction or textual interpretation. Studies by Long and Hartley do, however, indicate that there are some social practices and interpretive strategies that recur among many groups, and I am drawing upon their insights when I discuss colloquial reading practices in this article.

5   Also notable was the cultural authority accorded to Carrier as a writer, critic, and "national" figure by the other panelists (all women) who deferred to him, and commented upon his seniority.

6   For a list of spin-off activities relating to "Canada Reads" see Fuller and Rehberg Sedo 3031. Some of the postings are archived on the various "Canada Reads" websites (see n. ii).

7   Some examples of readers blogging can be accessed at <http://www.chekhovsmistress.com>; <http://lbc.typepad.com/blog/>;<http://noggs.typepad.com/the_reading_experience/>

8   The Red Tent discussion was facilitated by DeNel Rehberg Sedo, while Judith's Book group kindly recorded their discussion for us. Quotations are taken from transcripts of recordings. Names of participants have been changed for the Red Tent and removed for Judith's Book group.

Works cited

Barrs, Myra, and Sue Pidgeon, Eds. *Reading the Difference: Gender and Reading in Elementary Classrooms.* Markham, ON: Pembroke Publishers, 1994.

Bethune, Brian. "Correcting a Literary Deficiency: How the Judges in CBC Radio's Second Canada Reads Contest Chose a Toughie." Maclean's May 2003:52.

Carnell, Eileen. "Boys and their Reading: Conceptions of Young People About the Success of the 'Full On' Magazine." *Curriculum Journal* 16.3 (2005): 363–389.

Cavallo, Guglielmo and Roger Chartier. Introduction. *A History of Reading in the West.* Eds. Cavallo and Chartier. Trans. Lydia G. Cochrane. Cambridge: Polity, 1999:1–36.

CBC. Press Release for "Canada Reads 2003." 7 Nov. 2003.15 Jan. 2006. <http://www.cbc.ca/canadareads>.

Daspin, Elaine. "Experiencing literary hell: Book club victims break the silence." *Globe and Mail* 19 Jan. 1999: C1–2.

Davies, Gwendolyn. E-mail to the author. 12 Apr. 2005.

Dean, Misao. Online posting. 2 Mar. 2005. CanLit-L. 16 Sept. 2006. <listserv@infoserv.nlc-bnc.ca>.

Finkelstein, David, and Alistair McCleery. *An Introduction to Book History.* London: Routledge, 2005.

Forsyth, Louise. Online posting. 29 Apr. 2003. CanLit-L. 16 Sept. 2006. <listserv@infoserv.nlc-bnc.ca>.

Friends of Canadian Broadcasting. "Statistics and Trends on Canadian Broadcasting." 17 Aug. 2006. <www.friends.ca/news/stats.asp>.

Fuller, Danielle. "Strange terrain: Re-producing and resisting place-myths in two contemporary fictions of Newfoundland." *Essays on Canadian Writing* 82 (2004): 21–50.

—— and DeNel Rehberg Sedo. "A Reading Spectacle for the Nation: The CBC and 'Canada Reads'." *Journal of Canadian Studies* 40.1 (2006): 5–36.

Gordon, Charles. *Opinion. Niagara Falls Review*, 1 May, 2002: A4.

Hall, R. Mark. "The 'Oprahfication' of Literacy: Reading Oprah's Book Club.'" *College English* 65.6 (2003): 646–667.

Hartley, Jenny. *Reading Groups.* Oxford UP, 2001.

Henighan, Stephen. *When Words Deny the World: The Reshaping of Canadian Writing.* Erin, ON: Porcupine's Quill, 2002.

Hulan, Renée. "Blurred Visions: The Interdisciplinarity of Canadian Literary Criticism." *Essays on Canadian Writing* 65 (1998): 38–55.

Jones, Jami. "Priority Male: If We Want Boys to Love Books, It's Important to Recognize What They Want." *School Library Journal* 51.3 (2005): 37.

Judith's Book Group. Discussion of *Rockbound.* 13 Apr. 2005.

Kamboureli, Smaro. "The Culture of Celebrity and National Pedagogy." *Home-work: Postcolonialism, Pedagogy and Canadian Literature.* Ed. Cynthia Sugars. Ottawa: U of Ottawa P, 2004. 35–56.

Lesk, Andrew. Online posting. 2 Feb. 2005. CanLit-L. 16 Sept. 2006. <listserv@infoserv.nlc-bnc.ca>

Long, Elizabeth. Book Clubs: *Women and the Uses of Reading in Everyday Life.* Chicago: Chicago UP, 2003.

—— . "Textual interpretation as collective action." *The Ethnography of Reading.* Ed. J. Boyarin. Berkeley: U of California P, 1992.180–211.

Lynch, Gerald. Online posting. 30 Apr. 2003. CanLit-L. 16 Sept. 2006. <listserv@infoserv.nlc-bnc.ca>

—— . Online posting. 3 Mar. 2005. CanLit-L. 16 Sept 2006. <listserv@infoserv.nlc-bnc.ca>

MacSkimming, Roy. *The Perilous Trade: Publishing Canada's Writers.* Toronto: McClelland & Stewart, 2003.

McGinley, William and Katanna Conley. "Literary Retailing and the (Re)making of Popular Reading." *Journal of Popular Culture* 35 (2001): 207–221.

Moss, Laura. "Editorial: Canada Reads." *Canadian Literature.* 182 (2004). 10 Dec. 2005. <http://www.canlit.ca/archive/archive2004/182/182.edit.moss.html>

—— . E-mail to the author. 16 Aug. 2006.

Murray, Heather. *Come, Bright Improvement: The Literary Societies of Nineteenth-Century Ontario.* Toronto: U of Toronto P, 2002.

Niedzviecki Hal. "The Story of O." *This Magazine.* July/Aug. 2002:15–17.

Paterson, Janet. Telephone interview. 22 July 2003.

Petrucci, Armando. "Reading to Read: A Future for Reading." *A History of Reading in the West.* Eds. Guglielmo Cavallo and Roger Chartier. Trans. Lydia G. Cochrane. Cambridge: Polity, 1999. 345–367.

Price, Leah. "Reading: The State of the Discipline." *Book History?* (2004): 303–320.

Red Tent Book Group. Discussion of *Rockbound*. 29 Mar. 2005.

Rehberg Sedo, DeNel. "Badges Of Wisdom, Space For Being: A Study of Contemporary Women's Book Clubs," Diss. Simon Fraser University. 2004.

——. "Readers in Reading Groups: An On-Line Survey of Face-To-Face and Virtual Book Clubs." Convergence: *The Journal of Research into New Media Technologies* 9 (2003): 66–90.

Riegelhof, Terry. E-mail to the author. 15–16 Aug. 2006.

Rifkind, Candida. E-mail to the author. 17 Aug. 2006.

Robbins, Li. "Book Club Virgin (and Proud of It): The Scorn of the Solitary Reader." 14 Jan. 2005. Canadian Broadcasting Association. 31 Jan. 2005. <http://www.cbc.ca/arts/books/bookclubvirgin.html>.

Scribbling Woman. Blog. 20 Aug. 2006 <http://unbsj.ca/arts/english/jones/mt>.

Sugars, Cynthia. "Notes on a Mystic Hockey Puck: Death, Paternity, and National Identity in Wayne Johnston's *The Divine Ryans*." *Essays on Canadian Writing* 82 (2004): 151–172.

Taylor, Kate. "Cultural Contests Out of Control." *Globe & Mail* 23 Feb. 2005: R1.

Turner, Graeme. *Understanding Celebrity*. London: Sage, 2004.

Van Herk, Aritha. "Publishing and Perishing with No Parachute." *How Canadians Communicate*. Eds. David Taras, Frits Pannekoek and Maria Bakardjieva. Calgary, AB: University of Calgary Press, 2003. 121–141.

Vartanian, Talin and Jackie Carlos. Personal interview with DeNel Rehberg Sedo. 20 Feb. 2003.

—— and David Barnard. Personal interview. 7 July 2003.

Chapter 36

Rosalind Crone, Katie Halsey, Mary Hammond and Shafquat Towheed

THE READING EXPERIENCE DATABASE 1450–1945 (RED)

Why do we need RED?

MARY HAMMOND WRITES: I would like to approach this question through the use of an anecdote. When I was a child in the 1960s, our grandmother frequently looked after my sisters and me as our mother worked full time. Grandma's house was an adventure. I particularly loved the glass-fronted bookcase, which I was allowed to open and explore whenever I liked. Occupying a tall alcove in the unused parlour, it emitted a thrilling smell of old paper and furniture polish as the door swung ajar.

I believe I owe my sense of myself as a book historian to that bookcase. It sheds light on my family's reading patterns, and thereby perhaps on our lives and pleasures and concerns. The presence of old Sunday School prize books and cheap novels reveals my grandparents' roots in the Board-school educated working classes of the late nineteenth and early twentieth centuries. The later addition of encyclopaedias, classics series and more expensively bound novels marks their move between the wars from a two-up two-down terrace with a privy out the back to a larger house, indoor plumbing and the relatively prosperous lower-middle classes. Further additions in the shape of boys' adventure stories, collections of plays and short stories, and movie fan books show also the very different reading patterns of their offspring, my mother and her brothers. I didn't realize this, of course, as between the ages of six and sixteen I scoured the beautiful illustrations of the *Encyclopaedia Britannica*, dipped into Agatha Christie, tossed aside the once well-read but now arcane popular novels of an earlier age, and ignored the far less well-thumbed sets of classics.

But I realize it now. And how I wish I had asked questions, and taken notes. I remember that my grandfather read the *Yorkshire Evening Press* (for which his son, my uncle, ended up working as a compositor) and also that he sometimes used it to disguise the fact that he was actually dozing in his chair. I remember that my grandmother read the *People's Friend* every week without fail, but tolerated the newspaper only for its headlines, the obituaries and the crossword. I remember that she loved and sometimes reread Florence Barclay, the best-selling Evangelical romance novelist of the first decade of the twentieth century. I also remember that her favourite author – perhaps more surprisingly – was not one of those normally thought of as the preserve of women readers, but the adventure writer John Buchan.

I didn't ask questions, or take notes, and they were not great talkers at the level of the personal. I don't know why my grandfather despised any reading that ventured beyond headlines, sport and the stock market. I don't know which John Buchan books were my grandmother's favourites, or why. I don't know whether these reading patterns were typical of their respective genders, or of their class. The autobiographies written by other members of their class and generation are of limited use as they are unlikely to be representative; as Jonathan Rose has demonstrated (without quite acknowledging the problem), such autobiographies are usually written by the aspirational or the successful and therefore tend to trumpet an early, inherent propensity for 'serious' reading rather than admitting to a passion for popular trash.

Quantitative book history can help me here. It informs me that in the period when my grandparents were buying and reading books and magazines, popular novels sold more copies than literary fiction, and provincial dwellers tended to read the local paper more than newspapers which originated in the metropolis. Library records suggest that mostly middle-class women borrowed mostly popular fiction, and that the lower-middle classes most frequently consulted the reference works. Close analysis of the books produced for women, and the discourses surrounding their use, suggests that women's reading was of a specific character which both informed and was informed by distinctive publishing and advertising strategies. Feminist criticism suggests that women's books may have been politically subversive or in some way empowering, even if only because they were pleasurable. Postcolonial book history can tell me that some classics and some popular novels retained a large audience in colonial regions long after they went out of fashion in their country of production.

But these aspects of book history, invaluable as they are, are limited. They can't tell me whether the books taken out of libraries were actually read, either wholly or in part, or if they were, what their readers thought of them. Book publication statistics and sales figures gleaned from publishers' archives or from booksellers can't tell me whether a book marketed as a 'women's novel' was read even predominantly by women, or an adventure novel predominantly by men, or if these reading patterns were different in different geographical areas, or at different historical periods. My own family's reading history confirms some parts of this empirical evidence, but contradicts others. My grandmother read 'men's' books as well as – and sometimes in preference to – 'women's' books. My grandparents seldom if ever visited the library, and there was a sense among some members of the family (even by the time I came along) that visiting a library was a bit too much like showing off. But my grandmother did take part in an unofficial kind of reading club, through which novels and magazines (which she also called 'books') were passed around between family members, friends and neighbours, sometimes for the fictional serials, sometimes just for the crossword.

My grandmother's bookshelf, and the things I do and do not know – or can and cannot find out – about how it was used, point up some crucial questions for book historians. If we are to make even an educated guess as to what people read, and how, and why and when, we need some evidence of their patterns and their idiosyncrasies. Statistics can tell us what was published, sold and distributed, and in some cases what was remaindered, but they cannot tell us how much of this print output was actually read, how it was read, by whom, in what circumstances and by how many, nor – perhaps even more contentiously – what a text may have 'meant' to its readers. In order to begin to understand what print means in culture, we need to gather some basic pieces of information about readers and their reading, data which has too frequently been ignored, passed over, lost, put away for another day, or which has seemed so brief that it has been deemed insignificant.

Above all, we need to know the following things:

1.   Who the readers were – their age, sex, class, nationality, region – and anything else we can find out about them.
2.   What they read.
3.   Where they read it.
4.   When they read.
5.   Whether they read silently or aloud to themselves or to others.
6.   What they thought of what they read or had read to them.
7.   How often they read.
8.   Whether the reading matter was bought, borrowed or stolen, and from where. If all this information – the kinds of information which we all run across regularly as researchers – could be collated, we might have the beginnings of an important new resource.

This is where the *Reading Experience Database* (RED) comes in. Its aim is to collect as much data as possible on the reading habits of British subjects between 1450 and 1945 – on those readers who for the most part are no longer around to speak for themselves. Now that it is fully operational, we hope that RED will be able to fill in some of the gaps in our knowledge of readers and reading which cannot be supplied from other sources available to us. At the very least, RED will supplement these other sources. But it may even supplant some of them, surprising us with what it reveals about the reading practices of our ancestors.

Background to the project

The RED Team writes

RED was launched in 1996 by Simon Eliot, then of the Open University (OU). After several years of exploratory research and development, in 2006 the RED team secured generous Arts and Humanities Research Council (AHRC) funding with the aim of launching a freely available public database on the web and obtaining the critical mass in terms of data necessary for RED to be of use to researchers and to have a lasting impact on the field. In June 2007, the first version of RED was released for public access, and, by the end of the funding period in July 2009, two more updated versions had been uploaded on the web and over 25,000 individual records of reading had been collected. These are mainly in the form of quotations derived from published and manuscript diaries, letters, journals, autobiographies and marginalia with some evidence of provenance and/or identity of the reader, though some are much barer details of a reading experience. Our approach has been an inclusive one; we have mined the contents of more unusual sources not traditionally used for histories of reading, such as criminal court and prison records, which we hope will provide more valuable information about the elusive 'common reader'. Entries have been provided by researchers in the RED team, scholars from other institutions in the UK and abroad, and a large number of volunteers who have developed a special interest in the project. Quality assurance is central to our project; no piece of data entered into RED is made available for public searching without being double-checked for accuracy by the RED team. This has meant a huge ongoing editorial responsibility, as well as the vigilant support of our technical team.

Since the completion of the AHRC-funded period in July 2009, RED has been successful in securing further internal and external development funds in order to facilitate relationships with similar projects around the world. We hope that this model for a database cataloguing reading experiences will be copied and modified as necessary, and that soon it will be possible, through an umbrella search facility, to scan the contents of multiple national REDs at once. We also hope that, now live and very visible on the web as a research tool, RED should be able to generate its own publicity, with an exponential increase in the volume of both users and contributors. We continue to add new data fields, search functions, and links with other projects. The database is infinitely expandable, and the Open University has made an indefinite commitment to the project, both in terms of server space and supporting its use as a research and teaching tool.

Methodology: what we want (for the moment) and what we don't

The most common questions asked of the RED project team are:

- What is a 'reading experience'?
- How does one define it, or contain it?
- What information does the database contain?
- What does it not contain?
- Why have you left things out?

We try as far as possible not to ignore the context of the reading experience. Our chronological timeframe is wide (1450–1945) and our geographical scope reasonably generous: we are interested in readers born or resident in the British Isles reading pretty much anything, in any language whatsoever. Broadly speaking, we are seeking the following information:

1   What did British-born readers read in Britain?
2   What did they read when they went abroad?
3   What did other nationals read while they were in Britain?
4   What did the first generation of British or Irish emigrants read?

Of course, for logistical reasons there have to be certain restrictions. We are deliberately restricting our sense of what constitutes 'reading' to print culture, rather than thinking in terms of the 'critical reading' of a play or a film, though we would be interested in a reader reading a script, or a novelization of a play or film. We also differentiate 'reading' from 'ownership': a reader might own more books than he or she actually reads, so mere lists of books in libraries (whether public or private) will not be recorded. That said, we accept as a 'reading experience' evidence of the reading of most printed and manuscript matter, not just books, newspapers, magazines and religious tracts, but also advertisements, tickets, playbills, theatrical programmes and the like.

There are currently some types of information that we have decided not to include. We have not yet been able to include fictional references to reading, for example, and we do not often record the reading of private letters (though letters to newspapers and open letters are included, and we do include references to the reading of other materials found in letters). We do not record public performances (such as Dickens's public readings of his work). And we do not yet record the graphic evidence of reading found in woodcuts, engravings, illustrations, paintings and photographs. In this way we have tried to solve the problem of definition. At this stage we are sufficiently clear about what we want to avoid confusion, but we are acutely aware of the need for flexibility and very conscious that we should not overlook important evidence which might one day be useful.

The Contribution Form (www.open.ac.uk/Arts/RED/contribute.html)

RED is a very unusual academic project, in that it has, from its inception, encouraged contributions from the public, and our online contribution form has played a crucial part in allowing a wide variety of people to contribute material to our database. Over the course of the AHRC-funded period, over sixty volunteers, many from outside the academic community, worked through a large number of diaries, letters, autobiographies and memoirs (often from members of their own families) and entered the reading experiences contained in these sources into RED via the online contribution form.

The contribution form was designed with clarity, flexibility and ease of use in mind. It has had to be extensive enough to gather sufficient useful information, but brief and user-friendly enough to encourage those who hate forms. We have divided the form into three sections, each containing fields for information but arranged in a hierarchical order. Section one contains three compulsory questions that allow the editors to verify the entry – the name and contact details of the contributor, the evidence of the reading experience, which may be either a quotation from a source or a description of the trace a particular reader left behind, and the source where the evidence was found – as well as fields for those details contributors are most likely to have about the reading experience – the century and date of the reading experience, the name, gender and age of the reader, listener (when the identity of the reader is not known) or reading group, and the author, title and genre or subject matter of the text being read. Section two solicits some further information about the text; and section three asks for data contributors will probably be least likely to have but that is vital for histories of reading, including the occupation and religion of the reader and the place and time of the reading experience.

After each section, there is an option to submit the form. We also provide detailed accompanying notes which give guidance on completing each individual field. On completion of the form, contributors are asked briefly to review their entry before formal submission. Entries are stored in an edit buffer, which allows them to be checked by a RED team member before being released for searching. Aware that a single source, for example, a diary, memoir or collection of letters, often contains multiple entries, we have provided contributors with a choice after submission of an entry to continue to enter data using a duplicate form created from their previous entry.

The involvement of the volunteers has built a community based on shared interest in the history of reading, and ensures that the work of the project is widely known, as well as fostering (and sometimes teaching) some research skills. In this regard, RED actively promotes the social construction of knowledge: the RED team provides the guideline parameters but the contributors determine the content of the database. Volunteers often report that their work for the RED project has encouraged them to reflect on their own reading practices, and they comment on the amount they learn about both history and literature from their close focus on an individual's letters, diaries or autobiography.

Searching and Browsing (www.open.ac.uk/Arts/RED)

Since June 2007, visitors to RED have been able to search for entries which have been edited and released. In version 3.0 of RED (released June 2009), users are able to choose between a basic search, which looks for specified keywords in any text field of the database, and an advanced search, which searches for specific keywords or set values within specified fields. Almost every field in the RED contribution form has been made available for searching. And these can be searched in combination, not just individually. For example, we might be interested to know what type of fiction female servants in the nineteenth century read. Or perhaps which newspapers males in London of the clerk/tradesman/artisan/smallholder class read. The possibilities are extensive and the results often surprising.

On obtaining a list of hits, users of RED are able to select how those entries should be ordered: by the century of experience, or alphabetically by the author or title of the text. By using the check boxes on the left hand side of the table, users can generate lists of marked entries which can be printed, saved to a hard drive or portable device, or exported via e-mail. By clicking on the evidence of the reading experience, users can view the complete entry on that reading experience. Red hyperlinks within these individual records allow users to abandon searches in order follow a particular reader or author through the database. Finally, we have built a browsing page which contains automatically updated alphabetically arranged lists of the names of all the readers and authors in the database.

Early Findings: A challenge to or reconfirmation of existing histories of reading?

We have now reached our first major milestone: 25,000 individual records of reading, a collection we originally believed would provide enough critical mass to enable the data to be used to test some of the grand narratives used in the history of reading. But is it enough? What does RED contain at this point, and how might the data be usefully employed?

RED covers a long period in history, roughly 500 years between 1450 and 1945, and so it might be useful to start by examining the spread of entries over time, as illustrated by Graph 36.1. Immediately obvious is the massive concentration of data from the nineteenth century. This is in part explicable with reference to the terms of the AHRC award, which required us to focus on gathering data from the period 1800 to 1945. At the same time, we did not neglect evidence from other centuries. In fact the steep upward curve in reading activity from 1450 to 1899, which increases greatly between the eighteenth and the nineteenth centuries, reflects both the growth of literacy rates and the expansion of the reading public in Britain, as well as the tremendous proliferation of cheap print. Given that mass

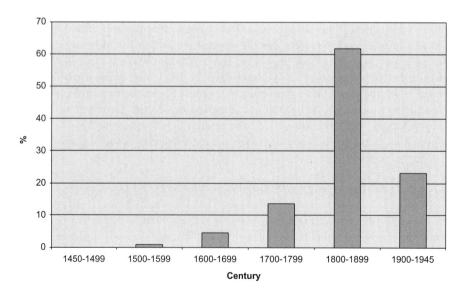

Graph 36.1 Distribution of entries across the centuries covered by RED.

literacy had been achieved by the period 1900 to 1945, the decline in the number of entries shown by the graph may be artificial. We must remember that we have only collected data over a fifty year period rather than a one hundred year period as for 1800 to 1899. The proportionate decrease in reading activity highlighted by RED might indicate the impact of other media, such as radio and cinema, which competed with printed matter for many people's leisure time, or it might gesture towards the decline of a particular type of reflective reading practice (such as the keeping of commonplace books and reading diaries) popular in the late-nineteenth century. Furthermore, as Richard Hoggart has argued, during the first half of the twentieth century, commercial imperatives began to limit the range of reading to which many people were exposed.

If we turn to look at the general characteristics of the readers featured in RED, again we find the replication of some key trends in the data collected. For instance, we have been able to specify the gender of the reader in 96 per cent of entries. Male readers account for 61 per cent of all entries, and female readers for 39 per cent – figures we would expect given the higher literacy of males for most of the period under question, as well as a sex-bias that would be likely to occur in the sources used for gathering material. Diaries and memoirs were most often written by men, and for a large part of the period, comments on the habits of women were largely excluded from observational sources as the presence of women within the public sphere remained very restricted.

Despite low expectations, surprisingly 93 per cent of all entries in RED describe the socio-economic group of the reader in some way. The distribution of this data is presented in Table 36.1. The largest concentration of readers is found in the professional/academic/merchant and farmer class, perhaps a predictable result, given both the sources used and the likelihood of access to print and incentives to read for this group across almost the whole period covered by RED. But we should also take some encouragement from the proportions registered for the lower socio-economic groupings, as these percentages represent very large numbers of entries. We have over 2,500 entries that cover the reading of the artisanal class, and more than 1,600 relating to labourers, agricultural labourers and servants. It could also be significant that more data is available on general unskilled labourers than agricultural labourers, given that many of the first were probably resident in towns or urban centres where both literacy rates and access to print were greater. We must also note that, when the identity of the reader is known, the entry relates to the experience of that individual, rather than any listeners who might have been present. This could be important in our assessment of the presence of servants in RED, who might have more often been listeners rather than readers, or at least as recorded in the sources available.

From the data on the genre or subject matter of the texts read, we should be able to

Table 36.1 Socio-economic groups of readers in RED

Socio-economic group	%
Labourer	5.1
Agricultural labourer	1.1
Servant	0.4
Clerk/tradesman/artisan/smallholder	10.5
Professional/academic/merchant/farmer	58.9
Clergy	4.8
Gentry	13.1
Aristocracy/Royalty	6

make some remarks about the popularity of particular types of reading matter. There are 36 different categories of subject matter, and contributors are able to select multiple categories to describe the text being read. Information on subject matter is available for almost every entry in the database, and the spread across the categories is wide and diverse. We have not yet found evidence of an individual or group reading an emblem book. But we do have multiple entries for every other category. Table 36.2 presents the number and proportion of texts identified as belonging to each category, from the smallest to the largest. Some of the categories are baggier than others, and the very specific nature of some may account for some of the small proportions. But there are some notable findings within the table. For instance, conduct books are only present in 0.4 per cent of all the entries in RED, which may have some bearing on studies which attempt to use these texts as an indication of how men and women lived at particular times. Conduct books were more often given as gifts, or regarded as a useful title to have in one's library; they were often indicative of tastes or values, rather than books which were actually being read. We can also combine socio-economic data with the data on subject matter to demonstrate the impact particular groups of texts may have had outside a particular profession. For instance, if we join religious matter, sermons and Bible under one category, only in 8.4 per cent of those entries was a member of the clergy (of any denomination) reading one of these texts.

Similarly, by adding in data on the century of the reading experience, we can get a sense of the rise and fall of particular genres over time. Graph 36.2 takes the four largest categories of subject matter, namely fiction, poetry, essays/criticism and religious works (a combination of Bible, sermons and other religious matter) and illustrates the proportion of works in each category for every century covered by RED. Because of the huge bulk of entries in the nineteenth century, and also taking account of the wide proliferation of print in that period, we have divided that century in two. Also, it might be wise to discard the data

Table 36.2 Genre and subject matter of texts in RED

Genre/Subject Matter	Entries	%	Genre/Subject Matter	Entries	%
emblem book	0	0	children's literature	402	1.6
crafts	12	0.05	science	417	1.6
cookery	15	0.06	social science	472	1.8
heraldry	30	0.1	reference/general works	599	2.3
technology	42	0.2	ephemera	780	3
sport/leisure	51	0.2	autobiography/diary	850	3.3
mathematics	76	0.3	Bible	879	3.4
astrology/alchemy/occult	79	0.3	philosophy	992	3.8
agricultural/horticulture/ husbandry	88	0.3	geography/travel	1026	4
conduct books	100	0.4	biography	1178	4.6
education	130	0.5	classics	1339	5.2
medicine	144	0.6	drama	1610	6.2
natural history	205	0.8	politics	1642	6.4
textbook/self education	220	0.9	other religious	1651	6.4
sermons	256	1	history	1910	7.4
arts/architecture	294	1.1	essays/criticism	2709	10.5
law	332	1.3	poetry	5244	20.3
miscellany/anthology	376	1.5	fiction	6062	23.5

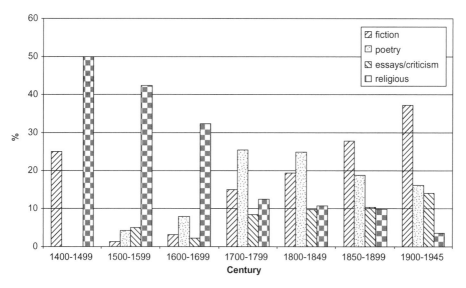

Graph 36.2 Rise and fall of genres/subject matter of texts read over time.

available for the period 1450–1499, as RED only contains four entries from that period. Data across the rest of the time tends to confirm some general patterns previously illumin-ated in studies of the reading of individuals or groups and in research on trends in publishing. The presence of religious texts declines with the advance of time. Fiction, on the other hand, grows to reach a predictable peak in the early twentieth century. Poetry peaks in the Romantic period, when poets were, P.B. Shelley claimed, the 'unacknowledged legislators of the world', while the essays/criticism genre reaches a fairly steady plateau in the nineteenth century, commensurate with the growing number of journals.

These statistics are illuminating. But are they reliable? There are certainly potential problems in their use and we want to be as upfront about this as possible. The first relates to the way in which specific reading experiences or entries have been collected and stored. While some sources have been worked through systematically, others have not at this stage. We might have all the recorded reading experiences of one individual but only one example of the reading of another. For some readers, every single mention of a reading, no matter how similar or mundane, has been entered into RED. For others, contributors have left a direction for users to advise that although an individual read a particular text over several days, only one of those incidents has been entered into RED as an example. Differences in the source material have some impact on the shape of the data as well. For example, a memoir may mention that an individual read a certain title, but a diary might give an account of every single day that the text was read. The memoir will generate one entry, the diary perhaps ten or more, depending on the speed and commitment of the reader. Over time, as data continues to accumulate in RED, we expect that such issues will be balanced out, that the critical mass will ensure a fairly representative picture of reading in the past emerges. Users of RED need to be aware that in many ways, the database may tell us much more about the sources available for reading, rather than about actual reading, and yet such a proposition in no way challenges the value of the collated data.

We should not underestimate the contribution of the individual entries contained in RED, in particular the way these continue to challenge theories proposed about reading in the past. Although many scholars have claimed that an important shift in reading practice occurred around the turn of the nineteenth century, whereby the growth in both print and skills led to an increase in silent reading and extensive reading, RED boasts an unprecedented body of evidence to demonstrate that this just was not the case. Many readers were still confined to a limited number of texts (often due to poverty or a lack of access to a wide range of material), and, either through choice or not, read these works repeatedly, some to the point of memorisation. The practice of reading aloud either to oneself or to family and friends is evident in all socio-economic groups during the nineteenth century. It was both a form of entertainment, and a method of sharing skills within groups where the ability to read was not universal. Reading could also have direct and powerful uses, many of which are not immediately evident. It would be appropriate to conclude this chapter with a somewhat unusual example of reading's utility, from an underused source in the history of reading: criminal court records. At the famous trial of James Greenacre and Sarah Gale for the murder of Greenacre's former paramour, Hannah Brown, whose body he chopped into parts then distributed around London, Gale's former landlord, Henry Wignal, was called to give evidence. He told the court that on 1 January 1837, he read the newspaper to his wife, Sarah. It featured a story about the discovery of a trunk of a body in Edgware Road, London. Greenacre and Gale were in the next room, and with the door ajar, heard everything. The very next day, the prisoners decided to move on.

WORKS CITED AND FURTHER READING

Works cited and further reading

General

Ainsworth, David, *Milton and the Spiritual Reader: Reading and Religion in Seventeenth-Century England* (London & New York: Routledge, 2008).

Altick, Richard, *The English Common Reader: A Social History of the Mass Reading Public* (Chicago: University of Chicago Press, 1957).

Cavallo, Guglielmo and Roger Chartier (eds), *A History of Reading in the West*, trans. Lydia G. Cochrane (Oxford: Polity, 1999).

Darnton, Robert, *The Kiss of Lamourette: Reflections in Cultural History* (London: Faber & Faber, 1990).

Davidson, Cathy (ed.), *Reading in America: Literature and Social History* (Baltimore: John Hopkins University Press, 1989).

Eliot, Simon, 'The Reading Experience Database; or, what are we to do about the history of reading?' (1994). http://www.open.ac.uk/Arts/RED/redback.htm.

Fadiman, Anne, *Ex Libris: Confessions of a Common Reader* (London: Allen Lane, 2000).

Fischer, Steven Roger, *A History of Reading* (London: Reaktion, 2003).

Flint, Kate, *The Woman Reader, 1837–1914* (Oxford: Oxford University Press, 1993).

Green, D.H., *Women Readers in the Middle Ages* (Cambridge: Cambridge University Press, 2007).

Hackel, Heidi Brayman and Catherine E. Kelly (eds), *Reading Women: Literacy, Authorship, and Culture in the Atlantic World, 1500–1800* (Philadelphia: University of Pennsylvania Press, 2008).

Hutner, Gordon, *What America Read: Race, Class and the Novel, 1920–1960* (Chapel Hill: University of North Carolina Press, 2009).

Jackson, Holbrook, *The Reading of Books* (London: Faber & Faber, 1946).

Jackson, Holbrook, *The Anatomy of Bibliomania* (London: Faber & Faber, 1950).

Jajdelska, Elspeth, *Silent Reading and the Birth of the Narrator* (Toronto: University of Toronto Press, 2007).

Johnson, William A. and Holt N. Parker (eds), *Ancient Literacies: The Culture of Reading in Greece and Rome* (Oxford: Oxford University Press, 2009).

Kaestle, Carl F. and Janice A. Radway (eds), Section IV, 'Readers and Reading' in *A History of the Book in America, Vol.4, Print in Motion: The Expansion of Publishing and Reading in the United States, 1880–1940* (Chapel Hill: University of North Carolina Press, 2009).

Kertész, André, *On Reading* (New York: W.W. Norton & Company, 1971).

Machor, James L., *Readers in History: Nineteenth-Century American Literature and the Contexts of Response* (Baltimore: John Hopkins University Press, 1993).

Manguel, Alberto, *A History of Reading* (London: Harper Collins, 1996).

Manguel, Alberto, *A Reading Diary, a Year of Favourite Books* (Toronto: Alfred A. Knopf Canada, 2004).

Palmer, Beth and Adelene Buckland (eds), *A Return to the Common Reader: Print, Culture and the Novel, 1850–1900* (Farnham: Ashgate, 2010).

Patten, Robert L. and John O. Jordan (eds), *Literature in the Marketplace: Nineteenth-Century Publishing and Reading Practices* (Cambridge: Cambridge University Press, 1995).

Pearson, David, *Books as History: The Influence of Books beyond their Texts* (London: British Library, 2008).

Raven, James, Helen Small and Naomi Tadmor (eds), *The Practice and Representation of Reading in England* (Cambridge: Cambridge University Press, 1996).

Sherman, William H., *Used Books: Marking Readers in Renaissance England* (Philadelphia: University of Pennsylvania Press, 2008).

St. Clair, William, *The Reading Nation in the Romantic Period* (Cambridge: Cambridge University Press, 2004).

Wakelin, Daniel, *Humanism, Reading and English Literature, 1430–1530* (Oxford: Oxford University Press, 2007).

Waller, P.J, *Writers, Readers and Reputations: Literary Life in Britain, 1870–1918* (Oxford: Oxford University Press, 2006).

Watling, Gabrielle and Sara E. Quay (eds), *A Cultural History of Reading* (Westport, CT: Greenwood Press, 2008).

Woolf, D.R., *Reading History in Early Modern England* (Cambridge: Cambridge University Press, 2000).

Woolf, Virginia, *The Common Reader* (London: Hogarth Press, 1925).

Woolf, Virginia, *The Common Reader, Second Series* (London: Hogarth Press, 1932).

Zaid, Gabriel, *So Many Books: Reading and Publishing in an Age of Abundance* (London: Paul Dry Books, 2004).

Section 1

Burke, Edmund Huey, *The Psychology and Pedagogy of Reading: With a Review of the History of Reading and Writing* (New York: Macmillan, 1908).

Chartier, Roger, *The Order of Books*, trans. Lydia Cochrane (Cambridge: Polity, 1994).

Clanchy, M. T., *From Memory to Written Record: England 1066–1307*, 2nd edn (Oxford: Basil Blackwell, 1993).

Darnton, Robert, 'What is the history of books?', *Daedalus*, III.3 (1982): 62–83.

Darnton, Robert, 'First Steps Towards a History of Reading' in *The Kiss of Lamourette: Reflections in Cultural History* (London: Faber & Faber, 1990): 154–82.

Goldhill, Simon, 'Literary History without Literature: Reading Practices in the Ancient World', *SubStance*, 28:1 (1999): 57–89.

Hall, David D., 'What was the History of the Book? A Response', *Modern Intellectual History*, 4:3 (2007): 537–44.

Howsam, Leslie, *Old Books and New Histories: An Orientation to Studies in Book and Print Culture* (Toronto, University of Toronto Press, 2006).

Jackson, Ian, 'Approaches to the History of Readers and Reading in Eighteenth-Century Britain', *The Historical Journal*, 47 (2004): 1041–54.

Leavis, Q.D., *Fiction and the Reading Public* (London: Chatto & Windus, 1932).

Lerer, Seth, 'Histories of Reading', *Raritan*, 20:1 (2000): 108–26.

Lyons, Martyn, *A History of Reading and Writing in the Western World* (Basingstoke: Palgrave Macmillan, 2009).

Martin, Henri-Jean, *The History and Power of Writing*, trans. Lydia G. Cochrane (Chicago: University of Chicago Press, 1994).

Miall, David, 'Empirical Approaches to Studying Literary Readers: The State of the Discipline', *Book History*, 9 (2006): 291–311.

Moorhead, John, 'Reading in Late Antiquity' in Carl Deroux (ed.), *Studies in Latin Literature and Roman History* (Brussels: Latomus, 2008).

Moretti, Franco, *Atlas of the European Novel 1800–1900* (London: Verso, 1998).

Price, Leah, 'Reading: The State of the Discipline', *Book History*, 7 (2004): 303–20.

Price, Leah, 'Introduction: Reading Matter', *Proceedings of the Modern Language Association*, 121:1 (January 2006): 9–16.

Rose, Jonathan, 'How Historians Study Reader Response', in *Literature in the Marketplace*, ed. J. Jordan and R. Patten (Cambridge: Cambridge University Press, 1995): 195–212.

Rose, Jonathan, 'A Preface to a History of Audiences,' in *The Book History Reader*, ed. Alistair McCleery and David Finkelstein (London: Routledge, 2002): 324–39.

Rubin, Joan Shelley, 'What is the History of the History of Books', *Journal of American History*, 90:2 (September 2003): 555–75.

Wittmann, Reinhard, 'Was there a Reading Revolution at the End of the Eighteenth Century?' in *A History of Reading in the West*, ed. Guglielmo Cavallo and Roger Chartier (Oxford: Polity, 1999): 286–306.

Section 2

Anderson, Benedict, 'The Origins of National Consciousness', in *Imagined Communities: Reflections on the Origin and Spread of Nationalism* (London: Verso, 2006): 37–46.

Bakhtin, M.M., *Problems of Dostoevsky's Poetics* (1963), trans. Caryl Emerson (Minneapolis: University of Minnesota Press, 1984).

Bakhtin, M.M., *The Dialogic Imagination*, ed. Michael Holquist, trans. Caryl Emerson and Michael Holquist (Austin: University of Texas Press, 1981).

Barthes, Roland, *The Pleasure of the Text* (1973) trans. Richard Miller (London: Cape, 1976).

Bleich, David, *Subjective Criticism* (Baltimore: John Hopkins University Press, 1978).

Bloom, Harold, *The Anxiety of Influence* (New York: Oxford University Press, 1973).

Calinescu, Matei, *Rereading* (New Haven: Yale University Press, 1993).

de Certeau, Michel, *The Practice of Everyday Life*, trans. Steven F. Rendal (Berkeley: University of California Press, 1984).

Eco, Umberto, *The Role of the Reader: Explorations in the Semiotics of Texts* (Bloomington: Indiana University Press, 1979).

Engelsing, Rolf, *Analphabetentum und Lektüre; zur Sozialgeschichte des Lesens in Deutschland zwischen feudaler und industrieller Gesellschaft* (Stuttgart: Metzler, 1973).

Engelsing, Rolf, *Der Bürger als Leser: Lesergeschichte in Deutschland 1500–1800* (Stuttgart: Metzler, 1974).

Felman, Shoshana, *What Does a Woman Want? Reading and Sexual Difference* (Baltimore and London: John Hopkins University Press, 1993).

Fetterley, Judith, *The Resisting Reader: A Feminist Approach to American Fiction* (Bloomington and London: Indiana University Press, 1978).

Fish, Stanley, *Is there a Text in this Class?: The Authority of Interpretive Communities* (Cambridge, Mass.: Harvard University Press, 1980).

Fish, Stanley, *Surprised by Sin: The Reader in Paradise Lost* (1967) (Berkeley: University of California Press, 1971).

Freund, Elizabeth, *The Return of the Reader: Reader-Response Criticism* (London: Methuen, 1987).

Goldstein, Philip, *Modern American Reading Practices: Between Aesthetics and History* (Basingstoke: Palgrave Macmillan, 2009).

Halsey, Katie, ' "Folk stylistics" and the History of Reading: A Discussion of Method', *Language and Literature*, 18.3 (2009): 231–46.

Holland, Norman, *The Dynamics of Literary Response* (New York: Oxford University Press, 1968).

Holland, Norman, *5 Readers Reading* (New Haven: Yale University Press, 1975).

Iser, Wolfgang, *Prospecting: From Reader Response to Literary Anthropology* (Baltimore: John Hopkins University Press, 1989).

Iser, Wolfgang, *The Act of Reading: A Theory of Aesthetic Response* (London: Routledge & Kegan Paul, 1978).

Iser, Wolfgang, *The Implied Reader; Patterns of Communication in Prose Fiction from Bunyan to Beckett* (Baltimore: John Hopkins University Press, 1974).

Jauss, Hans Robert, *Aesthetic Experience and Literary Hermeneutics*, trans. Michael Shaw (Minneapolis, University of Minnesota Press, 1982).

Jauss, Hans Robert, *Toward an Aesthetic of Reception*, trans. Timothy Bahti (Minneapolis: University of Minnesota Press, 1982).

Johns, Adrian, 'The Physiology of Reading', in his *The Nature of the Book* (Chicago: University of Chicago Press, 1998): 380–443.

Lewis, C.S., *An Experiment in Criticism* (Cambridge: Cambridge University Press, 1961).

Littau, Karin, *Theories of Reading: Books, Bodies and Bibliomania* (Cambridge: Polity, 2006).

Martindale, Charles, *Redeeming the Text* (Cambridge: Cambridge University Press, 1993).

Mills, Sara (ed.), *Gendering the Reader* (New York: Harvester Wheatsheaf, 1994).

Richards, I.A., *Practical Criticism: A Study in Literary Judgement* (London: K. Paul, Trench, Trubner, 1925).

Riffaterre, Michael, *Text Production*, trans. Therese Lyons (New York: Columbia University Press, 1983).

Riffaterre, Michael, *The Semiotics of Poetry* (Bloomington: Indiana University Press, 1978).

Rosenblatt, Louise M., *Literature as Exploration* (New York: D. Appleton-Century Company, 1938).

Saenger, Paul, 'Silent Reading: Its impact on Late Medieval Script and Society', *Viator*, 13 (1982): 367–414.

Suleiman, Susan R., & Inge Crosman, *The Reader in the Text: Essays on Audience and Interpretation* (Princeton: Princeton University Press, 1980).

Tompkins, Jane (ed.), *Reader-Response Criticism: From Formalism to Post-Structuralism* (Baltimore: John Hopkins University Press, 1980).

Section 3

Acevedo-Rodrigo, Ariadna, 'Rural literacy: the simulation of reading in rural Indian Mexico, 1870–1930', *Paedagogica Historica*, 44 (2008): 49–65.

Adamik-Jászó, Anna, *Literacy in Hungary, Past and Present* (Budapest: Dinasztia Educational Publisher, 2006).

Ballara, Marcela, *Women and Literacy* (London, Zed, 1992).

Baynham, Mike, *Literacy Practices: Investigating Literacy in Social Contexts* (London: Longman, 1995).

Blaak, Jeroen, *Literacy in Everyday Life: Reading and Writing in Early Modern Dutch Diaries*, trans. Beverley Jackson (Leiden: Brill, 2009).

Brayman Hackel, H. *Reading Material in Early Modern England: Print, Gender and Literacy* (Cambridge: Cambridge University Press, 2005).

Briggs, C. F., 'Literacy, Reading and Writing in the Medieval West', *Journal of Medieval History*, 26 (2000): 397–420

Burns, Alfred, *The Power of the Written Word. The Role of Literacy in the History of Western Civilisation* (New York: P. Lang, 1989).

Chartier, Roger, 'Measuring Literacy', in *Passions of the Renaissance*, ed. Chartier, vol. iii of *A History of Private Life* (eds), P. Aries & G. Duby, trans. A. Goldhammer (Cambridge, Mass.: Belknap, 1989).

Cipolla, Carlo M., *Literacy and Development in the West* (Harmondsworth: Pelican books, 1969).

Cobley, Alan G., 'Literacy, Libraries and Consciousness: The Provision of Library Services for Blacks in South Africa in the pre-Apartheid Era', *Libraries & Culture*, 32 (1997): 57–80.

Cornelius, Janet Duitsman, *'When I Can Read my Title Clear': Literacy, Slavery and Religion in the Antebellum South* (Columbia S.C.: University of South Carolina Press, 1992).

Cressy, David, *Literacy and the Social Order: Reading and Writing in Tudor and Stuart England* (Cambridge: Cambridge University Press, 1980).

Crone, Rosalind, 'Reappraising Victorian Literacy through Prison Records', *Journal of Victorian Culture*, 15 (2010): 3–37.

Daly, Mary E., and David Dickson (eds), *The Origins of Popular Literacy in Ireland: Language Change and Educational Development 1700–1920* (Dublin: Department of Modern History, Trinity College Dublin, 1990).

Davids, Karel, and Jan Lucassen (eds), *A Miracle Mirrored: The Dutch Republic in European Perspective* (Cambridge: Cambridge University Press, 1996).

Davies, W.J. Frank, *Teaching Reading in Early England* (London: Pitman, 1973).

Dobraszczyk, Paul, ' "Give in your Account": Using and Abusing Victorian Census Forms', *Journal of Victorian Culture*, 14 (2009): 1–25.

Fernandez, Jean, *Victorian Servants, Class, and the Politics of Literacy* (Abingdon: Routledge, 2009).

Finnegan, Ruth H., *Literacy and Orality: Studies in the Technology of Communication* (Oxford: Basil Blackwell, 1988).

Ford, Wyn, 'The Problem of Literacy in Early Modern England', *History*, 78 (1993): 22–37.

Fox, Adam, *Oral and Literate Culture in England 1500–1700* (Oxford: Clarendon, 2000).

Fox, Adam, and Daniel Woolf (eds), *The Spoken Word: Oral Culture in Britain 1500–1850* (Manchester: Manchester University Press, 2002).

Frandsen, Niels H., 'Literacy and Literature in North Greenland, 1791–1850', *Études-Inuit-Studies*, 23 (1999): 69–90.

Frijhoff, Willem, 'Calvinism, Literacy, and Reading Culture in the Early Modern Northern Netherlands: Towards a Reassessment', *Archiv für Reformationsgeschichte*, 95 (2004): 252–65.

Furet, François, and Jacques Ozouf, *Reading and Writing: Literacy in France from Calvin to Jules Ferry* (1977, Eng. trans. Cambridge: Cambridge University Press, 1982).

Gawthrop, Richard, and Gerald Strauss, 'Protestantism and Literacy in Early Modern Germany', *Past and Present*, 104 (1984): 31–55.

Gilmont, J.F. (ed.), *The Reformation and the Book*, trans. K. Maag (Aldershot: Ashgate, 1998).

Gilmore, W.J., *Reading Becomes a Necessity of Life: Material and Cultural Life in Rural New England, 1780–1835* (Knoxville: University of Tennessee Press, 1989).

Goody, Jack (ed.), *Literacy in Traditional Societies* (Cambridge: Cambridge University Press, 1968).

Graff, H.J., *The Legacies of Literacy. Continuities and Contradictions in Western Culture and Society* (Bloomington: Indiana University Press, 1987).

Graff, H.J., *The Literacy Myth: Literacy and Social Structure in the Nineteenth Century City* (New York: Academic Press, 1979).

Graff, H.J., *The Labyrinths of Literacy: Reflections on Literacy Past and Present* (Revised edn., Pittsburgh: University of Pittsburgh Press, 1995).

Graff, H.J., (ed.), *Literacy and Social Development in the West* (Cambridge: Cambridge University Press, 1981).

Graff, H.J., A. Mackinnon, B. Sandin and I. Winchester (eds), *Understanding Literacy in its Historical Contexts: Looking Backward and Looking Forward – Past Approaches and Work in Progress, Interchange* (Calgary), 34, nos. 2 & 3 (2003).

Gray, W.S., *The Teaching of Reading and Writing* (London: UNESCO, 1956).

Guttormsson, Loftur, 'The Development of Popular Religious Literacy in the Seventeenth and Eighteenth Centuries', *Scandinavian Journal of History*, 15 (1990): 7–35.

Hall, David D., 'The Uses of Literacy in New England: 1600–1850,' in *Printing and Society in Early America*, ed. William Joyce (Worcester: American Antiquarian Society, 1983): 1–47.

Hanna, Nelly, 'Literacy and the "Great Divide" in the Islamic world, 1300–1800', *Journal of Global History*, 2 (2007): 175–93.

Hoggart, Richard, *The Uses of Literacy* (London: Chatto & Windus, 1957).

Houston, R.A., 'Literacy and Society in the West', *Social History*, 8 (1983): 269–93.

Houston, R.A., *Literacy in Early Modern Europe: Culture and Education 1500–1800* (London: Longman, 1988).

Johansson, E., *The History of Literacy in Sweden* (Umea: Umea University and School of Education, 1977).

Kaestle, Carl F. et al. (eds), *Literacy in the United States: Readers and Reading since 1880* (New Haven: Yale University Press, 1991).

Kenez, Peter, 'Liquidating Illiteracy in Revolutionary Russia', *Russian History*, 9, 2–3 (1982): 173–86.

Kimberley, K., M. Meek and J. Miller (eds), *New Readings: Contributions to an Understanding of Literacy* (London: A & C Black, 1993).

Kirsch, I., and J.T. Guthrie, 'The Concept and Measurement of Functional Literacy', *Reading Research Quarterly*, 13, 4 (1977–8): 485–507.

Laqueur, T.W., 'The Cultural Origins of Popular Literacy 1500–1850', *Oxford Review of Education*, 2 (1976): 255–75.

Lindmark, Daniel (ed.), *Alphabeta Varia. Orality, Reading and Writing in the History of Literacy* (Umea: Umea University, 1998).

Lockridge, Kenneth A., *Literacy in Colonial New England: an Enquiry into the Social Context of Literacy in the Early Modern West* (New York: Norton, 1974).

Lyons, Martyn, 'What did the Peasants Read? Written and Printed Culture in Rural France 1815–1914', *European History Quarterly*, 27 (1997): 165–97.

Martin, Henri-Jean, 'The Bibliothèque Bleue: Literature for the Masses in the Ancien Régime', *Publishing History*, 3 (1978): 70–102.

Matthews, M., *Teaching to Read Historically Considered* (Chicago: University of Chicago Press, 1966).

McKitterick, Rosamond (ed.), *The Uses of Literacy in Early Medieval Europe* (Cambridge, 1990).

Merkel-Hess, Kate, 'Reading the Rural Modern: Literacy and Morality in Republican China', *History Compass*, 7 (2009): 44–54.

Mitch, David F., *The Rise of Popular Literacy in Victorian England: The Influence of Private Choice and Public Policy* (Philadelphia: University of Pennsylvania Press, 1992).

Mitch, David F., 'Literacy and Occupational Mobility in Rural versus Urban Victorian England: Evidence from the Linked Marriage Register and Census Records for Birmingham and Norfolk, 1851 and 1881', *Historical Methods*, 38 (2005): 26–38.

Monaghan, E. Jennifer, *Learning to Read and Write in Colonial America* (Amherst, MA: University of Massachusetts Press, 2005).

Nalle, Sara T., 'Literacy and Culture in Early Modern Castile', *Past & Present*, 125 (1989): 65–96.

Neuberg, Victor E., *Popular Literature: a History and Guide* (Harmondsworth: Penguin, 1977).

Nipperdey, Thomas, 'Mass Education and Modernization: the Case of Germany 1780–1850', *Transactions of the Royal Historical Society*, 5th ser., 27 (1987): 155–72.

Nunez, C-E., 'Literacy and Economic Growth in Spain 1860–1977', in *Education and Economic Development since the Industrial Revolution*, ed. Gabriel Tortilla (València: Generalitat Valenciana, 1990): 123–151.

Ong, W.J., *Orality and Literacy* (London: Methuen, 1982).

Rawski, Evelyn Sakakida, *Education and Popular Literacy in Ch'ing China* (Ann Arbor: University of Michigan Press, 1979).

Reay, B., 'The Context and Meaning of Popular Literacy: Some Evidence from Nineteenth Century Rural England', *Past & Present*, 131 (1991): 89–129.

Rees Jones, S., *Learning and Literacy in Medieval England and Abroad* (Turnhout: Brepols, 2003).

Resnik, D.P., *Literacy in Historical Perspective* (Washington: Library of Congress, 1983).

Reynolds, Suzanne, *Medieval Reading: Grammar, Rhetoric and the Classical Text* (Cambridge: Cambridge University Press, 1996).

Rowe, Steven E., 'Writing Modern Selves: Literacy and the French Working Class in the Early-nineteenth Century', *Journal of Social History*, 40 (2006): 55–83.

Rubinger, Richard, *Popular Literacy in Early Modern Japan* (Honolulu: University of Hawaii Press, 2007).

Schousboe, K., and Trolle Larsen, M. (eds), *Literacy and Society* (Copenhagen: Akademisk forlag [for] Center for Research in the Humanities, Copenhagen University, 1989).

Spufford, Margaret, 'First Steps in Literacy: The Reading and Writing Experiences of the Humblest Seventeenth-century Spiritual Biographers', *Social History*, 4 (1979): 407–435.

Stephens, W.B., *Education, Literacy and Society 1830–1870. The Geography of Diversity in Provincial England* (Manchester: Manchester University Press, 1987).

Strauss, G., 'Lutheranism and Literacy: A Reassessment' in K. Von Greyerz (ed.), *Religion and Society in Early Modern Europe 1500–1800* (London: German Historical Institute, 1984): 102–23.

Street, Brian V., *Literacy in Theory and Practice* (Cambridge: Cambridge University Press, 1985).

Thomas, Rosalind, *Literacy and Orality in Ancient Greece* (Cambridge: Cambridge University Press, 1992).

Torrance, Richard, 'Literacy and Modern Literature in the Izumo Region, 1880–1930', *Journal of Japanese Studies*, 22 (1996): 327–62.

Toth, I.G., *Literacy and Written Culture in Early Modern Central Europe* (Budapest: Central European University Press, 1996; Eng. trans. 2000).

Vilanova, M., 'Anarchism, Political Participation and Illiteracy in Barcelona 1934–1936', *American Historical Review*, 97, 1 (February 1992): 96–120.

Vincent, David, *Literacy and Popular Culture: England 1750–1914* (Cambridge: Cambridge University Press, 1989).

Vincent, David, 'Reading Made Strange: Context and Method in Becoming Literate in Eighteenth and Nineteenth-century England', in *Silences and Images: the Social History of the Classroom*, ed. Ian Grosvenor, Martin Lawn and Kate Rousmaniere (New York: Peter Lang, 1999): 180–197.

Vincent, David, 'The Progress of Literacy', *Victorian Studies*, 45 (2003): 405–31.

Watkins, Morris G., *Literacy, Bible Reading, and Church Growth through the Ages* (South Pasanda, CA: William Carey Library, 1978).

Webb, R.K., *The British Working Class Reader, 1790–1848: Literacy and Social Tension* (London: Allen & Unwin, 1955).

Section 4

Adams, J.R.R., *The Printed Word and the Common Man. Popular Culture in Ulster 1700–1900* (Belfast: Queen's University of Belfast, Institute of Irish Studies, 1987).

Allan, David, *A Nation of Readers: The Lending Library in Georgian England* (London: British Library, 2008).

Anderson, Patricia, *The Printed Image and the Transformation of Popular Culture 1790–1860* (Oxford: Clarendon Press, 1991).

Bennett, Scott, 'Revolutions in Thought: Serial Publication and the Mass Market for Reading', in *The Victorian Periodical Press: Samplings and Soundings*, ed. J. Shattock and M. Wolff (Leicester: Leicester University Press, 1982): 225–257.

Birn, R., 'Deconstructing Popular Culture: The Bibliothèque Bleue and its Historians', *Australian Journal of French Studies*, 23, 1 (1986): 31–47.

Brantlinger, Patrick, *The Reading Lesson: The Threat of Mass Literacy in Nineteenth-Century British Fiction* (Bloomington: Indiana University Press, 1998).

Breen, Katharine, *Imagining an English Reading Public, 1150–1400* (Cambridge: Cambridge University Press, 2010).

Brokaw, Cynthia J. and Kai-wing Chow (eds), *Printing and Book Culture in Late Imperial China* (Berkeley: University of California Press, 2005).

Brooks, Jeffrey, *When Russia Learned to Read: Literacy and Popular Literature, 1861–1917* (Evanston, IL: Northwestern University Press, 2003).

Coleman, Joyce, *Public Reading and the Reading Public in late Medieval England and France* (Cambridge: Cambridge University Press, 1996).

Comparato, Frank E., *Books for the Millions: a History of the Men whose Methods and Machines Packaged the Printed Word* (Harrisburg: Stackpole Co., 1971).

Crone, Rosalind, 'Cries of Murder and Sounds of Bloodshed: The Practice of Reading Cheap Fiction in Working-class Communities in Early Victorian London', in *New Perspectives in British Cultural History,* eds. Rosalind Crone, David Gange and Katy Jones (Newcastle: Cambridge Scholars Publishing, 2007): 203–213.

Crone, Rosalind, 'From Sawney Beane to Sweeney Todd: Murder Machines in the Mid-Nineteenth Century Metropolis', *Cultural and Social History,* 7 (2010): 59–85.

Donaldson, William, *Popular Literature in Victorian Scotland: Language, Fiction and the Press* (Aberdeen: Aberdeen University Press, 1986).

Engelstein, L., 'Print Culture and the Transformation of Imperial Russia: Three New Views', *Comparative Studies in Society and History*, 31 (October 1989): 784–90.

Fullerton, R.A., 'Creating a Mass Book Market in Germany: The Story of the "Colporteur Novel" 1870–1890', *Journal of Social History*, 10, 3 (March 1977): 265–83.

Gamsa, Mark, *The Reading of Russian Literature in China: A Moral Example and Manual of Practice* (Basingstoke: Palgrave Macmillan, 2010).

Ghosh, Anindita, *Power in Print: Popular Publishing and the Politics of Language and Culture in a Colonial Society, 1778–1905* (New Delhi: Oxford University Press, 2006).

Hammond, Mary, *Reading, Publishing and the Formation of Literary Taste in England, 1880–1914* (Aldershot: Ashgate, 2006).

Haywood, Ian, *The Revolution in Popular Literature: Print, Politics and the People, 1790–1860* (Cambridge: Cambridge University Press, 2004).

Henkin, David M., *City Reading: Written Words and Public Spaces in Antebellum New York* (New York: Columbia University Press, 1998).

Hindley, Charles, *The Life and Times of James Catnach (Late of the Seven Dials)* (London: Reeves and Turner, 1878).

Jacobs, Edward, 'Bloods in the Street: London Street Culture, "Industrial Literacy", and the Emergence of Mass Culture in Victorian England', *Nineteenth-Century Contexts*, 18 (1995): 321–47.

James, Louis, *Fiction for the Working Man, 1830–1850* (Oxford: Oxford University Press, 1963).

James, Louis, *Print and the People, 1819–1951* (London: Allen Lane, 1976).

Kaegbein, Paul, and Magnus Torstensson, 'The History of Reading and Libraries in the Nordic Countries', *Libraries and Culture* 28:1 (1993).

Kirsop, Wallace, *Books for Colonial Readers: The Nineteenth-Century Australian Experience* (Melbourne: Bibliographical Society of Australia and New Zealand in association with the Centre for Bibliographical and Textual Studies, Monash University, 1995).

Klancher, Jon, *The Making of English Reading Audiences, 1790–1832* (Madison: University of Wisconsin Press, 1987).

Lovell, Stephen, *The Russian Reading Revolution: Print Culture in the Soviet and Post-Soviet Eras* (Basingstoke: Macmillan, 2000).

Lyons, Martyn, with Lucy Taksa, *Australian Readers Remember: An Oral History of Reading 1890–1930* (Melbourne: Oxford University Press, 1992).

McAleer, J., *Popular Reading and Publishing in Britain 1914–1950* (Oxford: Clarendon Press, 1992).

Pedersen, Susan, 'Hannah More meets Simple Simon: Tracts, Chapbooks and Popular Culture in Late Eighteenth Century Britain', *Journal of British Studies*, 25 (1986): 84–113.

Price, Leah, *The Anthology and the Rise of the Novel: From Richardson to George Eliot* (Cambridge: Cambridge University Press, 2000).

Radway, Janice, *Reading the Romance: Women, Patriarchy and Popular Literature* (Chapel Hill: University of North Carolina Press, 1984).

Radway, Janice, *A Feeling for Books: The Book-of-the-Month Club, Literary Tastes, and Middle-Class Desire* (Chapel Hill: University of North Carolina Press, 1997).

Roldán-Vera, Eugenia, 'Reading in Questions and Answers: The Catechism as an Educational Genre in Early Independent Spanish America', *Book History*, 4 (2001): 17–48.

Rubin, Joan Shelley, *Songs of Ourselves: The Uses of Poetry in America* (Cambridge, Mass.: Belknap, 2007).

Sharpe, Kevin, *Reading Revolutions: The Politics of Reading in Early Modern England* (London: Yale University Press, 2000).

Smith, Erin A., 'How the Other Half Read: Advertising, Working-Class Readers, and Pulp Magazines', *Book History*, 3 (2000): 204–30.

Spufford, Margaret, *Small Books and Pleasant Histories: Popular Fiction and its Readership in Seventeenth-Century England* (London: Methuen, 1981).

Vincent, D., 'Reading in the Working-class Home', in *Leisure in Britain 1780–1939*, eds. J.K. Walton and J. Walvin (Manchester: Manchester University Press, 1983): 208–26.

Ware, Richard, 'Some aspects of the Russian reading public in the 1880s', *Renaissance & Modern Studies*, 24 (1980): 18–37.

Warner, Michael, *The Letters of the Republic: Publication and the Public Sphere in Eighteenth-Century America* (Cambridge Mass.: Harvard University Press, 1990).

Wild, Jonathan, ' "Insects in Letters": "John O'London's Weekly" and the New Reading Public', *Literature & History*, 15 (2006): 50–62.

Section 5

Andersen, Jennifer, and Elizabeth Sauer (eds), *Books and Their Readers in Early Modern England* (Philadelphia: University of Pennsylvania Press, 2002).

Aoyama, Tomoko, and Barbara Hartley (eds), *Girl reading Girl in Japan* (Abingdon: Routledge, 2009).

Baggs, Chris, 'How Well Read was my Valley? Reading, Popular Fiction and the Miners of South Wales, 1875–1939', *Book History*, 4 (2001): 277–301.

Bell, Bill, 'Bound for Botany Bay; or, What did the Nineteenth-century Convict Read?' in *Against the Law: Crime, Sharp Practice and the Control of Print*, ed. Robin Myers, Michael Harris and Giles Mandelbrote (New Castle, DE: Oak Knoll Press, 2004): 151–75.

Bell, Lady F., 'What People Read', *Independent Review*, 7 (1905): 27.

Blair, Ann, 'Reading Strategies for Coping with Information Overload ca.1550–1700', *Journal of the History of Ideas*, 64:1 (2003): 11–28.

Boyarin, Jonathan, *The Ethnography of Reading* (Berkeley: University of California Press, 1992).

Chow, Rey, 'Mandarin Ducks and Butterflies: An Exercise in Popular Readings' in *Woman and Chinese Modernity* (Minneapolis: University of Minnesota Press, 1993): 34–83.

Cohen, Matt, 'The History of the Book in New England: The State of the Discipline', *Book History*, 11 (2008): 301–23.

Colclough, Stephen, *Consuming Texts: Readers and Reading Communities, 1695–1870* (Basingstoke: Palgrave Macmillan, 2007).

Dick, Archie L., ' "To Make the People of South Africa Proud of their Membership of the Great British Empire": Home reading unions in South Africa, 1900–1914', *Libraries and Culture* 40:1 (2005): 1–24.

Fergus, Jan, *Provincial Readers in Eighteenth-Century England* (Oxford: Oxford University Press, 2006).

Gilmore, William J., *Reading becomes a Necessity of Life: Material and Cultural Life in Rural New England, 1780–1835* (Knoxville: University of Tennessee Press, 1989).

Grenby, M. O., 'Adults only? Children and Children's Books in British Circulating Libraries, 1748–1948', *Book History* 5 (2002): 19–38.

Griswold, Wendy, *Bearing Witness: Readers, Writers, and the Novel in Nigeria* (Princeton: Princeton University Press, 2000).

Hammond, Mary, and Shafquat Towheed (eds), *Publishing in the First World War: Essays in Book History* (Basingstoke: Palgrave Macmillan, 2007).

Hochman, Barbara, *Getting at the Author: Reimagining Books and Reading in the Age of American Realism* (Amherst: University of Massachusetts Press, 2001).

Holt, Elizabeth M., 'Narrative and the Reading Public in 1870s Beirut', *Journal of Arabic Literature*, 40 (2009): 37–70.

Johanningsmeier, Charles, 'Welcome Guests or Representatives of the "Mal-Odorous Class": Periodicals and their Readers in American Public Libraries, 1876–1914', *Libraries and Culture*, 39:3 (2004): 260–92.

Johnson, William A., *Readers and Reading Culture in the High Roman Empire: A Study of Elite Communities* (Oxford: Oxford University Press, 2010).

Joshi, Priya, *In Another Country: Colonialism, Culture and the English Novel in India* (New York: Columbia University Press, 2002).

Kallendorf, Craig, *The Virgilian Tradition: Book History and the History of Reading in Early Modern Europe* (Aldershot: Ashgate, 2007).

Kloek, Joost, 'Reconsidering the Reading Revolution: The Thesis of the "Reading Revolution" and a Dutch Bookseller's Clientele Around 1800', *Poetics*, 26:6 (1999): 289–307.

Long, Elizabeth, *Book Clubs: Women and the Uses of Reading in Everyday Life* (Chicago and London: University of Chicago Press, 2003).

Lyons, Martyn, *Reading Culture and Writing Practices in Nineteenth-Century France* (Toronto: University of Toronto Press, 2008).

Manley, K.A., 'Rural Reading in Northwest England: the Sedbergh Book Club, 1728–1928', *Book History*, 2 (1999): 78–95.

McDowell, Kathleen, 'Towards a History of Children as Readers, 1890–1930', *Book History*, 12 (2009): 240–65.

McHenry, Elizabeth, *Forgotten Readers: Recovering the Lost History of African American Literary Societies*, (Durham, NC: Duke University Press, 2002).

McHenry, Elizabeth, ' "An Association of Kindred Spirits": Black Readers and their Reading Rooms', in *Institutions of Reading: The Social Life of Libraries in the United States*, ed. Thomas Augst and Kenneth Carpenter (Amherst: University of Massachusetts Press, 2007): 99–118.

McNair, John, 'The "Reading Library" and the Reading Public: the Decline and Fall of "Biblioteka Dlia Chteniia" ', *Slavonic & East European Review*, 70 (1992): 213–27.

Monaghan, Jennifer E., ' "She Loved to Read in Good Books": Literacy and the Indians of Martha's Vineyard, 1643–1725', *History of Education Quarterly*, 30 (1990): 493–521.

Murphy, Sharon, 'Imperial Reading? The East India Company's Lending Libraries for Soldiers, c.1819–1834', *Book History*, 12 (2009): 74–99.

Naimark-Goldberg, Natalie, 'Reading and Modernization: The Experience of Jewish Women in Berlin around 1800', *Nashim: A Journal of Jewish Women's Studies and Gender Issues*, 15 (2008): 58–87.

Newell, Stephanie, *Literary Culture in Colonial Ghana: 'How to Play the Game of Life'* (Manchester: Manchester University Press, 2002).

Pawley, Christine, *Reading on the Middle Border: The Culture of Print in Late Nineteenth-Century Osage, Iowa* (Amherst: University of Massachusetts Press, 2001).

Petrucci, Armando, 'Reading in the Middle Ages' in *Writers and Readers in Medieval Italy: Studies in the History of Written Culture*, ed. and trans. Charles M. Radding (New Haven: Yale University Press, 1995): 132–144.

Rivers, Isabel, *Books and Their Readers in Eighteenth-Century England* (Leicester: Leicester University Press, 1982).

Rivers, Isabel, *Books and Their Readers in Eighteenth-Century England: New Essays* (London: Continuum, 2002).

Rose, Jonathan, *The Intellectual Life of the British Working Classes* (New Haven: Yale University Press, 2001).

Rothstein, Marian, *Reading in the Renaissance: Amadis de Gaule and the Lessons of Memory* (Newark, Del: University of Delaware Press, 1999).

Simpson, James, *Burning to Read: English Fundamentalism and its Reformation Opponents* (Cambridge: Cambridge University Press, 2007).

Stewart, Garrett, *Dear Reader: The Conscripted Audience in Nineteenth-Century British Fiction* (Baltimore: John Hopkins University Press, 1996).

Styles, Morag, and Evelyn Arizpe (eds), *Acts of Reading: Teachers, Texts and Childhood* (Stoke-on-Trent: Trentham, 2009).

Towsey, Mark, ' "Patron of Infidelity": Scottish Readers respond to David Hume, c.1750–c.1820', *Book History*, 11 (2008): 89–123.

Tsai, Weipin, *Reading Shenbao: Nationalism, Consumerism and Individuality in China, 1919–37* (Basingstoke: Palgrave Macmillan, 2009).

Wang, Juan, 'Officialdom Unmasked: Shanghai Tabloid Press, 1897–1911', *Late Imperial China*, 28:2 (2007): 81–128.

Williams, Heather Andrea, *Self-taught: African-American Education in Freedom and Slavery* (Chapel Hill: University of North Carolina Press, 2005).

Zboray, Ronald J., and Mary Saracino Zboray, *Everyday Ideas: Socioliterary Experience among Antebellum New Englanders* (Knoxville: University of Tennessee Press, 2006).

Section 6

Baker, Geoff, *Reading and Politics in Early Modern England: the Mental World of a Seventeenth-Century Catholic Gentleman* (Manchester: Manchester University Press, 2010).

Basbanes, Nicholas A., *Every Book its Reader: The Power of the Written Word to Stir the World* (London: HarperPerennial, 2007).

Brantley, Jessica, *Reading in the Wilderness: Private Devotion and Public Performance in Late Medieval England* (Chicago: University of Chicago Press, 2007).

Brewer, John, 'Cultural Consumption in Eighteenth-Century England: The View of the Reader', in *Frühe Neuzeit – Frühe Moderne? Forschungen zur Vielschichtigkeit von Übergangsprozessen: Herausgegeben von Rudolf Vierbaus und Mitarbeitern des Max-Planck-Instituts für Geschichte* (Göttingen: Vandenhoeck & Ruprecht, 1992): 366–91.

Cavell, Janice, 'In the Margins: Regimental History and a Veteran's Narrative of the First World War', *Book History*, 11 (2008): 199–219.

Chartier, Roger, *The Cultural Uses of Print in Early Modern France*, trans. L.G. Cochrane (Princeton: Princeton University Press, 1987).

Darnton, Robert, 'Readers Respond to Rousseau', in *The Great Cat Massacre and Other Episodes in French Cultural History* (London: Allen Lane, 1984): 215–56.

DeMaria, Robert, *Samuel Johnson and the Life of Reading* (Baltimore: John Hopkins University Press, 1997).

Fadiman, Anne, *Rereadings: Seventeen Writers Revisit Books They Love* (New York: Macmillan, 2006).

Ginzburg, Carlo, *The Cheese and the Worms: the Cosmos of a Sixteenth-Century Miller*, trans. T. and A. Tedeschi (London: Routledge & Kegan Paul, 1980).

Grafton, Anthony, 'Is the History of Reading a Marginal Enterprise?: Guillaume Bude and His Books,' *Papers of the Bibliographical Society of America*, 91(1997): 139–57.

Halsey, Katie, ' "Critics as a Race are Donkeys": Margaret Oliphant, Critic or Common Reader?', *Journal of the Edinburgh Bibliographical Society*, 2 (2007): 42–68.

Hayes, Kevin J., *The Road to Monticello: The Life and Mind of Thomas Jefferson*. (Oxford: Oxford University Press, 2008).

Hunt, L. (ed.), *The New Cultural History* (Berkeley: University of California Press, 1989).

Hunter, M., G. Mandelbrote et al. (eds), *A Radical's Books: the Library Catalogue of Samuel Jeake of Rye, 1623–90* (Woodbridge: D.S. Brewer, 1999).

Jackson, H.J., *Marginalia: Readers Writing in Books* (London: Yale University Press, 2001).

Jackson, H.J., *Romantic Readers* (New Haven: Yale University Press, 2005).

Meek, Richard, Jane Rickard, and Richard Wilson (eds), *Shakespeare's Books: Essays in Reading, Writing and Reception* (Manchester: Manchester University Press, 2008).

Pearson, Jacqueline, *Women's Reading in Britain, 1750–1835: A Dangerous Recreation* (Cambridge: Cambridge University Press, 1999).

Pooley, S. and C. Pooley, ' "Such a Splendid Tale": The Late-nineteenth Century World of a Young Female Reader', Cultural and Social History, 2 (2005): 329–351.

Ryback, Timothy W., *Hitler's Private Library: The Books that Shaped his Life* (Bodley Head: Knopf Publishing Group, 2008).

Sherman, William, *John Dee: The Politics of Reading and Writing in the English Renaissance* (Amherst: University of Massachusetts Press, 1995).

Stimpson, Felicity, ' "I have spent my morning reading Greek": The Marginalia of Sir George Otto Trevelyan', Library History, 23:3 (2007): 239–50.

Stock, Brian, *After Augustine: The Meditative Reader and the Text* (Philadelphia: University of Pennsylvania Press, 2001).

Towheed, Shafquat, 'Reading History and Nation: Robert Louis Stevenson's reading of William Forbes-Mitchell's *Reminiscences of the Great Mutiny, 1857–9*', Nineteenth-Century Contexts, 31:1 (2009): 3–17.

Towsey, Mark, ' "An Infant Son to Truth Engage": Virtue, Responsibility and Self-Improvement in the Reading of Elizabeth Rose of Kilravock, 1747–1815', Journal of the Edinburgh Bibliographical Society, 2 (2007): 69–92.

Willes, Margaret, *Reading Matters: Five Centuries of Discovering Books* (New Haven: Yale University Press, 2008).

Windscheffel, Ruth Clayton, *Reading Gladstone* (Basingstoke: Palgrave Macmillan, 2008).

Wright, Thomas, *Oscar's Books* (London: Chatto & Windus, 2008).

Zwicker, Steven N., 'The Reader Revealed', in *The Reader Revealed*, eds. Sabrina Alcorn Baron, Elizabeth Walsh and Susan Scola (Washington, D.C: Folger Shakespeare Library, 2001): 11–17.

Section 7

Aubry, Timothy, 'Afghanistan meets the *Amazon*: Reading *The Kite Runner* in America', *Proceedings of the Modern Language Association*, 124:1 (2009): 25–43.

Birkerts, Sven, *The Gutenberg Elegies: The Fate of Reading in an Electronic Age* (London: Faber, 1996).

Birkerts, Sven, 'Resisting the Kindle', The Atlantic, 2 March 2009.

Collinson, Ian, *Everyday Readers: Reading and Popular Culture* (London: Equinox, 2009).

Crone, Rosalind, Katie Halsey and Shafquat Towheed, 'Examining the Evidence of Reading: Three Examples from the Reading Experience Database', in *Reading in History: New Methodologies from the Anglo-American Tradition,* ed. Bonnie Gunzenhauser (London: Pickering & Chatto, 2010): 29–45.

Darnton, Robert, *The Case for Books: Past, Present and Future* (Philadelphia: University of Pennsylvania Press, 2009).

De Weerdt, Hilde, 'Maps and Memory: Readings of Cartography in Twelfth- and Thirteenth- Century Song China', *Imago Mundi: International Journal for the History of Cartography*, 61:2 (2009): 1–23.

Dobraszczyk, Paul, 'Useful Reading? Designing Information for London's Victorian Cab Passengers', Journal of Design History, 21 (2008): 121–41.

Elfenbein, Andrew, 'Cognitive Science and the History of Reading', *Proceedings of the Modern Language Association*, 121:1 (2006): 484–502.

Esbester, Mike, 'Nineteenth-Century Timetables and the History of Reading', Book History, 12 (2009): 156–85.

Fuller, Danielle, 'Listening to the Readers of "Canada Reads" ', Canadian Literature, 193 (2007): 11–34.

Garde-Hansen, Joanne, Andrew Hoskins and Anna Reading (eds), *Save As . . . Digital Memories* (Basingstoke: Palgrave, 2009).

Gerrard, Teresa, 'New Methods in the History of Reading: "Answers to Correspondents" in *The Family Herald*, 1860–1900', *Publishing History*, 43 (1998): 53–66.

Gunzenheimer, Bonnie (ed.), *Reading in History: New Methodologies from the Anglo-American Tradition* (London: Pickering & Chatto, 2010).

Gutjahr, Paul, 'No Longer Left Behind: Amazon.com, Reader-response, and the Changing Fortunes of the Christian Novel in America', *Book History*, 5 (2002): 209–27.

Halsey, Katie, 'Reading the Evidence of Reading', *Popular Narrative Media*, 2 (2008): 123–37.

Hartley, Jenny, *Reading Groups* (Oxford: Oxford University Press, 2001).

Henkin, David, *City Reading: Written Words and Public Spaces in Antebellum New York* (New York: Columbia University Press, 1998).

Hofmeyr, Isabel, *The Portable Bunyan: A Transnational History of The Pilgrim's Progress* (Princeton: Princeton University Press, 2004).

Jackson, H.J., ' "Marginal Frivolities": Readers' Notes as Evidence for the History of Reading', in *Owners, Annotators and the Signs of Reading*, ed. Robin Myers, Michael Harris and Giles Mandelbrote (New Castle, Delaware: Oak Knoll, 2005): 137–151.

Kirschenbaum, Matthew, *Mechanisms: New Media and the Forensic Imagination* (Boston, MA: MIT Press, 2008).

Lerer, Seth, ' "Thy Life to Mend, this Book Attend" – Reading and Healing in the Arc of Children's Literature', *New Literary History*, 37:3 (2006): 631–42.

McKitterick, David, 'Book Catalogues: Their Varieties and Uses,' in *The Book Encompassed: Studies in Twentieth-Century Bibliography*, ed. Peter Davison (Cambridge: Cambridge University Press, 1992): 161–75.

Manguel, Alberto, *Reading Pictures: A History of Love and Hate* (London: Bloomsbury, 2001).

Nafisi, Azar, *Reading Lolita in Tehran: A Memoir in Books* (London: Random House, 2004).

Piroux, Lorraine, 'The Encyclopedist and the Peruvian Princess: The Poetics of Illegibility in French Enlightenment Book Culture', *Proceedings of the Modern Language Association*, 121:1 (2006): 107–23.

Whitington, Teresa, *The Syllables of Time: Proust and the History of Reading* (London: Modern Humanities Research Association and Maney Publishing, 2009).

Index

Related titles from Routledge

Book History through Postcolonial Eyes
Rewriting the Script
Robert Fraser

This surprising study draws together the disparate fields of postcolonial theory and book history in a challenging and illuminating way.

Robert Fraser proposes that we now look beyond the traditional methods of the Anglo-European bibliographic paradigm, and instead learn to appreciate the diversity of shapes that verbal expression has assumed across different societies. This change of attitude will encourage students and researchers to question developmentally conceived models of communication, and move instead to a re-formulation of just what is meant by a book, an author and a text.

Fraser illustrates his combined approach with comparative case studies of print, script and speech cultures in South Asia and Africa, before panning out to examine conflicts and paradoxes arising in parallel contexts. The re-orientation of approach and the freshness of view offered by this volume will foster understanding and creative collaboration between scholars of different outlooks, while offering a radical critique to those identified in its concluding section as purveyors of global literary power.

ISBN13: 978–0–415–40293–4 (hbk)
ISBN13: 978–0–415–40294–1 (pbk)
ISBN13: 978–0–203–88811–7 (ebk)

Available at all good bookshops
For ordering and further information please visit:
www.routledge.com

Related titles from Routledge

The Book History Reader
Edited by David Finkelstein and Alistair McCleery

Following on from the widely successful first volume, this second edition has been updated and expanded to create an essential collection of writings examining different aspects of the history of books and print culture.

Arranged in thematic sections, bringing together a wide range of contributors, and featuring introductions to each section, this new edition:

- contains more extracts covering issues of gender, material culture and bibliographical matters

- has a brand new section on the future of the book in the electronic age

- examines different aspects of book history including: the development of the book, spoken words to written texts, the commodification of books and the power and profile of readers.

This pioneering book is a vital resource for all those involved in publishing studies, library studies, book history and also those studying English literature, cultural studies, sociology and history.

ISBN13: 978-0-415-40235-4 (hbk)
ISBN13: 978-0-415-35947-4 (pbk)

Available at all good bookshops
For ordering and further information please visit:
www.routledge.com

Related titles from Routledge

An Introduction to Book History
David Finkelstein and Alistair McCleery

'David Finkelstein and Alistair McCleery have written an excellent introduction to the history of the book. This concise volume covers the major aspects of book history to introduce the novice or to refresh the memory of the scholar ... the book as a whole provides a starting place for further discussion and exploration into the history of literacy, the book, and ideas about reading and text.' – *Millie Jackson, Libraries and the Cultural Record*

'...the tracing of history, historiography and competing views is engaging.' – *Journalism History*

An Introduction to Book History provides a comprehensive critical introduction to the development of the book and print culture.
David Finkelstein and Alistair McCleery chart the move from spoken word to written texts, the coming of print, the book as commodity, the power and profile of readers and the future of the book in the electronic age.

Each section begins with a summary of the chapter's aims and contents, followed by a detailed discussion of the relevant issues, concluding with a summary of the chapter and suggestions for further reading.

Sections include:

- the history of the book
- orality to Literacy
- literacy to printing
- authors, authorship and authority
- printers, booksellers, publishers and agents
- readers and reading
- the future of the book.

An Introduction to Book History is an ideal introduction to this exciting field of study, and is designed as a companion text to *The Book History Reader*.

ISBN13: 978–0–415–31442–8 (hbk)
ISBN13: 978–0–415–31443–5 (pbk)
ISBN13: 978–0–203–50555–7 (ebk)

Available at all good bookshops
For ordering and further information please visit:
www.routledge.com

Related titles from Routledge

The Routledge Concise History of
Nineteenth Century Literature

Josephine Guy and Ian Small

Nineteenth-century Britain saw the rise of secularism, the development of a modern capitalist economy, multi-party democracy and an explosive growth in technological, scientific and medical knowledge. It also witnessed the emergence of a mass literary culture which changed permanently the relationships between writers, readers and publishers.

Focusing on the work of British and Irish authors, *The Routledge Concise History of Nineteenth-Century Literature*:

- considers changes in literary forms, styles and genres, as well as in critical discourses

- examines movements such as Romanticism, Pre-Raphaelitism, Aestheticism and Decadence

- considers the work of a wide range of canonical and non-canonical writers

- views the period through gender studies, queer theory, postcolonialism and book history

- contains useful, student-friendly features such as explanatory text boxes, chapter summaries, a detailed glossary and suggestions for further reading.

In their lucid and accessible manner, Josephine M. Guy and Ian Small provide readers with an understanding of the complexity and variety of nineteenth-century literary culture, as well as the historical conditions which produced it.

ISBN13: 978–0–415–48710–8 (hbk)
ISBN13: 978–0–415–48711–5 (pbk)
ISBN13: 978–0–203–83941–6 (ebk)

Available at all good bookshops
For ordering and further information please visit:
www.routledge.com

Related titles from Routledge

Reading the Nation in English Literature:
A Critical Reader
Edited by Elizabeth Sauer and Julia M. Wright

This volume contains primary materials and introductory essays on the historical, critical and theoretical study of 'national literature', focusing on the years 1550 – 1850 and the impact of ideas of nationhood from this period on contemporary literature and culture.

The book is helpfully divided into three comprehensive parts. Part One contains a selection of primary materials from various English-speaking nations, written between the early modern and the early Victorian eras. These include political essays, poetry, religious writing and literary theory by major authors and thinkers ranging from Edmund Spenser, Anne Bradstreet and David Hume to Adam Kidd and Peter Du Ponceau. Parts Two and Three contain critical essays by leading scholars in the field: Part Two introduces and contextualizes the primary material and Part III brings the discussion up-to-date by discussing its impact on contemporary issues such as canon-formation and globalization.

The volume is prefaced by an extensive introduction to – and overview of – recent studies in nationalism, the history and debates of nationalism through major literary periods and discussion of why the question of nationhood is important.

Reading the Nation in English is a comprehensive resource, offering coherent, accessible readings on the ideologies, discourses and practices of nationhood.

Contributors: Terence N. Bowers, Andrea Cabajsky, Sarah Corse, Andrew Escobedo, Andrew Hadfield, Deborah Madsen, Elizabeth Sauer, Imre Szeman, Julia M. Wright.

ISBN13: 978–0–415–44523–8 (hbk)
ISBN13: 978–0–415–44524–5 (pbk)
ISBN13: 978–0–203–87303–8 (ebk)

Available at all good bookshops
For ordering and further information please visit:
www.routledge.com

Related titles from Routledge

The Handbook to Literary Research
Second Edition
Edited by Delia da Sousa Correa and W.R. Owens

The Handbook to Literary Research is a practical guide for students embarking on postgraduate work in Literary Studies. It introduces and explains research techniques, methodologies and approaches to information resources, paying careful attention to the differences between countries and institutions, and providing a range of key examples.

This fully updated second edition is divided into five sections which cover:

- Tools of the trade – a brand new chapter outlining how to make the most of literary resources;

- Textual scholarship and book history – explains key concepts and variations in editing, publishing and bibliography;

- Issues and approaches in literary research – presents a critical overview of theoretical approaches essential to literary studies;

- The dissertation – demonstrates how to approach, plan and write this important research exercise;

- Glossary – provides comprehensive explanations of key terms, and a checklist of resources.

Packed with useful tips and exercises and written by scholars with extensive experience as teachers and researchers in the field, this volume is the ideal handbook for those beginning postgraduate research in literature.

ISBN13: 978–0–415–49732–9 (hbk)
ISBN13: 978–0–415–48500–5 (pbk)
ISBN13: 978–0–203–87333–5 (ebk)

Available at all good bookshops
For ordering and further information please visit:
www.routledge.com

Related titles from Routledge

THE NEW CRITICAL IDIOM

Series Editor: John Drakakis, University of Stirling

The New Critical Idiom is an invaluable series of introductory guides to today's critical terminology. Each book:

- provides a handy, explanatory guide to the use (and abuse) of the term
- offers an original and distinctive overview by a leading literary and cultural critic
- relates the term to the larger field of cultural representation

With a strong emphasis on clarity, lively debate and the widest possible breadth of examples, The New Critical Idiom is an indispensable approach to key topics in literary studies.

'The New Critical Idiom is a constant resource – essential reading for all students.' – *Tom Paulin, University of Oxford*

'Easily the most informative and wide-ranging series of its kind, so packed with bright ideas that it has become an indispensable resource for students of literature.' – *Terry Eagleton, University of Manchester*

Available in this series:

The Author by Andrew Bennett
Autobiography by Linda Anderson
Adaptation and Appropriation by Julie Sanders
Class by Gary Day
Colonialism/Postcolonialism – Second edition by Ania Loomba
Comedy by Andrew Stott
Crime Fiction by John Scaggs
Culture/Metaculture by Francis Mulhern
Difference by Mark Currie
Discourse by Sara Mills
Drama / Theatre / Performance by Simon Shepherd and Mick Wallis
Dramatic Monologue by Glennis Byron
Ecocriticism by Greg Garrard
Elegy by David Kennedy
Genders by David Glover and Cora Kaplan
Genre by John Frow
Gothic by Fred Botting
Historicism by Paul Hamilton
Humanism by Tony Davies
Ideology by David Hawkes
Interdisciplinarity by Joe Moran

Intertextuality by Graham Allen
Irony by Claire Colebrook
Literature by Peter Widdowson
Magic(al) Realism by Maggie Ann Bowers
Metre, Rhythm and Verse Form by Philip Hobsbaum
Metaphor by David Punter
Mimesis by Matthew Potolsky
Modernism by Peter Childs
Myth by Laurence Coupe
Narrative by Paul Cobley
Parody by Simon Dentith
Pastoral by Terry Gifford
The Postmodern by Simon Malpas
The Sublime by Philip Shaw
The Author by Andrew Bennett
Realism by Pam Morris
Rhetoric by Jennifer Richards
Romance by Barbara Fuchs
Romanticism by Aidan Day
Science Fiction by Adam Roberts
Sexuality by Joseph Bristow
Stylistics by Richard Bradford
Subjectivity by Donald E. Hall
The Unconscious by Antony Easthope

For further information on individual books in the series, visit:
www.routledge.com/literature/nci

Related titles from Routledge

Routledge Critical Thinkers

Series Editor: Robert Eaglestone,
Royal Holloway, University of London

Routledge Critical Thinkers is designed for students who need an accessible introduction to the key figures in contemporary critical thought. The books provide crucial orientation for further study and equip readers to engage with each theorist's original texts.

- why he or she is important
- what motivated his/her work
- what were his/her key ideas
- who and what influenced the thinker
- who and what the thinker has influenced
- what to read next and why.

Featuring extensively annotated guides to further reading, *Routledge Critical Thinkers* is the first point of reference for any student wishing to investigate the work of a specific theorist.

'These little books are certainly helpful study guides. They are clear, concise and complete. They are ideal for undergraduates studying for exams or writing essays and for lifelong learners wanting to expand their knowledge of a given author or idea.' - Beth Lord, THES

'This series demystifies the demigods of theory.' – *Susan Bennett, University of Calgary*

Available in this series

Louis Althusser by Luke Ferretter
Theodor Adorno by Ross Wilson
Hannah Arendt by Simon Swift
Roland Barthes by Graham Allen
Jean Baudrillard by Richard J. Lane
Simone de Beauvoir by Ursula Tidd
Homi K. Bhabha by David Huddart
Maurice Blanchot by Ullrich Haase and William Large
Judith Butler by Sara Salih
Gilles Deleuze by Claire Colebrook
Jacques Derrida by Nicholas Royle
Michel Foucault by Sara Mills
Sigmund Freud by Pamela Thurschwell
Antonio Gramsci by Steve Jones
Stephen Greenblatt by Mark Robson
Stuart Hall by James Procter
Martin Heidegger by Timothy Clark
Fredric Jameson by Adam Roberts
Julia Kristeva by Noëlle McAfee
Jacques Lacan by Sean Homer
Emmanuel Levinas by Seán Hand
F.R. Leavis by Richard Storer
Jean-François Lyotard by Simon Malpas
Paul de Man by Martin McQuillan
Friedrich Nietzsche by Lee Spinks

Paul Ricoeur by Karl Simms
Edward Said by Bill Ashcroft and Pal Ahluwalia
Jean-Paul Sartre by Christine Daigle
Eve Kosofsky Sedgwick by Jason Edwards
Gayatri Chakravorty Spivak by Stephen Morton
Paul Virilio by Ian James
Slavoj by Tony Myers
American Theorists of the Novel: Henry James, Lionel Trilling & Wayne C. Booth by Peter Rawlings
Theorists of the Modernist Novel: James Joyce, Dorothy Richardson & Virginia Woolf by Deborah Parsons
Theorists of Modernist Poetry: T.S. Eliot, T.E. Hulme & Ezra Pound by Rebecca Beasley
Feminist Film Theorists: Laura Mulvey, Kaja Silverman, Teresa de Lauretis and Barbara Creed by Shohini Chaudhuri
Cyberculture Theorists: Manuel Castells and Donna Harroway by David Bell

Available at all good bookshops
For further information on individual books in the series, visit:
www.routledge.com/literature/nci